PRAISE FOR
NO SILENT NIGHT

"An exciting chronicle of the one day that changed the course of the war and the world . . . based on some extraordinary research and extensive interviews."   —Bookviews by Alan Caruba

"Leo Barron and Don Cygan have shed new light on the crucial siege of Bastogne during the Battle of the Bulge. *No Silent Night* is the product of in-depth research and a strong commitment to historical accuracy. Whether you are new to the topic or a confirmed expert, you will learn much from this book."

—John C. McManus, author of *Alamo in the Ardennes* and *September Hope*

"Bastogne has always figured large in any account of the Battle of the Bulge. In *No Silent Night*, Leo Barron and Don Cygan provide new insight into the climatic battle that raged for that small Ardennes market town on Christmas Day 1944. New sources, interviews, and thorough documentation grace this book, which will be a boon for those seeking to understand how Americans prevailed in one of their most famous World War II victories."

—Danny S. Parker, author of *Fatal Crossroads*

NO SILENT NIGHT

THE CHRISTMAS BATTLE FOR BASTOGNE

Leo Barron and Don Cygan

NAL
CALIBER

NAL Caliber
Published by the Penguin Group
Penguin Group (USA) LLC, 375 Hudson Street,
New York, New York 10014, USA

USA | Canada | UK | Ireland | Australia | New Zealand | India | South Africa | China
penguin.com
A Penguin Random House Company

Published by NAL Caliber, an imprint of New American Library, a division of Penguin Group
(USA) LLC. Previously published in an NAL Caliber hardcover edition.

First NAL Caliber Trade Paperback Printing, November 2013

NAL Caliber Trade Paperback ISBN: 978-0-451-41485-4

THE LIBRARY OF CONGRESS HAS CATALOGUED THE HARDCOVER EDITION OF THIS TITLE AS FOLLOWS:

Barron, Leo.
No silent night: the Christmas battle for Bastogne/Leo Barron and Don Cygan.
p. cm.
Includes bibliographical references and index.
ISBN 978-0-451-23813-9
I. World War, 1939–1945—Campaigns—Belgium—Bastogne.   2. Ardennes, Battle of the,
1944–1945.   I. Cygan, Don.   II. Title.
D756.5.A7B257 2012
940.54'219348—dc23   2012007136

Printed in the United States of America
10   9   8   7   6   5   4   3   2   1

Set in Granjon
Designed by Patrice Sheridan

PUBLISHER'S NOTE
While the author has made every effort to provide accurate telephone numbers and Internet addresses
at the time of publication, neither the publisher nor the author assumes any responsibility for errors,
or for changes that occur after publication. Further, publisher does not have any control over and does
not assume any responsibility for author or third-party Web sites or their content.

"Möge die Welt nie mehr solche Weihnachtsnacht erleben! Nichts ist schrecklicher, als fern von Mutter, Frau und Kinder, von Waffen niedergerestrckt zu werden. Entspricht es der Menschenwürde, der Mutter, einen Sohn zu rauben, der Gattin den Ehmann, den Kindern ihren Vater? Das Leben wird uns geschenkt, um einander zu lieben en zu achten. Aus den Ruinen, dem Blut und dem Tode wird wohl eine bruderlisch Welt geboren werden."

—Ein Deutscher Offizier

"Let the world never see such a Christmas night again! To die, far from one's children, one's wife and mother, under the fire of guns, there is no greater cruelty. To take away a son from his mother, a husband from his wife, a father from his children, is it worthy of a human being? Life can only be for love and respect. At the sight of ruins, of blood and death, universal fraternity will rise."

—Discovered by schoolmaster Monsieur Schmitz and
several Americans written on a chalkboard at the local school in
Champs, Belgium, after the Christmas Day battle.
The author was likely a German officer from the 77th Volksgrenadier Regiment.[1]

To Carl Koonsman, a teacher who sparked my interest in World War II

—DON CYGAN

To Blake Russell and all the other Screaming Eagles who made the ultimate sacrifice

—LEO BARRON

CONTENTS

ACKNOWLEDGMENTS

In writing this book, the authors compiled and reviewed extensive archival data, letters, written accounts, photographs, and maps from a vast number of sources. Both authors, veterans of the U.S. Army, walked the battle sites and conducted multiple simulations and field tests to help understand all the aspects of what transpired during the Christmas Day battle. Many interviews were conducted with noted survivors of the struggle.

First and foremost, this story is about the battalions that fought in the Christmas Day battle. Therefore, most of our attention focuses on the 1/401st Glider Infantry, 1/502nd Parachute Infantry, elements of the 705th Tank Destroyer Battalion, the 463rd Parachute Field Artillery Battalion, and the 406th Fighter Group. On the German side, we highlight the contributions of the 77th Volksgrenadier Regiment and the 115th Panzergrenadier Regiment. We also spend a great deal of time on the commanders who made the crucial decisions: *Oberst* Heinz Kokott, *General der Panzertruppen* Heinrich von Lüttwitz, Brigadier General Anthony McAuliffe, Lieutenant Colonel Steve Chappuis, Lieutenant Colonel John Cooper, Lieutenant Colonel Ray Allen, and *Oberst* Wolfgang Maucke.

We decided to tell the story of *No Silent Night* in as close to a narrative style as possible, as seen through the eyes of the participants, but grounded in this historical research. In several points in the book (primarily dialogue where actual quoted conversations were not available, or the actual account was brief and dry), we took the liberty of creating conversations or thought processes based on transcripts, notes, or accounts of what was said or done—particularly during some of the command briefings. Notes taken at these briefings were often written without elaboration, but when we compared the information from other sources, certain logical deductions could be made and constructed to create a more complete picture for the reader. In other words, we know what was discussed at these meetings, and we know what documents were produced as a result of what was discussed at these meetings. Therefore, we can infer from these primary sources the thought process involved. As a result, instead of presenting a dry and boring account of what was said, we decided to make it more engaging by presenting them as conversations between the participants. Do we know the exact words that were said? No. But the substance of the conversations is accurate, according to the historical record. An example of this would be the operations briefing for the German plan for the Ardennes offensive. Colonel Heinz Kokott, who was the commander of the 26th Volksgrenadier Division, attended the briefing in Kyllburg. We know that for a fact. We also know who else was there, thanks to Kokott's notes and those of others. Finally, we know what was discussed due to subsequent interviews with Kokott and his commander, General Heinrich Freiherr von Lüttwitz. To flesh out the operations briefing, we quoted from the operational order—named Christrose. Therefore, the staff officer's words are actually the contents of the order. The result is a balanced snapshot of the briefing: one that provides the reader context as well as the actual information from German records.

In most other situations, we let the extensive record of personal interviews, letters, and reports tell the story, particularly on the American side, where we were blessed with an abundance of this information. We also rely heavily on S. L. A. Marshall's combat interviews for the senior officers in the 101st Airborne. In the last few years, historians have called into question Marshall's research methods. We have found that his combat interviews tend to be accurate in our case, and so we used them throughout the book. In fact, many of the veterans in other interviews refer back to his book *Bastogne: The First Eight Days* as an honest account of the siege. Therefore, if it's good enough for them, it's good enough for us.

Moving on, serious historians will notice that we left some units off the various maps in the book. We did this on purpose so that the maps will include only the units directly involved in the Christmas Day battle. Therefore, the reader will not have to search endlessly for the various units on cluttered maps. Next, on these maps, the reader will discover that American companies are typically designated by letters (e.g., A Company, B Company, etc.). In addition, battalions usually received a numerical designation, such as 1st Battalion, 2nd Battalion, etc. On the other hand, the Germans typically numbered their companies. Hence, one of our main characters belonged to 6th Company, 2nd Battalion, of the 77th Volksgrenadier Regiment. We hope this will clear up any potential confusion for those who are not familiar with military organizational nomenclature rules.

Finally, we tend to use German and American rank equivalents throughout the book. This is on purpose, since many of the German ranks match their American counterparts. For example, an *Oberst* or colonel holds the same position in the American Army. An *Oberstleutnant* is a lieutenant colonel, and both typically commanded regiments at this point in the war. Hence, we used them interchangeably.

This book could not have been written without many others who took their personal time to help us with this story by acting as hosts, researchers, mentors, guides, primary sources, or just offering expert or practical opinion. We apologize in advance if we left anyone out; it was certainly not our intention. If you assisted us in some fashion with this book, we are grateful and in your debt.

The authors would especially like to thank the veterans who offered their time, memories, and information for multiple interviews spanning almost five years. We could not be in more agreement when Tom Brokaw referred to these men as "the Greatest Generation." They are true heroes, as the story will show, whether they would be willing to admit this today or not. Their humble spirit, candor, and friendliness went a long way in helping tell this amazing story. Sadly, so many are passing away at the time of this writing that capturing their accounts seems to be an even more urgent goal for historians and future generations.

First off, we must thank four gentlemen who were of invaluable help in this project—Anthony D'Angelo of the 705th TD Battalion (who, sadly, passed away during the writing of this book), Carmen Gisi of the 1/401st, Ken Hesler of the 463rd PFAB, and Charles Asay of A/502nd PIR. We would like to thank the Chappuis family and Joseph Pangerl, Willis Fowler of A/502nd, Paul Krick, Robert O'Mara and Robert Lott of 1/401st. Also, we offer many thanks to Trish O'Malley, daughter of Lieutenant "Gus" Ryan, for providing her father's diary and other information. From the 705th: Wayne Tennant, Frank McCurdy, Tom E. Toms, John "Jack" Dibble Jr., and Anthony Breder. From the 377th: Jim Robinson. From the 463rd:

Victor Tofany. Belgians: Michel Marecaux for providing a tour of McAuliffe's headquarters. Bernard Maus (the grandson of Madame Maus de Rolle) was of great assistance in showing off the Rolle Château grounds and nearby battlefield, and a wonderful host and guide. We would be remiss if we didn't mention Filip Willems, who has done extensive research on the 463rd and maintains a great Web site; and Pierre Henri-Darliguie, for his help in researching the 77th Volksgrenadier Regiment. Germans: Ludwig Lindemann of the 77th for his account, and his daughter Marion and granddaughter, Nina, for their assistance in translating. Thanks to Hannes Spreigl and Dieter Stenger for their help in translating German reports as well. To Benjamin Haas, who found those German records in the German Federal Archives that provided us with key answers to some of our more important questions. Others: Josh Coates, owner of one of the few working M18 tank destroyers left in the United States for answering our technical questions and letting Don crawl through the interior and even fire the main gun of his vehicle. Thanks to Jon Parshall, coauthor of the wonderfully detailed account of the Battle of Midway *Shattered Sword*, for his advice, experience, and mentoring on our project. Ditto for other authors who helped and encouraged: Kirk B. Ross, author of *The Sky Men*, and Michael Tolhurst, author of an outstanding guide to the Bastogne battlefields. We are greatly in debt to Jim and Lois Pawley Wick for their work on the history of the 705th, as well as Frank Knafelc, who also wrote about the 705th. In addition, we certainly would like to mention Jill Hughes and Jeanette de Beauvoir for their help in editing our submission chapters and developing our initial book proposal. Furthermore, we would like to thank Tim Frank and Susan Strange for their services in combing through the National Archives to find those after-action reports that were so crucial to our story. To Danny S. Parker and Lynn Gamma, both of whom provided valuable assistance in researching the air war over Bastogne. To Randy Black, who provided us some great photos of his father, Layton Black. To the folks at the U.S. Army Historical Education Center, who gave us access to the George Koskimaki collection to assist in the development of a training exercise, which we later used in our book. To the staff at the Donald F. Pratt Museum who provided us access to their archives and helped Leo write his first article. To George Bick, our agent, who adopted our vision as if it were his own, and to Mark Chait, our editor, who decided to give our story a chance.

Don Cygan would like to thank his wife and sons for their infinite patience, and Lou Zoughby, a local friend and Battle of the Bulge veteran of the 17th Airborne Division. Last, but certainly not least, my coauthor, Leo. Sharing a mutual passion for this story is what made the dream of writing this book a reality. Leo Barron would like to thank Don Cygan for pushing him to write a better tale than just a string of facts in a paragraph. To my friends and colleagues at the U.S. Army Intelligence Center, thank you for allowing me to use my Bastogne research to teach U.S. Army captains the valuable skills needed on today's battlefield. Finally, I would like to thank my wife, Caulyne, who allowed me to disappear and write for endless hours while she raised our son and did everything else. Without her support, this book would have remained a dream and not a reality.

NO SILENT NIGHT

★ ★ ★ ★ ★ ★ ★ ★ ★ ★ ★ ★ ★ ★ ★ ★ ★ ★ ★ ★

"Let the World Never See Such a Christmas Night Again!"

Sunday, Christmas Eve, 1944
6,500 feet over eastern Belgium

For the people of Bastogne, it was as if the Magi had brought bombs instead of gifts this Christmas. The harmless presents of gold, frankincense, and myrrh had been replaced with the far deadlier ones of five hundred pound high-explosive and fragmentation ordnance dumped on the American soldiers and hapless civilians below. These Magi were not wise men from the countries of Persia, but rather the crew members of Staffel 1, Kampfgeschwader 66 (KG 66), a Luftwaffe attack bomber unit based out of Dedelstorf, Germany. They flew twelve Junkers 88 medium bombers in tight formation. Each Ju 88 was carrying nearly seven thousand pounds of high-explosive munitions in its bomb bays, and each Ju 88 could deliver this payload with lethal accuracy.

On Christmas Eve, holiest of nights for the many Christian peoples of Europe, Adolf Hitler was unleashing the full fury of his remaining Luftwaffe bomber force on Bastogne. For Bastogne was the holdout city, center of Allied resistance to his *Wacht am Rhein* (Watch on the Rhine) offensive— the German surprise attack in the west that would become known among the Allies as the Battle of the Bulge. Frustrated with epic resistance from the U.S. forces trapped inside the Belgian city of Bastogne, Hitler had authorized a bombing mission that was debatably military in scope and nature.

Instead, it was more a punishment for the people of Bastogne. *Der Führer* had had enough of the American resistance in the encircled town and was preparing the outlying areas for a final ground assault to break the resistance and capture Bastogne. Civilian targets would be hit indiscriminately, and numerous Bastogne citizens would be killed on this Christmas Eve, buried in the rubble of their homes and shops. Collateral damage was not Hitler's concern, but to him, it was a fitting by-product for their support for the Allies.

Unteroffizier (noncommissioned officer) Karl Heinz Struhs was the bombardier for one of the pathfinder Ju 88s that night. His Ju 88, tail number Z6 FH, was part of the lead team of six aircraft. Their mission was to mark a target, which was the town of Bastogne, on Christmas Eve so that another team of bombers could release their payload accurately. As they approached their target, homing in on a radio transmission known as a Y-beam, Struhs stared through both the aircraft's Perspex nose and targeting reticule to precisely target his deadly payload, and then, instead of dropping bombs, he released bright magnesium flares to illuminate the target.[1]

Bomber Z6 FH had a young but experienced crew. At twenty-two years old, Struhs was the oldest crew member on a team of three. His pilot, *Leutnant* (Lieutenant) Peter Schulz, was the youngest, at twenty, while the radio operator, *Unteroffizier* Karl-Heinz Oldenburg, was in the middle, at twenty-one. These men had started their careers in KG 66 in May 1944, when it had become operational as part of a pathfinder unit to mark targets over England. Before arriving in France, the crew had been part of Staffel 4 of KG 54 and had flown seven missions in Italy. Now, as part of KG 66, they had already flown ten missions over England. After the disaster at Normandy, the crew had abandoned their base at Montdidier and eventually established themselves in the town of Dedelstorf. For most of the summer and fall, the crew had languished. Finally, on 4 December 1944, they conducted their first mission in months—a weather reconnaissance operation over the North Sea near the Thames estuary. After beginning with twelve aircraft, their Staffel now numbered only nine.[2]

Several days after making a weather reconnaissance mission over the North Sea, the crew of bomber Z6 FH had received the news that Hitler was planning a major winter offensive to steal the initiative from the Allies on the Western Front. This had rekindled morale among the crew, and now they were going to fly night operations against tactical targets, just as the older pilots had done during the heady days of 1940 and 1941. The pilots and crews were excited to once again be involved in a major offensive against the enemy.[3]

Despite the obvious dangers, the Luftwaffe bombing crews were highly motivated to participate in *Wacht am Rhein*. Allied daytime and nighttime bombings had battered and wrecked their country. The once proud cities of the Reich now lay in ruins as British and American bombs destroyed the resplendent landscapes. Berlin, Dusseldorf, Hamburg, and many other German cities all lay in rubble. In the eyes of many German soldiers and pilots, the Americans and the British were violating the laws of war, as they targeted innocent civilians, and now the Germans were given an opportunity to even the score. Major Schmidt, the commander of I/KG 66, had delivered the orders to the Staffel 1 and its commander, *Oberstleutnant* (First Lieutenant) Piota. The operations officer, *Oberstleutnant* Heberstreit, then typed up the mission. The mission would take place on Christmas Eve, and their target was a crossroads town in Belgium where the Wehrmacht (armed forces) had surrounded a lone American division currently defending Bastogne.

Twelve Ju 88s left the aerodrome at Dedelstorf and headed west. The sun had already slipped below the horizon as the aircraft assembled into an echeloned formation. When they had completed the mustering, the six pathfinder Ju 88s flew ahead. Struhs looked out over the horizon as he tracked his bomber's progress. The moon was three-quarters full, providing almost too much illumination as the planes raced through the clouds. From Dedelstorf they flew over Hannover, and then over Paderborn. From there they traveled over Bonn and finally south over Trier, where the Luftwaffe had erected a light beacon to guide the bombers and night fighters. The beacon also served as a reminder that they were fast approaching the front lines.

Inside the dark cockpit, the crew steeled themselves for combat, recalling the fate of previous Ju 88 crews shot down in the early days of the offensive. From Trier, Luftwaffe antiaircraft crews would mark the waypoints with flak star shells. Seeing the flak burst into a series of brilliant guiding lights, the crew of Z6 FH now commenced their path-finding run. After they passed the last starburst, they guided their plane for two minutes, using dead reckoning to reach the target area. Struhs looked ahead through the honeycombed windows of the Ju 88 and saw the quaint Belgian town nestled among the rolling hills of the Ardennes. The snow reflected the bright moonlight as they passed over the Belgian fields. As they closed in, he could make out the numerous roads that crisscrossed through the town that made it key terrain. The Ardennes region was a densely forested area with rolling hills, and for panzer units, it was severely restrictive terrain. You had to stay on the roads to drive through it. Therefore, towns like Bastogne were vital to any mechanized unit, since it was a major road hub. This mattered little to Struhs, busy preparing to drop the flares.

Dropping magnesium flares was a simple process. Struhs and the pilot, *Leutnant* Schulz, lined up the aircraft so that it would fly directly over the target in a straight line and cross over its center. Then, as the plane flew over, they dropped their flares at ten-second intervals. The plane would release a total of ten flares. After they completed their run, the Ju 88, a very maneuverable aircraft, swung around to observe the illuminated town. The flares burned brightly, like falling stars, flittering and sputtering to the ground. Struhs's aircraft roared over the target once again—this time to drop green marking flares. The green flares would provide the follow-on bombers a clear aiming point. Their mission completed, the crew of Z6 FH turned their Ju 88 and headed home.[4]

Struhs probably wondered why they were bombing this picturesque Belgian town on, of all nights, Christmas Eve. He knew it was a target, and that was all that mattered. He had his orders, and he followed them to the letter.

What Struhs did not know was that his pathfinder mission was only the first phase of a much larger effort to seize the vital crossroads town before the American general George S. Patton could relieve the surrounded garrison. Inside the town were the paratroopers and glidermen of the 101st Airborne, tank destroyers of the 705th, and other American units. To keep the Americans awake and on high alert, the German high command had planned for not one but two bombing raids that night. According to Hitler's plans, carried out by his generals currently encircling Bastogne, within just a few hours German tanks and soldiers would follow in the wake of the bombs and finally capture the town. The German commander had ordered the ground attack to start first thing on Christmas morning.

Much was at stake for the Germans. They knew if Bastogne did not fall, their entire Ardennes offensive would be at risk. The generals in charge of the attack realized that Hitler was dead serious about seizing Bastogne quickly, before the opportunity was lost. Hitler wanted Bastogne as a Christmas present, and now it was up to the thousands of Wehrmacht forces surrounding the city to make their leader's wish come true. The attack on Christmas would decide the fate of Bastogne, and Hitler and his generals knew that whoever controlled Bastogne would undoubtedly determine the success or failure of *Wacht am Rhein*.

The battle that would result from Hitler's orders would become the climactic event of the Bastogne saga: a rapid-fire, desperate assault by overwhelming German armored might, defended in bloody struggle by the ragged but determined GIs trapped in Bastogne. It would be either the last stand of the American defenders or the culmination of the German drive to capture the vital crossroads. Either way pointed to a climactic showdown— a desperate bloodbath in the snowy fields of Bastogne.

For hundreds of German and American soldiers facing off in the siege, the events of Christmas 1944 would destroy any sense of holiness and peace on earth. For the soldiers on both sides, and for the brave people of Bastogne, this would be no silent night.

CHAPTER ONE

★ ★ ★ ★ ★ ★ ★ ★ ★ ★ ★ ★ ★ ★ ★ ★ ★ ★ ★

"We Gamble Everything!"

"The enemy move more rapidly this way. . . . It was impossible for such a handful to make a stand against this superior force."

—Congressional delegate William Hooper at the
evacuation of Philadelphia, before the British
Army captured it in the fall of 1776[1]

Friday, 8 December 1944
Headquarters of the 26th Volksgrenadier Division
Waxweiler, Germany[2]

Oberst (Colonel) Heinz Kokott shook his head glumly as he glanced over the message from headquarters. It was the sixth year of the war, and as far as Kokott was concerned, Germany was losing. He was the commander of the newly designated 26th Volksgrenadier (or people's grenadier) Division, and like many officers in the Wehrmacht, he wondered how the war was going to end. His instincts told him the future did not look good, but despondency was something that the führer did not tolerate. A lack of will could end in a lack of life for those who were not careful with their thoughts. He forced down whatever feelings he had, trying desperately to purge the inklings of defeatism within his mind. Now was not the time to replay past decisions. Besides, he had a very important meeting to attend at the corps headquarters.

Kokott stepped out of his own division HQ in Waxweiler, Germany,

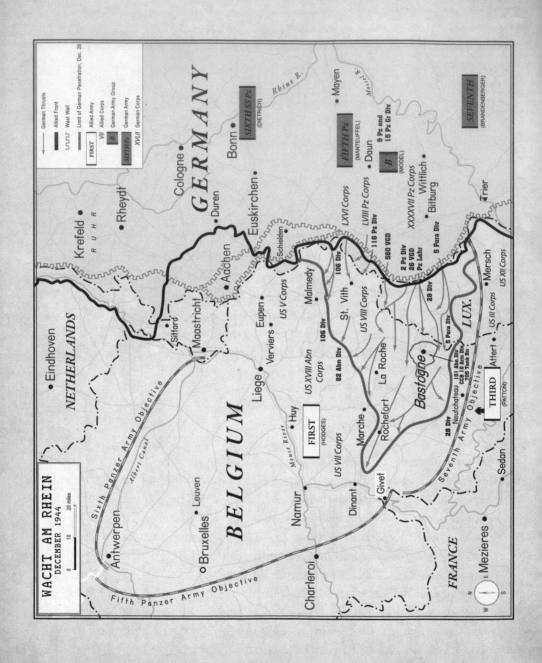

WACHT AM RHEIN
DECEMBER 1944

0   10   20 miles

German Thrusts
Allied Front
West Wall
Limit of German Penetration, Dec. 26

FIRST   Allied Army
VII   Allied Corps
B   German Army Group
SIXTH Pz. German Army
XVLII   German Corps

NETHERLANDS
• Eindhoven

GERMANY

Krefeld •
Rheydt •
RUHR
• Cologne
• Bonn
Duren •
Euskirchen •
Rhine R.
• Mayen
Mosel R.

SIXTH SS Pz.
(DIETRICH)

FIFTH Pz.
(MANTEUFFEL)
• Daun

9 Pz and
15 Pz Gr Div

B
(MODEL)

Aachen •
Maastricht •
Sittard •
Albert Canal

Eupen •
Verviers •
Schelden •
Malmedy •

US V Corps
106 Div
St. Vith
106 Div
US VIII Corps

LXVI Corps
LVIII Pz Corps
116 Pz Div
560 VGD
2 Pz Div
26 VGD
Pz Lehr

XXXXVII Pz Corps
Wittlich •
Bitburg •
5 Para Div

28 Div

• Trier
US XII Corps
Mersch •

BELGIUM

Liege •
Huy •
Meuse River

US XVIII Abn
Corps
82 Abn Div

La Roche
Marche
Rochefort

5 Para Div
Bastogne
101 Abn Div
CCB 10 Arm Div
705 Tank Bn

LUX.
US III Corps

FIRST
(HODGES)

US VII Corps

Namur •
Dinant •
Givet •

28 Div
Neufchateau •

THIRD
(PATTON)

Attert •

Sixth Panzer Army Objective

Antwerpen •
Leuven •
Bruxelles ○

Charleroi •

Seventh Army Objective

SEVENTH
(BRANDENBERGER)

FRANCE
Sedan •
• Mezieres

Fifth Panzer Army Objective

N
W E
S

breathing in the cool winter air that filled his lungs like a glass of ice-cold water. The cold was invigorating, and so was his view of the surrounding countryside. Nestled in the valley of the Prüm River in the Eifel region of Germany, Waxweiler in the early winter of 1944 still resembled a village from a Brothers Grimm fairy tale. Hills surrounded it on all sides like an amphitheater, and in the center of the town, a church spire reached to the heavens like a needle pointing directly to God. Many of the trees were spindly and leafless, but some evergreens dotted the hillsides, creating a natural patchwork quilt of verdant green and soiled brown. Though it was December, mud still covered much of the area, since rain was more common than snow in this region of Germany, but this did not detract from the rustic beauty of Waxweiler. It was a quiet and tranquil place—far removed from the sounds and sights of battle. It was also far from the nonsense that was Berlin, where staff officers plotted fictitious battles on maps and reported lies to their superiors. Berlin was more than four hundred miles (650 kilometers) northeast of Waxweiler, but the distance in reality was far greater. For the past two years, Berlin demanded the impossible from army units stationed on the western front. In short, Waxweiler's blessed isolation was also a curse.

Kokott smiled wistfully, remembering better times for Germany. So far, Waxweiler had escaped the ravages of war. Ironically, American soldiers had occupied the town after the Armistice of 1918—the very enemy Germany was facing once again. Waxweiler, fortunately for its denizens, had survived both this war and the Great War. Many towns in Germany could no longer claim such a fortunate status. Allied bombs had wrecked much of the Third Reich, and five years of costly battles had sapped the strength of the Fatherland. Even worse, the bones of Germany's sons lay scattered across the fields of Russia, Poland, Yugoslavia, Greece, North Africa, Norway, France, and Belgium, and with them the dreams of a generation of lost youth. Still, many in Germany believed that victory was not beyond their reach. The führer promised that the fortunes of war would look favorably on Germany again. Many still believed him. Kokott himself was far less sanguine.

That August, victory belonged to the Allies. For most of the summer, on both fronts, the Allies had a monopoly on success. Soviet armies rolled over German divisions in Poland and the rest of Eastern Europe, while in France, American and British units pulverized outnumbered German forces as if they were titans and the Germans were delicate sand castles. Then, as if the führer controlled a force field, the Allied juggernaut skidded to a halt at the western borders of Germany. Hitler had predicted such an event in August. Some of the generals probably thought Hitler was suffering from dementia due to the bombing that almost took his life in late July—the result of a failed assassination attempt. Few believed that the Allies would run out of gas at the German border so close to total victory. Hitler, though, was already preparing for the counterstrike.

For Nazi Germany, the Allied pause was a fortunate respite. It bought time for the Wehrmacht to reconstitute and reorganize. By mid-September, the Western Front had stabilized, and the Russian steamroller had also sputtered to a halt along the banks of the Vistula River in Poland. At the same time, an Allied airborne operation in Holland failed. Meanwhile, the Americans were hurling division after division at the German frontier. The American Army edged ever forward, but progress was now in costly inches instead of miles, and the human toll for the Allies was growing exponentially. Many German generals called the startling change of fortune *Das Wunder im Westen* ("the Miracle in the West").

Unlike his peers in the Waffen SS, Kokott looked nothing like the Aryan superman that Hitler held in such high regard. In fact, his countenance would remind an observer of Goofy, the Disney character, with his crooked smile and chipped teeth. In addition to his odd features, Kokott's vision was poor, and he wore thick, round, horn-rimmed glasses to compensate for this handicap. Furthermore, his high forehead and his dark slicked-back hair made him look more like a disheveled professor than a decorated officer in the Wehrmacht. In spite of his modest appearance, he was a successful and esteemed officer. Although Kokott was Heinrich Himmler's brother-in-law (and it's quite possible that a little nepotism may have had something to do with his standing in the Wehrmacht), the easygoing Kokott seemed naively unaware that such a relationship may have played any role in his advancement.

To be fair, Kokott was a professional soldier in his own right who had served admirably during the lean interwar years. He was born in 1890 in the town of Gross Strehlitz. Later on, he enlisted as a soldier in the 157th Infantry Regiment, but he did not see action in World War I. After the war, he earned his commission as second lieutenant in 1923 and served in the 7th Infantry Regiment for more than a decade.

At the outset of World War II, Kokott was an instructor at the Infantry School in Döberitz. His first major command was as a battalion commander for the Second Battalion of the 196th Infantry Regiment, and it was on the

Eastern Front where Kokott began earning his reputation. During the winter of 1941 Kokott assumed command of the 178th Infantry Regiment, and led the regiment for several months before attending a staff school. When he returned to the front, his superiors gave him another command in the 337th Infantry Regiment, where he served as its commander for a year. When he completed this posting, he returned to Germany to be the commandant of the Infantry School at Beverloo. A year later, he took over the command of the 26th Volksgrenadier Division in August 1944 while it recovered from operations in eastern Poland.[3]

In the first week of November 1944, the division received orders to ship out to the Westwall, along the Our River, as part of the buildup for *Wacht am Rhein*. After spending years on the Eastern Front, the 26th Volksgrenadier Division would face a much different enemy now—the Americans. By the first week of December, the 26th Volksgrenadier Division had also replaced most of its losses from the campaigns of the previous summer and fall, and now it was near 100 percent strength. Prior to its deployment in the West, Kokott had overseen the division's five-week shakedown period in the fall. During this time, it received former Luftwaffe airmen and Kriegsmarine sailors to fill its depleted frontline infantry units. The division's cadre of noncommissioned officers was a mixture of seasoned Eastern Front veterans and transfers from the German navy, air force, and rear-echelon army personnel who were of little value as soldiers, since they knew nothing about infantry tactics.

Fortunately, thought Kokott, the officers were of higher quality. The regimental, battalion, and company commanders were all veterans of the Eastern campaigns. In addition, the division had been busy repairing and acquiring new equipment to replace its losses. The most important were the new vehicles: fourteen Hetzer self-propelled tank hunters, small and speedy tanks armed with 75mm armor-piercing guns, that were the latest in German tank-destroyer technology. In addition, Kokott had trained the division hard all November. By midmonth he felt sure his men were ready for action.[4]

But by the end of the month, Kokott began to notice some subtle changes occurring in his command area. For starters, by mid-November his division began to assume a much larger frontage so that other units could pull back to the rear for rest and retraining. Next, his higher headquarters ordered him to cease all reconnaissance activity. Kokott thought this was most peculiar. He knew his sector was a quiet one; after all, his primary adversary, the U.S. 28th Infantry Division, located in front of the 26th VGD's lines and across the Our River, was recovering from a bloody stretch of fighting in the Hürtgen Forest. The Americans seemed none too keen to start much trouble with the Germans. Still, to Kokott, the idea of halting all reconnaissance and surveillance operations did not seem prudent, and he did not like the idea of ceding no-man's-land to the Americans. In disobedience, Kokott continued to send out his patrols and operate his observation posts. Orders might be orders—*Befehlen sind befehlen*, as the Germans said—but Kokott was smart enough to realize he still had an enemy to his front—a powerful enemy that he might soon have to face in combat.

In the last week of November, new units began to arrive in the rear areas, and as more arrived, traffic clogged the narrow country roads and highways. There were overcrowding problems in the nearby billets as well. The German army was stuffing unit after unit into the hamlets and villages that dotted the Eifel region. It was all very strange, thought Kokott. Something was definitely afoot—perhaps the army commanders were preparing for a major operation?[5]

That first week of December, Kokott learned that his suspicions were correct. He received a summons to meet with the corps commander, General Walter Lucht. Lucht told him that Hitler had decided to strike back, and he wanted to do it in the West—against the Americans. Hitler chose the Americans and the Western Front for several reasons. First, an attack of more than twenty divisions would have little impact against the Russian hordes. The number of enemy divisions along the Eastern Front was in the hundreds. The Russians would lose dozens of divisions trying to halt the German advance, but they would be successful in the end, because they could replace their losses. However, the German army could not.

On the other hand, along the Western Front, the Allies could field only a little more than fifteen armored divisions, and just over forty-five infantry and airborne divisions. A sudden successful attack by a force of twenty or more divisions would seriously jeopardize the entire Allied front, particularly if this attack was aimed at a thin sector of the Allied line. Moreover, the main reason Hitler chose the Americans instead of the British was overextension. The American Twelfth Army Group had the most divisions, but it also had the largest area of operations and was overextended. The Americans lines were brittle in some places, especially around the Ardennes. A massing of overwhelming combat power at one of these weak spots could result in a successful breakthrough and potentially a breakout.

The ultimate objective for the offensive was Antwerp, Lucht had explained. It made perfect sense. Antwerp had become the main port for Allied forces in northwest Europe after its capture in the fall of 1944. The majority of Allied supplies from England and the United States disembarked at Antwerp. If the Germans captured Antwerp, they would cut off a major artery the Allies used to resupply their forces.[6]

Lucht told Kokott that he knew little else. No one at corps had received the order yet, and so Kokott did not know his division's specific role, if any, in the overall plan. Finally, to maintain operational secrecy, Lucht informed Kokott that no one—not even his operations officer—could know about the operation. Kokott realized that he and many other senior officers in the Wehrmacht were signing statements of secrecy—punishable by death should it be determined later that someone divulged any details about the plan. To Kokott, it all seemed a little bizarre, particularly at this late stage of the war.

Now it was Friday, December 8. Cold, clear, but still no snow on the ground. It was only about two weeks before the holiday, and several of his senior officers were busy trying to scrounge up Christmas presents and food for family back home or comrades in arms. Kokott's orderly had brought him the message to report to the headquarters of the XXXXVII Panzer Corps in Kyllburg, Germany. Again, Kokott thought this was odd, as the XXXXVII Panzer Corps was not his higher headquarters. Perhaps now he would find out what role his division might play in this obviously highly important, top-secret operation.

Wisely, Kokott had the foresight to start a training regimen of three-day maneuvers for his troops and staff, just in case the 26th would play a defining role in the upcoming plans. While the officers had pored over map exercises, the men had done some training in the valley, practicing the fine art of blitzkrieg that the Germans had perfected. It was a rather subdued effort, for Kokott obviously did not want to attract attention from higher headquarters. Yet, as he stood looking out over the valley pondering the importance of the upcoming meeting, Kokott hoped it was enough.

While Kokott waited impatiently outside his headquarters, his driver brought up his command car, splashing through the mud. Kokott was careful to lift his immaculate wool overcoat high over his boots before stepping in. With one last look at Waxweiler, Kokott ordered his driver to head for Kyllburg.

The drive to Kyllburg took longer than usual since the Oberkommando Wehrmacht (the German high command, or OKW) had forbidden most vehicle traffic during the day, unless bad weather grounded all flights. Fortunately, the overcast weather had allowed him to safely attend the meeting, because overcast weather meant the dreaded and ubiquitous Allied fighter-bombers were grounded. All along the roads of the Eifel the preparations for this major offensive were visible. Crates of ammunition and foodstuffs crowded the woods, and tucked in between the various stacks he saw vehicles of all types: tanks, trucks, trailers, cars, and artillery. All of this remained hidden under a canopy of trees, safe from the prying eyes of Allied aerial reconnaissance. Moreover, military police units had established various checkpoints to control the flow of traffic up to six miles behind the front, while roving patrols provided security in the villages and woods. Nothing was being left to chance.

Kokott was transfixed by all the matériel. This was it. This must be the big operation—the great gamble. The lavish amount of supply and hardware amazed him, as he had believed, like many other of his colleagues, that Germany's vaunted war machine was being held together with bubble gum and baling wire. No one had seen such a gathering of Wehrmacht combat power in years. No one thought Germany could still produce such a vast amount of equipment, but the Reich Minister of Armaments and War Production, Albert Speer, had apparently produced a miracle.

As impressive as it was, Kokott also realized this massive buildup made operational secrecy almost impossible. Any *landser* (common German foot soldier) marching in the rear areas could see something was up. Besides the prodigious piles of supplies, men by the trainloads were unloading at the various railroad stations throughout the Eifel and marching to the front. Unfamiliar faces were showing up at the Westwall as new division staffs conducted their reconnaissance of the forward assembly areas, while at night, a never-ending parade of trucks and tanks rolled constantly toward the front. He sighed. It was too late to do anything about it now.

After several hours of driving along the winding roads choked with traffic, Kokott finally arrived in Kyllburg. Kyllburg, like Waxweiler, was a small town tucked away in the Kyll River valley of the Eifel. Hills hemmed in Kyllburg on all sides. Dominating the skyline was the Gothic *Stiftskirche* (Collegiate Church) complex and monastery, built in the fourteenth century as the region's parish church. Close by was the massive, baroque Marburg Castle, which was constructed in the early eighteenth century for the local potentate Johann Werner. Like many villages in the Eifel, Kyllburg so far had escaped the cruel hand of war. The only indicators that the townsfolk had suffered the ravages of combat were the widowed women and fatherless children who roamed the streets like lost souls. Kokott, though, hardly noticed. Although not insensitive to these scenes, he had been hardened by this war. These scenes were all too common now in Germany, especially in the large cities that had suffered at the hands of the Allied day and night bombing campaigns.

Pulling up to the XXXXVII Panzer Corps headquarters, located at an ornate building in the center of town, Kokott got out of his car and hurried inside. Several division commanders were already in the room, and on a large table in front of them was a map of the Ardennes. The usual smell of cigar and cigarette smoke assaulted Kokott's senses. Kokott recognized most of the commanders, congenially talking in pairs and groups of three or more, waiting anxiously for the meeting to begin. One of them was General Fritz Bayerlein, the commander of the vaunted Panzer Lehr Division. He had built his reputation as Field Marshal Erwin Rommel's chief of staff during the North African Campaign. Standing next to him was General Henning Schönfeld, the commander of the 2nd Panzer Division. Also in the room was General Walter Krüger, the commander of the LVIII Panzer Corps. Standing beside Krüger were two men who would become the masters of Kokott's fate in the next few weeks.[7]

One of them was *General der Panzertruppen* Baron Heinrich Freiherr von Lüttwitz, the commander of the XXXXVII Panzer Corps. He had a heavyset face that made him look like the friendly town butcher, but the monocle he wore over his right eye contradicted this jovial facade. He was a born-and-bred Prussian officer from Silesia. In short, von Lüttwitz was almost a caricature of the typical Nazi officer depicted in American propaganda films.

Kokott quickly learned from von Lüttwitz's staff that he and his division were now under the command of General von Lüttwitz and the XXXXVII Panzer Corps. Like Kokott, Baron von Lüttwitz had cut his teeth on the Eastern Front, but unlike Kokott, von Lüttwitz had experience fighting the Americans and British in Normandy. Similar to Kokott, von Lüttwitz was a career army officer who had taken an oath to defend his country, and had spent most of his life in the defense of Germany. Von Lüttwitz came from an old and well-known military family in Germany. His uncle, Walther von Lüttwitz, was well-known for having been jailed in the 1920s after a putsch failed to take over a post–World War I government that many saw as sympathetic to the Versailles Treaty.[8] Von Lüttwitz himself had seen the ravages of battle as a young man in the First World War as a second lieutenant in the 48th Infantry Regiment, which had seen action at the Somme in northwest Europe. Impressed by his service, his superiors had awarded him the Iron Cross, Second and First Class, for acts of bravery during several battles in 1917 on the Western Front.

When war broke out again in 1939, von Lüttwitz missed most of the action in Poland and saw no combat in the France campaign. It was in Russia where von Lüttwitz shone as a panzer commander. From 1941 on, he soared in rank from lieutenant colonel to major general. During this span of time, he commanded the 59th Rifle Regiment, the 20th Rifle Brigade, and finally the 20th Panzer Division when its division commander, Major General Walther Durvert, became ill. This time, his superiors also awarded him the clasp for his Iron Cross, First Class, in August of 1941 for heroic actions as the commander of the 59th Rifle Regiment as it fought the Soviet army that summer. From 1942 to 1944, paradoxically, von Lüttwitz's career continued to rise as the fortunes of Nazi Germany began to fall. In 1944, he was transferred to command the 2nd Panzer Division in France to prepare for the Allied invasion. Hitler wanted his best panzer commanders there to ensure the Allies would fail in their attempt.

On June 6, 1944, the Allies landed in Normandy, and OKW ordered the 2nd Panzer Division to the front. Because the Allies controlled the air, many Wehrmacht units spent weeks on the road trying to reach their destinations as they attempted to avoid the ever-present Allied fighter-bomber aircraft. Wisely, von Lüttwitz had trained his soldiers before the invasion on how to move stealthily and avoid the Allied air threat by moving only at night and during inclement weather. Using these tactics, the 2nd Panzer Division reached the front within days—not weeks. When his tanks arrived at the front, von Lüttwitz sent them into battle near Villers-Bocage. It was here on June 14 that they won an important victory, effectively halting the advance of the British 7th Armored Division. Although senior German commanders praised Lüttwitz for his aggressive action, unfortunately the celebration was short-lived.

Throughout the late summer of 1944, the Allies continued to pour men and matériel across the channel and into western France. Even though the 2nd Panzer Division inflicted serious losses on Allied units, the Allies could quickly replace their tanks and men. The Wehrmacht could not. By August, the German lines had disintegrated; the remaining Wehrmacht and SS units were staggering and faltering as they struggled to reach the safety of

Germany. Many German soldiers died in the desperate retreats, the Allies capturing many more.

Decimated by continuous Allied attacks, by August the 2nd Panzer Division was a panzer division in name only. All that remained in its panzer regiment were seven tanks. Even with this paltry force, von Lüttwitz led his division to freedom as the Allied pincers closed the Falaise Pocket behind him. Many other units and their commanders were not so fortunate. Trapped by Allied fighter-bombers, they were destroyed piecemeal.

The loss of so many commanders led to major shuffles in the panzer corps. The OKW promoted some and sacked others. Von Lüttwitz's performance had not gone unnoticed. On September 4, 1944, OKW ordered him to take command of the XXXXVII Panzer Corps, replacing General Hans von Funck, who had earned the ire of the führer because of his poor performance in the Normandy campaign (when von Funck received his dismissal order, OKW provided no particular explanation). Von Lüttwitz had his first challenge as corps commander, fighting a battle against General George S. Patton's Third Army in Lorraine in mid-September. During these battles, the XXXXVII Panzer Corps performed well at first, but once again, sheer Allied numbers and Allied airpower were too much to overcome, and the struggle in Lorraine ended with Patton victorious. In October and November, von Lüttwitz pulled the XXXXVII Panzer Corps off the front lines to undergo a refit. It had been a hard summer of fighting in Normandy and France, and von Lüttwitz's corps was now a shadow of what it once had been. Time was needed for the men to rest and recuperate, and for OKW to refurbish the XXXXVII Panzer Corps with whatever men, vehicles, and supplies they could scrape together.[9]

On this chilly day in Kyllburg, it was up to von Lüttwitz to brief his new division commanders on the operations order for the great winter offensive. Kokott nodded his head in concentration as he listened to von Lüttwitz, wondering whether this new commander would turn the sorry state of affairs around for the 26th Division and lead them to victory.

The other man in the room was Baron General Hasso von Manteuffel, the commander of Fifth Panzer Army, and, ergo, von Lüttwitz's boss. Von Manteuffel was a diminutive man (he barely topped five feet) who came from a traditional and honored Potsdam military family known throughout Germany. He had served competently as a junior officer during the Great War, and had also been a jockey and pentathlon champion. His military career had been stellar in this, his second war, leading to rumors and comparisons to the late Erwin Rommel. (Although still revered by the Wehrmacht command as a tactical genius and national hero, tragically, Rommel had committed suicide in early autumn after being implicated in the July bomb plot.)

In fact, because of von Manteuffel's successful leadership in Russia and North Africa, he had quickly become one of Hitler's rising stars. Like von Lüttwitz, he was also a member of the Prussian aristocracy; also like von Lüttwitz, his meteoric rise had more to do with his merits and skills as a leader than his family connections. He was one of the few field commanders who felt he could speak honestly and directly to *Der Führer*. Hitler, in turn, respected von Manteuffel enough to value his opinions over those of many other senior officers. Von Manteuffel had so impressed Hitler that the führer promoted him to army commander after he'd served only as a division commander, skipping the prerequisite corps command.

Years of constant warfare had etched the gaunt features of von Manteuffel's face, making him appear older than he was. Still, Kokott thought, as he watched the short ex-cavalryman stroll to the table, von Manteuffel was as feisty and optimistic as ever. The baron was known to be a risk taker and competitor, and was not one to be easily intimidated. Perhaps it was this energy and confidence that attracted Hitler and many others to him in these darker days of the war. In truth, Kokott could not have asked for better commanders.[10]

For the next few minutes, the various officers exchanged pleasantries. At a polite signal from a staff officer, the men extinguished their cigars and cigarettes and set down their drinks, and the briefing began. The commanders watched and listened as various operations officers of the XXXXVII Panzer Corps staff outlined the major points of the corps plan while pointing at various objectives on the large map. Meanwhile, von Manteuffel watched, like an overseer. He was there to make sure his subordinate commanders fully understood his intent.

The staff officers presented the strategic concept first. Hitler had titled it *Wacht am Rhein*, or "Watch on the Rhine." The name in itself was a ruse to make the Allies believe the operation was little more than a shoring up of the defenses on the Siegfried Line, which was an extensive line of pillboxes and dragon's teeth antitank obstacles that stretched along the western border of the Reich. There would be nothing defensive about Hitler's plan. It was designed to secure a crucial victory for the Reich.

According to the plan, on "Null Day" (the German version of D-day) a combined series of coordinated assaults would smash into an unsuspecting Allied line, using the Ardennes Forest along the Belgian border as cover. Hitler believed the Ardennes, thick with forested plots and hills and valleys, would be the area the Americans would least expect an attack to come from.

Field Marshal Walther Model, commander of Army Group B and overall operational commander, planned to hurl three armies into the Ardennes: the Sixth SS Panzer Army under General Sepp Dietrich, the Fifth Panzer Army under von Manteuffel, and the Seventh Army under General Erich Brandenberger. In these armies were seven panzer divisions, two panzer brigades, thirteen Volksgrenadier (or people's grenadier) divisions, and two Fallschirmjäger (paratroop) divisions. In addition, he could call on one panzer division, two Panzergrenadier divisions, and one Volksgrenadier division from the strategic reserve. In short, he would amass twenty-two divisions in the first wave and another four in the second wave.[11] Meanwhile, in the areas where tanks could not operate, Model would his use Fallschirmjäger and Volksgrenadier divisions. (A typical panzer division was composed of one panzer regiment and two Panzergrenadier regiments. A panzer regiment, at full strength, had more than a hundred tanks.[12] The standard Volksgrenadier division had three infantry regiments, and each regiment had two battalions each.)

To make up for the shortage of manpower, the Wehrmacht increased the firepower of the individual soldier in these divisions. Many of the grenadiers would carry the latest Sturmgewehr 44 semiautomatic assault rifle instead of the bolt-action Mauser K98.[13] In total, the German force would number more than 850 Panzers and self-propelled assault guns.[14] In terms of manpower, the numbers were staggering. A normal panzer division had a complement of anywhere from 14,000 to 17,000 soldiers, depending on whether it was an SS or a regular army unit. A Volksgrenadier division numbered around 10,000 men, while a Panzergrenadier division could muster 14,000 soldiers. Finally, a Fallschirmjäger division could field up to 16,000 paratroopers. Therefore, Model commanded more than 250,000 soldiers in the first wave and nearly 50,000 in the second.[15] Added to this, 1,900 pieces of artillery, both mobile and static, would be committed to providing an initial bombardment and follow-on artillery support as the offensive moved ever forward toward the goal of assaulting and seizing Antwerp. A front more than eighty miles wide through the Ardennes had to be selected in order to accommodate the massive forces involved.

Hitler had amassed quite a strike force, but in actuality, it had half the number of infantry divisions that Army Group A had on hand during the invasion of France in 1940. Hitler may not have enjoyed the sheer manpower and number of divisions that he did in 1940, but in terms of overall firepower, it was the largest German offensive ever on the Western Front. After all, Hitler had the same number of panzer divisions in the first wave in this new offensive that he had in 1940. That was the number that counted.

The officers in the room knew that to have any chance of success, *Wacht am Rhein* would need to be a quick and total surprise to the Allies—a blitzkrieg in the dead of winter. The attack would have to bulldoze through the Ardennes and achieve vital objectives rapidly. Four days would have to be sufficient for the combined armor and infantry forces to reach and cross the Meuse River. From there, the Sixth SS Panzer Army would seize the cities of Brussels and Antwerp, while the Fifth Panzer Army and Seventh Army secured its southern flank.[16] If the Wehrmacht could not meet this timetable, and if the Allies were able to react rapidly enough, the major portion of the German army would be caught in a vise—cut off from Germany, and stuck between the Americans and the British. In typical Hitlerian style, *Der Führer* had no backup plan. It was all or nothing. If the Allies surrounded his forces, he had nothing left in his panzer cupboard to throw at them. The Allies would encircle his armies and destroy them.

Kokott shrugged to himself as he glanced over the map. He knew the terrain of the Ardennes would be as much an enemy to his forces as to the Americans. Thick, impenetrable forest covered much of the region, while closer to the Our River, narrow draws and steep valleys cleaved through much of the landscape, making it terrible country for tanks and motor vehicles. This was the reason General Omar Bradley, who was the commander of the American Twelfth Army Group, felt he could leave only four divisions there to defend it. No one in their right mind would send large forces through the Ardennes in the dead of winter. Everything had to travel along the roads—especially tanks. The country opened up and flattened out beyond the Meuse River, but the terrain leading up to it was severely restricted. For von Manteuffel's Fifth Panzer Army, the Meuse would be critical. If von Manteuffel's forces could not reach this major river in time, the Americans would be able to easily deny a crossing, stopping *Wacht am Rhein* in its tracks. With such limited routes of travel toward the Meuse, road hubs like the Belgian towns of Bastogne and St. Vith became decisive terrain. Kokott sighed. He realized what many of the other officers in the room must be thinking, but were afraid to yet voice: If the Wehrmacht failed to seize those two towns early on, it would be almost impossible to reach the Meuse River in four days.[17]

The staff officers continued. To counter the overwhelming Allied airpower, *Wacht am Rhein* would commence during a period of bad flying weather. German meteorologists predicted that mid-December would provide a rare warm front, which would produce a perfect storm of low-level clouds and fog that would keep the Allied air forces on the ground and balance the odds for the German army. The once powerful German air force was now heavily emasculated, and American airpower dominated the skies. OKW realized it could not count on Hermann Göring's flyboys for support in this massive offensive. Winter weather would have to be the Luftwaffe this time. Luckily, the weather forecasters were some of the finest experts in the field. They had played a pivotal role in May 1940, when they had predicted the prerequisite five days of clear weather that allowed the Luftwaffe to wreak havoc on Allied airfields and supply lines in the crucial opening hours of Operation Fall Gelb that led to the downfall of France. The meteorologists predicted nasty weather for much of December, but were uncertain after that. The weather window was tight. If the operation was to be a maximum success, the time for the attack was now.[18]

The staff officers next predicted that the Americans would be unable to stop such an overwhelming force. They assessed that the Americans had only a handful divisions in the area of the Ardennes. Therefore the German forces would outnumber the Americans almost six to one. Where the Fifth Panzer Army planned to strike, the only division facing them was the 28th Infantry Division and elements of the 106th Infantry Division. In fact, in Kokott's sector, the XXXXVII Panzer Corps would face only one infantry regiment—the 110th Infantry. The Americans had long believed that the Germans were on the ropes, and therefore had concluded that the Wehrmacht could field only five hundred tanks and assault guns while supporting shrinking infantry divisions. Kokott smiled. The Americans were in for a shock.

The briefing droned on. While the staff officers talked, soldiers moved flags and cards across the map, as if it were a game of shuffleboard. Finally, the individual orders and plans were broken down by corps and division. This part would contain the pertinent information that Kokott was expecting—the details in what the 26th VGD was expected to do, what objectives lay ahead. As the briefers started to discuss the tasks of the

XXXXVII Panzer Corps, Kokott stood up from his chair to listen, while various assistants scribbled some notes on pads of paper. Now he would find out exactly what they expected him to do.

Von Manteuffel had called his portion of the *Wacht am Rhein* Operation Rheingold. The H-hour would be early in the morning, well before sunrise, so that Allied airpower could not disrupt the German assault forces. Instead of a long, drawn-out barrage like the one planned for the Sixth SS Panzer Army to the north of them, von Manteuffel was going to use a short but violent assault. The staff officers explained that a prolonged one would serve only to alert the Allied troops to a major offensive and provide time for forward troops to prepare and defend themselves for the expected attack. To prevent this, von Manteuffel planned to infiltrate his infantry as close as possible to the American lines before the artillery strikes, and once the barrage ended, soldiers would quickly overrun the American forward trenches before they could respond. Kokott nodded. This meant the 26th Volksgrenadier Division would be first in the fight, since his men would likely be the infiltrators that von Manteuffel needed. He continued to listen intently as the staff officer presented the plans for the XXXXVII Panzer Corps. Whereas von Manteuffel called his portion of the *Wacht am Rhein* Operation Rheingold, von Lüttwitz decided to name his piece Operation Christrose.[19]

One of the staff officers then tapped the pointer down on the map. Everyone leaned forward to see where he was indicating. He stated that the key task for Operation Christrose was for the XXXXVII Panzer Corps to reach the Meuse River at Namur and Dinant and seize the bridges there for follow-on forces. If they were successful, these forces could then protect the southern flank of the Sixth SS Panzer Army, whose task was to capture the port of Antwerp. For the Americans, this would be an unmitigated disaster. By capturing those bridges, the Germans would trap several American divisions east of the Meuse River. It might even alter the course of the war in the West.

In fact, one of the staff officers mentioned, it was *Der Führer*'s belief that this offensive could successfully stifle the western Allies if they could drive far enough through Belgium and deep into Holland. Intelligence had led Hitler to believe the British and American command staffs were at extreme odds on the course of the war. If successful, *Wacht am Rhein* would not only physically create a wedge between the Allied armies, but politically separate them as well. An overwhelming attack might force the Allies to seek separate negotiations with Germany and give up talk of Germany's uncondi-tional surrender.

To accomplish this mission, the operations officer continued, the corps must secure crossings along the Our River, between the towns of Dasburg and Gemünd. To add emphasis, he then traced the area with his pointer on the map. Kokott focused on the town of Gemünd. It was in his sector.

Von Lüttwitz peered through his monocle at the map, nodding, and then looked over at General Schönfeld, the commander of the 2nd Pan-zer Division. Schönfeld's face was a mask of intense concentration while the briefer confirmed that the 2nd Panzer Division had the task to secure the crossings at Dasburg. Schönfeld nodded to acknowledge that he understood his mission. Von Lüttwitz turned and told Kokott that it would be up to his division to secure the crossings at Gemünd. Kokott nodded in reply.

Gemünd would be a tough place to cross, Kokott thought, but it was the only place in his sector where he could do it. Thousands of years ago, glaciers had burrowed through the Ardennes, and the results were scores of rivers with steep banks. Thus the terrain favored the defenders, who held the higher ground, and because of this, as the Germans emerged from the for-ested border with Germany, they would be fighting while moving uphill. The briefing officer slid his pointer west across the map and stopped on a town that looked like the hub on a bicycle wheel.

To add emphasis, he tapped on it several times. Seven roads emanated from it like spokes. Kokott peered intently at the map, trying to make out the name of this town, but since the map was upside down to him, it took him a few seconds. *Bastogne.* Kokott muttered the name to himself, as if repeating it would etch it into his memory.

For a moment, silence filled the room. The briefer's eyes stopped on General Bayerlein and then he glanced over to Kokott. Once across, the 26th Volksgrenadier Division would allow the Panzer Lehr Division to pass through their lines. Next, the Panzer Lehr would dispatch a *kampfgruppe* (or combat team) to seize Bastogne through coup de main. A coup de main was a quick and powerful dash to seize a key objective before an enemy could establish a defense around it. If Bayerlein's panzers failed to reach Bastogne before the Americans reinforced it, then the 26th Volksgrenadier Division would surround the town and isolate it.

The speaker paused. Kokott now adjusted his glasses and moved for-ward to examine the map, as Bayerlein hovered close by him. He could see that the terrain between Bastogne and the Our River was awful. Forests had grown up everywhere like weeds, while creeks crisscrossed the landscape like spiderwebs. However, west of Bastogne, the ground opened up, allowing for unrestricted movement for tanks and vehicles. It was obvious to all: The capture of Bastogne would seriously hamper the Allies' ability to retaliate against the German offensive. On the other hand, if the Americans continued to hold Bastogne, the entire German offensive would be in jeopardy. If the Americans were tactically clever, they would use the town as a rallying point to disrupt *Wacht am Rhein*'s supply lines.

Von Lüttwitz lazily waved for his operations section to continue the briefing. Now the staff read from the order so that each commander would understand his task and purpose clearly. The staff first read off the tasks for the 2nd Panzer Division. After several minutes, the briefer next moved on to Kokott's division. In response, Kokott stiffened his back to show he was listening and paying attention.

The operations officer paused briefly to allow the staff stenographers to catch up and then he began: "Sir, the 26th Volksgrenadier Division." He stared at Kokott to ensure that the division commander was ready, and then began tracing the route on the map with his pointer. "Following your entry into your preparatory positions east of Fischbach, the 26th Volksgrenadier Division shall cross the Our River on D-day at 0500 hours. You will attack on a broad front with four battalions forward, and then the 26th Volksgrenadier Division will break through the enemy lines in the vicinity of Hosingen. You shall penetrate the enemy line quickly and proceed west to Drauffelt, and establish and hold a bridgehead there on the Clerf River. Concurrently, with follow-on forces, the 26th Volksgrenadier Division shall flush out any remaining enemy troops in the terrain between Lellingen and Holzthum. After securing the bridges along the Our River, the Panzer Lehr Division shall conduct forward passage of lines through the 26th Volksgrenadier Division. The 26th then shall fall in behind the Panzer Lehr Division and proceed to the area of Bastogne, and wait for further orders from the corps commander."

Then the operations officer glanced at General Bayerlein. "Sir, the Panzer Lehr Division will make available a forward battalion and deploy it in the area of Karlshausen. General Bayerlein, you will be located at the combat post of the 26th VGD. You will begin marching toward crossings at the bridges at Dasburg and Eisenbach after you have reconnoitered them. Then the bulk of the division shall penetrate the enemy lines across the Clerf in the direction of Bastogne. In addition, you will organize your division in such a manner that would allow the Panzer Lehr to prepare for movement within thirty minutes of receiving orders from the corps headquarters. The Panzer Lehr will then move through the designated exit point at Waxweiler, while passing through the sector of the 2nd Panzer Division. In the same manner, it shall move through the 26th VGD for the attack on Bastogne."

The briefer then mapped out the line of march for the Panzer Lehr, using the pointer. It went from Bastogne to the Meuse, a distance of eighty-five kilometers from east to west. He added in a louder voice, "The mission of the Panzer Lehr Division shall be the following: the forward battalion shall capture Bastogne and from there, in echeloned formation, travel through Rochefort-Leignon, and then across the Meuse River between Annevoie and Yvoir. From there, it will attack across the Sambre River between Basse and Floreffe and seize to hold open and defend the Meuse and Sambre river bridges."

Now the staff officer addressed Kokott. "Gentlemen, each unit will create one *kampfgruppe* to act as a blocking force. It will consist of a rifle company, an antitank company, an armored reconnaissance company, a pioneer platoon, and a battery of artillery. This team must be prepared to secure key terrain quickly and defend it, and it's essential that each division create one of these task forces, but especially the 26th Volksgrenadier Division."

At this point, General von Lüttwitz stood up and said to the audience in a booming voice, "The primary goal of all the divisions is this: We must have bridges across the Meuse at Namur." For emphasis, he pointed at the city of Namur on the map with his finger. His knuckles whitened as he pressed down on the table with intensity. Von Manteuffel nodded to show that he concurred with his subordinate's assessment.[20]

Von Lüttwitz continued. "Bastogne must be captured, if necessary from the rear." As he spoke, his eyes remained fixed on Kokott and Bayerlein. Both nodded in unison to show they understood the tasks. Then he issued a prophetic warning to all in the room. "Otherwise it will be an 'abscess' along the route of the advance, and it will tie up too many of our forces. Bastogne is to be mopped up first, and then the bulk of the corps will continue its advance. If the Panzer Lehr can't take Bastogne, then the 26th Volksgrenadier Division must take it."[21]

While von Lüttwitz spoke, Kokott watched General von Manteuffel. When von Lüttwitz mentioned how Bastogne had to be "mopped up" before the corps could continue to move forward, Kokott noticed von

Manteuffel was shaking his head. It appeared to Kokott that they were not in total agreement on this matter. He was right.

After the briefing ended, all the generals tried to hash out a solution for Bastogne. Von Lüttwitz felt that Bastogne needed his corps' full attention, while von Manteuffel argued that the panzers could leave Bastogne to wither on the vine. The conference ended without a satisfactory solution. Everyone hoped the Panzer Lehr could take it on the second or third day. No one wanted to contemplate what would happen if Bayerlein's *kampfgruppe* failed.

Kokott, though, did not have a choice. He had to mull over the question of Bastogne, since the issue had essentially been dropped in his lap. *Bastogne must be taken—Bastogne and then Namur*, thought Kokott. Even though the original mission of the Panzer Lehr was to capture the vital Belgian crossroads, he sensed that Bastogne would become his problem and his responsibility alone, thereby allowing Bayerlein and the Panzer Lehr to dash to the Meuse with the 2nd Panzer Division. Kokott then realized Christmas was just over two weeks away. Not very festive to conduct a major offensive during the holidays, he thought. None of which mattered, for as usual in Hitler's Reich, *befehlen sind befehlen*. . . .

It was clear to Kokott that his role was part of a final desperate effort to end the war on Germany's terms. His mission of taking Bastogne, this whole great plan in which he played a part, would have to come together perfectly. If it did not, he shuddered to think of the personal price paid for failure in Hitler's Reich.

As for Bastogne, it would soon become more than just Kokott's problem.

Evening, Tuesday, 12 December 1944
The führer's bunker
Wiesental, Germany

Kokott peered out into the evening darkness. The temperature had dropped since he had left OKW headquarters, and in this area an icy chill hung in the night air. He could see his breath and the breath of others nearby. The effect made everyone look like engine smokestacks, puffing away in rhythm as each officer stepped off the bus. Winter was definitely approaching central Germany.

Kokott was surrounded by scores of other corps and division commanders. Some of them he knew, and some he did not know, but they were all clueless as to their whereabouts. Hitler had kept it that way for security purposes. The führer's bodyguard detachment was still nervous and reactionary after the failed Valkyrie coup attempt on Hitler's life on July 20. Hitler's bodyguard units from the Waffen SS (Schutzstaffel) were taking no chances. Extreme precautions were in place to prevent another potential assassination attempt.

In this case, Field Marshal Gerd von Rundstedt, the overall commander in the west, gathered all the generals—including Kokott—who were participating in *Wacht am Rhein* at Ziegenberg, Germany, headquarters for OKW. From there, they had boarded several buses. Next, the bus drivers had seemingly driven around in circles to disorient them. For several hours, Kokott noticed, they drove around aimlessly. Finally the buses dropped them off in front of a nondescript barracks building. The designers had tucked it away on the side of a knoll and underneath an awning of trees in order to prevent its detection by Allied reconnaissance aircraft. It did not look very comfortable and inviting, Kokott thought, but Hitler was known for his austerity and Spartan lifestyle. Hence, it did not surprise any of the officers that this was where Hitler planned to live for the duration of the offensive.

After thoroughly checking the identification papers of each commander, the Waffen SS bodyguards herded the men together and led them into the bunker. Once inside, the officers entered a conference room, where they waited for the führer to arrive. Several minutes passed. When Hitler entered, Kokott gasped softly to himself in surprise, for the leader of Germany appeared sickly and drained. He walked around the room, looking like an aged and decrepit man. Inching his way toward a table that was in front of all the generals in the room, Hitler approached them. His steps were hesitant and unsteady, as if he were carrying a great weight on his shoulders. Once there, he sat down, pulled out a piece of paper, and took out his reading glasses.[22] Kokott and many of the others were shocked by Hitler's appearance, but kept their thoughts to themselves. This shell of a man was no longer the strong, energetic, and charismatic leader who mesmerized millions with his gift of oratory. Gone was the man who instilled a national will in the German people.

Still, it didn't stop Hitler from drawing on all of his strength for this meeting, and exhorting his generals to win one final victory. He started his speech by reminding his audience of the sacrifices of the German people and the successes of National Socialism, and, even more important, that after five years of an exhaustive total war, the Allies had not defeated Germany.[23]

Then Hitler told Kokott and the others that this was the final gamble, for the fate of Nazi Germany depended on the success of this offensive. He repeated the goal of Antwerp, and he insisted on the destruction of Montgomery's 21st Army Group. He explained how the Sixth SS Panzer Army was the decisive force in this operation. While the Fifth Panzer Army had to advance through Belgium to Antwerp, the Sixth SS would roll toward Liege with the ultimate mission of destroying the 21st Army Group.[24] Kokott and the other commanders listened. They knew that it was a long shot, and the chances of victory were slim. Despite these dark predictions, they also knew that they did not have a choice. They had sworn an oath to the führer. Perhaps history would repeat itself, and the Americans would break, as the French had done when the German panzers crossed the Meuse near Sedan in those heady days of 1940.

Hitler concluded his speech with these words: "Gentlemen, if we are successful, the victory belongs to you, the generals. However, if we fail, I will shoulder the blame. If our armies push through Belgium, I will find a way to get you the divisions so that we can continue into France. We still have divisions in Norway that we could send to you. But, gentlemen, I must warn you that our German industries have been preparing for this operation for months, and in doing so, we have neglected the Eastern Front. It will take too long to replace these losses if we fail."

Hitler's voice rose in volume and intensity as he emphasized the last statement.

"There is no second chance. If we fail, it will be terrible for Germany."

In response, the entire room erupted with a raucous, "*Heil* Hitler!"[25]

Kokott and the others could not predict it then, but the town of Bastogne would jeopardize all of Hitler's grandiose plans.

Wednesday, 13 December 1944
Headquarters of the 26th Volksgrenadier Division
Waxweiler, Germany

Kokott returned to his headquarters near the Our River late on the following day. The thirteenth was spent dissecting the corps operations order and going over the details with his staff officers. There was not much time before December 16—Hitler's "Null Day"—but Kokott wanted to make sure that he provided clear instructions and guidance to the commanders of the Volksgrenadier regiments before they crossed into enemy territory. On

December 13, he convened his staff for his own map rehearsal, and each of his regimental commanders was there. They all had heard rumors, but now he was going to reveal to them the mission that would determine the fate of Germany itself.

Since he commanded an infantry division, Kokott had a different plan of attack from his panzer comrades in the Panzer Lehr and 2nd Panzer divisions. His main effort would be the 77th Volksgrenadier Regiment. The 77th would attack along an east–west axis on the division's northern flank. The 39th Fusilier Regiment would conduct a supporting operation in order to secure the southern flank of the 77th. The third infantry regiment, the 78th Volksgrenadier Regiment, would be the division reserve, stationed at Affler, Germany.[26]

Kokott's workhorse regiment, the 77th Volksgrenadier, had a short but epic history. The Wehrmacht established the 77th Infantry Regiment in the spring of 1936. It grew out of the Wehrkreis VI Military District, and many of the men who joined the division came from the Rhineland region of Germany. As further evidence of its Westphalian, Hanoverian, and Rhineland roots, its 1st Battalion received its start-up funds from the German state police district of Dusseldorf, while the 2nd Battalion received its funds from the state police district of Essen. It remained on the Western Front, and like its parent division, the 26th Infantry, it participated in the invasion of France in 1940. When Operation Barbarossa kicked off in June 1941, it marched into Russia and fought several battles around Moscow and Smolensk. In 1942, OKW designated the 77th as a grenadier regiment, and it fought as part of the 26th Infantry Division along the Don River. In 1943, the 77th Grenadier Regiment fought several battles around Kursk, and for the rest of the year and well into 1944, the 77th Grenadier Regiment retreated with the rest of the German army and fought delaying actions along the way. By September 1944, the constant fighting had wrecked the 77th Grenadier Regiment, and OKW decided to reconstitute it, along with the rest of the 26th Infantry Division, into a Volksgrenadier unit. In the autumn it had returned to the Western Front, where it had undergone its baptism of fire several long years before.[27]

The commander of the 77th Volksgrenadier Regiment was *Oberstleutnant* (Lieutenant Colonel) Martin Schriefer, who had earned the Iron Cross while serving as the commander of the 168th Grenadier Regiment in June of 1944, when the Russians destroyed it in Hube's pocket, fighting in the Ukraine. The 1st Battalion commander was Captain Weber, and the commander of 2nd Battalion was Captain Josef Raab, who also had earned the coveted Iron Cross in October of that year.[28]

Kokott was too much of a realist not to see that the time line handed to him at the briefing was going to be impossible to meet. It would be risky, but perhaps a risk worth taking for the brother-in-law of Heinrich Himmler. In order to make this work with his division, he would have to disobey the orders of his army group commander. With this in mind, he began his presentation.

"Gentlemen," Kokott started as he directed their attention to the Our River on a nearby map of the Ardennes, "the engineers will move down to the river early, and then they will construct a sufficient number of infantry footbridges across so that our forces can traverse quickly. In addition, we will attach our mine locating and clearing detachments to the 39th and 77th regiments."

Schriefer nodded as he studied the map. Kokott continued. "Also, as per our instructions from the corps, we will build a partially motorized *kampf-gruppe* from our specially organized reconnaissance battalion. The battalion will be assembled in the Neuerburg area at the start of the attack, and it must be ready to move out with the Panzer Lehr Division as soon as the bridge near Gemünd is trafficable. This *kampfgruppe* will be a combined-arms unit, and it will have the following. . . ." Kokott now pulled out piece of paper and proceeded to read from it. "'. . . A company of Hetzers, a mechanized antiaircraft gun platoon with 37mm AA flak guns, a motorized engineer platoon, a motorized battery of towed 105mm howitzers, and a motorized platoon of 120mm mortars.'" Major Rolf Kunkel, the commander of the reconnaissance battalion, scribbled some notes, and then he traced the route of the battalion from Neuerberg to Gemünd.[29] When he was finished, he looked back at Kokott and back-briefed his task.

Kokott next outlined several key tasks for each of his maneuver regiments. "Gentlemen," he said, pointing to two circles on the map, "first, both the 77th and 39th regiments need to be in position in your forward areas west of the Our River before the start of our artillery barrage. Once the artillery opens up at exactly 0530 on the sixteenth, you will rush to your final attack positions. The barrage will last about twenty minutes, so make the most of it. Then your forward observers will radio in targets for targeted artillery strikes on those positions. Meanwhile, your assault battalions will rush westward over the Hosingen road along an extended front."[30]

Kokott wanted to overwhelm the Americans. He determined then that a frontal attack was the best way. He figured that if the 39th and the 77th stepped off at the same time, then the Americans would not be able to block a double breach in their defensive lines.

Kokott now paused to let the information sink in. When his regimental commanders looked up from the map, he resumed his brief. "From there, the two forward infantry regiments will proceed to their next objectives."

"Martin," said Kokott, who now directed his attention to Lieutenant Colonel Schriefer, "I want the 77th Volksgrenadier Regiment to bypass the town of Hosingen to the north and then isolate Hosingen from the west. After your regiment completes this task, I want the 77th to pass through Bockholz, then onto Drauffelt. Once there, it must seize a bridge on the Clerf River." Kokott pounded his fist on the map for emphasis.

Lieutenant Colonel Schriefer snapped back, "Yes, sir!" His voice was as sharp as his clicking heels.

"In addition," added Kokott, "I will give you priority of fires for the 77th. I will consolidate all the artillery and mortars from your regiment and the 78th and establish a series of batteries around the town of Affler."

Kokott had estimated that the 77th had the most important mission and would likely face the stiffest opposition on its advance to Drauffelt.[31] Therefore, he decided to provide the bulk of his artillery in a direct support role for the 77th Volksgrenadier Regiment. Removing his glasses and momentarily rubbing his eyes, Kokott went over the tasks for the 39th Fusilier Regiment, which had the mission to secure the southern flank of the 77th.

When he was finished, Kokott explained the role of the 26th Reconnaissance Battalion. "After the regiments have secured their objectives, the reinforced 26th Reconnaissance Battalion, together with 130th Reconnaissance Battalion from the Panzer Lehr Division, will then conduct a forward passage of lines, and exploit the penetration that the 77th achieved near Drauffelt."

While he spoke, Kokott traced a circle around the town of Drauffelt on the map. "Gentlemen, the next part is crucial. From Drauffelt, this *kampfgruppe* must race along these roads and seize Bastogne through a coup de main." He then mapped out the route and town on the map for his commanders, using a pointer.

After a brief pause, Kokott started again. "From there, the *kampfgruppe* will move westward on to Dinant. Its line of advance will be through

Eschweiler, then to Niederwampach, or through Doncols-Bras, and then onto Bastogne.[32] To ensure proper control, I will control both battalions of the *kampfgruppe* at the division level."

Kokott continued his briefing for another hour or so. When he finished, the officers went over each of their tasks to ensure they understood Kokott's intent. After that, the division commander reiterated that the key to the whole operation was speed and violence. Kokott could not afford delays, or Christrose would not work. Kokott indeed felt the pressure, for like a chain of dominoes, if Christrose did not work, Rheingold would also most likely fail. If von Manteuffel failed to reach the Meuse and cross it, all of *Wacht am Rhein* would collapse. Kokott knew his grenadiers needed to secure the crossing sites at the Our River, and that his improvised Panzer Lehr/26th Volksgrenadier *kampfgruppe* would need to race to Bastogne with utmost haste, regardless of its flanks. Kokott made it clear to his subordinates: The assaults must be rapid and use overwhelming force against the Americans. After all, the last thing Kokott wanted was to have to fight his way into Bastogne.

Evening, Friday, 15 December 1944
77th Volksgrenadier area of operations
Opposite the town of Hosingen, along the Our River

December 15 was a cold and misty morning among the hills and woods of the Ardennes. All was in place along the border of Germany, Belgium, and Luxembourg. The soldiers were fed and armed, the vehicles fueled and loaded, the officers informed of their routes and initial objectives. All that remained was the anxious wait for the order to attack—*"Vorwärts!"*

Ludwig Lindemann, a young *Unteroffizier* (sergeant) in the 77th Volksgrenadier Regiment, was one of the many German soldiers who were surprised by the news of the impending offensive. Nicknamed "Lutz," Lindemann had been a painter in the small town of Heyen, Germany, before the war. He had joined the Wehrmacht in October 1941. Now, more than three years later, in December 1944, Lindemann was already an experienced combat veteran who had been wounded fighting near the town of Woronesh in the frigid cold of the Russian winters of 1942 and 1943. He had also received the wound badge, close combat sword, and Iron Cross, First and Second Class, all before his twenty-second birthday.[33]

Recently, Lindemann had been forced to take over as *Kompanieführer* (company commander) of 6th Company, due to the death of his lieutenant right before the offensive. The promotion was unusual because of his NCO (noncommissioned officer) rank, but an indication of his experience and the manpower shortages in the German army. His unit, the 77th Volksgrenadier Regiment, was the main effort of Kokott's 26th Volksgrenadier Division. The 77th had arrived in the Eifel region in October 1944 after traveling across Germany by train. As the trains rolled through Germany, many of the soldiers had their first look at the devastation wrought by Allied bombers on their cities and factories. Lindemann recalled the impact it had on his morale. It was not rage that overtook him, but a deep sadness. The war was destroying Germany.

When the 77th arrived in the Eifel, Lindemann and his men occupied several Siegfried Line bunkers along the German frontier. While the concrete bunkers were built to withstand direct hits from heavy artillery, they could not withstand the biting cold that was typical of autumn in northwestern Europe. Every day seemed to bring more rain, and the conditions were nearly intolerable. The added danger of reconnaissance patrols reminded him the Americans were out there, waiting to kill him.

As October faded into November, and November dragged into December, Lindemann began to notice odd changes taking place. Behind his company's bunkers and back by his battalion headquarters, stacks of ammunition began appearing along the roads, in the nearby towns, and inside the woods. With each passing day, these piles multiplied, and some grew even larger. When he inquired about the piles at his battalion headquarters, no one knew anything, but unlike many of the replacements he was in charge of, Lindemann was a seasoned veteran. He figured something was in the offing, most probably another "push."

Toward the end of November, higher headquarters had ordered the cessation of patrols, a command that required all messages to be delivered via courier, as radio silence was the order of the day. Lindemann noticed other changes. Artillery had been presited and camouflaged in positions in the nearby forests. Straw had even been thrown on the *Rollbahns* (main routes chosen for the attack) to reduce the sound of marching boots. Massive searchlights on trailers had been moved into position to provide light for what he assumed would be night attacks.

"Only two commanding officers knew of the mission," Lindemann recounted in a recent interview, "the regimental commander of the 77th and the division commander [Kokott]. We, the regular troops, were informed the evening of December fifteenth during dinner."[34]

For men like Ludwig Lindemann and the rest of the 26th Volksgrenadier Division, the night of the fifteenth was the last opportunity to move
troops and equipment to the jump-off points. While Lindemann and his
company made their precombat inspections, *Oberst* Kokott came down to the
river to oversee the final preparations. Kokott felt the sting of the wind as
he checked the status of his troops moving through the forests of the Eifel.
Some of the unpaved roads were barely drivable due to the onset of ice, while
the darkness of night further hampered efforts to move the men and weapons of war. To prevent the Allies from detecting the movement of heavy
equipment, Kokott authorized his artillery to fire the occasional artillery barrage to drown out the sound of the revving vehicle engines. His tactic worked.

At this point, most of grenadiers were unaware of where exactly they
were going. As soldiers do, they followed orders, trusting their officers and
moving along the paths in a disciplined manner. They were good soldiers,
thought Kokott. Still, as vehicles, men, and horses jockeyed for position
along the narrow, winding roads, accidents happened, and congestion became an issue. The result was controlled chaos, but despite the massive number of men and matériel and the ever-present intermittent shelling from
the Allies, few casualties occurred. Later in the evening, most of the units
were in position at their specified time. While they waited for the next day,
the individual company commanders informed their men of the great gamble as they read a message from Field Marshal Gerd von Rundstedt.[35]

"Soldiers of the Western Front! Your great hour has arrived. Large attacking armies have started against the Anglo-Americans. I do not have to
tell you more than that. You feel it yourself. We gamble everything! You can
carry with you the holy obligation to give everything to achieve things beyond human possibilities for our Fatherland and our führer!"[36]

The soldiers received the news stoically, but without reservation. They
knew what Germany was demanding of them, and they were ready for the
task. Their morale and esprit de corps was excellent, and Kokott was confident that his division would succeed in its tasks. The spirit was becoming
infectious, even to many of the tired foot soldiers who had previously been
dubious of German victory.

Lindemann agreed, recalling, "Yes, in December 1944 I thought it was
a good idea to fight this battle and to win the war."[37]

The previous evening, Kokott had his staff move the division headquarters closer to the front, to a town called Herbstmuehle. From there, he could
direct the actions of his regiments more efficiently. At the same time, outposts

along the forward edge of the battle area screened the movements of the 77th and 39th regiments as they inched their way toward their final attack positions before the great artillery barrage. Kokott read over the final reports as he thought about the days ahead. It was all or nothing for Germany. They won, and they would deal a devastating blow to the Anglo-American alliance. They lost, and the war was lost. He knew that even though he drifted into skepticism, he would do his part. His division was ready to do its part for the Fatherland, and he would not let his men down. He wondered whether the Americans, across the way, would fight just as hard.[38]

"Lutz" Lindemann, however, had much more immediate concerns, as he and his men crept down to the banks of the chilly Our River. He wanted to be warm tonight. It was midnight, and it had started to drizzle. This added to Lindemann's general misery.

He looked around at his men. There was a sprinkling of surviving veterans like him who had made it this far in the war, having survived the dreaded Eastern Front. Unfortunately, there were even more of the younger men, brand-new conscripts from the *Heimat* (homeland). Here and there, a new face—previously a member of the emasculated Kriegsmarine (German navy) or Luftwaffe ground crew forced into the Wehrmacht.

"Many were ersatz [replacement] soldiers and were from flak [antiaircraft crews], naval, [and] excess personnel from the Luftwaffe," Lindemann recalled.[39]

Sadly, these men were proof that Hitler was indeed scraping the bottom of the barrel for everything he could throw into this massive effort. Many of these men had been handed a rifle, given rudimentary training as a soldier, and transferred without choice into the 26th.

Lindemann was much happier to see that his men had been well supplied. They wore white camouflage snowsuits, and most of them were armed with the new Sturmgewehr 44 assault rifles—the latest deadly surprise from Hitler's bag of tricks. Ammunition seemed plentiful, warm food was in their bellies, and there floated a certain excitement in the air, as if the victorious ghosts of 1940's blitzkrieg were surrounding them.

The same could not be said for many of the other German regiments and divisions tasked with supporting the great offensive. Several divisions of Volksgrenadiers were supplied with bicycles. Bullets, grenades, bombs, and artillery shells were rationed. Even captured equipment, including obsolete French, Italian, Russian, and Polish war materials, was used. In some panzer units trucks had to stand in for half-tracks or even tanks.

The engineers in Lindemann's unit had already erected a makeshift bridge from rafts and planks to span the river, which allowed the grenadiers to file across it. Once they were on the other side, Lindemann marched with his company westward toward a valley just east of Hosingen. By 0300, they had reached their assault positions. The entire company went into the prone position on the damp earth and waited for the opening artillery barrage to signal the beginning of the offensive. A remorseless chill gripped them as they waited like runners, straining in the starting blocks and waiting for the gun to go off.[40]

0530 hours, Saturday, 16 December 1944
77th Volksgrenadier area of operations
Opposite the town of Hosingen, along the Our River

All was set for Hitler's great offensive in the west. German Volksgrenadiers, panzer crews, artillery gunners, and engineers waited for the word to attack on the east bank of the Our. Some had even moved to the west bank in rubber boats and across rope bridges, getting the jump start on their assault positions near many vacant American forward observation posts. The artillery gunners had laid their barrels on their primary targets along the west bank, calibrating their first targets on hastily folded maps and opening the breeches of the 105mm howitzers. Meanwhile, nearby heavy mortar crews elevated their tubes skyward. Everything seemed to be going to plan. As predicted by the meteorologists, the sky was cloudy and would be an ally of Germany that day, grounding Allied airpower. Down on the earth below, the officers stared at stopwatches as the minutes clicked down to seconds: 10 . . . 9 . . . 8 . . . 7 . . . 6 . . . 5 . . . 4 . . . 3 . . . 2 . . . 1 . . . 0530 . . . *Feuer!*[41]

Suddenly night became day, as man-made thunder and lightning crashed and roared across the desolate winter landscape like a hurricane making landfall. Loaders shoved round after round into the breeches of the guns, while the gunners yanked the lanyard with each pass. Like a metallic mule, the barrel of each gun would kick back, and then return to its former position as the soldiers loaded still another shell. On the western side of the Our River, Volksgrenadiers crouched in their foxholes while the rounds whistled over their heads, relieved they were not on the receiving end of such a tempest of steel. In the sector of the 26th Volksgrenadier Division, a chorus of three hundred guns boomed their refrain, while the American side responded with only muted surprise. There would be no duet this morning.

To add to the maelstrom of confusion, the German soldiers switched on the antiaircraft searchlights. This effect created a cathedral of light as their rays bounced off the clouds above them and illuminated the ground below, providing the first waves of assault infantry with much-needed light. The initial barrage lasted seventeen long minutes, and then the guns fell silent. During the cannonade, the assault teams in both divisions had rushed from their starting positions to their next phase line. There, they waited. Forward observers, moving with the assault companies, radioed back to the fire direction centers that the initial waves had reached their first phase line. Then the next barrage opened up, this time lasting another ten minutes—ten minutes that provided enough time for most of the assault teams to infiltrate between the American positions.[42] These positions fell quickly and effortlessly.

Lindemann recalled the attack early the next morning as the German offensive in the Ardennes kicked off with a roar:

"Around 0530 artillery and *nebelwerfers* [rocket launchers] fired for about half an hour. We were woken up at 0600 and our company was ordered to march to engage the enemy. Our goal was to take over Hosingen."

Lindemann and his company then moved out. Each man slunk forward, hoping that his next tentative step did not trigger an American antipersonnel mine. They had lost track of their engineers who were supposed to clear the minefields they all thought were out there, becoming separated from them during the approach march. It did not matter, as the Americans had failed to mine this particular dismounted avenue of approach. As Lindemann closed in on Hosingen, he could make out the various buildings and, in particular, the water tower that dominated the skyline. When they reached the southern edge of town, several American soldiers appeared wearing only their undergarments. Before Lindemann and his men could react, the surprised GIs bolted off into the murky darkness through a garden. The grenadiers halted after this incident and waited for orders. They had already achieved their morning's objectives.

After several hours, Lindemann's company then moved westward toward the next town. His company had sustained only a few casualties in the initial assault, and the great counteroffensive was proceeding according to plan. Lindemann could not have known on December 16 what lay ahead at Bastogne. On Christmas morning, he would find out.[43]

CHAPTER TWO

"I Don't Think This Is a Feint."

"We should (not) leave a vast extent of fertile country to be despoiled and ravaged by the enemy, from which they would draw vast supplies and where many of our firm friends would be exposed to all the miseries of the most insulting and wanton depredation. A train of evil might be enumerated; these considerations make it indispensably necessary for the army to take such a position."

—George Washington, writing about his choice for the location of the Continental Army quarters at Valley Forge, 1777[1]

2030 hours, Saturday, 16 December 1944
Headquarters of U.S. Army VIII Corps, Heinz Barracks
Bastogne, Belgium

Major General Troy H. Middleton, the U.S. VIII Corps commander, certainly didn't look like a general. In fact, with his shock of pepper-gray hair and his horn-rimmed glasses, he looked more like a small-town doctor. His looks were deceiving, though. Middleton's corps had played an important part in the Allied breakout from Normandy and subsequent drive through France. By December, Middleton had three divisions resting and refitting on the frontier of Germany: the 28th, 4th, and 106th infantry divisions. Both the 28th and 4th had suffered horrendous casualties in the Battle of Hürtgen

Forest, while the 106th was a green division, newly arrived from the States. Middleton also had half of one armored division, the 9th, in reserve. Unbeknownst to him, the Germans had chosen his area of operations to launch a major counteroffensive.[2]

The morning and afternoon of the sixteenth, Middleton had spent much of his time in his tactical operations center (TOC) in Bastogne, the center of his corps area of responsibility. He had established his headquarters at the Heinz army barracks on the northern outskirts of town. Like many barracks, the Belgian buildings were austere affairs, constructed of dour sandstone and dull mountain-red bricks. Their previous occupants had been the Wehrmacht, and evidence in the form of painted Wehrmacht signs and unit symbols on the walls still abounded in several of the structures. Middleton had set up his TOC in one of the two-story buildings, located in the eastern end of the complex. Unlike the rest of the barracks, the building looked like an administration building—a fitting place for a corps staff.[3]

When the German offensive kicked off that morning, Middleton telephoned all his division commanders to get situation reports. As information came into his headquarters, the telephone lines on the switchboard buzzed with activity, and his staff handed him update after update. He and his staff continued this routine throughout the day and into the night.[4]

Middleton was closely monitoring the situation with his 28th Infantry Division. The "Keystone" Division, as they were known, was apparently being hit hard by the initial German attacks. At first, the news coming out of the 28th's sector was not serious. Middleton was more concerned with his green division, the 106th, to the north, which was also under enormous pressure. Around 1840 hours that night, the corps commander issued Sitrep (situation report) 505 to his division units and to his higher headquarters, First Army. In it, he passed on reports from his faltering 28th, which reported German units west of the Our River.

The complete picture, though, was still vague. The Allies had gone into December considering any German strategic offensive unlikely. For Middleton, the initial news indicated a large spoiling attack to upset Allied offensive operations like Patton's Third Army offensive to the south. Still, the size of the attack against his regiments in the 28th's sector was troubling: The 3rd Battalion of the 112th Infantry Regiment reported the enemy attack in their sector to number around three battalions, giving the Germans three-to-one odds.[5]

Staring at the map in his command center, Middleton wondered what the Germans were up to. An intelligence officer handed him his answer. A report found on a dead German officer showed the 116th Panzer Division was planning to capture St. Vith today and Bastogne tomorrow. To make this attack, the Germans had massed three panzer divisions in the central part of Belgium. The Germans were out to secure two major towns in Belgium, and probably points beyond. With this new information, Middleton realized this must be more than just a mere spoiling attack.[6]

Deep in thought, Middleton traced his finger along a line on the map. It was all becoming very clear now. If this was a German offensive, he had to slow it down so that SHAEF (Supreme Headquarters Allied Expeditionary Force) had time to send in reinforcements. Middleton realized his corps area was about to become the eye of the proverbial hurricane. The Germans had picked a good spot to mass their forces. Because supreme allied command thought this sector was "quiet," Middleton was defending an eighty-eight-mile front with only three infantry divisions and half an armored division.[7]

Now, if he didn't act soon, the Germans would have the full advantage of hitting unprepared units all up and down his line. Middleton dictated his orders to his alert staff scribes. He wanted it crystal clear that none of his divisional and regimental commanders were to withdraw unless their positions had become completely untenable. Looking at the map, he traced an imaginary line that bisected the towns of Holzheim, Setz, Maspelt, Bockholz, Colmar, and Wecker. The Germans must not be allowed to cross this line. If they did, they would be able to break out on the plains to the west of the Ardennes and tear freely toward Antwerp or Brussels.

"These towns will be held at all costs," he told his staff. The six communities stretched along a line several kilometers west of the Our River.[8]

On his operations map, two larger towns stood out. One was St. Vith, which was the road hub behind the 106th Infantry Division, and, more important, Bastogne, the location of his own headquarters. These were the two towns that intelligence had revealed were targeted by the Germans to be overrun tomorrow. Middleton knew the twin towns would soon become decisive terrain. He knew he had to hold them no matter the cost. If he held them, he might be able to bog down the entire German offensive, since both towns controlled the road networks east of the Meuse—likely the reason the Germans wanted them so soon. In his own sector, it was glaringly obvious from the map that Bastogne lay directly in the path of the German advance. Middleton clenched his jaw. *I would sacrifice a division to hold Bastogne*, he thought grimly. Having made up his mind, Middleton needed approval from his higher headquarters. More important, he had to find a division to sacrifice. Luckily for him, his bosses were thinking some of the same things.[9]

16–18 December 1944
Area of operations, U.S. Army VIII Corps
Northern Luxembourg/southern Belgium

Prior to late 1944, no one could have guessed the crossroads town of Bastogne would play such a crucial role in the war for Europe. In medieval times, Bastogne was the center of religious and economic matters in the pastoral Luxembourg province of Walloon. Numerous abbeys and monasteries dotted the rolling hills and fields about the town. Every Sunday, the tolling of bells in local churches brought the nearby farmers and their families to worship from the outlying towns.

By the 1200s, the Holy Roman Emperor Henry VII authorized the minting of coins in Bastogne. In 1332, his son, known as John I (John the Blind) of Bohemia, built defensive walls around the heart of Bastogne, part of which, known as the Porte de Trèves, can still be seen today. In 1602, John the Blind's construction efforts were appreciated by the populace, as the walls helped repel a Dutch invasion.

As a typical European feudal center, the quiet town became well-known for hosting cattle fairs during the sixteenth century. By the eighteenth and nineteenth centuries, roads and railway lines spider-legged out from Bastogne as the town's economy surpassed that of her neighbors. Even during its occupation by the Germans during World War I, Bastogne's population continued to grow and prosper right up until after the Great War.

On May 10, 1940, the Germans captured the city at the start of the blitzkrieg that swept through France and the Low Countries. For the duration of the war, the population of Bastogne endured Nazi occupation, most of her 3,500-some citizens waiting for the promise of Allied liberation. American forces liberated the town in September of 1944. Many of the Bastognards (as they call themselves) considered themselves lucky that the fortunes of war had spared their town. In December, their luck changed.[10]

After the war, German General Fritz Bayerlein commented, "Bastogne was a particularly indispensable point for German supplies, as a traffic hub and staging point. . . . A glance at the map is sufficient for someone with no military training to realize that Bastogne was vital for the offensive."[11]

The town was one of the largest urban areas directly in the path of Fifth Panzer Army's advance. Certainly von Manteuffel's tanks would be dependent on a firm road network in order for *Wacht am Rhein* to move quickly, especially in winter. Hitler and his commanders knew that control of the crossroads town would prove vital to keep the drive toward Antwerp intact.

Unfortunately for the Germans, almost immediately things started to go wrong for von Lüttwitz's XXXXVII Panzer Corps. According to Bayerlein, the dogged defense of the towns of Hosingen and Holzthum by the U.S. 28th Infantry Division stymied the German plans to capture Bastogne early—in one fell stroke. In fact, Bayerlein estimated the defenders of Hosingen had delayed his Panzer Lehr Division thirty-six crucial hours. Due to the fight put up by the Americans, the Germans' carefully calculated timetable was already starting to unravel.[12]

The Germans knew the work of the 28th would be in vain if VIII Corps, their higher headquarters, could not send them reinforcements. The next few hours would determine whether Bastogne would fall suddenly or through a protracted siege. That evening, the men on both sides who would decide the fate of Bastogne made the first of many difficult decisions.

Late afternoon to evening, Saturday, 16 December 1944
SHAEF (Supreme Headquarters Allied Expeditionary Force), Trianon Palace hotel
Versailles, France

Bastogne had been lucky. The war had wrecked many of the ancient cities of Europe, forever changing the landscape and history of the centers of Western civilization. Another, larger population center—the city of Versailles—had also survived two of the most cataclysmic wars in modern times. Amazingly, the early years of World War II had spared most of the city, as if God had deemed its fate too important to be left to the whims of capricious and vain men. As a result, the palaces of the Bourbons remained inviolate, even though much of France now lay in ruins.

Not far from the palace grounds was the Trianon Palace hotel, which housed General Dwight D. Eisenhower's (SHAEF) headquarters. Ike had chosen well. The hotel was a magnificent and luxurious edifice that was one of the finest buildings of Versailles, as if it were one of Louis XIV's own palaces. It opened in 1910, and during the First World War it served as a hospital. At the beginning of World War II, the Royal Air Force had turned it into their headquarters. When France fell, the victorious Nazis found the

British tastes agreeable, and the Luftwaffe became the new owners of the Trianon hotel. However, their tenancy was short-lived, and in 1944 the Allies returned, and this time it was the Americans and British who moved into the Trianon Palace. One of them was the supreme commander of all Allied forces in Europe, General Eisenhower.

That late afternoon, as Eisenhower stared out the window of his office in the Trianon, cold and gray weather blanketed the skies and the city below. The clouds and rain had grounded the Allied air forces. Without the crucial daily reconnaissance flights, the Allies were somewhat blind to Hitler's wild intentions.

Eisenhower's subordinate General Omar Bradley, the Commander of Twelfth Army Group, had visited Trianon to discuss infantry replacement issues. The two had just started conversing when a staff officer arrived with a disturbing announcement. The Germans had launched attacks at various parts of the VII Corps and V Corps sectors in the Ardennes, in some areas penetrating the American lines completely.[13]

After reviewing the initial information, Eisenhower saw clearly that the Germans were on the offensive. "This is no local attack," Eisenhower quickly surmised. "This could be a major counteroffensive or a feint to attract our attention elsewhere. Brad?"

Bradley answered, "I don't think it's a feint. Where would he hit us besides the Ardennes? Everywhere else we're pretty strong."

Eisenhower nodded in agreement. "I think you're right. . . . No, I think this is it. The Germans came out of here in 1940 and kicked the British off the continent, and now it looks like von Rundstedt is trying to repeat his earlier success." While he spoke, Eisenhower kept tapping the location of the Ardennes on a map with his finger.[14]

That evening, most of his subordinate commanders had no idea the Germans had unleashed a major offensive. Eisenhower had a feeling that something bigger was up. Instead of waiting for confirmation, Eisenhower seized the initiative and made the decision to commit his strategic reserve and shift several key divisions to the threatened Ardennes sector.

Fortunately, the Allied armies did not operate in the same fashion as the ponderous Wehrmacht. Eisenhower had total authorization to react as he saw fit. After the war, in interviews, many high-ranking Germans in the General Staff did not understand this. They could not foresee how quickly the Allies would react, and as result, there was little the Wehrmacht could do when the massive counterattacks came.[15]

Within no time, Eisenhower rounded up key members of his staff to plan a defense, and possibly a counterstrike to stymie the Nazi incursion. They quickly settled on shifting two armored divisions to support First Army. One was the 7th Armored Division and the other was the 10th Armored Division. The question then arose about the strategic reserve. Ike had only two divisions in it: the 101st and the 82nd Airborne divisions. Both units had seen hard fighting ever since D-day. The supreme commander sighed and shook his head as he stared at the map. He was reluctant to send these two divisions back into harm's way, but he had little choice.

Eisenhower knew both the 82nd "All-Americans" and the 101st "Screaming Eagles" were presently enjoying some downtime at Mourmelon-le-Grand near Reims, France, after bitter fighting in Holland that fall. The two divisions were part of General Matthew Ridgway's XVIII Airborne Corps.[16] After some discussion, Eisenhower decided to release the two airborne divisions to Twelfth Army Group the next morning.[17]

The race for Bastogne had begun.

0800–1800 hours, Sunday, 17 December 1944
Headquarters of the 101st Airborne Division
Mourmelon-le-Grand ("Camp Mourmelon"), France

Even though it was younger than its brother airborne division—the 82nd—the 101st had already gained a reputation for daring and audacity during D-day. That reputation was further enhanced by a sterling combat record in southern Holland in September during the Market Garden operation. Both airborne units had been made up of the cream of the crop, some of the best-trained men in America. By this time, any surviving veterans in both the 82nd or 101st were basically the experienced elite of the U.S. Army in Europe.

During their time at Camp Mourmelon, efforts had been made in the two divisions to inject replacements to make up for casualties from the previous campaigns. For the 101st, many of these "green kids" had yet to become fully integrated into the division prior to their deployment to Bastogne. Although each of the four infantry regiments of the 101st was at 91 percent manpower prior to Bastogne, a lot of these paratroopers were inexperienced soldiers from the "repple depples" (replacement depots for incoming new soldiers).[18]

The 101st consisted of three parachute infantry regiments. Each regiment had roughly 130 officers and 2,200 enlisted men. The regiments were the 501st Parachute Infantry Regiment, the 502nd PIR, and the 506th PIR. In addition, each airborne division carried one glider infantry regiment as its fourth infantry regiment. In this case, the 327th Glider Infantry Regiment (GIR) rounded out the infantry power of the 101st Airborne with its 140 officers and 2,800 enlisted men. The glidermen had the equally hazardous duty of riding to the ground in flimsy gliders as support for the paratroopers in both Normandy and Holland. In fact, one battalion of the 327th was carried over from an earlier regiment: the 401st. Since the "glider riders" (as they called themselves) of the first battalion of the 401st still held a significant amount of loyalty to their old regiment, they were typically referred to by their original designation.[19]

Once SHAEF made the decision to release the airborne units, it took several hours for the first warning order to reach the two divisional headquarters as the communiqué slowly wound its way down through the various chains of command. The 101st's G3, or operations officer, was Lieutenant Colonel Harry W. O. Kinnard. He was one of the first to learn the Screaming Eagles were moving out. He had received his initial instructions at 0800 hours the morning of the seventeenth, when the acting division commander, Brigadier General Anthony McAuliffe, got a phone call from the staff of the XVIII Airborne Corps telling him to prepare for an immediate departure to join Middleton's VIII Corps in the Ardennes. The news came as a shock to the usually calm and austere McAuliffe—a major enemy offensive had kicked off, and his troops were now some of the only Allied reserves to throw at the swelling German tide.

The biggest problem was that the 101st's commanding officer, Major General Maxwell B. Taylor, was in Washington, D.C., at the time to discuss organizational changes in the division. Moreover, Brigadier General Gerald J. Higgins (Taylor's assistant division commander) was also away in England, providing an after-action review of the Holland operation. It turned out that McAuliffe, previously the divisional artillery commander, was next in the 101st's chain of command.[20]

As the day dragged on, Harry Kinnard tried to disguise his knowledge of the impending deployment. Other than McAuliffe and the chief of staff, Lieutenant Colonel Ned D. Moore, no one else on the staff knew about the order. The staff officers were all on pass or attending various Christmas parties that day.

Harry Kinnard, twenty-nine, was young for a lieutenant colonel. His boyish face made him seem more so, and now he was the chief operations officer for a division that numbered more than twelve thousand men. Like many of his fellow officers, Kinnard was a West Pointer, and was only five years out from graduation. His clean-cut Boy Scout countenance hid his true strengths, which were a talent for planning and a brilliant organizational mind. His skills surpassed many of his older peers. He would need all of them today.[21]

Not all of the senior officers were completely in the dark. Kinnard's close friend and roommate, Lieutenant Colonel Paul A. Danahy, suspected something was going on. That was a good thing, since Colonel Danahy was the G2, or chief intelligence officer, for the 101st. Like a good spook, Danahy had kept his ear to the ground when the first reports started to filter down about recent German activity. At that point Danahy started collecting and reviewing the incoming information. Like Kinnard, Danahy was only twenty-nine years old, but unlike Kinnard, Danahy had been a civilian before the war. He was an Irishman from Buffalo, New York, and like many civilians-turned-soldiers in World War II, army rules did not agree with him. Despite his disdain for military regulations, Danahy was respected because he was gifted at intelligence work.[22]

At 1800 hours that night, during the evening Christmas party, Colonel Moore relayed to Danahy that General McAuliffe wanted to see him. Danahy reported straightaway to "General Mac." The acting commander's beetle brows furrowed as he peppered Danahy with questions about the Germans in the Ardennes. Danahy gradually spilled the beans that he had been collecting information about recent German movements there. Danahy explained that a German offensive had kicked off in an area where the Americans had only three and a half divisions. In addition, Troy Middleton's VIII Corps headquarters at Bastogne lay directly in the path of the German attack—if the Germans got that far. McAuliffe quietly nodded while Danahy briefed him on what he knew, which, at the time, was not a great deal.

After Danahy finished the skimpy intelligence dump, a somewhat preoccupied McAuliffe waved him away and told him to go back to the party. Danahy knew McAuliffe had plenty to think about. One question nagged him, though. Danahy wondered why his boss was so concerned with VIII Corps; after all, the 101st did not belong to General Middleton's corps.[23]

McAuliffe traveled back to his office that afternoon to plan for the divisional move-out. He was concerned, and struggling with the fact that not all of the 101st were at Mourmelon. Officers and enlisted men were scattered to and fro. Many soldiers were on leave. Some were hopping Paris nightclubs, or enjoying the attractions of the famed Pig Alley, as a generation of doughboys had done during the previous war.[24] GIs were excited that the war seemed to have paused for the moment, and took advantage of the lull in anticipation of the holidays. After all, Marlene Dietrich was visiting Belgium courtesy of the USO. It was even rumored that Glenn Miller, the noted band leader and Army Air Force captain, would be flying over from London to Paris for a special pre-Christmas concert. Some were conducting more mundane tasks, such as doing a little seasonal shopping for the family back home. It would become a huge effort to gather up these men away on leave. Many would have to be rounded up by jeeps scouring the streets. As a last-ditch effort, any troopers wearing the All-American or the Screaming Eagle patches would be rounded up by the MPs and brought in forcibly, if need be.[25]

Afternoon to evening, Sunday, 17 December 1944
Army/Army Air Force football game at Army Air Force base
Nancy, France

Not far from Camp Mourmelon was the French town of Nancy. Here, many of the Screaming Eagles were playing their annual divisional football game, a friendly if sometimes rough game against an Army Air Corps unit. The rivalry was tremendous within the U.S. Army, and many of the division's troopers had made the long ride to the air base just to watch and cheer on some of the more athletically inclined Screaming Eagles.

If there was one man in the division who knew football, it was Captain Wallace A. Swanson. "Swannie," as he was affectionately called by the men who served under him, was commander of Able Company of the 502nd. A large, stocky man, he had been raised on football, growing up in farm country near Sharon Springs, Kansas. At twenty-four years of age he had already completed an illustrious college career playing for Kansas State University. He had even been offered a contract with the Philadelphia Eagles after graduation, but had turned it down to pursue a career as an army officer. The military, though, could not ignore his talent. Swanson had been ordered to play on the Eastern Armed Forces All-Star football team in 1942. During that time, the AF team was a sort of short-lived NFL division that drew players from all branches of the military. Swanson remembered:

"After training for five weeks, with grueling two-a-day practices, we played three pro teams in eight days. We won two, lost to the Chicago Bears seven to zero. Then the team disbanded and we all returned to our separate units."

Football had left Swanson in peak physical shape and taught him about leadership. Shortly after marrying his sweetheart, Thelma Jeanne Combs, at Fort Bragg, North Carolina, Swanson was deployed to England. Swanson was made company commander in the 502nd and kept busy preparing his men for the anticipated invasion of Nazi-held France. He cut his combat teeth during the night jump on D-day and in bloody fighting by the 101st at the Norman town of Foucarville. Swanson had even been momentarily captured by some Germans, but during a truce in the fight was luckily freed by his captors. Action in Holland had also earned him accolades from his superiors for his leadership and decisiveness.

On Sunday afternoon, Swanson was at Nancy acting as the division's coach, trainer, and manager of the football team. He remembered the game was just wrapping up and the paratroopers had won by a touchdown or two.[26]

"We knew something was up," Swanson recounted. "The game was at an air corps base, and some of our fighter planes came in low, giving what we thought were victory rolls."[27]

During the football game, one of Swanson's star players, a strapping, twenty-four-year-old sergeant in C Company of the 502nd, noticed that several of the Army Air Corps's best players had suddenly left. Growing annoyed, Ohio-born Sergeant Layton Black Jr. heard call after call blare over the base loudspeakers, repeatedly interrupting the game.

"I played my heart out, and the game was going fast and furiously when suddenly the loudspeaker system we were using for our game would blast out a call for 'Major so-and-so,' 'Captain so-and-so,' 'Lieutenant this,' and 'Corporal that,' saying, 'You are to report to your squadron at once. On the double!'"

Black and the other 101st players exchanged quizzical looks in the huddle as players left the field and subs were brought in. "Coach Swanson called me over to him so he could tell me something. I knelt on one knee next to the coach, who was squatting by the sideline on our side of the field. He started to show me something on his clipboard when suddenly the lights went out for me!"

Black had been slammed into the ground by an opposing player. Briefly unconscious, he finally came to and, wobbly, walked back up to Swanson.

Black, who had been caught with his helmet off by a cheap shot from behind, had a broken nose and a bloody face. Swanson took one look at Black and ordered him sidelined and to be checked by the medic.

After the game, Black got caught up in the postgame celebration. The generous Army Air Force personnel wined and dined the 101st players. Pretty French girls were brought in from Nancy. Dancing and drinking went on all evening. Later, Black and some comrades collapsed in the upstairs bunks of a barracks at the base. He awoke to voices downstairs.

"'Hey, down there!' Black yelled. 'What's going on? Anything we ought to know about up here?'

"'Who in the hell are those guys upstairs?' someone replied.

"'They are those football players from the 101st Airborne, our paratroopers,' another said.

"'Paratroopers? 101st Airborne? They have been put on alert. Haven't they left yet? Go wake them up! They have got to get back to their camp!'"[28]

Black had a feeling his hangover was about to get a lot worse.

2100 hours, Sunday, 17 December 1944
Briefing room, headquarters of the 101st Airborne Division
Mourmelon, France

"All I know of the situation is that there has been a breakthrough and we have got to get up there," Brigadier General Anthony McAuliffe announced to his staff and regimental commanders, pointing to a spot on a map near the Ardennes Forest. Once again the Screaming Eagles would be going into combat, but this time they would ride into war on the back of trucks instead of leaping from planes. Their original orders were simple: Proceed to Werbomont and join up with VIII Corps to stop the German advance.[29]

As soon as he made the official announcement, McAuliffe was firing off questions, asking for status updates from each of his regimental commanders in attendance. From the information they shared, McAuliffe felt he had waited as long as he could to gather as many paratroopers and glidermen and bring them back to Mourmelon. He could no longer wait for those who were still stuck somewhere on leave. He didn't have time.

McAuliffe had concluded that the best way to move out was as regimental combat teams. With the reported speed of the German advance, it was highly possible his men would have to fight the moment they arrived. At the end of the briefing, McAuliffe chose a group of men from each regiment to be part of an advance party with Colonel C. D. Renfro as the commander. Their job was to take off immediately and hunt down the best forward assembly areas for each regiment. Danahy would also be on that team, McAuliffe decided. It would be a good idea to have his intelligence chief there to feel out the situation and have a report ready for when he arrived.[30]

For years, McAuliffe had wanted a division command, and now he had one. Unlike some of his peers, McAuliffe had missed out on serving in the American Expeditionary Force in World War I, having just graduated from West Point when the war ended. Like many army officers, he languished during the interwar years. In 1941, he was working at the Pentagon in the field of weapons development. When the United States entered WWII, McAuliffe transferred to the 101st to serve as the commander for its artillery. In fact, at the age of forty-six, he was older than General Taylor by three years, and sometimes referred to himself as "Old Crock" in front of his younger subordinates. Now, with the absence of General Taylor, the "Old Crock" would be leading the division back to combat on its most important mission of the war.[31]

McAuliffe would rely heavily on his regimental commanders. Luckily, most of them had served as battalion commanders in Normandy and Holland.[32] One of those regimental commanders was Lieutenant Colonel Steven A. Chappuis (pronounced "Chap-wee"), who commanded the 502nd Parachute Infantry Regiment.

At thirty years old, Chappuis was one of the youngest regimental commanders in the airborne. A Louisiana native and graduate of the prestigious military school at Louisiana State University, Chappuis had grown up in a hardworking Cajun family near the town of Rayne. Growing up in a farming family during the Great Depression was a struggle in itself. Because of the hardscrabble times, the entire Chappuis clan—including all six siblings—worked days and nights on the family rice and cotton farm. Incredibly, through scrimping and saving, his parents had managed to send all of the children on to college. It was this hard, sacrificial start to life that forged Chappuis' quiet, hardworking, and austere personality.[33]

At LSU, Chappuis became interested in the military life. As were many Depression-era young men who joined the military or civilian work programs, Chappuis was happy to have a roof over his head, regular work, camaraderie, and three square meals a day at LSU. He fell into the ordered life easily and, as a quick-learning cadet, never received a demerit. Ironically, his ROTC commandant during this time was none other than Troy Middleton.

In 1936, Chappuis graduated with a second lieutenant's commission, through a federal program called the Thomason Act that helped ROTC grads become commissioned quickly in the regular army. With war breaking out in Asia, and the threat of war in Europe, the U.S. Army was pushing to expand the ranks with young officers like Chappuis.

The lanky Louisianan was transferred to lackluster posts at Fort Sam Houston in Texas, Fort Huachuca in Arizona, and even Schofield Barracks in Hawaii within just a few short years. Chappuis was ordered back to the States after the Japanese attack on Pearl Harbor. Shortly after that infamous day, he volunteered for the airborne. Soon he found himself heading to the European theater.

Just prior to D-day, Chappuis was eventually promoted to command 2nd Battalion of the 502nd and won praise from his regimental commander at that time, Lieutenant Colonel John H. "Iron Mike" Michaelis.[34] When Michaelis was wounded in Holland in September, Chappuis took over as regimental commander.

"Steven was very smart and down to earth," his youngest brother, Charles, mentioned in an interview years later. "He was more of thinker and doer, not a talker. For one thing, even after the war was over he didn't want to talk about it," Charles Chappuis added.[35]

Perhaps Chappuis felt a bit uneasy being thrust into the role of regimental commander just before Bastogne. Nevertheless, Chappuis' rock-solid calm was just what the 502nd needed. He had earned a reputation in the 101st as a steady and dependable regimental leader. At the same time, some of the more extroverted officers of the 101st called him "Silent Steve." At one point during the siege, Kinnard, who knew Chappuis, decided he should clue in McAuliffe and his staff before it was too late:

"If Chappuis says he's in trouble, you'd better believe it and do something about it fast, because Silent Steve will be in real big trouble and he won't call back to tell you again."[36]

As he listened to General McAuliffe brief the upcoming operation, Chappuis lived up to his nickname, his mind already quietly planning. His regiment had been on the line for more than seventy days in Holland. When they arrived in Mourmelon, he had to absorb the replacements. Luckily, Chappuis and his company commanders had thrown together several days of individual training to help incorporate the new arrivals. This included lots of familiarization with their new command structure and heavy weapons. The hard work would reap huge dividends later.[37]

While McAuliffe spoke with his commanders at the end of the briefing, he failed to notice a short, cocky lieutenant colonel. The man's name was John T. Cooper Jr., the commanding officer of the 463rd Parachute Field Artillery Battalion, a unit that had just recently been sent to Mourmelon to rest and refit with the 101st. Unknown to many of the Screaming Eagles, Cooper's outfit was a blooded veteran battalion. The unit had seen intense combat in Italy, supporting and parachuting into Sicily with the 509th PIR and the First Special Service Force (the famous "Devil's Brigade"). The unit had also fought in the recent invasion of southern France. Now the unit was simply marking time until they would join up with the new 17th Airborne Division, which would soon be arriving in the ETO from stateside.

Many of the 101st paratroopers assumed the 463rd, which had arrived five days earlier, was just a bunch of green newbies from the States. The troopers of the 463rd, trained to parachute into battle with their 75mm M1 Pack howitzers broken down and parachuted in parts, were too proud to make much of a fuss about the issue. If the 101st boys wanted to think they were a bunch of rookies, then so be it.

As a matter of fact, Cooper had been in a discussion several days before at the mess hall with two 101st officers, Lieutenant Colonel Harry W. Elkins, the commander of the 377th Parachute Field Artillery Battalion, and Edward L. Carmichael, the commander of the 321st Glider Field Artillery Battalion. Both men, veteran artillery officers in their own right, were skeptical that a little 75mm Pack howitzer could take out a German tank. In a humble tone, Cooper told the crowd at the table that his unit had done just that at Biazza Ridge in Sicily, knocking out several panzer tanks. Cooper was immediately scoffed at and told, "The general [McAuliffe] said you could not knock out a tank with a 75mm pack. You could disable one if you got a lucky hit on a track, but not knock one out."

Now Cooper watched the frenetic commotion and shook his head. This whole situation was a mess, he thought to himself, and he was not terribly impressed with the 101st up to this point. His "red legs" (the traditional nickname of the artillery, due to the red-striped pants they wore in the Civil

War) would have called this a snafu, or "situation normal, all fucked-up." He was not surprised that McAuliffe had forgotten about his parachute artillery battalion. He decided to reintroduce himself, and knocked on McAuliffe's door and waited. Colonel Thomas L. Sherburne, who was the acting commander of the division artillery, answered the door and immediately recognized Cooper. McAuliffe was sitting behind his desk, signing forms for the move-out. The three discussed a possible course of action for the 463rd. McAuliffe scratched his chin in frustration and finally told Cooper, "I wish I could take you, as the 327th needs a direct support battalion."

That was all there was to it, and a disheartened Cooper left the room.

By design, each regiment of an airborne division was supposed to have an artillery battalion to support it. (Either the glider-landed M3 105mm "snub-nosed" howitzers, or the para-dropped M1 75mm Packs). At that time, the 327th Glider Infantry Regiment was the only regiment in the division that was lacking this support. Cooper quickly held an officers' call with the leaders of the 463rd, asking whether they wanted to be a part of the move-out of the 101st, or wait around indefinitely in Mourmelon to be reassigned. Cooper and his men figured the 101st was a veteran division, and the 17th was not. At the end of that evening, the overwhelming vote was to go with McAuliffe's men. If any man could finagle a way, it would be Cooper—he was too determined to give up at this point.[38]

Cooper left his men and made for the barracks of the 327th. Cooper and his cannon-cockers of the 463rd didn't yet know it, but even as tagalongs, they would play a pivotal role in the defense of Bastogne.

Morning, Monday, 18 December 1944
Army Air Corps barracks
Nancy, France

Layton Black could not believe they were back on alert. He looked at his watch and it was only minutes after midnight, early Monday morning. Other than a random voice, no one had officially alerted them. Sergeant Black and the other NCOs and officers then decided to send someone over to the local officers' club to find out what was really going on.

When the sergeant returned, he was mobbed. The NCO pushed them back and waved his hands in a downward motion to signal silence.

After several seconds, the men stopped speaking and the lone NCO reported: "We NCOs are to stay where we are for the night. Yes, there has been a German breakthrough. But it is way up north in a place called the Ardennes. Go back to sleep, because we are to move out early in the morning for Camp Mourmelon."

Another voice from the crowd then piped up: "What about the German paratroopers being dropped in the area?" Black was curious about that rumor, too.

The messenger quickly replied, nodding, "Yes, there's an alert along the whole ETO front. Someone said they were dressed like American GIs, and some even thought they might be trying to capture General Ike!"

Black shook his head. German paratroopers—saboteurs dressed like GIs? What the hell was going on?

Black and the small group of 101st football players spent the rest of the night trying to get some sleep. The next morning, the men boarded trucks to head back to Mourmelon and join the rest of the division for mobilization.

Before he left with the officers, Captain Swanson swung by the barracks to give Black and the others an update about the next twenty-four hours. He told them, "The 101st Division has been alerted to move up. Somewhere to the north in the Ardennes there has been a breakthrough. It is big enough to cause Ike to send in his reserves. And just in case you didn't know it, that's what the 101st and 82nd divisions have been since we left Holland, the ETO reserve."

Black could see the growing impatience and frustration in the soldiers' faces. He could see written in their expressions, *Why us?* Apparently Captain Swanson read the same thing.

"Because our two divisions are the *only* reserve. Everyone else is on the line!" And with that, Swanson hopped in a jeep with Colonel Chappuis, who had arrived earlier to collect his officers, brief them, and take them back to Mourmelon.[39]

In the car, Chappuis informed Swanson that the Germans had broken through. They were to report back to Mourmelon, pack up the 502nd, and prepare to move out. Where, Chappuis admitted, he didn't yet know. When Swanson arrived at Mourmelon, he was relieved that his company had started the process of moving out ahead of his arrival. Like good paratroopers, they didn't wait for orders to start moving. They took the initiative and followed their standard operating procedures. That self-sufficiency,

Swanson was proud to say years later, would get them through the terrible days ahead.[40]

Morning to 1800 hours, Monday, 18 December 1944
Marshaling area of the 1/502nd Parachute Infantry Battalion,
101st Airborne Division
Camp Mourmelon-le-Grand, Mourmelon, France

Throughout the day, the division headquarters at Mourmelon was buzzing with activity as McAuliffe oversaw the deployment of his division. Despite Colonel Cooper's misgivings about the apparent lack of organization and direction, the 101st performed a military miracle in how quickly it assembled and was ready to roll. Almost the entire division (close to 12,000 men) would be up and moving east in less than eighteen hours.[41]

The paratroopers of Layton Black's company were not the only ones feeling the heat. Sergeant Charles Verne Asay, a paratrooper in third platoon, A Company, 502nd, was busy trying to round up his squad. He had been raised for five years of his life in an orphanage in Sioux City, Iowa. The upbringing, austere and communal, had taught him to endure hardship and make do with less. Because he was one of the older boys, he was often responsible for getting his siblings and the younger lads dressed and fed. Such a sense of responsibility had led the blond-haired sergeant to quick promotion in the army as squad leader, and some sly jibes from his men for being a "mother hen."

Still, Asay, who had joined the Kansas National Guard in 1940, wasn't satisfied with training recruits at Fort Rucker, Alabama. As soon as he could, Asay transferred to the airborne. In England, Asay entered Able Company as a replacement squad leader, causing a bit of resentment from some of the longer-serving men. All was forgotten, however, after the D-day jump, in which Asay proved his worth as a leader. He jumped eighteenth in his aircraft that deadly night, ensuring that every man in his squad made it out the door safely.

On that fateful December night at Mourmelon, Asay organized his squad, ordering the men to grab whatever gear they could carry. Asay made sure men such as Corporal Willis Fowler, a former peanut farmer from Cordele, Georgia, loaded his heavy .30-caliber machine gun into one of the trucks, along with plenty of boxes of ammo.[42]

Large tractor-trailer trucks, with open trailers, were soon pulling into

Mourmelon in a long, curving line. "Huge trucks, we called them cattle cars, were showing up," Asay described. "[Soon] we all were trucked to the Ardennes."[43]

Asay's fellow troopers continued scouring the camp for supplies. As of December, the infantry regiments in the 101st had not been resupplied with the necessary provisions and war matériel for a big fight. Paratroopers and glidermen searched the camp for anything and everything. Boots, extra blankets, ponchos, helmets, bandoliers of ammo, grenades, bazookas, and machine guns were grabbed up. Paperwork was thrown aside as the regiment hurriedly packed the equipment helter-skelter into any available vehicle. Boxes were thrown onto the open-topped trailer trucks and filled the two-and-a-half-ton GMC trucks. It was concerning to the officers that so little could be found. (Troopers of the 82nd had more time after the Holland fighting to rest and refit, and with a full load of equipment and ammunition were able to start off on their journey a bit earlier.)

Meanwhile, Captain Swanson watched his NCOs like Asay count the men as they loaded onto the trucks. He would be one of the last to hop onto the trailer, because he wanted to make sure no one got left behind. He looked at his watch. It was almost 1800. Just as he was climbing up, an orderly handed him a telegram.

"The telegram stated that my wife, Jeanne, had given birth to our first child, Wallace Jr. He was born on December 13, and I received the telegram on the eighteenth as we were loading out at about six o'clock in the evening," Swanson wrote after the war. "That gave me a whole new outlook on life, how valuable our living and existing in freedom really was."[44]

Swanson took the note and shoved it into his pocket. He looked around at his paratroopers and quietly nodded. Soon the trucks carrying the 502nd Parachute Infantry Regiment rolled out. Many of them would never see Mourmelon again.[45]

Morning to 2130 hours, Monday, 18 December 1944
Marshaling area of the 1/401st Glider Infantry Battalion, 101st Airborne Division
Mourmelon, France

One of the last units to depart Mourmelon was the 1/401st Glider Infantry. Its commander was a veteran officer named Lieutenant Colonel Ray C. Allen.[46] Unlike the paratroopers in the 502nd, who were all volunteers, the soldiers of the 401st were glider riders, and some were even draftees.

Sometimes, in the airborne world, the paratroopers tended to look down on the men who rode into combat in gliders. In reality, the action was as dangerous as jumping from the sky, if not more so. Allen disagreed with those who looked down on the glidermen. He felt he had something to prove. He wanted to make his battalion the best in the 101st.

Unlike his polished peers from West Point, Allen came up through the army the hard way. In 1922, he enlisted as a private in the Texas National Guard. Several years later, he earned a commission as a second lieutenant. In 1941, about a year after President Franklin Delano Roosevelt mobilized the National Guard, Allen transferred over to the Regular Army as a captain. He briefly joined the 82nd as a battalion commander before it became an airborne division. In 1942, when the 82nd gave up some of its units to form the 101st, Allen went with those new units and became the commander of 1st Battalion of the 401st. Now he was leading his tough battalion in its third combat operation of the war.[47]

Allen trained his men hard. As a result, General William Lee, the first division commander of the 101st, declared that the 1/401st performed the best of all the infantry battalions at the Tennessee Maneuvers in 1943. Much to Allen and his glider boys' surprise, they had bested the paratrooper battalions. The 1/401st then went on to participate in D-day and wound up conducting its only glider assault of the war during the liberation of Holland several months later. The men were expecting a much-earned break after spending seventy days in Holland. Unfortunately, the Germans had other ideas.[48]

At the meeting the night before, Allen had been the acting regimental commander, filling in for Colonel Joseph H. "Bud" Harper. Hence, Captain Robert J. MacDonald, the B or Baker Company commander, had stepped up to fill in for Allen to prepare the battalion until Harper returned from England. MacDonald was the senior company commander of the 1/401st and had served in that position throughout all of Normandy and Holland.[49] Like many officers in World War II, MacDonald was relatively young for his rank. At twenty-three years old, he still had some growing to do. Though he was over six feet tall and was a giant compared to his commander, he weighed less than 150 pounds, so he always appeared gaunt and sinewy, like a high school basketball player who wasn't quite used to his new height.[50] Despite MacDonald's appearance, Allen could not have asked for a better temporary replacement than Bob MacDonald.

When Allen told MacDonald about the deployment order the night before, the Baker Company commander shook his head as he went over the numbers. Like the parachute units, their ammunition and supplies were far below the recommended amount for a combat deployment. Worse yet, nearly a quarter of the men were stuck in Paris on pass, including the battalion executive officer—the reason for MacDonald's ascension to temporary command of the battalion. Able Company was missing fully half of its manpower. The men were not notified in time and missed the transport to Belgium. Along with half the company, Able's commander, Captain Taze Huntley, was left behind in Paris. Command of the seventy-seven remaining men was left in the hands of First Lieutenant Howard G. Bowles, the young company executive officer.[51]

MacDonald had to make a snap decision the morning of the eighteenth. The 1/401st was just going to have to go with what they had in personnel and equipment. MacDonald issued his men their instructions: "Carry with you what equipment you came out of Holland with."[52]

One of the troopers in the 1/401st, Private First Class Carmen Gisi, from Orange, New Jersey, was woken up by his sergeant and told there had been a breakthrough. Gisi, known as "Geese" to his buddies, was a rifleman in MacDonald's B Company. He recalled specific orders to pack cold-weather gear as the rest of the glidermen were roused from their beds and given only minutes to pack as much warm clothing as they could scrounge:

"We got as much ammo and gear as we could, and then loaded up in trucks for the drive north to Belgium. I was wearing my long underwear, on top of that, my dress uniform, and on top of that, my combat uniform. Extra socks in my pockets, knit cap, gloves, and I was still freezing."

The men in the barracks grumbled when they heard all passes to Reims and Paris had been canceled. Gisi agreed with the others that the return to combat was disheartening. "Our reaction to this was despair; we had just come out of Holland after seventy-three days of combat. [But] [a]fter we heard about the American troops getting beat up, our attitudes changed."[53]

About a half hour before departure, Colonel Harper finally arrived and relieved Colonel Allen to assume control of the regiment. Harper had been in England with Colonel Robert F. Sink of the 506th when they got the word to return to Mourmelon. The two had quickly hopped on a cross-channel flight, making it back to Mourmelon in the nick of time.[54]

Colonel Cooper, the determined commander of the 463rd PFAB, wouldn't take no for an answer. He continued to search for Colonel Harper, hoping the 327th's commander would agree to take along the 463rd. Harper was already moving his glider fighters out by the truckload when Cooper finally found him.

The roar of ten-ton trucks chugging by forced Cooper to yell in Harper's ear: "Do you need some artillery?"

"Hell, yes, I can use a battalion; just follow my regiment out," Harper replied, smiling at his good fortune.

Cooper had the foresight and cocksure optimism to have ordered the 463rd to hook up its guns and load its ammo and equipment in the trucks the day before. He told Harper he could immediately give the order to his men to head out. Grinning, Cooper walked back to his command vehicle at the head of his convoy. At last, the 463rd might get a chance to show these 101st boys just what they could do.[55]

Before the war, Private First Class Ken Hesler, from Greenup, Illinois, had been a butcher for Kroger's. Now he was a veteran of Dog Battery of the 463rd. Hesler remembered the hubbub that sent so many of the 101st men tearing around the Mourmelon barracks, getting ready to move out.

"We were the 'bastard battalion' in that we were temporarily assigned to different divisions," Hesler recalled later. "We had an advantage moving out, as our ammo trucks were already loaded at Mourmelon. [Compared to the rest of the division] we were well supplied prior to setting out for Bastogne."[56]

The young artilleryman remembered loading up in the rear of a tarp-covered truck driven by an African-American of the famed "Red Ball Express." After years in the army, Hesler had a developed a useful knack for finding a place to sleep or making himself comfortable in almost any situation. This ride was a bit different. Nervously, he and the other troopers noticed the truck was full of five-gallon gasoline cans. For Hesler, it was a night of "fitful sleep with my legs stretched across the gasoline cans."[57]

As they said good-bye to Mourmelon, Hesler and the rest of his battalion watched from their trucks as the 327th Glider Infantry rolled by. At 2130 hours, after the 1/401st had passed, it was their turn, and with a wave of his hand Colonel Cooper led his wayward band of red legs to Belgium.[58]

Within hours of being notified, more than 380 trucks packed with airborne infantry started down the roads toward the Franco-Belgian border. From there, the endless train of vehicles was heading east over the Belgian border to a split at the fork in the main road. The convoy carrying troopers of the 101st snaked its way northward toward Werbomont.

1600 hours to evening, Monday, 18 December 1944
Headquarters, VIII Corps
Bastogne, Belgium

Fred MacKenzie never felt so lucky. As a reporter for the *Buffalo Evening News*, he was the only news correspondent in Bastogne with the 101st Airborne. MacKenzie had worked for several years for the Associated Press in Pittsburgh and the *Pittsburgh Sun-Telegraph*. He had met General McAuliffe several days prior to the news of the German breakthrough at the Scribe Hotel in Paris. Always one with a nose for news, MacKenzie asked to join the 101st at Mourmelon. An amused McAuliffe agreed; having a reporter on board might give the young 101st Airborne some good coverage for the folks back home. MacKenzie drove down with the general to the camp.

Things at Mourmelon were pretty dry from a reporting standpoint— the occasional personality piece on a particular trooper for his hometown or an awards ceremony. Then on December 17 came a stroke of incredible luck. Word came down that the 101st was moving out to counter the German attack, and MacKenzie wanted in. He did not want to miss out on a great story, and his senses told him there was one in the offing. At first, General Mac was reluctant. He had his hands full with organizing the entire division and getting it to Werbomont in one piece. (The division's original orders were to go to Werbomont and not Bastogne.) McAuliffe gave the eager reporter fair warning—where they were going, they were sure to see combat. MacKenzie said he didn't care. In the end, General McAuliffe acquiesced.[59] Now the intrepid reporter was driving along with the division commander, on their way to Belgium. Anyway, McAuliffe had more to worry about than a single reporter. He hadn't heard back from the advance party, and it was now Monday afternoon. Concerned, he decided to move out ahead of the division and seek more information for himself.

Just thirty miles south of Werbomont, McAuliffe glanced down at his watch and realized the trip took a lot less time than he had planned. Realizing he had time to kill, and still craving information, he looked over his shoulder at Colonel Kinnard and said, "Harry, I think I'll check up on the situation before we go on up there. There's a road junction ahead. We'll turn and go to VIII Corps headquarters at Bastogne to see what we can find out."[60]

McAuliffe's driver sped southeast toward Bastogne. Wisely, they approached the town from the west, where the roads remained relatively clear of traffic. Once inside of town, they found the roads choked with half-tracks, self-propelled artillery, and trucks. In addition to the heavy vehicle traffic, ragged and haggard GIs walked along the sides of streets, looking more like wayward zombies than combat soldiers.

McAuliffe and Kinnard instantly knew something was wrong. Even MacKenzie, the civilian, could see that things were amiss. To the horror of the officers in the jeep, it seemed the defense of Bastogne was falling apart.

Kinnard finally voiced what everyone was thinking as the jeep weaved its way through the masses of vehicles and humanity: "Sir, unless these people are having a premature case of jitters, I'd say the Germans must be barreling this way pretty fast."

McAuliffe nodded. "So I was thinking. We'll soon find out."[61]

McAuliffe and his retinue arrived at Heinz Barracks at 1600 hours that evening. Inside the headquarters, chaos reigned. No one knew where the Germans were. Worse yet, no one seemed to know where the Americans were either. All that could be discerned was that part of the 10th Armored and 9th Armored divisions were somewhere east of town, fighting the Germans, but no one had any idea as to their exact locations or status. In contrast to his staff, Middleton was calm, a lighthouse standing tall amid the crashing waves.[62]

Middleton informed McAuliffe that per 12th Army Group, his orders were changed. The Screaming Eagles would be redirected to Bastogne. General Bradley had concurred with Middleton when Middleton had called earlier, telling him that Bastogne could be important to holding up the German offense, and he needed a division, pronto.

"Tony, there's been a major penetration here," Middleton said as he pointed to the region between St. Vith and Gemünd on a Belgian map. "Certain units of mine are shattered, especially the 106th Infantry Division and the 28th Infantry Division."

Middleton waved his hand over the area east of Bastogne. "Somewhere in this area, 9th Armored and 10th Armored divisions are heavily engaged with the enemy. Combat Command B of the 10th Armored Division has established roadblocks to the northeast, east, and southeast of here. I believe the enemy is just outside of town."

The news hit McAuliffe like a brick.

There was a pause. Middleton concluded by telling McAuliffe that unfortunately he had to depart. First Army General Courtney Hodges had ordered Middleton and his staff to leave Bastogne to the 101st and make haste for Neufchâteau, approximately sixteen miles to the southwest. There

Middleton was hoping to reform the VIII Corps HQ and start planning for the immediate counterattack to drive the Germans back.[63]

As McAuliffe peered over Middleton's shoulder at the map, he knew he had to get the word to the rest of the 101st column and let them know that Bastogne was their destination. He chose an assembly area for his men in the fields around the town of Mande Saint-Etienne, about three and a half miles to the west of Bastogne. It was close and accessible by road, as well as open enough to accommodate the mass of troopers and vehicles that would soon be arriving. With Middleton's help, he began to pick out areas around Bastogne where he might first have to commit his men to battle as soon as they arrived. Most of this area, the two generals agreed, was, for the time being, to the east. Luckily, the Screaming Eagles wouldn't be alone in defending the town. They would have help from others.[64]

CHAPTER THREE

"Come Any Way Possible to Bastogne, but Get There."

"Associate with men of good quality if you esteem your own reputation: for 'tis better to be alone than in bad company."

—Attributed to George Washington[1]

1200–1600 hours, Sunday, 17 December 1944
Headquarters of the 513th Fighter Squadron of the 406th Fighter Group
Mourmelon-le-Grand ("Camp Mourmelon"), France

The legendary status of the 101st Airborne often overshadows the fact that so many other units helped defend Bastogne. Parts of the 9th and 10th armored divisions, parts of two tank destroyer battalions, and survivors of the various divisions shattered by the initial breakthrough (such as remnants of the 28th Infantry Division, who took sanctuary in Bastogne after being pitched back early on December 16) played key roles.

Airpower, too, was an important and overlooked weapon in the effort to save Bastogne from the German advance. Missions flown by the pilots and crews of supply aircraft and fighter-bombers contributed as much to Bastogne's salvation as did the hard-pressed ground troops.

One fighter-bomber unit in particular forged a lasting bond with the Screaming Eagles prior to their deployment to Bastogne. Based at Mourmelon were more than 320 fighter pilots and ground crew of the 513th

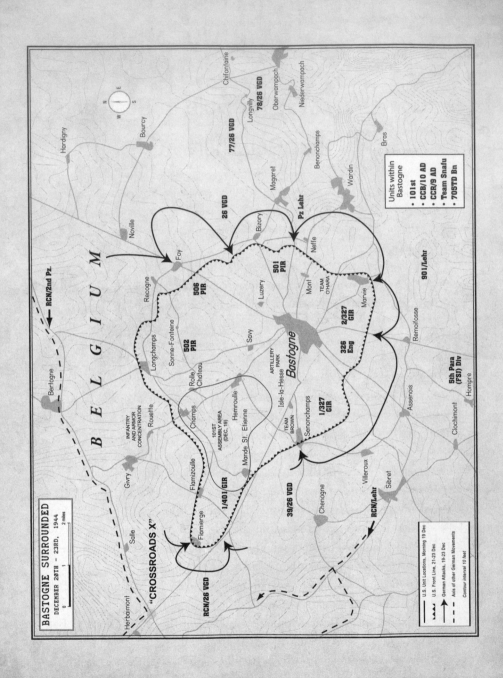

BASTOGNE SURROUNDED
DECEMBER 20TH – 23RD, 1944

0   1   2 miles

Units within Bastogne
• 101st
• CCB/10 AD
• CCR/9 AD
• Team Snafu
• 705TD Bn

U.S. Unit Locations, Morning 19 Dec
U.S. Front Line, 21–23 Dec
German Attacks, 19–23 Dec
Axis of other German Movements
Contour interval 10 feet

B E L G I U M

"CROSSROADS X"

RCN/2nd Pz.
RCN/Lehr
RCN/26 VGD

Herbaimont
Salle
Givry
Rouette
Flamizoulle
Flamierge
Chenogne
Villeroux
Sibret
Clochimont
Hompre
Assenois
Remoifosse
Wardin
Bras
Niederwampach
Oberwampach
Chifontaine
Longvilly
Magaret
Benonchamps
Bizory
Neffe
Marvie
Mont
Luzery
Savy
Sonne-Fonteine
Longchamps
Recogne
Foy
Noville
Bourcy
Hardigny
Bertogne
Champs
Hemroulle
Monde St. Etienne
Senonchamps

502 PIR
506 PIR
501 PIR
2/327 GIR
326 Eng
I/327 GIR
1/401 GIR
TEAM BROWN
TEAM O'HARA
901/Lehr

Bastogne
ARTILLERY PARK
Isle-la-Hesse
INFANTRY AND ARMOR CONCENTRATION
101ST ASSEMBLY AREA (DEC. 19)
Rolle Chateau

26 VGD
Pz Lehr
77/26 VGD
78/26 VGD
39/26 VGD
5th Para (FSI) Div

N E S W

Fighter Squadron of the 406th Fighter Group. The Army Air Force men had inhabited the buildings of the old French army barracks for some time before the first units of the 101st had arrived from Holland. They had been using the nearby airfield to fly the occasional ground-support mission or escort the lumbering C-47s that would fly in supplies and troopers all during the month of November.[2]

At first there was some grumbling from the paratroopers about having to share a post with the fighter pilots and their crews. As the men from both units got to know one another, a friendly rivalry matured into many friendships and mutual respect. The airborne troops admired the dedication of the "fighter jockeys," whose typical missions during the early part of December involved taking off in almost zero visibility and destroying armored vehicles and transports on the ground. The paratroopers could respect this "roll-up-your-sleeves" warfare, which helped them do their job on the ground, more than if the 513th were just made up of a bunch of "Hollywood flyboys" trying to scratch another Messerschmitt kill on the side of their cockpit.

In turn, the pilots and crews of the P-47 Thunderbolts were awed by the stories of ground combat the paratroopers shared over beers at the local watering holes. Screaming Eagle veterans relished telling stories of furious combat against the Nazis in Normandy and Holland to the eager air corps men.

A writer for the *406th Occupier*, the 406th Fighter Group's unit paper, wrote about the relationship with the 101st troopers: "A certain amount of friendly barter went on between the two organizations and all the C-47s used to fly in equipment to them landed at our strip."

First Lieutenant Howard M. Park of International Falls, Minnesota, was a veteran fighter pilot. He had flown a mix of ground-attack and escort missions since arriving in England in April, and was wounded during one mission in September. Upon his successful convalescence and return to active duty, his squadron was based in October to Mourmelon-le-Grand.[3]

Park busied himself with training several of the new replacement pilots, taking up flights of "Jugs"—the nickname for the powerful Republic P-47 Thunderbolt fighters—and familiarizing the rookie pilots in poor-weather flying. Park would teach the new pilots how to fly a straight course using instruments and how to fly their aircraft in tight formation. The training was timely, as the area was typically socked in with thick cloud cover on a daily basis.[4]

The day of the 101st Airborne Division/Army Air Force game, Park was too busy to attend it. He worked closely on the flight lines with his ground crews, making sure the massive Jugs were armed, fueled, and ready for action, whenever and whatever the next mission might be.

Already that morning there was a buzz afoot on the flight lines. A group of sixteen P-47s of the 513th had taken off from Mourmelon and mixed it up in a dogfight with several German Me (Bf) 109s over the town of Zülpich. The mission was flown in support of the U.S. 8th Infantry Division, which was being pushed hard by the Germans. Fliers like Park were excited. When the pilots returned that afternoon, they claimed they had shot down seven German fighters.[5]

Park knew something big was up. Since D-day, the Luftwaffe rarely challenged the American fighter-bombers. It was too costly for them, and when did they come up, it was in small numbers. Now here was a flight of forty Messerschmitts trying to contest the skies over western Germany. Why the sudden change? He would soon find out. By 1415 he was pulling his P-47D "Big Ass Bird II" into the air, hoping to bag some 109s of his own.

Strapped to his wings were two five-hundred-pound bombs—an early Christmas present for some hapless German soldier. Once aloft, Park and his squadron mates were heading 120 degrees, flying southeast into Germany for a ground support mission. As was typical this time of year, the sky was overcast and the cloud cover was at 12,000 feet.[6]

It didn't take long for Park to find his German fighters. His flight of twelve P-47s saw a group of P-38 Lightnings tangling with six Focke-Wulf 190s near the western border of Germany. After seeing the bandits, the squadron leader gave the order. Park and the rest of his squadron jettisoned their bombs to make their planes more maneuverable, and then dived into the scuffle.

In seconds, Park had one FW-190 hugging his tail like a hungry yapping dog at his heels. This dog, though, had four 20mm cannons mounted in its wings that had enough bite to bring down a B-17 Flying Fortress. Park nervously watched the tracers from the cannons zip past his canopy. He jinked his Thunderbolt to the left, and the great big plane barely responded with a snap roll. It was acting sluggish. Desperately, Park swiveled his head around in all directions and quickly discovered why. One of the five-hundred-pound bombs was still attached under his wing. Park was sure he was a dead man as he desperately tried to shake the bomb loose. Luckily, his wingman fired some bursts and chased the FW-190 off Park's tail. Meanwhile, eddying all around him, the battle continued. As Park frantically struggled to release the bomb, parachutes drifted past him like dandelion seeds. Finally the Germans broke off, leaving the skies to the Americans.

Park sank back in his seat, not believing his good fortune. After all, not everyone in his squadron made it back home that day. The flight had lost one pilot who bailed out after colliding with a diving P-38 during the aerial fracas. On the other hand, the Luftwaffe suffered losses, too, and three of Park's buddies each shot down an FW-190. As Park flew back to Mourmelon, he wondered what got the Luftwaffe buzzing again.

The next morning, Park and his fellow fliers would learn about the German offensive, as they watched their comrades and friends in the 101st Airborne load up on trucks. Unfortunately, for the next five days bad weather would ground the 513th Fighter Squadron. Due to the inclement weather, Park and his frustrated squadron mates could do nothing but sit and wait, hoping to soon fly in support of their friends in the 101st.[7]

Late Monday, 18 December, to late Tuesday, 19 December 1944
705th Tank Destroyer Battalion convoy
Kohlscheid, Germany, to Bastogne, Belgium

Another lucky ace up McAuliffe's sleeve was a fast-moving tank destroyer unit that managed to slip into Bastogne at the last minute. It was the 705th Tank Destroyer Battalion, a veteran unit that had fought through France after D-day. The 705th had arrived in the ETO (European theater of operations) with the lethal M18 "Hellcat" tank destroyer. The M18 was rather new to the allies in Europe, and represented an interesting take on the tank destroyer tactical philosophy. TDs (tank destroyers) were primarily designed for defensive operations, to destroy enemy tanks. The M18 was a perfect example of this. The tracked vehicle had a powerful 76mm gun designed for penetrating thick German armor. But most incredibly, the Hellcat was one of the fastest military vehicles ever designed. It could travel on good roads at speeds over fifty-five miles per hour powered by its 460-horsepower radial aircraft engine.[8]

Unlike an M4 Sherman tank—the standard tank of the U.S. Army—the M18 was designed to "shoot and scoot." In other words, instead of getting into a head-on, tank-versus-tank battle, the Hellcat was supposed to race ahead and ambush German armor, and then race away before the German tanks could return fire. The downside was that return fire on an M18 was devastating. Its designers had made sacrifices in order to give it such great speed. The vehicle was lightly armored (only one-half to one inch of steel protected the crew, compared to a Sherman's 2.5-inch thick frontal armor and a German Panzerkampfwagen Mark IV's typical three or more inches).[9]

Anthony C. Breder, a member of the 705th, bluntly summed up the chances of surviving an armor-piercing hit to an M18. "They were pretty good tanks—the best the Americans ever made. Fast, you know—fifty-five miles per hour. No armor, though. If a German gun shot at you it went right through that armor like paper."[10]

The 705th was holding the line at Kohlscheid, Germany, with the U.S. Ninth Army, when it received orders on the eighteenth to head south for Bastogne. In command of the 705th was Lieutenant Colonel Clifford D. Templeton. That night, he ordered First Lieutenant Richard B. Miller's 1st Platoon, Reconnaissance Company, to scout ahead and find the fastest and safest route into Bastogne.

Miller, like many of the soldiers during those first harrowing days and nights of the Battle of the Bulge, did not know much about the upcoming mission. He knew the Germans had broken through and that he needed to lead his battalion to Bastogne. They were driving in blackout conditions. All he could see in front of him was from the cat's eyes on his jeep's headlights. At 0001 hours, the morning of the nineteenth, the 705th Tank Destroyer Battalion reached Liège.[11] Continuing on from Liège, at one point Miller peered into the night and saw tiny flashes bouncing off the road in front of him like Chinese firecrackers. He looked closer as the flashes approached his vehicle, wondering what it was. He soon found out. The roar of a piston engine warned him that it was a low-flying aircraft strafing the road, and it was too late for him to take cover. He sat in his jeep, frozen and helpless. The flashing and popping stopped as the aircraft passed over his head, leaving him and his platoon unscathed.

Miller later recounted in an interview, "God really was with me."

Templeton then ordered Miller to push forward to Houffalize and then to Bastogne. It was a straight shot, and it should have been a short trip. Unfortunately, the roads were clogged with human flotsam and jetsam as Miller ran smack into the remnants of American units that had fallen victim to the winter blitzkrieg. Retreating men, too tired to walk, lined the roads like sleeping corpses underneath the trucks that were supposed to take them somewhere. Some were still awake, and Miller asked them about the Germans. The news was not good. The Germans had taken Houffalize, blocking the route to Bastogne. Miller decided to bypass Houffalize and make for La Roche. The time now was between 0700 and 0800 hours.[12]

Several minutes after Miller took off for La Roche, Templeton lost communications with him. Templeton knew there were roving German patrols, and he worried that his advance guard was in trouble. He ordered a section from 2nd Platoon, Reconnaissance Company, to link up with Miller's platoon and determine whether they needed assistance. The officer in charge was First Lieutenant Claude W. Duvall. Unfortunately, Duvall and his scout group of armored cars and jeeps were unaware that Miller had taken a detour. As a result, Duvall and his team drove straight into Houffalize and into the mouth of the German advance. After a close encounter with a German tank blocking that town's main street, Duvall finally received the corrected info: Miller had found an alternative route into Bastogne. Leaving the harrowing journey behind him, Duvall and his men were able to link up with the main force outside of Bastogne later that day. The two recon units had done their job well, radioing back the quickest routes for Templeton and his tank destroyers to travel in order to safely make it to Bastogne.[13]

On his way through La Roche, Templeton also discovered the crossroads was a mess. Retreating American units were in complete disarray—confused, disorganized, and no one was making any effort to defend the area from the Germans. Smartly, Templeton detached one tank destroyer platoon and one reconnaissance platoon from his unit to set up a roadblock near town, in order to help momentarily hold the town and secure the rear of his column as it passed through.[14] Then Templeton, along with a section of reconnaissance vehicles, headed out in advance to find VIII Corps headquarters.

Along the way, Templeton discovered that VIII Corps had moved their headquarters to Neufchâteau. When he arrived there, Middleton immediately ordered him toward Bastogne, stating that he was now under McAuliffe's command. A slightly confused Templeton nodded, saluted, and backtracked on the double toward Bastogne and to report to McAuliffe.[15]

In hindsight, this was one of Troy Middleton's best decisions that day. Faced with the potential of overwhelming German armor, McAuliffe was thrilled to hear he would have tank destroyers to defend the woods, hills, and streets of Bastogne.

Far behind Templeton, Miller, and Duvall, the rest of the 705th (minus two platoons—eight M18s—from A Company left to guard a bridge at Ourtheuville) was rolling down the roads deep into Belgium.[16] Sergeant Anthony D'Angelo was a young tank destroyer commander in the 705th. As his C Company moved out, he recalled better days before the war working as a laborer for the Civilian Conservation Corps and the Pennsylvania Railroad Company near his hometown of Wellsville, Ohio.

Now he was leaning back in the open turret of his Hellcat as it sped down the road toward Bastogne, one of the last M18s in the column. D'Angelo's M18 had the nickname of "No Love, No Nothing" painted on the side of the hull by his crew, after a popular radio hit sung by American sweetheart Ella Mae Morse. Blowing on his hands to keep them warm, D'Angelo witnessed the shocking roadside scenery near La Roche. It would remain forever seared in his memory.

"We were ordered to Bastogne December 18, 1944. The lines were fluid. We saw the 82nd Airborne going one way; we were going the other. I remember seeing burning German and American armor and wrecks alongside the road. I remember that well. Looked like the fires of hell to me," D'Angelo said in an interview years later.[17]

To D'Angelo and his crew, the blazing vehicles seemed a stark warning of things to come.

The next few hours were terrifying ones for Colonel Templeton. On his way north to coordinate the arrival of his tank destroyers, his small reconnaissance section ran into a German roadblock near the town of Bertogne. At a bend in the road, the Germans had hidden a small but lethal team of some heavy antiaircraft guns, two heavy machine guns, and even a Sturmgeschütz (StuG) III self-propelled gun. The result was predictable. The Germans got the drop and opened fire, immediately destroying one of the jeeps and wounding several soldiers. Realizing the German roadblock outgunned them, Templeton decided to fall back and seek an alternate route for his TDs around the pesky roadblock. Within minutes, they discovered that one of their six-wheeled M20 armored cars was trapped. The crew quickly abandoned the vehicle. Luckily, Templeton still had an M8 Greyhound armored car, which was armed with a 37mm cannon. Though it lacked the punch of the 75mm cannon on the StuG, it could fire a lot faster. It might at least provide enough covering fire to make good their escape. The Greyhound gunner let loose with a string of volleys. For a moment, the Germans were stunned, allowing the small command detachment to safely withdraw.

Templeton immediately radioed the incoming column of 705th armor to be ready for a possible "hot reception" on the road in. With the advance warning, Templeton felt confident his TDs could either deal with the German roadblock, or take the less risky option of bypassing it. Either way, the roadblock was reportedly not a problem for the 705th. After all, Templeton's orders to his tankers had been crystal clear: "Come any way possible to Bastogne, but get there."[18]

By 2100 hours, Tuesday, December 19, Templeton was in Bastogne. The M18s and their support vehicles came rumbling in shortly after.[19]

D'Angelo recalled the careful entry into Bastogne, slipping through just as many of the roadways were being closed off by the Germans. "I remember we arrived at Bastogne at night. We swung around several hot spots in order to get into Bastogne. We came in from the south, the only way in. My TD was the last one in."[20]

To say that Templeton's tank destroyers, with their long, 76mm armor-piercing guns, would come in handy defending Bastogne from von Manteuffel's panzers would be a huge understatement. By the second day of their arrival, they were already proving their worth, successfully defending the northeastern approaches to town. For Templeton, Miller, Duvall, and D'Angelo, the fighting had just begun. They would see a lot more on Christmas morning.

Early to midmorning, Tuesday, 19 December 1944
101st Airborne Division assembly area
Mande Saint-Etienne, Belgium (just west of Bastogne)

Early on Tuesday morning, December 19, thousands of windburned and frozen Screaming Eagles clambered over the sides of their trucks at a roadside west of Bastogne. The men complained and stamped their feet in the cold. They had traveled 107 miles in more than eight hours through freezing sleet and icy-cold rain. Many were in poor spirits, having been almost fully exposed while huddling in the back of the open-topped "cattle cars."[21] Bob MacDonald, commander of Baker Company, 1/401st, summed up the feeling well: "The whole trip was miserable. It was foggy, it was cold, and occasionally snowing en route. The men were so crowded in the trucks that only half of them could attempt to sleep on the floor, while the remainder stood and took it."[22] It was not how they wanted to spend their days leading up to Christmas.

Trucks full of paratroopers were still arriving in the Mande area as Middleton departed with his VIII Corps headquarters to Neufchâteau.[23] The first regiment of the 101st to arrive was Lieutenant Colonel Julian J. Ewell's 501st. They had rolled into the area of Bastogne the night before. They were followed by Sink's 506th. The final regiments to "close the back door" and arrive in the marshaling fields near Mande Saint-Etienne on the nineteenth were the 502nd under Chappuis and Colonel "Bud" Harper's 327th (plus the 1/401st) Glider Infantry Regiment, which arrived at 0930 and 1015, respectively.[24]

As the cold and nervous paratroopers of Ewell's 501st heard the distant gunfire, they hiked up their pack straps, shouldered their weapons, and marched off through town to the east. With barely a pause, the 101st Airborne Division had just joined the battle for Bastogne.

Afternoon, Tuesday, 19 December 1944
101st Airborne Division Headquarters, Heinz Barracks
Bastogne, Belgium

Colonel Danahy finally reached Bastogne after an odyssey that took him to Werbomont and back. Upon learning that the 101st was actually redirected toward Bastogne, a frustrated Danahy finally arrived later that morning with the so-called advance party, which, ironically, was one of the last divisional units to show up.

Kinnard and the rest of the division staff had decided to relocate the makeshift division headquarters from the schoolhouse in Mande Saint-Etienne to the Heinz Barracks, where VIII Corps was in the process of vacating. McAuliffe and his staff eschewed the two-story building the corps had utilized for its operations center for the more unassuming basement of a barracks building on the southern side of the main courtyard near the main gateway. Kinnard and the others felt that if they had to defend the headquarters, this building would make a better spot, being partially underground and having access to an entrance. To emphasize their determination to fight it out at the headquarters, the paratroopers even rolled in a towed anti-tank gun to cover the entrance in case a panzer decided to show up.[25]

Upon his arrival, Danahy went immediately to work, trying to glean whatever information he could from VIII Corps holdouts and any of the latest intelligence reports coming in from the fighting to the east of town. Danahy strolled down to the very end of the hallway of McAuliffe's HQ. Finding the operations center label, he stepped inside and walked over to his section. Fortunately, his NCOs were on the ball, running the shop even while he was away.

Danahy glanced at the operations map where his staff section plotted known and suspected enemy locations around Bastogne. He had to admit it was a pathetic affair; at thirty inches wide, it was downright minuscule, but it was the only one available that showed the region around Bastogne in any detail. Despite its size, it was enough to show Danahy that the Germans were closing in fast. It was only a matter of time before German forces traveling north and south of town would link up to the west and surround Bastogne.[26]

Danahy grabbed the radio log and quickly went over the morning's reports. The Germans seemed busy as bees around Bastogne.[27] Next he flipped through the divisional logs for that morning. Stepping right out from the marshaling area, Ewell's 501st had run into the Germans to the east of Bastogne in the town of Neffe between 0800 and 0900.[28] In addition, Colonel Sink, the commander of the 506th Parachute Infantry Regiment, reported that his battalion started their attack to the north of Noville at 1400 hours to assist Task Force Desobry, one of the armor teams from Combat Command B, 10th Armored, that was holding the line against the Germans to the northeast of town.[29] Meanwhile, Task Force Cherry, another unit from Combat Command B, was fighting for its life around a château in Neffe, east of Bastogne.[30] Danahy's analysts were doing all they could, even poring over captured German documents and personal effects from German dead and prisoners.[31] The various reports were telling. *We are throwing everything we've got at them to save Bastogne,* he thought to himself, *but at least the Germans aren't west of Bastogne yet.*

Danahy didn't know it at the time, but the Germans were already there and looking for a fight.

1700–midnight, Tuesday, 19 December 1944
502nd Parachute Infantry Regiment area of operations
Northwest of Bastogne, Belgium

At 1700 hours, Colonel Steve Chappuis received word from division to establish a defensive position near Longchamps and Rolle, northwest of

Bastogne.[32] Chappuis was also ordered to give up a total of two battalions for the division reserve. Chappuis had to pull 1st Battalion back, leaving 2nd Battalion on the line. He placed 1st Battalion in a cluster of woods called the Bois de Niblamont, which was behind Rolle Château. As a result, 2nd Battalion now had a frontage of nearly 7,000 yards that stretched from the town of Champs to the town of Recogne. [33]

For Captain Swanson, Sergeant Asay, and the rest of the men of Able Company, the nineteenth was a frustrating day of digging and walking and digging again. After arriving in the regimental assembly area that morning, they were immediately ordered to dig foxholes. Grunting and panting, the paratroopers stripped off their field jackets as they quickly overheated in the misty woods. Like the rest of the regiment, they remained there until 1715 hours that night, when they received their orders to move out. Cursing, the Screaming Eagles left their freshly dug foxholes and set off to a different location to dig more.

They arrived in Longchamps around 1925 hours that night and then moved up to Monaville. Swanson had both 2nd and 3rd platoons on the line, while he had 1st Platoon as the company reserve. Private Ted Goldmann remembered the frustration of not knowing where they were or where they were going all that Tuesday. Goldmann was a member of Asay's squad and had spent a week at bazooka school in December with his friend and squad mate Private John C. Ballard. Soon they were on their way to Bastogne. When they got off the trucks the next morning, they had no clue as to where they were. Goldmann wrote:

> We could have been in China for all we knew. We hadn't seen any towns because practically everyone had managed to drop off to sleep. We marched two miles to a bare hill (it seemed a hell of a place to us) and sat down. We dug shallow holes, filled them with straw, built fires and ate K-rations. After many stops and starts and at about 11 o'clock at night (darkness at 5) we stopped outside a small village and were given a squad area and told to dig in and set up a MG and try to get some sleep. We had a tree-lined gulley so we didn't do any digging, threw the MG up on the edge of the gulley, set one at a time on guard and to hell with the Germans [and] went to sleep.[34]

For Goldmann and the others, that first night at Monaville was a cold and damp one, as sleet fell down around them. Fortunately, though, it was

also an uneventful one. Still, the paratroopers could hear the noises of combat to the east, where the Germans were battling with Sink's 506th. Goldmann, Asay, Ballard, and other veterans of the 502nd sensed their moment
would come all too soon.[35]

Afternoon to evening, Tuesday, 19 December 1944
463rd Parachute Field Artillery Battalion gun line
Hemroulle, west of Bastogne, Belgium

Colonel Cooper's "Bastard Battalion" arrived at Bastogne the morning of
the nineteenth. Between 1400 and 1500 hours, Cooper directed his cannon-
cockers to set up their gun line near the village of Hemroulle, behind the
327th GIR and the 502nd PIR. As instructed, the 463rd would fire in direct
support of the 327th.

Surveying the area around Hemroulle, Cooper set up his command
post in a nearby farmhouse with the Fire Direction Center (FDC). In the
U.S. Army during World War II, an FDC was the brain of an artillery battalion. There, radio operators and artillerymen plotted and directed the
various artillery strikes on the enemy. The Americans had learned during
World War I that to accurately plot, destroy, and assess the success of massed
gunfire, communication was the key. The FDC was one of the chief reasons
the Americans had such an overwhelming advantage in artillery in World
War II. No one could match the U.S. Army's accuracy and ability to mass
fires at a single point on the battlefield at the same time. A lot of this advantage lay in the fact that the Americans could supply communications equipment all the way down to the platoon level. Therefore, a mere platoon
leader—lieutenant or sergeant—could relay information back to a battalion
FDC and bring dozens of shells on a single target in practically no time. No
other army of its time could do that.[36]

Across the road, the medics set up their aid station in the town chapel.
Cooper then oversaw the setup of his 75mm Pack howitzers throughout the
area, the four batteries spread out to give a maximum amount of coverage
to the area around the village. In an indirect-fire mode, his guns would
be able to fire in a 360-degree defense of the perimeter if called upon. The
gun teams were also instructed to start working on direct-fire positions for
antitank work. At 1700 and 1725 hours, both Able and Dog batteries, respectively, registered their guns. Satisfied with his setup, Cooper waited for
the requests for fire missions he knew would soon be coming.[37]

2345 hours, Tuesday, 19 December 1944
327th Glider Infantry Regiment Headquarters
Mande Saint-Etienne, west of Bastogne, Belgium

At 2245 hours, a report came in to Colonel Harper's headquarters that a supply convoy had been ambushed on the road to Hargimont at a crossroads not far from Salle. At 2345 hours, the regimental radio operators received another report from division. Someone had seen a burning truck at the location of the reported ambush. In addition, that someone claimed hearing small arms fire in the area where the 326th Medical Company had set up their field hospital at the crossroads of the Marche and Salle roads, an area known to locals as the Barrière Hinck.[38] It was growing obvious to Harper and his men that the Germans had moved quicker than thought, and they were already about six miles west and closing.[39]

Close to midnight, Tuesday, 19 December 1944
101st Division Headquarters, Heinz Barracks
Bastogne, Belgium

Lieutenant Miller and his reconnaissance platoon had pulled up to the division headquarters and parked their vehicles in the barracks courtyard. The lights were out because of blackout restrictions, and an eerie quiet settled over the foggy barracks, much like a ghost town, save for the nervous sentries who challenged anyone and everyone who approached them. Miller could see that most of the men on staff were trying to catch some sleep.

Templeton and the headquarters staff of the 705th were inside discussing the deployment tasks for the battalion with McAuliffe and his headquarters crew. Miller decided not to interrupt Templeton with his report until later. Everyone in Miller's platoon was tired but edgy. One of his men whispered, "I never thought we'd make it, Lieutenant."

Miller nodded and replied, "We almost didn't," remembering his brush with death when the German plane nearly strafed their column that morning. He shook his head in disbelief. They had all been incredibly lucky today. He hoped their good fortune would hold out.[40]

Danahy's intelligence boys had been earning their pay: acquiring information from the few German prisoners who had been captured, interviewing active patrols, grilling the departing VIII Corps staff, and going over reports from the staffs of the 9th and 10th Armored, as well as some of the 28th Division stragglers, who had already been up against the enemy's forces.

Danahy prepared a quick intelligence summary. Before he turned it in to the "boss," he decided to read over his work one more time: Elements of the 101st had already reported contact with the Germans at Noville, Margeret, and Neffe. Prisoners had been captured by the 501st and 506th from the 2nd Panzer Division, as well as the 902nd Panzergrenadier Regiment of the Panzer Lehr. Disturbingly, Danahy noted that the prisoners mentioned that their units had received replacements and new equipment before the attack. Reports from the interrogators mentioned another sobering fact: Morale among the Germans, because they were once more on the offensive, was excellent. Danahy read more bad news. The Panzer Lehr Division, one of the finest German armored units, was pushing against Bastogne. Also, according to a captured map, the 26th Volksgrenadier, a large division in its own right, had been tasked with capturing Bastogne.

Danahy had concluded the report by mentioning that at this point, it seemed there was little holding the Germans back from grabbing Bastogne. Reserves and lines of supply for the Germans seemed adequate. Combined with the reconstitution of the enemy divisions and the spirit of the men, this did not bode well for the Americans.[41]

It was clear to all that the Germans were going to keep up the pressure until Bastogne broke under the weight. For the commanders and the staff, the question now was how to keep the Germans from cracking Bastogne like a fragile nut. Satisfied with his report, Danahy typed up the final administration data at the bottom and went to hand it to McAuliffe in person. It didn't paint a pretty picture, Danahy knew, but in wartime, the truth was typically pretty ugly.

Setting up his new office at the barracks that evening, McAuliffe ruminated over the next day's operations. To McAuliffe, the best way to deal with the oncoming Germans was artillery. Particularly because of his background in that branch, he had made sure to take stock of the 101st's own artillery as it arrived from Mourmelon. The divisional artillery's field guns were smaller versions of their big cousins, but just as lethal, and light enough to be dropped by parachute or delivered in gliders. In total, the 101st had two battalions of the light 75mm Pack howitzers (Elkin's 377th and Cooper's recently added 463rd) and two medium artillery battalions of "snub-nosed" 105mm howitzers—the 321st and 907th Glider Field Artillery. These units were typically assigned the role of support for one of the four infantry regiments. More powerful defensive fire would have to come from the few large-caliber artillery units that Middleton had left him.[42]

Middleton had attached two heavy field artillery battalions and the remnants of one, the 755th and 333rd Field Artillery Group (333rd and 969th Field Artillery battalions) to McAuliffe's command. Some of these guns were the massive towed 155mm "Long Toms." In addition to those guns, Combat Command B, under Colonel Roberts, had the 420th Armored Field Artillery Battalion, which included the mobile M7 "Priest" 105mm tracked Howitzer Motor Carriages. Combined with the 101st's artillery, McAuliffe now had a total of eight artillery battalions under his direct control. All of these guns could fire from central Bastogne and hit almost anything in any direction within a seven-mile radius.

Actually, in terms of gun tubes, McAuliffe had nearly a hundred pieces by December 20, which during most of the siege would actually outnumber the German artillery facing him.[43] This was a tremendous advantage, particularly in a defensive position. With this in mind, McAuliffe decided to create an "artillery park" near the western portion of the city and the outlying town of Savy. Here he could keep several of the guns and some of the ammo available and limbered, ready to respond wherever they were needed the most.

By Wednesday, McAuliffe was guessing he held an advantage in artillery. Danahy's report mentioned that the Germans were using self-propelled guns as artillery to the northeast of Bastogne. *Why would they use self-propelled guns as artillery unless they didn't have the artillery in the first place?* He knew that most German divisions, even in 1944, still relied on horse-drawn artillery, and therefore, on the offensive, were too slow to move and deploy. The panzer divisions had motorized and mechanized artillery, but they were the exception and not the rule. On the other hand, almost all American artillery was motorized, and could move to any hot spot a lot quicker than its German counterparts.[44]

To defend Bastogne, Colonel Kinnard recommended that McAuliffe assign each regiment to protect a sector of the perimeter. The perimeter would be based on the ordinal directions spreading out from Bastogne, with the town center as its hub and headquarters. Each unit would be responsible for that sector's outlying villages or one of the seven roads leading into the city. McAuliffe and his staff knew that the Germans would try to seize these roads and towns for lines of attack into Bastogne. To McAuliffe, Kinnard's idea made sense. The German tanks would be forced to use these inroads, as the open fields around Bastogne were soft and muddy. Any remaining land was either too hilly or thick with woodlots—impossible for armored vehicles to penetrate.

In addition, McAuliffe created a centralized designated reserve that could reach any part of the perimeter quickly, as well as instructed each regiment to maintain a local reserve to plug holes or be used for a counterattack if the opportunity presented itself.

Most of all, McAuliffe wanted to use his artillery and the available armor to separate the German infantry from their tanks. McAuliffe's plan was for the paratroopers to kill the Panzergrenadiers while the tanks, tank destroyers, and antitank guns took care of the panzers.[45]

With the regiments in place and the artillery ready, the division staff waited for the inevitable German attacks that were sure to start Wednesday morning. The Americans must have felt as if they were reliving ancient European history and "gazing from the ramparts," like some throwback to a medieval siege. Bastogne was their fortress, with the roaring armor and approaching men of Hitler's vaunted Wehrmacht gathering like barbarians from all four directions to surround them.

Unfortunately, the Germans had struck the first deadly blow hours earlier. The reports that reached the 327th of gunfire and burning vehicles to the west were true. The 326th Medical Company's field hospital had been set up northwest of Flamierge in an open field at the intersection of the Marche road and the Barrière Hinck, nicknamed "Crossroads X" by the GIs. The medical company had set up there upon arrival, because at that time no one thought the Germans were close to the western approaches.[46] Now reports were filtering in that a supply convoy had also been ambushed in the area. Kinnard and McAuliffe wanted Colonel Ray Allen's 1/401st men, closest to the crossroads, to check it out. Perhaps a firefight had broken out between the Americans and a passing German patrol. In fact, it was worse than that. Early the next morning, Allen's glidermen would be the first to discover the grim truth—the hospital was gone. Moreover, the Germans were now west of Bastogne. It would be only a matter of time before Hitler's henchmen would have the town completely surrounded.

CHAPTER FOUR

"If You Don't Understand What 'Nuts' Means, in Plain English It Is the Same As 'Go to Hell. . . .'"

(DECEMBER 20–22)

"The officers and soldiers, with one heart, and one mind, will resolve to surmount every difficulty, with a fortitude and patience, becoming their profession, and the sacred cause in which they are engaged. . . ."

—George Washington, Orders of the Day,
Valley Forge, 1778[1]

16–22 December 1944
Bastogne, Belgium

The sudden shock of the German offensive had caught the people of Bastogne unawares. The city had been occupied and controlled by the Germans twice in two wars. Worse yet, the population had only recently celebrated being liberated in September, as the Allies had confidently sped through Belgium on their way to the German frontier. Now it looked to its denizens as if German jackboots would once again be heard marching through the streets, for a third time.

On December 16, though German tanks and troops were poised to

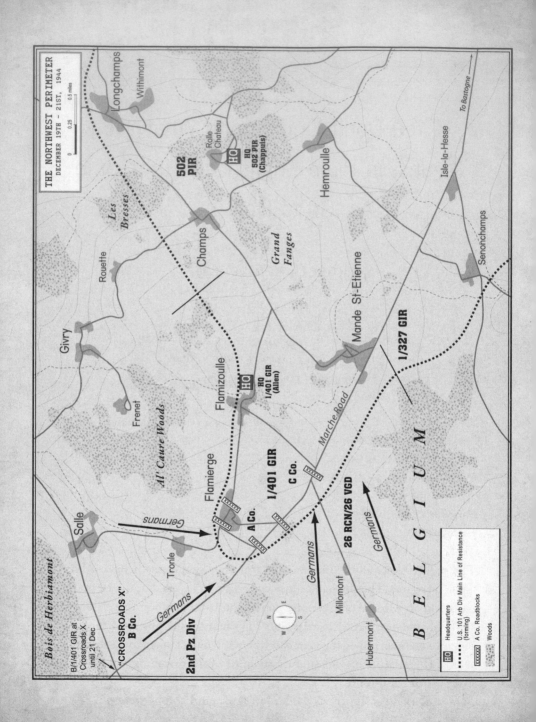

THE NORTHWEST PERIMETER
DECEMBER 19TH – 21ST, 1944

0   0.25   0.5 miles

Bois de Herbiamont

B/1/401 GIR at
Crossroads X
until 21 Dec

Longchamps
Withimont

Rolle
Chateau

502
PIR

HQ
502 PIR
(Chappuis)

Hemroulle

Isle-la-Hesse

Les
Bresses

Champs

Grand
Fanges

Senonchamps

Rouette

Givry

Frenet

Al' Caure Woods

Flamizoulle

HQ

HQ
1/401 GIR
(Allen)

Mande St-Etienne

1/327 GIR

Marche Road

Salle

Flamierge

Germans

1/401 GIR
C Co.

26 RCN/26 VGD

Tronle

A Co.

Germans

"CROSSROADS X"
B Co.

Germans

Germans

Millomont

B E L G I U M

2nd Pz Div

Hubermont

N
W   E
S

HQ   Headquarters

....   U.S. 101 Arb Div Main Line of Resistance
            (forming)

XXXXXX   A Co. Roadblocks

            Woods

To Bastogne

launch their attack only twenty miles from town, and rumors of the buildup were flying through the farmsteads of eastern Belgium, the townspeople went about their daily routines. It was going to be the first Christmas since liberation, and many were excited to celebrate the holiday. The muffled blasts of artillery emanating from the east troubled only a few. It was the usual distant sounds of war that most had simply gotten used to over the past years. If there was a minor probe by the Germans or a shelling from the German border, certainly the Americans would deal with it.

Some, though, were not so sure. Xavier Gaspard, a local pharmacist, continued to go about his business at the Bastogne Apothecary serving the needs of the local townspeople. At the same time, he nervously noticed the buildup of American forces in town. Farmers from the outlying villages whispered nervous chatter when they visited his shop, mentioning conversations with Belgian relatives they had spoken with farther to the east. Those relatives had reported troubling sounds of vehicle movement from just over the border with Germany.[2]

After December 16, the sounds of battle continued to grow in intensity in the distance. By Sunday morning, the seventeenth, the Bastognards began to worry about what was happening east of their town. Alas, the American soldiers of VIII Corps had more pressing issues, and information was scant. As a result, greater rumors started to fly. Was the Boche (The Germans) launching a grand attack? The local GIs of General Middleton's headquarters were irritable and provided no real information when questioned by some of the inhabitants.[3]

By Sunday night, it was clear to the townspeople that something was amiss when the electricity went out. The Germans had cut the power lines between Malmedy and Bastogne. To add to the restlessness and uncertainty, Middleton's civil affairs officers declared a curfew for all civilians that would begin at 1800 hours that night. Despite the curfew and power outage, some of the local schools continued with their winter exams, which began that Monday morning.[4]

However, the business-as-usual attitude changed dramatically as Monday morning wore on. The first indication of disaster that day was the crush of refugees coming from Luxembourg with frantic tales of panzers and retreat. Around 1500 that afternoon, the first artillery shells slammed into Bastogne near the Chapel of Ste. Thérèse, announcing to the townspeople that the Germans were back. As a result, the schools canceled their exams and promptly sent the students home. That afternoon, when McAuliffe and his staff were driving into Bastogne, the first Bastognards were attempting to escape before their town was invaded or surrounded. Few were able to make good their escape. To add to their frustration over the lack of information, the townspeople were never officially told to evacuate. It seemed the American authorities had never taken an evacuation of Bastogne into account, and therefore didn't really have a plan to deal with thousands of civilians fleeing to the west. Realistically, there was no way to evacuate all the civilians. Hence, no word went out.[5]

By Tuesday, the nineteenth of December, it was almost too late to leave. As the first trucks from the 101st rolled into Mande Saint-Etienne, Belgian gendarmes and MPs were forced to establish checkpoints to prevent people from leaving and jamming the roads west of Bastogne. It was vital to keep the roads open for the American paratroopers, glidermen, tanks, and supplies heading in the opposite direction—arriving in Bastogne. A few intrepid individuals attempted to leave the town anyway, but now their chief obstacle was not the gendarmes but machine gun fire. Some were seen precariously riding on the outside of U.S. supply trucks, or hitching rides in American jeeps. The whole scene, many civilians recalled, was terrifying, reminding the older citizens of the exodus of refugees that followed the Nazi invasion four years earlier.

On the other hand, many Bastognards chose to wait it out in the cellars and basements of their homes. Nearly a third of the population decided to settle in one of three community shelters throughout the town. The Institute of the Sisters of Notre Dame housed nearly six hundred people, including the one hundred young female students who had been unable to escape. The Franciscan fathers took an additional 150 into their church and stuffed them in the shelter beneath their chapel, while the Récollets (the French branch of the Franciscans) sheltered around a hundred more in their seventeenth-century monastery. By Wednesday, nobody else was leaving Bastogne. Their cellars and shelters would become their homes for the foreseeable future.[6]

For the Americans, several thousand civilians trapped in Bastogne needed more than a few civil affair officers to calm and oversee them, and since most of the town officials had fled, the Americans were forced to appoint an interim town leader. They were lucky to find Léon Jacqmin, who was a World War I veteran and a well-known businessman in town. More important to the Allies, he was also a superb organizer. He quickly set about the task of feeding and housing all of the civilians. First he established a medical section: Two local doctors volunteered to treat the civilian wounded and sick. Then Jacqmin designated the Institute of the Sisters of Notre Dame as the central node for food preparation and distribution. The bakers were Louis Renquin and Justin Gierens, who prepared and baked all the bread. In addition, Jacqmin could provide ample meat to the populace, since they had carefully sent out teams of young men from farm families to collect scores of abandoned pigs from the surrounding countryside. As a result, the civilians were actually well fed during the siege.[7]

If anyone in Bastogne doubted that the Americans were willing to fight for every block and every building, the buildup of forces on December 19–20 dispelled these notions. Xavier Gaspard remembered the Sherman tanks from Combat Command B parked in the main town square on Wednesday. One of them was stationed right outside his pharmacy. Gaspard, like many Bastognards, briefly debated the option of leaving, but many of his customers warned him against it. Still, his parents, who were older, would be less likely to survive a long siege. Gaspard wanted to send them to Hemroulle, where he had family. Hemroulle was a smaller village on the northwestern periphery of town.[8]

Xavier Gaspard and many others like him felt these villages that lined the perimeter were havens from the impending combat. They were wrong. Some of these villages would become a virtual no man's-land between the lines. Others would quickly be occupied by the Germans as they completed their encirclement of the American forces in Bastogne. Unknown to Gaspard and many others, these villages would be the scenes of the heaviest fighting, because it was there that the Americans planned to stop the Germans.

The villagers learned this bitter lesson shortly afterward. On December 21, a German patrol stumbled into an American patrol in Rouette while the villagers had gathered in the center of town to find out what was going on. The shoot-out was brief, and the Americans won, killing a German officer. Despite the storm of bullets, none of the townspeople were killed in the cross fire. However, it served as a warning to them that these tiny outlying villages were key terrain in the battle for Bastogne. Over the next couple of weeks, major battles would occur in places like Champs, Marvie, Noville, and elsewhere. In those hotly contested engagements, scores of civilians would be killed—a lasting reminder that the casualties in war were not always from the two armies fighting for possession of Bastogne.[9]

Wednesday, 20 December 1944
Area of operations, 101st Airborne Division
Bastogne and environs

December 20 was a rough day for the Americans. The 2nd Panzer Division was pushing hard into Noville and Foy, while to the east elements of the Panzer Lehr and the 26th Volksgrenadier, respectively, continued to pound their way past Wardin and into the villages directly east of Bastogne. For the men of Baker Company of 1/401st Glider Infantry, their search of Crossroads X resulted in a grim discovery. After destroying a small German force left at the crossroads, the glidermen cleared the area and searched for survivors. It was to no avail. The 326th Medical Company field hospital was gone, with all its men and equipment. The Germans had left little but empty tents and bodies. As a result, the division had little in the way of medical supplies. More important, it had lost many of its surgeons, who were either dead or prisoners of war. The only bright spot of the day was the discovery of several .50-caliber machine guns in the wrecked convoy trucks near the hospital. The glidermen grabbed them up, knowing they might come in handy later.

Despite this devastating setback, Captain Robert MacDonald's Baker Company had a mission to secure the crossroads, since it was the last major road junction west of Bastogne still under American control. So long as the Americans controlled it, the Germans would have to go around it, thereby increasing their tenuous supply lines. It wasn't long before the 2nd Panzer Division tried to take it back. Later that day, a pair of Panther tanks rumbled toward the crossroads, only to turn around, since they had no infantry accompanying them. MacDonald knew it wouldn't be long before the Germans returned. Moreover, his company was out on a limb, and if the Germans forced the issue, Baker Company had no one to reinforce them.[10]

Northeast of Allen's battalion, the 502nd Parachute Infantry Regiment was locked in combat with the advancing Wehrmacht for control of Noville. As the 2nd Panzer Division began to overwhelm the defenders—chiefly the 506th PIR and Team Desobry of Combat Command B, 10th Armored, Colonel Chappuis was positioning his regiment to the southwest of Noville to prevent the Germans from penetrating the Bastogne perimeter in that area. The key to his defense was the area around the village of Recogne, which was about a mile southwest of Noville.

The battle in and around Recogne lasted all day, as 3rd Battalion of the 502nd PIR fought to keep the Germans from establishing a firm foothold just north of Bastogne. Several tank destroyers from C Company of the 705th helped out. Sergeant Lazar Hovland, one of Sergeant Tony D'Angelo's platoon mates, destroyed one Mk IV and damaged another. Despite these successes, Lieutenant Colonel John P. Stopka, 3rd Battalion's commander, decided the best course of action was to leave Recogne a no-man's-land. Instead, his battalion withdrew and deployed along high ground to the southwest of Recogne, where they could still observe the town.[11]

That night, Fred MacKenzie watched as General McAuliffe and his staff looked over the reports of the day and scrutinized the few they had of the Bastogne area. At thirty-nine years of age, MacKenzie was an educated and experienced man. He knew that he was privileged to be witnessing something historical and was determined, come what may, to capture every bit of it for posterity. At the same time, MacKenzie had his doubts. Maybe coming to Bastogne with the Screaming Eagles was not the best decision. Though safe within the division's bustling headquarters, he could hear the dull thunder of German artillery in the distance.

In his famous account of the siege, *The Men of Bastogne*, written decades after the war, MacKenzie captured the atmosphere: "In the Division Operations Room, the deepening gloom darkened the shadows cast by the figures of its occupants."[12]

MacKenzie listened in as McAuliffe's staff—which included Brigadier General Gerald J. Higgins, the assistant division commander; Lieutenant Colonel Carl W. Kohls, the G4, or chief supply officer; and the ever-busy Kinnard—discussed the events of the day.

The trio conversed about how, earlier, less than two miles to the southeast of Bastogne at Marvie, Colonel Harper's 2nd Battalion of the 327th Glider Infantry had thwarted an assault from Panzer Lehr. The news that day was a tradeoff. By late afternoon, reports had arrived that the battle for Noville had been lost. By 1400, units of the 506th were retreating pell-mell toward Foy. Elements of the 2nd Panzer Division had almost turned the retreat into a bloody rout.[13]

There had also been the report of the field hospital debacle. This was a tremendous blow to the entire division, and dramatically pointed out a weakness in the "backdoor" defense of the hastily created American perimeter. As the regiments had disposed themselves and divided up to cover the various 360 degrees around Bastogne, McAuliffe emphasized to his staff that constant communication and flexibility would be key to defending the seven roadways into the town.

McAuliffe worked with his staff to grasp the full situation and fully assess all of the information available, but in the end, he knew the decision would be his and his alone. The decision would likely be the toughest one of his career, and it would define him for the rest of his life. Should the 101st Airborne stay and fight in Bastogne or withdraw to the southwest?

If they decided to withdraw, they had to do it now. The Germans, like a great python, were coiling their way around the town of Bastogne. Within hours they might encircle all of the American forces in a suffocating death grip. A withdrawal from town, though, was fraught with risks and, in the face of intense enemy pressure, could lead to a rout and disaster. The Germans had plenty more vehicles than the Americans, so the likelihood was high that the Wehrmacht could easily catch up with the paratroopers, who would mostly be marching out on foot. The near disaster that day at Noville had pointed out that it was almost impossible for a predominantly infantry-heavy force to break contact and retreat in the face of a predominantly panzer-heavy force.

McAuliffe and his staff were not afraid of being surrounded. Paratroopers and glider troops were trained and expected to fight completely surrounded and cut off from friendly forces. This was nothing new. If they were to stay put and let the Germans surround them, the big question was how they would be supplied so they could continue to hold Bastogne. Food, ammunition, medical supplies, and fuel would be used up quickly.

The most pressing issue, as far as McAuliffe was concerned, would be the artillery ammunition. He knew he had the guns, but worried about having enough rounds for a protracted siege or sustained artillery action.

McAuliffe discussed the issue of resupply with his staff. For now, they were relying on a thin stream of trucks traveling on a single road to the southwest. If that was cut, resupply would have to come from the air. McAuliffe was gambling that the weather would clear enough in the near future for aerial resupply, but the forecasts were not good. The weather would apparently get a lot worse before it got better. For now, the defenders of Bastogne would have to make do with what they had brought and what they could find.[14]

He still needed more information. *What are we up against, exactly? What do the Germans plan to do?* He needed to know these answers before he made such a critical decision. For several minutes, indecision reigned in McAuliffe's mind.

Then there was a knock at the office door. Colonel Danahy had returned from Crossroads X and the overrun field hospital. He immediately filled in McAuliffe as to what he had seen.

"Sir," he announced to General McAuliffe with confidence, "they are using our equipment because they need it." Danahy had found eleven dead Germans wearing various articles of American uniforms and civilian clothes. Danahy doubted this was being done as a ruse, because it seemed inconsistent and random. In addition, he had received reports that the Germans were also using American tanks. It all meant only one thing to Danahy—the Germans were scrounging for stuff because they didn't have it themselves. The Germans were evidently not well prepared for a siege.

Hearing Danahy's assessment helped McAuliffe make his decision. "I'm staying," he declared. None of the men in the room knew it at the time, but their commander had just committed them to one of the epic stands in American military history.[15]

MacKenzie had witnessed the incident. Years later, he wrote of the stirring moment after the war. "The tenor of the General's voice marked what he said as the considered, unalterable decision of their commander, and the staff members experienced the thrill that command decisions always sent coursing through them in situations where their courage was challenged and where their lives could be forfeited. The bit of drama that General McAuliffe had furnished was needed. . . ."[16]

The Americans were staying in Bastogne. The staff responded, nodding. The officers and MacKenzie knew what the stakes were. They were taking a stand. Success meant victory and, more important, survival. Defeat meant probable death. McAuliffe's single-minded decision could turn out to be the most famous decision for the 101st Airborne, or it could turn out to spell their doom.

With that, McAuliffe made plans to make one last trip to meet with General Middleton and make sure that if they stayed in Bastogne, somehow they'd be supplied.

Later that night, General McAuliffe made a risky but necessary trip southwest down the last open road to Neufchâteau to meet one last time with General Troy Middleton, the VIII Corps commander, and inform him that the 101st Airborne was going to stay and fight in Bastogne. Unbeknownst to McAuliffe, the German 26th Reconnaissance Battalion was slowly making its way westward from Remoifosse. Several hours after McAuliffe returned to Bastogne, Major Rolf Kunkel's scouts cut the road to Neufchâteau, severing Bastogne's lifeline to the outside world. In short, had

McAuliffe returned several hours later, he would have been a prisoner of war instead of an American hero.[17]

Morning to afternoon, Thursday, 21 December 1944
Area of operations, 101st Airborne Division
Bastogne and environs

The morning of the twenty-first started out with a successful ambush at Crossroads X west of Bastogne. Baker Company of the 1/401st Glider Infantry destroyed an entire column of German vehicles traveling south from Salle. As a result, the 2nd Panzer Division had to commit more combat power to clear out the intersection. In addition, Baker Company's tenuous hold on the crossroads continued to disrupt German supply lines.[18]

Later that afternoon, the Germans started to pressure the isolated glider company. Around 1200 hours, after another probing attack of panzers, Lieutenant Colonel Ray Allen decided to pull back B Company, ordering Captain MacDonald to withdraw from Crossroads X. MacDonald's men reached the battalion lines at Flamizoulle that evening. Since the morning of December 20, this lone company had held up the supply lines of an entire panzer division.[19]

Since MacDonald's men had been pulled back to the north of C Company, it now fell on Charlie Company to watch the Marche road. The men knew that if they hadn't already, the Germans would probably try to seal this avenue or try once again to use it as an inroad to Bastogne.

Sergeant Robert Bowen, the leader of C Company's understrength 3rd Platoon, recalled the situation:

"Company C held a very vulnerable sector of the defense line with the greatest gaps between it and the other companies. The 2nd platoon held the westernmost roadblock in the division, dug in on the slope of a rise among some trees, with rolling hills and patches of woods to the front."[20]

Even with Baker Company's redeployment, in protecting this "back door" to Bastogne, the entire 1/401st was still spread much too thin. The dangerous salient that thrust out like a sore thumb from the perimeter surrounding Bastogne still existed.[21]

Because of this, Captain Preston E. Towns, Bowen's company commander, grew nervous. Like many of the other company commanders, he had heard the discomfiting noises of German vehicles and men moving near the road that morning. Towns, an extremely tall, lanky officer with a misleading baby face, had relayed this information to Allen. Allen told him to stay put for now.

When the word got back to him, it was no consolation to Towns. Sitting at his headquarters in a farmyard garage, his six-foot-seven frame squeezed into an old car, the Georgia native cursed when he received the response. Like MacDonald, Towns was frustrated with his position. He knew what was expected of his company, but for the next few days and nights, the glidermen would be dangerously exposed, spread out in a thin line almost five miles from the established perimeter.[22] To help out, McAuliffe agreed to send over some armor support in the form of two M18s from Templeton's 705th and a Sherman tank from the 10th Armored Division. In addition to that, the glidermen set up a 37mm antitank gun in the woods nearby.[23]

In the 502nd's area of operations, things were much quieter. 1st Battalion, under the command of Major John D. Hanlon, was on standby to support 3rd Battalion in case the Germans attacked Bastogne from the direction of Recogne. Later that day, Chappuis shifted Able Company from the area around Monaville to south of Longchamps to block any German infiltration emanating from Givry and Rouette. In addition, Chappuis started to send out reconnaissance patrols northwest toward Givry to probe and find the German lines. Other than a small run-in with a German patrol, the front was relatively quiet.[24]

All around the northwestern perimeter of Bastogne, from the Marche road to Champs in the north, the glider fighters of the 1/401st and paratroopers of 502nd sat in their exposed positions. Fortunately, all was quiet that night. Several of the soldiers on watch smoked cigarettes low in their foxholes, where the enemy couldn't see the glow. Others gnawed on K ration bars, or checked their weapons and counted ammunition. Large flakes of snow fell at first, which became smaller and icier as the evening turned into morning.

By morning, a virtual carpet of white blanketed the fields in front of them. It was going to be a white Christmas this year. Unfortunately for the soldiers around Bastogne, they didn't have much reason to celebrate.

Evening, Thursday, 21 December 1944
Area of operations, 26th Volksgrenadier Division
Bastogne and environs

Earlier that day, Colonel Kokott had decided to move his headquarters to the village of Hompre. This was not just on a whim. Kokott needed to be closer to where the fighting was breaking out, and today that had primarily been the areas to the south of town. On the twenty-first, his division had sustained 300 to 350 casualties fighting to secure the ground to the south of Bastogne. The 26th Reconnaissance Battalion incurred most of those casualties, but the price was worth it. Kunkel's battalion had tied the noose around Bastogne from the south. Now, Kokott hoped, it would be only a matter of time before the garrison in Bastogne withered and died.

Kokott was proud of his division. They had fought well, and now they were reaping the benefits of their efforts. Kokott had heard *Wacht am Rhein* was once again picking up steam. North of his division, almost an entire American division (two regiments of the 106th Infantry Division) had just surrendered in the Schnee Eifel on Tuesday. He wanted to repeat that feat here in Bastogne.

Scanning his operations map, which showed the various positions of his units, Kokott noticed that most of the enemy activity had been in the south and southwest. To him, it seemed the Americans were trying to break out somewhere on this side of the perimeter. In contrast, to the north and east, the lines had been remarkably quiet. It seemed to support his theory that the Americans were trying to escape toward Neufchâteau. Therefore he knew he should concentrate the bulk of his forces on the southwest side of the perimeter.

Just then an orderly arrived and handed him a piece of paper. It was the latest instructions from von Lüttwitz. Kokott read the instructions. The orders came as a shock. The first part informed him that the XXXXVII Corps commander was leaving the Bastogne mission to the 26th Volksgrenadier Division. This came as no surprise. Responsibility for keeping the Bastogne garrison surrounded would now fall on Kokott's shoulders. He realized the rest of Fifth Panzer Army would have to move on if *Wacht am Rhein* had any chance of success. It was the second portion that floored him. Although von Lüttwitz was handing off Panzer Lehr's 901st Regiment and giving him a corps artillery battalion for support, he was now ordering Kokott to *capture* Bastogne as well!

Kokott could not believe what he was reading. *Capture Bastogne!?* It was one thing to use his division to surround the town, but to capture it seemed a stretch. Did von Lüttwitz know something he didn't know? Perhaps the corps intelligence sections estimated that the Americans holding Bastogne had sustained greater losses than previously thought and, as a result, their morale was suffering? Still, Kokott thought, it was ludicrous to think that one division could defeat another division in a deliberate attack, especially when the enemy division was dug in and firmly emplaced in a major urban center. Military logic dictated that you needed at least a two-to-one advantage in combat power before you even contemplated tackling a foe who was in a prepared defense. All this and he faced an American armored combat command in addition to an elite airborne division—some of the toughest fighters the Amis had (The term *Amis* was German slang for Americans).

Von Lüttwitz did not have a choice. He had to keep pushing to the Meuse River, and he could not allocate any more forces to the reduction of the Bastogne garrison. He was under pressure from von Manteuffel, who was growing impatient with von Lüttwitz's corps, and needed to quickly seize the bridges at the Meuse if *Wacht am Rhein* were to succeed. He realized that Bastogne was what was dragging at the tail of his momentum. To von Manteuffel, *Wacht am Rhein* was running behind schedule, and Bastogne was merely a sideshow. The 101st was an American Fallschirmjäger division, not usually supplied or suited for long operations. The corps commander believed in a siege, and when the conditions were ripe—when the *Amis* ran desperately short of ammunition and supplies—it would be time for Kokott's men to drive in for the kill.

The problem was that there was no way for the Germans to predict when the American garrison in Bastogne would break. It could happen in days or weeks. The paradox was von Manteuffel had to have Bastogne as soon as possible, but he didn't have the forces to take Bastogne and reach the Meuse simultaneously.[25]

Outside in the streets of Hompre, the wind had kicked up, and the snow was coming down more rapidly than before, falling on the roofs of the farmhouses and barns. The snow was actually starting to stick, Kokott noticed. It reminded him of more peaceful Decembers in Germany—many a Christmas spent watching the beautiful blanket of snow out the window of his home, enjoying the company of friends and family. Now the weather seemed an enemy—as in Russia—a hardship. It was destined to make matters worse tomorrow, especially in light of this news.

Frustrated but determined, Kokott and his operations officer, Major Hans Freiherr von Tiesenhausen, went to work by lantern light, drafting up the next-day orders for the regiments. For Colonel Martin Schriefer's 77th Volksgrenadier Regiment, the mission was simple: Relieve the security detachments from the 2nd Panzer Division and head west. Looking at the map, Kokott could see that the 77th would eventually have to march to Mande

Saint-Etienne to link up with the rest of the division. In addition, Kokott wanted the 77th to concentrate its decisive operation around the tiny town of Champs. He could see that Champs also controlled a vital avenue into Bastogne from the northwest. As a matter of fact, Kokott noticed that the road here traveled through German-held Rouette and straight into Champs. Although his patrols had checked out this route, there had been no serious attempts at probing it and finding whether it was, in fact, the way into Bastogne.[26]

Friday, 22 December 1944
Area of operations, 101st Airborne Division
Bastogne and environs

Although it did not come as a shock, the first major snowfall of the season was certainly an unpleasant experience for the Americans dug in around Bastogne. Soldiers shivered as they woke up from their foxholes, shaking off the snowflakes and brushing their tarps and weapons clean. The ground was now rock-hard, making it almost impossible to build new positions or expand trenches. Water had frozen in canteens, and the cold remnants of K rations had no appeal as an early morning breakfast. Fingers and toes were still numb after the bitter-cold night, and many of the GIs were already reporting cases of frostbite.

Temperatures had dropped so low the night before that many of the men had slept on top of one another in bundles, using their own body heat to keep from freezing. Usually two to three soldiers were crammed into a foxhole. As they crawled out of their cramped holes to urinate, the paratroopers stretched stiff muscles and cracked their backs. Here and there a cigarette was lit and shared.

There wasn't much holiday cheer. Any thoughts of Christmas were buried under jobs to do, and the pure struggle to survive the cold and their predicament. Men grumbled and cursed the snow. They pulled their jacket collars up to protect their chins and necks and tried to warm their hands under their armpits. Some even stayed in their bedrolls, wearing the sleeping bags and wool blankets as makeshift parkas. Flurries continued that morning, driving the men to huddle around their small stoves for the little warmth they provided. Those who could find shelter in a barn or farmhouse quickly did so. It was clear to both armies now that they would be fighting a brand-new enemy for survival—Mother Nature.

The Germans didn't wait long that morning. Elements of the 26th Reconnaissance Battalion struck the overextended lines of Charlie and Able companies of the 1/401st Glider Infantry, west of Mande Saint-Etienne. Sergeant Robert Bradley and Sergeant Robert Bowen from Able and Charlie companies, respectively, rounded up some troops and a Sherman tank to evict the German intruders. After a brief firefight, they restored the lines with minimal casualties, while inflicting severe losses on the German grenadiers. Bowen, though glad they were victorious, knew the Germans would soon try again.[27]

Morning, Friday, 22 December 1944
Area of operations, Able Company, 1/502nd Parachute Infantry Regiment
Champs, Belgium

Like any old soldier, Private Ted Goldmann was used to being left in the dark concerning the bigger picture. But Friday morning, as the wind continued to blow snow through the tree lots and down the gullies near the town of Champs, Goldmann was starting to wonder just what the hell was going on. Once again A Company was ordered up and marching. When they first arrived near Bastogne, Able Company had dug in around the town of Monaville. Then, on Thursday, the company was told to desert their freshly dug foxholes and head eastward to reinforce the 506th. Goldmann had been part of the group that had gone to Recogne. While they had waited in their assault positions, word had come down to Captain Swanson, Goldmann's company commander, that Able Company and the rest of 1st Battalion were no longer needed. Picking up his rifle, bedroll, and musette bag, Goldmann marched with the rest of the Able boys to another position outside of Longchamps in some nearby woods. There the men spent the day digging new holes.

Now it was Friday morning, and once again A Company was ordered to move. Where, Goldmann had no idea. All he knew was that once they arrived they would have to dig more foxholes again, and this time it would be worse. They would first have to dig through the snow, then the ground, which had frozen rock-hard since yesterday. The small entrenching tools the paratroopers had carried with them since D-day were not up to the task.[28] Now he was trudging through the snow to another town. Where or why, he had no clue. All he could guess was that the Germans might be coming, having finally picked on the boys in the 502nd for a fight. The rumors flying around among the "dogfaces" were so bad that a few days ago he thought the Germans had surrounded and isolated part of the 502nd. It wasn't until the next morning that he found out to his relief that he wasn't alone: It was the entire division the Germans had surrounded. The news was no big deal to the paratroops. Goldmann shared the grim humor and spirit expressed by another soldier in a different regiment that had been making the rounds: "So they've got us surrounded, the poor bastards!"[29]

When Goldmann arrived in Champs, he found the townspeople incredibly friendly. They were hard-pressed like everyone else, but despite this adversity, they managed to scrape and scour to provide the paratroopers with bread, butter, and chicory for coffee.[30] While Goldmann enjoyed some Belgian hospitality, Captain Wallace Swanson, his commander, surveyed the area on the outskirts of the town. Swanson decided to place his 2nd Platoon on the southern flank, 1st Platoon on the northern flank, and 3rd Platoon would occupy a position in the center, but on the western outskirts of Champs. Like a good zone defense in football, Swanson had also ensured that he had backup in the form of solid artillery to cover the bowl-shaped vale encompassing Champs. The 377th PFAB sent him a forward observer so that his company would have immediate communication and on-the-spot artillery support. At 1015 hours, he radioed to Rolle that his company had established a roadblock in Champs. Luckily for Swanson, Chappuis had made sure that more help was on the way.[31]

For the past twenty-four-hour period, Lieutenant Claude Duvall's platoon (minus one section) of tank destroyers had been waiting for a new set of orders. The twentieth had been a day of frantic action, as Duvall had tangled with panzers in support of Lieutenant Colonel John P. Stopka's 3rd Battalion in Recogne, but on Thursday, Duvall's truncated platoon remained south of that town, sitting around, observing and reporting enemy movements.

At 1000 hours Duvall received an order to vacate his current position and link up with Captain Swanson's Able Company of the 502nd at Champs. Duvall was responding to the urgent call for armor that had gone out from Swanson that morning. When Duvall's M8 rolled into the town, he was pleased to find two M18 tank destroyers from Charlie Company of the 705th already there. Although this section of TDs had originally belonged to Lieutenant Paul Long's 3rd Platoon, it would now be considered under his command, since he was the senior 705th officer at that location. Luckily for Duvall, the TD commanders were both top-notch: Sergeant Tony D'Angelo and Sergeant Larry Vallitta.

Duvall quickly went to work establishing a defense. First he sent one Hellcat to occupy a battle position just to the south of Champs adjacent to a building. Next he directed the other TD to a spot on the main north–south road running through town so that it could watch over the first one and provide direct fire support against any vehicle coming down the Champs road from Rouette. In addition to Long's section, the division allocated one M18 tank destroyer from the 811th Tank Destroyer Battalion.

The story of this lone tank destroyer and its adopted crew was an interesting orphan's tale. The M18 was originally from 3rd Platoon, Charlie Company, of the 811th. The five-man crew had lost its original TD, fighting in support of Combat Command Reserve, 9th Armored Division, during the battle of Longvilly on the nineteenth. Then, by a stroke of luck, the crew discovered an abandoned M18 the next day. The remnants of their platoon and the rest of the company found themselves attached to Combat Command B of 10th Armored Division, which directed several Hellcats to man one of the many roadblocks east of Bastogne. On the morning of the twenty-second, CCB, 10th Armored, relieved the adopted M18. The crew decided on their own initiative to head west to Champs. It was a crew with a borrowed vehicle, in a unit that had borrowed them. They didn't know anyone else, but were willing to help defend Bastogne to the best of their ability. In Champs, Duvall positioned the "orphan" M18 by the village church to cover the approaches to the northwest.[32]

Satisfied with the positioning of the tank destroyers, Duvall drove his own M8 to a spot on the northwest side of town so that he could fire 37mm canister rounds anywhere in Champs to help break up any potential infantry attack. He knew the additional firepower would help Swanson and his boys feel a little better about their precarious hold on the town. With three TDs, an M8, a towed 57mm AT gun, and a slew of extra machine guns, Swanson had amassed enough firepower to beat back any probe with relative ease. But what if the Germans attacked with something more than a probe? Neither Swanson nor Duvall would know that answer until Christmas morning.[33]

Morning, Friday, 22 December 1944
Headquarters, 1/502nd Parachute Infantry Battalion
Hemroulle, Belgium

It was snowing again in the small Belgian village of Hemroulle. So much flurried from the skies that it clung to the spire of the local church. In house billet number thirteen near the end of the village, Major John Hanlon, 1st Battalion commander of the 502nd, kept his headquarters. A native New Englander, Hanlon, twenty-six, was nicknamed "Long John" for his skinny build. A top graduate of his 1940 ROTC class at the University of New Hampshire, Hanlon, like so many young officers in the airborne, had initially wanted to join the paratroopers when he heard they made fifty dollars more a month than the average soldier. But it was more than the money to Hanlon; it was the chance to play an important part in the war. Hanlon had served with the 502nd in Normandy and Holland. A German sniper had wounded him in Holland that September. It was a close call. He was shot in the back, and doctors were at first concerned that he was paralyzed, but luckily that was not the case. Shortly after his recuperation, Hanlon found himself heading out for Bastogne.[34]

Hemroulle was a small town with about a dozen farmhouses and less than a hundred inhabitants, and most of them had been sheltering in the basements of their homes since the beginning of the siege. There was not much in the way of cover nearby. There were some patches of trees near the town, a few hedgerows, but to Hanlon his men seemed terribly exposed. Their dark olive drab uniforms seemed conspicuous against the newly fallen snow.

Hanlon held an impromptu staff huddle.[35] During the brainstorming session, one of his staff suggested procuring bedsheets from the local villagers for camouflage. Hanlon nodded. It was worth a shot. He sent Captain Edward Fitzgerald, the battalion executive officer, and several members of his headquarters staff to contact the burgomaster of the town, Victor Gaspard, who had seen the Germans occupy his town twice (once in 1914 and again in 1940) in the seventy-some years he had lived near Bastogne. Gaspard, grinning behind a large white mustache, agreed to help the Americans. The two men rang the Hemroulle church bell. When villagers arrived to investigate the commotion, Gaspard explained to his people the need for white linen: anything—bedsheets, pillowcases, tablecloths, even window curtains—that would help the Americans hide their positions and vehicles.

Hanlon was moved when he saw the villagers disperse quickly, and then return with their arms full of white linen—more than forty-eight sets, individually some two hundred or more sheets, which were all the citizens owned, were turned over to "Long John" and his staff without a complaint. None of the Belgians even asked when the items would be returned. As

Gaspard explained to them, the Americans were here to save their town from the Nazis. Anything they could give that could help in that goal was worth the sacrifice of a few bedsheets.

Hanlon searched in his field jacket pocket for a receipt to write the mayor. Finding none at the moment, he felt embarrassed as his troopers carted the linen away. Gaspard smiled and touched Hanlon's hand. "Long John" promised he would reimburse the villagers after the war.

Soon paratroopers of the 502nd sported pillowcases for helmet covers; mortar and machine gun pits were blanketed under linen; and great white sheets helped disguise the hoods and frames of trucks, half-tracks, and jeeps.[36]

Morning, Friday, 22 December 1944
Headquarters, 115th Panzergrenadier Regiment
Roggendorf, Germany (111 kilometers northeast of Bastogne)

Earlier that morning, as Colonel Heinz Kokott pondered how he was going to take Bastogne, a middle-aged Wehrmacht *Oberst* (colonel) with thinning hair stepped out onto a darkened street in the town of Roggendorf, Germany. Like most towns in the *Heimat*, Roggendorf's homes and buildings were under strict blackout orders from the Reichsminister to keep Allied bombers from using the lights to guide them to their targets.

To Colonel Wolfgang Maucke, the whole atmosphere was deathly depressing. He glanced down at his leather riding boots. He noticed how quickly the bottoms had become caked in ice and snow. During the night, snowstorms had covered much of northwest Germany, Luxembourg, and Belgium. Now the soft white snow created a scene reminiscent of Christmas paintings and postcards. Maucke knew deep in his heart that once again, as in the past few years, there would be no Christmas rest. There would be no chance to spend time with family and friends in, for once, a peaceful Christmas season. No, for Maucke, commander of the 115th Panzergrenadier Regiment, Christmas would likely be another day of war.

It was still dark in the town of Roggendorf that morning as he hopped into his staff car. Snow continued to fall, and the warmth of the car was welcome as he leaned back in his seat and recalled the events of the last few days. Maucke had arrived in Roggendorf the night of the twentieth with the rest of his regimental staff. He waited in Roggendorf that day for his orders, which he assumed would dictate the role he and the 115th would play in the great offensive now under way. Finally, during the night, the commander of the 15th Panzergrenadier Division (and Maucke's superior), Colonel Hans Joachim Deckert, issued instructions for each of its regiments to move down to the town of Prüm, Germany.[37] The movement would have to be made during hours of limited visibility in hopes the American fighter-bombers would miss the convoys.[38]

For Maucke, this was not the first time he had led his men into battle against the American army. Unlike his brethren in the 26th Volksgrenadier Division, who had fought mostly against the Russians prior to the Bulge, the 15th Panzergrenadier had fought in Italy against both the American and British armies. The veterans of the division were well-versed in American tactics. They knew the Americans preferred to use firepower over manpower. They also knew the American eagle was faster and cleverer than the Russian bear on the battlefield. For the German soldiers of the 15th Panzergrenadier Division, Italy had been a crash course in learning to defend against an enemy who ruled the air, moved in unexpected ways, and typically had more firepower.

Luckily for Maucke, the 15th Panzergrenadier was a different kind of division. It was neither a panzer division nor an infantry division, but a bastardization of both—a balance of mobile infantry and armor. Whereas Kokott's 26th Volksgrenadier was heavily reliant on trains and horses to move its men and supplies around, the 15th Panzergrenadier was almost completely motorized, to the point that OKW considered it a mobile division. The only downside to being mobile was that Maucke's division had to rely completely on trucks, making it roadbound.

By 1944, the Wehrmacht's Panzergrenadier divisions had only two infantry maneuver regiments. In the case of the 15th Panzergrenadier, these were the 104th and Maucke's own 115th Panzergrenadier Regiments. The 15th also had a battalion of tanks and self-propelled assault guns, and almost an entire battalion of self-propelled tank destroyers (Panzerjägers). In the case of the 15th, two of these companies of Panzerjägers were self-propelled, and one company had towed Pak 40 antitank guns. Finally, like most infantry divisions, it had an antiaircraft battalion, an artillery regiment, and a reconnaissance battalion. In short, the typical Panzergrenadier division packed significant punch for getting the job done and going head-to-head with any Allied infantry division.

As Wehrmacht divisions went, the 15th Panzergrenadier was relatively new. It was born in the summer of 1943 on the island of Sicily from the remnants of the 15th Panzer Division. From there, it fought the Allies up the Italian peninsula. In August of 1944, OKW transferred the division northward to help stem the collapsing front in France. The division didn't get there in time to help prevent the Allies from liberating France. Instead, it wound up fighting in the Aachen campaign, where it suffered serious losses slogging it out with the U.S. First Army. As a result, OKW withdrew it from the front lines to refit the division in October 1944 in preparation for *Wacht am Rhein*.[39]

Like his division, Wolfgang Maucke was a survivor. At forty-four years of age, Maucke was aware that he was getting a bit long in the tooth to be an *Oberst* in the Wehrmacht. From photos, he bore a bit of a resemblance to the famous Afrika Korps commander, the Desert Fox—Field Marshal Erwin Rommel. Like Rommel, Maucke had proven a steady and reliable officer, but unlike Rommel, he had led a fairly lackluster career in the German army. His career had not enjoyed the meteoric trajectory of von Manteuffel's; nor did he enjoy the nepotistic relationship to high offices that Kokott did. Still, he was a trustworthy battle leader held in regard by his superiors. He had taken command of the 115th Regiment in April 1943 and successfully led it through various battles in Italy.[40]

Maucke first heard of the big push on December 14. Ironically, his regiment had been preparing for another operation in the area northeast of Aachen. In fact, his division staff had already briefed the regimental commanders on the twelfth of December, so purely by luck, his men, equipment, and vehicles were ready, stocked with ammo and supplies, and fueled. When the Aachen operation was postponed, Maucke was hoping his men could relax for the holidays, before the anticipated Allied spring offensive. On the fourteenth, Maucke and the rest of his fellow commanders received a summons to meet with the division staff the very next day. As with Kokott, the message piqued Maucke's curiosity, especially when he was informed that only commanders could attend the highly secretive meeting.

During that meeting, a mere two days before the date set for the attack, Maucke learned of *Wacht am Rhein* for the first time. Like his comrades in the 26th Volksgrenadier Division, Maucke had to sign a document swearing secrecy punishable by death. He also got the customary reading of Hitler's speech, and a staff officer's emphasis on how this effort would be all or nothing. For the original plan, the 15th Panzergrenadier Division was going to advance toward the town of Liège from the town of Roermond. This evening, however, there had been a change in orders, and to Maucke's chagrin, the 15th Panzergrenadier would now play a backup role, supporting the offensive as part of a secondary wave.

Maucke's 115th Panzergrenadiers received the news of *Wacht am Rhein* on the sixteenth. They understood the gravity of the situation, and perhaps had a better understanding of how hard the enemy (the *Amis*) could fight than many in Kokott's division. Most of the men hailed from the region around the city of Darmstadt, and the unit was one of the oldest regiments in the German army. It had served the kaiser before it had served the führer, and the men knew they had a distinctive and proud heritage to uphold.

As the column of vehicles began to move down the roads out of Germany, a nervous Maucke was just relieved to be on the move. While his command vehicle weaved its way along the snow-covered roads, Maucke wondered where OKW would eventually direct his portion of the division. Little did he know at the time that generals and staff officers were making decisions that would send his regiment to a fateful Christmas meeting outside Bastogne.[41]

Morning, Friday, 22 December 1944
Headquarters, XXXXVII Panzer Corps
Château de Roumont, Belgium[42]

Sitting in his temporary headquarters, General Baron von Lüttwitz marveled at his new abode. He couldn't have asked for a better building to house himself and his staff. The château at Roumont was built in 1912, near the town of Libin. With its conical spires and landscaped forests, the château resembled the mighty Renaissance châteaus of the Loire region in France. The freshly fallen snow had given the palatial home a fairy-tale appearance, as if it were caked in frosting. Now it was von Lüttwitz's headquarters.[43] Despite the luxurious and spacious surroundings, von Lüttwitz could not relax and enjoy them. He had an offensive to manage and a great many problems to solve.

One problem in particular was Bastogne, and Bastogne was quickly becoming the biggest problem. He needed to solve it, and quickly. As he sat in a fine chair in the luxurious château, von Lüttwitz mentally ticked off the disadvantages that the Americans must now be confronting: They were surrounded, could not get resupplied, and were cut off from the rest of the Allied army. The artillery fire seemed to have slackened. That could mean the *Amis* were running out of shells. There had been no major reports of clashes with American armor, so it was logical to suspect that they had only a scant number of tanks. Von Lüttwitz knew the 101st Airborne Division, the unit the Allies called the "Eagle Division," was the primary unit ensconced behind Bastogne's walls. A Fallschirmjäger unit was not designed to fight very long without supplies, armor, or additional infantry support. Also, the recent turn in the weather could only be making the situation miserable for the Americans.

He casually fingered the reports that lay on the table next to his chair. There was another option—a gamble at best, but a gamble backed with some power and based on some good news that had recently been received. Finally bending to von Luttwitz's request, von Manteuffel had asked OKW for reinforcements to divest Bastogne. Von Manteuffel knew there were few to come by, and such a commitment of releasing reinforcements to Fifth Panzer would have to be approved by Hitler himself. Also, Fifth Panzer Army had reported to him that almost an entire American division had surrendered in the Schnee Eifel four days earlier after the LXVI Corps surrounded them in a whirlwind attack reminiscent of the early days of blitzkrieg. There was also the recent news that the American attempt to defend St. Vith, a town north of Bastogne, was failing. It looked like the Americans would be lucky to withdraw their forces in time.

Von Lüttwitz was well aware that Kokott had successfully closed off Bastogne the previous day, so it was not impossible that the Americans might be desperate and running out of supplies, possibly in the same situation as the Ami troops at the Schnee Eifel or St. Vith. *He knew what he would do. It could o*nly be wise to give it a try first before committing Kokott's forces to an all-out attempt to break into Bastogne. He would throw the dice and see whether the Americans were willing to see things the German way. He would formally request the American garrison at Bastogne to surrender that afternoon. If it worked, it would free up the entire 26th Volksgrenadier Division and a regiment of Panzergrenadiers from the Panzer Lehr Division to continue the drive west.

The corps commander concluded that it was worth a shot. The day before he had already ordered the Panzer Lehr Division to be prepared to send an emissary to Bastogne, demanding its surrender sometime today. He knew Kokott would carry out these orders, whether he was in agreement with them or not. (News of the impending ultimatum traveled fast, and Colonel Kokott mentioned hearing about it on the twenty-first in his interview after the war. The bespectacled division commander even remarked that the possibility of a looming capitulation raised the morale of his men.)

Von Lüttwitz gave the responsibility to one of his staff, a Major Wagner, and together with Lieutenant Hellmuth Henke, the personal adjutant of General Fritz Bayerlein (commander of the Panzer Lehr Division), he would deliver the ultimatum sometime around noon today. Von Lüttwitz expected to hear back from the party soon. Hopefully the Americans would be sensible and they would agree to capitulation.

The general slumped back into his chair. Von Lüttwitz realized that he was issuing this ultimatum without General Hasso von Manteuffel's approval. He hoped his gamble would work, for if it did, he would probably be hailed as a hero. If it didn't, von Manteuffel, and probably all of Germany, would unleash their wrath on him instead of the Americans.[44]

1205 through early afternoon, 22 December 1944
101st Division Headquarters, Heinz Barracks
Bastogne, Belgium

About the time that Maucke's regiment was heading toward Bastogne, Major Alvin Jones, Colonel Joseph H. Harper's S3, took an incoming call from the 2/327th at Marvie. A trooper from Fox Company manning a roadblock had reported a bizarre sight: A group of four Germans—two officers and two enlisted men—carrying a white flag, had approached the 327th's outposts near Remoifosse. The Germans had walked right up to the American foxholes on the Arlon road leading straight south out of Bastogne.

The glidermen blindfolded one of the German officers, *Leutnant* Henke, who spoke English, and escorted him back to their command post.[45] The word was relayed to divisional headquarters at the Heinz Barracks. As headquarters staff and duty officers went to notify McAuliffe, the GIs in the know tried to guess the nature of all the excitement. Were the Germans surrendering? Had they had enough of American tenacity? Or were they asking the *defenders* to submit? The rumors and unanswered questions spread.

Major Jones carried the message to the division headquarters and McAuliffe.[46] When Jones arrived, McAuliffe was with Lieutenant Colonel Kinnard. The two men were discussing the success of Allen's 1/401st in holding the Marche road roadblocks. The day had started well, so McAuliffe was surprised to hear the news that the German commanders were demanding that the Americans surrender. A member of his staff read the typed message aloud:

December 22nd 1944

To the U.S.A. Commander of the encircled town of Bastogne.

The fortune of war is changing. This time the U.S.A. forces in and near Bastogne have been encircled by strong German armored units. More German armored units have crossed the river Ourthe near Ortheuville, have taken Marche and reached St. Hubert by passing through Hombres Sibret-Tillet. Libramont is in German hands.

There is only one possibility to save the encircled U.S.A. Troops from total annihilation: that is the honorable surrender of the encircled town. In order to think it over a term of two hours will be granted beginning with the presentation of this note.

If this proposal should be rejected one German Artillery Corps and six heavy A.A. battalions are ready to annihilate the U.S.A. Troops in and near Bastogne. The order for firing will be given immediately after this two hour's term.

All the serious civilian losses caused by this artillery fire would not correspond with the well known American humanity.

The German Commander [47]

McAuliffe could not believe it. He knew that his men were beating back the Germans every time they attacked. Not one German had made it into Bastogne, and yet the Germans were seeking their surrender. He laughed as the staff officer finished reading the message. "Aw, nuts," he blurted out. Without missing a beat, he left the command post for a jeep ride to congratulate members of the 1/401st on their work recapturing the roadblock near Mande.

When he returned a short time later, McAuliffe was reminded by a staff officer that the German officers were waiting for a reply. McAuliffe realized that protocol required that he provide an answer to the German demands. He looked back at his operations officer, Kinnard, and asked his subordinates what they thought would be a satisfactory response, knowing there was no way he would ever consider surrender.

"That first remark of yours would be hard to beat, General," Kinnard said.[48]

And with a grin from McAuliffe, one of the shortest, yet most famous military quotes in history was born. A staff sergeant typed up the formal reply:

> To the German Commander:
> N-U-T-S
> —The American Commander

While they waited, "Bud" Harper arrived at McAuliffe's headquarters after inspecting his defenses to the south of Bastogne. Located in the dark basement of the Heinz Barracks, staff wags had taken to calling the 101st's HQ the Cave. McAuliffe told the 327th's commander about the surrender ultimatum and handed it to him to read. He asked Harper what he thought might be a good answer to the German demands. Before Harper could respond, a clerk handed him another sheet of paper. Harper looked down and read it himself.

Harper laughed and told McAuliffe he would be more than happy to deliver it in person on his way back to the 327th's command post near the Arlon road. He wanted to see the faces of the German officers when they read the note. "I will deliver it myself. It will be a lot of fun."[49]

When he arrived at his own F Company's battle positions, Harper placed the folded piece of paper in the German major's hands. "I have the American commander's reply," he announced.

The guards removed the lieutenant's blindfold. Henke read the message, translating it for his major. Hearing the response, the puzzled major spoke briefly to the lieutenant, who then asked for his superior. "Is the reply in the negative or affirmative? If in the affirmative, we have the authority to negotiate further your surrender."

The lieutenant spoke perfect English with a British accent. Harper thought the German's tone dripped with condescension. He emphasized that it was clearly a refusal: "The reply is decidedly not affirmative. If you continue this foolish attack your losses will be tremendous."

The negotiations were over. With the deadline fast approaching, Harper rode with the German officers in a jeep, driving them back to the front line, where they met up with the two German enlisted men carrying the white flag, who were being watched by the men of Fox Company. As he removed their blindfolds, Harper felt his face flush with anger. He still wasn't sure the Germans got it, so he decided to make sure the message was understood loud and clear.

"If you don't understand what 'nuts' means, in plain English it is the same as 'Go to hell.' I will tell you something else—if you continue to attack, we will kill every goddamn German that tries to break into this city."

The German officers saluted stiffly. "We will kill many Americans. This is war," Henke allegedly retorted.

"On your way, Bud," said Harper, pointing the envoys down the road. As they stepped smartly away, Harper called after them, "Good luck to you."

Harper and the glidermen of F Company watched the emissaries trudge through the snow, back to their own lines. For years, Colonel Joseph H. Harper would always wonder what at that moment could have possibly possessed him to wish his enemies good luck.[50]

Von Lüttwitz had gambled and lost. Bastogne would have to be crushed, and he knew he was running out of time. General George S. Patton and the U.S. Third Army were coming up from the south, and fast. He knew he had only a few more days before they reached Bastogne. The next forty-eight to seventy-two hours were critical.

The defenders inside Bastogne agreed: Von Lüttwitz's estimate was correct. They were running out of supplies, chiefly artillery shells. Without artillery support, the paratroopers and glidermen had little chance to defeat the panzer onslaught that was surely coming.[51] Moreover, the division staff reckoned that the next major German push would be from the west, against the 1/401st Glider Infantry and perhaps the 1/502nd Parachute Infantry. Reconnaissance had indicated a buildup in those sectors.[52] The frozen terrain in the northwest was perfect for large-scale armor operations, perfect for panzers.[53]

Unknown to the Americans, General Heinz Kokott's troops were having supply problems of their own. Kokott, who was still stressed about his recent and confusing directive to both envelop and capture Bastogne, was having difficulty restocking ammo for his big guns and mortars. In short, the clogged supply lines were beginning to seriously hamper the German operations, particularly around the massive Allied-held roadblock known as Bastogne. For the Germans, the town was like a giant boulder that had become dislodged, falling into a small stream of water. German forces were forced to swing wide around the town, taking backroads many miles out of their way to continue the drive west. Moreover, the siege of Bastogne had become truly medieval when the besiegers were suffering as much as the besieged, Kokott mused. The only good news in terms of supply was his small-arms ammunition, of which he still had plenty on hand.[54]

Kokott heard later that day from his corps headquarters that the American commander had rejected the surrender ultimatum. It only added to his level of stress. Now Kokott was forced to back up the threat with firepower that didn't, at the moment, really exist.

In an interview after the war, Kokott wrote, ". . . the commander in charge of the Bastogne forces had declined a surrender with remarkable brevity." According to Kokott, McAuliffe's forces also backed up their general's insolence with dogged resistance.[55]

That morning, as Kokott's forces had jabbed here and there, especially down the Marche road approaches, the Americans seemed as strong as ever. In the battles around Villeroux, Senonchamps, and Assenois, Kokott's grenadiers were inching forward, but the Americans seemed to have an inexhaustible supply of artillery, which always seemed to hit at the right place and right time with the right amount of concentrated fire.[56]

Still, despite the failed surrender attempt, and despite all the losses and shortages, Kokott believed the initiative remained with his division. As Kokott looked over the map and read the reports, he believed they were getting closer and closer to finding a way into the American defenses and breaking the hard shell that surrounded Bastogne. Most important, he knew that supplies and reinforcements were on their way, even if it might take them some time to arrive. The additional artillery battalions from corps had already arrived, which would provide him the necessary firepower to match the American advantage in that arm. Moreover, his regiments that had not seen much combat had accomplished their respective missions that day. To the north, the 77th Volksgrenadier Regiment was still in the process of assuming the security mission of the 2nd Panzer Division in the northwest sector in the vicinity of Champs, as the panzer division moved on. Colonel Martin Schriefer reported that his regiment would complete this task sometime next morning.[57]

Kokott then looked up and asked himself, *What are the Americans trying to do?* The heaviest American effort in the last few days had resulted in the fighting in the southwestern/western sector around the town of Mande Saint-Etienne. Everywhere else the Americans had remained quiet. Kokott nodded to himself. He was more convinced than ever that the Americans were trying to break out from the Bastogne *kessel* (cauldron), and the most likely area for such an operation would be along the Marche or Neufchâteau highway.[58]

To Kokott, the reports of panic within the city of Bastogne, the Americans' desperate use of the Marche–Bastogne highway despite the exposure to German fire, and the lack of aerial resupply coupled with the continued resistance in the south meant the Americans were trying to find a way out of Bastogne.[59] In essence, just like what had occurred at St. Vith the day before, the Americans must be planning some way to execute a massive retreat from Bastogne. Basically, it was an escape. The only difference was that Bastogne was completely surrounded. The Americans would be in for a slaughter if they tried now, Kokott thought. He smiled. Unlike the American forces who had withdrawn from the pocket at St. Vith, for the defenders of Bastogne, it was far too late.

Acting on this assessment, Kokott reached a conclusion that night. He would use the 26th Volksgrenadier Division to choke off those western areas, and when the reinforcements arrived, he would be in position to use them for an all-out attack. Kokott sent instructions out to Schriefer's 77th Volksgrenadier Regiment to attack south from the Champs area while Kunkel's 26th Reconnaissance Battalion would strike north toward Mande Saint-Etienne. Von Lüttwitz's operations staff agreed with Kokott's conclusion and green-lighted his plan to cinch the knot even tighter. Furthermore, as a gesture of his faith in Kokott's new optimistic assessment, the corps commander ordered 2nd Panzer Division to give up one panzer *kampf-gruppe* to assist the 26th Reconnaissance Battalion's attack on Flamierge and Mande Saint-Etienne.[60]

However, Kokott knew that choking off Bastogne was only the start. He had realized, ever since his communication with von Lüttwitz the other day, that higher headquarters demanded he figure a way to take Bastogne, and take it soon. At the time, Kokott figured the 101st Airborne would try to break out to the southwest. He decided he could tie down the effort by the Americans simply by attacking Bastogne directly, forcing the Americans to shore up that part of their defensive line. He would attack from the southeast, through the outlying village of Marvie. The ground was not great, but the 901st Panzergrenadier Regiment had reported that the enemy forces there were also weak. Moreover, the 901st had seen little action in the last thirty-six hours and were still relatively fresh.

Kokott sent orders out that evening. The 901st would attack late in the day so that the 26th Reconnaissance Battalion and Schriefer's 77th would have completed their operation and thus could participate in an all-out attack if the 901st succeeded in seizing Marvie. One had to plan for such possibilities. If the Americans collapsed here, the Germans would have to move quickly to take advantage of the route in. The infantry and panzers of the 901st would attack shortly after sunset the evening of the twenty-third. The objective would truly be to take Bastogne. Kokott knew it was a stretch to take Bastogne with the forces he had under his command. It was a gamble that the American defense here was weak and faltering without supply. But his comrades to the north had done the same thing against the 106th Infantry Division. It was certainly worth a shot.[61]

Kokott, though, had either forgotten or ignored an important fact. His troops were not facing a green division whose soldiers had recently arrived in Europe. He was not facing a unit that had been demoralized and cut up in those first few hours of *Wacht am Rhein*. It would not be a showdown against line infantry low on supplies. He was facing a veteran airborne division whose paratroopers and glidermen had already fought and won some of the toughest battles on the Western Front. Furthermore, they were not alone. With them in the Bastogne pocket were a seasoned armored combat command and almost an entire battalion of tank destroyers—American tanks that had already inflicted serious losses on the 2nd Panzer Division.

Truth be told, both Kokott's and von Lüttwitz's assessments were off—way off. They would need more than a Volksgrenadier division to deal with the stubborn Americans in Bastogne. Luckily for them, help was on the way in the form of the 115th Panzergrenadier and its seasoned commander, Colonel Wolfgang Maucke.[62]

CHAPTER FIVE

"This Is Our Last Withdrawal.
Live or Die—This Is It."

(DECEMBER 23)

"To see our poor, brave fellows living in tents, bare-footed,
bare-legged, bare-breeched, in snow, in rain, on marches, in
camp and on duty without even able to supply their wants is
really distressing."

—Sergeant John Brooks of Pennsylvania at Valley
Forge, writing to a friend[1]

On Saturday, December 23, the stubborn American defenders of Bastogne
had reached their most desperate moment. That morning, many of the
hard-luck paratroopers of the 101st—the tankers and tank destroyers of
the armored units and the artillerymen manning their guns in the frozen
gun pits—were growing exhausted. They were cold, hungry, and running
out of everything.

Just two days short of Christmas, the lack of ammo was now being
compounded by the lack of cold-weather clothing and a shortage of medical
supplies. Men on outpost duty or patrols were having a difficult time keeping warm. On the MLR (main line of resistance), after the first snowfall the
merely uncomfortable nights turned deadly as temperatures dropped below
freezing. Men were constantly shivering, just trying to make it through each
frigid night. Christmas cheer was in short supply for the miserable GIs on
the MLR.

During the day, with the heat and movement of the men in the foxholes,

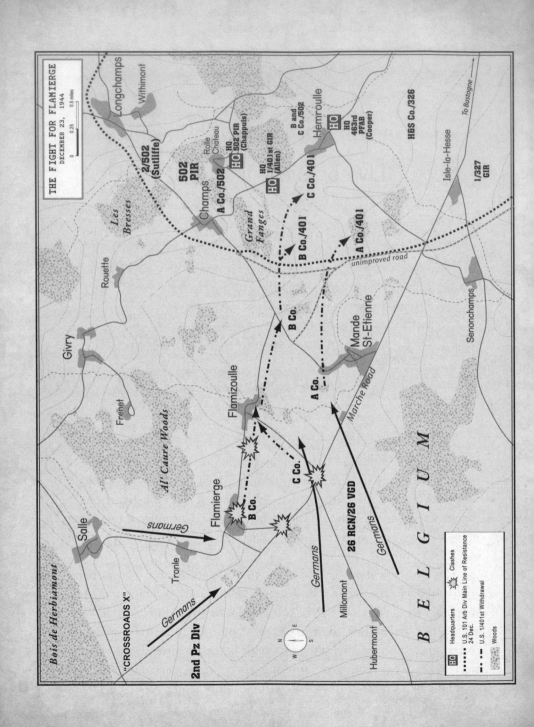

THE FIGHT FOR FLAMIERGE
DECEMBER 23, 1944

0   0.25   0.5 miles

Longchamps
Withimont

2/502
(Sutliffe)

502
PIR

Rolle
Château

Champs

A Co./502

HQ 502 PIR
(Chappuis)

HQ
A Co./502

HQ 1/401st GIR
(Allen)

HQ

Grand
Fanges

Les
Bresses

Rouette

B Co./401

B and
C Co./502

Hemroulle

HQ

HQ
463rd
PFAB
(Cooper)

H&S Co./326

C Co./401

A Co./401

unimproved road

Isle-la-Hesse

To Bostogne

1/327
GIR

Givry

B Co.

Frenet

Flamizoulle

Mande
St-Etienne

Senonchamps

Al' Caure Woods

A Co.

Marche Road

C Co.

Flamierge

Salle

Germans

B Co.

26 RCN/26 VGD

Tronle

Millomont

Germans

Bois de Herbiamont

"CROSSROADS X"

Germans

2nd Pz Div

Hubermont

B E L G I U M

N
W   E
S

Headquarters

Clashes

U.S. 101 Arb Div Main Line of Resistance

U.S. 1/401st Withdrawal
24 Dec.

Woods

snow and frozen mud would often melt and form a pool of water at the bottom of the foxholes. As the troopers bedded down for the night and tried to catch some valuable sleep, their soaking-wet clothes would often freeze as stiff as cardboard. Hundreds of men watched the skin on their feet literally peel away from what the military termed "immersion foot" but the GIs still called trench foot. Bare fingers froze to the metal on weapons. Faces went numb from frostbite caused by the windchill at night.

To make do, many of the Americans continued to scrounge and adapt. Some enterprising soldiers happened upon a barn full of burlap bags. Before long, the men were bundling the burlap over their shoes to provide an extra layer of insulation. The effect of an entire unit clad in this fashion must have resembled something from Valley Forge.[2]

Fortunately, the Americans had discovered a warehouse full of flour in Bastogne. The flour was used by the divisional cooks to make pancakes, which greatly supplemented the GIs' rations for the next few days. There were more examples of resourcefulness. Captain Jim Hatch remembered that Chappuis, as befitted a good regimental commander, was concerned about his men getting enough to eat. "Silent Steve" ordered his headquarters men to save one of their three rations a day to take up to the front line. On one occasion, Hatch decided to check in on how the men were eating, and found that one squad was dining on a preholiday dinner of fried potatoes and steak scrounged from a nearby farmer.[3]

Waking up outside of Flamierge, Sergeant Robert Bowen, the acting platoon leader for 3rd Platoon, Charlie Company, 1/401st Glider Infantry, was not so lucky. He remembered how his squad had suffered through the cold the night before, shivering in the winter air.

"The snow began covering the ground and quickly got deeper. Foxholes now became freezers, and no amount of stamping around could get one's feet warm," he said. "The cold had more serious effects, too. The actions on our weapons froze and all the lubrication had to be removed. Men who had foolishly discarded their overcoats and overshoes now suffered horribly. They spent a miserable night wrapped in blankets, shelter halves, and sleeping bags and still cold. I checked my squad several times during the night, mainly to keep warm."[4]

The tank destroyer crews fared better. Not that tanks were any warmer (the inside of a tank, with ventilation fans going and everything made out of steel, is actually quite a frigid home), but most of the men of Templeton's 705th had arrived in Bastogne fully supplied. Tank destroyer men gave much of their food, ammo, and warm clothing to the airborne troops. Tony D'Angelo remembered a particular incident:

"When we left [Germany] we were pretty much fully supplied with ammo, gas, rations, clothes. I remember we were always giving stuff to the 101st guys. See, they didn't have as much. I remember throwing a guy a pair of socks from my tank and he said thanks—like it must have been Christmas!"[5]

For the next few days as the soldiers were forced to endure the brutal winter conditions, any man who became a victim of trench foot, frostbite, or sickness meant a valuable warrior removed from the line of defense. On Saturday, McAuliffe realized the situation was becoming critical. Unfortunately, there was little he could do except tell his men to hold on. Hopefully supplies and Santa Patton would soon arrive.

Saturday, 23 December 1944
Area of operations, 502nd Parachute Infantry Regiment
Northwest of Bastogne, Belgium

Near the twin hamlets of Longchamps and Champs, Saturday morning found the Screaming Eagles of Chappuis's 502nd (nicknamed "the Deuce"[6]) still digging in. It had been a rough morning for Able Company. Swanson had sent out a small patrol late the night before, and he hadn't heard from them since. In addition, his forward observation post had opened fire on a German patrol, killing one of them.[7]

Still, compared to MacDonald's glider fighters and the men of the 506th, the men of the 502nd had escaped most of the fighting so far. Life was a bit more pleasant for the paratroopers. After all the marching around of the last couple of days, the men were finally able to place their machine guns and mortars, trail communications wire, throw some straw down in the bottom of their trenches, and start up the portable stoves for a little warm breakfast.[8]

Sergeant Layton Black recalled, "The sounds of war were muffled and far off, but growing closer and closer in the east. We were waiting."[9]

For Black, the operation started on a sour note. "When I woke up in the morning [on the first day] in a slit-trench foxhole, water was already settling in. The day started with rain and remained foggy and misty most of the day. It seemed to me that nothing had changed from the way things were three weeks earlier! [In Holland] [o]nly the terrain was different; now there were hills. Same Germans, same noise of war, the same dirty foxhole for a home. We were back in combat."[10]

Fortunately, the terrain was different. It was far more defensible than anything the 502nd had in Holland. Chappuis, the introspective commander of the 502nd, had picked a good spot to establish his defensive battle position. Almost directly between the 502nd and the forward positions of the 1/401st ran the Champs–Hemroulle road, running diagonally from the northwest to the southeast. On the northwest end rested the town of Champs; on the southeast end, approximately a mile and a half away, was the slightly larger village of Hemroulle, where Cooper's 463rd had established their headquarters. Although the ground to the west of the road was mainly made up of gently rolling fields, around the towns on either end and behind the road the terrain became hilly, wooded, and divided by small rivers and frozen ponds. This road (today the N854) was considered one of the best of the seven hard roads running into Bastogne. Chappuis and the other commanders in Bastogne knew such hard roads would be important to the Germans if they tried to force their way into Bastogne.

Heading southeast from Champs, a driver on this route would notice a meticulously groomed lane of trees that bisected the road roughly halfway between Champs and Hemroulle. To the right, the trees were elms, more than fifty feet in height, and extended in an almost perfect line for about a hundred yards. At that point, the trees became pines. To the left of the Champs road there were more pines, standing almost twenty feet tall and paired on either side of another lane. This road, known as the Dreve de Mande (usually referred to as the "Lane of Trees" by the Americans), angled northeast from the main route (to the left) and continued about six hundred yards into the woods and hills, ending at a postcard-perfect château called Rolle.[11]

In this beautiful seventeenth-century stone château surrounded by trout ponds, and located adjacent to the ruins of an earlier tenth-century castle, Chappuis had planted his headquarters. From this location, Chappuis believed he could best direct his regiment and cover the northwest sector.

Those first days after arriving at Bastogne, Chappuis struggled personally with the cold. As a native Southerner, he had trouble adapting to the frigid conditions typical of a European winter. On the ride in from Mourmelon, Captain James J. Hatch, his S3 (operations and training) officer, remembered how Chappuis had sat in the back of the jeep for the entire trip, bundled in blankets.[12]

Captain Joseph Pangerl, Chappuis' intelligence officer charged with interrogating POWs, was stationed at Rolle Château for most of the action.[13] In a letter home to his parents (written during the siege), he commented on the picturesque location:

"The setting here is much like a Hollywood one," he noted. "We are on a small hill with hills all around us, covered with pine forests. There are small lakes and rushing brooks that you always associate with such a setting and the fact that it snowed over a week ago and all the snow is still on the ground makes everything look like a Xmas postcard."

The practical Chappuis had clearly not chosen this location for its romantic appeal. Pangerl described how the stone walls made the headquarters men feel more secure:

"It has been modernized," he continued in the letter home to his family, "but, naturally, still has the three-foot-thick walls all around and you know what that means in combat dad."[14]

In front of the château was a typical French-style courtyard, with walls and an iron gate. Within these grounds there existed two long stone buildings, one on each side. On one side were former servants' quarters; on the other were stables and a barn. The staff of the 502nd's headquarters company—a polyglot of engineers, radio communication experts, intelligence officers, cooks, and medics—set up housekeeping in this area.

T/4 Robert J. Hale, one of Chappuis's radio operators, dug in with a buddy near a wall of firewood in the courtyard. From his vantage point, he watched the comings and goings during the daylight hours of the twentieth and twenty-first:

> Captain (James C.) Stone (the headquarters captain) would come and go, twirling his thin, but elaborate mustache. He holed up in a cellar under one of the stone buildings. Communications people occupied every available nook and cranny—barns, attics, basements and haystacks in the compound sheltered a wide variety of troopers. Wounded took up a large area in the stables; S2 (Military Intelligence) people and demo personnel shared available space with medics and men from the wire (communications) gangs. Parts of existing supplies were spread out under tarps on a sloping hillside, just outside the walls. I seem to recall at least one 6 X 6 truck parked just outside the main gates and under it one or two deep foxholes had been dug.[15]

Mixed in with the Screaming Eagles were several civilians. Rolle was the traditional center of much of the local community. There was the family, including Madame Nicole Maus de Rolle, twenty-seven years old at the time, and her children. The family had owned the land since 1902. Their take on this bizarre invasion of American personnel was at first mild bemusement. Later, as the château became the focus of German artillery attention, the madame opened up her massive home as a shelter for many of the nearby Belgian families caught in the deadly cross fire. Her generosity would be remembered by the locals for many years after the war.[16]

0950 hours, Saturday, 23 December 1944
3rd Platoon, Reconnaissance Company of
the 705th (one squad of Baker Company attached)
Outskirts of Flamierge, Belgium

Privates first class Carmen Gisi and Richard V. Bostwick had already spent two harrowing days at Crossroads X, the site of the field hospital ambush, and now they were going back into battle again. The two men grumbled, feeling that they were carrying more than their share of the fighting. Their mission was to force the German patrols back out of Flamierge, which the Germans had taken without much of a fight earlier that morning.

Bostwick remembered the particular mission and wrote about it after the war. He recounted the event: "In the morning, Captain Mac summoned our squad to the CP. It seemed that our squad's number had been coming up too darned often. When there was a dirty job to be done, we were the ones to do it. Mac didn't waste any words and we were soon prepared to go to the village on a 'combat patrol.' This meant being prepared to fight."[17]

Once again, MacDonald had picked their squad to team up with Lieutenant Rudolph Voboril's 3rd Platoon, Reconnaissance Company of the 705th Tank Destroyer Battalion.

Voboril would lead the combat patrol in his jeep. Following him would be four jeeps, two M8 Greyhound armored cars, and then a Howitzer Motor Carriage (HMC) M8, which was a small, converted M5 Stuart tank mounting a 75mm howitzer. The glidermen had found it stalled out and abandoned on a road. Bringing it back to life, they had commandeered it for the mission. With the glidermen riding along on the jeeps like migrant workers, overcoats and scarves flapping in the cold wind, the motley patrol moved out.[18]

As they started off, the men finally noticed that a minor miracle had occurred over Bastogne. The clouds that had blotted out the sun for the last five
days were gone. As the men glanced up, they noticed the skies were showing
some rare patches of blue. Better yet, the sun was actually shining. They knew
this was a good portent: The fighter-bombers would soon be back.

Within minutes, the American artillery opened up from behind them.
Carmen Gisi instinctively hunched over as the 75mm rounds screamed over
his head and the heads of his comrades, Richard Bostwick and Francis
Walsh. The three men then watched as the rounds impacted in Flamierge,
the tiny little crossroads town sitting in the dip of land and across from
the snowy hills they were facing. It was a memorable scene, as fountains of
earth and snow sprayed up in the air, the shells bursting amid the hamlet
of houses and showering the area with deadly shards of steel.[19] They knew
the Germans were there. Walsh and his platoon had already skirmished
with them the night before, and the Americans wanted as much steel as
possible on the target.[20]

Unfortunately, the barrage was a short one. In fact, to the men of 3rd
Platoon, it seemed that almost as soon as the barrage started, it stopped.
Colonel Allen had desired to pound with artillery the Germans deployed in
and around the town, but for some reason the effort was coming up a bit
short. Unknown to the glider fighters, Cooper's gunners were merely following McAuliffe's instructions from the day before. At that time, the general
had given specific orders to his artillery battalions. Since the vital artillery
ammo could rapidly run out, McAuliffe limited his artillery commanders
to conserve ammo and only fire barrages on priority targets. Basically, any
enemy position that was a direct threat to the American defense of the
perimeter.

Gisi recalled the bouncy and bumpy ride as the glidermen rode into
Flamierge on the back of the jeeps, armored cars, and a light tank. After the
shelling lifted, Rudolph Voboril's jeep stopped just outside the town. With a
wave of his hand, Voboril motioned two machine gun teams to set up and
start spraying the edge of the town like Chicago gangsters. Red tracers spit
out and lanced into the sky above the village.

Suddenly the belch of a German rapid-fire weapon answered the American machine gunners from the edge of the village. The men leaped to the
ground for cover as a German machine gun returned fire, pelting the road.
Almost instantly, several rounds slammed into the lead jeep, shattering the

glass windshield and hitting the young driver, Technician Fifth Grade Donald Kreider. Kreider slumped over and screamed in pain—a German slug had busted open his kneecap like a grapefruit on a firing range. Bostwick remembered the horrifying sight: "The jeep that was leading our parade was hit and the driver wounded, maybe killed. He was hanging half out of the jeep on the driver's side, some forty or fifty feet in front of me."

German lead continued to slash down the entryway to Flamierge, kicking up great spouts of snow and chips of rock from the road. Francis Walsh, watching Kreider bleeding and writhing in agony in the jeep's front seat, stood up and sprinted toward another jeep. Jumping into the driver's seat, Walsh stomped down on the gas and jerked the stick into first gear. The jeep lunged forward, spewing snow from the tires. Walsh deftly pulled the jeep parallel to Kreider's, huddling behind the dashboard for safety. Crawling over into Kreider's jeep in a prone position, he pulled himself over Kreider's screaming form and grabbed the wheel of that vehicle. He managed to pull the jeep around, and together, the two men drove back down the mile-long road to Flamizoulle.

The heroics impressed all who witnessed it, but the glidermen were still pinned down in the center of the street and in the icy ditches bordering it. Gisi was one of them. When the firing started, he dived onto the road and tried to make himself the size of a pea as bullets cracked all around him.

As he lay there hugging the pavement, Gisi looked over and saw one of his squad buddies staring at something up the road. Gisi turned his head and saw what it was: a hand grenade that someone had dropped during the initial barrage. Gisi recalled, "A few feet away a grenade was lying there. We thought that it would get hit by a machine gun bullet and hit [kill] both of us."

In a nearby ditch, Bostwick ducked for cover with Private First Class Norman Blimline, whom the men in 3rd Platoon affectionately called "Blimp." The two glidermen lay there, helpless, as the German machine guns stitched the road with a blistering fire. From close by, Voboril knew he had to get his men up and moving again. He waved for the 75mm M8 light tank to move forward and blast the German machine gun crews out of the buildings. The M8 HMC chugged forward, its howitzer flashing and booming. The crew of the little tank was firing at every house in Flamierge as if the Germans were everywhere. From his position on the ground, Bostwick watched the tank enter the town. Even with the pesky machine guns silenced, he and Blimline took no chances. They crawled down the ditch, carefully following the tank.[21]

Gisi got the short reprieve he needed. He scrambled to his feet and scurried to cover along the road. After several seconds, he looked up and noticed a statue of the Virgin Mary, who was staring down at him. It was one of the many roadside religious icons that were common throughout Belgium and France.

"Being Catholic, I made the sign of the cross," Gisi recounted, feeling especially religious at the moment.[22]

Ahead of Gisi, Blimp and Bostwick started to clear the houses in town. The two glidermen stood up and jogged to the nearest building. Standard procedure was to first toss a hand grenade through a window or a door. The men felt sure the Germans could be the only occupants of these buildings, as the locals had either left some time ago or were huddled in deep basements for cover.

Together, Blimp and Bostwick started lobbing fragmentation grenades into the houses, like a paper boy tosses a morning paper. Just then, something came back at them with force.

"I crawled into my helmet again. There was one hell of a 'wham!'" Bostwick recalled.

The Germans had responded with mortars. Bostwick continued his account. "I could hear the hollow 'choonk' sound of the shells leaving the mortar tube, indicating the krauts weren't far from us." Suddenly everything around them burst and exploded as a salvo of mortar rounds dropped down upon them like deadly baseball-size hailstones. The two leaped for cover, down to the earth and behind any concrete structures of the houses. Bostwick and Blimp were quick enough this day. Though the brief pattern of mortar bombs pounded the street and houses, leaving Bostwick's ears ringing, it did little else. As soon as there was a break, the two got up, dusted themselves off, and cautiously continued their task of clearing houses.

Their teamwork soon paid off. After they assaulted another house, five German soldiers appeared in the doorway, with their hands firmly placed on the backs of their heads. The duo then enlisted the aid of one of Voboril's Greyhound armored cars, which blasted away at the cellar windows of the next house with its .30-caliber machine gun.

The group repeated this a few times, steadily advancing deeper into

Flamierge. Chucking his last grenade into a window, Bostwick heard screaming, too high-pitched to be a man's voice.

"I ran into the house, to the head of the stairway leading to the basement, and held my rifle ready as the sounds of footsteps ascended the stairs. Sergeant [Hubert] Watson and some of the others joined me just as an old man and three women, all civilians, appeared. Two of the women were elderly and one appeared to be about twenty years old. The old man had a terrible gash over his right eye and the skin was hanging down over the eye. My grenades had done this."

Bostwick felt terrible. He recounted what happened next: "The young girl asked if we were Americans; we assured her that we were. She bawled and bawled and kissed every one of us on the cheek. The old man was attended to by the medics. They were loaded onto a vehicle and returned to our lines."

Using a flashlight, Sergeant Watson, Bostwick's squad leader, led the pair into the smoke-filled basement, weapons ready. He discovered a passageway that clearly led to another room. Bostwick motioned to Watson that he wanted to toss a hand grenade into the room, but Watson shook his head. He didn't want to injure any more civilians. Instead, the sergeant took a deep breath and plunged into the dark room while the other two covered him.

Bostwick later wrote, "Watson had guts. He entered the room with that stupid flashlight throwing a feeble glow before him. Suddenly, the light fell upon a German uniform. It was incredible. There were seven others, fully armed, standing with their backs to the wall, standing in the darkness, with their hands over their heads."

Eight more Germans joined the tally of prisoners the glider fighters were acquiring. After they relieved them of their weapons, Bostwick and the others then led them outside for questioning and processing. By the end of the short block, they had four more prisoners, Germans who had stumbled out of another house, shocked and dazed from the M8's cannon shells that had turned the basement into a lethal kill zone.[23]

Despite the lackluster artillery prep, the fight for Flamierge, though intense, had turned out well for Ray Allen's men. Regiment got word about 1050 that Voboril's force had pretty much regained the town.

But the truth was that Kokott's panzers were coming. Their orders were simple—take Flamierge, wipe out the glidermen there, and slice up Allen's extended line.[24]

Late Saturday morning, fortune was finally going to reward the stubborn GIs holding Bastogne. Lieutenant Colonel Carl W. Kohls's hard work had paid off. For several days he had been desperately trying to arrange the aerial resupply mission that could be the salvation of the Americans in Bastogne.

It came as a relief to Kohls when the weather cleared Saturday morning. Like so many groundhogs, GIs crawled from their foxholes to warm their faces and gaze in wonder at shadows they could finally see on the ground.

It only got better. Out of the sky, like guardian angels, two groups of pathfinders arrived that morning. The drone of an IX Troop Carrier Command C-47 aircraft split the sky around 0945. Several more followed. Through the clear, cold air, the pathfinders, whose mission it was to parachute in and prepare drop zones, tumbled out of the aircraft, surprising even the Germans who were on watch around Bastogne.

As the men gently settled into the snowy fields close to Bastogne, pathfinder leader First Lieutenant Gordon Rothwell unhooked his parachute harness and quickly found the division headquarters. He linked up with an overjoyed Colonel Kohls, the two planning the particulars of the scheduled supply drop.

This was great news for the headquarters team, who perked up almost instantly. At last, resupply! The weather had cleared, and the news reenergized the G4 staff as they rushed to work.

Rothwell informed Kohls that the first flight would arrive over the drop zone within an hour and a half. Kohls wasn't worried. He had long ago designated the planned drop zones, and he directed Rothwell and his team out to the area west of town. In short, the DZ would be almost in Colonel Allen's and Major Hanlon's backyards.

The pathfinders were greeted with smiles and grins by the headquarters types. The newcomers were regarded as heroes. They quickly found a large, ten-foot-tall stack of bricks belonging to a Belgian woman named Mrs. Massen. It was on the highest point in the area, perfect for setting up their radio and signal equipment to help guide the aircraft in. The brick pile also had the double advantage of offering possible cover, in case the enemy spotted them and opened fire.

Within minutes Rothwell's men were transmitting. A little after eleven in the morning, they had established contact with the first wave of resupply planes. When Kohls heard the news, he breathed a great sigh of relief. Around 1150 hours, the pathfinders had a visual on the massive air armada and began to direct them toward the drop zone. For General McAuliffe and the others, the armada meant the paratroopers would soon have what they needed to continue defending Bastogne.[25]

Noon–1230, Saturday, 23 December 1944
26th Volksgrenadier Division Headquarters
Hompre, Belgium

Until that noon, Colonel Heinz Kokott thought things were going well. The 26th Reconnaissance Battalion, together with some panzers from the 2nd Panzer Division, had commenced their attack to the west of Bastogne. Initial reports claimed that Major Kunkel had captured Flamierge, though the report was still unconfirmed as of noon. In addition, Colonel Schriefer's 77th Volksgrenadier Regiment was moving steadily southward to attack the American units west of Bastogne.

While he stood over the operations map and listened to reports coming in on the radio at his headquarters in Hompre, Kokott heard a sudden commotion from outside. At first, he ignored it, but then he noticed as more and more of his staff stepped outside to see what was going on. Curious, he too stepped out into the cold.

What greeted him was a disaster in the making. Leaderless mobs of German paratroopers—Fallschirmjägers—many discernible by their squared-off helmet rims and Luftwaffe smocks, were streaming past the division headquarters. Kokott knew they belonged to the 5th Fallschirmjäger Division, part of the Seventh Army to the south. The Seventh Army had the task of blocking General George Patton's Third U.S. Army as it was driving northward to the relief of Bastogne. Obviously things did not appear to be going so well. Kokott could see the looks on their faces. They seemed a beaten and demoralized force. One of his staff officers shouted at the paratroopers, asking what had happened.

A frightened soldier responded, "The enemy has broken through! He moved to the north with tanks and has captured Chaumont!"

Soon Kokott learned that Patton's tanks and infantry had wiped out the Fallschirmjäger battalion defending Chaumont. The remnants were now stumbling past him. Most of the officers and NCOs had died fighting the American forces, leaving their soldiers leaderless, panicked, and lost. Meanwhile, horse-drawn vehicles were showing up around Hompre, starting to tie up traffic as supply and support elements of the broken paratroops tried to escape the American tidal wave arising from the south.

For a moment, Kokott felt sorry for the men who were retreating. Like many *landsers*, these men were not hardened infantry soldiers. Though many were young and fit, a majority of them had served most of the war in rear echelons units as clerks, cooks, and technicians. In the case of the 5th Fallschirmjäger Division, most of these men had never actually participated in a parachute jump or been parachute trained. They were Fallschirmjäger in name only, much less knew the first thing about being a soldier, let alone a Fallschirmjäger. Now they were told to stop General George S. Patton's Third Army, one of the finest Allied armor-heavy forces. It was no wonder that so many of them broke.

Despite his sympathies, Kokott had to whip them into shape. They were no longer Luftwaffe clerks. They were going to have to be soldiers now, which meant they had to turn around and fight. If they didn't, Patton's forces would not only overrun the 5th Fallschirmjäger, but, without protection to his southern flank, Kokott's 26th Volksgrenadier Division would be overrun too. Kokott ordered his staff officers to start organizing the masses into cohesive units.

Suddenly Kokott heard the ripping fire of machine guns and the chunking sounds of 20mm flak cannons pounding skyward. He stared into the midday sun and saw winged dots screaming down from the heavens like mythical Harpies. He knew instantly what they were. The American fighter-bombers had returned. The traffic jam of disorganized men, plodding horses, wagons, and idling vehicles moving along at a snail's pace in the bright sun was just too easy and attractive a target for the Allied pilots. Once again, Kokott braced for destruction.[26]

1206–1430, Saturday, 23 December 1944
514th Fighter Squadron
Over Sibret, Belgium

It wasn't even noon, and the 514th Fighter Squadron had already seen a great deal of action that day. Now, miles from their base near Mourmelon, another flight of P-47s was diving through the thin cloud layers and into combat over Bastogne. Originally this flight had the mission to provide security to the lumbering procession of C-47s that were heading to Bastogne to drop supplies. Like sheepdogs, the stubby P-47s protected the herd of Dakotas from any Luftwaffe wolves that might be hunting for easy prey. The fighters, faster than the big transports, would fly lazy Z-shaped patterns over the flight in order to keep pace and watch all possible attack angles. The fighters had left Mourmelon at 1206 hours, but because the distance was so short, they reached their rendezvous point over western Bastogne at 1230.

Within minutes of linking up with the procession of C-47s, the pilots of the 514th spotted a worthwhile target to the southwest between Sibret and Hompre. It was a convoy of more than twenty German vehicles. Some of them were trucks pulling artillery, and some were staff cars driving along the road. The flight commander gave a "Tallyho!" With a roar from the huge turbo-charged Pratt & Whitney engines, the fighters peeled off and started to line up to strafe the convoy. For the pilots of the 514th, it was a turkey shoot. Howling down from the skies over Bastogne, scores of silver jug-shaped fighters dived on anything German around the perimeter.

Down below, Kokott's men were unprepared for the "*Jabos*" (German slang for Allied fighter-bombers). The Germans had grown complacently comfortable with the absence of Allied fighter-bombers due to the poor flying weather. Little was done, initially, in the way of setting up a thorough antiaircraft defense. Terrified German soldiers dived into icy ditches for cover. Vehicles were perforated or blasted apart as their gas tanks ignited from the aerial assault. It seemed there was no place to hide. The Thunderbolts were relentless, like jackals picking apart the Germans below. In minutes the convoy was reduced to a smoking and burning wreckage of metal and flesh. Later the pilots claimed they destroyed twelve vehicles and damaged another eight in only six passes.

As they turned for home around 1400 hours, one of the pilots noticed a vivid scene far below. Across the white fields, puffs that looked like little exploding kernels of popcorn were erupting to the west of Bastogne. It appeared the American positions in that area were under a sustained German artillery bombardment. Indeed, they were. The targets were Allen's bold glider-fighters around Flamierge, and their situation had taken a decided turn for the worse.[27]

1230–1300, Saturday, 23 December 1944
26th Volksgrenadier Division Headquarters
Hompre, Belgium

Colonel Kokott witnessed the wrath of the *"Jabos"* as they screamed down from the sky and visited death and destruction on the convoys between Hompre and Sibret. Vehicles vanished in clouds of fire and ash, while crumpled and bloody forms that once resembled German soldiers lay scattered along the roadways, some burned horribly beyond recognition.

Kokott watched as his officers and NCOs went to work. With the efficiency that the Wehrmacht was known for, they rounded up the survivors and began to organize them to care for the wounded and prepare for a possible ground attack. Meanwhile, antiaircraft crews continued to fire away at the spots in the air, brass shells rattling out of their guns with the fury of rapid fire.

Many of Kokott's men were so shocked by the savagery of the attack that they failed to notice the arrival of the transports, focused as they were on trying to reorganize. From the southwest came a steady, ominous drone. A procession of cargo planes started to arrive over Bastogne—an aerial parade. When the slow-moving air trucks began to disgorge parachutes by the hundreds, perhaps thousands, the Volksgrenadiers realized what was happening, Kokott most of all.

Watching with his mouth open, Kokott suddenly received a message from his operations center. He read it to himself as he watched in despair. "Enemy parachutists [are] jumping and landing in our rear," it read.

Curiously, no one in the German high command ever contemplated the Allies' reinforcing their trapped airborne troops with more paratroopers. In all their meticulous planning, the possibility had never been discussed.

Now Kokott also had to change his thinking. If they were being enveloped by fresh Allied airborne troops, he would need to arrange some immediate defense. He issued orders for all men, regardless of military occupation, to set up defenses around Hompre and as far west as Sibret and Clochimont. In addition, several of the division artillery batteries turned their guns 180 degrees to face southward. He also called up the reserves to buttress their defenses. There was little he could do about the airdrop, but he had to stop Patton from coming up from the south. Fortunately a platoon of four Tiger tanks was passing through Hompre. These tracked behemoths were one of the most lethal tanks in Hitler's arsenal of destruction. They weighed more than fifty-six tons and mounted an 88mm cannon that could outshoot any American Sherman Tank. Evidently they had become separated from their parent unit.

Kokott wrestled with his thoughts for a moment. They weren't his for the taking, but he needed them badly. Seizing the opportunity, he commandeered the platoon of Jagdtigers and, together with a detachment of grenadiers from his Division Combat School, he sent the *kampfgruppe* south to Grandrue and Remichampagne to stop Patton's 4th Armored Division. It was all he could do. Kokott returned to his command post and waited. If the Americans in Bastogne had, in fact, been reinforced, and Patton's tankers were making jabs to the south, then the next few hours would be crucial.[28]

Noon, Saturday, 23 December 1944
101st Airborne Division Headquarters, Heinz Barracks
Bastogne, Belgium

McAuliffe and his staff had watched from the front entrance to the Heinz Barracks as the welcome sound grew in volume from the southwest. The pathfinders had done their job well. As the men nearby hollered in joy, the C-47s from Troop Carrier Command spread over Bastogne like angels with olive drab wings. From each aircraft dropped packages ("parapacks") that blossomed with red, green, and blue parachutes and drifted lazily to the ground. Typically, red parachutes signaled ammunition, green was rations, and blue, water and other items.[29] The parapacks mainly fell on the low and open ground the pathfinders had marked as a drop zone about a quarter mile due west near the town of Savy. To many watching the drop, the gently falling parachutes reminded them of the falling snow the day before.

Fred MacKenzie also witnessed the drop that day from the division headquarters. Outside, he had noticed a group of men steadily growing. MacKenzie, with the typical reporter's nose for a story, followed the men. He overheard members of the division staff saying, "Wait and see," and scanning the sky as if Santa and his sleigh would suddenly appear.

It was every bit as good. MacKenzie described what happened next: "Low over the field and town then swarmed objects so dear to their straining eyes they might not look upon [an] angel band with greater wonderment and joy. The objects were the foremost planes of a mass flight of 240 C-47 cargo carriers bringing them supplies. Here were messengers of tidings that the world of friends and decency had not forgotten the defenders of Bastogne."

MacKenzie heard the men cheer and scream as if they were at a sporting event, watching each large plane float overhead with a roar. With a flair for the drama of the moment, MacKenzie later described the men's glee as each aircraft passed, dropping bundles to the hard-pressed GIs below.

"Upturned faces in the headquarters courtyard were transfigured with rapture as the planes came on and on like great immortal carriers of good from heaven. . . ."

MacKenzie noted one paratrooper among the group exclaim as he danced a little jig of joy, "We'll beat the krauts now, sir."[30]

In a letter written years later, Kinnard also shared his emotions:

"In my mind's eye I recalled a soldier who saw his shadow on the snow. He began an Indian war dance whooping, hollering, jumping and stomping. He fully realized the importance to us of a break in the weather, which would permit air operations. Then I saw all the retrieval teams running for the precious bundles, which they correctly interpreted as assurance that we could, and would, hold Bastogne. It was a once-in-a-lifetime occasion, which all who were there will never forget."[31]

The GIs watched German antiaircraft fire lash several C-47s as they entered and exited the drop zone. Here and there a plane would start to smoke as some of the flak hit home. Several aircraft crashed into snowy fields within the American lines, or the aircrew bailed out of a smoking Dakota. Unfortunately, a few wound up on the wrong side of the lines and were quickly made prisoners by the Germans, but the main body of the flight did not deviate. The brave pilots kept a steady hand and continued to plow forward through the storm of bursting flak. The courage of the pilots won them new respect among the paratroopers, who had been somewhat critical of Troop Carrier Command's reputation after the Normandy drops, where many paratroopers had been dropped and scattered way off target.

Because of the airdrop, the various regimental S4s collected nearly 4,000 rounds of 75mm howitzer ammunition, more than 1,400 rounds of 105mm ammunition, 3,300 rounds of 60mm mortar ammunition, 1,100 rounds of 81mm mortar ammunition, more than 410,000 rounds of .30-caliber machine gun ammunition, almost 900 bazooka rockets, and more than 56,000 rounds of .50-caliber machine gun ammunition. In addition to all the ammunition, the logistic crews amassed more than 16,000 K rations for feeding the troops. Not all of the parapacks fell where the Americans could recover them, but enough did to help resupply the dangerously diminishing essentials: artillery ammunition and medical supplies.[32]

The drop had been a tremendous success. Certainly more drops would be required, but it was a good start. The headquarters crew hoped that SHAEF's best meteorologists could forecast similar weather tomorrow, Christmas Eve. If that was the case, perhaps, McAuliffe's staff thought, another air supply mission could get through.

1200–1600, Saturday, 23 December 1944
3rd Platoon, Reconnaissance Company of
the 705th (one squad of Baker Company attached)
Flamierge, Belgium

Like Sergeant Layton Black in the 502nd, Carmen Gisi was glad to see the planes overhead. From his position at Flamierge, Gisi could count the parachutes dropping from the C-47s. The men knew what that meant: "There were parachutes dropping with ammo. I will never forget it; we were yelling and screaming with joy."[33]

Meanwhile, the men of 3rd Platoon, Reconnaissance Company, had run into a problem. Their commandeered HMC M8 had decided to stop working. Some of the crew reckoned it had run out of gas. Worse yet, it was out of ammunition.[34]

As the men tinkered with the broken-down tank and tried to hunt up some jerry cans, Bostwick heard Blimline call to him from a nearby house. Blimp was upstairs, looking out a window. Bostwick ran over to the house and clambered up the stairs. An excited Blimp was gesturing. He had spotted a group of German soldiers moving back into Flamierge from the west. Using binoculars he had pilfered from one of the German POWs, Bostwick spied a German truck hiding behind a copse of trees several hundred yards from town. Grenadiers were pouring out the back and fanning out to attack Flamierge.[35]

German mortars pounded the town. The Americans went scrambling for cover. Voboril realized the Germans were coming in force again, and knew he and his men would need help. He ordered one of his armored car commanders to return to Flamizoulle and get more reinforcements or the town would be lost. The M8 sped out onto the roadway, driving for nearby

Flamizoulle. Already other armored cars from Voboril's recon unit were ferrying reinforcements into the growing melee in Flamierge.[36]

Rifle and machine gun fire echoed through the streets and off the tall houses and buildings in Flamierge. With the addition of reinforcements from both sides now, the fight between the Americans and the Germans was growing in intensity. The men of 3rd Platoon fought tenaciously to hold on to the town.

Back in Flamizoulle, Francis Walsh decided it was time to get back to his platoon. He had dropped the wounded Kreider off at the aid station and, upon hearing the renewal of gunfire back at Flamierge, hopped in the jeep and drove back. As the little jeep sped down the mile of road separating the two towns, Walsh could hear mortar fire. Ditching the jeep for safety's sake, he decided to make the rest of the run into town on foot. Grabbing his M1 carbine and web gear, he had just started off when he heard the familiar but frightening whooshing sound of incoming mortar rounds, dropping very close.

Walsh dived to the wet ground as several rounds burst near him, showering him with dirt. Nonplussed, he brushed himself off and continued into town. It was then that he noticed a formation of white-clad German grenadiers behind him, moving toward Flamizoulle. Walsh recalled the incident after the battle. He had observed ". . . the Germans moving down the road in an infantry formation. Headed down the road toward the area of Flamizoulle and they're in white camouflage uniforms . . ." The Germans were apparently trying to cut the road, and cut off the Americans in Flamierge from the rest of the battalion in Flamizoulle. Walsh knew he had to get to Flamierge, find Lieutenant Voboril, and warn him. Time was crucial.

After several minutes of dodging and diving, he finally reached Voboril's strongpoint. Panting, Walsh told the lieutenant the news that the Germans were about to cut them off. Voboril cursed. Whether he liked it or not, now he had to fall back. He shouted to the men, "Load up. We're moving back to Flamizoulle."

Voboril's plan was simple. He was going to use the jeeps and armored cars to move the men back to the 1/401st roadblock outside of town. From there, they could reestablish some semblance of a defensive line before Flamizoulle.

The armored car sergeant Voboril had sent back to Flamizoulle returned by this time, bringing gas to try to fuel up the M8 HMC. Unfortunately, the gas didn't help. When the crew pressed the ignition, nothing happened. Perhaps the lines were frozen by now, or perhaps the old tank had just given up the ghost. The men realized they didn't want the tank to fall into German hands, so they tossed a white phosphorous grenade into the engine. The engine compartment smoked and caught fire. As the men turned and walked away, they cast a last look at the brave little gun carriage that had helped them out in their struggle to hold Flamierge. Now, though, it left them with one fewer means of transport for Voboril's fall-back plan.[37]

Bostwick, guarding the German prisoners in a stable that was attached to a house, heard the news they were leaving. By now German mortars were raining down, pummeling the town, and Bostwick could see a huge number of German *landsers* sprinting across an open area nearby. Sergeant Watson—Bostwick's squad leader—told them about the armored car shuttle service waiting with engines running outside. Voboril said to move out the wounded first. While they ferried the bleeding troopers out, Bostwick, Gisi, and the others could do nothing but wait for the motorcade to return. In his account written after the war, Bostwick remembered his wait in the stable: "While in the stable, I stood between two horses and was surprised at the heat given off from their bodies. It was a bitterly cold day."

When the armored cars came back, the men sensed this would be the last trip. Instead of attempting two more shuttle runs, Voboril and Watson realized time had run out. German gunfire was already so close it was "tearing chunks out of the buildings," according to Bostwick. This time it would have to be all or nothing—as many could fit on the vehicles, and then the rest would have to take their chances withdrawing on foot.

The German grenadiers were only a few blocks away when 3rd Platoon started to move out. The men were leaning forward in the doorway of the building, preparing to sprint. Bostwick vividly described what happened next:

"This was it. A half dozen of us, together with the armored car and twelve prisoners, made a run for it. We ran and ran. The cross fire was murderous. Tracer bullets cut red patterns all around us and behind us. One soldier made the mistake of climbing atop the vehicle. A single bullet through his head and he toppled without a sound into the ditch. One of the prisoners was shot through the jaw; he didn't make a fuss, just kept on running. After running the longest three miles of our lives, we literally stumbled into the company area."

When the exhausted men reached the roadblock, it was 1600 hours. Unfortunately, Flamizoulle wasn't much safer than Flamierge by that point—still easily within striking distance of the German lines and extending far from the American lines. While the men of 3rd Platoon had been fighting for Flamierge, an even larger German force had attacked to the south of the 1/401st and was about to overrun the entire battalion. For Ray Allen and his men, the nightmare had just begun.[38]

1200–1330, Saturday, 23 December 1944
Area of operations, Charlie Company, 1/401st Glider Infantry
Just west of Mande Saint-Etienne, Belgium

Captain Preston Towns needed help, and he needed it now. Not long after the planes had dropped tons of supplies in his backyard, Kokott's *kampfgruppe* from the 2nd Panzer Division commenced its attack on his understrength C Company. At about noon, outposts first reported panzers and white-clad troops emerging from the Bois de Valets woods, south of the main road leading to Saint-Hubert.

Towns forwarded the news up to Allen's HQ. The observation post had counted five tanks and an undetermined number of infantry. Within minutes the armored column fell on Towns's 2nd Platoon, which was manning a roadblock on the Mande Saint-Etienne–Hargimont road. Towns once again called up Bowen, his acting 3rd Platoon leader, to come to his command post in the old garage. Towns was in a quandary. He knew that Allen could not spare him any men from A and B companies, as the two were currently engaged in the battle for Flamierge. He would just have to keep shuffling around his platoons in the hope that would be enough.[39]

After several interminable minutes, Bowen arrived, panting, having plowed through the snow. The young sergeant's face was rosy from gasping for air and the cold. Bowen poked his head inside the car.

"Bowen, 2nd Platoon's under heavy attack. They don't know if they can hold. They've had some casualties and need help. I want you to take [Elmer] Felker's and [Joseph A.] Kloczkowski's squads and move to 2nd Platoon's roadblock to support them. Lieutenant Wagner will meet you near the intersection of the main road and the one out front of here and lead you into position. I don't have to tell you to hurry. Good luck and do whatever you can."

To Sergeant Bowen, Captain Towns looked tired, worn down, and despondent. The constant fighting and lack of sleep had taken their toll on his lanky commander, wearing lines in the typically youthful face. For Towns, Bowen was one of his best soldiers, and he was someone he could rely on when the chips were down, but he sensed he was sending Bowen into a hellstorm. Little did either man know it, but they would never see each other again.[40]

1330–1400, Saturday, 23 December 1944
1st Platoon, Reconnaissance Company, 705th Tank Destroyer Battalion
Approaching Mande Saint-Etienne, Belgium

First Lieutenant Richard B. Miller was thankful for a brief respite. Miller and his men were able to catch a breather after some hard work supporting Allen's beleaguered battalion over the last few days. Like Voboril, Miller was the commanding officer of a recon platoon in the 705th's reconnaissance company. Unlike Voboril's crew, right now the men of his 1st Platoon were spending their time relaxing, smoking, and grabbing some grub. It was also a good opportunity to check the vehicles and restock ammo and supplies.

Earlier in the week, Miller's recon platoon had been busy helping the 501st and conducting various reconnaissance work for Allen's glidermen near Mande Saint-Etienne. Saturday morning Miller was told by the 705th headquarters to remain on a fifteen-minute alert in Bastogne.

Miller was a high-strung type, and though he was thankful that his men could grab some R & R, he felt it was time to get back into action. That afternoon, he got his wish. At 1330 hours, his platoon received orders to move out to Monty, the town across from the Marche road and on the edge of the 1/401st's sector. Captain Towns's cry for help was about to be answered. According to initial reports, German tracked vehicles had attacked the southern and western lines of Towns's Charlie Company. On the way out of Bastogne, Miller's force joined up with a larger unit, including six M18 tank destroyers under the command of First Lieutenant Morris Klampert of A Company of the 705th. (Two of the tank destroyers were actually under the command of First Lieutenant James W. Crudgington of C/705.)

On the edge of town, the caravan stopped for a quick planning session. Amid the idling vehicles, the officers and senior NCOs met to discuss their strategy. Donald "Moe" Williams, first sergeant of the C/705th, was in attendance, making sure his tank commanders got the latest information before they headed out. Suddenly the familiar screech of incoming artillery shells split the sky. The men jumped off the road or behind buildings for cover, steadying their helmets with their hands as they ran.

The first few shells came in fast. Williams was thrown to the ground by the blast, which instantly filled the air around him with a cloud of dirt. The explosion rang in his head like a bell. Sergeant Ralph "Shorty" Vining of C Company ran to his aid with several others. Vining noticed that Williams was "knocked over by a blast and could hardly speak or breathe. I pulled him over to a building while the rest of our group started to move out."

Williams eventually came to. He was okay, though he had a hell of a headache as a result of a severe concussion. For a while all he could do was sit against the wall of the building and shake. Miller, meanwhile, watched as the heavy vehicles fired up their engines and rumbled down the frozen highway. It was obvious to him that this was something big. The TDs were precious and few—the threat in this sector must be something serious if the division was sending this many into the area.

As Klampert's makeshift platoon drove down the road, the crews did not know that actually several German panzers had beaten them to the punch while advancing toward Mande Saint-Etienne. Like an Old West ambush in a dark canyon, the Germans were going to have the first shot, and in armored warfare, tanks that got the first shot usually won.

Beyond Mande Saint-Etienne, the Marche highway entered a deep cut that was nearly 550 yards in length. On the western end of the cut was the hamlet of Cocheval, while to the south were several patches of woods. The panzer commanders had selected these groves to conceal their tanks as they were driving toward Mande Saint-Etienne. Being on higher ground, it was fairly easy for the Germans to spot the column of blind Hellcats as they emerged from the road cut. By the time the Americans spotted the panzers, it was too late. When the last of the Hellcats crawled out of the cut, the German tanks opened fire.

The result was predictable. Soon German tank shells screamed in and had reduced one of the M18s to a smoldering wreck. Corporal Henry A. Ruotanen, of Ontonagon, Michigan, the commander of the lead M18, fired several 76mm shells at the Mk IVs, which had merely bounced off their thicker armor. A gliderman was helping to act as a spotter, but as Ruotanen attempted to climb up the berm to the side of the road for a clear shot, his TD was fatally hit. Ralph "Shorty" Vining witnessed the tragedy:

"He got off one shot and then backed back into the cut bank. They claimed that they had hit the German tank but the shell may have glanced off. The 101st Airborne guy was looking through his binoculars and told me he didn't think they had hit the German. He passed me the binoculars. When he did, that German tank turned and was facing us. I slid down the bank and was going to go over and stop the tank destroyer from going up for another shot, because the German could knock it out face on. I hollered to them. I couldn't climb up on the tank destroyer because they had started to move. He went out for a second shot. He got a shot off all right, but he got one back. It went right under the barrel of the tank destroyer."[41]

There was a sudden flash and an impact like the open turret had been whacked with a giant sledgehammer. A 75mm shell had sliced like a bolt of lightning through the Hellcat, killing Ruotanen's gunner, Corporal Charles J. Mayeux, a native of Bunkie, Louisiana. The blast had also severely injured Ruotanen and another crewman. Klampert leaped from his vehicle and helped drag the wounded crew to safety. A dismayed Miller quickly tossed a white phosphorous grenade into the engine. Miller knew it would be impossible to recover the damaged tank destroyer under enemy fire. (Later that night, the platoon armorer crawled up and removed the breechblocks so the Germans couldn't use the abandoned Hellcats.)

Klampert's convoy was still stuck in the road, which was rapidly becoming a death trap. He ordered the remaining vehicles to sprint out of the cut bank to the right and make for the safety and concealment of the streets and houses of Cocheval. The Hellcat drivers would take advantage of the vehicle's greatest combat advantage—its quick speed.

The M18s gunned their engines and popped into gear. Within seconds they had raced out of the cut and veered right down the embankment toward the town. One of the panzers tried a parting shot at the Hellcat taking up the rear. The German round let out a horrendous crack as it split the air—a near miss. Klampert established a roadblock with two Hellcats on the eastern side of Mande Saint-Etienne. There was little else he could do but take up a defensive position in town. With the panzers covering the road, the TDs were not going to get through to Towns.

The western defenses of Bastogne were crumbling. The men of Allen's battalion were becoming strained, and German tanks were just adding to their misery. Towns's Charlie Company had been fending off the Germans for hours, and now they were starting to break. Klampert's TDs couldn't get through to them in their hour of need. All that mattered to the exhausted glider-fighters was who would escape from that shrinking pocket with their lives.[42]

Midafternoon, Saturday, 23 December 1944
Area of operations, 2nd Platoon, Charlie Company, 1/401st Glider Infantry
Just west of Mande Saint-Etienne, Belgium

Bowen arrived at 2nd Platoon's position, exhausted. He had run a gauntlet of fire from Captain Towns's command post. Along the way, he passed by some foxholes. In one of them he made a gruesome discovery—the bits and pieces of a body. A mortar round had impacted directly in the hole, vaporizing the occupant. "I didn't know it then, but it was all that remained of my close friend Homer Johnson," Bowen wrote years later.

As Bowen counted his men, he quickly realized that some of them were missing. The heavy snowdrifts had turned running into an exhausting exercise—damp boots slipped and failed to find traction in the thickening snow. Bowen suspected that many of the men had fallen behind, struggling to keep up while carrying some of the heavier equipment. One of the missing was his radioman. Because of this, Bowen never got the word that Towns had now changed his mind, ordering Bowen's platoon to stand down.

Bowen finally linked up with First Lieutenant Robert A. Wagner of 1st Platoon at 2nd Platoon's command post in a "sunken courtyard" next to a stone house just north of the Mande Saint-Etienne highway.

Wagner and Bowen quickly took stock of the situation. A Sherman tank that had provided crucial fire support earlier had been knocked out. Nearby in a stand of fir trees stood a 37mm antitank gun, but it, too, was useless. The biting cold had frozen the wheels to the ground as if it had been welded in place. German shells continued to shriek and pound the earth nearby, causing the glidermen to flinch with each near miss. Bowen counted eleven German tanks and scores of Panzergrenadiers several hundred yards away, pouring a blistering fire into the courtyard.

One Hellcat, commanded by Staff Sergeant Chester Sakwinski from Milwaukee, Wisconsin, was turning out to be C Company's guardian angel. As Sakwinski's TD slammed shells toward the Germans, a second Hellcat was in a bit of a fix. Apparently the ice-cold temperatures were affecting more than just 37mm guns that morning. The turret on the M18 had frozen, and the tank commander could not get it to rotate.

The tank destroyer scooted out of the courtyard and raced back to Bastogne to get it fixed. As it rumbled away, a Mk IV took a shot at it. Several men recalled watching the German shell knock a pile of bedrolls off the turret, but that was the sum of the damage done. Again speed had saved one of the little M18s.

Meanwhile Sakwinski was playing a game of hide-and-seek with the panzers. He would order his driver to pop up from the courtyard onto a slight berm and shoot at the Germans. Before they could retaliate, Sakwinski would quickly roll back down. Having no clue how many tank destroyers were defending the house, the German tankers hesitated, instead of bum-rushing the house with their superior numbers. Sakwinski's charade was helping buy time for Allen's glider-fighters.

Towns's men were falling left and right in the fields near the house. As Bowen lay there in the cold snow, the sound of gunfire started up again, reaching a crescendo of intensity as the Panzergrenadiers closed in. Bowen looked around at the dark forms of the dead and dying, bright red blood spilling into the snow. He knew almost all of them. Bowen might have wondered whether he too would soon be joining them.[43]

1200–1500 hours, Saturday, 23 December 1944
Headquarters, 1/401st Glider Infantry
Flamizoulle, Belgium

Back at his command post in Flamizoulle, Allen could tell the Germans were trying to penetrate his lines north of the Mande Saint-Etienne highway and bypass his battle positions. If they did that, Allen reasoned, he would have little to throw at them. There was a huge gap between his battalion and the 502nd to the north. If the Germans found that gap, it would be a serious threat to the western perimeter. Using that avenue of approach, the Germans could sweep around and cut off his entire battalion from Bastogne. Worse, from there, the door to Bastogne would be left wide-open.

Allen knew his best chance for success was artillery, and although he had been scrimping for rounds earlier, he had also witnessed the airlift. He knew there had to be more mortar and artillery rounds available somewhere. At 1500 hours he requested artillery. He also asked for six hundred rounds for his mortars. In addition, he asked his regimental headquarters to send as much small arms ammunition as they could spare.[44]

Allen's prayers were soon answered. Almost immediately he got more artillery, and he got a lot of it. Evidently the high command felt this was as good a reason to justify a massive artillery support mission as any other. Now the infusion of resupplied 75mm rounds enabled Cooper's 463rd to provide prodigious amounts of indirect fire in support of Allen's beleaguered battalion.

"Keynote, this is Five Baker." First Lieutenant Henry L. Smither's voice broke through the static. "Fire mission . . . Grid . . . 475598 . . . Break . . . 482592 . . . Ten enemy tanks and personnel."

The battle staff quickly made the calculations and then sent the fire solutions to the gun line. Since they had more ammunition now, the FDC staff allocated two entire batteries, Baker and Dog—eight guns total—for the fire mission. This was first time that day that two batteries were tasked with supporting one unit.

Cooper's little Pack howitzers banged to life as they fired salvo after salvo. By 1610 that afternoon, they had fired fifty-eight rounds of high explosive at the enemy.[45] Soon, their brothers in the 377th PFAB had joined in with their guns and nearly a hundred rounds landed in one square kilometer southwest of Cocheval. The airborne gunners were doing what they did best—supporting the infantry with massed firepower.[46]

Late afternoon to early evening, Saturday, 23 December 1944
Area of operations, 2nd Platoon, Charlie Company, 1/401st Glider Infantry
Just west of Mande Saint-Etienne, Belgium

To Bowen and Wagner, crouching in the cold near Mande, the rain of steel falling on the German positions was welcome, but not enough to drive the Germans back. In his memoirs, Bowen claimed that division had denied all requests for artillery support. Obviously that was not the case; it is more probable that the German fire was so intense that Bowen never noticed his own artillery.

The situation was deteriorating rapidly beyond all control. Neither Bowen nor Wagner had communications with Captain Towns. They were clueless as to how long he expected them to maintain their positions.

The most pressing problem was the panzers. Sergeant Sakwinski was fighting off one group of German tanks with his tank destroyer, but another group of Mk IVs had edged their way forward, and from a distance had managed to curve around and enter a small draw where Sakwinski couldn't get them. Bowen recalled seeing a bazooka in the back of a lone CCB 10th Armored half-track that had been abandoned by its crew nearby. Bowen figured he or one of his men might be able to sneak up on one of the panzers and help even the odds for Sakwinski.

Bowen darted off, running in a crouch. He returned a moment later with the great steel tube over his shoulder. Wagner helped him load one of the rockets and then tapped Bowen on the helmet. Bowen took a deep breath and headed back out across the snow to get a better fix on the flanking panzers. In his memoir, he described what happened next.

"I had to cross the front yard of the house that was being swept by small arms fire. However, I managed this without being hit, even though my heart was in my mouth the whole time. I settled behind the embankment and looked through the trees for a target. A tank was sitting in a little draw some 200 yards out. I set the sights, took a long careful aim after making sure the pin was pulled in the rocket, and pulled the trigger. Without a shield on the weapon or protective glasses, the blast from the rocket nearly blinded me. However, I kept my eyes on the tank. The rocket it grazed it without exploding. The tank hurriedly backed out of sight."

Bowen wasn't satisfied, but wisely decided to get out of there before the panzers pinpointed his position and unleashed their fury upon him. He returned to the command post and reported back to Wagner. He told the lieutenant, "I'd like to go back in case the tank moved forward again."

Wagner said no. He showed Bowen that there were only two rockets left. "I think we should save the rockets. We might need them later."

The sergeant nodded in agreement. A few minutes later, Staff Sergeant Louis A. Butts arrived from his squad. Butts was one of the 2nd Platoon squad leaders, with an unshaven face that resembled the dogface stereotype of a GI from the Bill Mauldin cartoons. Bowen could read the frustration and anger in his expression. Butts was clearly wondering why his men were fighting and dying for what seemed like an impossible position to hold.

"Half of my squad is either dead or wounded. And we're nearly out of ammunition. The rest of the platoon is no better off. I think we should pull back," Butts said in a growl.

For a moment Lieutenant Wagner said nothing, quietly considering the various options available to him. None of them were good. Finally he looked back at Butts and snapped, "Sergeant, my orders are to hold this position. Until there is a change in those orders, that's what I plan on doing. Now go back to your men. You'll be notified if we are to pull out."

Bowen later wrote about Butts, "Even though his face flushed with anger, he gritted his teeth, turned and somehow got back to his squad's position."

For the next hour or so, the panzers continued to slam round after round into the 2nd Platoon battle positions while German mortars hammered away at the survivors. Amidst the carnage, Sergeant Joe Damato of Wagner's platoon arrived at the makeshift CP. Second Lieutenant Leonard E. Gewin, Sakwinski's commander, Wagner, and Bowen were all there to speak with him. Damato brought bad news: The whole line was collapsing.

Bowen recalled, "Suddenly the whole world seemed to explode in my face. I felt myself being tossed aside as if a giant bubble had violently burst at my feet."

A German mortar round had detonated within ten feet of their location. All four of the men suffered wounds. Gewin was a mess. Bowen and Damato were both injured but conscious. Luckily, Wagner had sustained only a minor wound to his foot. The lieutenant didn't have time to worry about it. Once the medic wrapped his foot, he hobbled off, trying to maintain what was left of 2nd Platoon and the roadblock. Meanwhile, the medics determined that Bowen and Damato were out of the fight. They were taken to a basement of a nearby house. To ease the pain, a medic gave them morphine.

Wagner didn't get very far when he realized the Germans had come up from behind, cutting him off from 2nd Platoon. He limped over to 1st Platoon's position. When he got there, he discovered that his own platoon had left, falling back to the main American positions beyond the road.

For Bowen and Damato, lying in the basement, the next few hours were a morphine haze. Damato had suffered a huge gash in the back of his right leg. Bowen had been lucky. His suspenders had helped deflect the force of a chunk of shrapnel, but the piece had still stuck in his ribs. The medics were able to remove it, but not another jagged chunk that was sticking out of his wrist. By now it was dark. It had been a while since they had spoken with Wagner, and Damato sensed something was wrong. The two men contemplated a run to try to find Wagner, but Bowen knew Damato would never make it.

Outside, the constant chatter of gunfire had begun to peter out, as Bowen recalled. He reached down and checked to see whether he still had his pistol. By now most of the men knew about the massacre at Malmedy.

The prospect of capture by the Germans did not sound good. From the news of Malmedy, it seemed the Germans often arbitrarily executed captured GIs. Bowen and Damato lay huddled in the cellar, resting in some hay with other wounded men, including the intrepid crew of Sakwinski's M18, who had finally been forced to give up their single-handed duel with the German armor. Several civilians were also sitting in the dark basement, shivering with fear and cold.

"[The basement] . . . had become complete chaos. The civilians were hysterical, crying, praying, and screaming. The medics were unable to quiet them," Bowen remembered. "The door was shoved in with a kick and a big German in a snowsuit came in, machine pistol leveled. He had a flashlight, which he shone on the medic and the litters."

Bowen heard one of the medics say in German, "Nothing but wounded." The grenadier pointed the machine pistol at the Americans. Fortunately, he was only checking to see if the American medic was telling the truth about the wounded. Using a flashlight, he shone a beam around the room, examining each soldier to confirm that he was indeed out of the fight. As the German did this, Bowen gripped his pistol even tighter and started to raise it up. In his morphine-induced haze, his first reaction was, *I'm not going down without a fight*. Quickly and wisely, he reconsidered. Sense had come back into his head, and he tucked the pistol away.

"Yes, they are all wounded. That's good." The German spoke in English. He then looked right at Bowen and remarked, "For you the war is over."[47]

1840–2200 hours, Saturday, 23 December 1944
Headquarters, 1/401st Glider Infantry
Flamizoulle, Belgium

Ray Allen knew it was past time to go. All day he had listened to C Company's desperate struggle to hold open the Mande corridor. By evening the bad news had arrived—the Germans had retaken the town of Flamierge. Voboril's force had come back pell-mell, the same way they had gone out, riding on the jeeps and Greyhounds. This time, though, they brought wounded.

At 1700 hours, a platoon of tank destroyers arrived from the 705th's B Company. These Hellcats were under the command of First Lieutenant Robert Andrews. Andrews had positioned his four tank destroyers south of Flamizoulle, and angled their fire to the south and southwest to block the Germans if they attempted to approach the American lines from that direction.

The news got worse as darkness descended and the cold night swept in around Flamizoulle. Around 1800 Allen got a call from Towns that the Germans were swarming over his lines to the south. The words were short, but the meaning was clear: "1810—Enemy tanks reported to have overrun Blue Charlie." Not long after that disastrous report, division radioed to all units that enemy tanks were rolling down the Marche road east of Monty. The time was 1835 hours.

At 1840 hours, Allen knew he had to put plan A into effect. He had held out as long as he could. Allen knew that ever since their arrival several days ago, the glider-fighters of the 1/401st had fought tooth and nail to protect the "back door" to Bastogne. Lots of American blood had been spilled in that effort.

Fortunately, Allen's three company commanders—Towns, MacDonald, and Bowles—knew what plan A was, and how to execute it. They had discussed it after MacDonald returned from Crossroads X on the twenty-first. Each company would leapfrog backward, allowing another to cover it as it moved. Allen remembered the Germans had a vote in this matter too. If they were as spent as the Americans from fighting all day, the glidermen had a good chance of pulling back unmolested and reconsolidating their lines. If not, or if the Germans had fresh reinforcements, well, Allen didn't want to think about it.

Baker Company was to stand fast, since it was the designated rear guard. Meanwhile, the tattered remnants of Charlie Company, all of Weapons Company, and the battalion headquarters would pull back through Flamizoulle. Able Company had to take a different route, since it was the closest to Bastogne, withdrawing north and then east past Mande Saint-Etienne.

For a short time Flamizoulle was a tangled mess, as various units had to thread the needle. Charlie Company had the most difficult time, since a good portion of Captain Towns's company was still in contact with the Germans. Furthermore, several vehicles from the 705th Tank Destroyer Battalion were also in the mix. The result was a temporary logjam at the Flamizoulle chokepoint. Compounding the situation, Allen didn't have enough trucks and jeeps to carry all the wounded, ammunition, and equipment. The glidermen had to destroy some of the equipment to keep it from falling into German hands.

Despite this, most of the battalion managed to pull back to a new main line of resistance that was east of Mande Saint-Etienne and parallel to the Champs–Hemroulle road behind it. By 2200 hours that night, Allen informed Harper and McAuliffe that he had established his new command post near Hemroulle.

That night, more snow was falling—soft flakes at first, which became smaller and more like ice pellets as the dark of night spread into the pink stain of morning. The weather was uncomfortable for the exhausted men of the 1/401st, but in a way a blessing. The snow and fog would help to mask their movement as they continued to break contact and withdraw. The bulk of the men retreated almost two miles closer to Bastogne. As the drained glider fighters of C Company threw A6 machine guns, mortar plates, and ammo over their shoulders and quietly moved out, they took one last glance at Flamierge and Flamizoulle in the distance. The villages were largely quiet and, in the softly falling snow, resembled something from a peaceful Currier and Ives print. Allen's men guessed by now that the twin towns were completely occupied by German soldiers.

MacDonald's B Company (to the north) and Bowles's A Company (to the south) quickly emplaced on a ridgeline near a farm road overlooking Mande Saint-Etienne. Now the lines of the 1/401st were a bit safer and more compact, though as they dug new foxholes through the fresh layer of snow that morning, the men noticed they were in positions not much closer to one another than before.

Allen figured Towns's hard-fought C Company could use a bit of a break, so he put them in reserve. Towns's men retreated to a mile-and-a-half-wide open field behind the others. This new line of defense was on the gradual downward slope of a broad, forested hill above Hemroulle. The ground before his men was open and flat, void of much in the way of natural cover or concealment.

Regardless, Allen let all of the men know they could pull back no more. That night he told his men, "This is our last withdrawal. Live or die—this is it."[48]

1630 to early evening, Saturday, 23 December 1944
26th Volksgrenadier Division Headquarters
Hompre, Belgium

"Mande Saint-Etienne taken, communication established with Grenadier Regiment 77 in Flamizoulle area!" was the report that Colonel Heinz

Kokott received that night from his subordinate units that had forced the issue in the Mande area all day. It was the first good news Kokott had heard in a while. Soon after, he received another piece of good news—some of his men had seized the American equipment bundles, verifying that what Kokott had seen falling from the sky was not American paratroopers, but supplies. True, the aerial resupply could mean the Americans might hold out longer, but at least he didn't have to contend with another division of American paratroopers. Kokott was learning the hard way that one was more than enough.

The best news, however, came from the south. It certainly had not started out that way Saturday morning. Around 1630–1700 hours, the four massive Tigers and accompanying troops struck the Americans in Chaumont. The attack was apparently a bit of a surprise for the Americans, especially the giant tanks. The *Amis* had failed to seize the high ground to the north of town, and that turned out to be the support-by-fire position for the Tigers. From that position they had a superb field of fire. The tanks used their huge 88mm guns to wreak havoc on the Americans. In no time, they had destroyed or disabled eleven of Patton's Sherman tanks, forcing the Americans to retreat.

When Kokott heard the news, he was pleased. Things seemed to be taking a turn for the better. He had finally forced back the American lines to the west of Bastogne. He had dealt a stinging rebuke to the American forces coming up from the south. Most important, these actions were buying him a great deal of time. Now he could concentrate his forces, use any fresh reinforcements currently on their way, and choose a place somewhere along the Bastogne perimeter to mount the major armored-infantry attack—the *Panzer Angriff* that could seal the fate of the Americans in Bastogne.

Kokott then looked at the time. The 901st Panzergrenadier Regiment's attack on Marvie was about to begin.[49]

Late evening, Saturday, 23 December 1944
Headquarters, XXXXVII Panzer Corps
Château de Roumont, Belgium[50]

As evening blackened the sky over Belgium, for once, *General der Panzertruppen* Heinrich von Lüttwitz had many reasons to be optimistic. True, the American commander at Bastogne had rudely snubbed his surrender demand, but elsewhere, matters were progressing in his favor. After all, Kokott's division had successfully driven in part of the American perimeter surrounding Bastogne.

At the same time, the hard fighting that day proved to von Lüttwitz that Kokott's division would not be enough to capture Bastogne. Obviously the Allied forces were putting up a greater fight than had previously been anticipated. He had already learned earlier that evening from Kokott that the attack on Marvie had stalled, and it was not likely to achieve its goal. Kokott would require more combat power to capture Bastogne.

Fortuitously, that same evening the corps commander received news that the Fifth Panzer Army was sending him more divisions. In fact, two of them—the 9th Panzer and 15th Panzergrenadier divisions—would arrive sometime tomorrow and pass through the town of Noville, to the north of Bastogne.

Von Manteuffel had given von Lüttwitz his choice—he could use the divisions either at Bastogne or to secure crossings at the Meuse River. However, after the war, the chief of staff of the Fifth Panzer Army, Carl Wagener, wrote that he had strongly suggested that XXXXVII Panzer Corps use the divisions for the Meuse crossing. Von Lüttwitz, though, rejected that notion. He never liked the concept of leaving Bastogne behind as von Manteuffel's forces barreled toward Antwerp. He would divert whichever division showed up first to Kokott. For von Lüttwitz, it was finally time to lance the Bastogne boil.[51]

CHAPTER SIX

"I Was Just Here to Wish You a Merry Christmas."

(DECEMBER 24)

"Poor food—hard lodging—Cold Weather—fatigue—Nasty Cloaths—and nasty Cookery—Vomit half my time—smoak'd out of my senses—the Devil's in't—I can't Endure it—Why are we sent here to starve and freeze—What sweet Felicities have I left at home. . . . Here all Confusion—smoke Cold— hunger & filthyness—A pox on my bad luck! Here comes a bowl of beef soup—full of burnt leaves and dirt, sickish enough to make a Hector spue,—away with it Boys!—I'll live like the Chameleon upon Air."

—Surgeon Albigence Waldo, Connecticut Line, Valley Forge, 1778[1]

All around the Bastogne perimeter, the sons of the Third Reich marked time and waited. As the snow intermittently fell that Sunday, Kokott's Panzergrenadiers were suffering similar hardships to the Americans'. For the Germans, living in frozen holes with wrapped feet and faces to prevent frostbite, food, medicine, and ammunition were also starting to run thin.

A few enjoyed the amenities of being the besiegers instead of the besieged. With the freedom to move about the outlying towns, some of the German soldiers could afford to scrounge for food, firewood, and warm housing. Many a Belgian farm, barn, or town hall was taken over by German

151

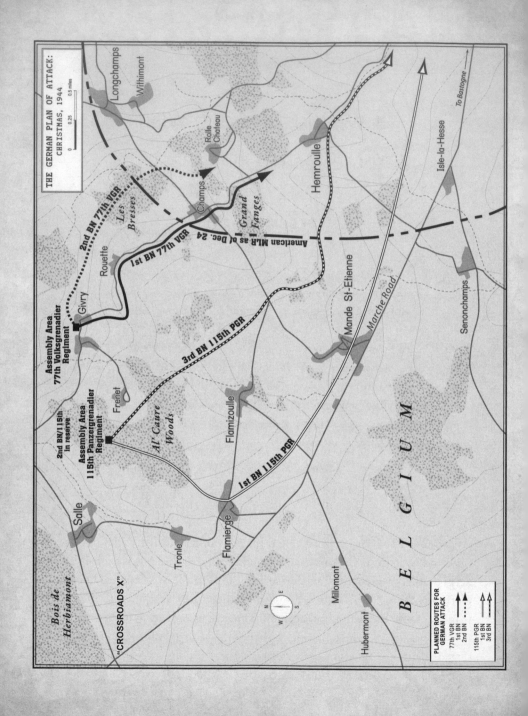

THE GERMAN PLAN OF ATTACK:
CHRISTMAS, 1944

0   0.25   0.5 miles

Bois de
Herbiamont

Salle

Tronle

"CROSSROADS X"

Assembly Area
77th Volksgrenadier
Regiment

2nd BN/115th
in reserve

Assembly Area
115th Panzergrenadier
Regiment

Frenet

Al' Casse
Woods

Flamierge

Hubermont

Milliomont

Longchamps

Withimont

Rolle
Chateau

2nd BN 77th VGR

Les
Bresses

Rouette

Givry

Champs

1st BN 77th VGR

1st BN

Grand
Fanges

American MLR as of Dec. 24

Hemroulle

3rd BN 115th PGR

Flamizoulle

1st BN 115th PGR

Mande St-Etienne

Marche Road

Isle-la-Hesse

To Bastogne

Senonchamps

B E L G I U M

N
W   E
S

PLANNED ROUTES FOR
GERMAN ATTACK
77th VGR
1st BN
2nd BN
115th PGR
1st BN
3rd BN

troops and converted into a warm dormitory or *brötkuchen* (bread kitchen) for the soldiers of Kokott's army.

Near Rouette that morning, "Lutz" Lindemann recalled the cold nights he had already spent around Bastogne. Even for a veteran of the freezing winters of Russia, Lindemann and his men found the land around Bastogne Spartan:

"The winter in Russia was stronger. Very, very cold—minus forty degrees [Celsius]," he recounted in an interview. "In these days [Bastogne] terrible weather, rain, snow and fog [temperatures approximately six degrees]. We always slept outside with a tarp over us. No fire, no blankets, no warmth, no food, since the field kitchen could not reach us. The only food was captured, unused American rations."

Exhaustion was also treating the Germans with as heavy a hand as it had laid on the Americans. The German soldiers of the 26th Volksgrenadier Division had moved about the perimeter on foot or vehicle, and from town to town so many times that many had lost count. The fighting had taken place each day as unit after unit had attempted to punch through the American defenses. The constant get up and go had left the soldiers drained, cold, and frustrated. Even the few veterans of winter campaigns of the Eastern Front, like Lindemann, were starting to feel it, especially as temperatures dropped below freezing the last few days before Christmas.

Morale was faltering. Purposely left out of the main drive, the grenadiers were unable to share the glories and victories with their brothers in 2nd Panzer and Panzer Lehr as they shattered American divisions and aimed for the Meuse.

The day before, Lindemann had been in the woods near Foy with his 6th Company. The men raised their heads at the sound of aircraft engines and were witnesses to the 101st pathfinders dropping from the sky and landing in the snowy fields outside Bastogne. He specifically instructed his men not to shoot at the helpless soldiers as they swung in the air on their parachutes. He told his men to wait until they hit the ground. To Lindemann, shooting a defenseless paratrooper hanging in the sky just did not seem particularly sporting. Still, as they watched the spectacle of the resupply planes dropping the parcels that afternoon, it must have been a depressing spectacle for him and his men.[2]

Christmas, such an important holiday for Germanic people, was turning into a bloody affair. This would be the sixth consecutive Christmas in which Germany was at war. Soldiers' thoughts turned to their homes and

families, which many had not seen for years. Far from the *Heimat*, they suffered once again, as all Germany was, for Hitler's twisted ambitions.[3]

2330–1200 hours, Saturday to Sunday, 24 December 1944
Traveling with the headquarters element of the 115th Panzergrenadier Regiment
Heading west from Prüm, Germany, to Houffalize, Belgium

Early Christmas Eve, *Oberst* (Colonel) Wolfgang Maucke, commanding the
115th, lead regiment of 15th Panzergrenadier Division, was making his way
dutifully to an area around Houffalize, Belgium. Maucke stood in his open
command vehicle to better spot any Allied aircraft. His men and vehicles
had already been savaged earlier along the road to Houffalize, north of Bastogne, by the ever-present *Jabos*.

Left and right, Maucke was losing vehicles. The day before at Prüm,
Maucke had stopped to receive orders. During the pause, he had requested
that his forward units, including an artillery regiment, be able to deploy to
safer defensive positions outside of town. His superiors had told him it was
unnecessary, as his men would soon be moving on.

Unfortunately, roaming Allied fighter-bombers caught the guns and
crews out in the open around 2330 hours that night and destroyed much of
the equipment in his regiment's infantry gun company. It got worse. There
were other factors that seemed determined to whittle away at Maucke's
shrinking force.

Maucke recalled that time after the war:

> The weather throughout the period was dominated by uninter-
> rupted fog until sunlight broke through around midday on 23.12.44
> [Saturday]. . . . It was relatively cold. The roads were frozen and
> slick as mirrors, which created excessive difficulty for the heavy
> vehicles. The familiar serpentines caused significant vehicular
> losses when vehicles slid off the roads and crashed after entering a
> curve.

Maucke realized that the worst fears of the German high command
seemed to be coming to fruition. Now that the weather had improved, it was
almost impossible to move reinforcements for *Wacht am Rhein* up the roads
during daylight hours. Simply moving his force to Belgium was becoming a
major battle within itself.

Later that morning, a single Allied fighter-bomber swept in and attacked 1st Battalion, which was strung out along a road like a bunch of schoolchildren, innocently standing in a queue. The losses from the attack were severe. The solitary *Jabo* had destroyed 1st Battalion's field kitchen and more than 60 percent of the vehicles and medium mortars as they were lined up in the van of the column. Luckily casualties were minimal. Still, Maucke knew he couldn't afford to lose any more equipment before he arrived at his assault position somewhere in Belgium.

As much as he would have preferred to move by night, his one thought now was to get whatever was left of his tanks and men to Belgium in all haste. After the war, Maucke remarked in an interview, "Any thoughts not to travel during the day were not acknowledged. It was said repeatedly, 'Orders from the top—we will march,' and we marched and overcame adversity. Countless unknown drivers fulfilled their duties and followed their orders, but many did so unto their deaths."

As a senior field commander, he could see with his own eyes the reality that the war was not going the way Adolf Hitler imagined it was. The truth was very obvious this Christmas Eve, as he watched what was left of his column rumbling along behind him. The scars showed with the damaged and missing vehicles, and the fear in the faces of his grenadiers, scanning the air for the next deadly attack.

He knew that even with a limping force, he would be expected to play a key role in the upcoming operation—whatever that was. Despite the attacks on his regiment, his men were ready. Unlike some other units that the OKW had thrown into the Bulge, the 115th Panzergrenadier Regiment was well prepared. As opposed to the divisions that had served on the Eastern Front and suffered catastrophic losses as a result, a sizable number of older veteran NCOs and experienced junior officers were still serving in the 115th. Hence, as Maucke put it, ". . . [They] formed a fundamental nucleus of the division. They endured their combat trials and crisis in a positive manner." Maucke's division also had another advantage over some of its fellow divisions. Unlike Kokott's 26th Volksgrenadier, the 15th Panzergrenadier had a well-trained and organized Feldgendarmerie, or military police unit. These specialists excelled in traffic control, and they proved their expertise during the movement of the 15th Panzergrenadier Division to Belgium. In spite of the constant aerial harassment and the twisting, icy roads, the Feldgendarmerie controlled the traffic flow and ensured that the division would arrive at its appointed time. Around noon, Maucke's regiment and the rest

of the division finally arrived at their assembly area southeast of Houffalize. Maucke then went to report to Kokott for his next set of orders.[4]

Morning, Sunday, 24 December 1944
Headquarters, 26th Volksgrenadier Division
Gives, Belgium

The battle for Marvie petered out early Sunday morning, with the Americans holding half of the town, and the Germans the other. It certainly was
not the conclusive and key engagement Colonel Heinz Kokott had sought.
He could tell by looking over the reports from the 901st Panzergrenadier
Regiment, which had spearheaded the attack on Marvie. Once again the
stubborn *Ami* paratroopers had refused to yield to common sense. Reluc-
tantly, Kokott began to feel some admiration for his adversary, and he decided that everyone, including his higher headquarters, had underestimated
the pluck of the GIs trapped in Bastogne.

The attack on Marvie had foundered relatively early. Kokott knew by
2200 hours the previous night that the assault had become mired in the
streets of the small Belgian hamlet. Indeed, the operations center of the 901st
reported to him at that time, "[T]he attack had been halted by increased
enemy resistance and . . . there were no longer any reserves for continuance
of the attack with any hope for success." Kokott knew it was senseless to
continue reinforcing failure. Besides, he had a good reason to call off the
attack.

About the same time the Panzergrenadiers were starting to navigate
the tortuous streets of Marvie, Kokott received an order directly from the
Fifth Panzer Army. When he opened it and quickly perused it, he knew
how serious the situation had become. It read: "26th Division prepares large-
scale attack on Bastogne. Objective: capture of Bastogne. Time: 25 December. 15th Panzergrenadier Division being brought up—will be
subordinated to the 26th Division for this attack." Kokott nodded and
smiled to himself. At last he was getting what he needed to take care of
Bastogne—reinforcements. General Hasso von Manteuffel was allocating
an entire division to him, and it was a division with teeth—a Panzergrenadier division. That meant tanks and motorized troops. In addition to that
piece of good news, Kokott had finally figured out exactly where to utilize
this additional combat power.

Earlier, Kokott had made a personal reconnaissance of the western roads to Bastogne. He was well aware of the strong resistance put up by the Americans near Mande Saint-Etienne and Flamierge. However, he was inspired when recon elements reported the early morning retraction of the American lines in this sector. After four days of stubborn resistance, the *Amis* had finally pulled back their forces here. Perhaps, thought Kokott, this was a clear indication that the Americans were stretched too thin in Bastogne's western approaches. Furthermore, he had struck the Americans everywhere but in the northwest sector. Kokott reckoned that to defend the other areas, such as Marvie and Mande, the Americans most likely pulled forces from around Champs.

During his personal scouting trip, Kokott was also encouraged by the ground here. Not only were the roads good, but now that the temperature had dropped, the fields had frozen firm enough to ensure that his tanks would not bog down if they had to move cross-country. There was an abundance of gently rolling farm fields in this area, and only a few woodlots that could break up his forces or be used as ambush points by the American infantry. All in all, Kokott was finally convinced that the northwestern approaches—that snow-covered land between Longchamps and Hemroulle—were the Achilles' heel of the enemy's defense. Here, he figured, was what he had been looking for all along—the perfect place for a *Panzer Angriff* to crack the Bastogne nut.

Now that he had a place, a deadline, and a formidable force, Kokott knew he needed to sketch out a plan. Kokott decided the 15th Panzergrenadier Division, since they would arrive new and refreshed, would form the *schwerpunkt*—or spearhead—of the main effort. This armored force would punch through the thinned Allied lines along the axis between Hemroulle and the highway to Mande Saint-Etienne. In addition, other German units would fix the American forces on the flanks of the main effort to protect the flanks of the penetration and confuse the Americans as to the actual point of attack. To the north, the 77th Volksgrenadier Regiment was the primary supporting effort. *Oberstleutnant* Martin Schriefer's Volksgrenadiers would push out from Rouette and seize the town of Champs and then Hemroulle, thereby tying down the paratroopers defending that area. Meanwhile, to the south, the 26th Reconnaissance Battalion would advance from Mande Saint-Etienne and capture the heights in the vicinity of Isle-la-Hesse. If all went according to plan, these two supporting efforts would prevent the American forces in Bastogne from shifting units along their perimeter to counter the attack. Kokott would isolate Allen's battalion so the glidermen would face the panzers alone, without support. At the same time, he hoped to make significant inroads in the area of Champs and the Marche road entryway to Bastogne.

.   In addition to the main operation, Kokott tasked the other German regiments surrounding Bastogne to fix their respective adversaries. In other words, most of the units would put up a determined, simultaneous attack of some sort to keep the Americans facing them busy—too busy to come to the aid of the northwestern perimeter, Kokott hoped. If it worked, even forces like the 501st Parachute Infantry Regiment, defending the front door at Neffe, could not possibly come to the aid of one of the units in the threatened area. More good news reached Kokott that morning. Fifth Panzer Army and the XXXXVII Panzer Corps would be providing additional fire support in the form of 105mm and 150mm howitzers. To ensure effective fire control, Kokott concentrated most of these batteries in the area around Flamierge and Givry. To orchestrate such a concentration, and perhaps show von Manteuffel's seriousness concerning the planned attack, Fifth Panzer Army sent their senior artillery officer to oversee the entire operation.

For Kokott, the timing of the operation was also crucial. As on the twenty-third, the weather for Christmas Day was expected to break sunny about noon. No doubt the American fighter-bombers would return with the good weather, wreaking their destruction on German soldiers and vehicles alike. Even with good weather and nearby bases in France, Kokott knew it would take some time for the Americans to get their *Jabos* launched and over Bastogne. It was a narrow window of time, but in order to beat the impending hellstorm, the panzers would need to be inside Bastogne by midmorning. If not, they would be out in the open and vulnerable.

Kokott knew the 15th's panzers would have to roll out right before sunrise. It would be dark, and a night attack would pose some difficulties in coordination, but the half-moon and snowy fields would certainly aid visibility. Starting off early would give the 15th Panzergrenadier Division two to three hours to get into Bastogne. Once they were there, the close-quarters fighting would prevent the Americans from using their aircraft for fear of hitting their own forces, civilians, and command posts.

Kokott wiped his glasses. He read over the various notes associated with the plan, and knew that once he had ironed out the details, he would call his commanders in later to go over the operation. In some ways, Kokott believed the depressing events of the twenty-third had been fortunate. The airdrops, the fighter-bomber attacks, the brutal resistance put up near Mande and in the town of Marvie had, hopefully, opened the eyes of his senior commanders—namely von Manteuffel. Added to that, Patton's spearhead, the 4th Armored Division, was barreling northward a lot quicker than everyone thought was possible, and the day before Patton's forces almost had a breakthrough at Chaumont. He could not believe the fortuitous decision to grant him the 15th Panzergrenadier. Perhaps—Kokott stroked his chin, deep in thought—the high command finally understood that without their sending him some help, Bastogne was going to take a long time to capture.

But the town had to be taken, and soon. Now, he figured, he finally had the forces on hand to do just that.[5] *The 15th Panzergrenadier Division*, Kokott thought to himself. *An entire Panzergrenadier Division handed over to me.* Fortune, he thought for a moment, certainly favored the brave. And for Kokott, Christmas Eve—*Heilige Abend*—was turning out to be a very fortunate time indeed.

Morning to noon, Sunday, 24 December 1944
Headquarters, XXXXVII Panzer Corps, visiting the
headquarters, 2nd Panzer Division
Bande, Belgium

General Heinrich von Lüttwitz stepped out of his command car, placed his monocle to his eye, and marched into the command post of the 2nd Panzer Division. He had requested the meeting to hear *Oberst* (Colonel) Meinhard von Lauchert's status report on the drive to the Meuse River.

The news was bad. The division staff officers immediately brought to his attention the desperate plight of their unit. The 2nd Panzer Division was fighting for its life. All morning long the staff had received calls for assistance from the various subordinate units. They all reported the same things: no gas, no ammunition, and no Luftwaffe to defend them against the American *Jabos*. The corps commander shook his head in disgust.

Von Lüttwitz turned to the commander of 2nd Panzer, who broke even more bad news. Von Lauchert's division was under extreme pressure outside of Marche as it beat back constant American attacks. Meanwhile, the Americans' 2nd Armored Division was squeezing the tiny salient near Foy-Notre-Dame, which was the farthest point of penetration for the Germans. Von Lauchert had exhorted his men to hold on and keep fighting—he had heard help was on the way in the form of the 9th Panzer Division. It might be too late. The Americans had isolated various parts of 2nd Panzer, which were now forming tiny pockets of resistance against the Allied pressure. As a consequence, the Americans could concentrate on and destroy each one in detail. The main body of von Lauchert's division, stuck outside of Marche, could not send reinforcements to elements fighting at Foy-Notre-Dame or outside of Conneux, Belgium. Finally von Lauchert admitted to von Lüttwitz that many of his units had run out of gas. If they were not resupplied with fuel, and soon, they would have to make their way out on foot.

Fuel . . . fuel had been the item that had cost them. Von Lüttwitz leaned forward, dropped his head into his hands, and slowly shook it. *Wacht am Rhein* was coming to a sputtering halt because the Germans could not get enough fuel for their gas-guzzling tanks, half-tracks, and trucks. The fuel couldn't be brought forward to the units spearheading the advance because transportation along the narrow and clogged routes took too much time. On top of that, they had to contend with the Allied fighter-bombers circling overhead like birds of prey. Fuel and supply vehicles were conspicuous targets. Most of all, the bulk of the fuel and supply vehicles could not take a direct route. Obviously, as wheeled vehicles, they required hard roads to travel upon, particularly with the recent snow. They were confined to the roads, and the major road hub in that sector was the town of Bastogne.

Bastogne! Von Lüttwitz gritted his teeth in frustration. Snapping his monocle away from his eye, he looked around at the sorry faces of the 2nd Panzer staff around him. The Americans, as Kokott had reported, still retained an iron grip on Bastogne.

Von Lüttwitz had warned his boss that Bastogne would be the problem if the Germans didn't take it in the initial advance. Instead, von Manteuffel had ordered him to leave only the 26th Volksgrenadier Division behind to invest the town, while the two Panzer divisions drove headlong to the river. Now the 2nd Panzer Division, on account of unprotected and overextended supply lines, had come to a halt.

He desperately needed the reinforcements. Fifth Panzer Army kept telling von Lüttwitz that 9th Panzer Division was coming, and it would arrive sometime that evening. He wasn't convinced. In addition, his entire corps was out on a limb. No other German units were guarding his flanks. To the north, the 116th Panzer Division had come to a halt far from its intermediate objective, while to the south the 5th Fallschirmjäger Division was rapidly buckling under the constant blows from Patton's Third Army. The overextended German flanks of the "bulge" were fragile. With Patton coming up from the south, there was a very real danger the entire German offensive could be decapitated.

Still, von Lüttwitz knew he had to make the best of the situation and keep the remainder of his corps moving forward. The most he could do for 2nd Panzer Division was to redirect the Panzer Lehr's axis of advance to clear the roads of American forces between Rochefort and Marche. If the roads were unclogged, maybe they could then send supplies to his belea guered units west of that area.

At last, it seemed he could finally do something about Bastogne. The lead units of the 15th Panzergrenadier Division had finally reached the area of operations of the XXXXVII Panzer Corps. Almost immediately he put the newly arrived division under the temporary command of the 26th Volks-grenadier Division. Tomorrow, with these potent reinforcements, he figured Kokott could make no more excuses not to take Bastogne. After all, a general like Heinrich von Lüttwitz always made damn sure he got what he wanted.[6]

Midday to late afternoon, Sunday, 24 December 1944
Headquarters, 101st Airborne Division, Heinz Barracks
Bastogne, Belgium

As Christmas Eve dawned around Bastogne, the Americans had reasons to celebrate and feel the worst was over. Another air supply had come in that morning, right on cue, courtesy of more than 160 troop carrier C-47s. Besides ammunition, the Air Corps dropped several containers of K rations. This time eleven of the flimsy CG-4 cargo-carrying gliders also came in, their spectacular landings in the snowy fields fascinating the GIs around Bastogne. Several skidded to a halt just outside the artillery positions near Savy and Hemroulle.

Like manna from heaven, the gliders were loaded with 105mm and 75mm shells for the big American guns. The arrival of the rations, something most of the GIs would grouse about at any other given moment, helped raise morale tremendously. The K rations, in cardboard boxes about as large as a cigarette carton, gave the troopers a much-needed break from the constant menu of pancakes.[7]

Along with the troop carriers came the ever-present fighter-bombers. The skies roared with the sound of the P-47s dropping bombs pointedly on the Marvie area and knocking the Germans back. Due to a few deadly "friendly fire" incidents, the paratroopers were much more industrious this morning when it came to laying out the orange marker panels in front of their positions. The panels were used to mark friend from foe, but even then were not always easy to see from a cockpit, speeding overhead at four hundred miles per hour.

Spirits were picking up among the GIs. The headquarters types—spared the constant shivering and huddling in some muddy hole—had picked humor as the best weapon to fight the war. After all, it was Christmas Eve.[8] In the Cave at Heinz Barracks, a wisecracking Danahy had written a sprawling "Merry Christmas" in green crayon across the red lines of the German positions portrayed on the large operations map.[9]

That afternoon, as the Marvie battle was ending, McAuliffe had personally radioed General Middleton at Neufchâteau, saying; "The finest Christmas present the 101st could get would be a relief tomorrow."[10]

"I know, boy, I know," was all Middleton could reply, frustrated that he couldn't do more.[11]

McAuliffe's basement headquarters had picked up a message relayed by VIII Corps from General Patton and the Third Army. Patton's Third was still fighting their way north to the city, and now was only eight miles away.

"Xmas Eve present coming up. Hold on," the message said.[12]

Like any good commander, McAuliffe wanted to nip any morale issue in the bud before it became problematic—especially on the holiday. Even if he was starting to have his own concerns, he wasn't about to let on to any of his staff or soldiers. On this Christmas, he knew that many of the hard-pressed GIs would start to worry about home and family. It would be important to remind them why they were here. In a widely circulated flyer, Colonel Kinnard wrote the following Christmas message. McAuliffe approved it and had it distributed to all of the men in and out of the frozen foxholes:

Merry Christmas!
What's merry about all this you ask? We're fighting—it's cold—we aren't home. All true, but what has the proud Eagle Division accomplished with its worthy comrades of the 10th Armored

Division, the 705th Tank Destroyer Battalion and all the rest? Just this: We have stopped cold everything that has been thrown at us from the north, east, south and west. We have identifications from four German panzer divisions, two German infantry divisions and one German parachute division. These units, spearheading the last desperate German lunge, were heading straight west for key points when the Eagle Division was hurriedly ordered to stem the advance. How effectively this was done will be written in history; not alone in our Division's glorious history but in world history. The Germans actually did surround us, their radios blared our doom. Allied troops are counterattacking in force. We continue to hold Bastogne. By holding Bastogne we assure the success of the Allied armies. We know that our Division commander, General Taylor, will say: "Well done!" We are giving our country and our loved ones at home a worthy Christmas present and being privileged to take part in this gallant feat of arms are truly making for ourselves a merry Christmas.[13]

At the bottom of the page was a reprint of the German surrender demand on Friday and McAuliffe's stubborn and already-famous reply: "Nuts!"

Regardless of the jovial mood from headquarters, the next twenty-four hours would sorely test the Christmas spirit of both the men in command and the men on the front lines. Meanwhile, as the headquarters staff joked and laughed, several miles west of Bastogne a pair of GIs saw that the Germans were bringing something far worse than coal for the Americans this Christmas.

Afternoon, Sunday, 24 December 1944
Area of operations, Alpha Company, 502nd Parachute Infantry Regiment
Near Champs, Belgium

Christmas Eve found an American officer and a sergeant gazing in shock at the sight before them. Standing on the crest of a snow-blanketed hill near Longchamps, the two men were stunned. Down the hillside and over a short valley less than a mile away stood nearly a battalion of German tanks, engines throbbing and clouds of exhaust rising in the afternoon cold.

To the German soldiers starting to take notice, the two GIs presented an odd contrast: The officer was Captain Wallace Swanson, the Kansas State University football player—big and burly. The other man was Tony D'Angelo, dark, Italian-American, and in his own words "short and scrawny," compared to Swanson.

Tied around Swanson's neck was a cardboard sign cut out from a box of rations, with the words "Don't Sky-Line Yourself" scribbled in pen. His helmet was wrapped in a white pillowcase for camouflage. It was ironic that both men were in such a state of shock since that was exactly what they were doing: silhouetting themselves on the top of the hill. "We stood there like a bunch of idiots, just staring for a minute," D'Angelo recalled of that moment. "That whole damn hillside was just loaded. There must have been a parking lot full of German tanks, in ten or eleven lines, and there we were just looking at all that armor sitting there."

It didn't take long for the Germans to respond. Shouting commands and jumping into their vehicles, they quickly loaded their weapons and aimed at the Americans. D'Angelo recalled how, at first, his legs seemed frozen, unable to move.

"That paratrooper captain and I just watched as they fired at us."

Nearby was a brick-and-stone religious shrine used by the residents of the neighboring village of Longchamps. The structure was about six feet wide and ten feet tall. Swanson, hearing the shriek of the incoming rounds, suddenly straightened up and slapped D'Angelo on the shoulder, telling him to run. "We both dived behind that shrine, I tell you," D'Angelo said.

A German shell screamed in and blasted the top of the shrine, knocking brick fragments over the heads of the men. The two ran down the back side of the hill, D'Angelo back to his tank destroyer and crew, Swanson to warn headquarters of the German buildup they had just discovered in this northwest sector of Bastogne.

Now the rumors were set to rest. Now they had visual proof. The Germans were massing for an attack on Champs.

"The captain fell down and I swear, I ran right over the back of the poor guy trying to get out of there," D'Angelo remarked. "I got the hell out of there fast."[14]

D'Angelo devised a clever ruse to keep the panzers at bay. He figured that, since most of the American fighting positions were on a reverse slope, the Germans probably didn't have an accurate estimate of American armor.

D'Angelo reckoned that if he popped off a couple of shots from his tank destroyer, it would warn the Germans that the Americans had some fire-power on the other side of the hill waiting for them, even if it was only one TD. D'Angelo had his crew lob a few rounds at the Germans. There was no response. Fortunately, the newly arrived German tankers from the 15th Panzergrenadier Division were still organizing and by no means ready for a German all-out assault on any American positions.[15]

Seeing that no attack seemed imminent, Sergeant D'Angelo and the crew of "No Love, No Nothing" returned to Champs. D'Angelo had teamed up with the other gun in his section: an M18 commanded by Sergeant Law-rence Vallitta. The two sergeants set themselves up in a little farmhouse in Champs for the evening, believing for the moment that they would see little action that day.

"I didn't have any time to think about Christmas or home," D'Angelo said. "There was too much happening—seems like we were too busy just trying to stay warm and stay alive."[16]

The M18 crews had taken to warming their hands on the backs of the vehicles, where the exhaust came up in torrents of hot air from the large nine-cylinder Continental radial aircraft engine. Through trial and error, the tank destroyer men had also learned another trick—to dig a shallow foxhole, and then drive their Hellcat over the hole, straddling it. With about fourteen inches of clearance under the vehicle, this would make a comfy and well-protected—if somewhat claustrophobic—"bunker" for the crew to sleep in.[17]

Generally most soldiers preferred the quaint stone farmhouses to truly escape the cold nights, but there were just not enough of these available. D'Angelo noted how many of the Belgian home owners were perfectly will-ing to give up their upstairs accommodations to the soldiers, preferring to stay in the basements and shelter for the duration of the siege.

As he tossed and turned, trying to get some sleep that Christmas Eve, D'Angelo couldn't help worrying about the massive amount of German ar-mor he had seen earlier that day with Swanson. Even though HQ was aware of it, to D'Angelo it still felt like some monster just waiting over the hill to pounce on the American lines. Unable to sleep, D'Angelo decided to hunt up some food for his men for Christmas Eve fare. The men were tired of K rations, and had given many of their rations away to paratroopers earlier that day near Longchamps.

"One [civilian] guy butchered a cow, and gave us and the 101st guys some. We were very grateful."[18]

The tiny village of Champs, in the northern sector, lay in a bowl-like depression, with hills to the north and south. Here Swanson's A Company kept their vigil, with orders to watch the ground to the north, particularly the high road to Rouette. The men of Able Company knew something was up. All that afternoon, the noises of German vehicles had come to them loud and clear from that general direction.

The cold paratroopers of Able Company had a long line to watch. In a crescent shape, their line snaked from Longchamps to the northeast (where they attempted to connect with their brothers in Lieutenant Colonel Thomas H. Sutliffe's Second Battalion) in a broad curve before Champs and terminated at a hill on their left flank. At this hill, the line was supposed to join airtight with B Company of the 1/401st, but gaps made this more wishful thinking than reality.

Christmas Eve was spent expanding their foxholes or cleaning weapons. Corporal Willis Fowler, the .30-caliber M1919A4 machine gunner from Georgia, stripped his weapon and cleaned each part on a ground cloth. Fowler wanted to make sure the machine gun—complicated and with many moving parts—would not freeze up that night when it might be most needed. He checked and rechecked the head space on the bolt and wiped off belts of .30-caliber bullets, ensuring that each link was free of ice, snow, or grit. Trying to prepare for anything, as well as keep his mind off of home and hearth, Fowler figured it, "seemed like the smart thing to do."[19]

Fowler occupied his mind thusly while waiting in his position on the left side of the Rouette road. Fowler's platoon was entrenched behind a potato shed used as their squad CP. Across the road to the right, the rest of 2nd Platoon was situated along the slope of a hill, occupying several other farm buildings. Swanson's headquarters was behind this position in a house in Champs near the intersection of the Rouette and Longchamps roads, just behind a school and a stone church. In the waning light of evening, Fowler kept a steady watch over the fields ahead of them for any sign of German activity.

To the east side of the road, Sergeant Charles Asay, the squad leader from Sioux City, Iowa, had a similar notion. His 3rd Platoon was placed in foxholes spread down the slope into Champs. Forward of his position, up the incline and in the woods, were several outposts. These positions would basically serve as "speed bumps," slowing down the enemy and giving advance notification of any attack.

Captain Swanson had already made his rounds as the sun set, sharing with Asay and the other squad leaders what he had seen with D'Angelo earlier that day.

"Swannie—Captain Swanson, that's what we called him—he told the guys on outpost that night to stay awake," Asay recalled. "German activity was pretty deep." Asay, in turn, made sure his squad kept focused on the woods ahead. He checked his own M1 clips in his ammo belt, each packed with eight bullets, wishing he had more. Overall, he didn't think too much about it being Christmas. "[As an orphan] my family was the army. As for Christmas in the orphanage, if you were a boy you got to pull a blue ribbon from under the tree. Not much to say there."

One thing the orphanage did give Asay was responsibility. He had to take care of many of the younger boys, so the role of sergeant and squad leader came naturally. That evening, he checked and rechecked his men to make sure they were warm as could be and had enough ammunition for the coming fight. "I was a bit of a mother hen," he wrote about that night.[20]

1730–1800 hours, Sunday, 24 December 1944
Command element of the 115th Panzergrenadier Regiment at
26th Volksgrenadier Division Headquarters
Gives, Belgium

That evening, when a tired Colonel Wolfgang Maucke finally arrived at the command post of the 26th Volksgrenadier Division near Gives, he immediately started looking for his new boss, Colonel Kokott, to get his orders. Kokott was elsewhere. Maucke was forced to get his briefing, for the time being, from the division's operations officer—Major Hans Freiherr von Tiesenhausen. Von Tiesenhausen did not waste time with formalities, cordialities, or reminiscing about the holidays. All of Kokott's staff knew about the new directive to take Bastogne with the all-out *Panzer Angriff* on Christmas Day.

Von Tiesenhausen immediately outlined the plan and informed Maucke of his role in it. Maucke's 115th Panzergrenadier Regiment would assemble in the area around Salle. Maucke's panzers would spearhead the attack. It would be a classic combined armor-infantry thrust bearing southeast from the Flamierge vicinity and then east into Bastogne. In addition, Maucke would receive support on both of his flanks from Schriefer's 77th Volksgrenadier Regiment to the north attacking Champs and the 26th Reconnaissance Battalion to the south. To Maucke's surprise, von Tiesenhausen informed him that the attack would commence at first light the next morning. This, he explained, was to fully exploit the element of surprise. To accomplish this, Maucke would have to have all of his men and hardware in position that night. The final assembly time would be 0300 hours tomorrow (Christmas) morning.

As Maucke stood before von Tiesenhausen and reviewed the orders, he could not believe what he was hearing. Most of his regiment had not arrived in the Bastogne area yet. His regiment was being thrown piecemeal into an attack, in the dark, without maps, reconnaissance of the area, or any time for careful coordination. Many of Maucke's soldiers, artillery, and tank crews were exhausted from the toil and strain of moving at breakneck speed to Bastogne over the past two days. Because of the loss of a field kitchen, shot up by the American fighter-bombers, one of his battalions had no rations. Mail, which could have been a great morale boost that Christmas Eve, had not caught up with his unit.

Now he had to disseminate orders and prepare his men for an attack that was roughly twelve hours away. Moreover, he hadn't seen the ground his tanks were supposed to seize in daylight. Maucke would be literally seeing the area in the dark for the first time, and there was little to guide him in carrying out an incredibly crucial attack plan. The veteran commander, who had fought hard in the Italian Campaign, was incredulous. *Verrückt*—crazy! *This won't do at all*, he thought to himself. To plan an attack without having the time to effectively put his force together, fully brief his men, and properly reconnoiter the ground seemed to be asking for trouble. Now Kokott was ordering him to do just that. He knew that his men would carry out his orders. They were good and loyal soldiers, but to Maucke, this whole thing seemed thrown together and haphazard, and reeked of disaster.

As Maucke started to leave, von Tiesenhausen reminded him, "At 2200 hours you are to report to the command post of the 26th VGD, where you will receive your orders personally from the divisional commander."

Maucke nodded. Kokott was coming. At least he would have a chance to protest his orders to the man who signed them. Maucke wondered, however, what chance he would have. It all seemed so desperate.[21]

1700–1800 hours, Sunday, 24 December 1944
Headquarters, 502nd Parachute Infantry Regiment
Rolle Château, Belgium

Southeast of Swanson's A Company positions at Champs, the main road led out of town and passed over a small bridge fording the river Grand Etang. The road gradually climbed and continued to a bend between the woods. From here, as the ground leveled out, it was only four hundred yards to the "Lane of Trees" (Dreve de Mande) that marked the intersection with the Rolle Château road. Following this wooded lane to the left would guide someone directly to the front gateway of the Rolle Château—the headquarters of the 502nd.

Here, Chappuis' signalmen were finishing their work, making sure communication was solid between the 502nd HQ and the various battalions and companies nearby. The cold signalmen had finally tied in all the units with communication wire. The herculean task had taken all day, and the men were exhausted from working in the snow. Outside of the château, demolition teams were placing charges underneath the two stone bridges around Champs. In addition, the engineers planted mines along the road between Champs and Longchamps and provided antitank chain mines to prevent panzers from crossing the bridges. Finally, these teams left two men at each of the bridges to ensure that they would blow them if and when the time came—a last desperate act if the headquarters was in danger of being overrun. Demolitions Sergeant Schuyler "Sky" Jackson was one of the soldiers attached to headquarters who was on one of these teams.

"The temperature, though, was around zero," he wrote after the war. "There were a couple of replacements who actually froze to death on duty. I would always have two guys go out there to keep the men awake and prevent them from freezing."[22]

Back inside the château, the intelligence staff received a terse message from division at 1735 hours. It read, "Be on alert for a possible enemy attack from the west tonight." Undoubtedly the radio switchboard operators laughed when they heard this. Division didn't need to tell them what was coming, since it was they who had reported this information in the first place.[23]

Early evening, Sunday, 24 December 1944
Assembly area, Charlie Company, 1/502nd Parachute Infantry Regiment
Hemroulle, Belgium

The Champs-Hemroulle road runs straight as it continues southeast from the intersection of the Rolle Château road to Hemroulle and then directly into Bastogne. Along this section, thick woods patchworked the valleys and hills carved by the Rau Rolle directly to the east. At one point, these woods almost touched the road, lined with concrete telephone poles and wire cattle fencing.

Just a few hundred yards south of where the woods came to the road, a double-structure, two-story stone farmhouse stood on the west side. Colonel Ray Allen had chosen this whitewashed building as his new headquarters after executing plan A the day before.

Another hundred yards farther south, the road forked at the entrance to the town of Hemroulle. Hemroulle itself, composed of a small church and about ten to fifteen buildings, is only a little more than a mile from the entryways to Bastogne proper. Colonel : "Silent Steve" Chappuis had instructed Major John Hanlon to position both Baker and Charlie companies of the 502nd as a reserve in and around Hemroulle that night. The idea was that if either Allen's glidermen or Chappuis' headquarters needed help, Hanlon could be there in a jiffy.

Christmas Eve, Sergeant Layton Black's 2nd Platoon found themselves lodging in a warm but dilapidated barn on the outskirts of Hemroulle. As the men bedded down in the hayloft, Black remembered "[We] covered ourselves with the loose hay. I was never that warm again in the Bulge."

Nervous young soldiers in Black's squad kept asking whether they would fight soon. Black knew the 502nd was overdue for its share of defending Bastogne. He and the other NCOs tried to calm the men so they could all get a sound rest, but few were sleeping.

At one point, a voice asked aloud, "Sergeant Black, are you asleep yet?"

"No, not yet," Black replied.

"When do you think we are going up?" the paratrooper then inquired.

"Maybe tonight. Better get some sleep." Black tried to steady his voice to sound like the self-assured NCO his soldiers thought he was. Black, though, knew their time was coming, and he didn't want to scare his men.

After the war, Black recalled that night. "I thought about home, about Christmas in the States, about Mom and Dad, about my best girl, my three brothers and my sister. Also, I thought about the very first Christmas, the barn, the hayloft, in a far-off time. What did it all mean?"

Fortunately for Black's squad of "Screaming Eagles" that night, there would be a welcome break in the Christmas menu and a real boost to his squad's morale. Black described the event. "Maybe it was 2000 [eight p.m.] when someone came into the barn, yelled, 'Santa Claus is here!' and passed out a box of cookies to each of us. They just might have been the best cookies I ever ate."[24]

Early evening, Sunday, 24 December 1944
Area of operations, 1/401st Glider Infantry Regiment
West of Hemroulle, Belgium

Almost due west of Hemroulle the ground gradually climbed and flattened out into large, open fields. It was in this broad, snowy area before Allen's headquarters that Towns's hard-fought Charlie Company had entrenched some distance behind their brothers in Able and Baker companies.

For one of Towns's men, Private First Class Robert Lott, squatting in a foxhole, Christmas Eve just meant colder weather. The temperature had dropped again, and Lott and his fellow glider troopers of Charlie Company did their best to stay warm. One of Lott's buddies, Jack Gresh, was getting sick from the cold. The GIs took him to a nearby barn for protection from the elements. Inside the farmhouse, Lott remembered a welcome sight:

"There was this woman in the house making soup. She let us stay and eat. We had several guys all crammed under that dining room table, sleeping, just to keep warm in there." Lott appreciated the Belgian woman's gratitude and found it "the best Christmas gift any of us could have asked for at that time."[25]

After the beating it had sustained the previous day, mercifully, Captain Towns's company was now in reserve. Shivering in their foxholes, some of the glidermen could hear the sound of gurgling panzer engines in the distance, coming from the direction of Salle and Tronle. For many, there was a sad resignation—they felt it was going to be their last night on earth. Ray Allen said in an interview after the war:

We had seen the Germans building up west of our lines for two days, and the men knew that division was expecting the Germans to attack on Christmas Day. They knew division believed our area was the most likely area to be attacked by tanks, and division didn't think our thinly spread line could hold if we were attacked by tanks. The men felt this could be their last night together—and their last Christmas Eve. Some of them felt they probably wouldn't live to see dawn. So they climbed out of their carefully prepared foxholes, shook hands with one another and wished each other a Merry Christmas. Then they got back in their foxholes and waited.[26]

Farther west, on the newly established 1/401st lines stretching north from the Marche road, and pushed back almost a mile from Mande Saint-Etienne, was the rest of Allen's battalion. Entrenched on a slight ridge were Bowles's Able Company to the south and MacDonald's Baker Company to its north. Here, spread more than two miles in length and almost reaching the outskirts of Champs was Allen's "do or die" main line of resistance: the only thing between the road to Bastogne and Kokott's forces.

In an open position along these gently rolling hills, New Jersey native Carmen Gisi was mulling over the previous day's desperate fighting and retreat from Flamierge. Although he was cold and tired, incredibly, Gisi's spirits were still high. He had heard about the surrender request from the Germans, and like many of his comrades, had to laugh at McAuliffe's response.

"We all thought it was a joke," he recalled. "Because we felt like we were knocking the hell out of them."

Still, not every soldier shared Gisi's foxhole optimism. Gisi remembered that Benny Cohen, a young Jewish soldier in the foxhole next to him, had quietly disposed of his dog tags when he got news the 101st was officially surrounded.[27]

As some shivered in their holes, others celebrated the holiday with the little cheer and ceremony that could be arranged.

Early evening, Sunday, 24 December 1944
Headquarters, 463rd Parachute Field Artillery battalion
Hemroulle, Belgium

Just a few yards slightly southwest of Hemroulle was a large, split hill. The hill was crested by a hedge running diagonally along the top, and a few bordering trees. At the southern base of this area, and along a low creek called the Rau de Petite Fontaine, sat Colonel Cooper's artillerymen of the 463rd. Here Cooper had positioned his four batteries (Able, Baker, Charlie, and Dog).[28] The remaining units were dispersed south of Hemroulle and west of Savy in a sharp curve. This careful disposition, overseen by the veteran Cooper, allowed the gunners to fire on multiple targets around the American perimeter. The guns could also be moved up into the antitank positions that Cooper had the men build several days before. To their left, the rest of Harper's 327th was responsible for the part of the perimeter that extended through the crossroads of Isle-la-Hesse and continued southwest of Bastogne.

Major Stuart Seaton, the 463rd's executive officer, fondly remembered a Christmas service held in Hemroulle. He wrote after the war, "The division chaplain came out to our town for a Christmas Eve service. We had the service in a stable. Somehow, that service had a distinct significance. A rather humble setting, somewhat reminiscent of an event some 2,000 years previous." The artillerymen ended the service by singing "Silent Night." Seaton noted that it was the setting that would cause him to remember that Christmas service over all others for many years.[29]

Ken Hesler, the twenty-year-old artillery communications man from Greenup, Illinois, attended the same service in the stables that night. "I didn't think about Christmas. It was just another day—tomorrow would be another day. All you could do was just wait and find out what happens."

Hesler had spent most of the day relaying messages from forward observers to his HQ in Hemroulle, and he was tired. Nevertheless, he drew guard duty that night along the Hemroulle-Savy road. After the service, Hesler donned his overcoat and shoepacs, grabbed his M1 rifle, and spent the remainder of Christmas Eve on a lonely and cold patrol in a long foxhole south of town.

"You always heard noises in the distance, it seemed, gunfire, explosions, machine gun fire—those kind of sounds were not that unusual in the background on or off all night. [But] it was one of the more quiet evenings in between."

The only saving grace was a warming tent erected by the 463rd near the road and some trees south of Hemroulle. Heated by a small coal stove, it was a convenient place to dry out, warm up, and get some rest. As it got dark, Hesler was given a break from his duty and sent to the tent to rest up for his next round of sentry duty.[30]

Early evening, Sunday, 24 December 1944
Headquarters, 502nd Parachute Infantry Regiment
Château Rolle, Belgium

At Rolle, Chappuis removed his helmet and sat in on a Christmas Eve Mass given in the ancient chapel by the 502nd's chaplain, Father Joseph Andrejewski.[31] Still suffering from the cold, Chappuis did his best to stay alert for the service. Any soldiers who could be relieved off the line for a few moments were in attendance, rotating in and out, receiving communion and singing Christmas hymns. The chapel, located on the second floor of the ancient turret of the structure, was small and cramped. Only the top brass could squeeze into the cylindrical room; the rest lined the hall outside, straining to hear the padre's words. The altar was a fantastic array of medieval finery, including linen banners from the early seventeenth century adorned with gilt crosses and figures of the savior and virgin.

Captain Joseph Pangerl, the 502nd's prisoner interrogator, was a faithful Catholic. He attended the service and described it years later:

"Christmas Eve we had a midnight Mass in the chapel which is in the tower of the castle. The chapel is round, like the tower. It had rough stone walls and was fitted out with rustic but beautiful furniture and had pine boughs all around. The chaplain was our own and we filled the chapel. In fact, there were many who couldn't get in. The family of the house was also present, of course." Pangerl remembered that his parents had sent him a package of holiday gifts. In a gesture of goodwill, he gave the package to Madame Maus de Rolle, who distributed them to the local children.[32]

1800–1900 hours, Sunday, 24 December 1944
Headquarters, 101st Airborne Division, Heinz Barracks
Bastogne, Belgium

The time was 1800 hours, and Colonel Joseph "Bud" Harper was relieved to have Ray Allen's battalion back under his control. However, it came with a price tag. The assistant division commander, General Higgins, informed him that he owned a rather large chunk of real estate to defend. Looking at the map, Harper could see where the long line that Allen had established with his battalion was spread before the rolling fields west of Hemroulle and Rolle.

"Look at it; this is half of the division perimeter!" Harper exclaimed.

Higgins was unmoved. He replied, "It's all yours; do what you can with it. There isn't any other solution."

Harper knew, like everybody else, that McAuliffe didn't have a choice. *That's the problem with being on the defensive*, Harper thought. *You don't set the tempo because the enemy has the initiative. Therefore, all you can do is merely react to your opponent's moves.*[33]

Meanwhile, life in the operations room continued. Fred MacKenzie, the reporter from Buffalo, watched the men as they went about their duties. Oddly, a few of the headquarters orderlies caught naps on a pile of coal sitting at the end of one of the halls. In the background, distant German artillery rumbled like thunder on a summer night. MacKenzie looked at his watch. It was almost seven, and he remembered that the division chaplain was hosting a Catholic Mass at 1900 hours. He decided it was a good place to be, especially if this might wind up being his last Christmas.

The young chaplain was holding the service in a converted barracks room. Nearly a hundred paratroopers and soldiers crowded into the tiny space while a field organ droned as the men sang Christmas carols. MacKenzie described the scene in his book: "The simple service and the dimly lighted room were wondrously appropriate to this place where the human spirit sometimes seemed recognizable, a naked and vibrant thing, apart from fleshly woes. It was as though one was dying, or being born, in travail."[34]

After Mass ended, the participants filed out of the room and made their way back into the Cave. MacKenzie could feel the fatalism in the air. To the commanders, it didn't make sense. However, the men felt that this was it; something about Christmas Eve brought out the strong, sober, and sorrowful emotions. As the men went back to work, they quickly did everything they could to put the depressing thoughts out of their minds. One thing was for sure: They weren't going down without a fight.[35]

According to Bastogne lore, General McAuliffe left the headquarters early that evening to walk around town for some fresh air. As he walked past the police station, which held several hundred German prisoners, he heard them singing Christmas carols in German: "*O Tannenbaum*," and "*Stille Nacht*."

Impressed, McAuliffe ducked inside, followed by the guards. When the Germans noticed an American general in their midst, they could not help taunting him in English.

"We shall be at Anvers [Antwerp] in a few weeks," heckled one of them.

"We'll soon be freed, and it is you who will be the prisoner," another prisoner predicted.

"You will like it here, General; it is most comfortable and cozy," a third prisoner added.

McAuliffe waited until the bravado had stopped, and then softly spoke.

"I was just here to wish you a merry Christmas."

McAuliffe then left in his jeep that evening to go see his men on the lines and encourage them with those very same words.[36]

CHAPTER SEVEN

"Hark, The Herald Angels Sing!"

(DECEMBER 24)

"I am sorry to hear your brigade has been fatigued or alarmed. You may be assured that the rebel army in Pennsylvania . . . does not exceed eight thousand men who have neither shoes nor stockings, are in fact almost naked, dying of cold, without blankets, and very ill supplied with provisions. On this side of the Delaware they have not three hundred men. These stroll about in small parties under the command of subaltern officers none of them above the rank of captain, and their principal object is to pick up some of our Light Dragoons."

> —British general James Grant in Brunswick
> writing to Hessian commander Colonel
> Johann Rall at Trenton, December 21, 1776[1]

1925–1945 hours, Sunday, 24 December 1944
Bastogne, Belgium

Those who survived the terror bombings of Bastogne—thousands of feet beneath the bomb bays of *Unteroffizier* Karl Heinz Struhs and the other Junker bombers on their Christmas Eve mission of destruction—recalled how the planes came in like a flight pattern, one after another.

The first reports of approaching German aircraft came over the radios around 1925 hours, and within minutes bombs were falling in the center of Bastogne.[2] Adolf Hitler had unleashed his fury and frustration on the little Belgian town. Snarling like fat mosquitoes, the bombers and the eruptions of their payloads—high-explosive, fragmentation, incendiaries, and bright magnesium flares—blasted the still winter night.

The citizens of Bastogne hid in their basements, shivering with cold and fear. As each Luftwaffe plane buzzed over, more flares fell, sputtering and photo-flashing against the stone facades before thudding to the streets. The flares, as much as the bombs, created a freakish effect—strobe lights in the hellish night.

The concussions could be felt easily for miles around the perimeter of Bastogne. The earth pounded and rocked for the men crouching in holes dug in the frozen earth. The 81st Antiaircraft Battalion, armed with .50-caliber machine guns, could do little to stop the bombing. The gunners estimated the Ju 88s were between 900 to 1,800 feet in altitude and roaring in at full speed. Since the bigger antiaircraft guns were oriented toward ground targets, they were powerless. For what seemed like forever to those on the ground, the bombers had a free rein of destruction over Bastogne.[3]

To the Nazi propagandists, it was just reward for the garrison's insolence. Several hours before the bombs were falling, leaflets shot from artillery tubes fluttered down into the city. Their message was clear:

HARK the HERALD ANGELS sing! Well soldier here you are in "No-Mans-Land" just before Christmas far away from home and your loved ones. Your sweetheart or wife, your little girl, or perhaps even your little boy, don't you feel them worrying about you, praying for you? Yes old boy, praying and hoping you'll come back home again, soon. Will you come back, are you sure to see those dear ones again. . . . Man, have you thought about it, what if you don't come back . . . what of those dear ones?[4]

Little attention was paid to the leaflets. No one was surrendering. The Germans concluded that Bastogne was now a legitimate military target. The weapons of war had shattered this Christmas, and with it the many lives of the soldiers and civilians holding out in Bastogne.

1925–1945 hours, Sunday, 24 December 1944
Headquarters, 101st Airborne Division, Heinz Barracks
Bastogne, Belgium

Fred Mackenzie was down in the Cave when the bombs hit. No one had heard the first one fall. It just exploded. To the reporter, they seemed to hit in quick succession, like a series of blows. Outside was chaos. MacKenzie described the scene:

> An all but imperceptible movement swept along the passage. It seemed to begin at one end, pass through each man, and go on down the corridor. It was like the stirring of leaves through which a vagrant wind passes; they were drawing their physical parts into tight knots to resist the shock. A thin, shrieking whistle and a thunderous roar beat down their senses. The cellar rocked. They crouched along the walls. A second shriek, almost instantaneously after the first, pierced benumbed senses. But the shattering blast of the second bomb blotted out the sensation its falling produced, benumbing them anew. A man seemed to be buffeted between the heaving walls. The third bomb of the stick came down mercifully fast to fracture violently again the ties between conscious mind and body pressing desperately against the unyielding concrete to escape.

As the men tried to regain their senses, Colonel Ned Moore appeared, like the captain of a ship strolling onto the bridge during a violent storm.

"Steady, men. Keep calm. Don't crowd," the acting chief of staff commanded, like Christ calming the waters.

One of the men started to panic. "Let's get out of here," Corporal Daniel Olney said as he grabbed his blanket and stumbled up the stairs. MacKenzie decided to follow the soldier into the moonlit night. As he stepped outside, he felt the cold, invigorating air. In a sense, he was like someone on the Great Plains emerging from the cellar after a tornado had roared through the town, wondering what had just happened. MacKenzie could still hear the bombing in the distance as the drone of the Ju 88s faded into the night. In front of him were several blazing fires. The flames cast strange, flickering shadows across the taller buildings in the town center down the road from the barracks. One monstrous conflagration caught his attention, and the intrepid reporter ran toward the blaze like a moth drawn to a flame.

As MacKenzie hustled down the Rue de Neufchâteau, he ran into Colonel Curtis Renfro, the 101st's "spare" colonel, who was heading toward the same fire. Together the two men dashed off to the center of town. Finally, after several minutes of jogging down snow-covered cobblestone avenues, they passed the town square and arrived at the scene. What was once a building was now twisted, burning embers and smashed masonry.

Several troopers were trying to put out the fire using only buckets. It was a losing battle, but they tried anyway. Other men dug furiously, desperately trying to help their buddies out of the rubble. It was dangerous work. All around them the building continued to burn and crumble. The Buffalo reporter could only watch, helpless.

"There were thirty-two wounded men in there," a shocked lieutenant cried out, pointing at the monstrous, consuming inferno. On the way to the site, MacKenzie had learned that the holocaust in front of him had been the medical aid station for Combat Command B of the 10th Armored Division. Finally, disgusted and defeated, the diggers retreated and yielded to the growing fire.

The lieutenant then pointed at the debris and remarked, "One of the men told me that a Belgian nurse was caught under a falling timber just as she was nearly out," said the lieutenant. "She was taking care of the wounded."

To the war correspondent, it was bad enough to lose young men, but to hear that a young woman had passed away was even worse. MacKenzie later learned that her name was Renée Lemaire, daughter of Gustav Lemaire, a village merchant. She was a nurse, in a sense, tending to the wounded in the aid station. Lemaire had already become something of a legend to the wounded Americans. Her tending to their every need, her basic medical abilities, and her compassion as she dispensed dollops of brandy as a painkiller all endeared her to the soldiers of the 101st. Indeed, her nickname became "the Angel of Bastogne." Equally important was the work of another nurse, Augusta Chiwy, an African from the Belgian Congo, who cared for the wounded side by side with American medics and doctors.[5]

What seemed callous could have been accidental. Perhaps it was a rogue German bomb, or perhaps it was intentionally triggered by the Ju 88 bombardier. It certainly was a fat and tempting target: The medical aid station was located in a three-story building on the edge of town. Half-tracks and jeeps were parked outside to deliver the evening's load of wounded and frostbitten. To a Luftwaffe bombardier at almost 2,000 feet, zipping by at more than two hundred miles per hour in the dark, it could have appeared to have military value—perhaps a headquarters or some other important target?

The single bomb had penetrated through the aging timber roof and then detonated on contact with the station floor. The ensuing explosion had shattered the glass windows for blocks as smoke and flame erupted from the openings. Captain John "Jack" T. Prior, an army medical officer who was there that night, recorded the experience years later:

> I was in a building next to my hospital preparing to go next door and write a letter for a young lieutenant to his wife. The lieutenant was dying of a chest wound. As I was about to step out the door for the hospital one of my men asked if I knew what day it was, pointing out that on Christmas Eve we should open a Champagne bottle. As the two of us filled our cups, the room, which was well blackened out, became as bright as an arc welder's torch. Within a second or two we heard the screeching sound of the first bomb we had ever heard. Every bomb, as it descends, seems to be pointed right at you. We hit the floor as a terrible explosion next door rocked our building.

Prior had rushed outside, trying to pull away the planks and bits of stone. He could hear the cries of the wounded, trapped underneath. More bombers started strafing the area with their machine guns. Several times, he and the enlisted men had to duck under nearby vehicles for cover, reemerging to continue their rescue work.

Prior wrote, "A large number of men soon joined us and we located a cellar window (they were marked by white arrows on European buildings). Some men volunteered to be lowered in to the smoking cellar on a rope and two or three injured were pulled out before the entire building fell into the cellar."

When the ground floor had collapsed into the basement, dozens of wounded soldiers were instantly buried, killed, or entrapped. Prior believed that Renée Lemaire was one of them. He later remarked, "It seems that Renée had been in the kitchen as the bomb came down and she either dashed into, or was pushed into, the cellar before the bomb hit." Prior wrote:

"Ironically enough, all those in the kitchen were blown outdoors since one wall was made of glass."

Chiwy was more fortunate. She survived, being one of those flung from the adjacent building when the bomb detonated. The tragedy would hang heavy on the hearts of the soldiers that evening. It was just another cold, cruel reminder of the senselessness of war. Prior continued in his account: "Before our unit left Bastogne we dissected the hospital rubble and identified the majority of the bodies, including Renée Lemaire." Tenderly, Jack Prior brought the remains to her parents, wrapped in a silk parachute cloth that she had wanted for a wedding dress. He also wrote a posthumous commendation for Lemaire and forwarded it to McAuliffe.[6]

Not only was Lemaire's death a symbol of Bastogne's martyrdom that night, but it was also a clear indication to the Americans as to what they were fighting for. This tragic Christmas Eve news only proved that Bastogne and the sacrifices of her brave people would not be in vain. The Americans were now, and ever more so, determined to hold their ground and keep the Germans out.

The word of the score of wounded soldiers and Lemaire's death reached the outposts that evening, even as Bastogne's HQ runners delivered what little mail and hot food they could to the men in the outlying towns. As the soldiers whispered prayers in their cold foxholes, the brave little Belgian nurse and the casualties would not be forgotten, certainly not on this most holy night.

1925–1945 hours, Sunday, 24 December 1944
Headquarters, 327th Glider Infantry Regiment
Bastogne, Belgium

The aid station was not the only target that night. Colonel "Bud" Harper, commander of the 327th GIR, remembered the Luftwaffe attack on his headquarters. Harper and his executive officer had dug a slit trench in the HQ for protection from German bombs. They had lined the inside of the trench with parachute silk, and the two had dragged a dirt-filled footlocker over the top to provide some measure of overhead protection. Finally, Harper had posted an enlisted man outside and instructed him to blow three blasts on a whistle if he heard or saw any German aircraft flying over.

"My exec had been down to Marvie making an inspection. He went in a house down there and in the cellar they had a whole lot of sugar-cured hams hanging up," Harper said. "He came back with a ham and we were sitting there eating ham sandwiches."

Before Harper could take another bite, he heard the soldier blast three times on the whistle. Skeptical, Harper stepped out into the night air. The soldier mutely pointed up into the sky.

"The Germans had dropped a flare right square over us and that was the signal we were the target."

Harper turned to his executive officer. "You know who's the target?" he asked.

The XO replied negatively.

Harper then declared, "We are. Let's get down in that foxhole."

With that, the colonel jumped down into his foxhole with seconds to spare. Suddenly bombs burst around his command post as he and his HQ staff took shelter. Even though bombs penetrated the roof of the building and collapsed the floors above his S2 and S3 office, casualties were minimal.

"They dropped the five-hundred-pound bomb and right across the street from where we were was the cemetery. That five-hundred-pound bomb hit in the cemetery and a piece of tombstone came right through the window. I thought that was kind of sad." The next day, Harper moved his headquarters. He wasn't about to take any more chances.[7]

1925–1945 hours, Sunday, 24 December 1944
On the outskirts of Bastogne, Belgium

In the farmhouse near Champs, Sergeant D'Angelo's sleepless night was only getting worse. He recalled how he was "banged and bounced" around in his bed, as the Luftwaffe repeatedly bombed the area during the night.[8]

Others, too, figured something big was going to happen that night. Layton Black, comfortable with his squad in the Hemroulle barn, woke to the noise of bombing. He wrote in his memoir, "What woke me up was the terrible shaking of our old barn and the noise of German bombs falling nearby," he recalled. "Our guards told us that the Germans had bombed Bastogne at midnight and the fires could be seen from outside our hayloft."[9]

Twenty-one-year-old Private Anthony Breder, the "floater" for the 705th, was told there was little need for an assistant TD driver that evening. Breder found himself in Bastogne, running errands for the 705th's HQ.

This included guard duty outside the building that Colonel Templeton was using as his headquarters, and frequent trips running messages out to the outlying regimental command posts.

The bombing and shelling could be relentless, and lest anyone think the headquarters types were perfectly safe or had it easy in Bastogne, Breder's experience that night might prove them wrong. At one point he was assigned to help one of the aid stations.

"I would carry arms and legs from the hospital and put them in a pile," He said. "We would burn them later. It was god-awful."

Breder had to return to his pit under a truck for protection as the German planes conducted a second bombing run later that night. As bomb after bomb hit the streets and buildings around the town square, Breder and several other soldiers dived for safety under the truck. Breder prayed that a bomb would not score a direct hit on the vehicle. When it was over, he was relieved when he was placed on food duty, running hotcakes out to the TD crews.[10]

Bruce Middough, a trooper with the 463rd, was standing guard duty near the gasoline dump at Hemroulle. Fortunately, the planes ignored his area, but from the hillside where he stood he caught a panoramic view as the aircraft passed over Bastogne and other parts of the perimeter, dumping their deadly payloads in the night.

"I could watch the bombing of Bastogne. I heard the planes coming over and watched them drop their flares. I could actually see the bellies of the planes when they dove over Bastogne from the reflection of the flares."[11]

Evening, Sunday, 24 December 1944
Area of operations, 6th Company, 77th Volksgrenadier Regiment
Near Flamierge, Belgium

Ludwig Lindemann had established his makeshift command post in a tank dugout south of Flamierge. "As at Irssin [Russia] we were told to keep fighting that day and on Christmas Day," Lindemann recounted. "I would have preferred to take a break; instead we had nothing to celebrate Christmas, no food or anything like that. I don't think it registered to us that it was Christmas."

From there, the veteran *Unteroffizier* organized his company. Like most of these nights, Lindemann blew on his hands to keep them warm. He could see his breath in the cool night air, and like many of his men he felt pangs in his stomach. It had been some time since many of them had eaten. His unit had sustained serious losses over the last eight days fighting these stubborn *Amis*, and now, he learned, he was going to take his company in for another attack. The mission was simple—avoid the villages and take Bastogne—but Lindemann sent a runner to get the full set of orders from battalion. The young man he sent dashed off into the night and returned later with the new set of more complete orders.[12]

Lindemann scanned the order for relevant data that pertained to his unit. According to the regimental directive, his battalion must be in its assault position by 0215 hours, in a forest more than five hundred yards east of Rouette. Lindemann looked at his watch. He didn't have a lot of time to get his men ready and up there. Lindemann's battalion would be required to secure the northern flank of the regimental attack, as another armor-infantry unit would make the main assault. *Oberstleutnant* Martin Schriefer, the regimental commander, tasked the battalion to seize Château Rolle, the 502nd PIR's headquarters, southeast of the woods. Their axis of advance would take them through the woods, north of Champs, and then back up a ridge to attack the château from the north.

Schriefer's plan was textbook infantry infiltration tactics. Under the cover of darkness, his entire regiment would use the Les Bresses woods to the north of Champs to conceal their movement. Their objective was to cut the Champs–Longchamps road at the base of a hill and attack the American lines here. If successful, they would separate the 1st of the 502nd from its sister battalion, the 2nd, to the northeast. Here, the connection between "Long John" Hanlon's 1st and Lieutenant Colonel Thomas Sutliffe's 2nd was thin.

At 0255 hours, the attack would commence. First the various artillery batteries and mortars would lay down a blanket of suppressive fire to pin the American machine guns and artillery. It would be a short but violent barrage that would last five minutes. Then both battalions would move out. 1st Company would lead the advance of 1st Battalion, which had the mission to move down the Rouette road, through Champs, and reach the woods to the southeast of Rolle. There it would conduct a tactical pause while 2nd Battalion, Lindemann's unit, would catch up after severing the American lines after exiting the woods, and moving up the slope to take Château Rolle. The whole time both battalions would be moving through either villages or forests to provide cover and concealment.

After completing their initial missions, both battalions, acting in concert with Maucke's portion of the 115th Panzergrenadier, would continue their advance toward Bastogne. Both battalions of the 77th would then seize the towns of Hemroulle and Savy. Once they had accomplished that operation, Schriefer hoped he could mass his combat power with that of the other German units and take the northwest sector of Bastogne itself.

Schriefer relied on other parts of his regiment to provide firepower and support. For artillery support, the infantry gun company would move behind both battalions as they advanced southeastward. Furthermore, each battalion would receive an additional antitank platoon that would provide more than a dozen Panzerschrecks (shoulder-borne rocket launchers similar to American bazookas). One antitank platoon would remain with the regimental headquarters to act as a reserve with the AT company commander. Moreover, each battalion would receive flamethrowers from the 26th Pioneer Company. Hence, if the Americans would not leave their foxholes willingly, Schriefer would have the ability to burn them out. If the Americans counterattacked with armor, Kokott allocated an entire troop of Hetzers—small but deadly 75mm-equipped tank destroyers—to the 77th. To make matters worse for the Americans, once they had secured the area, the engineers would lay antitank minefields to block any counterattack. Finally, an entire battalion of artillery would support the 77th's attack with an initial barrage.

In short, Kokott had given Schriefer an extraordinary amount of firepower.

To Lindemann, desperately trying to stay warm that night in the tank trench, huddled with his men around a small fire, the code word would be "Nurnberg." Once he heard that over the radio, around 0215 hours, he knew that the regimental commander had commenced the operation, and he would lead his company forward into the woods. The young *Unteroffizier* had been instructed to fire a white flare into the night sky to signal when he had seized each of his objectives. That was it. Lindemann folded up the order and slipped it into his pocket. He looked at the tired faces of his men around him. Some he had known since Russia. Then there were the new replacements. Even though they were only a few years shy of his own age, they seemed babies compared to him and the other veterans.

Lindemann was tired, but he knew sleep would have to wait. For the veteran *soldat* and ex-painter from Heyen, it would be another miserable Christmas far from home. Once again, in the grand service of Hitler's Reich, Christmas was turning out to be just another day at war.[13]

2200 hours, Sunday, 24 December 1944
Headquarters, 26th Volksgrenadier Division
Gives, Belgium

At roughly 2200 hours on Christmas Eve, *Oberst* Wolfgang Maucke was a picture of frustration. Trapped by the rigid demands of the German military system, he found himself standing before his commanding officer in the little warming hut in Gives, once again being told to follow impossible orders.

Maucke, like many midlevel officers during *Wacht am Rhein*, had found himself caught between a rock and a hard place. Pressured to simply carry out orders from above, even if in all good conscience, he knew they stood little chance of success. Now, standing before his superior, Colonel Kokott, Maucke could hold back no longer. He had to speak.

"What about reconnaissance?"

Kokott glared at Maucke from behind his wire-rimmed glasses. Kokott responded. There was no time for a thorough reconnaissance. The attack must go forward Christmas morning. Kokott emphasized to Maucke why that was so important—the better to surprise the *Amis* and evade the Allied fighter-bombers before the men and armor were caught in the daylight. Bastogne simply *must* be breached before daybreak, Kokott told him, and Maucke's combined armor-infantry attack *must* be in Bastogne before the reappearance of the *Jabos*. If Maucke were stalled, held up by resistance, or otherwise late, the Allied airpower would catch the Germans at their most vulnerable point and quickly put an end to the attack.

Maucke clenched his jaw. Daybreak was a mere eight hours away. Even one day of sending an armored car patrol to Rouette, or allowing the time for some of his snowsuit-clad soldiers with optics to crawl up among the hills surrounding Champs or Hemroulle, would be of some help in planning the assault. There were too many unknowns. Did the Americans have artillery support in this sector, and how much? Where were they entrenched? Had they placed mines in the surrounding fields? Did they have antitank guns or tank destroyers? How many? Those last two points were of great interest to Maucke's tank commanders. Kokott's staff could provide little help and few answers to his questions.

Kokott smiled artificially. He wished to set Maucke at ease as much as he could. Maucke and the 15th were highly regarded in the Wehrmacht. Unfortunately, when Kokott had heard of the arrival and Maucke had reported in to him, Kokott was crestfallen. He had expected an entire division—the vaunted 15th Panzergrenadier—to lead his attack. Instead OKW had given him only one regiment from that division, which he considered to be under-strength. Either someone had forgotten to tell Army Group B and its com-mander, *Generalfeldmarschall* Walther Model, that the 15th Panzergrenadier Division was not at full strength, or *Wacht am Rhein* was indeed turning out to be as desperate as many German commanders had secretly feared.

Well, that didn't matter now. Nothing could be done at this point—it would soon be Christmas. He explained to Maucke that the Americans, it was hoped, would be too distracted, thinking of their holidays away from their loved ones, to organize much of a resistance at the supposedly weak Champs–Hemroulle sector—Kokott's planned attack route into Bastogne. Seeing the distance, Maucke quickly counted the number of kilometers on his own map. It was more than eight kilometers (almost five miles) from the assembly point to the final objective. He shook his head in disbelief.

After the war, Maucke wrote that it was ". . . [an] attack with tanks in the dark, across unfamiliar terrain, and against a well-entrenched en-emy that belonged to well-known elite troops of the American army."[14]

Maucke figured he had protested as strongly as he dared. There were still many limitations, even with his rank and experience highly regarded by the high command. The attack seemed to Maucke to be at best a halfhearted gesture ordered by von Manteuffel to get the führer off his back about Bas-togne. These thoughts he kept to himself. Unfortunately, he and his men were going to have to pay the price for it if it failed. Unhappily, he about-faced and left Kokott's headquarters. Maucke had lodged his protest; now, as any German officer knew, there was only duty, even if that duty smelled like failure. There was no time to waste. He had to set about developing a plan. *Befehlen sind befehlen*—orders were orders.

As he strolled outside in the cold night, Maucke pulled on his gloves. He thought about his piecemeal unit. He could not wait for any others and would have to go into battle with whatever parts of his three battalions had arrived in the Bastogne area by now. About two hours earlier, Maucke's battalions had moved out to their initial start positions. His divisional com-mander, *Oberst* Hans Joachim Deckert, had buttressed Maucke's regiment with a company of Mark IV Panzerkampfwagens and a company of smaller, but just as lethal 75mm-equipped tank destroyers (Sturmgeschütz III). Un-fortunately, the tank destroyers had no radios, which made coordination and communication problematic. In addition, even though Deckert was giving him the entire company of seventeen panzers, only eleven would be available. (By this time in the war, German operational readiness had suffered due to a lack of spare parts, so it was rare when an entire panzer company could deploy with all of its tanks.) Fortunately, Deckert understood the crucial role Maucke's regiment would be playing. Like Kokott, he had given most of his artillery to support Maucke's regiment for the assault.[15]

Maucke glanced at his watch. There was little time for him to convey this information to his battalion commanders. He had to return to his own headquarters as soon as possible. There was no time to waste. It would be close to midnight when he would finally give them their final orders.[16]

Kokott heard the rumble of Maucke's command vehicle driving off outside the warming hut. He, too walked outside to clear his head. Despite the woefully inadequate *kampfgruppe* from the 15th Panzergrenadier Division, he knew had no choice but to continue with the attack. At least the *soldaten* of the 15th were known throughout the Heer to be some of the finest troops, with a gallant and successful combat record. That was why Kokott was thrilled when he had originally heard the entire division would be under his temporary command. Kokott rubbed his glasses clean with his sleeve and sighed. Now he had only one regiment with bits and pieces of a few Panzergrenadier companies to deliver what was expected by German high command to be the decisive blow on the American forces holding Bastogne.

It would simply have to do, he thought.

In an interview after the war, Kokott said, "Changes could no longer be made regarding the attack itself, i.e., the time for the attack and the details of the execution. It had to be started and brought to a successful conclusion."[17]

Kokott then remembered it was Christmas Eve. In a few hours, his men would begin their attack on the Americans in Bastogne. He hoped fortune would be on his side, because now the plan relied on it.

Late evening, Sunday, 24 December 1944
Headquarters, 101st Airborne Division, Heinz Barracks
Bastogne, Belgium

Lieutenant Colonel Paul Danahy finished typing his nightly report. It was his sixth nightly report since the beginning of the operation. He had already finished his overlay showing the various enemy units that surrounded the division, and it caused quite a jovial stir when he wrote "Merry Christmas" on it. Still, there was a decidedly serious nature to the overlay. It was grim evidence of what they faced. According to his intelligence reports, the 101st was surrounded and in direct contact on all sectors of the perimeter with eight different enemy regiments. These included three Volksgrenadier regiments, four Panzergrenadier regiments, and one SS Panzergrenadier regiment. Basically, that Christmas Eve, the Germans outnumbered his division and its attachments by nearly two to one. (In fact, Danahy's estimates were off. The 2nd Panzer Division and most of the Panzer Lehr Division had left, leaving only three Volksgrenadier regiments and two Panzergrenadier regiments.)

Moreover, the Germans showed no signs of giving up. After the bombings were over and the initial excitement had died down at the Heinz Barracks, Danahy had basically determined that the Ju 88s had done very little damage. Most of the losses the division suffered were the result of those killed at the 10th Armored Division's aid station. According to the personnel officer, 123 casualties were in the aid station at the time. Danahy sighed. It seemed cold, but it was a military reality—from a tactical standpoint, the bombing had been a failure. The Luftwaffe had managed to inflict casualties on people who were already casualties. Furthermore, from a psychological standpoint, the deaths of their helpless comrades and Lemaire had only infuriated the GIs more. The night bombing may have been terrifying, particularly to the Bastognards who had endured it, but from a military standpoint, the Germans had accomplished very little harm to the American defense of Bastogne.

Of course, there was the possibility that the bombing was just the warm-up for the large-scale German attack that they had all been waiting for. What *did* the bombing presage? To Chappuis' 502nd men near Champs and Allen's bloodied 1/401st crew outside of Hemroulle, the answer was obvious. All day they had been feeding reports up to Danahy. To the men of those two units in the northwestern sector, it was clear the Germans were gearing up for one last effort to take Bastogne before Patton arrived. To Danahy, it was a good analysis. It was the sector they had figured would be hit next. Now the only question was when. The Germans would answer that in a couple of hours.[18]

Midnight to 0200, Monday, 25 December 1944
Temporary headquarters of the 115th Panzergrenadier Regiment
Troismont, Belgium, several kilometers west of Mande Saint-Etienne

Oberst Maucke stood inside a small, rustic farmhouse just east of the town of Salle at a place called Troismont. The farmhouse was small, but warm and cozy—hardly a fitting place where commanders planned a major attack on Christ's birthday. No matter. He now had his orders, and had devised an overall game plan based on the scant maps and information Kokott's headquarters could provide.

He reviewed the latest reports one more time before he spoke with his subordinates. According to the intelligence he received from the 26th Volksgrenadier, the Americans still had forces in the vicinity of Flamierge. Other than that, Maucke could make guesses, but he was unsure of the exact location of the American main line. All he had was a crude map with question marks on it. Maucke gritted his teeth in frustration. He truly had no idea as to the disposition of the American forces.

As the hour approached midnight, the various commanders filed into the quaint Belgian home in a scuffling of boots and a shaking of snow from their shoulders. They were all dressed in their cold-weather gear, wearing long coats or the padded Russian winter parkas. He studied their grim faces. They were good men, several whom he had served with before, such as Major Richard Wörner, who would lead the attack from the Al'Caure Woods with his first battalion as the spearhead. Maucke would attach the panzer company to his battalion to furnish the powerful *Panzer Angriff* that Kokott had been hoping for. In a supporting role was Major Adam Dyroff, the commander of 3rd Battalion, who would team up his men with the platoon of StuG III assault guns. Dyroff was already a legend of sorts in Maucke's regiment, and Maucke's shining star: Born in Langstadt bei Dieburg, Germany, Dyroff seems to have been born a military leader. He had been awarded the Knight's Cross only several weeks prior, and had served in the division for several years, fighting in North Africa, Sicily, and at the bloody battle for Monte Cassino. Maucke wanted him in the attack, but he felt it might be time for someone else to lead the charge. Besides, it would be good to have a dependable, veteran leader for the follow-up. As for 2nd Battalion, its commander was Hauptmann Ernst Weichsel, and he was new to the job. In addition, many of his men were replacements. Therefore, Maucke thought it wise to place his battalion in the rear as a reserve, south of Salle in the Bois de Herbaimont woods.

There were other lesser commanders there, as well, including a *Hauptmann* Schmidt, the twenty-nine-year-old commander of the panzer unit attached to Wörner's battalion, headphones dangling around his neck.

Maucke unfolded the map and began to outline his plan to his commanders. He made motions with his hands to indicate the direction of travel and attack for each unit. He was proud to see that his officers, a few who had served with him since Italy, seemed to put their unswerving trust in their commander, fully realizing the urgency and importance of this all-out attack.

"First," Maucke said, pointing to a spot near Flamierge, "I want the commitment of two battalions in the forwardmost line."

Maucke then looked over at Wörner. "On the right, I want your battalion mounted on tanks attacking in the direction of Bastogne via Flamizoulle, then onto the northern fringe of Saint-Etienne. Make sure your right wing is traveling along the road to Bastogne."

Wörner nodded. His commander continued to explain. "Next to Wörner's battalion, I want 3rd Battalion, staggered somewhat behind, but attacking past the northern rim of the village of Flamizoulle. From there, skirt south of the drainage here and then onto the northern portion of Bastogne." As he spoke, Maucke traced the route on the map with his finger.

"The tank destroyers [StuGs] are to follow Dyroff's battalion, in order to engage and neutralize any enemy tanks." Maucke knew the morning would be dark and foggy, so communication would be vital. "Radio contact must be between every individual tank and with Wörner's battalion."

"Finally," he instructed, "I want *Hauptmann* Weichsel's battalion in reserve. Understood?"

In closing, Maucke emphasized that there would be no preparatory bombardment prior to the attack. Unlike Schriefer, Maucke wanted to keep the element of surprise. As soon as the two lead battalions were engaged and had a better idea of the American strongpoints, artillery support could be brought to bear on any problematic American positions.

The three commanders nodded and muttered their acknowledgment. They were all veterans. To them, it was another operation.

"Everything must be ready by 0230 hours," added Maucke. They all looked at their watches. It was already past midnight. Before the war, he would have added, *Fröhliche Weihnachten*—Merry Christmas—but now all he could add, looking at the grim and determined expressions of his officers, was, "Good luck."[19]

From Givry to the north down to Flamierge to the south, the entire western sector of Bastogne's road network was alive with the movement and sound of German might and muscle.

As the hour approached, Maucke climbed aboard his own command car that was sputtering to life and coughing out great puffs of exhaust in the frozen December air. Earlier that evening, he had seen the men of his regiment as they arrived and set up in their positions, loading equipment, topping off the fuel tanks of the panzers and StuGs, and gathering ammunition for the attack.

Many of Maucke's grenadiers, artillery, and tank crews were exhausted from the strain of moving at breakneck speed to Bastogne over the past two days. Because of the loss of a field kitchen, shot up by the American fighter-bombers, one of his battalions had no rations. As the engines came alive on the self-propelled guns and tanks lining the farm trails and roads, the Panzergrenadiers cursed in the dark as they helped one another hand over hand onto the tanks and low-slung StuGs until each vehicle was loaded with some fifteen or more soldiers. Maucke took a long look at his brave men.

He would never see many of them again.

Midnight, Monday, 25 December 1944
Basement of the Pensionnat des Soeurs de Notre-Dame
Bastogne, Belgium

As the might of Hitler's vengeance prepared to make a final, concentrated push upon Bastogne, the peacefulness of Christmas Eve was about to be shattered in a terrifying battle of steel, fire, and blood.

Despite the bombings and shelling, the people of Bastogne refused to surrender to this fear and give up hope. As fires consumed several buildings in Bastogne, many of the people continued to celebrate midnight Mass. In the basement of Notre-Dame, a boarding school, students and wounded soldiers sang Christmas carols together. A priest, who was also a professor at the nearby college, presided over the services. The basement was stuffed from wall to wall with people. One section was filled with students and nuns, while the other section was mainly filled with the wounded U.S. soldiers, many lying on stretchers. In the middle of a corridor, between the two groups, was a Christmas tree brought in for this occasion. Outside, the fires continued. A couple of hours after the Mass ended, the German bombers returned; as if in response to the defiant and brazen courage of Bastogne's inhabitants, the Germans bombed Bastogne again.[20]

CHAPTER EIGHT

"All I Know Is That I Wish We Were Out of Here."

(CHRISTMAS MORNING)

"Grant writes me the enemy are naked, hungry and very weak and that it is not necessary to place troops (sentries)."[1]

—Colonel Johann Gottlieb Rall, Hessian commander
at Trenton, to his officers upon receiving a letter from
British General James Grant on December 21, 1776

"Let them come. We want no trenches. We will go at them with the bayonet."

—Rall's written reply to Grant, 1776[2]

0300 hours, Monday, 25 December 1944
Headquarters, 101st Airborne Division, Heinz Barracks
Bastogne, Belgium

Fred MacKenzie couldn't sleep. He had managed to snatch only three hours after witnessing the drama and violence of that Christmas Eve in Bastogne. The images were still seared into his consciousness, in particular the burned and smoking rubble of the hospital and the dreadful bombing that night. *How, in God's name,* he wondered, *will I ever be able to write about all of this?*

It was still dark at 0300 hours in the morning when MacKenzie decided to go outside for a stroll and talk with the MPs who guarded the entrance

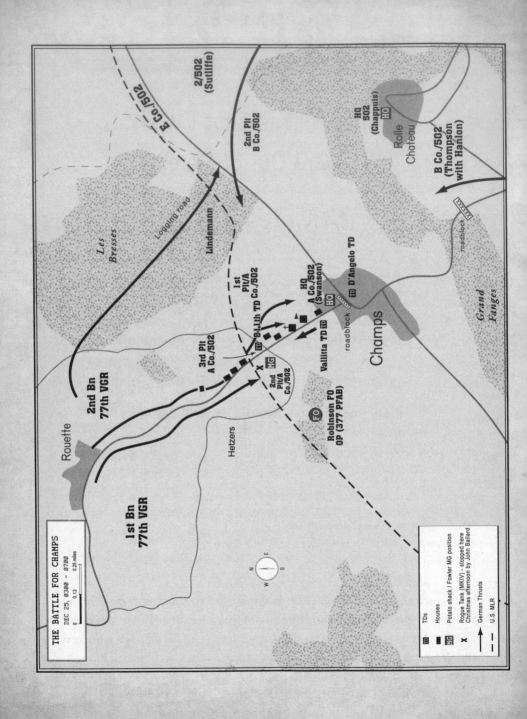

THE BATTLE FOR CHAMPS

DEC 25, 0300 – 0700

0   0.12   0.25 miles

Rouette

Les
Bresses

Logging road

E Co./502

2/502
(Sutliffe)

2nd Plt
B Co./502

HQ
502
(Chappuis)

Rolle
Chateau

B Co./502
(Thompson
with Hanlon)

roadblock

Grand
Fanges

Champs

D'Angelo TD

HQ
A Co./502
(Swanson)

roadblock

Vallitta TD

1st Plt/A
811th TD Co./502

3rd Plt
A Co./502

2nd
Plt/A
Co./502

MG

Hetzers

Robinson FO
OP (377 PFAB)

FO

2nd Bn
77th VGR

1st Bn
77th VGR

Lindemann

N
W   E
S

TDs

Houses

Potato shack / Fowler MG position

Rogue Tank (MKIV) - stopped here
Christmas afternoon by John Ballard

German Thrusts

U.S. MLR

to the Heinz Barracks. They were statuesque sentinels, carefully keeping watch, particularly on the night sky now. MacKenzie had developed a good rapport with the men of the 101st, enduring and sharing what many of the soldiers were going through in the bitter siege. MacKenzie wondered how the exhausted guards managed to stay awake. When asked, the men replied that, like himself, after the shock of the early evening bombing, they had no problem staying up.

One of the sentries asked him, "If you had known what we were getting into, would you have come along?"

MacKenzie replied, "I don't know. All I know is that I wish we were out of here." Sometimes getting the story was not worth your life, he realized. It was a lesson he had to remind himself of over and over again.

MacKenzie pondered all that had happened since his arrival, and that of the Screaming Eagles, in Bastogne. A lot had happened since that Monday, now only a week ago. As MacKenzie stood, alone in his thoughts, he noticed that for the most part, the night was quiet. Quieter than usual. Sure, there was the typical sound of occasional distant shelling that the ears had grown so used to as to render it background, but it seemed fainter now. As he blew on his hands he could hear the sound of his own shoes on the paved grounds of the barracks, stepping up and down as he walked in place to keep warm.

Then, far off, he started to hear the familiar sound of an airplane engine overhead. The still night amplified it so the droning seemed like it was only a hundred feet above his head. MacKenzie's heart started to race with the fear of another bombing ordeal.

As if reading his mind, one of the guards looked at him. "They are ours," he declared.

"They are Black Widows, looking for Jerries," added another. (Black Widows were U.S. twin-engine P-61 night fighters.)

To MacKenzie, recovering from a sudden cold sweat, they didn't sound like American planes, but he kept his thoughts to himself. A second later, his worst fears were realized. The group of men heard a dreadful whistling that was the telltale sound of bombs falling. It had immediately answered the question of whether the planes were friend or foe.

"In here, sir!" one of the soldiers yelled, pointing to a foxhole.

MacKenzie didn't need any directions. He knew where to go. In his book *The Men of Bastogne*, MacKenzie wrote:

The unsheltered bystander, [MacKenzie] too had heard the first note of Death's Christmas Hymn. Instantly he was in the foxhole with them. The three watchmen of the night jammed themselves down in the hole's depths. The bomb, and more bombs, crashed; how many and for how long the foxhole occupants did not know. At the beginning of each descent, if the bombs did not fall upon another, the three collapsed in the hole. And after the infernal things were down, each with agonizing roar, they expanded and rose as upright as they might until the next.[3]

Though it lasted only a few minutes, to the men stuffed inside the tiny foxhole like sardines it seemed an eternity. With each blast the ground heaved and the concussion whipped up a cold wind on the ground, blowing dirt and snow over the foxhole. When it finally ended, the four men cautiously peered over the edge of the hole to see what had been hit. To the west, MacKenzie saw a light show of green and white flares, careening tracers, and blinding explosions.

Suddenly a panicked GI appeared near the gates of the division headquarters. He exclaimed, "I'm getting out of here."

He stepped out into town and then turned to face the men in the foxhole. He was clearly lost, like a boy wandering aimlessly in a large store, looking desperately for his parents. "Can I go this way?" he asked MacKenzie and the sentries. His voice sounded hesitant and shaky. Obviously the stress and the bombing had broken the man. The soldier was not a paratrooper but one of the many men who had filtered into town during the first few days, joining Team SNAFU. His unit had vanished, a victim of the German attack days before. What horrors he had experienced during the destruction of his unit, MacKenzie could only guess and sympathize.

MacKenzie finally answered the soldier's question. "That way goes into town. Be careful."

One of the sentries then looked over at MacKenzie and remarked, "You shouldn't have said that, sir. You will scare him."

The young soldier, realizing the folly of his actions, then turned around and walked back through the gate. By now the American artillery had joined the noisy night party, adding to the cacophony with scores of outgoing shells. Feeling the bombing was over, MacKenzie crawled out of the foxhole to watch the light show. It was a careless move on the part of the reporter. The foxhole was the safest place. Another soldier thought so too.

He was a friend of the sentries and joined them, taking MacKenzie's place and turning the already crowded foxhole into a human sandwich.

It didn't take long for the reporter to realize the folly of his curiosity. The blazing fireworks display was hypnotizing, and despite the crash and boom of artillery, MacKenzie detected the dreaded but now familiar sound of airplane engines returning, once again zooming in above their heads. It was too late to jump into the foxhole he had just vacated. Caught in the open, he could hear the telltale shriek of the stick of bombs falling. All he could do was duck behind a stone pillar that was part of the gate entrance.

"You had better get into a hole on the other side," one of the sentries shouted to MacKenzie over the din.

"I will as soon as I can make it," the reporter screamed. The next string of bombs was already on its way.

MacKenzie scrambled into another foxhole that reminded him of a grave, which was even more unsettling, since the Bastogne cemetery was just across the street from the barracks. The bombs were exploding all around him, rattling his head and sucking the breath from his lungs with each thunderous blast. The next few moments were a hellish, terrifying blur as he dashed from one foxhole to the next, searching for some semblance of haven. Writing in the third person, MacKenzie described the scene in his book thusly:

> Knees drawn up under chin and enfolded in his arms, he wound himself into a slight ball of which he was acutely conscious as his body, composed of flesh, blood, bones. This body was vulnerable. How he treasured it. He had a sensation of warm, friendly intimacy with the earth. At last he was unable to preserve the last vestige of self command. It seemed that the interminable shrieking from the black unreality around him must be funneled inevitably to burst on the bit of reality that was partly his body and partly the dear inches of earth that encompassed it. A flood of terror, vile and contaminating, washed away the little stability to which he had clung, and he could only think, or feel, or cry out, *Thy will be done. Thy will be done. Thy will be done.*

While MacKenzie prayed for an end to the apocalypse, the men in the operations room of the Cave sensed that this was the big push. Colonel Ned

Moore was the senior officer on duty that Christmas morning. Everyone else, including General McAuliffe, was trying to catch a few hours of sleep. Moore could hear the artillery fire intensifying to the northwest. He immediately got on the phone to call Chappuis over at the 502nd's sector and see what was up.

Before he could get a word out, the switchboard operator, a young enlisted soldier, told him the bad news: The lines to Château Rolle had been cut, most likely as a result of the artillery barrage. Without a telephone line, the fallback was to use radio. Moore ordered the operator to try to raise Kickoff (the 502nd Headquarters call sign) over the radio. After several tries, the radio operator shook his head. No one was answering the radio at Rolle Château, either.

Moore was convinced this was serious. It certainly sounded like the German attack they had been dreading, but awaiting, for days. It also seemed to be in the sector they had guessed it would arrive in.

"We had better wake the old man," he said to the staff. Not long afterward, a slightly groggy McAuliffe entered the ops room. Despite the arrival of the division commander, it was clear to all in the room that for the next few hours, the men of the Deuce were going to be on their own.[4]

0300 Hours, Monday, 25 December 1944
Area of operations, Able Company, 502nd Parachute Infantry Regiment
Champs, Belgium

At 0300 hours up and down the sector, the German guns opened up. Shells screeched through the cold night and landed along Chappuis's lines, blasting the frozen earth into the air. German 105mm howitzers proceeded to pour in on the beleaguered GIs, especially in the area near Champs. Shell after shell pocked the ground in great flashes and blasts of heat. The Germans were prepping for the attack, and now the Americans knew it was coming, and where. Overhead, sporadic German bombers unloaded their deadly payloads.[5]

Within three minutes, Captain Wallace Swanson, the Able Company commander, had lost communication with all three of his platoons.[6] Swanson chose to send out runners—a pretty dicey plan, considering the shards of steel filling the night air. He didn't relish the decision of endangering the lives of these men, but he had little choice.

"All of our communications were destroyed from our CP to the platoons. The only way we could get messages in or out was by runner—and that was dangerous because of the barrages but that was something we had to keep doing out of necessity," Swanson later wrote.[7]

The former football star was no newbie to the battlefield, but even he was impressed by the intensity of the rain of German steel coming down around Champs. He described it as ". . . an all-out barrage, artillery, cannon, mortar and other firepower. It was raining, snowing, hailing down on our Company A positions. This was the strongest, most extensive, continuous barrage I was ever in. Their goal was to devastate our main line of resistance and all connections from the front to the back and around our strong points."[8]

From the small house that he was using as his command post, Swanson could see the flashes in the night sky. His command post was centrally located in Champs, leaving Swanson with an all-around view of the devastation. Shell after shell screamed in, creating fountains of snow and hurling frozen sod with each detonation. Luckily, his men were well dug in on the outskirts of the little village, hunkered down in their cold foxholes, waiting for the bombardment to end.

To Willis Fowler, trying to sleep in the potato shed, the shelling was loud, but "didn't last too long. The shells were going over [our positions] and hitting the town." Fowler, like the others in his squad nearby, immediately took cover, crouching on the ground. He suspected this was the preamble to the long-awaited attack. "We knew something was up."[9]

At the same 2nd Platoon outpost, the situation went from bad to worse in seconds. Private George J. Hodge Jr. was manning a .30-caliber machine gun with his buddy, a Private Snyder. Hodge had been manning the outpost off and on since the beginning of the siege. Like many of the paratroopers that morning, he was relatively new to the unit. He had not jumped into Normandy, and had joined the company toward the end of the Holland campaign. He had seen little combat. Tonight that was about to change.

Within seconds of the first explosions, Snyder suddenly slumped back in his muddy foxhole. Hodge looked over at him and saw that he was wounded in the back. The wound was ghastly, and Hodge knew Snyder needed a medic or he was going to bleed to death. With the German shells still coming in, Hodge knew it would be impossible to carry Snyder out of there. Desperate to get help for his friend, Hodge took a deep breath. Scrambling out of the foxhole, he tore off in the direction of the platoon command post to get help.

It was a long sprint to the 2nd Platoon CP, more than three hundred yards behind the outpost position. Hodge ran over fields and cattle fences, his breath forming puffs of vapor in the night air. Shells slammed into the ground nearby, the shock wave almost knocking him off his feet.

Hodge reached 2nd Platoon's main line of foxholes in front of the town. Lieutenants John Harrison and Albert Wise had prudently placed the men on the reverse of a slight slope. Their CP was another hundred yards behind the trench line and inside a farmhouse. Like many of the men, Wise and Harrison had only a few hours of sleep. They had been up partaking in a meager Christmas celebration at midnight, and had just fallen asleep when the barrage startled them awake.

Outside the windows of the tiny home, the partial moon shone off the snowy fields surrounding Champs. As each German shell impacted, a bright orange flash lit up the dark room, followed by the thunderous echo. Watching the bombardment outside, a groggy Wise and Harrison tried to make sense of the chaos while ducking down in their CP. Suddenly Hodge slammed open the door and stumbled inside, panting and wheezing. Gasping, he told the two officers what had happened and asked for a medic for Snyder. Harrison knew Wise could stay in contact with Captain Swannie's runners and handle the shop while he was gone. Harrison decided he and a medic would go out to the outpost. Hodge would lead them there. Just in time, the artillery fire seemed to be slackening. The three men yanked open the door and prepared to dart out into the cold night air. If they were to rescue Snyder, it would have to be now or never.

The battle had barely even started, and with Snyder down, 2nd Platoon had already suffered its first casualty.[10]

0300 hours, Monday, 25 December 1944
Headquarters, 502nd Parachute Infantry Regiment, Rolle Château
Rolle, Belgium

Insomnia abounded that evening. Because he couldn't sleep after the Christmas Eve service, Lieutenant Colonel Patrick F. Cassidy (nicknamed "Hopalong" by his fellow officers) was the self-appointed duty officer. It had been a late night in Rolle Château, with the service and all, so Cassidy had let Chappuis sleep, giving his commander a few hours of rest to help him stave off the cold. Cassidy was on one of his periodic checks with the single regimental telephone operator in Rolle when he heard the artillery barrage begin. As Cassidy stood near a window, he could hear the pounding of incoming artillery rounds nearby. Most of the noise seemed to be coming from Champs.

Sure enough, Cassidy quickly got a call from Swanson. Over the noise of gunfire, Swanson told Cassidy that the enemy could be seen moving en masse from the direction of Givry and Rouette and that his "front had become active." Cassidy asked whether Swanson could determine the strength and objective of the enemy attack. The big Kansan replied negatively to both questions. At this point, none of A Company's men knew exactly what was going on.[11]

While Cassidy waited on the line to hear more, there was a terrific explosion. The blast seemed to shake the very foundation of the château. It rattled the windows and illuminated the courtyard outside. A single bomb had detonated in the courtyard of the château, sending a jeep flying through the air as if it were a toy. Nearby, the remnants of a serving line for hungry soldiers lay scattered about like a tornado had swept through the area. Luckily, the walls of the château yard had shielded the soldiers from the flying shrapnel, and as a result no one was injured.

Meanwhile, the 502nd HQ received messages from other units, while the German artillery pounded away outside. Only minutes after the barrage had started, a patrol from Lieutenant Colonel Thomas H. Sutliffe's Fox Company called in and reported German soldiers in a nearby copse north of Rolle. They didn't stay there long. A machine gun near one of the bridges chased them off. The infiltrators were apparently German engineers who had defused the explosives underneath the bridge, allowing their armor to cross the bridge if the need arose.[12]

As the artillery bombardment tapered off, the headquarters men in Rolle Château heard another sound. It seemed as if all the machine guns in Sutliffe's 2nd Battalion, spread between Champs and Longchamps, had opened fire at once, firing into the Les Bresses woods. 2nd Battalion's mortars soon joined in the fight.

Sutliffe's machine gunners and their assistants began to call in on any available line, spotting concentrations of the German troops moving through the logging trail along the wooded hill and acting as spotters for the mortars farther back. The switchboard operator at Rolle relayed the info to the mortar team leaders so they could adjust their fire in the night. The mortarmen moved their tubes so they would drop bombs at 1,600 mils, or due north, deep into the Les Bresses woods. With fingers trembling from the cold, the mortar crews dropped the 60- and 81mm rounds down each tube and hopped back as each round pounded up skyward into the night.

North of Champs, the target area exploded as rounds burst like high-velocity popcorn kernels among the trees. The terrifying noise of the explosions mixed with the screams of the Volksgrenadiers who had tried to infiltrate by that route. At this same time, the staff officers at Rolle began to yell for the support personnel—cooks, clerks, jeep drivers, etc.—who were promptly ordered to be prepared to buttress 2nd Battalion's lines in case any Germans made it to the château. Everyone braced for a collision.[13]

0300–0319 hours, Monday, 25 December 1944
Command post, Able Company, 502nd Parachute Infantry Regiment
Champs, Belgium

Swanson's A Company positions outside of Champs were some of the first to be hit, and hit hard, by the 77th Volksgrenadiers. German recon soldiers, wearing white parkas, had managed to sneak into the western portion of the Les Bresses woods in front of A Company's foxholes. Rising up from the snow, the Germans attacked the forward outposts. To the startled Americans, the Volksgrenadiers seemed to glow with an ethereal quality emphasized by their white parkas reflecting the waxing moonlight. Firing short bursts from submachine guns, the Germans charged at each position, forcing the outpost men to fall back toward Champs.[14]

From his CP, Swanson heard the last few artillery rounds bursting in front of him. The echoes of German artillery fire seemed to come straight from Givry, precisely where he and D'Angelo had spotted the enemy buildup the other day. Swanson knew that his troopers, out in the dark ahead of him, were fighting for their lives. However, it would do no good to play Chicken Little. If he started screaming for reinforcements before he determined exactly what the Germans were up to, he could wind up launching the whole regiment in the wrong direction, which could open a dangerous gap somewhere else on the line.

Swanson knew he had to hold tight. He would watch to see exactly where the Germans hit his line, and request reinforcements only if it seemed Champs was in danger of falling. Now was the time to keep cool and use his coach's intuition to measure just what this new offensive line was made of.

As the Germans crept closer to Champs, gunfire suddenly erupted from the American lines. By 0319 hours, less than twenty minutes into the attack,

Swanson realized he was in trouble. Looking out from his window, he determined that the Germans had penetrated between the 1st and 3rd platoons' battle positions. In addition, the 2nd Platoon command post was on fire. Swanson had his answer. It was time to act.[15]

With telephone communication down between Champs and Rolle, Swanson preferred to wait before using the radios. The batteries were not entirely trustworthy in the cold. He would have to send out more runners to Chappuis, knowing full well that if the Germans started the bombardment again, the runners might not make it.

0300–0330 hours, Monday, 25 December 1944
2nd Platoon command post, Able Company, 502nd Parachute Infantry Regiment
Champs, Belgium

Inside the CP, First Lieutenant John Harrison, the 2nd Platoon leader, was getting ready to dash out into the snow with a medic and bring back a wounded Private Snyder. Just as Harrison and the medic started to leave on their rescue attempt, the men noticed a group of figures darting around in the yard. The enemy had surrounded the building. To their right, they noticed more Germans attacking 1st Platoon's CP. Quickly Harrison yanked the medic back indoors. The Germans saw the movement and fired a machine gun from almost point-blank range.

Bullets blasted through the nearest window and chewed up the interior as the three men hit the floor. Glass shattered. Plaster exploded from the walls. A small stove in the corner of the room was knocked over and started the room on fire. To make matters worse, a second German machine gun opened up from the other side of the house, raking the back of the structure and preventing the men from escaping out that door.

Wise could hear the Germans shouting outside. Several Panzerfaust rounds came crashing through the walls. Now the room was on fire and thick with smoke. If they didn't abandon the CP, Harrison knew they would be burned alive.

As Wise lay on the ground, he couldn't help thinking that the German attacks seemed to focus their fire on the farmhouse. It was as if the enemy knew exactly where the platoon CP was located.

When there was a break in the fire (the Germans were probably reloading), the men made a run for it. They darted into the attached barn. Harrison suggested letting the cows out of the barn and using them as cover.

When the cows were released and not fired upon, Harrison, Wise, the medic, Hodge, and several other soldiers made a break for it, leaving boot prints in the snow as they ran for their lives. Running another twenty-five yards southeast, they hid in a tall hedgerow behind the house.

From there, the two officers watched as their CP went up in flames, lighting up the cold night. Just a few men had time to grab their weapons. Harrison eventually crept forward to try to collect more survivors of 2nd Platoon and organize some sort of defense. Wise stayed at the hedge with a small group taking potshots at the Germans as they continued their attack into town.[16]

0300–0330 hours, Monday, 25 December 1944
Machine gun section, 3rd Platoon, Able Company, 502nd Parachute Infantry Regiment
West side of the Rouette–Champs road, Champs, Belgium

Through the wisps of smoke and fog rising from the ground in the moonlight before him, Corporal Lewis Fowler saw the lines of white-coated soldiers approaching. He had just walked out of the potato shed to man his foxhole located on the corner of the wooden structure. To the left of the Rouette–Champs road was the gentle slope of snow-covered, fallow field leading up to a ridge a quarter mile to his front.

German armored vehicles appeared on the ridge. In the cold silence, Fowler could hear his breathing, the distant rumble of the tanks, and the nervous shifting of Private Bill Emerson, his assistant gunner, who was manning the .30-caliber machine gun. Even though Fowler knew for certain his gun was working, it now seemed that Emerson had frozen up.

"He hadn't been firing the machine gun. I knew I had to get that gun into action."

The former peanut farmer from Georgia hopped down into the pit and pushed Emerson aside, taking the gun from him. He set the sights on the white figures silhouetting themselves on the ridge as they advanced ten or more abreast.

"I told him, 'I'm going to whup up on that column.'" Fowler reassured the frightened Emerson with as much bravado as he could muster himself.

Fowler squeezed the trigger. His obsessive work that night cleaning the weapon paid off. The machine gun burst to life, spitting out red tracers with a deadly chatter. The weapon worked "like a charm." As the white-clad soldiers began to fall in front of him, Emerson had finally come to life, rapidly feeding belt after belt into Fowler's hungry gun.[17]

To Fowler's right, across the road, and to his left, the machine guns of 1st, 2nd, and 3rd platoons were largely silent. The cold that night had frozen up the bolts, and ice had built up in the actions. Several soldiers desperately tried urinating on the mechanisms to get them to thaw.[18] Meanwhile, the riflemen opened up with staccato fusillades of fire, flashing across the snowy ground.

0300–0330 hours, Monday, 25 December 1944
3rd Platoon, Able Company, 502nd Parachute Infantry Regiment
East side of the Rouette–Champs road, Champs, Belgium

Right after the bombardment had ceased, Sergeant Charles Asay was moving. Asay—the self-admitted "mother hen"—was out of the potato shack and sprinting across the road, encouraging his men to hold off the attack. Private Ted Goldmann had a hard time keeping up with Asay. Years later, he remembered how the outpost to their front was quickly overwhelmed by German Volksgrenadiers:

> The squad on the right side of the road wasn't so lucky. Four men were in the house with the barn, and two men were in a haystack when the Germans infiltrated. Only two men were on their MG [machine gun]. The Germans brought up two tanks to the outpost along with infantry, and since there was no telephone, they had no orders to withdraw. Anyway, the tanks had them covered. The corporal, Jimmy Goodyear, who escaped in March, said these six men on the outpost were also captured, that he had seen them all, which substantiated our beliefs.

Goldmann went on to mention that "Fowler was a miracle man with that LMG [light machine gun]." He credited Fowler with saving their left flank and keeping the main German thrust at a standstill down the left side of the Rouette road.[19]

Asay was more concerned about the right flank. He could hear sporadic firing and the occasional oaths of men shouting in hand-to-hand combat. It seemed to him that the troopers of 1st and 2nd platoons and his own platoon CP were being overrun. Grabbing several of his men, he started across the road, firing and chucking grenades at the oncoming figures, who were still pouring down the hillside and making for the houses to his right. It didn't take long for him to realize his platoon had lost an entire squad on his flank. To someone at higher headquarters, those missing men would be only numbers, but to him they were comrades—Lunde, Gorde, Howard, Edwards, Begonyi, and Summerford. Now, completely overwhelmed by the determined Volksgrenadiers, they were gone.[20]

Private First Class Werner C. Lunde, one of the captured soldiers, wrote about the event after the war. "I should have gotten back to our line. I feel bad about that. I still don't know how so many Germans could get past our guard posts without being seen. By the time the guys on guard woke us up, we were completely surrounded. There were several tanks right outside the door. That was the beginning of the worst four months of my life."[21]

0300–0330 hours, Monday, 25 December 1944
Mortar section, 1st Platoon, Able Company, 502nd Parachute Infantry Regiment
Champs, Belgium

Mortar section sergeant Louis Merlano had taken brief shelter with several of his men in a cellar near the 1st Platoon's CP during the short bombardment. When the firing let up, he told the men trapped with him to get ready for an attack.

"Hustle up!" he exhorted.

The sudden bombardment had separated Merlano from his mortar team. To get back to them, he chose to sprint from the cellar with his rifle in his hands and beeline for their last-known position. As he momentarily glanced up, Merlano saw several Germans heading his way. He changed directions and rolled out of a cellar window instead, dropping out into an alleyway. He could hear the firing as some of his men took on the Germans at point-blank range.

When he finally made it back to his mortar section, Merlano ordered his men to start hanging rounds into the tube. Panting, his breath making clouds of condensation in the cold air, Merlano knelt in the snow and watched the figures darting around the dark houses of Champs. He heard the sporadic, amplified gunfire in the still night air, the crackling of the fire burning the roof of the nearby CP, and the desperate shouts in German and English. From where he sat, it didn't look good.

"At that point, it looked like we were totally overrun. . . ."[22]

0300–0400 hours, Monday, 25 December 1944
Down in the cellars of various homes
Champs, Belgium

The soldiers weren't the only ones caught up in the Christmas-morning maelstrom. The townspeople of Champs, those brave souls who had decided to stay, were also trapped inside their homes, while German Volksgrenadiers and Hetzer tank destroyers roamed free outside. For the soldiers, the line of buildings running along the east side of the road was merely cover and concealment. To the townspeople, the buildings were their homes, many families having lived in the area for a century or more. In fact, the initial penetration passed between Victor Raviola's and the Rieses' houses, east of the Rouette–Champs road. Down in the cellars, the huddling Belgians could hear the shouts of German soldiers calling out to one another over the sounds of battle.

A few minutes later, the civilians heard chugging and popping sounds emanating from the Longchamps road where the Americans had dug in. Some of the more patriotic probably smiled, knowing now that the Americans were not rolling over, but putting up a fight to save their town. Suddenly Madeleine Séleck, one of the younger residents, watched as the Poncelet farm burst into flames. The farm was also on the east side of the Rouette–Champs road, and lay between German lines and Asay's squad. As the roof of the building began to burn, it resembled a huge orange torch in the night. The fire produced an unexpected dividend for the Americans. The blazing farm silhouetted the advancing German soldiers. Now, with better targets, the paratroopers had begun to rally and fight back. From positions in ditches, behind buildings, and in hedgerows like the one commanded by Albert Wise, the Screaming Eagles opened up with a fury of rifle and automatic weapons fire.

In response, the German Volksgrenadiers barged into the stone homes to escape the deadly and now accurate fusillades. Several groups occupied the chapel and the local schoolhouse, just down the road. The group of grenadiers who occupied the chapel sent a soldier scurrying up the stairs of the blocky stone bell tower. He immediately mounted an antenna atop the steeple so the squad could communicate back to regiment.

Glancing from a cellar window, Mademoiselle Séleck noticed some Germans approaching their farmhouse. Like many in the town she was hiding with twenty others who had joined her family deep in the cold cellar. They could hear the Germans on the floor above them as they burst through the door and rummaged around the farmhouse. Madeleine's godfather, a brave and perhaps foolhardy man, decided to find out what was going on upstairs and left the group. Several minutes later, he returned with two Germans dressed in white smocks. At first Madeleine didn't know who they were, but when they removed their winter tops and she heard them speak, she knew they were the enemy. Curiously, the two soldiers sat down and laid their weapons by their sides. They did not seem too concerned about the ongoing battle or that they were surrounded by Belgian civilians. As a matter of fact, Séleck could see they were there only to catch their breath. The two Germans had no intention to harm them. After a few minutes, the two picked up their weapons and, without a word, climbed back up the stairs to rejoin the battle raging in the streets. Just like that, the Germans were gone.

A little later, several more of Schriefer's grenadiers returned and climbed down into the now-crowded Séleck cellar. This time, though, it was mostly German wounded. One of them, suffering from a horrible bullet wound to his jaw, still managed to ask the civilians for a cigarette. This time, Séleck noticed, two German grenadiers posted themselves by the stairway, pointing their Schmeisser submachine guns up the stairs. Outside, the battle noises continued unabated.[23]

0319–0330 hours, Monday, 25 December 1944
Command post, Able Company, 502nd Parachute Infantry Regiment
Champs, Belgium

Now Swanson was getting nervous. Peering out the frosted window of his farmhouse, he could see the flames and hear the gunfire coming from the two A Company platoon CPs located past the school. This was only a scant hundred yards to the northwest. Just then Cassidy called back on the line to check in. It was 0330 hours.

Cassidy wanted another update. Swanson, trying not to sound worried, still had to convey the seriousness of the situation. "The krauts are on top of us," the Able Company commander replied. Before he could say anything more, a Krupp artillery shell cut short their conversation, severing the phone line. Swanson's line to headquarters at Rolle had just gone dead.[24]

0330–0400 hours, Monday, 25 December 1944
Headquarters, 502nd Parachute Infantry Regiment, Rolle Château
Rolle, Belgium

To Chappuis, listening carefully to the communications and gunfire to the north and west of Rolle, it seemed like all hell was breaking loose. The commander had raced into the communications center after the barrage to see what was going on. Now he drummed his fingers on the table where the telephone and radios lay. Like Swanson, Chappuis was quickly debating whether this could be the main German thrust at Champs or a mere feint. At that moment, German artillery interrupted his thoughts. The German gunners had shifted their attention to Rolle itself. A shell screamed in and exploded nearby. Spurred on, "Silent Steve" knew he'd need to make a decision and act quickly, before the entire A Company line was penetrated and the krauts came rolling down the road to Bastogne. Every few seconds Chappuis ducked as another round came shrieking down and exploded outside.

Cassidy stood nearby, tension on his face. Chappuis was aware of Cassidy's presence, waiting for his commander's decision. Chappuis, ever the man of few words, simply told Cassidy to call for Hanlon down in Hemroulle. The communications operator, an enlisted man, quickly determined that the phone lines to Hemroulle had also been cut. Once again the radio was the only option.

When "Long John" answered the radio, Chappuis ordered him to report immediately to Rolle and prepare his other two companies (B and C) for battle. When "Kickoff" signed off, Chappuis, still wrapped in the wool blanket he had been sleeping in, started considering his next move while he waited for Hanlon.

When he arrived, the 1st Battalion commander informed Chappuis that Baker Company was on the road from Hemroulle moving up to Champs, and C Company would be following shortly. When Hanlon learned that Chappuis had lost contact with Swanson and Able Company, Long John requested that he go and reestablish contact with his lead company. Swanson was one of his best commanders, and the major felt a sharp sense of responsibility to the Kansas football player.

Chappuis told him to wait. Having his 1st Battalion commander rush off without a clear idea of the situation, especially with communication so choppy, would not be in anyone's best interest. Chappuis knew they needed to determine right now whether the attack was big enough to commit all of the battalion at this time in order to hold Champs. Or Champs could even already be lost, in which case it didn't make much sense to send Hanlon off willy-nilly until a strategy to retake the town could be devised. Chappuis and "Hopalong" went over to the map and quickly discussed the potential enemy courses of action. To Chappuis, the Germans' main effort would either be pushing through Champs or southwest of it. Once again, the ground to the south of Champs seemed more suited for armor, if the Germans were mounting a serious attempt that morning. Hanlon nodded in agreement. The best solution would be a second line of defense behind Champs, which could potentially react to either enemy course of action. Hanlon, seeing the logic, immediately called back down to his Baker Company and ordered them to move forward and occupy the roadblock behind Champs. Satisfied that he had done all he could, Hanlon snapped a quick salute and left in his jeep to go find "Swannie" and the rest of A Company.[25]

0400 hours, Monday, 25 December 1944
Command post, Able Company, 502nd Parachute Infantry Regiment
Champs, Belgium

Throughout the desperate struggle for Champs, Swanson had sent out runners to check on his platoon commanders, but so far all had failed to come back. He was about to send one as far as Rolle when his radio operator suddenly picked up a message from Chappuis: Cassidy had woken the regimental commander, who wished to check the situation first, but promised to get right back to him. It had been minutes since he had spoken with Cassidy, but those minutes felt like hours. Swanson felt relief to hear the soft, deliberate Louisiana accent come over the earpiece of the "handy-talky." Chappuis asked Swanson to tell him more about the situation.

Shouting into the radio over the noise of gunfire, Swanson told him the fighting was furious and house-to-house, but the Americans seemed to be holding Champs, if barely. Chappuis assured Swanson that Hanlon was sending help in the form of Lieutenant Clarence J. Thompson's B Company and Captain George R. Cody's C Company, both units called up from their bivouacs outside of Hemroulle. Already the two companies were moving up the road toward Champs. Swanson expressed his concern that in the dark, and with the battle in full swing, his boys might not be able to distinguish between friend or foe. He suggested that Hanlon keep the rest of his battalion outside of Champs.

Swanson signed off, listening to the continuous rattle of an American machine gun, strong and singular, firing somewhere in the dark ahead and to his left. He hoped Chappuis would consider his recommendation. It could be a disaster if Able's paratroopers opened fire on their comrades in Baker Company, but with the dark and chaos running rampant in the town, it was a very real possibility.[26]

0330–0400 hours, Monday, 25 December 1944
Machine gun section, 3rd Platoon, Able Company,
502nd Parachute Infantry Regiment
West side of the Rouette–Champs road, Champs, Belgium

Two of A Company's abandoned command posts were burning, casting a flickering orange glow into the night, but from his foxhole position next to the potato shed across the road, Fowler was still firing. The .30-caliber was banging away, and German soldiers were going down in droves. Caught moving down the Rouette road or in the open field advancing, persistent Volksgrenadiers found no cover. Fowler watched his deadly work as the enemy dropped in writhing groups to the snowy ground. In between bursts he could hear their shouts and screams. He paid no mind to the possibility that the Germans might be sneaking by on his right, preparing to flank his position; Fowler was too focused on what was in front of him to care. All he knew was that he seemed to be the only machine gun in action, and his bullets were holding up the attack in front of him.

As Fowler finished a belt, he would yell for Emerson to reload the gun. The muddy bottom of the foxhole was filling with spent brass as the two men continued to work. By now, other members of the platoon were crawling up to their position and dropping off the extra ammunition from the frozen machine guns. During one break, Fowler happened to notice a German tank on the ridge. In the dark it was a sinister, monstrous shape moving back and forth. For the life of him, Fowler couldn't understand why the tanks didn't just come charging down on his position.

"That probably would have been the end of us," he later noted in an interview.[27]

To Fowler's right and left, the situation was desperate. Able Company's

1st and most of its 2nd Platoon had been forced to withdraw and give up the farmhouses and barns that dotted the road from Champs to Rouette. The Germans had moved quickly, and were now in possession of those buildings and foxholes the Americans had been squatting in about an hour before. And to the far right of A Company's flank, the situation was about to get worse.

0330–0400 hours, Monday, 25 December 1944
Forward line of troops, 6th Company, 77th Volksgrenadier Regiment
Les Bresses woods, Champs, Belgium

True to Kokott's orders, *Unteroffizier* Ludwig Lindemann and others from the 2nd Battalion of the 77th Volksgrenadier had moved through the cover of the Les Bresses woods, following the Rue Rouette streambed and a parallel logging trail. Their objective was to cut the Champs–Longchamps road at the base of the slope, and thus separate the 1st of the 502nd from its sister battalion, the 2nd, to the northeast.

For the past few days, Lindemann's commander, Martin Schriefer, had been able to exercise a distinct advantage over Maucke: He was able to reconnoiter the American positions and determine that here, indeed, the American line was thin and weak. Creeping stealthily through the snow and trees Lindemann's company had advanced carefully most of that night. The partial moon dimly reflected through the snowy woods as the Volksgrenadiers moved in, weapons ready.

Lindemann recalled the first contact as his men crept forward in the thick woods, hugging the trees along the broad logging trail. "As we moved through the woods quietly, we saw the American positions about sixty meters away," he recalled.

Clutching his Sturmgewehr 44 automatic rifle, Lindemann used hand signals as best he could in the dark. The Germans, dressed in white overcoats and helmets covered in white cloth or painted white, crawled through the snow. Yards from the first American outposts, the men leaped up and attacked, many firing from the hip as they charged.

Lindemann continued his account, "I saw a few of the Americans; they were everywhere and they ran at first. I hoped we would win the battle. Many of the Americans retreated."

After the Volksgrenadiers successfully drove in the outposts, they reached a sharp dropoff in elevation as the woods made contact with the

Longchamps–Champs road. The American line here was somewhat alert, having heard the fighting to their left. Just yards away from each other, both sides erupted in gunfire. Great chunks of wood were blasted from tree trunks. The smell of tree sap was strong in the air. Lindemann and the other Volksgrenadiers dived for cover behind the trees and logs.

Gunshots echoed back and forth through the once-peaceful woods.[28]

0400 hours, Monday, 25 December 1944
3rd Platoon, Able Company, 502nd Parachute Infantry Regiment
Along the Longchamps–Champs road, Champs, Belgium

Meanwhile in Champs, Sergeant Charles Asay was moving back from house to house with his squad. As he did so, he would occasionally empty a clip from his M1 at anything moving from doorway to doorway or following him down the street.

Moving with Asay, Private First Class Goldmann noticed that the Germans were starting to make mistakes. "They shot flares into a totally dark sky and we took advantage of them. They fired haystacks and then got in between us and the blazes to form perfect silhouettes and down they went."[29]

Asay noticed the same. He hurled more hand grenades to his right to keep the Germans at bay as they moved through the fields and the abandoned 1st Platoon and 2nd Platoon positions in an attempt to flank the town and hit the intersection of the Rouette and Longchamps road, near where Swanson had his company HQ.

Chased behind buildings, the GIs continued to fire at any German who silhouetted himself against the fires. Machine guns chattered, and bullets ricocheted and slapped into the stonework Belgian houses. The right flank was indeed falling back, but as Asay hurled another grenade at a cluster of Volksgrenadiers rounding a building, he could tell his squad was fighting back with everything they had.

0400 hours, Monday, 25 December 1944
2nd Platoon, Able Company, 502nd Parachute Infantry Regiment
West of the Rouette–Champs road, Champs, Belgium

The battle in Champs had degenerated into a pell-mell street fight. House-to-house—and in some areas hand-to-hand—was reported. Typical of the violent struggle on the right flank was Staff Sergeant Robert Barnes's experience that night. During the attack on the right, Barnes was in a slit trench near a machine gun position. He heard gunfire and then saw movement:

> Suddenly, I heard what sounded like a moan from the direction of the machine gun. I looked over and saw a figure in white making arm motions. I ducked down in the foxhole, not knowing if other Germans were around. I heard another moan that was real low. My first thought was that a bayonet or knife was being used. I suppose this helped put me to use as I raised up, pointed my rifle, could not see the sights, and fired. The figure in white fell, and at the same time a grenade went off. Shots were fired at me from my flank. Four or five of the shots were fired and then all was quiet. I went over to the machine gun and the figure in white was a German officer, shot in the head. The grenade was a concussion type and was dropped by the officer when hit. As there were only two, I assumed that it was a reconnaissance patrol trying to pick up a prisoner. The two men on the machine gun received slight wounds from the grenade but [that] didn't put them out of action, which was good, as we only had seventeen men left in the 2nd Platoon at this time. The German who had fired at me from the flank made a getaway.[30]

Already Swanson could tell he had lost part of the town to the Germans, but he was not ready to desert Champs just yet. He continued to hear American rifle fire, and knew that many of his men were holding their own just in front of his position, past the schoolyard and the church. In the cold night distance, he could also hear Fowler's machine gun firing away in burst after reassuring burst.

Maybe he remembered his encounter with D'Angelo the previous day, when the two men had spotted the buildup and been shot at. Swanson recalled how the tank destroyer sergeant had moved his Hellcat up and shot back. Or perhaps there was something else that came into play; regardless, he quickly grabbed the radio from one of his men.

True, a TD was not quite a tank, but what they needed now was any sort of heavy firepower, and Swannie remembered right where to find it—about four hundred yards behind him.[31]

0400–0415 hours, Monday, 25 December 1944
2nd Platoon, Reconnaissance Company, 705th Tank Destroyer Battalion
East of Champs, Belgium

The paratroopers of Able Company were not the only ones feeling the pressure of the German attack. First Lieutenant Claude W. Duvall and his 2nd Platoon, Reconnaissance Company, had dug in a line of defense behind Champs three days prior. He had dismounted his four .30-caliber machine guns to provide covering fire while his own M8 Greyhound occupied a position on the northwest side of town. Duvall had established his command post in a house on the southwest side of town. To protect it, he had his men set up their lone .50-caliber heavy machine gun in the yard. From this position, the machine gun could lay down suppressive fire over most of the western side of Champs. In addition to his own platoon, Charlie Company had allocated a section of tank destroyers to strengthen Duvall's platoon, which spent most of Christmas Eve rotating between roadblocks around the town.

When the attack started, the machine gun teams opened up on the enemy infantry while Duvall's M8 fired round after round of 37mm canisters into the German ranks. It didn't take long for Duvall to realize that he might need the two tank destroyers from Charlie Company. Swanson had been thinking the same thing. Sometime around 0400 hours, Swanson called up Duvall and ordered the Hellcats into the fray.

Tony D'Angelo gave up on sleeping. He heard the bombardment and then rifle gunfire in Champs, and figured wisely that he would soon be needed. The usual morning routine was for the four TDs in his 3rd Platoon to move into Champs, turn left, and take the road down to Rolle. From there, one section (two TDs) would set up near the woods or at the château's "Lane of Trees" (Dreve de Mande), which gave them a good position from which to cover both Rolle and Champs.

Today, however, the action was clearly in Champs. Leaving the warmth of the farmhouse in the early morning dark, D'Angelo and his chilly crew posted aboard "No Love, No Nothing" and, using the cold-weather engine turnover crank on the back, fired the M18 to life.

As soon as both Hellcats were warmed up, the section rumbled off down the short hill and toward Champs. They had not gone far when a radio call came in, confirming D'Angelo's suspicions. Swanson was asking for tank support in the town to help root out the attacking Germans.

"We stayed out waiting if they needed us. TDs are not supposed to do that job for a tank, but we had to make do," D'Angelo recalled in an interview.

First Sergeant Don "Moe" Williams agreed that one TD should stay just out of town for backup. D'Angelo and his crew stood in reserve at the first intersection. For now, Vallitta's TD went into town, loaded for bear. D'Angelo felt nervous for his fellow tank commander and friend. Although the little M18s could negotiate the narrow streets well enough, a heavily built-up town was not the ideal environment for a Hellcat. One or two shots from a Panzerfaust and Vallitta and his crew would be cooked.

Clanking through the main road in Champs, Vallitta's M18 was quickly put to work. Using the tank destroyer to fire on buildings, Swanson's men quickly attempted to retake the town. Ted Beishline, A Company's first sergeant, hopped on and off of Vallitta's Hellcat to point out enemy positions in the houses ahead. Vallitta was also instructed to fire several rounds up the ridge above town to scare the German vehicles that Fowler had been watching since earlier that morning. Although in the twilight and fog no one was sure whether Vallitta's TD hit anything, amazingly, it seemed to have worked.

Several of the paratroopers pointed out another position ahead. A machine gun nest in the basement of a house on the right side of the road was playing hell with the paratroopers. Vallitta had his gunner, Corporal Lewis Clark, fired point-blank into the house's windows and doors. The structure collapsed, and the machine gun was heard from no more.

Moving down the main street toward the schoolyard and church, the counterattacking Americans stayed close to the walls of the houses, and when gunfire or movement was seen in a house, the paratroopers would back up have Vallitta's TD fire point-blank into it.

The force of the 76mm gun on the German positions was having a telling effect, as Vallitta's driver, Corporal Paul "the Greek" Stoling, vividly remembered: "We blew up a house [with one shot]," Stoling recalled. The paratroopers recorded later that some thirty Volksgrenadiers were eliminated with one round.

From time to time that morning, Vallitta's crew and the other two TDs would rev their engines and gear down the road, eliminating German position after German position until the German return fire was silenced.

The A Company troopers noticed that some of the Germans, typically older ones, would run from the houses or attempt to surrender. Some of the younger, perhaps more fanatical Volksgrenadiers, however, stood their ground and died at their positions. Vallitta would destroy his fourth house at around 0530 hours. By that point, the battle for Champs was beginning to swing back in the Americans' favor.[32]

0350–0420 hours, Monday, 25 December 1944
Gun line, 377th Parachute Field Artillery Battalion
Savy, Belgium

Several kilometers east of Champs, the cannon cockers of the 377th cussed and grumbled as they prepared their tubes for battle. *Leave it to the Germans to spoil Christmas morning,* many thought as they adjusted the elevation cranks and traversing wheels on their Pack howitzers. The Fire Direction Center had alerted the crews around 0330 hours that there was a major attack on Champs, and now the men were poised to put the guns back into action. Within minutes, the FDC relayed the first fire missions of the morning:

"Target . . . Infantry . . . Grid coordinates . . . 530 . . . Break . . . 652." It didn't take long for the crews to respond, and by 0350 the first few guns began to blast away, sending deadly Christmas presents toward the German lines.

After the first fire mission, the next one was not long in coming. The target was the Les Bresses. The crews quickly adjusted their tubes and fired round after round into it. The forest suddenly ripped apart in bright flashes as high-explosive shells detonated with lethal effect, scattering deadly metal shards and splinters of wood everywhere. By 0420 hours, the crews had hurled more than 120 rounds from their howitzers at the Germans. For Schriefer's men of the 77th on the receiving end, the 75mm rounds were having a deadly effect.[33]

0350–0420 hours, Monday, 25 December 1944
Area of operations, 1st Battalion, 77th Volksgrenadier Regiment
Northern Section of Champs, Belgium

Now the tide was starting to turn. In the northern section of Champs, the Germans were discovering they had penetrated too far into town, and there was no support from any reinforcements. For the Germans hiding in the cover of the houses, the American artillery came on pretty thick. They could do nothing other than cower with the civilians and hope that a shell didn't explode on top of them. One of the Volksgrenadier companies, under the command of *Leutnant* J. Hüsken that morning, was trying to consolidate their gains under the incessant barrage. Their initial attack had met with some success, but Hüsken noted that the American shelling and gunfire were increasing in intensity and becoming more accurate, probably due to day starting to break. Certainly his men had occupied several homes on the northern end of Champs, but now, as each *Ami* shell thundered down, the homes could quickly become their mausoleums.

Hüsken recalled the bitter combat in a letter written a month after the battle: "The company had to endure very heavy fighting after the enemy, repeatedly, dug in and fought a stubborn defense. Often the enemy strongholds had to be taken by storm. During an attack against Champs, the company managed to first enter the village, but was then forced to withdraw back to the start-point, after hitting stiff enemy resistance. The most heavy artillery and mortar fire struck the block of homes occupied by our company."

When the bombardment began, many of the Germans had no choice but to fall back to their start positions. As Hüsken counted up the survivors, he quickly realized that some of his men were missing, including one of his NCOs, Sergeant Anton Adorf. At first he thought Adorf had simply become separated, and perhaps the absent NCO had linked up with another company. After several days, Hüsken knew deep down in his gut that this was not the case, and Adorf was either dead or a prisoner of war. Toward the end of January, Hüsken figured Adorf was likely dead. The Americans were good about notifying the Red Cross about POWs, and he had received no notice from them. That January 25, weeks after the battle, Hüsken wrote the dreaded letter to Adorf's wife. The last words of the emotional missive were:

> Following the severity of the fighting, the company presumed that your beloved husband was picked up either as a straggler with another unit, or he was wounded and admitted to a field hospital. However, considering that a significant amount of time has already passed, the above-mentioned possibilities are highly unlikely. The company regrets very much the terrible loss, considering that your

beloved husband proved himself to be a brave and exemplary soldier. On behalf of his comrades, I wish to extend our warmest sympathies to your most difficult sorrow, by which this travesty has afflicted you. With my most sincere condolences, I greet you Heil Hitler!

Sadly, this Christmas Hüsken would not be the only German officer writing letters of condolence to distraught widows and mothers. For the Germans, the stubborn Americans would provide many opportunities to practice their writing skills after Christmas morning.[34]

0400–0500 hours, Monday, 25 December 1944
Command post, Able Company, 502nd Parachute Infantry Regiment
Champs, Belgium

Forward observer Lieutenant Jim Robinson of the 377th PFAB was on attached duty to Swanson's A Company in Champs. He had spent much of the morning near Swanson's headquarters watching the battle unfold. Now, with a brief lull in the fight, he was desperately trying to get to his observation post on the hill above Champs. He knew that if he could get back to this vantage point, he could direct artillery fire down on the attacking Germans. From this point over the previous days, Robinson had determined that he had one of the best views of the entire sector. He could see unobstructed for miles in an almost 180-degree arc around the area. Starting north, he could watch German movement in the village of Fays, and, turning to his left, he could keep an eye on the German base at Givry. He could even see all the way to his left, heading almost due east, where he could just make out the snow-covered rooftops of Flamizoulle and the lines of the 1/401st. Such a post could be vital to winning the battle.

The trick was getting to it.

Robinson crunched through the snow, M1 in his hands, heading down a cart path about a hundred yards to the left of Fowler's machine gun position. Nervous, he could see his breath in the cold air. Sure, it might seem suicidal to try, but he also felt responsible for the four men he had left up there, and wanted to know their fate.

As he climbed the slope, he came upon a short hill. On the other side, there were bushes on each side of the path. From the opposite side he heard German voices.

A squad of German soldiers, half-asleep and awaiting orders to continue the fight, was behind the shrubs. Before they could react, Robinson stood up and fired on them repeatedly. Hit by the big .30-06 rounds, the soldiers fell to the ground, screaming in pain.

Reloading another clip after his M1 ejected the last, he slapped the bolt forward with the palm of his hand and pumped eight more rounds into the figures. "Where there was movement, I fired until they stopped moving or screaming," Robinson recounted.

After a third and final clip, Robinson wheeled around, boots crunching through the snow, and ran back toward Champs. When he got to town, he found one of his enlisted men. Tossing him a carbine, he told the soldier to follow him. The two found the spot later that morning, with the bodies of the dead Germans lying about, blood soaking into the muddy cart path. The young soldier, sickened by the sight, vomited. Robinson, going through the bodies, found a backpack full of cookies on the body of one of the dead Germans. He was so hungry he remembered eating some of the cookies right then and there.

"I learned something about myself that day."

Later that morning, as the fighting tapered off near Champs, Robinson was able to make it back to his OP. Robinson knew now that he could call down some fire from the 377th's 75mm Pack howitzers, positioned near Rolle, and do some real damage to the pausing Germans.[35]

0400–0500 hours, Monday, 25 December 1944
2nd Platoon, Able Company, 502nd Parachute Infantry Regiment
Champs, Belgium

Back at the hedge behind his burning post in Champs, Al Wise and the survivors huddled in the dark. Lieutenant Harrison returned, having organized a few stragglers from both 2nd and 1st platoons. Wise and the medic had not forgotten about the wounded Private Snyder left back on the ridge. Now that the German gunfire seemed to abate, Wise recruited a few others, including Hodge, the trooper who had originally told them about Snyder. Moving quietly and at a crouch, the rescue group trotted past the burning command post. Scattered gunfire erupted in the darkness as they sneaked back up the ridge.

The medic was able to pinpoint the location of Snyder, lying in the snow and half-dead. Carrying him over his shoulder, the medic started back for the hedge. The others followed cautiously, rifles and carbines at the ready. Wise and his patrol carefully skirted the former command post, hearing the voices of Germans nearby. The group safely returned to Harrison's position in the hedge. In the end, Snyder survived.[36]

0440 hours, Monday, 25 December 1944
Headquarters, 502nd Parachute Infantry Regiment
Rolle Château, Belgium

Chappuis could hear the gunfire not far from his headquarters. Sutliffe soon called in on the radio. He reported that the Germans had infiltrated past his 2nd Battalion and were now east of Champs. He added that to seal this group off, he was shifting some of his units to cover his southern flank. In response, Chappuis looked back at the map and tried to figure out how he could best help Sutliffe. The answer was a lone platoon from Baker Company that was already manning a roadblock behind the fighting. The platoon was anchored on the zigzag woodlot that crossed the Champs–Hemroulle road just immediately northwest of Rolle and the Dreve de Mande. Here the road climbed as it leveled out on the plain near the château grounds. A single platoon wasn't much, but Chappuis knew every little bit could make the difference for Sutliffe's perforated line. He could easily move that platoon to cover down on the skimpy seam between Swanson's Able Company and 2nd Battalion. Chappuis gave the order and let Sutliffe know help would soon be approaching his southern flank.[37]

0500–0530 hours, Monday, 25 December 1944
Command post, Able Company, 502nd Parachute Infantry Regiment
Champs, Belgium

After speaking with Colonel Chappuis, Hanlon left Rolle, driving quickly in his jeep past the many headquarters types hustling about in the château courtyard. The jeep sped away down the Lane of Trees and hooked a right, heading for Champs.

When Hanlon arrived at the wooded zigzag ridge on the road between Rolle and Champs, he was able to see into the embattled village. His paratroopers were shooting at everything, and he could see fires burning and smoke rising from the farthest parts of town. In the dark, "Long John" definitely was concerned that B Company might be mistaken for Germans and shot by their own men as they entered Champs from the rear. He found Swanson's CP and walked in to find his company commander in control of the situation. Swanson agreed that it would be dicey to send new troops into Champs right now. He admitted that after this morning, his men were jittery and prone to shoot at anything moving through town in the dark.

Hanlon got the handy-talky from the jeep and contacted Chappuis again. Telling Chappuis that he hesitated to send in his men, and also commit a valuable reserve to what appeared to be a stabilized situation, Hanlon was able to convince "Silent Steve" that sending Baker Company into Champs would be a costly mistake. "Silent Steve" agreed with his subordinate commanders. Besides, Chappuis had by now decided that the main attack, complete with armor, must be coming someplace else. It didn't make sense for the Germans to send it down the extended Champs road and through the tight confines of the village, some three miles or more from Bastogne proper. He also knew that Swanson was feeling confident once again, now that he had some infantry and artillery backup and rolling firepower in his hands in the form of the tank destroyers.

For now, Chappuis ordered Hanlon to have B Company dig in at the roadblock at the midway point in the zigzag of the woods. From here he could fortify Swanson's men in Champs just in case something broke through. They could also quickly join his fighters in the town if need be. In addition, Chappuis still wanted C Company moved up closer to Champs in case they were needed. "Long John" acknowledged the order and got into his jeep for Hemroulle to find Captain Cody and Charlie Company.[38]

0500–0530 hours, Monday, 25 December 1944
3rd Platoon, Able Company, 502nd Parachute Infantry Regiment
Champs, Belgium

By 0500 hours, Asay and others, though exhausted, were counterattacking. The Sioux City sergeant remembered charging back up the road with his squad, made up of Goldmann, Ballard, and others. "Even later, I was still carrying grenades," Asay recalled.[39]

Asay and his squad made for the old command post, its smoldering ruins being used as a holdout by the Germans now. "The Germans, in their eagerness and self-confidence, even set up an aid station in the house with the barn attached," Goldmann remembered.

The big sergeant ran up and threw grenades into the group of Germans, "scattering them like a busted vase," according to Goldmann.

As the rest of his men charged in, firing, shrapnel hit Asay in the ribs and left cheek, possibly from his own grenades, possibly from a German mortar round hitting the bricks nearby. The wounds were relatively minor and Asay continued to do his job, albeit bleeding. Regardless, the house was soon liberated and prisoners taken. Asay and his men discovered a strange but relieved mixture of inhabitants.

"That house was an odd one—four Americans hiding upstairs, a German aid station on the main floor, and eighteen Belgian civilians hiding in the basement," Goldmann recalled years later.

While Asay's squad continued to clear the homes in Champs, two Hetzers once again appeared along the skyline to the northwest of Fowler's position. A lone M18 tank destroyer, left behind by the 811th Tank Destroyer Battalion, was able to destroy one of the distant Hetzers and damage the other, driving the pair off.

At this point, a lull settled over Champs. The Germans were still trying to move men and armor into the area they had captured, but the best trail—the roadway that ran down from Rouette—was still being held up by the single machine gunner from Cordele, Georgia.

Fowler's gun was now steaming hot, and he and Emerson threw snow on the barrel to cool it. They welcomed the break in the fighting, taking advantage of the time to reload the weapon and stand the boxes of .30-caliber ammo nearby for ready use.

It was almost 0530 hours when Emerson and Fowler noticed the group of four more German armored vehicles appear on the ridge ahead of them, front-on. They ducked as they saw the tanks fire into Champs.

"Those were some pretty good-sized German tanks," Fowler said.

Fowler decided his best course of action was to stay low and continue to let the gun cool. Unfortunately, he wasn't going to get much of a break. "We'd be very quiet and inconspicuous," he said. "I'm sure the tankers could probably see us, but whether they did or not, I was looking at them when a column of German soldiers came darting out from behind the tanks. They started down the ridge toward our location. I told Emerson to stay low; I was going to fire on them and then the tanks would open up on us. I caught the column from front to rear and every man fell. I'm not sure whether I killed every one of them or not but I'm sure I killed some."[40]

Sure enough, as Fowler hopped up and started firing the .30-caliber at the German troops, the tanks answered in kind. Out of the corner of his eye, Fowler caught the muzzle flash from one of the tanks. He dived back into the foxhole. The shell hit the corner of the potato shed, ripping out great splinters of wood. The concussion from the passing shell threw the two men back against the cold ground of their hole. When the two shocked paratroopers had recovered and checked each other for wounds, Fowler told Emerson it would be wiser now to stay down and play dead.

"I told him that if they see any movement, they'll fire again."

After a while, Fowler took off his helmet and peeked over the foxhole edge, exposing just the top of his head. He could tell that the flying pieces of potato shack had damaged the machine gun, blasting it off the tripod. Now the tanks had them pinned, and they had no way of fighting back. Fowler looked at his machine gun and noticed that it appeared damaged. Meanwhile, the rest of the squad hunkered down. The German tanks were too far away for a bazooka shot, and therefore the Screaming Eagles couldn't return fire.

"I thought we were really in trouble then," Fowler recalled.[41]

The gunners in the little Hetzers found the single tank destroyer and disabled it with a series of blows. The crew tried to restart the engine, but it was dead. Realizing they were sitting ducks, the crew bailed out of the doomed TD and sought cover in the houses and foxholes nearby. The German tankers were far from finished, though. Peeking out of his foxhole, Fowler realized he and the others needed help, and soon. Luckily, help was on the way.[42]

0530 hours, Monday, 25 December 1944
Fire Direction Center, 377th Parachute Field Artillery Battalion
Savy, Belgium

While 3rd Platoon and the rest of Able Company dug deeper into their foxholes to escape the German armor, forward observers, like Lieutenant Robinson, were calling in fire missions on the meddlesome German tank destroyers. At 0530 hours, the FDC at Savy received another fire mission from an observer in Champs (possibly Robinson).

Within seconds the men of Able Company could hear the outgoing mail as it screamed over their heads, sounding like a freight train. The targeted area this time was the ridge between Rouette and Champs, and the targets themselves were the Hetzers. It didn't take long for the observer to radio back the results to the FDC. For the German tank destroyers, the twenty-two rounds of high-explosive forced them to withdraw behind the hill, thereby, saving 3rd Platoon. Later on that morning, four P-47s made a deadly strafing and bombing run, ensuring the Hetzers wouldn't return.[43]

Private Goldmann later wrote about the incident, feeling the battle for Champs was finally over: "Lovely artillery, beautiful TD's, wonderful Air Corps; we had been hurting for sure and now we had won."[44]

0600–0630 hours, Monday, 25 December 1944
Area of operations, Able Company, 502nd Parachute Infantry Regiment
Champs, Belgium

Able Company soldiers noticed the chatter of Willis Fowler's machine gun finally went silent around daybreak. He had been in nonstop action, firing for close to three hours. During the battle, Fowler had played a key role in beating the Germans back. Equally important, by slaughtering so many of the foot soldiers, Fowler had also held up the German armor.

A humble Fowler said in an interview with one of the authors, "I was told later, by my CO, that the German tankers were timid. They didn't want to go in [to Champs] without infantry support, and, well, we had taken care of that."[45]

The townspeople of Champs also noticed that the sounds of battle had started to fade following 0600 hours that morning, after the men of Able Company had executed their counterattack. Madeleine Séleck was still hiding in her cellar. After the war, she and the others remembered the moment as the battle for her village drew to a close:

> The Germans were at the end of their ropes by now; grenades and submachine gun fire were beginning to slow down. Little by little the bursts came with longer and longer delays. Suddenly there was the sound of footsteps stopping outside the cellar (where some Germans still were hiding, one of whom was an officer). The footsteps belonged to Edward Ries, and there were American soldiers with him: they spoke German and ordered the Germans out of the cellar and demanded that they surrender. For a few seconds (that felt like they went on forever) the German officer looked around the cellar, at the terrified civilians and the moaning wounded

soldiers. Then, suddenly, he stood up, paced to the cellar door, pulled it open, and threw his gun at the Americans' feet. Immediately thereafter the Americans got the wounded out of there, disarming them; and then the Americans descended into the cellar. They noticed an empty holster and immediately set about looking for the missing gun; as one of the civilians had hidden it in a pile of potatoes while the Germans were still there. The GIs were angry and yelled a lot, and Achille—who didn't move quickly enough for them—was kicked in his derriere. They finally left without finding the gun, which was actually discovered much later by a pig rooting about for food! Everyone was relieved, but no one dared go outside.[46]

Out in the streets the Americans continued to clear the various houses to see whether any Germans were hiding in the cellars and closets of the smashed homes. The paratroopers had decided to turn Victor Raviola's farm into a holding area for prisoners. Mr. Raviola even helped the men of Able Company in sorting and processing the vanquished.[47]

Besides the prisoners, the dead required sorting out too. Joss Heintz, in his book, *In the Perimeter of Bastogne*, wrote about the dead: "The village heights resembled a necropolis. Ninety nine German corpses were strewn over the grounds. The number of wounded was even greater. Torn arms, slashed legs, gaping wounds flooded with blood the Raviola kitchen where dozens of the injured awaited aid."[48]

As the sun rose dimly through the fog that morning, the Americans once again strolled through the devastated streets of Champs, ushering prisoners to the rear. Outside of Bastogne, the bodies lay scattered across the roads and fields. As they passed at a somber gait, the soldiers on both sides realized that tragically, for so many of their comrades, this was their last Christmas.

0500–0600 hours, Monday, 25 December 1944
Headquarters, 101st Airborne Division, Heinz Barracks
Bastogne, Belgium

Thanks to a reconnaissance section from the 90th Cavalry, perched on a hilltop overlooking Champs, the men of the division staff had been kept up-to-date and now knew the battle in Champs was basically over, the town back in American hands. By 0530 hours, the division staff learned that at least one German armored vehicle was destroyed, and that the Screaming Eagles of Able Company had "the situation well in hand." As the morning progressed, the news only improved.

At 0600 hours, the reconnaissance section reported that only a few Germans remained, trapped in several houses along the perimeter. To the cavalry scouts, sitting in their observation post, "Situation [was] quieting down [and] 6 or 8 Germans trapped in town will be mopped up at day light."[49]

For McAuliffe and his staff, it was a good thing that the fighting was settling down in Champs, because things were just getting interesting elsewhere around Bastogne.

0700 hours, Monday, 25 December 1944
Headquarters, 502nd Parachute Infantry Regiment, Rolle Château
Rolle, Belgium

As sporadic fighting continued, A Company continued to take each house to reclaim Champs. Every once in a while, German artillerists located near Givry would send a few mortar rounds into town, forcing the paratroopers to dive for cover into the cellars or behind anything made of stonework.

It was now daybreak. As he stood quietly in the stone château, listening to the radio, "Silent Steve's" moment of relief wouldn't last long. At that very moment, about two miles to the southeast, unknown to Chappuis, a train of German tanks was driving right toward his headquarters.

CHAPTER NINE

Panzer Angriff

"God grant that we may never be brought to such a wretched condition again!"

—Nathanael Greene, Valley Forge, 1778[1]

2200–0430 hours, 24–25 December 1944
Able Company, 1/401st Glider Infantry
Battle positions between Bastogne and Mande Saint-Etienne

In the dark of Christmas Eve, eleven American soldiers ran for their lives, leather boots crunching through the thin layer of snow, the sound of their breathing the only other noise in the night. Lieutenant Jack Adams sprinted at the front, his squad of glidermen from Able Company straining to catch up with their leader.

The muscular Oklahoman flashed back to what he and his men had witnessed earlier. For the past few hours, they had crouched and crawled through ditches and culverts, miserably hiding in freezing cold water as German soldiers hunted them like animals, trying to find and kill the American infiltrators in the dark. A hell of a way to spend Christmas Eve, Adams thought. Panting, he plowed on through the snowy field.

It had been a dangerous mission, Adams knew, but he accepted that danger. At 2200 hours, Lieutenant Bowles had been instructed by division to destroy a culvert near Flamizoulle, approximately one mile to the front of the 1/401st's main line. Demolishing the culvert would block any German

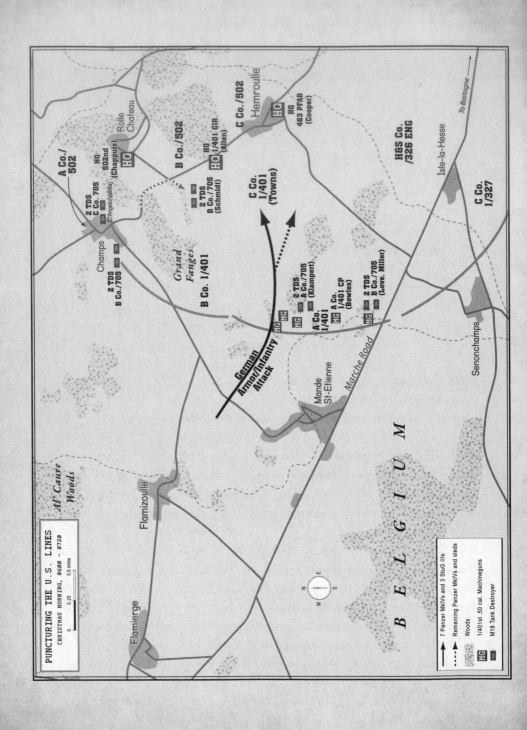

PUNCTURING THE U.S. LINES
CHRISTMAS MORNING, 0600 - 0720

0   0.25   0.5 miles

Al' Caure Woods

Rolle Château

A Co./ 502

HQ 502nd (Chappuis)   HQ

2 TDS C Co. 705 (D'Angelo/Valitta)

Champs

2 TDS B Co. 705

B Co./502

HQ 1/401 GIR (Allen)   HQ

2 TDS B Co./705 (Schmidt)

C Co./502   Hemrouille   HQ

HQ 463 PFAB (Cooper)

Grand Fanges

B Co. 1/401

C Co. 1/401 (Towns)

H&S Co. /326 ENG

Isle-la-Hesse

C Co. 1/327

German Armor/Infantry Attack

2 TDS A Co./705 (Klampert)

A Co. B Co.1/401 CP 1/401 (Bowles)

MG MG MG MG

A Co. 1/401   MG

2 TDS B Co./705 (Love, Miller)

MG

Mande St-Étienne

Marche Road

Senonchamps

Flamizoulle

B E L G I U M

Flamierge

N E W S

To Bastogne

7 Panzer MkIVs and 3 StuG IIIs

Remaining Panzer MkIVs and sleds

Woods

MG   1/401st .50 cal. Machineguns

M18 Tank Destroyer

tanks from using the road that ran from Flamizoulle to the intersection of the Champs–Mande Saint-Etienne road. Though it was a mission fraught with risk, after the battles the other day, it made good tactical sense to deny the Germans any avenue for their armor. Shortly after nightfall, Bowles gave Adams ten volunteers, including eight of the best engineers in the company, with the order to dynamite the culvert.

Creeping slowly to dampen the sound of their movement, and using the fog for camouflage, Adams and his patrol moved toward their objective. The young lieutenant measured their progress in inches, and several hours passed before the squad finally reached the culvert, only a hundred yards outside of German-held Flamizoulle. When they arrived, they started to drill holes near the base. While the engineers furiously dug, throwing piles of dirt onto the bridge, the riflemen maintained security on top of the culvert. Adams's men quickly shoved sticks of dynamite into the holes. They had been working for forty minutes, and Adams estimated they needed just a few more to complete their job.

Then they heard it. Through the thick fog, Adams detected the crunching sound of boots approaching through the snow. Since none of his own men were up and moving, he knew that those boots could belong only to German soldiers. At almost the same instant, the Americans heard the ominous sound of grinding gears. Just as they had done in battle drill, Adams and his patrol scrambled into the ditches that lined the road and watched while seven German tanks rolled onto the culvert bridge. Now there was no way to finish wiring the charges. Adams and his men noticed the watchful Panzergrenadiers who rode the tanks like spearmen on a chariot.

When they reached the culvert, the lead panzer commander noticed the strange mounds of dirt the engineers had left. The Panzergrenadiers hopped off to investigate. One of the Germans shot a flare into the night sky. Sensing the enemy was around, the Germans let loose with their submachine guns, spraying the cold night air. Using the sputtering cracks of the MP40s and the Kar 98s to mask the sound of their movement, the Americans used the cover of the roadside ditches and creeks to sneak away. When Adams believed his patrol was clear of the enemy, they stood up and broke into a run.

Adams knew he had to warn headquarters. Like Swanson and D'Angelo earlier that afternoon, Adams had stumbled upon a massed force of German armor that shocked him with its scale and power. Colonel Maucke had launched the column of *Hauptmann* Schmidt's panzers right at the heart of the 1/401st's fragile defensive lines.

It was after 0400 when the slightly frigid soldiers finally cleared the outposts (upon giving the proper password) and reached Bowles's CP behind a grove of trees. Puffing and panting, Adams told Bowles more than just the bad news that his group had failed to blow up the culvert. Out of breath, cheeks ruddy from the night cold, Adams could only point at the map. "Plenty of armor," he said, putting his trembling finger on the town of Flamizoulle.[2]

Now they all could hear the rumble of engines and the clanking of tank treads in the distance and closing. The tanks were heading right for their lines. Huddled in their foxholes carved from the frozen farmland east of Mande Saint-Etienne, Bowles's glidermen knew the sound was the unmistakable approach of the attack they had been anticipating for days. Kokott's desired *Panzer Angriff* was on its way—the führer's Christmas present would be delivered on time, as promised.[3]

Bowles desperately needed artillery to disrupt the rapidly assembling German force. He rang up Cooper's gunners, supporting the 1/401st that morning. Adams and Bowles figured that the Germans had moved their forces after Adams had bumped into them earlier on his patrol, so they adjusted the fire mission to drop rounds northeast of Flamizoulle.[4] At 0405 hours the 463rd unleashed a salvo of three rounds of high-explosive on the suspected enemy position. It was a bit of a shot in the dark. Because no observers were present, no one could adjust fire or conduct battle damage assessment on the target. For the Germans, the inaccurate rounds were a nuisance and did little to slow down their preparation for the attack.[5]

Bowles informed his higher command of the presence of German panzers near Flamizoulle.[6] Receiving the news at his HQ, Colonel "Bud" Harper was irritated. It was Christmas morning that the enemy had decided to strike in an area Harper predicted. *Christmas morning, for God's sake!* Harper could do nothing until he knew more about the German intentions. For now, the outcome of the battle would depend heavily on the decisions and actions of his subordinate commanders.

0430 hours, Monday, 25 December 1944
2nd Platoon/Able Company/705th Tank Destroyer Battle positions
East of Mande Saint-Etienne

Colonel Allen's hardy troopers were not alone. About two hundred yards behind Bowles's headquarters were two M18 tank destroyers under the command of Lieutenant Klampert of A/705. Two more TDs were another four hundred yards farther to the south under the command of Lieutenant Richard Miller. Between the two sections, using overlapping fields of fire, the TDs could roughly cover the area where Klampert had anticipated the Germans would strike.

Klampert had established these positions with Miller shortly after the bitter fight near Cocheval, where he lost the two tank destroyers. At 0430 hours the southernmost section detected four panzers moving east from the town of Monty. The two sections (four TDs) backed into the firing position to watch over the road. Coordinating with 2nd Platoon, B Company, within minutes, the Americans reported they had destroyed two panzers, causing the enemy infantry to scatter. Unfortunately, no one else could confirm 2nd Platoon's kills, especially the Germans.[7]

0500–0645 hours, Monday, 25 December 1944
The columns of 1st Battalion and 2nd Battalion of
the 115th Panzergrenadier Regiment
Traveling from Al'Caure through Mande Saint-Etienne and Flamizoulle

Bearing down on A Company were eleven Panzerkampfwagen Mk IVs and at least three StuG III assault guns of the 115th Panzer Battalion, and two Panzergrenadier battalions from the 115th Panzergrenadier Regiment. *Hauptmann* Schmidt, Maucke's tank commander, had formed his tanks into two snakelike columns, the better to navigate through the many woodlots once outside of Flamierge and the Al'Caure woods. All of Schmidt's panzers were attached to Major Wörner's 1st Battalion; Wörner had arrayed his forces into two *kampfgruppes*. Lagging behind 1st Battalion was 3rd Battalion, under the command of Major Adam Dyroff, whose role was to provide northern flank security for Wörner's decisive operation. Though Dyroff had no armor, he did have a platoon of StuG IIIs to provide a base of fire against any American tanks.[8]

Rumbling along, the German tanks ground the snow underneath, as great clots of ice dropped from the treads. The Panzergrenadiers, nervous with the anticipation of combat, clung to the backs of the tanks and kept their heads low in preparation for the coming fight. Within a half hour, the northern column of Wörner's battalion traveled through Flamizoulle, while the southern column passed through Monty.[9]

Through the thick fog and the dark, the Germans could only guess when they were approaching the forward American positions. As they closed the distance, the men begin to shout and cheer over the growling engines. Some, still feeling the effects of a bottle of schnapps passed around earlier to celebrate the holiday, were especially loud—drunk, or *blau*, as the Germans called it. The German officers and NCOs must have realized that Maucke's orders for a silent assault were by now impossible to enforce.[10]

The operation proceeded according to plan. Wörner's column radioed around 0405 hours that they had passed Flamizoulle without making contact with the enemy.[11] When the southern column emerged from Mande Saint-Etienne, it received flanking fire from an unidentified antitank gun, which likely damaged one of the tanks, but did little else to the oncoming armor.

As the panzer columns dipped down into pockets of the terrain, the fog was like a curtain. Maintaining interval distances became difficult, especially for the troops trudging behind on foot. Maucke's soldiers, tired and weary from the forced march to Bastogne, had gone without sleep or food as they prepared all Christmas Eve for the attack. The men had no opportunity to get their bearings in the dark. Coordination between the infantry and armor started to fall apart. As the distance increased, the foot soldiers began to lose sight of the vehicles, and soon the men following behind had to listen for the tanks just to keep up. Gaps as large as two hundred yards began to appear as the tanks outraced the remaining foot soldiers of Wörner's 1st Battalion, while the Panzergrenadiers of Dyroff's 3rd Battalion fell even farther behind. For the Germans, the combined armor-infantry attack, upon which Kokott had staked so much, was getting off on the wrong foot.[12]

0645 hours, Monday, 25 December 1944
115th Panzergrenadier Regiment command post
Near Flamizoulle

Though he was still angry with Kokott for denying him the opportunity to perform a proper reconnaissance, Colonel Maucke grew more confident as the reports gradually poured into his command post that morning.[13] His 1st Battalion had rolled through the perceived American security zone near Mande Saint-Etienne, and his 3rd Battalion had marched through the American screen line north of Flamizoulle without a hitch. The only perceivable threat came from intermittent artillery fire and an unidentified antitank battery southeast of his front lines near Isle-la-Hesse.

Kunkel's 26th Reconnaissance Battalion radioed in, confirming the presence of several American armored vehicles near Isle-la-Hesse soon after Maucke's columns had received the flanking fire.[14] Kunkel was once again playing an important role by screening the southern flank of the attack, near Isle-la-Hesse. If the recon troopers failed to contain any American attacks from that direction, it could spell disaster for Maucke's assault. Initial reports in this sector, though, were good. Here, both the 26th Reconnaissance Battalion and the 39th Fusilier Regiment were advancing steadily to pin Harper's glider troops.[15]

The truth was that the initial reports were exaggerated. Instead of near-simultaneous actions, the attack in Champs and to the south near Isle-la-Hesse had started to peter out long before the main attack had even begun.[16] Instead of the hoped-for enemy stumbling like a dazed boxer, Maucke's forces would march into the ring against a boxer who was primed, alert, and ready.

At first Maucke was ignorant of all of this. He'd had virtually no contact with much of his force since the operation got under way hours earlier. While the panzers and the Panzergrenadiers tried to assemble for the final push, Maucke waited. Finally, at 0645 hours he received the optimistic report from his 1st Battalion, which announced, "Standing before west rim of Bastogne!"[17] The decisive phase of the attack was about to begin.

0630–0710 hours, Monday, 25 December 1944
1/401st Glider Infantry
Battle positions west of Bastogne

Private Allie Moore, an outpost sentry, came tearing through the snow to Bowles's command post in a small grove of trees. Moore blurted out that he had seen the line of enemy tanks, and now they were heading straight toward Able. Bowles immediately reported this information to Allen and Harper, who spread the news to McAuliffe's HQ that the sector was under attack by enemy troops and armor.[18]

To Bowles's men, the approaching column sounded like some great, growling, serpentine creature. The first instinct for many of Bowles's shivering glidermen in 2nd Platoon was to bolt from their forward positions and run. Once they stifled this urge, aided by the professionalism of veteran NCOs, their next urge was to get mad and fight back.

"Scary" was how Carmen Gisi of MacDonald's nearby B Company later remembered the sound of the advancing tanks. He had been just to the right of Bowles's A Company. "But we had heard German tanks before, and you did what you had to do."[19]

Bowles dashed forward to the outpost on his left flank to see for himself. The tanks and German infantry were in a single column heading toward the center of A Company's line. Bowles hurried back to his command post near the plot of trees.[20] He rapidly discussed the situation with Adams, his 3rd Platoon leader, and his command post officer in charge, Lieutenant Ralph Nelson. Klampert, the tank destroyer platoon leader, was also there, eager to give his unit their orders. The three officers decided that the best course of action was to allow the panzers to pass through their lines and to withhold their fire. This would give Klampert's tank destroyers an excellent rear shot on the tanks.[21] To disrupt the German formations, Bowles requested another artillery fire mission to try to break up the German attack before it could gain the momentum to break his line.[22]

At the little stone farmhouse on the Champs–Hemroulle road where Ray Allen had his headquarters, Major Hershel E. Angus, Allen's executive officer, took the call. He sent another duty officer upstairs to rouse Allen. Asked whether he wanted to order the artillery into action, an awakening Allen responded, "No, that will start the whole front firing." When Angus heard the response, he doubted the aggressive Allen was fully coherent, but before he could question it, Allen came down the stairs, throwing on his overcoat to ward off the chill. Allen repeated the instruction to "tell the men to hold their fire."[23]

Allen knew he had to make some rapid-fire decisions. He backed up Bowles's plan to move his men out of the way as best he could and let the tanks pass through. Allen was gambling. He reasoned that the thick fog and thin light would prompt the bunched-up panzers to pass through the company battle positions. If they missed the positions of his glider-fighters, they would continue on and leave their infantry lagging behind them. If his men opened fire prematurely, the Germans would be able to discern, even in the dark, the positions of both Able and Baker companies. From there the German armor would run straight over the meager resistance of Bowles's men, whose only defense against the tanks was a few bazookas and machine guns.[24]

January 1945: Major General Maxwell Taylor, Commander of the 101st Airborne Division, congratulates Brigadier General Anthony C. McAuliffe, Deputy Commander, for his work in defending Bastogne.

Screaming Eagle leaders in the snow: McAuliffe (*center*) with two of his staff: Lieutenant Colonel Paul A. Danahy (*left*) and Lieutenant Colonel Harry W. O. Kinnard (*right*). Kinnard helped McAuliffe come up with his famous "Nuts" reply.

Lieutenant Colonel Clifford D. Templeton, Commander of the 705th Tank Destroyer Battalion, is awarded the Silver Star by Major General Maxwell Taylor in a ceremony shortly after Bastogne. Colonel William L. Roberts, commander of the 10th Armored Division, looks on. Templeton's M18 tank destroyers played a key, but often overlooked, role in the defense of Bastogne.

Photo U.S. Army
Military History Institute

Four M18 commanders of C/705th Tank Destroyer Battalion in Germany. All four played key roles in the defense of Bastogne: (*left to right*) Sergeant William T. "Bully" Boldt, Sergeant Anthony "Tony" D'Angelo, Sergeant Lawrence "Larry" Vallitta, and Sergeant Lazar J. Hovland.

Photo courtesy of the family of Anthony D'Angelo

The stalwart commander of the 1st Battalion, 401st Glider Infantry Regiment, Lieutenant Colonel Ray C. Allen in front of the regimental colors.

Photo courtesy of Carmen Gisi

To My Dear Friend
Carmen Gisi,
a great combat Soldier
who did his part
to bring fame and
glory to this flag
and who was the
last Soldier to handle
this flag in its
Official capacity.
Sincerely,
Ray C. Allen,
Colonel, U.S. Army
Ret.

Private First Class Carmen C. "Geese" Gisi,
3rd Platoon, B Company, 1/401st G.I.R.

Photo courtesy of Carmen Gisi

A photo of Allen's glider fighters around Bastogne taken
with a camera Gisi found at Crossroads X: (*left to right*) Al
Vaughn, Gisi, and Private First Class Ed Beneturski.

Photo courtesy of Carmen Gisi

Captain Robert MacDonald's glidermen of B Company, 1/401st. MacDonald is seated, second row,
eleventh from the right. Lieutenant "Gus" Ryan is immediately to his left. This photo was taken in
Reading, England, before D-Day.   *Photo courtesy of Patricia A. O'Malley, daughter of Lieutenant Ryan*

Officers of the 502nd Parachute Infantry Regiment outside of Rolle Château: (*left to right*) Lieutenant Colonel "Silent Steve" A. Chappuis, Lieutenant Colonel Patrick F. "Hopalong" Cassidy, Lieutenant Colonel John P. Stopka, and Major "Long John" D. Hanlon.

Photo courtesy of the Don F. Pratt Museum, Fort Campbell, KY

Corporal Willis H. Fowler, A/502nd PIR. Fowler's deadly work with a .30-caliber machine gun helped hold off the German attack Christmas morning. By the end of the war, Fowler would be promoted to staff sergeant and earn the Silver Star, Medal of Gallantry, and Purple Heart.

Photo courtesy of Staff Sergeant Willis H. Fowler; 502 Regt - 101st Airborne Div. Recipient of Silver Star Medal for Gallantry and Purple Heart

First Sergeant Layton Black, C/502. Black witnessed the German attack on Colonel Ray Allen's headquarters on Christmas morning. He also witnessed the expert shooting of the tank destroyers as they helped stop the assault.

Photo courtesy of Randy F. Black,
© 1998 ISBN 0-0665140-0-4

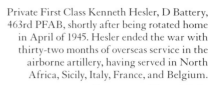

Private First Class Kenneth Hesler, D Battery, 463rd PFAB, shortly after being rotated home in April of 1945. Hesler ended the war with thirty-two months of overseas service in the airborne artillery, having served in North Africa, Sicily, Italy, France, and Belgium.

Photo courtesy of Kenneth Hesler

Lieutenant Colonel John T. Cooper, Commander of the 463rd Parachute Field Artillery Battalion, the "Bastard Battalion."

Photo courtesy of Kenneth Hesler

First Lieutenant Howard M. Park, P-47 fighter pilot in the 406th Fighter Group in the cockpit of his aircraft, "Big Ass Bird II."

Photo courtesy of the Pima Air and Space Museum, Tucson, AZ

Unteroffizier Ludwig "Lutz" Lindemann. Lindemann's unit attacked early Christmas morning through the Les Bresses woods near Champs.

Photo courtesy of Ludwig Lindemann/Marion Otto/Nira Krause

December 18th—The Road to Bastogne

Camp Mourmelon, Mourmelon-le-Grand, near Reims, France. This was the base camp for the 101st Airborne Division in early December. Nearby was an Army Air Corps Base.

The call goes out. Paratroopers of the 101st Airborne load up on the large "cattle car" trucks the afternoon of December 18 for the trip to Bastogne. The 107-mile-long journey in the open trucks would be miserable, with little room to sit or otherwise escape the cold.

Bastogne from the air, looking southeast. This aerial view shows the seven key roads and one rail line intersecting at the Belgian town.

All photos this page courtesy of the Don F. Pratt Museum, Fort Campbell, KY

The Americans Defend Bastogne

The entrance to the 101st Airborne's divisional headquarters in Bastogne—the former Belgian Army Heinz Barracks. McAuliffe's HQ was quickly moved to a basement of a building farther to the right in this photo, which became known as "the Cave." To the left, a signalman strings communication wire, while a machine gun team posts guard to his right.

Carting their belongings, civilians abandon Bastogne. Many Belgians thought they would find refuge in outlying towns, which unfortunately became the focus of intense struggles between the Germans and Americans.

All photos this page courtesy of the Don F. Pratt Museum, Fort Campbell, KY

Troopers of the 101st Airborne Division cover a road outside of Bastogne with a .30-caliber machine gun. In the foreground, an M1 Garand rifle fitted with a rifle grenade on the muzzle rests in a two-man foxhole fighting position.

A bazooka team on the Bastogne perimeter. This photo, though most certainly posed (the Mark V Panther tank in the background is already knocked out), gives a good idea of the close teamwork between the rocket launcher and loader.

One of Colonel Cooper's 75mm Pack howitzers in its indirect fire position near Savy. The 463rd was equipped with the versatile little guns. In the background, a CG-4 Waco glider that brought supplies to the 101st Christmas Eve day.

The Early Christmas Present: Resupply Airlifts, December 23–25

Screaming Eagle pathfinders set up homing equipment to help guide in the first wave of supply aircraft on December 23. The brick pile was considered a relatively safe, and high, place to transmit from.

Photo courtesy of the National Archives

Manna from heaven. C-47s continue to fly over Bastogne after delivering their parachute and glider loads to the GIs below. This photograph was taken from the Heinz barracks, the 101st Airborne's headquarters.

Photo courtesy of the Don F. Pratt Museum, Fort Campbell, KY

Resupplied and ready to fight. Two troopers from the 101st drag a parapack full of supplies and carry the parachute back to their positions.

Photo courtesy of the Don F. Pratt Museum, Fort Campbell, KY

Christmas Eve: No Silent Night

U.S. soldiers scan the sky for signs of the Luftwaffe. At least twice on Christmas Eve, the Germans bombed Bastogne. This M3 half track is camouflaged in white linen sheets, possibly provided by the generous citizens of Hemroulle.

Photo courtesy of the Don F. Pratt Museum, Fort Campbell, KY

A Christmas Eve church service somewhere in Bastogne. Most of the GIs out on the line were not so lucky, having to spend Christmas Eve in their frozen foxholes, with growing apprehension the Germans would attack first thing in the morning.

Photo courtesy of the Don F. Pratt Museum, Fort Campbell, KY

The Rolle Château today. This view is looking north, through the courtyard and court buildings towards the château house and turret. Colonel Steven Chappuis set up the headquarters of the 502nd here, shortly after arriving in Bastogne. Today, the château name is spelled Rolley. *Photo by author Don Cygan*

Madame Maus de Rolley (*right*) speaks with an officer in the 101st, showing him the small chapel inside the turret of the ancient château. Colonel Chappuis and his staff spent Christmas Eve here. The chapel has changed very little today.

Photo courtesy of the Don F. Pratt Museum, Fort Campbell, KY

Wounded soldiers are treated in one of the makeshift aid stations in Bastogne. By December 23, with Bastogne surrounded, there was a distinct lack of medical personnel and supplies available to treat both the wounded and the victims of the harsh weather.

Photo courtesy of the Don F. Pratt Museum, Fort Campbell, KY

The tragic Christmas Eve bombing of the 10th Armored Division's hospital in Bastogne. Twenty wounded GIs and a Belgian nurse were killed when the upper floors collapsed into the lower. Here, days later, German POWs are being used as labor to remove debris from the site.

Photo courtesy of the National Archives

The Christmas Day Battle

Sergeant George N. Schmidt's M18 Hellcat, knocked out on the Dreve de Mande by one of Maucke's panzers. Behind the tank destroyer is possibly one of the large haystacks the Hellcats were using for concealment that morning. Notice that the barrel of the M18's 76mm gun is still pointed towards the Champs-Hemroulle road and possibly, one of its last victims.

Paratroopers examine a StuG III of Maucke's unit that has been hit and knocked out near the Champs-Hemroulle road, identified as StuG #2 on the maps. Due to the location of the penetration hole in the left armored skirt (*schuerzen*), it is believed Schmidt's TD may have knocked this vehicle out, or perhaps damaged it, prior to Schmidt's own demise.

The intersection of the Dreve de Mande and the Champs-Hemroulle road, facing southeast toward Hemroulle. Three destroyed StuG IIIs and other wrecks can just be made out in the far distance beyond the ridge. The woods where D'Angelo's and Vallitta's TDs fired from are to the distant left.

All photos this page courtesy of the Don F. Pratt Museum, Fort Campbell, KY

The same crossroads today. The woods where the TDs ambushed the German tanks have thinned over the decades. So has the Dreve de Mande, though a few of the trees still remain to the right.

Photo by author Don Cygan

Another view of the crossroads from the opposite direction, looking toward Champs. The lane of firs leads to Rolle Château on the right. Two GIs pose behind StuG #1, while, in the distance, the Mk IV knocked out by Schuyler Jackson burns, recently bombed by American fighter-bombers.

Photo courtesy of the Don F. Pratt Museum, Fort Campbell, KY

The crossroads weeks later. Soldiers move up the road towards Bastogne. Near the Dreve, we see one of the haystacks that Schmidt and Wans used to conceal their TDs Christmas morning. The StuG wrecks have been blasted apart, perhaps by overzealous fighter-bombers or engineers tasked with clearing the roads. *Photo courtesy of the Don F. Pratt Museum, Fort Campbell, KY*

The dramatic demise of Jackson's Panzer Mk IV. In the past, this photo has been misidentified as showing a tank blasted apart by a TD round or a bazooka during the battle. It is improbable that either weapon could have produced such destruction, and photos exist of the tank days prior in near perfect condition. It was probably finished off by a U.S. fighter-bomber days after the Christmas battle.

Photo courtesy of the Don F. Pratt Museum, Fort Campbell, KY

Another view of the gutted Panzer Mk IV. The steel hull has been sheared off and the turret basket floor can be seen, along with the top of the driver's compartment.   *Photo courtesy of Joseph Pangerl*

U.S. soldiers move down an icy road towards the outlying town of Marvie. These are probably glider troops from Colonel Joseph Harper's 327th Glider Infantry Regiment. Harper's glider fighters fought hard to hold open the southwestern approaches to Bastogne several days prior to Christmas.

Photo courtesy of the National Archives

The second of Maucke's Mk IVs we can account for is *Lustmolch* (Happy Salamander). This is the panzer that turned toward Hemroulle after attacking Colonel Allen's headquarters on the Champs-Hemroulle road. The tank was captured by "Booger" Childress of the 463rd after being hit by one of Colonel Cooper's 75mm howitzers. Here it is in front of the pump house in Savy, once again being explored by an ever-curious GI.

Photo courtesy of the Don F. Pratt Museum, Fort Campbell, KY

The tragic cost of Hitler's insistence on taking Bastogne: Some of Maucke's Panzergrenadiers who would never see another Christmas. The authors believe they have determined the location of this photo after visiting Bastogne. Using aerial photos and maps, the view is identified as looking southeast at the extension of firs of the Dreve de Mande. To the immediate left, and beyond the Dreve, a corner of D'Angelo's woods can just be made out.

Photo courtesy of the Don F. Pratt Museum, Fort Campbell, KY

German prisoners of war, probably captured after the failed Christmas Day assault, are marched past the Bastogne cemetery by a guard. Several were put to work burying American, German, and Belgian corpses in the walled cemetery.

Relief! December 26–On

All photos this page courtesy of the Don F. Pratt Museum, Fort Campbell, KY

General McAuliffe, Lieutenant Colonel Chappuis, and General George S. Patton talk outside of the Rolle Château. Chappuis has just been awarded the DSC by Patton. Patton was reportedly quite pleased after viewing the German tank wrecks. He spent that night as a guest in the château.

Letting the tanks pass through his lines was more difficult than it sounded. It would take tremendous discipline from the glidermen. Per Allen's instructions during Saturday's execution of plan A, Bowles had spread out his seventy-seven men over a thousand yards on a low ridgeline facing Mande Saint-Etienne. He had anchored his right flank near a small pine plantation and had positioned his left flank in a small forest lot. Between the two flanks was where he had located his CP on the eastern side of a copse of trees. Farther to their right were more than 150 men of MacDonald's B Company. The German column was heading almost directly between the two companies and would soon penetrate Allen's thin line, splitting it as with a blade.[25]

For a young lieutenant who had certainly not expected to be a company commander until several days ago, the situation must have caused Bowles considerable anxiety. Although he knew he had backup with four tank destroyers, C Company of the 1/401st in reserve on the sloping field behind him, and two companies of the 502nd farther behind him, Bowles's most immediate concern was his front. It was too late to move his men out of their positions and fall back. Once his men were caught out in the open, the panzers would slaughter his men as they tried to escape.

While Bowles could do little about the tanks now menacing his front, he had a solution for the infantry. At carefully selected positions all along the line, the glidermen had set up nine machine guns. Bowles had arranged the guns so they could provide overlapping fields of fire. At least five of these guns were the big, belt-fed .50-caliber M2s on tripods. These were the guns Gisi and others had secured at Crossroads X several days earlier, and they were about to come in handy.[26]

Captain MacDonald and his men had also heard the Germans approaching early that night. Because the Panzergrenadiers had left their equipment unsecured, the glidermen could hear the clinking, clattering, and banging of canteens and gas masks in the draw as the Germans moved into their attack positions near MacDonald's left flank. MacDonald's radio operator, Edward Garrett, then reported, "The krauts are attacking with lots of tanks to our left front."[27]

The B Company unit closest to Able was 1st Platoon, under the command of First Lieutenant John T. O'Halloran. Like many of the units in Bastogne, 1st Platoon was understrength, with only fifteen soldiers and one officer on its roster. MacDonald realized it was dangerous for this platoon to remain on the line, so he had borrowed a squad from Towns's Charlie

Company. Though the platoon was still woefully undermanned, almost all the soldiers were grizzled veterans, and morale remained high.[28] They waited as the German tanks, spewing snow behind their tracks, blue exhaust faintly visible in the dim light, slowly advanced toward them.

Finally, at 0645 hours, the ground shuddered and shook, and the tanks were on top of them. The single column was an armored fist heading straight for Able Company and its 2nd Platoon. Self-preservation became the standing order for many of Bowles's 2nd Platoon men, who crawled out of the holes and darted over to Adams's 3rd Platoon positions until the tanks had passed. No one wanted to be ground into the snow beneath the treads of a twenty-five-ton steel monster on Christmas.[29]

While the soldiers of 2nd Platoon scurried for cover, Bowles watched the procession wind its way through the copse of trees in the center of 2nd Platoon's positions. The plodding metal behemoths spent thirty minutes tentatively passing through the lines. Bowles stood, awestruck. Most of his men remained silent and concealed as the enemy drove on past their foxholes. Not all could remain quiet, however. Off to the left, Sergeant Tom McLaughlin, disobeying orders, opened up on the column of tanks with his .50-caliber machine gun. This singular action might have deceived the Germans into thinking they were only passing through another screen line of outposts.[30]

Unlike the men in 2nd Platoon, those in the headquarters section could not scamper out of their foxholes in time. For them, the panzer parade had several terrifying moments. Lieutenant Ralph Nelson led this group, and they fought back hopelessly with mere rifles and carbines.[31] The big Mk IVs, like steamrollers, crushed equipment into flattened metal pancakes as their treads clanked onward. Harold R. Hansen, an Able Company private, remembered a particularly close call: "An enemy tank rode over our foxhole in which my buddy and I squatted down, hoping it would keep going. It did, but destroyed my M1 and our bazooka. My buddy's helmet got smashed."[32]

Another glidermen, Private First Class Paul E. Krick, was a runner for Able Company. As he approached an embankment near the company foxholes, tracers screamed by him. Krick ducked behind the little ridge. When he dared to look up again, he watched his company scatter before his eyes as the glidermen split up in the face of the oncoming tanks. According to Krick, scores of soldiers were scampering across an open field, looking for cover. One tracer found its mark, and a gliderman crumpled to the ground. Another soldier ran over and knelt by him. Before Krick could see what else happened, a Mk IV rolled too close for comfort and he ducked back behind the embankment to hide.

Trotting on the heels of the tanks, Wörner's Panzergrenadiers moved through Able Company. Looking ghostly in their white suits, the Germans began firing their weapons randomly, sometimes into the air, to see whether they could scare the Americans into revealing their positions. As they came over the ridge, they used the flamethrowers for the same purpose, not realizing they were squirting the hot flames at empty foxholes. The frozen ground also acted as a retardant, and, fortunately for the Americans, nothing—and no one—caught fire.

In a foxhole not far from Hansen, Sergeant Joseph Rogan, a forward observer with the 463rd PFAB, watched the tidelike procession of rolling steel. Rogan had seen the tanks emerge from the fog at 0630 hours. He quickly shook his friend Rester Bryan awake. Grabbing their rifles, the two FOs started firing at the infantry on the tanks. The bullets pinged off the armor of the Mk IVs as they rolled past their foxhole. The two men then turned their attention on the infantry marching behind the armor. While Bryan plugged away at the Panzergrenadiers, Rogan reached for the phone to call back to the 463rd's FDC in Hemroulle. He expected to hear static, but instead heard nothing—the phone line was dead. He quickly grabbed for his fallback—a radio he had wrapped in blankets the previous night to keep the batteries from freezing. It worked.

Rogan's call reporting that he was overrun to Major Victor Garrett, the 463rd's operations officer, gave barely enough time for Cooper's gunners to move most of their Pack howitzers into the colonel's preplanned antitank positions. The other guns opened up in the indirect-fire mode, showering the oncoming Germans with 123 rounds of high-explosive. Directly in front of Able and Baker companies, the thunderous blast of 75mm high-explosive shells pounded the snowy fields, drowning out the screams and cries of the dying Panzergrenadiers unlucky enough to be caught in the barrage.[33]

Suddenly Rogan noticed Bryan had stopped firing. He looked over his shoulder and saw the body of his partner slumped over the side of the hole. He touched the body but saw no reaction. Bryan was dead, but Rogan did not have time to think about it. The Germans were swarming around the nearby foxholes, and an enraged Rogan decided he was not going down without a fight. He reloaded a clip and continued to fire his rifle at the enemy.[34]

Bursts from German rifles killed two other members of the 463rd: Howard Hickenlooper and John T. Hall. A German submachine gun shot the fatal 9mm round that slammed into Hickenlooper's neck, while Hall fell as the result of a burst of fatal fire from an MG 42, which caught him in the chest. Five more men suffered wounds—even burns from boiling flame-thrower fuel oil that, fortunately, failed to ignite.[35] Overall, the casualties could have been far greater had the Germans stopped or continued to search for the remaining GIs in both of Allen's forward companies. Instead, anxious to keep pace with the tanks, Wörner's troops walked on toward their objective.[36]

On Able Company's right flank, a group of men under the stalwart Oklahoman Lieutenant Adams had positioned a .50-caliber on the slope of the ridge.[37] This machine gun opened fire on the clustered groups of German infantry. Repeatedly they fought back countless assaults by the white-coated Panzergrenadiers. Finally the Germans moved up and unleashed the flamethrowers on Adams's .50-caliber machine gun position and the rest of his platoon, forcing many of the glidermen to fall back. Eventually only three men from Adams's platoon remained on the line, rapidly moving over to join Baker Company's positions.[38]

As he watched the tanks roll over A Company's positions, MacDonald kept relaying messages around the battalion, as he had the only working SCR-300 "walkie-talkie" radio. MacDonald informed Allen that about four hundred German infantry had occupied the field where Able Company had previously held the line. Allen asked him to relay a message to Captain Towns and Charlie Company, who were right in the path of the oncoming Germans. Preston Towns's exhausted men, basically recuperating from Friday's fight and sitting in reserve, were not too far from Allen's HQ. Allen wanted them warned as to what was coming their way. Via MacDonald, Allen instructed Towns to see whether he could bring the men of his company up and counterattack.[39]

From his foxhole, a startled Gisi watched the panzers "shooting their [main] guns point-blank" at the American positions. Some of the men fought back, but, realizing the futility, most stayed in their holes and prayed the Germans did not spot them. "There wasn't much else we could do," Gisi remembered.

"It happened pretty quick," Lieutenant Clarence "Gus" Ryan, MacDonald's executive officer, recounted years later in a letter he wrote to Gisi: "We could hold the infantry, but not the tanks, so I told the platoon leaders to let the tanks through and they would get 'em in the rear but to knock every Jerry on foot."[40] Luckily the men in Baker Company had also equipped themselves with a few of the .50-caliber machine guns from Crossroads X. The men had removed the guns from the trucks and emplaced them in a manner similar to what Able Company had done across their front.[41]

One of these units was Lieutenant O'Halloran's platoon. While Mac-Donald was busy relaying information back to Allen, O'Halloran's troopers opened up on the swarming German infantry to prevent them from flanking Baker Company's battle position. The enfilade fire was having a telling effect, turning the German Panzergrenadiers to the east.[42]

As the tanks and foot soldiers continued to overwhelm his line, Bowles could only hope the others had received the warnings and would pass them on, especially to the tank destroyer and artillery units. For the time being, he ducked down in the woodlot command post and, like Rogan, waited for the worst to pass.

As *Hauptmann* Schmidt led his force forward, an Mk IV passed just fifty feet from a B/705th tank destroyer located behind Bowles's 1st Platoon CP. The German tank commander could only wonder why this particular tank was parked at a right angle to his own and, within the cover of a tree plantation, stood out of formation. He shouted something in German, perhaps ordering the crew to get back in line and stop dallying. In the fog and dark, the German commander mistook the vehicle for a German tank. Standing stock-still and holding their breaths, the American crew remained silent until the panzer moved on. Only then did they dare breathe again.[43]

Close by, in the same patch of woods, Lieutenant Miller, the 705th's 1st Platoon reconnaissance leader, waited with his men. His scouts saw the attack coming their way at 0630 that morning. As a precaution, Miller had ordered many of his men to dismount and to occupy the foxholes near the copse of trees. Like the glidermen, the scouts allowed the panzers to pass by them without firing a shot. Straining to see in the dim light and fog, Miller finally saw the German soldiers and tanks when the column halted only seventy-five yards from his command post, so close that Miller could hear the Panzergrenadiers yelling in German. From his position, Miller counted seven German tanks east of the woods.

Not far from Miller, Private First Class Edward R. Lamke sat in the turret of his M8 Greyhound armored car. When the German tanks rolled by his position, he ducked down in the steel turret, sure that the tanks would see his vehicle. Luckily his armored car was backed far enough into the wood line that the panzers missed it completely. Besides, Lamke realized, if a firefight broke out, the 37mm "popgun" in the Greyhound's turret would be about as much use as a peashooter against the Mk IVs. Worse, Lamke noticed, he had put himself in a bad position in the dark, and could kick himself for what he'd done. He could not even turn the turret on his M8, because nearby tree trunks blocked his gun barrel from rotating. Lamke's only option was to stay quiet and hope the German tanks would stop idling near his position and move on.[44]

0330–0715 hours, Monday, 25 December 1944
1/502nd Parachute Infantry tactical assembly area
Near the 1/401st headquarters, outside of Hemroulle

Along the road outside Hemroulle, Sergeant Layton Black and the rest of Captain Cody's Charlie Company were preparing to move out toward Champs. Shortly after 0330, Cody had been alerted by the call from Hanlon after his discussion with Chappuis.

Black was still grumbling to himself about having to desert his warm hayloft bed so early that morning. Word had come down that the boys of Company A were in trouble in Champs, and Charlie Company had been ordered two thousand yards up the road to bail them out. Baker Company, Black heard, had already headed that direction.[45] "We got ready in a hurry with few words. Everyone knew it was coming—the fighting. What upset me the most was that Jerry wasn't going to take Christmas off!"[46]

Now the men huddled and shivered together in the dark, waiting to start the march. Some stepped out onto the Champs–Hemroulle road. They kicked and stamped their feet to stay warm. Some cussed at the weather. Typical of the army, many of the soldiers joked that this was just another round of hurry up and wait for the next orders. The paratroopers blew into their hands, checked their weapons, and chatted in low tones.

Finally, with many stops and starts, C Company began to move in a column of twos up the road toward Champs. When they halted again, they had traveled only a half mile.[47] Captain Cody had gone forward to conduct an area reconnaissance while his platoon leaders established a perimeter defense along the road. Frank Miller, another member of C Company, remembered the thick fog that swept over the fields to their left and just beyond the farmhouse: "It was early in the morning, about six o'clock in the morning, just getting light; it really didn't get too light until about eight o'clock or so, till the fog cleared."[48]

As the men stopped by the last few farms marking the northern limits of Hemroulle, the paratroopers took notice of the farmhouse headquarters of the 1/401st. The door of the building and the opening of the high wall surrounding the courtyard both faced the road on which they were moving. Since they were once again waiting, Black's platoon wandered into the courtyard, where one of the men started to brew coffee. The paratroopers wondered at the stirrings of excited voices and activity within the glider fighters' headquarters.

Black noticed the tension in the men's faces as they stood around: "Our C Company moved halfway up the road. My 2nd Platoon, in close order marching formation, held up on the road next to the farmhouse that was the command post of the 327th [1/401st]," Black remembered. "There we were halted and stood in full battle dress, loaded down with heavy ammo, machine guns, mortars and bazookas. . . . We were jumpy," he admitted.[49]

Like any good NCO, Sergeant Black knew that just standing around was not the best plan. He began to organize a hasty defense for his squad. His first task was to establish his crew-served weapon, an M1919 .30-caliber machine gun, near the perimeter. Black picked out a spot near the courtyard gate and told his gunner to aim the machine gun to the west at a hilltop eight hundred yards from his position. While he was doing this, Black noticed that the rest of the 2nd Platoon men were standing around a fire. Black was pretty sure his soldiers had not started the fire and wondered who had. As he watched, more GIs emerged from the farmhouse.

Suddenly it all became clear. Black realized Allen's headquarters men were burning maps and other papers. The glidermen of the 401st were leaving, and leaving in a hurry.[50]

0710–0720 hours, Monday, 25 December 1944
Charlie Company/401st
Battle positions south of Hemroulle

Schmidt's panzers rumbled eastward. The low-silhouetted StuGs kept pace on the left. Ahead were the foxholes and trenches of Towns's Charlie Company, in reserve after the hard fighting near Mande in which the Germans had captured Sergeant Bowen the day before. Now they were in the last battle positions before their battalion commander's HQ and the Champs–Hemroulle road.

Private First Class Robert O'Mara, a rifleman in Towns's 2nd Platoon, recalled seeing the enemy tanks that morning. "I saw three of them coming over a hill. One was pulling a cart with people in it." The carts were large sleds that carried nearly a platoon's worth of Panzergrenadiers. In the early morning hours, before the sun came up, many Americans thought the sleds were additional tanks; now with the sun starting to shine, the GIs could make out several sleds being towed behind the rumbling tanks.[51]

Captain Towns had just called twenty-one-year-old Private First Class Robert Lott over to his foxhole that morning to congratulate him on the work he had done staving off a tank attack near Mande two days ago. Ironically, just as he was reminding Lott that he had promised a pass to Paris for any man in his company who knocked out an enemy tank, someone shouted that German tanks were heading their way.

To their front, Lott and Towns had heard the firefight between their sister companies and the Germans. They could even see flashes of gunfire in the fog. Shortly after, Towns received the message from MacDonald to "come up." Doing so, with the armor bearing down on him right now, was going to be quite difficult. Before he could truly get his men in motion, the tanks were upon them.

The lanky Towns ducked down to grab his radio and then turned to Lott: "Pass the word out—not any soldier is to take a shot."[52] Lott crawled through the snow and along a low hedge to spread the word. In each foxhole position, the men of Towns's company passed the message along. Quietly, the men of C Company did the same, as their brethren in A and B companies had done. The panzers sped through their area, some, like the whitewashed Mk IV that passed near Lott and Towns, only fifty feet away. With nerve-racking self-discipline, Towns's men hunkered down. The Germans passed by and the glidermen remained unharmed. Lott later called it "a miracle on Christmas Day."[53]

Maucke's tanks had completely broken through the outer American positions and were now almost astride the Champs–Hemroulle road to Bastogne. Suddenly the oncoming force split up. Several tanks in the line went to the north; others turned to the southeast. The glider troops thought this was odd, to say the least, and might just play right into the Americans' hands. "We wondered why the Germans went in opposite directions," recalled Lott, who witnessed the split with Towns.[54]

To this day, no one is sure why Schmidt's force suddenly split up into two parts and went in two separate directions. This was clearly not part of Maucke's or Kokott's original orders, and tactically it made no sense to weaken the drive toward Bastogne. Without the benefit of Maucke's much-argued-for reconnaissance, and in the thick fog, the tanks may simply have driven off course, unable to recognize where they were. On the other hand, perhaps the American fire was intense enough to divert some of the German tanks to make for the north (Champs) to link up with the friendly units of the 77th Volksgrenadier, engaged at that time with Swanson's Able Company. Other theories abound. For whatever reason, one half of the German assault that Kokott had staked so much on this Christmas Day was now heading in the complete opposite direction from Bastogne.

0710–0720 hours, Monday, 25 December 1944
Hauptmann Schmidt's Panzer section
Heading toward Hemroulle

In Flamierge, Maucke impatiently listened to his radio net. His last transmission from 1st Battalion was garbled. He received another report from 3rd Battalion, informing him that they had reached the ridgeline west of Hemroulle. He knew, though, that time was running out, and if Wörner was not in Bastogne by 0900 it would be too late.[55] At 0900 hours, the Allied fighter-bombers would arrive over the battlefield, and they would destroy the tanks caught in the open.

For the nine or ten German vehicles turning north, the Champs–Hemroulle road was now in view. The infantry fire from their rear had slacked off as they cleared Towns's Charlie Company positions. The drivers of the German tanks squinted through the thick glass of their periscopes. In the carpet of snow they could tell they were approaching the road from the concrete telephone poles that paralleled its path. Immediately before them stood the pale stone farmhouse that was Allen's headquarters. The German tankers saw the GIs racing out of it in panic. Beyond the road and farmhouse loomed a large section of dark woods.

Obviously the tanks would not be able to penetrate this thick wood line. They would have to turn to the right or left and use the road to go either north to Champs, or south to Hemroulle. The commander of this unit decided, like his counterpart to the right, to stop and wait for more infantry to catch up to the tanks. He ordered his driver to make for the farmhouse and capture it. So far the attack had gone as planned, and they had reached their initial objective—the Hemroulle road.[56] For the time being, the courtyard would be an excellent place to halt, regroup, and wait for the infantry.

As the other Mk IVs turned to the right and headed for the small forest lots and hills above Hemroulle, the nine to ten tanks in the northern column (five or six Mk IVs and at least three StuG IIIs from 3rd Battalion) drove straight toward Allen's headquarters. The StuGs were possibly in the lead. Inside the two-story farmhouse HQ, Allen and his staff were oblivious to how quickly the attack had covered ground since Bowles's report earlier.

Now, as the dawn light began to illuminate the fog-shrouded scene from the east, Towns and Lott were dumbstruck. They could see the entire force driving straight toward Allen's HQ from their recently bypassed position. Towns knew he had to warn Allen immediately. "Tanks are coming toward you!" he radioed tersely to his commander in the farmhouse.

"Where?" Allen asked.

"If you look out your back window now," Towns answered, "you'll be looking right down the muzzle of an 88."[57]

When he peered out of the farmhouse, Allen learned that Towns was not exaggerating. An approaching panzer fired its main gun at the building. As Allen and his staff hugged the floor, the shell splintered the roof and passed through the structure, setting it afire.

Allen shouted for Major Angus to get the men to burn any important papers and then get the hell out. *Thank God*, he thought as he heard the sound of the 463rd's guns engaging the tanks. *That might buy us a little time!* Grabbing the radio, he quickly contacted Colonel Harper to let him know that the battalion HQ was displacing and that the Germans had penetrated the American lines. When asked how close the German tanks were to his farmhouse, Allen responded: "Right here! They are firing point-blank at me from 150 yards' range. My units are still in position, but I've got to run."[58]

When there was a break in the firing, Allen told the last two men remaining, Captain James Pounders and Captain Joseph S. Brewster, to "come on." He grabbed an armful of papers, threw a piece of white parachute silk over his shoulders for camouflage, and bolted out the door just as a German tank picked him up in its sights. "The books say the tank was leading me with its fire, giving me credit for more speed than I possessed," Allen recounted with grim humor in an interview years later. "But I met an officer later who had just topped a hill when the tank started firing, and he saw the whole thing. I asked him if it was true the gun was leading me. He said: 'No. You were definitely leading it.'"[59]

0715–0720 hours, Monday, 25 December 1944
Charlie Company/502nd Parachute Infantry tactical assembly area
Inside the 1/401st Headquarters in Hemroulle

Sergeant Black knew the burning of the maps was not a good sign. He turned to warn his men, but it was too late.

"German tanks!" a voice shouted out.

"All hell broke loose," Black remembered.

There was a flash, a bang, and Black watched as a 75mm tank shell blew his .30-caliber machine gun into the air. Black yelled, "Every man for himself! Get the hell out of here! Head for the trees!" and the scene was one of chaos. The Germans seemed to close in from out of the fog and sweep down and surround the farmhouse. Men were flailing in the snow as the tank machine guns swept the courtyard and 75mm rounds blasted the walls into chunks of stone and clouds of masonry. Many of Black's men sprinted after Allen's headquarters section and made for the safety of the woods across the road.[60] Others, pinned to the ground in fear, became prisoners as Wörner's Panzergrenadiers leaped from the tanks, weapons ready.

There were shouts in German, rifle and machine gun fire, and in no time the Germans had captured Allen's headquarters. The fire on the roof of the structure was growing. Schmidt's tank crews pulled four of their tanks around the side of the whitewashed walls and paused as the German soldiers policed the area. Just like the GIs moments before, several grenadiers stopped to warm their hands over the fire in the courtyard.

Across the road, the men in C Company beat a hasty retreat into the woods. Some described it as an organized withdrawal, weapons and all, but others considered it a near rout.[61]

Private First Class James Flanagan was one of the paratroopers who barely survived the initial German onslaught. Like Black, he was waiting along the road to Champs when the tanks unleashed on the spread out paratroopers. Flanagan remembered that bedlam was the result, as every man dashed for the safety of the distant wood line. While he sprinted past an officer, a 75mm shell suddenly pulverized a tree that was between them. Flanagan dodged the trunk as it came crashing to the ground. His feeling of relief, though, was short-lived. He did not hear the next round when it hit. Without warning, he was hurled into the air, his legs pumping wildly, as if on a bicycle. Flanagan was thrown into a water-filled ditch. He looked around and saw the Mk IVs and the assault guns were just hitting the road, but many of his comrades were no longer running. C Company was starting to turn around and fight from the wood line, firing back at the Germans. "As my trusty M1 was frozen due to my dunking, I couldn't do much more than act as a cheerleader," Flanagan admitted.[62]

Caught at the farmhouse, Layton Black tried to run for cover into the building, dodging the Germans among the ancient stables attached to the burning structure. He finally sneaked through the haymow overhead to a door out the front, dropped down, and sprinted across the road to safety with many of his men. As he left, he caught sight of Colonel Allen doing the same.[63]

As Ray Allen and two of his headquarters staff ran to the road, aiming for the woods, some C Company men mistook them for Germans hot on their heels. The paratroopers wheeled about and fired at the hapless CO of the 401st. As Allen dived into the snow for cover, he swore under his breath. Inching back up, he told his men to follow and took off at a ninety-degree angle along the road and hedge, ducking low and heading for Hemroulle. The three officers dodged through some trees and a little valley, making their way south. Unfortunately for Allen, as soon as he entered that area, riflemen of Cooper's 463rd fired upon him. It seemed everyone was frantic and jumpy with the approach of the German tanks. Winded and exasperated, Allen and his group started waving a white handkerchief (possibly the parachute silk) as they sheltered in a roadside ditch. Finally the troopers around Hemroulle let them come forward, and Allen made it safely to American lines.[64]

Black still had a hundred yards to go before reaching the wood line. Lying on his back in the snow, he had disposed of his long overcoat so he could move faster. Hiding behind a pile of potatoes, Black watched as whitish green German tracer rounds zipped over his head. He picked an opportune moment and sprinted across the road to the woods, ducking for cover. Black also admitted later that the withdrawal of Charlie Company was more of a panicked run for cover than an organized retreat. On the positive side, Black noticed the men were keeping their wits and weapons about them, and that Captain Cody was quickly rallying them in the woods.

"Halfway up this long hillside, already in the open past the tree line, I looked up. There stood Captain Cody with his arms raised high. 'Hold up there!' he said. 'This is as far as we're going to run. Turn around! We are going back and fight the bastards!'" With Cody's growth of beard, long overcoat, and dramatically raised arms exhorting his men, Black noted, "You know something? For a moment there, he looked a lot like Jesus Christ to me."[65]

Black and his fellow NCOs began counting heads, organizing the men for a counterattack, and taking stock of what weapons they had. As they prepared themselves for the attack, other men from 1st, 2nd, and 3rd platoons began to arrive in driblets. Unfortunately, if they were going to counterattack, it would have to be with small arms. With all the commotion at the farmhouse, many heavy weapons had been left behind, and now there were hardly any machine guns, mortars, or bazookas. When Cody finally counted his men, he had most of 1st and 2nd platoons with him on the hill. Most of 3rd Platoon remained near the 401st Headquarters, either locked in combat for the courtyard or captured by the Germans.

In the end, the soldiers quickly noticed that two of 3rd Platoon's squads had escaped. The last squad had not made it. Black admitted that this was an added incentive. He and the others knew the men left at the farmhouse were now prisoners of the Germans.[66]

"The thought of the other men—were they killed or captured?—spurred us on," Black recalled.[67]

0715–0720 hours, Monday, 25 December 1944
B/502nd Parachute Infantry tactical assembly area
Near Rolle

By now, any other Americans along the road to Champs had either heard the ground-shaking cracks as the tank destroyers exchanged fire with the Germans, or had seen the German tanks emerging from the fog, heading for the road. In fact, as the sun spread on the horizon and burned through the cloud cover, the rumbling Panzers and StuGs were hard to miss.

Earlier that morning, after checking with Chappuis at Rolle, Major John Hanlon had brought Baker Company of the 502nd almost a mile to the north, ready to move into Champs if needed. At Chappuis's urging, Hanlon had already sent a platoon forward to help Sutliffe's 2nd Battalion on the line between Champs and Longchamps, where the 77th Volksgrenadiers had attacked through the Les Bresses woods and clashed with Sutliffe's men. The rest of B Company was digging in as reserve, to back up Swanson's company in Champs if need be. The troops reached the bushes and trees along a low hill near the zigzag of woods west of Rolle. As they started to dig their foxhole positions, the paratroopers grumbled and complained, doubting they would see any action. From the tapering off of gunfire in Champs, and from Swanson's radio reports, it looked like Able Company was getting things under control there. Now, as the sun rose in the east, Hanlon used one of Baker's platoons to set up a roadblock on the Withimont road north of Rolle.[68]

About that time, D'Angelo's and Vallitta's M18 Hellcats sped by, treads crunching the soft snow on the road as they headed toward Rolle. Sergeant "Moe" Williams had ordered Sergeant D'Angelo to head in that direction and help out. Since Swanson had released his and Vallitta's TDs from the close-quarters fighting in Champs, the two headed to their typical morning position near the Dreve de Mande, the "Lane of Trees." The two Hellcats rumbled past, turned to the left, one after another, and vanished from sight beneath the slope of land to the east, taking a trail through the woods.[69]

The Baker Company troopers probably wondered where the two TDs were going in such a hurry. They had their answer shortly when several soldiers nearby shouted, "German tanks!" and pointed to the southwest. In the distance, spread out like the fingers of a great armored claw, the dark and prowling forms crawled across the snowy slope to the south. Several seemed to be heading up the road, toward B Company's positions and straight toward Champs.

Hanlon was nowhere near a radio at this time. Hanlon's S2, First Lieutenant Samuel B. Nickels Jr.—who had been at Champs with A Company and had seen the German attack that morning—went scurrying to warn the regimental HQ.[70]

Automatically, several of the troopers guarding the roadblock turned the other way to face this new danger to their rear. Armed with rifles, two bazookas, and a machine gun, this small force of men, a platoon in size, now believed they were all that stood between this German assault and their brothers in arms at Champs. With no time to dig in, the soldiers found a ditch in the snowy ground edging the woodlot. As each man picked out a fighting position, the Screaming Eagles of Baker Company checked their weapons and prepared to deal out death and destruction.[71]

After "No Love, No Nothing" had passed the bend in the road, a burst of German machine gun fire over D'Angelo's head alerted him to the approaching German menace. Following the elevated Champs–Hemroulle road would just make his tank destroyer a perfect target, outlined against the rising sun to the east. Popping up in the open turret, D'Angelo raised his arms over his head to signal Vallitta. "I told him to follow me. We had fire coming in, so I went to follow the contour of the land," D'Angelo related. "We went to the left, where we were behind the ridge, and I saw all of these paratroopers up on this hill there, digging in and getting ready to fight." The two tank destroyer commanders knew this position. Lieutenant Long had assigned their section to the Champs sector for the last few days, and D'Angelo had already staked out the position near the tree line as a good ambush spot.

A paratrooper, happy to see the arrival of the "big guns," ran up to "No Love, No Nothing" and told D'Angelo that German tanks were attacking up ahead. "I got off my tank destroyer so doggone fast that I left my field glasses on board." He did not need to see the enemy—D'Angelo would hear from them soon enough.

At that moment, one of the German tanks let loose with a 75mm shell. The shell passed over D'Angelo and his crew as the paratroopers hit the earth. It crashed into the bushes and tree lot behind the vehicles, sending up geysers of snow. Having been shot at twice by tanks in the past twenty-four hours, D'Angelo felt very lucky as he picked himself up. "It was probably my closest call of the war," he admitted. The fire had come from one of the German tanks that had parked near the woods and Allen's recently abandoned HQ. D'Angelo's first sergeant, "Moe" Williams, shouted from his nearby Jeep to get the TDs around behind the Panzer and take it out from the rear. Williams put his Jeep in gear and drove ahead to scout the way.

Just then a 101st lieutenant ran up to his M18, ordering D'Angelo and Vallitta to go up the hill and attack the oncoming tanks. D'Angelo recalled the conversation:

"I told him, 'We can't fight like that. We ain't got no doggone armor!' He started swearing, calling me every name in the book."[72] Corporal Paul "the Greek" Stoling, the driver of Vallitta's tank, overheard the argument. "I remember the lieutenant who threatened to court-martial us. I said [if he had sent us straight at the German tanks], 'There, five men killed! You happy?'"[73]

It was a common problem during the Bastogne defense, as so few of the paratroopers had ever worked with tank destroyers before. D'Angelo realized there was no time to educate the young officer on tank destroyer tactics. Instead, he decided to appeal to the lieutenant's common sense. Even without his field glasses, D'Angelo could see the German tanks making for the Champs–Hemroulle road. He quickly noticed the woods south of Rolle, across the field in front of him, where Williams had indicated he should attack. He also noticed the tree line was adjacent to where the panzers would proceed on their present course. To the veteran tank destroyer commander, the site looked like the perfect firing position—concealed and offering an almost point-blank solution on the passing German armor. A perfect flank attack! D'Angelo knew that all he had to do was use the wooded trail to zip over to the woods in time, and with the speedy M18s that would be no problem.

"Look, Lieutenant," D'Angelo told him. "We'll fight our way, the way we were trained. We'll go around behind, back in the woods, and come out on them." The young officer gave his reluctant consent. D'Angelo hopped aboard his Hellcat and signaled the two tank destroyers to head out.[74]

0715–0720 hours, Monday, 25 December 1944
502nd Parachute Infantry Regiment command post
Rolle Château, Belgium

Colonel Chappuis sensed the German attack had stalled in Champs. He ordered Hanlon to prepare for a counterattack once the sun was up. Now "Silent Steve" was growing convinced that the German attack in Champs was only an attempt to contain U.S. forces and that the main German effort was coming somewhere else, nearby. Chappuis' staff officers, James J. Hatch, and Captain Ivan G. Phillips, the regimental communications officer, were able to send a message via radio to McAuliffe's headquarters at 0715 to inform them of the 502nd's plans to retake Champs.

As Hatch departed for Champs to plan the operation, a bright flash and shock wave blasted through the command center. Another explosion quickly followed and everything went dark. The switchboard operator, though stunned, was unharmed, but the switchboard itself was a different story. The blast had destroyed it, and with that, all communication with division headquarters had ceased. Phillips dispatched several parties to repair the lines.

At about this time, a very winded and flushed Lieutenant Nickels burst into the regimental HQ at Rolle just as the 502nd commander was picking up the radio. Chappuis had been expecting another call from Swanson at Champs, filling him in on the latest developments there. Instead, Nickels, standing in the doorway and catching his breath, blurted out more pressing news:

"There are seven enemy tanks and lots of infantry coming over the hill to your left," he said in a gasp.[75]

Chappuis now knew that the Germans had broken through Allen's positions and were literally in his front yard. The German tanks were approaching down the road, the first two StuGs about five hundred yards from the château front. He turned to Cassidy and the other officers present. In his calm drawl, "Silent Steve" ordered them to get everyone out who could carry a gun and fight.

Immediately, Captain Stone started gathering up men—radio operators, cooks, clerks, drivers, chaplains, engineers, and so forth—and headed out the château gate to do battle with the Germans. Stone decided the best place to establish his hasty defense was along the Dreve and the slight incline that overlooked the Rolle crossroads. It was a motley crew, but they were all that remained on the château grounds.[76]

Divisional surgeon Major Douglas T. Davidson told First Lieutenant Henry Barnes, a medical evacuation officer, to watch over the wounded men in the stable opposite the château. In this primitive, candlelit building, Barnes had been taking care of the more severely wounded. Davidson then took all of the wounded who were able to hold a rifle and, arming the men, left to follow Stone up the road.

Barnes, meanwhile, attempted to make the more severely wounded more comfortable. At one point, as soldiers darted past his aid station, he heard that "seven tanks were practically in the courtyard" of the ancient château.

"The noise of firing, explosions and shriek of incoming shells increased with daylight," Barnes recalled years later. "A medical officer ran over to me and told me to get ready to burn all the medical books of tags so the enemy couldn't know how many men we had lost." Barnes did everything within his power to keep the wounded calm. When he heard more gunfire outside, he started a small fire to burn the tags.[77]

Chappuis and Cassidy kept the one radio operator with them to maintain contact with their men. It was now only the three of them occupying the château, as Stone had scraped together every able body, including Davidson's twenty or more "walking wounded."

Chappuis knew that if he could coordinate the movements and actions of his 1st Battalion, which Hanlon had stretched out along the front from

Hemroulle to Champs (luckily, in exactly the place the Germans were at-tacking), he would have a fighting chance of blocking the German advance. In addition, if the officers could get the men to hold their ground—dig in and fight where they were—Chappuis could close the break in the line before any of the Germans reached Bastogne or the valuable artillery park to the south. To make this happen, Chappuis told Cassidy to radio B Com-pany to stand firm, and to get C Company turned around to face the attack from the west.

The radios were still the only way to communicate. Cassidy was not having trouble reaching the three companies, but getting hold of their com-manders was a different story. Swanson, for instance, had his hands busy in Champs. Chappuis could guess that. What "Silent Steve" did not know was that Baker and Charlie companies were in the same boat. Cassidy had already sent a runner to alert the two tank destroyers nearby and then go on to C Company with the message, but by the time the runner reached Cody, his men had already figured out on their own what to do. Cassidy was able to reach Hanlon by handy-talky and told him to face both companies around immediately to meet the German advance on the road. Unfortu-nately, neither he nor Chappuis realized that the two company commanders, frantically trying to save the line, never got the word.

As much as Chappuis was trying to organize the defense, the well-trained veterans of the 101st and 705th were typically one step ahead of their commanders. The average soldiers, NCOs, and junior officers reacted in-stinctively to the attack, and reacted well. Those vaunted airborne and ar-mor traits, and a little bit of luck, might just save Bastogne.[78]

CHAPTER TEN

"A Small Lesson in Tank Warfare"

"We have not so merry a Christmas."[1]

—Henry Dearborn, a private at Valley Forge

0710–0720 hours, Monday, 25 December 1944
1/401st battle positions
East of Mande Saint-Etienne

The men of Able and Baker companies of the 1/401st may have felt a little like they had been run over and left for dead, but they still had plenty of fight left in them.

Just minutes after the German tanks had passed through their positions, the angry glider-fighters of Bowles's 2nd Platoon slid back to their holes, turned their weapons around, cocked the charging handles on their machine guns, and prepared to deal with the German infantry that was trailing the panzers. These men did not need orders. They knew what they had to do.[2]

Back at Harper's command post, word had arrived that Allen had been forced out of his CP and sent running to Hemroulle. Communications, with the severing of the telephone lines throughout the sector, had almost completely broken down. Harper knew he had to get back in touch with Allen and find out what was happening, quick. Harper sent his S3, Major Alvin Jones, with a radio to the 463rd's command post in Hemroulle to help relay information about the breaking situation.

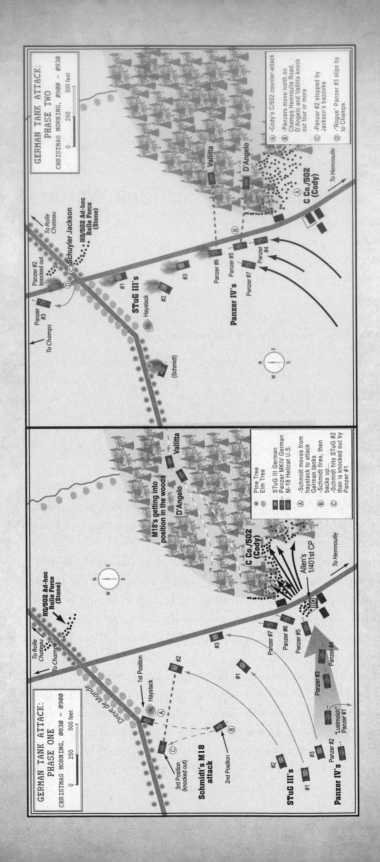

GERMAN TANK ATTACK: PHASE ONE

CHRISTMAS MORNING, 0830 - 0900

0   250   500 feet

To Rolle Chateau

HQ/502 Ad-hoc Rolle Force (Stone)

To Champs

Drève de Monde

1st Position

Haystack

#2

Ⓐ

3rd Position (knocked out)

2nd Position

Ⓒ

Ⓑ

Schmidt's M18 attack

STuG III's

#1

#2

Panzer #2

#3

"Lustmolch" Panzer #1

Panzer #4

Panzer #3

N

#3

Panzer #7

Panzer #6

Panzer #5

Panzer IV's

To Hemroulle

C Co./502 (Cody)

Allen's 1/401st CP

HQ

M18's getting into position in the woods

D'Angelo

Vailitta

Pine Tree
Elm Tree
STuG III German
Panzer MKIV German
M-18 Hellcat U.S.

Ⓐ - Schmidt moves from haystack to attack German tanks

Ⓑ - Schmidt fires, then backs up...

Ⓒ - Schmidt hits STuG #2 then is knocked out by Panzer #1

GERMAN TANK ATTACK: PHASE TWO

CHRISTMAS MORNING, 0900 - 0930

0   250   500 feet

To Rolle Chateau

Panzer #2 knocked out

Schuyler Jackson

HQ/502 Ad-hoc Rolle Force (Stone)

Panzer #3

To Champs

Ⓓ

Ⓒ

STuG III's

Haystack

#1

#2

#3

Panzer #6

Panzer #5

Panzer #7

Panzer #4

Panzer IV's

(Schmidt)

N

Ⓑ

C Co./502 (Cody)

Ⓐ

D'Angelo

Vailitta

To Hemroulle

Ⓐ - Cody's C/502 counter-attack

Ⓑ - Panzers move north on Champs Hemroulle Road. D'Angelo and Vailitta knock out four or more

Ⓒ - Panzer #2 stopped by Jackson's bazooka

Ⓓ - "Rogue" Panzer #3 slips by to Champs

Both Bowles and Towns, of course, were out of contact with the battalion—not that it mattered, because the battalion HQ was now swarming with Germans. Towns had a gut feeling the German armor that sped past his position had overrun the battalion command post.

Over the radio net, they heard Captain MacDonald. The voice of the more experienced commander on his flank helped set Bowles at ease.

"Here's the situation. The battalion commander has had to get out," MacDonald said. "I can see you from where I am. Your best bet is to stay where you are. Hold tight to your positions and fight back at them."[3]

MacDonald then radioed Towns. "Speck, this is the time for a counterattack. You come out at them over the route we followed yesterday, and we'll move in on this side. We can take them right where they are."[4]

Far behind the panzers was the infantry of Maucke's 3rd Battalion, under the command of Major Adam Dyroff. Dyroff's mission was to mop up the pockets of resistance the tanks had left behind. The soldiers trudged through the fields of thick, heavy snow, still yelling and firing into the air. Some of the grenadiers were in formation, and bunched up as they began to climb up the ridge toward Able and Baker companies' battle positions. To some of the men of the 1/401st, the German infantry looked like ghosts in their pale winter camouflage. Leveling their weapons and squinting down the sights, the determined glidermen prepared to fire.[5]

Suddenly the Panzergrenadiers heard a loud thump. Several of the older veterans of Italy knew that sound. It was the sound of a mortar round leaving its tube.

With keen foresight, Bowles had brought his lone 81mm mortar to bear on the clumps of German foot soldiers, who had made the fatal mistake of presenting the enemy with large, slow-moving targets. Before the Panzergrenadiers could react to the incoming rounds, Able Company's machine guns opened up. From their occupied trenches and foxholes, the glider-fighters poured .50-caliber and .30-caliber rounds into the soldiers. Red tracers ripped through the fog as if from nowhere, and the Germans dropped in droves, pools of crimson appearing in the snowdrifts. Caught out in the open with no cover, and in a deadly cross fire, the soldiers could do nothing but fall, screaming, as belt after belt of ammo lanced into their lines.[6]

The slaughter had only just begun.

Rifle fire rent the air. Now men from MacDonald's Baker Company joined in the cacophony of gunfire. Gisi and others emptied clip after clip of ammo from their M1 rifles as the Germans approached to their left, crunching through the snow on foot. Cut off from the armor, the Germans were shot down left and right. B Company's machine guns added to the awful chatter as bullets sliced through air and flesh. Caught out in the field between the two tree clumps, more grenadiers fell in heaps.

"It was a hell of a fight," Gisi recalled. ". . . the Germans we didn't kill, we captured . . . it was pure hell."[7]

Gisi remembered firing in "almost every direction" from his foxhole to the left, right, and upslope of A Company's position.[8]

Lieutenant Ryan's memory was similar: "We just piled the Jerry dead up and they did a good job on us too, but we got the most in the long run."[9]

Now, from their carefully dug-in positions behind the slope, MacDonald's 81mm mortar section chimed in, lobbing shells into the masses of German infantry. "In effect, we had bottled up the krauts. Towns was coming up from the rear, the 81s were plastering the front, and we were pouring in plenty of lead from the [right] flank," MacDonald reported after the war.[10]

"Finally, as dawn broke the enemy panicked and attempted to cross the 300 yards of open ground to our front. They never had a chance. We had our whole front well covered with mortar barrages and as they would move from one concentration area to another we would merely shift the fires," MacDonald remembered. "The riflemen were standing out of their holes bracing their rifles against the fir trees for better aim." For the duration of the morning, MacDonald's mortarmen played a horrific game of cat and mouse with the surviving German soldiers, hunting them this way with mortar and gun.[11]

With this move, the door had swung shut behind the armor, and the glidermen slaughtered most of the cutoff Panzergrenadiers who were on foot. Those who survived chose to surrender. By day's end, the A/401st would count ninety-two German prisoners of war. Many more lay still or twitching in the fields of snow.[12]

0710–0720 hours, Monday, 25 December 1944
Baker Company/705th Tank Destroyer section
A hundred yards behind Bowles's command post, west of Bastogne

From his position in the woods behind Able Company's foxholes, Lieutenant Richard Miller, the 705th reconnaissance leader, watched quietly as seven German tanks rolled past his position. A few minutes later, in the dim light, it appeared as if one of the Mk IVs apparently stalled or broke down.

To Miller, it looked like the Panzertruppen quickly hooked up cables and began to take the vehicle under tow. What he was probably witnessing, though, was the attachment of a large wooden troop sled being towed into battle behind the tank.

Like hunters carefully watching their quarry from the woods, Miller and his gun section—two B Company M18s led by Sergeant Clyde J. Love, from Sugar Grove, North Carolina—figured they would use the opportunity to even up the numbers.

Sergeant Love had his driver inch the olive drab TD out of the wood line. Although the whitewash some of the Mk IVs were painted with was an effective camouflage for the snow, the Americans were discovering that the dull green of their own vehicles was actually working well in the dark woods and shady tree lots.

To Love and Miller, it appeared that three German panzers were now heading eastward, one towing the other up the draw. The third vehicle was alone and providing rear security. Their lumbering speed made them easy targets for Love's gunner.

The crew probably never knew what hit them. The solitary Mk IV guarding the other was the first target. Love's Hellcat rocked backward as its 76mm gun fired. The first round hit home. The German tank brewed up, belching smoke. The other Mk IV, towing the large sledlike object, tried to escape, lurching forward, desperately trying to reach the crest of the hill in front of it. The sleigh behind it was an anchor, slowing down the metal beast as the two struggled up the hill.

The panzer would not find safety at the summit of the ridge. Like a swarm of bees, engineers from the Headquarters and Service Company of the 326th Engineers attacked the beleaguered vehicle. The company, under the command of Captain William J. Nancarrow, had been in reserve south of Colonel Allen's headquarters. Not long after the German tanks had penetrated the line, Nancarrow had received a warning from Allen that tanks had bypassed Miller's position and were heading his way. When the tanks reached a position three hundred yards north of the H&S Company, they opened fire on the American artillery batteries to the east near Savy. Nancarrow squinted, but in the dark was able to make out the oncoming vehicles as they crested a snowy rise. He noted that about fifty foot soldiers were accompanying the German armor. Placing three of his machine guns to provide covering fire, the gutsy Nancarrow grabbed a squad of men—privates Joe J. Berra, Stanley W. Wieczorek, Romer L. Williams, Joe

H. Douglas, Jacques Levan, Cort L. Paine, and Technician Fifth Grade William H. Hussey—to help him take on the tanks.

While the rest of his company prepared to attack, Nancarrow sneaked toward the closest Mark IV with his team. About two hundred yards from the tank, Nancarrow ordered the bazooka team to fire. Removing the safety pin, one engineer slid the 2.36-inch rocket into the back of the tube and wrapped the tiny wires from the rocket into the magneto clamp on the top of the bazooka. He patted the engineer in front of him as the signal he was loaded. The gunner fired. With a sharp blast, the rocket smoked toward the tank.

The round bounced harmlessly off the Mark IV's three-inch armor. To the engineers, it seemed the rocket merely angered the tank. Like a bear swatting at bees, the tank began to blindly fire its machine guns.

Nancarrow's three machine guns replied, killing several of the Panzergrenadiers who were on or around the tank and scattering the others. In the flashes of automatic gunfire rattling back and forth through the misty morning air, two of Nancarrow's men were killed.

Though the stalwart engineers had not killed the tank, they had distracted it. While it struggled to defend itself against the infantry, the German crew failed to notice Love's Hellcat lining up the furious panzer in its sights. Love's gunner tripped the electric trigger. The 76mm armor-piercing round slammed into the back of the Mark IV. Fire and smoke spewed out of the dark hatches and engine openings.[13]

0720–0830 hours, Monday, 25 December 1944
327th Glider Infantry Regiment command post
Inside Bastogne, Belgium

Back at his command post in Bastogne, Colonel Harper was frustrated. Although only a section of his widespread line had been attacked, it was obvious that part had been completely penetrated by Maucke's early morning daggerlike attack.

The initial, broken reports being relayed by radio were encouraging. Apparently, from what he could make out so far, the Germans had penetrated his MLR, but had not broken it. If the glidermen could take care of the enemy infantry, then the tanks would be vulnerable to antitank ambushes deeper within the perimeter. Until Major Jones reestablished contact with the rest of the 1/401st, though, Harper had no idea of what was happening on the battlefield. He was blind to the events occurring along the Hemroulle–Isle-la-Hesse road. He knew that with only bazookas, his men were vulnerable to just this type of enemy armor attack. Immediately, Harper called division HQ and requested armored reinforcements to plug the gaps.

Back at the Cave, McAuliffe was just starting to get a feel for what was happening in the northwest sector. "Mac" had to balance his trust for his subordinates. That is, to make sure they were feeding him real-time, immediate information, but also not overreacting to a situation that was still developing. After all, this could merely be part of an overall assault on the perimeter, or a feint prior to a larger attack somewhere else. McAuliffe carefully deliberated, as moving huge groups of infantry, armor, and artillery pell-mell around the perimeter could invite disaster. McAuliffe personally knew the caliber of "Bud" Harper, and because of that, he quickly granted Harper his wish. By 0735 hours, a tank and armored infantry team from Roberts's 10th Armored Division received orders to move out and buttress the northwest flank of the Bastogne perimeter. Unfortunately, it would take some time to get there.[14]

0720–0858 hours, Monday, 25 December 1944
115th Panzergrenadier Regiment command post
Near Flamizoulle

Across a great distance of smoke and fog that Christmas morning, Colonel Wolfgang Maucke was sharing much of the same frustrations as Colonel Harper. Maucke had also lost contact with some of his battalions. The last transmission from 1st Battalion was unintelligible, but he was able to make out that his 3rd Battalion was pinned down just west of Hemroulle. To find out what had happened to 1st Battalion, Maucke decided to send *Leutnant* Gaul, the regimental ordnance officer, in search of Wörner or his men. Gaul left Flamizoulle on a *kettenrad* tracked motorcycle and drove down the Marche road toward Isle-la-Hesse.

When the young officer pulled up near the crossroads at Isle-la-Hesse he found only Americans, who chased him off with heavy machine guns. Gaul was disturbed to see that there was no sign of his comrades in the area. He turned the *kettenrad* around and drove back to Flamizoulle to report to his commander. As he did, American artillery had started to pound Flamizoulle and Flamierge with high-explosive shells, disrupting German troop movements in the area, while Panzergrenadiers of 3rd Battalion, in vain, attempted to entrench in the nearby icy ground.[15]

At 0800 hours, Maucke finally received a communication from Dyroff and 3rd Battalion. It read, "0800 Hours . . . I and III Battalions stand 2.5 km west of Bastogne and encountering strong enemy resistance. The III Battalion has received heavy flanking fire from Hill 514, 505, and from the village of Hemroulle. 10th Company has occupied Hill 514 and has made no additional gains. The 11th Company, in position in front of the forest south of Hill 514, has received heavy tank and machine gun fire."[16]

Now Maucke knew something was wrong. Time was running out. By 0900 the skies would clear, meaning the return of the pestilent Allied fighter-bombers. Just in case, Maucke felt he had to be prepared if the tables were to turn. He ordered his engineer platoon to establish a defensive position on Hill 510 to the southeast of Flamizoulle. If the Americans were going to counterattack, Hill 510 might be the objective, since it dominated the surrounding terrain. In addition to this, he ordered his 2nd Battalion to back up his engineers and set up another defensive position north of Flamierge. To prevent American armor forces from overrunning them, Maucke used two Pak 40 AT guns from his 2nd Battalion to cover the area east of Flamizoulle and the road leading to Bastogne. Finally, for responsive artillery support, Maucke positioned his infantry gun company southwest of Flamizoulle. Their target would be Isle-la-Hesse. If things went wrong with the attack, Maucke knew he would now, at the least, have a sturdy rallying point.

Maucke's superior was also growing impatient with a lack of information. The abrupt manner in which Maucke had stormed off during the meeting the night before had Kokott wary of the good colonel and his determination to see this attack through. Kokott wanted to know whether panzers were inside Bastogne yet. Like most aggressive commanders, Kokott was impatient, and felt the need to pester his subordinate for constant information and updates, as if this would make a (by now somewhat) resentful Maucke work harder and faster.

But all of Kokott's exhortations and radio calls could not move 3rd Battalion. Unknown to him, Dyroff's Panzergrenadiers were dying. They lay defenseless in the snow while the glidermen of the 1/401st poured lead into their peppered ranks. Bullets were only part of the slaughter. The guns of the 463rd and the 377th had now zeroed in on the masses and were thoroughly decimating the ranks of the *landsers*. The artillery also happened to find Maucke's headquarters, whether by chance or the skill of a clear-eyed

American spotter will never be known. Regardless, several rounds slammed into it, knocking out all communications with his higher command. Maucke probably considered this a hidden blessing.[17]

At 0858 hours, Gaul returned from his hellish ride. He wasn't the bearer of glad tidings. Apparently, according to the officer, Major Wörner's 1st Battalion had been cut off. Moreover, no one in 3rd Battalion remained in contact with them. Even worse, the Americans had sealed the breach behind them. Maucke sensed that his 1st Battalion was gone, swallowed up, and all the men in it.[18]

0800–0830 hours, Monday, 25 December 1944
26th Volksgrenadier Division command post
Near Givry

Feeling his own pressure from von Manteuffel above, Kokott wanted answers. Any news of success would be something promising to pass on to his higher commander. He had also not heard a word from Schriefer's 77th since they'd launched their attack on Champs earlier that morning.

What is going on with the 77th Volksgrenadier Regiment? Kokott wondered.

In the small farmhouse at the Givry crossroads, eventually Kokott's young radio operator called out the details, adding information as it trickled in through his headset.

"Heavy fighting around Champs, to the south, penetration into the wooded sections west of Rolle. Fierce enemy counteraction."

Kokott paced. The 77th needed to do more in order for the operation to succeed. Kokott asked the radio operator where Kunkel's reconnaissance battalion could be.

His operator announced loudly, "Enemy counterthrusts repelled. Reconnaissance Battalion 26 continues attack in direction of Isle-la-Hesse."

Oddly, Kokott had not even heard from the commanders of units who were playing a smaller role in the assault—units that were being used to attack other portions of the American lines to basically serve as a distraction. Evidently these operations were not having the desired impact. Why? Kokott wanted to know. Surely these units, with less on their hands, would have reported by now. "What about the 39th Fusilier Regiment?"

The operator responded, "Despite strong enemy defense and heavy losses, attack in direction of Isle-le-Pre-Halte makes slow progress."

Kokott probably hoped for better news from the 901st Panzergrenadiers.

His operator could not oblige him, as he read the message aloud from the attached Panzer Lehr unit. "'Own assault troops approaching—advancing west of Marvie–Bastogne road. Strong enemy defense, heavy losses on our own side, final reserves committed.'"

Meanwhile, the news was not much better with the 78th Volksgrenadier Regiment and their attack. The report stated, "Own assault troops—advancing on both sides of Bastogne–Bourcy railroad line—approaching forest exit (1,400 meters) northeast of Luzery. Strong enemy fire."

All of these attacks were needed to fix the American forces in their respective areas in order to allow Maucke's regiment to break through the American forces in the northwest sector. If they failed to tie down the other American forces, McAuliffe's men, with their interior lines of communication, could rush reserves to block Colonel Maucke's armored thrust into Bastogne. The *Panzer Angriff* would fail.

Once again, Kokott tried contacting the 15th Panzergrenadier Division command post to find out the status of Maucke's attack. Finally some news, but it was a mixed answer. "Armored attack gains ground against strong enemy defense, come up close to Champs–Hemroulle road. Hemroulle and wooded sections to the north thereof held by the enemy. High losses on own side." Kokott sensed this must be the decisive moment of the operation, when everything hung in the balance. He was wrong. As the Panzergrenadiers continued to get cut down by Allen's men near Mande, and the tanks were continuing on, oblivious, victory was already slipping through his fingers.[19]

On the German gun line, the howitzers of the 26th Artillery Regiment shot salvo after salvo toward the American positions in order to support the ground forces. The main target areas were near Hemroulle, north of Hemroulle, and the roadway near Isle-la-Hesse. It mattered little. The American gunners, now using plenty of ammo, since this was obviously a major attack, pounded the German gun positions with pinpoint accuracy. The counter battery fire chewed up the earth in the areas around Champs, Grandes Fanges, Givry, Frenet, and Flamizoulle. Like Maucke, Kokott knew time was short.[20]

Kokott also realized that McAuliffe had far more guns—guns that could fire more accurately and were much more mobile in many respects than his own. In the war of artillery, the Americans would be the eventual winners. If he could not get into Bastogne Christmas morning, he would never get into Bastogne at all. If the Americans could hold Bastogne for another day or two, Patton would reach them.

0800–0900 hours, Monday, 25 December 1944
1st Platoon, B Company, 705th Tank Destroyer Battalion battle position
Near Rolle Château

At 0800 hours in the morning, the fog was still thick and sunrise was still half an hour away. The blankets of fog seemed to spread in the field that stretched before the Dreve de Mande—facing Hemroulle. Sergeant George N. Schmidt of Pardeeville, Wisconsin, took advantage of the opportunity to creep along the lane unobserved and find his tank destroyer section a perfect ambush spot. Schmidt's 1st Platoon section of B Company—his TD and that of Sergeant Adam Wans—had been called up by First Lieutenant Robert Andrews from Champs earlier that morning when the first word had spread of the German assault hitting the glidermen. Now he was going to try to do something about it.

Several feet taller than the German Mk IVs and StuG IIIs, the M18 Hellcat provided a bit more height for an observer standing in the turret. Schmidt and Wans had their drivers gun the twin M18s up from the Rolle courtyard and down the Lane of Trees before concealing themselves behind a set of ten-by-fifteen-foot haystacks. Even though Schmidt was looking down at Hemroulle from his position, due to the fog he still could not make out what was happening in the town.

He told his driver to head out into the field just southeast of the lane. The M18 rolled out about a hundred yards toward Hemroulle to get a better look. All of a sudden, Schmidt could see them rapidly poking through the fog—six or so of the Mk IV panzers and two or three of the squat little StuGs loitering around Allen's farmhouse headquarters. The veteran tank commander decided to fire several rounds at the tanks. The gun pounded as each round fired away, but because of the poor visibility, he could not tell whether he scored any hits. Now that he had the Germans' attention, Schmidt immediately ordered his driver to reverse the Hellcat and return to the concealed position near the haystack and trees.

Schmidt reported to Andrews about what he saw in Hemroulle. It was almost 0900, and the sun was beginning to burn off the fog. The curtain was rising. The second act of this deadly Christmas pageant was about to begin.[21]

No one had told Maucke that as far as the Americans were concerned, the final act was yet to come. Maucke's men who had ridden along with the tanks were taking a break only long enough to signal headquarters, wait for the infantrymen of Wörner's and Dyroff's battalions behind them, regroup, and push on into Bastogne.

Staring from the dark of the woods, the members of Captain Cody's C Company of the 502nd were catching their breath and preparing their weapons for the attack to regain Allen's HQ. As he prepared his squad in the woods across the road from the former headquarters, now owned and operated by the Germans, Sergeant Black and others noticed how nonchalant the Panzergrenadiers were as they milled about the burning farmhouse. Some even appeared to be making breakfast, oblivious to the counterattack that was about to happen.

The question holding up the Germans was, *Where to go from here?* It seemed they had penetrated the American positions. Again, now that light was breaking over the scene, the German tank commanders were perhaps confused. Were they in Bastogne? If not, how close were they to the town's entrance? Where was the rest of the infantry support? Remembering Maucke's meeting the night before, the officers certainly knew that Champs was to their left, up the road, and Bastogne, well . . . how far to the right? Without Maucke's requested reconnaissance, problems of orientation were starting to arise. Unsure of the ground or the American defenses here, the Germans found it unwise to press on to Bastogne without the infantry support. For the next hour, the tanks and infantry at the farmhouse just sat there, waiting for the foot soldiers to catch up.

As the German officers and tank commanders debated, their vehicle engines idling, the tired and hungry soldiers took advantage of the stop. Feeling cocksure that they had driven off or defeated the *Amis*, the hungry Panzertruppen started breaking out rations and eating. Others stood guard over the American prisoners they had just captured in the courtyard.

They had no idea that the glidermen had slaughtered the Panzergrenadiers from 3rd Battalion, who were supposed to be providing the bulk of the
infantry support for the attack. Those German troops, lying dead in the cold
snow hundreds of yards behind them, or taken prisoner by Allen's men,
would never catch up.

Captain Cody had organized the counterattack with as much firepower as
the paratroopers were able to muster. His plan was to use the farmhouse as a
point of fire, aiming everything at the courtyard and four tanks. Black remembered, "Halfway back to the farmhouse command post, we were cocky
about our chances of taking on all those German tanks. Out of nowhere
appeared two 705th U.S. TDs that showed up in the woods [D'Angelo's and
Vallitta's]. When we were within two hundred yards of the farmhouse, we
could see four of Jerry's tanks sitting there with their infantry milling
around the house."

Not all the paratroopers knew about the two M18s on their right, hidden in the trees. Apparently Cody was ignorant of their existence until after
the battle. Those who saw the sleek lines and deadly guns of the Hellcats
were emboldened now, knowing they could deal with the German armor.
Black believed the Germans had made a serious mistake in not coming after
them.[22]

Meanwhile, the Hellcats from Charlie Company girded themselves for
battle. Sergeant D'Angelo had noticed the frantic scramble of paratroopers
as his tank destroyer sped over to the woods. Dismounting, D'Angelo guided
first his and then Vallitta's M18s down the hidden firebreak trail, which
served as a cart path. Walking ahead of "No Love, No Nothing," he signaled the driver, June "Jeeps" Schultz, to bring the tank destroyer up a hill
about ten to twenty feet, close to the tree line, with a great view of the
Champs–Hemroulle road. Vallitta's driver, Paul "the Greek" Stoling, remembered Vallitta parking his tank parallel and about fifty yards to
the right of "No Love, No Nothing." Vallitta's tank was up a bit more
on the ridgeline, with a better view of the field before Rolle that they had
just crossed. Stoling remembered that the hiding place was good concealment, in the woods and on a little knoll, the long 76mm gun of their TD set
far back enough to be unseen from the edge of the woods. The height would
allow the two TDs to fire up to the ridgeline above the Champs–Hemroulle

road, but not be seen in turn. The loaders on both Hellcats then drew armor-piercing rounds from the turret ready racks and slammed the shells into the breeches, loading the guns for bear.

At about that time, First Sergeant Don "Moe" Williams, D'Angelo's Connecticut-born first sergeant, drove up in a Jeep to talk with the TD commanders. To keep a better eye on the approaching Germans, he and D'Angelo decided to stay outside the M18s and stroll the wood line. Williams knew where the panzer was that had shot at them earlier, and he wanted D'Angelo's Hellcat to surprise the tank from the rear. While they finalized their plans, explosions echoed in the distance. Looking up, they watched as a group of C Company paratroopers started their counterattack on the farmhouse across the road. Before D'Angelo and Williams could even finish their conversation, the boys in C Company had already started the battle.[23]

0850–0930 hours, Monday, 25 December 1944
502nd battle positions
Near Rolle Château and along the Champs–Hemroulle road

Maucke's 1st Battalion had to move. Their expected reinforcements had not shown up, and now they were in enemy territory with less than a battalion of infantry to support them. The sun was up, the fog had lifted, and they were out in the open, silhouetted against the pearl-white snow. If the *Jabos* showed up, the American fighter-bomber pilots could not have asked for better targets.

Without relaying their decision to Maucke, the German officers at the farmhouse arrived upon their own course of action. The first to move out were the StuGs. The platoon of three or four assault guns pushed northwest toward Champs in an apparent attempt to link up with the 77th Volksgrenadier Regiment.

Meanwhile, still hiding behind the haystack near the Dreve de Mande, Sergeant George Schmidt and his two Hellcats noticed the first two StuGs heading for the Champs–Hemroulle road. Schmidt's TD fired just as the lead vehicle crested the ridge, several hundred yards up the field and to his left. One StuG shuddered and died on the road. The second one, trailing behind it, had additional armor side skirts, or *schuerzen*, but they were of little use. The Hellcat was shooting at almost point-blank range. The round slammed into the side of the vehicle, dealing it a fatal blow.

Schmidt had claimed another tank, but now the jig was up. The Germans quickly located the pair of M18s as Schmidt ordered his crew and Wans's vehicle to back up from the haystack and take up a better position. Outnumbered, and before the Americans could reload, the panzer gunners coming across the field had them in their sights. The trail Mk IV closest to Hemroulle drew a bead on Schmidt's Hellcat. With a deafening crash, the TD erupted in flames. The impact of the 75mm *Panzergranate* (armor-piercing) round was so strong that the little Hellcat rolled backward. Crew members bailed out of the burning wreck. Inside the turret, Schmidt and a member of his crew, Private Manuel Rivas Jr., of Tombstone, Arizona, were both killed instantly. Wans's TD was hit soon after, its crew also bailing out, some with grievous injuries. Under small arms fire, the survivors crawled and dragged their wounded to the nearby trees and gullies near the lane.[24] In no time at all, the German tanks had blasted two American tank destroyers without missing a beat.

The rest of the German tanks, including at least four Mk IVs, started to move out from the farmhouse in the same direction, driving right for the approach to the Lane of Trees intersection to Rolle Château. Along the parallel tree line, several of Cody's troopers desperately dug into the snow and cold earth with helmets, entrenching shovels, or even their bare hands. The majority, however, simply lay down where they were, sighted their weapons, and opened fire.

The firing along the line seemed to move from the south to the north up the woods, following the moving Germans. Black and his men opened up as if on cue, pouring rifle, grenade, machine gun, and bazooka fire into the Germans directly across the road. Frank Miller remembered the attack well: "So when they [the Germans] started firing, they [officers] said 'fire at the flashes,'" Miller recounted. "Then they were firing and we were firing, we just kept shooting back and forth, it seemed like everybody was firing at once, and there were lots of flashes, you'd fire at flashes."[25]

Making for the road, the tank drivers had turned their flanks to the woods where Cody's men and Williams's TD section were hiding. The panzer turrets slowly rotated to the right, letting loose at the trees, but the Germans could see little in the way of targets. The paratroopers were staying low in their quickly constructed scrapes and holes, and Vallitta's and D'Angelo's Hellcats were set well back. German machine guns raked the woods, splintering fir trees left and right, but the fire was clearly random and panicked. The Americans, by contrast, were dropping by the dozens the

German soldiers caught out in the open and around the farmhouse without the protection of the tanks.[26]

"We opened up at the same time," Black said. "We poured all our rifle fire into that old farmhouse. All four [German] tanks took off north, headed down the road toward Champs, one right behind the other, as if the only thing that mattered was saving the tanks."[27]

One panzer, the Mk IV responsible for destroying Schmidt's Hellcat, turned in the opposite direction of its comrades and headed south toward Hemroulle, leaving a total of four or five Mk IVs bearing northwest toward Champs. This tank, nicknamed *"Lustmolch"* ("Happy Salamander") by its crew, attempted to make good its getaway toward Hemroulle.[28]

Not so for the others. C Company and Captain Stone's ad hoc headquarters force that had raced out from Rolle down the Dreve de Mande thoroughly raked the panzers with a storm of small-arms fire. They shredded the tanks of the last few infantrymen riding on the backs of the vehicles and then proceeded to pour fire into anything that moved on the ground.

Using the slope near the road for protection, the Americans dived to the ground and fired from a prone position at anything coming on, across, or diagonal to the road.[29]

Baker Company's platoon, under Hanlon's command in the zigzag tree plantation to the north, opened fire. Even though they were firing from a much longer range, they strafed the oncoming Germans with machine guns from a new direction. Just as the 1/401st had done, the paratroopers and tank destroyers had caught the Germans in another trap as they hit them from three sides: the west, the north, and the south. Panzergrenadiers fell backward in the snow, literally in heaps of bodies. There was no cover, and the German tanks started racing farther away from the panicked soldiers. Hanlon was so close to the tanks and infantry, he could read the various stencils on the panzers and see the intense expressions on the Panzergrenadiers' faces. As he walked by one of his paratroopers, he asked the man how the Germans had managed to penetrate their lines.

The paratrooper replied, "Beats me. But they'll have a hell of a time getting out." Hanlon knew this man was right. The carnage was confirming this soldier's prediction.[30]

Near the regimental headquarters, two 81mm mortar crews had pooled their resources. There was a shortage of mortar parts and ammo. One group had supplied the tripod and baseplate, while another crew brought the tube. Then, using radios, they linked up with forward observers who performed call-for-fire missions on the panicked Germans near the captured farmhouse. Within minutes, the crews had fired 102 rounds of ammunition on the German infantry. The result was a rain of devastation on the remaining German troops.[31] As a result, the last remaining grenadiers started to run from Allen's captured headquarters and out into the open.

Black watched the bedlam as some of the Germans raced from the farmhouse to catch up with their comrades riding on the back of the tanks. Unfortunately, almost as fast as they could do so, they were being shot, pitching off the decks of the panzers and falling into the snow.[32] Gunfire continued to reverberate through the air. By now the battle around Allen's former HQ had turned into a one-sided affair, with the Americans in possession of the farmhouse once again. The German soldiers, some hunkered down in the open field nearby, were unable to mount much of an attack. Others tried brave assaults in the direction of the woods, but that only made it easier for the Americans to cut them down in groups. Bazooka rounds lanced out from the woods like arrows of fire trailing smoke, trying to find a moving tank as it sped down the road, spewing snow and ice in its wake. Now that the panzers had exposed their flanks to the American TDs, the perfect opportunity presented itself.[33]

Black remembered walking the tree line, encouraging the men of his squad to keep up their fire. He crouched close to one of the two tank destroyers in the woods. He overheard "Moe" Williams and Tony D'Angelo talking near him. Williams guaranteed Layton that his M18s would "get those sonsabitches for ya."[34]

"Williams asked me to hold up my men while he taught the Germans a small lesson in tank warfare," Layton recalled.[35]

D'Angelo could not believe his eyes. There in front of him, at a range of about three hundred yards, were four German Mk IVs, with their lightly armored flanks exposed, grinding along the road toward the Dreve de Mande and the town of Champs beyond. The Germans had not seen him in the woods. As he had told the paratrooper lieutenant, this was the way it was supposed to be done in the tank destroyer corps. In fact, this was a picture-perfect, textbook position for an attack.[36]

The 76mm could penetrate the German armor, but only at close range. Unlike the German 8.8cm KwK 43 and the 7.5cm KwK 40 L/48 tank guns, the American 76mm penetration performance dropped off considerably at long range. The tanks, D'Angelo noted, were perfectly within the 550-yard range for maximum penetration with the armor-piercing rounds he had. At close range like that, D'Angelo knew his rounds could get through the two-inch side armor on the StuGs and Mk IVs. That is, if they hit. There could be no misses. The firing had to be fast, furious, and accurate, for if the panzers located their position, D'Angelo's and Vallitta's tank destroyers would join the fate of the other two M18s earlier that morning.[37]

A Mk IV or two had already slipped past, but D'Angelo would be damned if the others would get away. Right before him, traveling one after another at a speed of about fifteen miles per hour, were two Mk IVs. The tanks' camouflage was mixed and mottled with a sloppy application of white paint. Smoke arose from the panzers' exhaust as the engines revved and the drivers shifted into a faster gear.[38] Another clot of white-coated infantry soldiers fell from the back of one of the tanks, several twitching in the snow as Stone's group and C Company continued to fire. Over the noise of the gunfire, the rumbling engines of the tanks, and the shouts of the men in combat, it was, thankfully, hard to hear the screams of the dying and wounded Panzergrenadiers. Bullets ricocheted and spun off the tank armor in strange sparking flashes.

Standing under "No Love, No Nothing's" gun, D'Angelo shouted to his gunner, Sam Dedio. "I told him to take the last tank first, and then one at a time on up the line and fire when ready."[39]

Vallitta shouted a similar command to his crew. Tucked into the driving compartment of his M18, but with a good view of the action, Stoling heard Vallitta working off D'Angelo's plan to box the Germans inside the trap. "He [Vallitta] told us to take the lead tanks," Stoling remembered.[40]

D'Angelo's gunner, Dedio, set his sights on one of the tanks and fired first. There was a deafening *crack!* from the 76mm gun. Mesmerized by the sight of the enemy, D'Angelo had forgotten he was right underneath the gun. "Because of that, my left ear is dead from that battle."

The round struck the rear of the last panzer, where the armor was thin. The German tank slewed to a halt, smoking furiously. D'Angelo noticed Dedio had popped up from the turret to look.

"I told him to get the hell down, there's two more!"[41]

Vallitta's tank destroyer fired to the right of "No Love, No Nothing," hitting one of the German tanks, but the others kept coming.

D'Angelo's adrenaline was pumping now. He had Schultz back up the

Hellcat and reposition it, angled a bit more to the right, as some of Dedio's shots were hitting trees. Vallitta's gunner, Corporal Lewis M. Clark, was a bit more experienced than Dedio—his shot had been a direct hit.[42]

Nevertheless, the rest would have to be up to Dedio, as Vallitta's gun went down. The last round had overheated and stuck in the chamber, Stoling recalled. Stoling had to reverse Vallitta's M18 into the woods and the trail so the crew could take out the rammer and knock the shell casing out. To Vallitta's frustration, he had lined up his Hellcat on one of the best shots he would ever have during the war, but the jammed round had rendered his vehicle hors de combat.[43]

This was not the case for "No Love, No Nothing." Dedio fired the main gun repeatedly. D'Angelo's crew worked fast, loading each round like they were on an assembly line. Loader James P. Proulx would slide the long brass round in the breech of the angled 76mm gun. Once the breechblock snapped closed, he would shout, "Up!" Dedio, on the left of the turret, would line the target up in the single-lensed gunsight. When the crosshairs were on target, Dedio would depress the electric gun trigger—a foot pedal on the turret floor. With a great blast, the gun would fire, the recoil knocking the spent and smoking shell out into a canvas bag on the turret floor. Proulx would then pull another round from the rack in front of him, shove it in the breech, and the whole cycle would repeat.

By the last of six or more shots, four German tanks were burning wrecks just short of the lane to Rolle.[44] Sergeant Black, who witnessed the action, proclaimed:

"The TD next to me fired six shots. Two hit big trees, four hit tanks, and four were knocked out. It was the best I ever saw."[45]

One of Dedio's shots was thrown at the rear of an Mk IV that was making for the intersection at the Dreve. The TD crews saw the brief glow of the reddish orange tracer in the back of the AP shot as it sped away. D'Angelo swears that if Dedio had led the German a bit more, it would have gone right up the back and into the fuel tank. Unfortunately, it missed, and the tank motored past.[46]

The last panzer struggled to steer around the wrecks of the others. The Panzergrenadiers had been cleared from its deck a ways back. D'Angelo remembers watching the vehicle flare up after Dedio, his gunner, hit it in the rear. There were intense, white-hot flames as the vehicle's ammo ignited inside the steel tomb.

"I saw something come out of the top and roll onto the back of the tank there, jeez, I thought it was an animal or something," he said. "It was a German crewman engulfed in flames."[47]

Although two Mk IVs had now slipped past, heading for Champs, D'Angelo and Vallitta had accounted for four of the German tanks and blunted the last of the German drive. The 502nd had taken care of the infantry. The paratroopers rapidly silenced any pockets of resistance still trying to fight on in the trampled snow. Teams of paratroopers from B and C companies, as well as Stone's group, cautiously moved out to take prisoners. The *landsers* seemed all too willing to surrender, realizing that without their armor there was no hope now.

The pair of Mk IVs that had escaped D'Angelo and Vallitta's ambush was now passing the Rolle intersection at the Dreve de Mande. Up ahead, part of Baker Company and the 1st Battalion's commander were waiting for them. Hanlon was aware that the other German tanks behind were being shot up by something in the trees to the south. He knew that the demolition-trained paratroopers had placed antitank mines on this part of the road, but had dragged them off the road the other day when rumors surfaced that Patton's tankers were coming through to link up. Now Hanlon and his troopers could only hope one of the tanks would miss the road or veer enough to run into one of the ditches.[48]

The first German tank kept coming, heading straight for his men.

Sergeant Schuyler "Sky" Jackson ran as fast as he could in the snow through the Rolle courtyard as soon as he had heard the news that the Germans were attacking. Along the way, he had passed the many stacks of provisions and equipment, some of it under tarps along the short stone wall leading out of the courtyard gate. Jackson's expertise was combat engineering. He did demolitions for the regimental HQ, and combat engineers knew how to use bazookas. Seeing one leaning against the wall, Jackson took it, hoping the soldier who was chasing after him would be a good loader. Up ahead, over the cusp of the hill and along the Lane of Trees, Jackson could hear gunfire and the growling noise of German vehicles changing gears. Other men from Stone's group had gone to ground just short of the road and were opening up a fusillade on any remaining German infantry. Jackson was more intent on a tank.

"We had mined the bridge leading to the château," Jackson remembered years later. "But it was so cold that everything froze and we couldn't blow it up."

He continued. "I ran out the door and saw five tanks coming through the snow with the German infantrymen riding on them. I ran and got a bazooka as the rest of our guys ran out and reinforcements starting coming in from the town."

Several troopers recognized Jackson as he ran past, already a well-known figure in the 502nd, since he had been decorated for action in Normandy, and he had served as Colonel George Van Horn Moseley Jr.'s bodyguard after D-day. The identification would help later.

Jackson was hot on the heels of the slow-moving Mk IV, which now was bereft of its riders. He rounded the Rolle Lane of Trees, keeping the tall pines on his right for cover, and stood behind the second tree trunk before the road intersection. The German tank had chugged past menacingly. Jackson had a perfect line on it, and brought the bazooka up to his shoulder. The shot was less than a hundred yards, he recalled: "I was behind this tree. Right after it passed, I stepped out and let him have it with my bazooka."

Jackson watched as the rocket shot into the tank's engine compartment. There was a brief blast and oily smoke billowed out of the back of the tank. The Panzer rolled to a stop in the roadside ditch about twenty-five yards north of the intersection. The German crew immediately began to bail out through the hatches. "The crew came out fighting. They did not surrender," Jackson said. Because they were armed, "we had to shoot them," he said. As they evacuated their smoking vehicle, Stone's men poured a fusillade of fire into the five crewmen until they fell from the tank and stopped moving.[49]

Seeing the second tank driving up the rise toward Champs a bit farther on, Jackson tried to pull a double. Shouting at his loader above the gunfire, he told the man to reload a new rocket. Unfortunately, the nervous headquarters trooper forgot to pull the curved safety pin before clamping the ignition wires of the rocket to the bazooka tube. As Jackson shouted, "Clear!" and the second rocket whooshed from the barrel, he already had a feeling it would be a "one-in-a-million shot."

Unbelievably, the rocket hit the turret of the second tank but, unarmed, simply bounced around inside the *schuerzen* turret armor until the rocket engine burned out. Jackson swore at his assistant as the panzer continued around the corner, out of view, toward Champs.[50]

Hanlon's men were unable to locate this missing or "rogue" tank. Strangely, and almost mystically, this single tank seemed to then disappear for several hours.[51]

Barnes, the medical evacuation officer, remembered the scene: "One soldier [presumably Jackson or his loader] pounded me on the back, kept shouting that he hit one tank with his bazooka, but in the excitement had not armed it and all that happened was a loud clang when it hit the tank."

Walking through the crowd of happy troopers slapping one another on the back and whooping it up, Barnes noticed the carnage in front of the château. "Four German tanks were in sight, smoking, and the ground was strewn with bodies, some clothed in white."[52]

0930–1100 hours, Monday, 25 December 1944
502nd Battle Positions
Near Rolle and along the Champs–Hemroulle road

In the area around the Rolle Château, the Baker Company's zig-zag plantation position, and the woods where Charlie Company and the two tank destroyers had parked, the battle began to wind down.[53] Germans who were trying to hold out in the field—which was strewn with the bodies of their comrades and burning tanks, and had not an ounce of cover—opted to surrender. When the firing slackened, groups of grenadiers walked forward, hands in the air, as select patrols of paratroopers carefully stepped into the woods and hollows to disarm the enemy and march them toward Bastogne.

The paratroopers were taking no chances, and if a command of "*Hände hoch!*" ("Hands up") did not get an immediate response, then the Screaming Eagles would shoot first and ask questions later. Some of the more curious Americans waited until the fires had died down in the tanks and went to examine their handiwork. Remembering the crew member burned to death on the back of the tank, D'Angelo declined.

"I didn't want to see that." He said, "I mean, that was still some mother's son."[54]

For others, the end of the battle was a relief. When the Germans had overrun Allen's headquarters, they captured several men of 2nd Platoon. Now, as Layton Black and others collected the German prisoners, they discovered their comrades still in the farmhouse where Black and his soldiers had left them. For some of the liberated men, revenge gripped their senses. Black remembered one such awful incident:

After the fight, we "mopped up" the battleground area—the thick trees, hillside, farmhouse, barn and yard. Now freed, our 2nd

Platoon men who had been captured and held by Jerry wanted some sort of revenge. Our round-up was like a fox drive, where you drive all the foxes into a small circle and then capture or kill them. W.O. "Big" Holly [Sergeant William "Holly" Hollingsworth] and I went hunting together. We found a badly wounded German soldier at the edge of the fir trees. He was wounded too badly to speak or move. Seated with him in the snow was a soldier that couldn't have been more than fourteen years old. He was half frozen and scared to death. We saw that the boy was not going to be able to move his wounded friend, so I went for help.

When Black returned, they took the wounded man and boy to a group of German prisoners under guard by members of the 101st. The boy had struggled to try to help move the injured comrade. The other German soldiers were berating the boy and blaming him for the wounded man's certain death. Just then:

"At this moment one of our own troopers walked out of nowhere, moved into the circle and dropped to one knee. He took aim with his rifle and fired point-blank, shooting the boy through the head. He was dead before he hit the ground."

Black admitted he had become somewhat numb to the killing as well. He wrote: "The sick and disgusted feeling I had was only for the way our officer had killed the boy, not that he had done so."[55]

Now that the sun was out and the morning fog had burned off, the scene before the Americans was bright and vivid. About their positions lay the bodies of German soldiers, twisted and still, staining the snow red with their blood and viscera. In some places where the cross fire had been intense, the corpses were stacked on top of one another in piles, as if some great being had dumped a load of rag dolls in the snow. The still hulks of German tanks dotted the landscape. Some poured smoke out in a great black spiral that rose to the sky. Others merely steamed and sizzled in the snow.

Black and the rest of Charlie Company counted some thirty-five German prisoners and sixty-seven Germans killed in their sector.[56] There were very few casualties among the Americans. By 1100, it was clear to both the Americans and Germans that paratroopers and tank destroyers had stopped dead Maucke's armored attack.

In the woods across from the farmhouse, D'Angelo felt "relieved."[57] He still had no interest in taking a closer look at his deadly work. He was tired from being up all night and day, and his ears were still ringing from "No Love, No Nothing's" gun blasting so close to his head.

To this day, D'Angelo still believes the action was a validation of the training and intense gunnery practice the 705th had been put under by Colonel Templeton. While stateside, the men of the 705th had earned a reputation at Fort Hood, Texas, as some of the best shots in the tank destroyer corps.[58] He admitted, however, that luck, or something else, played a part in the outcome Christmas Day.

D'Angelo said, "By the grace of God, we got our rounds off before the Germans, or it would have been a different story."[59]

D'Angelo and Vallitta made sure the ready rack in both turrets was restocked with ammo, and then took a moment to smoke a cigarette and relax with their crews. Around them, the Charlie Company paratroopers were digging in and enlarging their fighting positions along the wood line, in anticipation of another attack. Others were rounding up and counting pale and shocked German prisoners. A short time later, D'Angelo remembered Colonel Templeton driving up to his TD with First Sergeant "Moe" Williams and a bottle of scotch: "Colonel Templeton came up to me and said, 'Job well done! Here sergeant, give your boys a drink.'" The Wellsville, Ohio, native took a swig and passed the bottle around to his crew. Templeton then handed out the first warm meal the tank destroyer crews had seen in days. "That meal was hot cakes. It tasted every doggone bit as good as turkey did when you're into your K-rations!" D'Angelo recalled.

D'Angelo was glad to be alive and glad things had quieted down in his area. Nonetheless, he had orders to stay in the Rolle sector and work with the 502nd in case of any further attacks that day.

"We had no more problems the rest of the day. As a matter of fact, I had a good [Christmas] day after that."[60] Although the 502nd paratroopers and Templeton's TDs had eliminated Maucke's northern column, the rest of the German force was still barreling towards Hemroulle to the south. The threat to Bastogne was not over yet, and all that stood between the town and the Germans was Cooper's "Bastard Battalion" of artillerymen.

CHAPTER ELEVEN

"Let the Shit Hit the Fan!"

(CHRISTMAS DAY)

"One saw men lying nearly everywhere who were mortally wounded and whose heads, arms, and legs had been shot off. . . . Likewise on watch and on post in the lines, on trench and work details, they were wounded by the fearfully heavy fire."[1]

—Account by a Hessian soldier

0730–0900 hours, Monday, 25 December 1944
Along the 463rd Parachute Field Artillery gun line,
Able, Baker, and Dog batteries
Hills east of Hemroulle, Belgium

The Americans could not have possibly guessed where the rest of Maucke's attack force was going. Stalled on the hills above the town of Hemroulle, the tanks and infantry seemed to pause, engines rumbling, exhaust rising over the woods. They waited, ready to pounce, hundreds of yards from the American defenders dug in around the village. The force was still only a mile or so from the outskirts of Bastogne.

To Ken Hesler, the twenty-year-old who had been on sentry duty for the 463rd just outside of Hemroulle all night, the foreboding sense of attack was overwhelming. After witnessing the bombing of Bastogne and being woken up to pull guard duty twice that night, he had quickly "gone horizontal" again in the warming tent off the Hemroulle road.

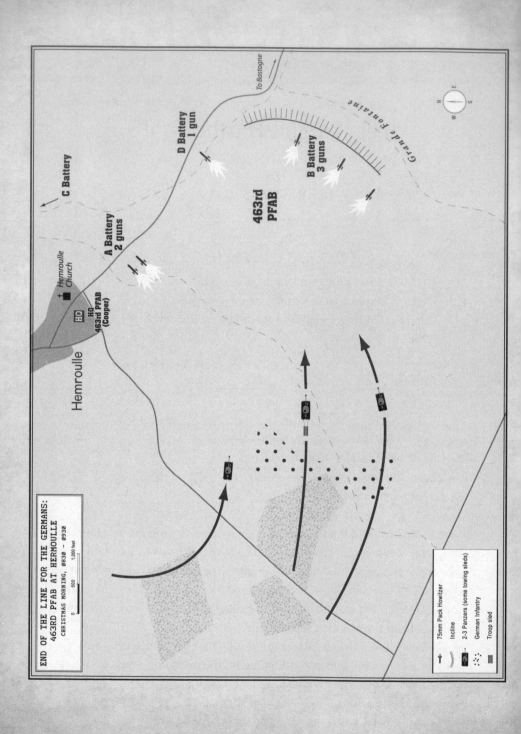

END OF THE LINE FOR THE GERMANS:
463RD PFAB AT HERMOULLE

CHRISTMAS MORNING, 0630 - 0930

0   500   1,000 feet

Hemroulle

Hemroulle
Church

HQ
463rd PFAB
(Cooper)

A Battery
2 guns

C Battery

D Battery
1 gun

To Bastogne

Grande Fontaine

B Battery
3 guns

463rd
PFAB

N
W   E
S

75mm Pack Howitzer

Incline

2-3 Panzers (some towing sleds)

German Infantry

Troop sled

"I think it was about six-seven Christmas morning, I heard a commotion that woke me up. I pulled on my boots—shoepacs with the felt lining. We always took them off in the warming tent to dry. I grabbed my M1 and went out with one to two others. We knew something was going on, but we didn't know what. We just went out, ran up to this ridge overlooking Hemroulle and took up positions. I got there when B Battery was just about to move its guns."

To add to his anxiety, it suddenly occurred to Hesler that if the German tanks made it to his position, there wasn't much he and his comrades could do. ". . . [I]t wasn't enough to stop anybody if they were coming—we only had rifles."[2]

The Germans were regrouping before they decided to roll down into Hemroulle. At this point, the German tank commanders might have mistaken Hemroulle for the outskirts of Bastogne. Unknown to the Germans, they were about to become trapped in a net of fire. It was the brainchild of Lieutenant Colonel John T. Cooper.

"As it began to snow and ammo decreased to critical conditions, we organized our battalion for the possibility of stand and fight, for there were no other places to go," Cooper wrote after the war. "We posted, dug in outpost guards with telephone communications to battalion HQ as well as to the battery they represented. Guns covering all tank approaches were dug in and prepared. Our guns were mutually supporting. Banking on the fact that a tank will attack a gun head on, we had another gun that would have a side shot at the tank."

Cooper continued to describe his setup: "The preparation for the tank attacks we received on Christmas Day had been planned and set up for several days. Snow had covered the gun positions. All we had to do was move our gun section in and start shooting."[3]

To the American command in Bastogne, Colonel Cooper's foresight was remarkable. His work prepping the 463rd's area of operations for antitank defense was a godsend. Days earlier, he ordered his men to dig out U-shaped berms from the frozen earth, located about fifty to a hundred yards ahead of the regular direct-fire positions. With the small guns wheeled into these positions, the profile of both gun and gun crew was kept to a minimum, and the barrels of the 75mm Packs could be lowered to shoot straight and true at any tank that closed on them. Cooper's plan, as laid out and practiced by the gun crews, was to have one of the guns in each battery fire at the first tank in an assault, while the other guns went after the rest. Hesler described the crew responsibilities and positions on each gun:

> There were generally four to a crew, and usually about four to five more. The other four to five were ammo carriers. The gunner [on the left] would set the azimuth at zero traverse and set the elevation. The assistant gunner [on the right] would set and open the breech, close it, and fire it by pulling the lanyard. The third guy would place the ammo in the breech. The fourth guy was back a bit and he was the fuse-setter.[4]

To protect the flanks of the guns, Cooper had his men dig foxholes on each side of the battery positions, occupied by machine gun and bazooka teams. These were the battalion security crews—members of the 463rd who were specifically delegated with the responsibility of protecting the batteries from enemy infantry.

Those busy days before Christmas, Cooper's experience from combat in Sicily was showing. His command and coordination, outposting of his forward observers (FOs), and communication structure were among the best-organized parts of the American defense in that sector. For the doubting Thomases and those who were still under the impression that his unit was made up of greenhorns, watching the batteries of the 463rd set up around Hemroulle had impressed them, to say the least. That Christmas Day, the veteran gunners of the 463rd were about to impress them even more.

It would be hard to determine exactly how many German vehicles reached Cooper's trap. By 0730 hours, members of the 463rd security teams, emplaced in foxholes in the fields and farmyards to the southwest of Hemroulle, were firing bazookas, heavy machine guns, and basically anything they could get their hands on as the Germans entered their lines near the woods. Noise and confusion were rampant. Some of these bazooka hits may have taken a toll on the German tanks. It was this gunfire that woke Hesler up that morning.

Wisely, Klampert's and Love's tank destroyer units that had been firing repeatedly since Maucke's *schwerpunkt* had punctured Allen's lines had backed off just short of the long hill west of Hemroulle. It would not be a good idea to follow in too closely, lest the Hellcats be mistaken by their own artillery as part of the German force.

Long-range artillery fire may have scored a direct hit or two on several of the German tanks as well. Regardless of the number of remaining German tanks in the southern column, obviously the threat to Bastogne was still very real. The best that can be figured is that as the gunners of the 463rd were moving their howitzers into the antitank positions, probably three to four German Mk IV panzers (some towing infantry sleds) and accompanying infantry were staring right down on them.[5]

The word had reached Cooper earlier that even with the valiant work of his artillery barrages, the 1/401st troopers, and the tank destroyers, enemy tanks and infantry were still heading his way. In fact, Cooper told his men to stack their barracks bags in a big pile and be prepared to burn them if the Germans broke into Hemroulle. Later, as the German tanks closed that gap and got even closer to his HQ, Cooper was nervous enough to order all classified documents and the M-209 cryptographic machine destroyed.[6]

That morning, on command from Major Victor Garrett, the fire operations officer, the artillery crews of Baker Battery manhandled their stubby guns into the special dug-out antitank positions they had prepared. The guns numbered one, three, and four were wheeled around 180 degrees from their position along the bank of the Rau de Petite Fontaine creek and pushed up a steep embankment. First Lieutenant Joseph Lyons, executive officer of Battery B, explained the need for repositioning the 463rd's guns:

A little after dawn on Christmas morning, we got a call from the officer of number one gun in Baker battery. He reported that tanks were visible about six hundred yards from his position. Baker Battery was equipped with six guns; however, we had only three guns that could shoot in that sector. The guns were numbered one through six, and guns numbered one through three were pointed towards the enemy tanks. According to the orders from headquarters, we had to have the guns shoot 360 degrees; just in case the Germans did break through, we could have guns covering any field of fire.[7]

Through field glasses, Lyons and his commanding officer, Captain Ardelle E. Cole, kept a nervous eye on the dark shapes ahead as their men prepped the guns for antitank work.

One of the gun crews from Dog Battery—the battery to the right of B and aligned on the Hemroulle road—heaved one of their weapons into an antitank position near the other three guns. This was to fill in for B Battery's fourth gun, which was still positioned for indirect fire. Instantly the mission of these four weapons had changed from the FO's earlier demands for indirect artillery barrages to straight-up antitank defense.[8]

At 1,339 pounds and well balanced, the M1A1 75mm Pack howitzer was a wonderful—if, by comparison to its bigger brothers, small—gun. The Pack howitzer was easy enough to move—it could be physically pushed into place by its four-man crew or towed by a jeep; it was for this reason that it was specifically chosen by the airborne divisions. The gun was designed to be taken apart and loaded in a glider, or even para-dropped in pieces to be assembled on the ground. The mobility of the little guns was about to save the day.[9] "The [M8] pack howitzer was well balanced and fairly easy to move with those big tires," Hesler acknowledged. "Several men could do it—it had that ring in the front to help."[10]

Private First Class Walter J. Peplowski, part of B Battery, gun number three's crew, also remembered moving the guns that morning: "The number 3 pack howitzer with [Clifford] Wolfenberger, Silvas and Peplowski as a full gun crew was used. If it wasn't for the powerful George Silvas of Corpus Christi, Texas, I don't know if we could have made it up hill through the soft snow to the gun pit."

The men threw open the wooden ammo chests containing the special M66 antitank rounds, (fortunately still in abundance, since the guns had been called on rarely in the antitank role since their arrival near Hemroulle) and loaded each gun for bear.

Peplowski wrote a description years later. In an exciting present tense, he described the action on his own gun: "Now the howitzer is in the pit—all ammo is taken out of the cases. The bare shells lined up in perfect order: HE, WP, HE, WP, HE, WP, etc. The barrel is traversed to the tanks on the extreme left. We wait knowing to fire now would invite disaster, powder snow, smoke, a real give away."[11]

As each loader slammed the breech on his weapon closed, the gunners spun the small elevating wheel, drastically lowering the muzzle. The men sat quietly behind each gun, waiting for the Germans to make their move. In the dim light of dawn, the four guns were now pointed at the shapes of the German tanks idling on the hill.

In a position forward of Baker Battery was an atypical young tech sergeant from Tennessee with an even more atypical nickname. He was ducked down in a hole behind a ridge of snow. The German Mk IVs had parked only about a hundred yards from Carson "Booger" Childress's position.

Childress and his security team, armed with rifles and a machine gun, had been quietly keeping an eye on the Germans for more than an hour. Childress was so close that he could hear the Germans talking, and could smell the coffee the cocky Panzertruppen were making as they sat and prepared— of all things—breakfast.[12]

Behind the forward positions, Claude D. Smith, B Battery's first sergeant, had grown tired of Captain Cole waking him up early each morning, ordering him to rouse the men and prepare the guns in case of a tank attack. Smith was starting to feel his commander was like the boy who cried wolf a few times too often. This morning—Christmas—Smith decided to sleep in. Cole called Smith in his foxhole near Hemroulle and told him to get up immediately:

"Sergeant Smith, if you are going to get up, it had better be now!" Cole barked into the radio. Recognizing the urgency in Cole's voice, Smith threw off his wool blanket and ran toward his lieutenant (Lyons) and the B Battery positions.[13]

Lyons crouched near his number one gun, which was to the left of Peplowski's number three gun and the number two gun (4th Section) commanded by Sergeant William D. Wood. The D Battery howitzer that had joined them to their far right was commanded by Sergeant Russell Derflinger. Two A Battery guns were also brought in for support, several hundred yards to the north and just alongside the Hemroulle road.[14]

One of Lyons's men, Private Merle W. McMorrow, shivered in the cold morning as he got the alert. McMorrow was a replacement who had served in the First Airborne Task Force in the invasion of southern France. When the panzers showed up along the ridgeline in front of the battery, he had been in the rear when a message came in over the phone, ordering them to head to the guns. McMorrow dashed over to one of the howitzers in B Battery. When he arrived he could hear the panzer engines in the darkness. As the sunlight finally crept over the horizon, the young paratrooper could make out several tanks along the ridgeline in front of him.

Later on, McMorrow recalled, ". . . there was more excitement than fear in the group. We usually never had an opportunity to see the enemy we were firing at." Each weapon had to be bore-sighted, because the German tanks were so close. In other words, the gunners could not use the sights, but opted for looking straight down or through the bore, much like a pheasant hunter would do with an antique shotgun. McMorrow remembered the process. He wrote, "It involved direct fire and the gun had to be moved down the slope slightly to get the tube depressed sufficiently to get the tanks in the gun sight."[15]

With everything in place now, the tension mounted. Everyone was waiting for Cooper's order to open fire. Lyons shivered in the morning cold. "Joe," he said to the gunner on one of his howitzers, "when you start firing, for God's sakes don't fire over." Lyons explained his reasoning later: "If you fire short, at least you get a ricochet shot. I was really wasting my time telling him that because he was such a good gunner. I knew he would instinctively do it. We waited about three or four minutes."[16]

The gunners wondered why they were waiting. Lyons passed on the message from the 463rd switchboard: Cooper wanted to make dead sure the tanks were German and not friendly armor. It was rumored that Patton's own tanks were nearby, trying their hardest this morning to bust into Bastogne. Cooper asked Lyons to see if he could tell whether the tanks had a muzzle brake (a knobby device on the end of German tank barrels to help eliminate the effects of gun flash. American tanks, at least in late 1944, typically did not have muzzle brakes).[17]

No sooner was Lyons peering through his field glasses to confirm this in the dim light than the Germans suddenly started to move. The panzer crews crawled back into their vehicles with the clanging of hatches slamming shut. Maybach engines roared to life. Some of the German soldiers started strolling forward cautiously, while others climbed back onto the tanks and sleds as the vehicles began a slow crawl down the hill.

Peplowski continued to narrate his anxious wait in the present tense: "The snow is melting as we kneel this Christmas morning. My knees are wet. We talk about the range and decided that a lead of 2 ¼ to 2 ½ tank lengths would be just right; also to drop rounds, aim lower so there would be no overs. The leading tank swerves, others follow just like in the book. We joke a little—the tension is broken. We know soon firing will commence and will move like hell. Wolfenberger is gunner, a cool, calm, efficient and accurate one."[18]

The German tanks and infantry seemed to be heading to the south and east of the 463rd's positions, rumbling across the field, trying to drive wide around Hemroulle and head into Bastogne. Cooper's men realized the Germans had to be stopped. The machine guns and bazooka men on security were the first to open up.

Corporal Nicholas Bellezza, Private First Class Aloysius Fredericks, and an unnamed green recruit were manning a .50-caliber machine gun near the Baker Battery gun line. They opened fire at the German soldiers as they advanced:

"On Christmas Day, at daybreak, I noticed through the haze, approximately 350 yards, the outlines of tanks which were located directly in front of my position," Bellezza recounted in a letter years later. "I immediately called the switchboard for verification to find out if they were our tanks. The response was negative."

As the Germans around the tanks began to move, Bellezza pushed the butterfly trigger on the M2 and started firing. "German fire was returned (white tracers) at my position. The recruit had said 'Don't fire, they may see us!' He was so scared that he left the gun position leaving Fredericks and me to keep firing. The barrel got so hot we had to stop and change it. Fredericks in his haste grabbed the barrel instead of using asbestos gloves. His burns were minor."[19]

By this time, First Sergeant Smith had reached Lyons's position, but not without difficulty. "I came out of my foxhole on the run and all I could see was a bunch of tracer bullets flying from all directions . . . there was a lot of lead flying around. I made a mad dash for the command post and found Captain Cole and Lieutenant Lyons already there. From the information I was able to obtain, the Germans had us in a circle and had launched their major attack."

Smith was just in time to witness that, "One of our machine gun crews noticed a bush that appeared to have grown larger overnight: Just to limber up their guns, they fired at the bush and it began to move and out came three German tanks. I was able to locate and identify them through my field glasses and requested Capt. Cole order our guns to open fire. He said no, they may be our tanks. I knew from the muzzle break [sic] they were German tanks, because our tanks don't have them. A few seconds later, the tanks fired on the three of us." Cole quickly changed his mind at that point, and ordered his men to open fire.[20]

Cooper finally had his confirmation. Lyons and the other battery commanders could see the muzzle brakes and low silhouettes easily now. There was no mistaking it—these were not Patton's Shermans—but German Mk IVs. Cooper had set up a previous code for the batteries. From his command post in a stone farmhouse across from the Hemroulle chapel, Cooper told Major Garrett to relay the radio order: "Let the shit hit the fan!"[21] With that blunt and earthy command, the battery commanders for Baker and Dog batteries whispered the order to their gun crews, spurring the gunners to pull the lanyards almost simultaneously on four gun breeches.

There were multiple shots. Some of the rounds tracked over; some of the lower rounds hit the snow and sent up jets of ice as they skipped like a massive stone on a pond. Several, though, struck home, slamming into the panzers with audible cracks that echoed across the great field. From his position on the hill overlooking the Hemroulle road, Hesler knew the fight was on:

"I couldn't see the action from where we were; because of some trees near us, our view was limited." But he could definitely hear the action, and he knew the difference between the 463rd's guns and the German guns. "The 75mm is a barker, not a boomer, so I could make out our guns firing," Hesler remembered.[22]

The machine gunners and bazooka men continued to add their destructive fire to the scene. Riflemen joined in, knocking any remaining German soldiers to the ground like bowling pins. The Germans, for their part, reacted poorly. Several of the vehicles began moving forward, apparently still trying to make for Bastogne or spot the gun positions and lay their own weapons on them. Unfortunately for the Germans, this just moved them closer to the gunners and further into the "kill box" the 463rd had established. It was a trap that none of the tanks would escape.

The 75mm rounds thumped into the frontal armor of several of the Mk IVs, and the tanks began to brew up—flames spewing from open hatches as the munitions cooked off in the intense heat. The American gunners could hear the detonations. Machine gunners and riflemen in their pits opened up on the infantry, targeting the German soldiers running about in confusion. By now, in the light of dawn, they made easy targets, and in contrast to the fight they had put up around Rolle, these men chose to run or surrender. For many, there was no longer a choice, as they lay still and bleeding in the snow next to the burning tanks.

One of the rounds from Lyons's and Cole's section of guns hit the nearest panzer, stopping it cold. The crew bailed from the burning wreck and ran for the woods. Another gun launched a white phosphorus round at the next tank, scattering the infantry riding on its back and turning the tank into a torch, lighting up the field. Hesler, though, still believes today that the WP round, usually used for gun registration (finding where to center your barrages), was intentional, mentioning that gunners were also taught to aim and light up the back section of a German tank.

"Well, we were taught that the back of the German tanks were greasy," he explained years later. "The German tanks had their gas tanks there."[23]

John Mockabee, a machine gunner from D Battery, also had a vivid recollection of the action. He was manning one of the .50-caliber machine guns that morning when the attack began:

> During the battle word came that tanks were coming up from the rear. A howitzer was then moved to the left and west of the 50 cal. machine gun and put into position to fire south. Also the 50 cal. that was covering the left flank of the battery was moved up and to the left side of the howitzer to fire south. As I remember there were three tanks and I think they were pulling sleds with troops. As I remember a lieutenant (probably Lieutenant Lyon) was directing the firing of the howitzer upon the tanks. After a few rounds the first tank was knocked out. At that time the 50 caliber started firing and then the howitzer directed their fire on the second and third tanks. There were other tanks but they stopped and turned and went back in the direction from which they had come.[24]

Mockabee then swept the field south of him with the M2 machine gun, chugging away at the hapless German dismounted troops.

It was the third panzer that would be most memorable to the men of the 463rd. The 75mm round cracked into the front left side of the turret, right as the crew was posting in their vehicle and attempting to back away from the firing. The crewman who was scrambling to enter the hatch at that unfortunate moment was killed instantly. The Americans watched as the tank commander, wounded, dropped from the tank into the snow, crawling to the nearby trees for cover. The driver of the vehicle threw it into reverse, down a ravine, and accidentally backed the tank into a clump of trees out of sight, effectively trapping the tank. With no place to go, several of the surviving members of the crew burst open through the hatches and, like the others, attempted to make it to the woods.

This vehicle was so close to "Booger" Childress's foxhole that he and his men leaped up, sprinted a mere fifty yards or so, and fired point-blank with their rifles into the crew compartment of the smoldering wreck. Straddling the front portion of the tank, pointing his rifle over the driver's and machine gunner's hatches, Childress found two of the crewmen dead. Childress then leaped back down, pouncing on the tank commander, who was nearby, leaning against a tree and obviously in great pain.

Childress and the men accompanying him—Private August F. Hazzard, Private William L. Justice, Private John T. Faria, Private Stanley M. Levendosky, Private Gordon L. Ballenger, and First Lieutenant Ross W. Scott—found the other members of the crew, and, shouting, *"Hände hoch!"* took them prisoner. Scanning the nearby woods with their rifles pointed and ready, the men captured another two officers and twelve enlisted men. Another group of five security men from Baker Battery sprinted from their positions and took on a German machine gun crew that was attempting to fight back from the same trees. Overwhelming the German MG with small-arms fire, the Americans killed one and captured eight enlisted men.[25]

Best yet, the tank that Childress had "captured" was still running. As he hauled the bodies out of the tank, he convinced the others around him that the panzer would make a fine trophy to show off at division. With a grin, Childress dropped inside the driving compartment and started trying to move it up and away from the trees.

The tank was none other than one of the lead panzers that had spearheaded the attack that morning, the tank with the name *"Lustmolch"* ("Happy Salamander") written on its barrel. According to some of the American witnesses, this was the same Mk IV that had knocked out both George Schmidt's and Adam Wans's M18s near the haystack as it rolled its way toward the Champs–Hemroulle road. It then turned right from Allen's headquarters when C Company attacked the farmhouse. (Evidently, the crew decided to take a chance and make for Hemroulle instead.) That's how the crew of this vehicle had joined up with the tanks assaulting the 463rd, only to be knocked out of commission just a little bit later.[26] *"Lustmolch"* had just become "Booger" Childress's prize of war.

The two Able Battery guns also fired from their position near the eastern hills above Hemroulle. These gunners claimed a tank or two. A Battery's captain, J. F. Gerhold, recalled how the two guns (numbers two and three) from his battery were turned to fire down from a hill, homing in on the approaching armor with a mixture of armor-piercing and white phosphorus rounds: Gerhold's sergeant told the gunner on the howitzer to remove the panoramic sight on the left of the breech and, like the men in

B Battery, simply bore-sight the gun on the nearest panzer. Gerhold remembered, "The sound of the tanks was definitely west of me and south, but very close. I ran to [Sergeant Raymond F.] Gooch's #2 gun and we could just about identify them when Col. Cooper screamed over the phone, 'Fire at the SOBs—kill the SOBs. They're Krauts. Open Fire!!'"

The assistant gunner pulled the lanyard cord on the right of the weapon. The next few rounds hit home. One round hit one of the large wooden sleds a panzer was pulling through the snow, loaded with troops. Gerhold witnessed the devastating effect: "Gooch . . . hit it or just below it and blew it to smithereens. I think that troop carrying sled was all wood. There wasn't much left of it or the Krauts on and around it."[27]

Excited and with their blood up, many of the 463rd security men abandoned their foxholes and ran after the German soldiers fleeing for the nearby trees in panic. As rifle shots split the air, the remaining Panzergrenadiers, having lost their armor support, and realizing that the assault had failed, either surrendered, ran back toward Mande Saint-Etienne in retreat, or died in place, fighting a hopeless fight.

Able Company's first sergeant Joseph F. Stolmeier remembered that morning with a touch of grim humor in a letter written after the war. "We had a real Christmas Day Turkey Shoot. That's the only time I had fun in combat. I hit one those dirty buggers with a shot from my Garand rifle, and I saw his boots go back up over his head, so I passed the word that you can't count a hit, unless you see his boots go up higher than his head."[28]

For the 463rd, it was an artilleryman's battle, and the veteran gunners proved their mettle, stopping the last of the German assault cold, just short of the entrance to Bastogne. As the last few rounds flashed out and struck home, oily smoke billowed from at least two of the German tanks, knocked out of commission, and one was captured. Back at the B Battery gun pits, First Sergeant Smith remembered being so mesmerized by the action while watching it through his binoculars that his bare hands had ". . . frozen to my field glasses." Smith had to have a buddy pry his hands off the binoculars and help him put his gloves back on.[29]

Cooper picked up the telephone to report the attack to division. Someone on the line had the nerve to ask, "Cooper, are you making this up?"

Cooper responded with satisfaction. "Hell no—look out your window and you will see five smoke columns, each a burning tank. No, make it six, there goes another one!" Cooper may have been exaggerating the number or possibly confused by the fires from other German vehicles destroyed nearby, but his crews had definite claim to stopping several of the last panzers to attack that day.

As things quieted down in his sector, Cooper's gunners took a break, but kept the armor-piercing shells unpacked and next to each gun pit in case of another attack.[30]

After 0900 hours, Monday, 25 December 1944
Along the 463rd Parachute Field Artillery gun line,
Able, Baker, and Dog batteries
Hills east of Hemroulle, Belgium

"Booger" Childress was a quick learner. To his amusement, he had *"Lustmolch"*—the captured Mk IV—moving, and in no time figured out how to steer the war trophy using the two large handles on each side of the driver's seat. With the driver's hatch open, just enough of his head was exposed so that he could see where he was going. A smiling Childress, accompanied by First Lieutenant Ross W. Scott and the others marching the German prisoners behind the tank, drove the tank toward the B Battery positions. The move was a bit foolhardy—luckily Cole and Lyons told their gunners to hold their fire, recognizing the GIs accompanying the tank and calling out.

"Our machine gun section drove the captured tank near our positions," Lyons recalled. "Meanwhile, the German prisoners were disarmed and marching behind the tank toward the number-one gun. Sergeant Childress and Gus Hazard [sic] of the machine gun section were riding the tank and stopped in front of my position. At that point I said to them, 'Get that tank out of our area, because if the skies ever clear they'll see the German tank and we'll catch hell from our own airplanes.' I said, 'Why don't you take them up to battalion.' So they took the German prisoners and operational German tank up to battalion."

Lyons remembered that one of the German prisoners, an officer with his hands on his head, spoke English. He directed his comment at Lyons, recognizing him as a fellow officer. "Lieutenant, you're wasting your time all around the perimeter," the German said cockily. Lyons looked him in the eye and replied, "You're the prisoner, I'm not."[31]

Someone from Baker Battery had already contacted Cooper. Anxious to see the trophy and the prisoners, Cooper told the men at the gun positions to tie a white T-shirt to the antenna or gun muzzle and he would soon be there. Hopping in his jeep with his driver, Private Walter Scherl, Cooper sped down and had to smile at the sight greeting him: his happy troopers clambering around the vehicle and scores of dejected German prisoners being searched by several guards.

This tank and these men, Cooper decided, needed to be taken to McAuliffe. That would forever silence those doubting Thomases who said his little guns and their crews couldn't stop German armor. Cooper led in his jeep, and Childress once again started up the Mk IV. Together they led a parade of captured grenadiers into Savy, for the division staff and all others to see the fruits of their labor. For many years, the soldiers of the 101st and other units in Bastogne would not forget the captured tank *"Lustmolch,"* which became an object of interest, photographed, examined, and regarded as one of the 101st Airborne's best trophies of the war.[32]

The 463rd lists three soldiers killed during the Christmas battle: Rogan's friend Corporal Rester W. Bryan, who was posthumously awarded the Bronze Star, Private Ollie S. Butts of HQ Battery, and Private First Class John P. Hall of the medical detachment. Two enlisted men were wounded—Private First Class Richard A. Carroll, A Battery, and Tech 4 Marlyn W. Havig, HQ Battery.[33]

The fire logs for Christmas show three fire missions during the period of 0700 to 0930, of which at least one was direct (antitank) fire. A Battery fired sixty-four rounds; B Battery fired 180, of which around thirty-one were AP; and Dog Battery fired seven rounds, and four AP from its one gun that was brought into play against the tanks later.

Christmas had indeed been a busy day, with the gun crews of the 463rd working like Santa's little helpers. For the entire December twenty-fifth, the battalion had fired off 884 rounds of HE, 51 rounds of WP, and 35 rounds of AP. The total of 970 rounds was the highest daily number the 463rd would fire for the entire Bastogne siege (December 18 to January 1).[34] Cooper's carefully laid-out plan had indeed brought a rain of steel upon Maucke's panzers.

Later that afternoon, General McAuliffe, Colonel Sherburne, and other division officers drove out in jeeps to see the 463rd's handiwork in the fields southeast of Hemroulle. With each smoking wreck, the staff officers took pictures and examined the devastation, carefully watching the skies overhead to ensure that no lurking American fighter-bombers would mistake them as a target of opportunity.

Much like the scene near Rolle, the sights that greeted the command were grisly. One of the men with Colonel Sherburne, Corporal James L. Martin, Sherburne's security, described the scene that midafternoon: ". . . there was a German tanker burned to a crisp hanging upside down on the right side of the tank. His foot was caught in or near the opening on top of the tank. . . . The other tank that I remember had made a mad dash into a thick patch of pines to escape. The trees were 6 to 8 inches in diameter. The tank plowed into the woods 75 to 100 yards, making a path about 10 feet wide until it hit a bank about 4 feet high at a 45 degree angle."[35]

Cooper was pleased that Colonel Elkins and Colonel Carmichael were also in attendance. He quietly relished the looks of surprise on their faces as McAuliffe gave the 463rd credit for three of the Mk IVs: the one Childress captured, and two others reduced to burned wrecks by the gunners of the three batteries.

"He [McAuliffe] would approach a burnt out tank and say, 'What gun hit this one?' It so happened that two tanks were hit in the side and were burned out. There was a streak in the snow that went directly to a gun aimed on those two. The general said, 'I'll give you credit for these two and the one you captured, but this other cannot [sic] positively be identified as being knocked out by your guns.'"

McAuliffe then added, "Anytime a tank is hit and burns up, it is destroyed and knocked out."

Hearing that, Cooper then inquired whether he could use that term in his after-action report.

The general shot back with a grin, "Hell, yes!"

Cooper turned to an awestruck Elkins and said with great satisfaction, "I got my tanks today!" He was more than pleased to get the official recognition for three tanks, although Cooper remained convinced that the 463rd actually accounted for destroying several more near Hemroulle that day, either with 75mm Pack rounds, bazookas, or determined "tank-stalking" infantry.[36]

Like D'Angelo and his crew near Rolle, the 463rd gunners were relieved the action was over and that they had stopped Maucke's right hook from getting through to Bastogne. As they relaxed and continued the restocking of ammo in the gun pits, the men, Hesler remembers, were once again served the typical fare for Christmas dinner—hotcakes with sugar.

After 0900 hours, Monday, 25 December 1944
Area of operations, Able Company, 502nd Parachute Infantry Regiment
Champs, Belgium

As late morning arrived, the fighting in Champs was starting to sputter out. Still, with many of the Germans still sheltering in the town, the houses and streets had the potential to explode into a deadly killing ground. Swanson's A Company had to go house-to-house to evict the last few stubborn Germans. It was during one of these actions that Sergeant Asay, the "mother hen" of his squad, almost lost his life.

The men would approach with rifles at the ready and surround the building. Usually one or two would have a grenade ready to hurl into the structure just in case there was resistance. Otherwise, it was hoped a few demands in German would help the enemy realize the hopelessness of their situation, drop their weapons, and come out peacefully. Asay remembered a tense moment. "Sergeant Zweibel and I were cleaning out houses. He went in the back door while I was backing him up."

Asay recalled that some sixth sense told him to turn at that moment. There stood a German coming around the corner, only a few feet away. "I shouted, *'Hände hoch!'* three times. He had a Schmeisser [submachine gun]—we were only two and a half feet apart from each other." After what seemed like an eternity of a standoff to Asay, the German finally dropped his gun and put his hands over his head. "Well, he yells into this house and out of this building come sixteen more, so I had seventeen prisoners." Asay and his men marched the Germans back into Champs.[37]

After dealing with the prisoners, Asay then approached a woodshed located on the right side of the Rouette–Givry road, the area of buildings that had been captured by the Germans and then evacuated as the Americans regained control of the road north of Champs. A group of Asay's men were in the structure, taking a break from the intense fighting. Still bleeding from his wound in the face, Asay walked over to the shed.

"As I entered the house, a shot rang out and hit the doorjamb near my head," Asay said. He ducked inside the shed and asked whether any of the men had seen where the shot came from. The men cautiously slid outside and noticed a dead German in the snowy field across the road. Rifles ready, Asay and his troops walked right up to the German soldier, dressed in white and lying facedown with his rifle near his hands.

"I gave him a few kicks in the ribs," Asay recalled. The German leaped up and lunged for his rifle. Asay fired twice from his M1, killing the grenadier instantly.

"He had been playing dead when we spotted him, and was the one who had taken a potshot at me." With that, Asay led his men back to the houses. A bit more determined, he continued the hunt for remaining Germans.[38]

Wallace Swanson recognized that things were starting to simmer down in Champs. He radioed Chappuis at Rolle and verified that he would not need Hanlon to bring B Company into play. Swanson decided to take a look at the situation for himself and, with an armed escort, left his CP and strolled cautiously toward the Champs church and the schoolyard nearby. The occasional burst of rifle or automatic fire confirmed that his men were still mopping up German resistance ahead. Prisoners were brought by him, marching in groups, and shed of their weapons, belts, and helmets, with their hands over their heads. To Swanson, the vaunted "*Übermensch*" of the Third Reich's 77th Volksgrenadier simply looked forlorn, cold, and tired.

The paratroopers continued to search the farmhouses, sheds, barns, and haystacks in Champs. Other Able Company men were ordered by Swanson to check the church tower and make sure there were no German "holdouts" still in it. Swanson knew that when the Germans had occupied it earlier that morning, they had used it to call in fire on his own position nearby.

Swanson asked one of his troopers whether he had searched and checked every part of the church and schoolyard. The sergeant answered affirmatively, so Swanson decided to climb the church tower and see what he could see of the situation in his area. Swanson recalled: "As I was going up, I ran into a curve in the stairway and steps and as I was moving I happened to glimpse out of the corner of my eye the movement of a white sheet lying in the corner of the floor area behind some paste board and boards leaning against the wall."

Drawing his weapon, Swanson shouted in the little German he knew for the figure to come out. "The object under the sheet moved again and it turned out to be a German officer who had been in command of some of the troops who had entered Champs. I retrieved a pistol which he had in his hand and told him to move on down stairs. As I came out of the church doorway, the sergeant who had told me everything was clear, was almost flabbergasted when I brought a German officer from that church steeple area."[39]

By late in the morning, the connection between A Company and Sutliffe's 2nd Battalion to the right had been reestablished; the Germans, including Ludwig Lindemann and the surviving members of his company, had apparently vacated the Les Bresses woods and retreated back toward where they had come, leaving their dead behind. The American positions around Champs, at least for the time being, appeared safe once again.[40]

Approximately 1000 hours, Monday, 25 December 1944
Possibly southwest of Champs, Belgium

Where precisely the tank had hidden for so long, and why, would remain a great mystery for years for the men of the 502nd. This single Mk IV would become known as the "rogue tank" to the Americans. Somehow, in the mad and frantic fighting that took place around Rolle that day, the tank had been forgotten. Unaccounted for, it had slipped past the American defenses. It had lunged at the Champs–Hemroulle road after surviving the fire of D'Angelo's and Vallitta's M18s. It survived Schuyler Jackson's second bazooka round, which had bounced off its turret. It had then motored on down the road toward the zigzag woods. The Mk IV panzer seemed to be either impervious or just plain lucky.

Shortly after the machine gunner in the bow of the tank had killed a private from Baker Company near the roadblock, the tank seemed to disappear. For hours it hid, probably deep in some woods, its crew by now realizing they were one of the last German units left intact within the American line, desperate to get back to their own lines. Hearing—or, as daylight broke, possibly seeing—the fighting in Champs, the tank commander decided to make his move. Perhaps he thought that if he could link back up with the 77th Volksgrenadier in Champs, he could get out of the American pocket alive.

As the panzer driver pushed the vehicle into gear, the tank pulled out of the snow and onto the road just southeast of the town. Smoke poured from the exhaust and muffler as the vehicle churned the mud and snow on the road, emerging from the woods and bearing straight into town.

Swanson was taken completely by surprise. He had just returned to his CP and was being visited by some of the 1/502nd's HQ brass; Major "Long

John" Hanlon, Captain Joe Pangerl, and Jim Hatch, the S3. Swanson remembered the shock:

"We heard a loud rumbling sound outside the house we were using as the company CP."

Swanson and Hatch went to the door and opened it. They were shocked to see a German tank roll right past their position on the street outside.

"We saw this German tank go by from our rear toward our front lines. We realized we had no weapons that would do any good. We shut the door and Hatch said, 'this is no place for a pistol!'"[41]

Discretion being the better part of valor, the officers decided to evacuate the house from the other side. Pangerl recalled the commotion years later: "I was telephoning with my back to the door, looking out of the window. About four men, including one of my majors, climbed over me to get out of the window. The last one said 'Scram—there's a German tank outside the door!' In my imagination, I could see the 88mm gun pointing through the door ready to fire so, needless to say, I went out that window, telephone and all. Nothing, however, happened so I went around the front of the house and saw it disappearing up over the hill with men running after it shooting but of course not doing any damage."[42]

Near the potato shed and the Rouette road, Corporal Willis Fowler and several other men from Asay's squad were finally relaxing, enjoying the tiny amount of sunlight that had burned off the fog, providing a small bit of warmth on their faces. Fowler was trying to fix the tripod on his machine gun. The other troopers were eating near the potato shed or cleaning weapons. Some of the men had scrounged bread and butter and other victuals from the German prisoners they had searched—a simple reward for the hungry victors. It almost made up for the three chickens Fowler, Ted Goldmann, and the others had killed, plucked, and stored in the potato shed for a planned Christmas feast. The chickens had become combat casualties, blown to pieces by the German tank shells that had blasted the wooden structure during the battle.

The men were chatting, recounting the part they had played in the morning battle, when someone suddenly yelled out that a German tank was approaching from behind. Fowler recalled the shock at seeing this holdout tank, guns blazing, heading toward them. "It was right there before we knew it, coming up the road."[43]

Ted Goldmann was also in disbelief: "Johnny [Ballard] was in his hole cleaning his rifle; Fowler and [Private Harold] Curry in theirs. Lenz, Williams and I were slicing bread with a bayonet. I had a slice fixed when Johnny yelled to ask me to fix him one, which I started doing."

The "rogue tank" veered slightly to the left after it passed Swanson's HQ, following the road out of Champs, just across from the church. As the paratroopers ducked between houses and dived out of the way, the tank continued on, climbing the incline, its commander apparently determined to reach Rouette.

Goldmann continued. "Fowler yelled, 'Here comes a German tank behind you!' Sure enough, a light-medium tank was coming up behind us with its machine gun blazing away. We [Lenz, Williams and myself] ducked behind what remained of the potato shack doorway."

A quick-thinking Johnny Ballard picked up his bazooka and waited until the Mk IV had passed his foxhole. There was a German soldier hanging onto the back of the tank who was quickly dispatched with a rifle shot from one of the paratroopers. Ballard leveled the bazooka, took aim, and fired at the back of the tank from less than fifty yards away.

The first bazooka shell slammed into the back of the motor—just under the turret—causing the tank to stall. It rolled off the left side of the road, grinding to a halt in front of the potato shed and some trees. Ballard reloaded and, firing again, hit the panzer squarely in the back. The tank's engine stopped dead and flames shot from the rear. Fowler, Goldmann, and the others whooped, then crouched back down as they saw the German crew bailing out. Aiming their rifles and carbines, they opened up.

"The crew came piling out to be met by a volley of lead from all of us. No more tank and all the crew was killed except one who had a radio on his back that Sgt. Bud Zweibel wanted to get intact," Goldmann recalled.[44]

As the wreckage of the tank sizzled and crackled, burning, the men were amazed at how close a call it had been. The "rogue tank"—although it had almost made it back to its lines—was little more than a stone's throw in front of their positions. So close the men had to back up as the wreck continued to burn that afternoon, in case the ammunition cooked off.

Walking back into Champs, Fowler and the others hoped they might finally be able to get some food and relax. They were handed K rations. It wasn't much, but for the time being, it satisfied Fowler's empty gut.

As Captain Swanson and the others regained their composure after the surprise from the rogue tank, "Swannie" was happy to see that communication lines had been repaired and he was back in touch with Rolle and

Bastogne via landline. Prisoners were tallied. According to Able Company records, more than a hundred or more Volksgrenadiers from both battalions of the 77th were accounted for. Meals were brought in for his exhausted troopers, who had been up all night fighting for the tiny little town. Christmas was more like Thanksgiving, in many ways, as many of the paratroopers had a warm meal and appreciated the very fact that they were alive for another day. Actually, casualties among Swanson's company were light, considering the ferocity of the German attack and the hard work of evicting the enemy from the town that morning. The company suffered only one killed in action, a Private Steinback, six missing in action, and thirteen wounded.[45]

Chappuis and Allen, as well as their company commanders, also took stock. Although the battle appeared to be won for now, up and down the 502nd's perimeter, there would be more fighting in the near future.

Midafternoon, Monday, 25 December 1944
West of Bastogne

All around the northwest sector, on a line from Champs in the north, past Rolle and the Dreve de Mande, and heading farther south past Hemroulle to the gun pits of the 463rd, the wreckage of the Christmas-morning battle lay dark and smoking.

Maucke's failed attack was evident. Bodies of *landsers* lay in clumps in the bloodstained snow. German prisoners, searched by guards from the 502nd, 463rd, and 1/401st, dropped their weapons in piles and marched toward Bastogne with their hands held over their heads.

Tanks, in various stages of wreckage, littered the area. The wreckage was thick, particularly along the Champs–Hemroulle road near D'Angelo's and Vallitta's positions. Some were burned black, their hulls crumpled down and still pouring smoke from the hatches. Inside, the charred remains of their crews sat at their posts where they had died. Some wrecks simply showed the small penetration hole of an armor-piercing shell, the snowy ground nearby scattered with the still bodies of the crew. Others were knocked about and pointing in all directions like a careless child's toys.

Impact holes—dark smears in the snow with earth thrown up around them—were everywhere, as were burn and scorch marks here and there. Brass shells, large-caliber and small-, glittered in the sun, scattered or in tight piles dumped in the snow. Hanlon provided his own description:

"Suddenly, as if on signal, the fighting ended; an eerie calm broken only by the crackling of burning tanks, came over the field."[46]

As the sun rose, warming the frozen fields, shadows began to appear. Christmas started to take on an air of hope for the GIs who had battled all night and morning. The survivors noted that the action seemed to have reached its crescendo, the Germans having apparently blown their attempt to gain Bastogne. The sight of so many German prisoners was indeed heartening to the defenders of Bastogne.

By noon, Chappuis had reestablished communications with all units in the area. To maintain the initiative, "Silent Steve" decided to seize the key terrain to the west of Champs in order to deny that territory to the Germans. It was vital that the Americans take advantage of the failed German assault and regain the ground lost that morning. Captain Hatch, the regimental operations officer still in Champs, orchestrated the attack.

At 1230 hours, the attack commenced. Baker Company had the task of clearing the eastern side of Champs, while Charlie Company, the decisive operation, pushed west to high ground. Unfortunately, not all the Germans had left Champs. Somewhere in town, a German forward observer had set up a hide site, and from there he called down artillery fire upon Baker Company's men as they attempted to push through the village. As a result, Baker's 3rd Platoon suffered severe casualties, including its platoon leader. Tragically, Lieutenant Porter C. Little of B Company was one of the last Americans to be killed that day. As the men of the 502nd moved up to try to retake the hill and Robinson's OP above Champs, the Germans fired a few parting shells. Lieutenant Little was hit and died shortly thereafter.[47]

Despite the losses, the attack continued. By 1500 hours, the two companies had achieved their missions. The Germans attempted a halfhearted counterattack, but it fell short. The paratroopers would keep their gains. After the counterattack, Chappuis pushed Baker Company toward the Bois de Nibelmont after a patrol from 3rd Battalion stumbled into some Germans in Recogne. Their mission was to secure the Longchamps–Bastogne road. The perimeter now secured, Chappuis and Cassidy spent the evening in Rolle, chewing on a Christmas meal of sardines and crackers.[48]

While they munched away on their Christmas dinner, the S2 staff pored over a captured order from one of the prisoners. It came from the 77th Volksgrenadier Regiment. The intelligence analysts realized that Able Company had taken on two German Volksgrenadier battalions that morning, while to the south, the 1/401st and 705th's tank destroyers had grappled with the entire 115th Panzergrenadier Regiment.[49] It was only then that the paratroopers realized how much the Germans had thrown at them in this Christmas attempt to end the siege. The Wehrmacht had concentrated two regiments against two battalions. In addition, one of the regiments had a company of panzers and assault guns to support it. Chappuis, Cassidy, Hanlon, and Swanson shook their heads in disbelief. By the standards of any military logic, this should have been more than enough to overrun the American lines. Instead, the attack had failed.

By the time the attack had stalled, the Germans had lost that entire company of panzers and a battalion of Panzergrenadiers; they were decimated by the stubborn 502nd's paratroopers and the glidermen of Allen's 1/401st. In addition, two battalions of Volksgrenadiers had been mauled by the American defenders in their failure to take Champs. Colonel Kokott had risked his newest armored forces to end the siege, and had wound up almost destroying Maucke's regiment. In essence, Kokott had gambled everything on the Christmas attack, only to lose it all.

Midafternoon, Monday, 25 December 1944
327th Glider Infantry Regiment area of operations
Southwest of Bastogne

Hearing the tapering off of the noises of battle near his sector, Colonel "Bud" Harper felt immense relief. It had been close, but his lines had held. The Germans had tried one more time to attack Able Company of the 401st's lines shortly before noon, but it was little more than an unenthusiastic attempt to stave off total defeat. Allen confirmed that, indeed, the repaired lines would hold.

Allen's battalion was not the only spot where the Germans had struck. The town of Marvie, in Harper's area of operations, also witnessed more fighting that day. But at the end of the day, when Captain William Abernathy, the Regimental S2, completed his roll-up report, the 2/327th had captured 117 Germans.[50] Thanks to prisoners of war, the intelligence officers at division now had a strong sense of whom they faced in Harper's part of the perimeter. Prisoners from the 1st and 2nd battalions of the 39th Fusilier Regiment, the 6th, 10th, and 11th companies of the 901st Panzergrenadier Regiment, and the 1st Battalion of the 77th Volksgrenadier Regiment had been captured. Furthermore, several prisoners revealed the location of the 77th regimental headquarters. Schriefer's HQ was in Rouette.[51] Overall, with the capture of so many Germans, the Americans were realizing an unexpected benefit—loads of information on the status and shape of the German forces still facing them. All in all, it was a good day for the interrogators.

The victory, though, was not without cost. During the rollover by Maucke's force that morning, Allen's 1/401st suffered twenty-two casualties. Many of these men sustained only light wounds, and would probably return to battle shortly. Others, however, were not so lucky. Bowles's Able Company had four men killed in action: Private First Class Frederick W. Bader, Staff Sergeant Seeber Crawford, Technical Sergeant Frank Evans, and Sergeant Roy W. Sprister. Towns's Charlie Company suffered only one man killed in action: Private First Class Amos Damron from Kentucky. Headquarters Company did not lose a single soul.[52]

Midafternoon, Monday, 25 December 1944
P-47 close air support mission from the
513th Fighter Squadron, 406th Fighter Group
Skies over Bastogne

First Lieutenant Howard M. Park glanced over his shoulder at the ground below. Somewhere dug in and around the town of Bastogne were his comrades in the 101st Airborne Division. Just a short time earlier, before Park and his fighter pilots arrived on station over Bastogne, the resupply aircraft had reappeared. Even if Patton's tanks had not arrived yet, Supreme Allied Command was going to make damn sure the defenders of Bastogne would receive a Christmas present. The sky once again filled with the shapes of C-47 transports, parachutes billowing from the aircraft and fluttering to the ground. The little fighters swept the sky before the next serial of Dakotas thundered overhead, delivering more goods to the GIs below. Now, with the supply birds gone, the fighters could once again ply their deadly trade on the German forces on the ground.

For P-47 pilots like Park, this was to be their finest hour. The weather that had sided with the Germans for the past week was gone. The clear skies beckoned the pilots to take to the air, and their rivals in the Luftwaffe seemed almost nonexistent.[53]

On the downside, Park had never experienced such flak before these missions, and he had been flying almost nonstop since spring. The intelligence staff had warned the pilots the Germans had more than nine hundred 20mm and 40mm flak guns pointed skyward, ringing Bastogne like a crown of thorns. This concentration of firepower gave the Germans the ability to throw a dome of hot lead and bursting shrapnel over the battle-field. No aircraft was safe over Bastogne, but that was where Park and his fellow pilots were needed.[54]

The 406th had given McAuliffe's boys constant coverage throughout the daylight hours, starting on the twenty-third. Park's 406th had three squad-rons, and each squadron flew four missions daily. For each mission, the squadron would send up two flights of four aircraft each. According to the flight records, the 406th averaged 105 sorties daily between December 23 and 27. Park himself had flown one mission each day so far. Today his air-craft had gone wheels up at 1400 in the afternoon. The typical flight to Bastogne, loiter time, and back lasted around two and a half hours.[55] The missions were becoming something of a blur to Park. Although the pilots were being worn and pushed to their limits, the men knew the work was vital to stopping the Germans' Christmas drive and helped relieve some of the pressure on the hard-pressed Americans in Bastogne.

Park's squadron, the 513th, had been pulverizing German positions outside of Bastogne since Christmas morning. A typical mission over Bas-togne was anything but typical. Once he reached the ten-mile exclusion zone around Bastogne, Park and his fellow pilots would receive a call from Captain James E. Parker, the forward air controller for the 101st. Parker, stationed on the ground near McAuliffe's headquarters, would provide the target and the location. Park would then search for the bright orange mark-ing panels that the airborne troopers had used to designate the forward line of troops, or FLOT. From there, Park would know where the friendlies were. He just had to avoid strafing or bombing anything on the Bastogne side of those markers.

Park and his wingmen would climb to a decent altitude for an overall view of the area on the ground, and to try to keep out of the range of the flak. Pushing over, the men would line up any targets in their crosshairs— the P-47 "Jugs" diving to the deck like chubby ospreys. As Park watched the snowy ground rise up from below, he looked for the telltale tracks of Ger-man vehicles on the enemy side of the perimeter. Meanwhile, he would "jink" the stick to avoid the exploding flak. The P-47's wings would dip and arc as he hurtled his eight-ton aircraft toward the ground. All around him, tracers passed over and beneath his wings, whipping by his canopy like supersonic fireflies. At the last second, Park would level out to deliver his payload and strafe the target. His mission complete, he would then pull up, repeating his jinking tactic as his plane pulled away. He knew that good stick handling was important to his survival, but whether his plane got hit or not would always be a matter of luck—the ultimate deciding factor.

Park remembered the tracers: "The flak tracers were like garden hoses with projectiles arcing lazily thru air toward one. I remember so vividly my slipping and skidding as streams of flak fire reached for me, sometimes within three feet of my wing surfaces."[56]

Down on the ground, Captain Parker, code-named "Ripsaw," directed the planes as if he were directing traffic at a busy intersection. Every morning he would consult Colonel Danahy's G2 map and vector in the aircraft to the locations where the infantry and tankers had reported enemy activity. His tactical operations center was a simple jeep with a high-frequency radio he'd borrowed from 10th Armored. Most of the time, his TOC, or tactical operations center, was in the courtyard of the Heinz Barracks, so he could be in close communication with McAuliffe's staff. He also wanted to be in the best place to observe the P-47s and P-51 Mustangs visually, as they whisked and wheeled over the battlefield.[57]

Throughout the morning and afternoon, the P-47s of the 406th Fighter Group continued to pound the Germans surrounding Bastogne. In total, the 406th flew 115 sorties on Christmas Day. The 512th and 513th fighter squadrons each flew six missions, while the 514th flew five. The 406th claimed that they struck forty-seven gun positions, nineteen armored vehicles, one mobile gun, eleven buildings, 128 motor transports, and ten tanks. The 512th Fighter Squadron also sent Thunderbolts to attack convoys outside of Givry, tanks near Lutrebois, vehicles outside of Assenois, enemy forces in Hompre, and field guns near Villeroux.

Park's own squadron directly assisted in the destruction of the German forces that had attempted to penetrate Chappuis's line. They attacked tanks outside of Marvie, troop concentrations south of Bourcy, enemy forces near Tintange, Wehrmacht units south of Bastogne, and especially enemy forces outside of Flamierge and antiaircraft units in Salle. Park's squadron winged over again and again and powered down on the northwestern sector, made conspicuous by the funeral pyres of so many burning tanks. Chattering .50-caliber bullets tore up the German positions where the Panzergrenadiers were trying to regroup and lick their wounds.

Park's sister squadron, the 514th, added to the devastation around

Bastogne. The pilots of the 514th flew over to Noville, where they quickly discovered a group of German motor transports and tanks, vulnerable and in the open; the column didn't stand a chance. 514th fighter jockeys also strafed troops outside of Bertogne and Sibret. In addition, they struck motor transports in Morhet, and attacked German units in Rouette.[58] A pilot from the 406th later remarked to General McAuliffe when asked about Christmas Day from the air, "This was better hunting than the Falaise pocket and that was the best I ever expected to see."[59]

Still, the hunting came with a stiff price tag. Tragically, the 513th lost two pilots flying over Bastogne that Christmas. Both First Lieutenant Myron A. Stone and Second Lieutenant Fred M. Bodden lost their lives providing close air support for McAuliffe's infantry in Bastogne.[60] Park, reflecting on who was killed in the 406th and who survived that deadly winter in the air, believed the difference was experience. Most of the pilots who died during the period between December 23 to 27 were the newer pilots who had not learned how to conduct ground missions in a hostile air environment. The veterans, with more flight time under their belts, fared better. In total, the 406th lost ten pilots in that five-day period.[61]

There were American deaths on the ground as well. True, McAuliffe's GIs had thrown out the orange panel markers in front of their positions, but these didn't always work. There had been several tragedies in which friendly fire from the fighter-bombers had already claimed several paratroopers, artillerymen, and TD crews. These "friendly fire" incidents were tragic, but often unavoidable. Try as they might, for the fighter pilots it was next to impossible to pinpoint with accuracy every marker panel while flying overhead at almost five hundred miles per hour.

In the 463rd, First Sergeant Claude Smith recalled a pilot who flew his aircraft right over the road that afternoon, firing at the 463rd's headquarters and mess kitchen in Hemroulle: "All the pots and pans had holes in them. Sgt. Thomas Spivey [the mess sergeant] was mad as a wet hen."[62]

In a tragic turn of events, Captain Preston Towns, Ray Allen's tall, courageous leader of C Company of the 1/401st since D-day and Holland, was killed the next day by a strafing P-47 during a friendly-fire incident near Hemroulle. The news of Towns's death was devastating to men like Allen, who considered Towns one of his best company commanders.[63]

(The veterans of the 101st Airborne who were at Bastogne seem to universally understand the price of the ground-attack missions that helped them defeat the Germans and break the siege. There are very few hard feelings, understanding that the occasional tragedy was the price to pay in the age of primitive ground-to-air communications in warfare.)

The sacrifice, however, reaped dividends and probably did more to break and demoralize the German effort around Bastogne than has been previously publicized. Through December twenty-third to the twenty-seventh, the 406th Fighter Group flew 529 sorties. During those missions, the 406th alone was credited with destroying or damaging "thirteen enemy aircraft, 610 motor transport, 194 tanks and armored vehicles, 226 gun positions, 59 fortified buildings, 43 horse-drawn vehicles, 12 bridges and 13 ammunition and fuel dumps."[64]

Just as Kokott had predicted, the *Jabos* were everywhere Monday, enjoying the fair and clear flying weather and pinpointing the men and vehicles of the Reich who were still trying to carry out their orders that Christmas Day. Kokott realized his effort to break in before they appeared had failed miserably and his worst fears were realized—he had known that if Maucke's attack failed to penetrate Bastogne by 0900 Christmas morning, the *Jabos* of the 406th Fighter Group would ensure that the Germans would never get a second chance. The Americans once again owned the airspace over Bastogne, and after Christmas, it would never again be contested. Simply put, it spelled disaster for any further large-scale German attempts to attack Bastogne during daylight or good weather.

Captain Parker realized the same thing—how valuable an asset the Americans had in their fighter-bomber squadrons that day at Bastogne. He later said, "According to Intelligence of the 101st, the 406th group alone gave air strength comparable to the combined striking power of four armored and infantry divisions. The Thunderbolts flew in above the tree tops and tackled every target assigned to them."[65]

For Lieutenant Park, Bastogne was personal for him. "We went out on the mission determined to help our ground forces, especially as we had developed a relationship with the men of the 101st who were bivouacked with us at Mourmelon."

Park continued in a postwar account: "On each of those missions I think back and believe that I just took a fatalistic turn of mind, figuring I'd do my damnedest to evade the flak but knowing the odds were pretty tough in carrying out the needs of the ground. As Capt. Parker notes . . . he suggested our target, and we [speaking for myself] never shirked regardless of flak or feelings. Summing up, the Bastogne period was the most significant time in my combat experience of 11½ months and two Purple Hearts."

The bond between the Screaming Eagles and the fighter pilots was strengthened that December at Bastogne. Dashing flyboys and rough paratroopers had a new level of respect for one another that now transcended the football field or local officers' club. The 101st Airborne had a partner in victory at Bastogne, and would never forget the valuable service the fighter pilots carried out putting the final deadly touches on the Germans' Christmas attack.[66]

Midafternoon, Monday, 25 December 1944
Rouette, Belgium

For some of the German units that decided to hide in the various villages circling Bastogne, Christmas brought a hellish storm from the skies above. Rouette was one of those unfortunate towns. The American pilots above could see the line of German soldiers below like they were a stream of ants marching off a hill. Many of them were wounded survivors of the morning debacle and had sought refuge in the home of a Mr. Féron.

Like the Ju 88s over Bastogne, it was hard for the American pilots to discern that the men below were injured noncombatants. The Thunderbolts dived on the column caught in the open streets of the town. For fifteen long minutes, the people of Rouette huddled in their cellars with the German soldiers as bombs exploded and shook the ground around them. Several bombs detonated harmlessly outside the town, chewing up earth and sod.

Some, though, found their mark, blasting apart eight homes. Indeed, the American pilots dropped not only fragmentation munitions but white phosphorous, too. As a result, several more homes burned. Some of the villagers were killed as well. Some died in the fires, while one, Lydie Gaspard, died as she ran to her home for shelter. A P-47, flying at treetop level, had cut her down with machine gun fire. She collapsed in her doorway in a pool of blood.

People were not the only victims. The Germans had housed their horses, used for pulling much of their artillery and supply trains in the town stables, and they were unable to set them free before the bombs hit. The helpless beasts perished in the flames.[67]

It was a cruel reminder to the people of Rouette that in war, death made no distinction between soldier, livestock, or innocent woman.

Midafternoon, Monday, 25 December 1944
Headquarters, 26th Volksgrenadier Division
Givry, Belgium

It was clear to Kokott by afternoon that Hitler would not get his Christmas wish. Bastogne was still standing in defiance. By now he knew that his *Panzer Angriff* had failed. All of the reports he received that afternoon painted a picture of failure. Though the attacks of the 77th and Maucke's Panzergrenadiers had started with promise—momentum, power, and surprise—nowhere had they achieved the breakthrough his division so desperately needed to end the siege. Erroneously, Kokott believed that his forces had inflicted terrible punishment on the 101st Airborne Division, but it was somehow not enough to penetrate the American lines. He reasoned that Maucke's watered-down forces had been too weak, despite the massing of these and other German units at what he was certain were the weakest points of the American line. Instead of victory, it had become a costly defeat. The one best chance the Germans had was now gone.

Kokott slowly realized that with the failed Christmas assault, the tipping point in the struggle for Bastogne had been reached. The Americans would now, most probably, hold all the cards. The Germans had lost their best opportunity to seize Bastogne, and soon Patton's forces would be slicing up from his division's rear, making straight for Bastogne like an unstoppable tidal wave of steel.[68]

Kokott turned his thoughts to defense. Patton's Third Army was hitting the Seventh Army hard to his south, and Kokott worried that the Fallschirmjägers protecting his boundary would buckle and break under the intense pressure.[69] If this happened, Kokott's southern unit, the 39th Fusilier Regiment, would have to conduct an about-face to counter Patton. In addition, the paratroopers in Bastogne might coordinate a counterattack while his own forces were disorganized, demoralized, and spread thin to the south of Bastogne. Therefore, Kokott knew he would have to put an immediate halt to the day's attack and readjust his lines so that his forces would occupy good defensible terrain in anticipation of American counterattacks.[70]

American fighter-bombers and artillery quickly frustrated his plans. Since midmorning, the Allied fighter-bombers had started their campaign to lay waste to the now exposed German forces around Bastogne. Closer to the front lines, Colonel Maucke reported that the *Jabos* had struck his own regimental command post. For the grenadiers caught out in the open that early evening, the terror from above dispelled any final hopes that their attack might have succeeded.[71]

The *Jabos* were not the only problem as the German troops withdrew to huddle in defensive positions. American artillerymen, restocked with ammo and emboldened from the morning's repulse, had unleashed a terrific barrage.

Cooper's 463rd soon had its Pack howitzers back in action, firing in the indirect support role from their positions near Hemroulle. Between 1100 and 1700 hours, the 463rd Parachute Field Artillery Battalion fired more than two hundred rounds of high-explosive shells at German targets along the southern and western perimeters.[72] Despite the furious shelling, the Americans chose not to follow up their artillery with an aggressive counterattack, and Kokott managed to stabilize his lines before nightfall.[73] And to his south, the 5th Fallschirmjäger Division had briefly checked Patton's advance—for now.[74]

With a heavy heart, Kokott used that evening to radio the bad news to General von Lüttwitz. Soon even Hitler would learn that *Festung* Bastogne remained in American hands.

Midafternoon, Monday, 25 December 1944
Area of operations, Able Company, 502nd Parachute Infantry Regiment
Outskirts of Champs

To Lieutenant Jim Robinson, observing a large group of Germans massing on the hill above Champs where he had been forced to desert his outpost, it appeared the enemy was taking advantage of the lull and planning another attack into town. The 377th FO watched as the German medium tanks and infantry were milling about on the hill and the outskirts of Rouette, apparently preparing to renew the assault and take Champs back from Swanson's tired men.

Looking through his field glasses, Robinson knew what to do. Coordinating with First Lieutenant Wise in Swanson's CP, he relayed a call to the 377th batteries. Giving the coordinates, he suggested using the brand-new radio proximity fuses, delivered in gliders during the ammo resupply the day before. This artillery round, which had never been used in combat in the European theater of operations, was a remarkable leap forward in artillery accuracy. After the shell was fired, a radio beacon signal emitted from the fuse could determine a preset cue to detonate the shell at whatever altitude or distance was desired.

Within minutes, the telltale shriek of "outgoing mail" passed over Robinson's head: "Like giant thunder claps 'Battalion—four rounds!' of time fire enveloped the dugouts and foxholes of our old OP. Gone for the moment was the pent-up frustrations of days of counting our scant ammo supply as massed artillery converged on the target," Robinson recalled.

Wise witnessed the scene as well: "We fired one round for range, which by luck was excellent and fired four rounds for effect. I never saw a more beautiful sight," Wise commented. "All four bursts detonated approximately 100 feet over the Jerries and I guarantee the hill was cleared."[75]

The effect, for the Germans, was murderous. Great bursts of snow and dirt flew up from the hillside. German soldiers ran for cover; tanks raced off the hill and defiladed for cover on the other side. It was too late, as more Volksgrenadiers died by the score, torn apart and consumed in the great blasts. The group was completely broken up and scattered, leaving behind a spread of corpses in the snow.

The deadly work was witnessed by Captain Swanson. Swanson later heaped accolades on both Vallitta's and D'Angelo's actions for helping his men regain control of Champs during the crucial aspects of the battle, as well as Robinson and other FOs for their yeoman work in directing fire on German troop concentrations afterward:

"During this Christmas Day encounter with the enemy, the field artillery observer, 1Lt. Jim Robinson and his radio operators gave me terrific support by calling in the needed artillery shelling on the advancing enemy. As daylight came to our area, men of 'A' Company were able to pick off a lot of enemy infantrymen who were moving towards our line."[76]

Up until the end of Christmas Day, as darkness once again enveloped the cold killing grounds around Bastogne, FOs like Robinson would continue to call in accurate artillery fire on clots of German soldiers near Rouette and Givry. The devastating American artillery, aided in accuracy by a startling new technology—the radio proximity rounds—would hammer the final nail in the coffin of Kokott's ambitious Christmas attack.

Midafternoon, Monday, 25 December 1944
Remnants of 6th Company, 77th Volksgrenadier Regiment
Somewhere west of Champs

Lindemann stared in shock at what remained of his company. *Nur dreissig soldaten!*—only thirty men! His Volksgrenadier company had started the offensive with a hundred men. In the beginning, he thought they stood a chance to take Bastogne, but now he felt they would never enter the cursed Belgian town.

The attack that had started that morning through the Les Bresses woods had ended in defeat. Meanwhile, people all around the Christian world celebrated Christmas while his men bled and died in the snow. Above him, American fighter-bombers relentlessly strafed and bombed their positions, circling overhead that afternoon like a flock of vultures. Several American bombs exploded near him.

"I also remember the American bombers dropping bombs Christmas Day. Some came near my position. I was lucky, though, [but] many of [my] soldiers died. About ten to thirteen were killed. So many were killed or captured."

Now all he had remaining in his company was the thirty soldiers, now looking at him in desperation and fear.

He recalled later, "No one recognized that it was Christmas. Every day was the same—carry out our orders. Our only wish was to stay alive that Christmas."

Lindemann sensed that the war for the Fatherland was over. This was, after all, as he and his men had been told so often over the last few weeks, the final push—the big gamble. He remembered it was at Bastogne that he realized Germany could not win the war. His only duty now was to save as many of his men as he could, get them home, and survive.[77]

Midafternoon, Monday, 25 December 1944
XXXXVII Panzer Corps headquarters
Château de Roumont, Belgium

General von Lüttwitz received the news of Kokott's defeat with shock. Listening to the reports over the field phone in his warm château, he realized all was not going well. The reports on *Wacht am Rhein* and the Fifth Panzer Army were no better than the news from Kokott at Bastogne: West of Bastogne, the spearhead of the Panzer Corps, the 2nd Panzer Division was dying. Its panzers had penetrated the farthest of all the German units, but by Christmas Day many of its vehicles had sputtered to a halt due to a fuel shortage—a fuel shortage that was the result of the Americans holding the vital road junction at Bastogne.

Because of Bastogne! Von Lüttwitz was starting to hate the very name.

Because of the failure of Kokott's Christmas attack to take Bastogne from the Americans, the 2nd Panzer Division had now rolled to a stop near Foy-Notre-Dame, Belgium—less than five miles short of the Meuse River. Now von Lüttwitz was more concerned with saving his forces from certain destruction as the Allies, having reacted with determined force to the initial German attack almost ten days ago, prepared to overwhelm the "bulge" in their lines and completely wipe out the German units trapped there. Allied units would soon envelop them, and the destructive end they had planned in Hitler's Wolf's Lair weeks ago would turn out to be their own doom. As von Lüttwitz dined on American K rations, which had fallen into his hands thanks to American airdrops near Bastogne, he dreaded the discussion he would have with his superior, von Manteuffel. He went over and over the operation again in his head, mulling over what went wrong.[78]

To add to the gloom, that night the 2nd Panzer's reconnaissance teams had reported the sound of tanks north of Conneux. The men of 2nd Panzer discovered that the tanks belonged to the American 2nd Armored Division, and they were the spearhead for the U.S. VII Corps, under the command of Major General "Lightning Joe" Collins. This meant the worst possible news, von Lüttwitz thought: The Americans had brought in another corps to blunt the German attack, punching it right in the nose of its farthest extension.[79]

Von Lüttwitz was hoping that von Lauchert's division would continue to batter its way through and make it to the Meuse. At the same time, he hoped that Bayerlein's Panzer Lehr would have equal success. It was a forlorn hope. Once again the American fighter-bombers struck with a fury. Vehicles by the score were turned into burning wrecks alongside the road as the Allied planes caught the columns like sitting ducks. By nightfall, the Panzer Lehr Division had withdrawn from Humain and Havrenne. Elements of 2nd Panzer attempted to link up with the stranded reconnaissance teams near Custinne. Like Panzer Lehr, they made some initial progress as they pushed through Ciergnon, but in the end, they too failed. As for the fate of the men of both divisions, many became Allied prisoners of war, and many more ended up in shallow graves. Few reached German lines.[80]

As day gave way to twilight, von Lüttwitz received the final reports. Because of aerial resupply to the 101st Airborne, Bastogne now was beyond the capabilities of the 26th Volksgrenadier Division alone to divest. Furthermore, the 5th Fallschirmjäger Division was barely holding the line south of Clochimont. In addition to this, von Lüttwitz learned that the Sixth Panzer

Army failed to advance past their lines, leaving the Fifth Panzer Army's northern flank in the air and unsecured.

To von Lüttwitz, it was clear the offensive was over. Survival of his forces was the paramount concern of the corps commander, but due to Hitler's intransigence, he could not order a general withdrawal. Frustrated, and in a sense realizing that he was now only fighting for time, he ordered his men to dig in and hold on while the rest of the final 5th Panzer Army reserve—the 9th Panzer Division—trickled in to bolster their lines. Seeing that west of the Meuse was now a dead end, he directed his attentions southward toward his greatest threat—Patton's Third Army. If Patton reached Bastogne and then pushed on to Houffalize, his tanks could slice the XXXXVII Panzer Corps into two halves, allowing the Allies to encircle the western portion of the Fifth Panzer Army and destroy it piecemeal. Bastogne would inevitably hold out until Patton reached it, and the town would provide Patton with a springboard for launching more American forces into the heart of the German offensive. Now that the battle for Bastogne was basically lost, von Lüttwitz had only one last option—to try to keep Patton from reaching the town.[81]

As he finished the last morsels of his meal and placed his monocle back in his eye socket to review the latest written reports thrust into his hand by a nearby staff officer, von Lüttwitz knew he was not the only high-ranking Wehrmacht general who could foresee an impending disaster. What they decided to do over the next few days as *Wacht am Rhein* ran out of steam would determine their careers, futures, and probably their lives. One thing was for sure: Capturing Bastogne, for now, seemed an impossibility, an opportunity that had quickly vanished, much like the foggy weather, the fuel in so many panzer tanks, the chance for a peaceful Christmas, and the lives of so many German soldiers.

1900 hours, Monday, 25 December 1944
Headquarters, 115th Panzergrenadier Regiment
The heights near Isle-la-Hesse, south of Bastogne

Making plans to continue *Wacht am Rhein* mattered little to a distraught Colonel Maucke. He had lost one-third of his men. He had tried to warn Kokott that the attack stood a good chance of failure without time and reconnaissance, and he had been proven right. Now his men had died in droves on the snowy fields outside of Bastogne, or burned to death inside their tanks, littering the roads, hills, and farm lots near the Champs–Hemroulle road.

To senior officers like von Manteuffel, von Lüttwitz, and even Kokott, those men were mere numbers. To Maucke those men were his soldiers. Many he had known since Italy. Several hundred men in his 1st Battalion had marched out with eleven tanks that morning, and not one panzer or Panzergrenadier had returned. At sundown, Maucke decided to drive down the Marche road to the heights just west of Isle-la-Hesse to find any survivors. When he reached the heights, gunfire drove him off, just like the hapless *Leutnant* Gaul earlier.

Discouraged, Maucke could only speculate as to what exactly had befallen his men that fateful Christmas morning. He knew firsthand that the attack had turned into a disaster. He had witnessed most of it that day. He could now see the aftermath as he left his vehicle after returning from his drive down to Isle-la-Hesse. The wounded were stacked up near his command post on a short hill near Givry, the overworked medical officers frantically tending to horrific wounds.

He knew the late and piecemeal arrival of his battalions precluded any advance planning. As he had warned Kokott and protested, he truly knew his unit could not successfully spearhead an attack over ground he had not seen, or take enemy positions that he did not have a clear picture of. All Christmas Eve, Maucke had held back the gnawing feeling that his men would suffer terribly, trying to keep a positive front for his soldiers. By Christmas afternoon, the reports and the lack of contact with any of his 1st Battalion had confirmed his worst fears.[82]

Now he had to prepare for another assault. He brought up his reserve and visited Major Adam Dyroff at the 3rd Battalion headquarters around 1535 hours. He shifted this 2nd Battalion to Mande Saint-Etienne and received from division a further six assault guns. At 1900 hours, Colonel Kokott arrived to oversee the final preparations. Seeing what was in front of him, Kokott then decided to postpone the attack until the following morning. The Americans had already tried to counterattack that afternoon with negligible results. Kokott doubted another one was in the offing.[83]

Now Maucke could only wait. He also doubted the Americans would try a counterattack. That would prove fortunate, because there would be little his men could do to fight it off. Surveying the wounded and exhausted men on the hilltop, he could tell there was no real fight left in them. Christmas had brought nothing but defeat and death to his regiment.[84]

For the division staff of the 101st Airborne Division, Christmas dinner was a welcome diversion from the chaos of Christmas morning. The headquarters men felt that Hitler's best shot had dropped well short of the target. For the kitchen cooks of the 101st Signal Company, the Christmas festivities had left an indelible mark on the barracks walls in the form of pockmarks from stray rounds. A Christmas meal was prepared for General McAuliffe, Colonel Roberts, and the rest of the staff officers of the division headquarters. Somehow a master sergeant had scrounged up some decorations, and in the center of the square table he erected a makeshift Christmas tree from several spruce branches, tied together. Atop it, he had even placed a paper star.

The staff sat down quietly, still wearing their coats, as if they were waiting to dash out at a moment's notice. The air seemed filled with a palpable sense of relief, mixed with exhaustion. Their meal, like Chappuis' and Cassidy's at Rolle, was paltry. It was ersatz coffee, canned salmon, and biscuits. For dessert, the sergeant had somehow worked a miracle and brought out some lemon meringue pie. A staff photographer snapped a photo to commemorate the historical event. McAuliffe did not even bother to flash a smile. He had too much on his mind, thinking about how close the day's events had come to spelling disaster for the defenders of Bastogne. As he sat there, brooding, with his arms folded across his chest and his eyes looking down at the table, a nearby explosion rattled the room.

"Let's get out of here," General McAuliffe ordered. Hearing the command, the staff hurriedly herded once again toward the cellar. Danahy, still holding his pie in his hand, tried to squeeze through the doorway without losing his dessert, but to no avail. Most of the pie ended up on Danahy's face, which elicited some chuckles from those present.

It was Christmas night, and they were all still alive. Bastogne had held, and it seemed to all at headquarters that the roughest parts might well be behind them. Earlier, Danahy had compiled his daily roll-up, and it was impressive: The 101st Airborne Division had captured more than six hundred enemy prisoners of war to date. In addition, his intelligence staff estimated that the division had destroyed or damaged 144 tanks and twenty-five half-tracks during the previous week's worth of fighting.[85] More important, relief was on the way. Danahy had spoken with McAuliffe earlier, and he had informed him that Patton's frontline trace was a thousand yards south of his lines. Because of this and the morning victory, the mood had lifted somewhat since last night. Everyone sensed that the Germans had made their big push, and the 101st had thrown them back. True, Patton had not yet arrived, but he was close, and he was getting closer every hour.[86]

Throughout the day, McAuliffe had demanded up-to-date information on Patton's whereabouts, specifically the 4th Armored Division. Earlier, McAuliffe had even sent one of his scout aircraft—a fragile little L4 Piper Cub—aloft to reconnoiter the battlefield and find it. The pilot, First Lieutenant Ben F. Wright, took off with his copilot, First Lieutenant George Schoneck. They circled the town, cataloging all the various positions, both friendly and enemy. When they returned, Wright marched over from the makeshift airfield to brief the general.

Wright later recalled the incident. "I went to his [McAuliffe's] headquarters and started on a long dissertation on every position. He said, 'Hell, I know that! I want to know where the 4th Armored is.'"[87]

The next day, around 1640 hours, the 326th Parachute Combat Engineers would find the 4th Armored Division and the rest of Patton's Third Army making their way into Bastogne.[88]

Supplies were once again air-dropped, and would continue to come in for the next few days until the corridor that Patton had forced his way through was safe enough for trucks and supply vehicles to transit. Soon a train of ambulances drove up from the south and arrived in town to help evacuate the severely wounded. Nothing could have been more appreciated for the overworked medical staff of the division, having done their best with short supplies to treat the wounded under some of the most challenging circumstances. A total of 652 wounded were taken to XII Corps hospitals that day. By the twenty-eighth, more than a thousand stretcher cases would be removed, even as the fighting continued; many men would return to their families alive—a belated Christmas present for many a soldier who might otherwise not have survived the siege.[89]

True, very few Screaming Eagles would ever admit they needed to be "rescued," but it is certain that at times the situation in Bastogne grew desperate for the Americans during that Christmas of 1944. The relief was appreciated, and just as Patton had predicted, the linkup with McAuliffe had now put the Americans in a strong position to counterattack and put an end to the German drive. Victory, however, is never so clean-cut. Over the next few days, around the perimeter, the Germans would continue to press the issue and harass the American lines. Both the 502nd and the 1/401st would be involved in stiff combat through January to keep out of German hands the territory they had gained at such a cost on Christmas.

One thing was certain: The men who fought and defended the town agreed that the Christmas Day attack was the pivotal episode of the siege. At no other point did the German forces outside Bastogne hold so many high cards in this bloody high-stakes poker game, and at no time was McAuliffe's situation as fragile as it was on that weekend of December 23–25.

It took a day or two, but it eventually dawned on the Americans that the major German attempt to take Bastogne had failed. Christmas had brought a present for both the citizens of the town and the American defenders. Patton's breakthrough was just the gift wrap that made it that much better. The Americans finally realized that the battle that determined Bastogne's salvation had actually been fought that dark Christmas morning. The Germans had been stopped by the paratroopers, tank destroyer crews, and Cooper's gunners less than a mile and a half short of McAuliffe's headquarters. For the men and women who lived through it, for many years afterward they would agree that it was the closest call of the siege and, for so many of them, a Christmas miracle.

For Tony D'Angelo, Larry Vallitta, Morris Klampert, Donald "Moe" Williams, and the other officers and men of the 705th Tank Destroyer Battalion, the fighting would continue on into Germany and Austria. The unit, which typically receives little credit for its role in the defense of Bastogne, was honored time and again by McAuliffe and the Screaming Eagles who fought beside them. It was estimated by Lieutenant Colonel Clifford Templeton that at Bastogne, the Hellcats of the 705th managed to destroy thirty-nine German vehicles. The ratio was calculated; basically, for every M18 lost, seven German tanks were put out of action. Templeton himself was awarded the Silver Star for his leadership. Sadly, the battalion would lose its steadfast commander, the man who had drilled them in gunnery back in the States until the 705th were some of the best shots in the ETO—Templeton fell victim to an artillery shell in Germany in March of 1945.[90]

In his sector, Colonel Allen credited both Love's TDs and Nancarrow's engineers with destroying five tanks that morning, some of which, in the poor light, were probably towed troop sleds mistaken for vehicles. For Captain Nancarrow's brave engineers who dared to take on a Mark IV, each man received a Bronze Star for valor.[91]

For the 101st Airborne paratroopers and glidermen who had fought side by side with the tank destroyer men, the 705th had earned their overwhelming respect during those bitter December days.[92]

Likewise, those tough glider-fighters of Allen's battalion, men like Carmen Gisi, Bob Lott, Robert Bowen, Robert O'Mara, and Robert Mac-Donald, had played an equally important role in stubbornly fighting inch by inch for the ground northwest of the perimeter. There would be little break for Allen's battalion, who throughout January would continue to engage in combat with the German forces threatening to once again seize the Marche road. As additional U.S. reinforcements were brought forward to widen the corridor in this area and beat back the German advances, the fighting would get especially bloody in this part of Belgium and Luxembourg during the start of 1945.

And, of course, there had been the contribution of the Army Air Corps, another unsung hero of the Battle of Bastogne. Without the valuable and determined work of the cargo aircraft and fighter-pilots such as Howard Park, the air over Bastogne would have been dominated by the Germans. Worse, the supplies would have never made it through, bad weather or not, and the terrifying firepower of the Allied fighter-bombers would never have reined back the armored tempest trying to strangle the Belgian town.

By the end of 1944 Allied airpower reigned supreme in the skies over Europe and was feared by the Wehrmacht on the ground. Hitler managed to launch one more aerial offensive in January—Operation Bodenplatte, which was a failure—spending the last of the Reich's valuable Luftwaffe fighters in a frivolous effort to knock back the encroachment of Allied airfields in Belgium and France.

For Ken Hesler, Claude Smith, Victor Garrett, and John Mockabee, as well as the many other members of the 463rd, there was very little Colonel Cooper's veteran gunners of the 463rd could do to add to their unit battle honors and streamers. After valiant service in Italy and southern France, the 463rd was probably one of the most "blooded" units in the airborne. After the Christmas Day battle, the gunners had the opportunity, as a surely smug John T. Cooper must have enjoyed, of proving to their airborne brothers just what their little guns and steady gun crews could do. Never again would there be doubts from paratroopers as to the tenacity and effectiveness of the

75mm battalions. Like the 705th, the Red Legs of the 463rd, through their disciplined fighting around Bastogne, had garnered the full respect of the Screaming Eagles. In March of 1945, Cooper's battalion would be formally attached to the 101st Airborne. The "Bastard Battalion" had found a home. The unit would remain so throughout the war, into Germany, and beyond.

For his role, and for the role of the 502nd's gallant defense of Champs and Rolle that Christmas, "Silent Steve" Chappuis received the Distinguished Service Cross, pinned on his chest by none other than General George S. Patton himself. Patton was reportedly delighted to see the destruction of so much German armor in the fields between Champs and Hemroulle when he toured the battlefield.

Like their brother glider-fighters in the 1/401st, the men of the 502nd continued to hold the line around Bastogne through tough fighting that January. Soldiers like Willis Fowler, who received the Silver Star for his action with the machine gun outside of Champs; Charles Asay; Ted Goldmann; and Schuyler Jackson, who earned a second Silver Star for knocking out the tank near Rolle, continued to hold the area around Champs through the bitter winter weeks until the German effort around Bastogne was completely spent.[93]

EPILOGUE

"Out of Blood and Death . . ."

Madame Maus de Rolle spent many quieter years after the war rebuilding her property and walking the peaceful grounds of the ancient château. After that dreadful battle on Christmas, two impish local teenagers, Gaëtan and Thierry de Villenfagne, left Rolle and clambered over the wrecked German tanks. They scrounged some items from two of the StuG IIIs that were stopped near the Dreve de Mande, and found the radio still worked in one of them.

Other family members, including Madame Maus de Rolle's son, Jean-Michael Maus, collected spent cartridges, rifles, and helmets left over from the Christmas battle. At one point he scavenged several bolt-action Mauser rifles from the inside of the StuG wreck closest to the Lane of Trees. The boys (Gaëtan, Thierry, and Jean-Michael) would go to the forest and shoot the Mausers. Upon returning home, Jean-Michael's parents would always ask him whether he had heard the sound of gunshots in the woods and whether he knew anything about them. Jean-Michael would, of course, deny that he had heard anything at all.

In 1967, the jig was up. Jean-Michael's father found the weaponry and, at Madame's request, dumped the Mausers and several other items down the château well to prevent the children from playing with them. The grand dame was none too happy. Not only did she not want to be reminded of that awful time years ago when both the lives of her family and her property were in jeopardy of being destroyed, but she knew that no good could come from kids playing with weapons that were still highly dangerous.

In 2008, Jean-Michael's son, Bernard Maus, and some other locals recovered two rusting Mausers, several clips of bullets, and a mortar shell from the well. Maus plans to display the items in a museum he hopes to open one day with Pierre Godeau on the château grounds. It is hoped that the museum and château will serve as a permanent reminder to Americans and Belgians alike of the fierce battle that took place mere yards away—the battle that decided the fate of Bastogne one Christmas so long ago.[1]

In the years after the war, Major "Long John" Hanlon felt an incredible sense of debt toward the people of Hemroulle. It had been their sacrifice and selfless charity that had helped his men survive the Bastogne siege. By giving up their priceless white linens and cloth, they had saved the lives of untold numbers of his soldiers who used the cloth for camouflage and warmth.

Hanlon—who returned to his hometown of Winchester, Massachusetts, married his sweetheart, Joan, and became a successful journalist—could not stop thinking about the people of Hemroulle and their noble sacrifice. After the war, he spoke to the clergy and congregation of his church, St. Mary's of Winchester, and told them the amazing story. Organizing volunteer efforts, the church sparked people in the town into donating more than seven hundred bedsheets, pillowcases, and other linen to take back to Bastogne and replace that which the Belgians had so willingly given up.[2]

In February of 1948, Hanlon flew back to Belgium with several members of his town and church. The story garnered national headlines, including coverage in *Life* magazine. As they traveled by bus to Bastogne, Hanlon was amazed at how quickly the Belgian countryside was rebounding from the war. Gone were the wrecks of tanks and weaponry, the shell craters were filled in, and in town, the rebuilding had already begun.

In Bastogne, the town was decorated with colorful flags, trimmings, and posters of appreciation for Hanlon and the other Americans who had saved Bastogne. To Hanlon, it seemed every child in Bastogne was waving a small American flag on each street corner. In a moving ceremony that day, the town leaders made Hanlon an honorary Belgian citizen.

The American delegation was also warmly greeted at Hemroulle. Once again Hanlon was given the honor of ringing the chapel bell. The townspeople had heard that Hanlon was coming back, but the American hero who had saved their town from German attack on that dark Christmas morning was humble. He was the one who had the debt to pay. As the Americans produced armfuls of folded sheets and blankets to give to the people, the town mayor, Victor Gaspard, embraced Hanlon in a warm reunion.[3]

It was hard to say who was more grateful; after all, the people of Bastogne and Hemroulle returned these favors years later by sending a surprise shipment of boxes to all of the churches in Winchester, regardless of denomination. In 1951 an elaborate ceremony was held at the crowded Winchester High School auditorium. As church bells rang throughout the town, the consul of Belgium—Dr. Albert Navez—presented the contents of the boxes to representatives of Winchester's ten churches. Inside each carefully packed crate, the clergy found a beautiful oil painting on a large wood frame. Each of the paintings represented a station of the cross from the Passion. The ten paintings had been hanging in the Hemroulle chapel since 1906. Before that, they had been in the possession of the sisters of Notre-Dame in Bastogne, possibly as early as 1820. Four previous paintings were damaged or destroyed, and several of the ten had the marks of shrapnel and bullets, but miraculously the ten works had survived both world wars, even the destructive Christmas Eve bombing.

In a brief speech, Dr. Navez communicated the appreciation of the people of Hemroulle and, in a wider sense, Bastogne and Belgium, for all the Americans had done in saving their city. Navez also expressed a fond sense of brotherhood between the people of Hemroulle and the people of Winchester that he hoped would be remembered by all who viewed the paintings in the ten Massachusetts churches for years to come.

The delicate yet simple representation of Christ's sacrifice, told in the beautiful gift of hand-painted Walloon woodcarving, was a gift from the Bastogne congregations to the congregations of America—a humble thank-you for saving their town. It was also an act of appreciation for the generosity of the reimbursed linen, and a reminder that the people of Bastogne would not forget the sacrifice made by so many Americans on that fateful Christmas in 1944.

More important, the paintings were a token of hope that the true meaning of Christmas, temporarily forsaken in those bloody and desperate days of 1944 among the people of Belgium, Germany, and the U.S., would once again never be forgotten.

The artwork adorns the churches of Winchester, Massachusetts, to this day.[4]

WORKS CITED

*College Park, Maryland refers to the U.S. National Archives Annex.

28th Infantry Division Headquarters. *G-3 Journal from 160001A, December 1944, to 162400A, December 1944.* Daily Journal, College Park, MD: Department of the Army, 1944.

28th Infantry Division Headquarters. *G-3 Journal from 170001A, December 1944, to 172400A December 1944.* G3 Journal, College Park, Maryland: Department of the Army, 1944.

28th Infantry Division Headquarters. *G-3 Journal from 180001A, December 1944, to 182400A, December 1944.* Daily Unit Journal, College Park, MD: Department of the Army, 1944.

501st Parachute Infantry Regiment. *Action for the 501st Regiment at Bastogne, 18–21 December.* Unit Narrative, College Park, Maryland: Department of the Army, 1945.

A Company Headquarters Section, 502nd Parachute Infantry. *Operation Bastard, 18 December 1944 to 18 January 1945.* Radio Log, Department of the Army, 1945.

Abernathy, William L. *Journal of the 327th Glider Infantry Regiment.* Intelligence Summary, Donald Pratt Museum, Fort Campbell, Kentucky: WWII Operations Reports, December 1944.

Abernathy, William L. *S-2 Periodic Report for the 327th GIR—from December 181800 to December 191800.* S-2 Periodic Report, College Park, MD: Department of the Army, 1944.

Abernathy, William L. *S-2 Periodic Report for the 327th GIR—from December 191800 to December 201800.* S-2 Periodic Report, College Park, MD: Department of the Army, 1944.

Abernathy, William L. *S-2 Periodic Report for the 327th GIR—from December 211800 to December 221800.* S-2 Periodic Report, College Park, MD: Department of the Army, 1944.

Alexander, Larry. *Biggest Brother: The Life of Major D. Winters—the Man who led the Band of Brothers.* New York: New American Library, 2005.

Allen, Ray C., interview by John G. Westover. *401 Withdrawal and 401 Road Block Action* (March 13, 1945).

Altermatt, Raymond C., Q.M.C. "Aerial Delivery of Supplies, The Quartermaster Review." Army Quartermaster Museum—Fort Lee, Virginia. September–October 1945, http://www.qmmuseum.lee.army.mil/WWII/aerial_supplies.htm (accessed September 26, 2011).

Anderson, J. Aubrey. "Presentation of the Overhanging Rock." *Historic Valley Forge.* 2010. http://www.ushistory.org/valleyforge/history/rock.html (accessed April 30, 2011).

Andreas Altenburger. "Die Träger des Ritterkreuzes R." *Lexikon-der-Wehrmacht.* 2011. http://www.lexikon-der-wehrmacht.de/Orden/Ritterkreuz/RKR-R.htm (accessed March 25, 2011).

———. "Panzer 35(t) und 38(t)." *Lexikon der Wehrmacht.* 2011. http://www.lexikon-der -wehrmacht.de/Waffen/pz38-R.htm (accessed March 25, 2011).

Andreas Düfel. *www.das-ritterkreuz.de.* 2006. http://www.das-ritterkreuz.de/index_ search_db.php4?modul=search_result_det&wert1=4045 (accessed July 9, 2011).

Andrews, Robert, interview by A. J. Webber. *1st Platoon, Company "B," 705th Tank Destroyer Battalion at Bastogne* (January 1945).

Arend, Guy Franz. *The Battle for Bastogne: If You Don't Know What "Nuts" Means.* Bastogne, Belgium: Bastogne Historical Center, 1987.

Aron, Paul. *We Hold These Truths . . . and Other Words that Made America.* Williamsburg, Virginia: Rowman & Littlefield Publishers, Inc., 2009.

Asay, Charles, interview by George Koskimaki. *Individual Action Report for Bastogne* (April 7, 1990).

Asay, Charles, interview by Don Cygan. "Interview with Charles Asay" (March 2009).

Astor, Gerald. *A Blood-dimmed Tide: The Battle of the Bulge by the Men Who Fought It.* New York: Dell Publishing, 1994.

Awards and Decorations for the 326th Airborne Engineer Battalion. Awards Report, Bastogne: Department of the Army, 1945.

Bando, Mark. *101st Airborne: The Screaming Eagles in World War II.* St. Paul: Zenith Press, 2007.

———. "E-mail from Mark Bando." June 21, 2011.

———. "The Bulge at Bastogne—the Battle of Champs." *Trigger Time,* August 2000. http://www.101airborneww2.com/souvenirs3.html (accessed October 8, 2011).

———. *Vanguard of the Crusade: The 101st Airborne Division in World War II.* Bedford, Pennsylvania: The Aberjona Press, 2003.

Barrett, Ben and Bob. "460th Parachute Field Artillery Battalion and 463rd Field Artillery Battalion." *517th Parachute Regimental Combat Team.* 2012. http://www.517prct .org/bios/merle_mcmorrow/merle_mcmorrow.htm (accessed October 28, 2011).

"Bastogne and the 101st Division." *The 406th Occupier vol. 1, no. 13,* September 28, 1945: 16.

Bayerlein, Fritz. *Bayerlein: After Action Reports of the Panzer Lehr Division Commander, From D-Day to the Ruhr.* Atglen, Pennsylvania: Schiffer Military History, 2005.

Bellaza, Nicholas. "Letter to Colonel John Cooper." Staten Island, New York, December 13, 1988.

Berger, Florian. *Mit Eichenlaub und Schwertern. Die höchstdekorierten Soldaten des Zweiten Weltkrieges.* Selbstverlag Florian Berger, 2006.

Berra, Joe, interview by George Koskimaki. *Individual Action Report for Bastogne for Joe Berra.*

Black, Layton. *The Last First Sergeant.* Caldwell, Idaho: Griffith Publishing, 1998.

———. "The Unedited Manuscript of Layton Black's Memoirs to George Koskimaki."

Boggess, Charles. "A Story by Charles Boggess." 1984.

Bostwick, Richard. "Diary of Private Richard V. Bostwick, Company B, 401st Glider Infantry Regiment." 1946.

Bowen, Robert. *Fighting with the Screaming Eagles: With the 101st Airborne Division from Normandy to Bastogne.* London: Greenhill Books, 2001.

———. *Fighting with the Screaming Eagles: With the 101st Airborne from Normandy to Bastogne.* London: Greenhill Books, 2004.

Bradley, Omar N. *A Soldier's Story.* New York: The Modern Library, 1999.

Brandenberger, Erich, interview by H. G. Elliott. *Ardennes Offensive of Seventh Army (16 Dec 1944–25 Jan 1945) 3 Vols.* Translated by W. B. Ross. National Archives, College Park, MD: Foreign Military Studies (July 6, 1946).

Breder, Anthony C., interview by Don Cygan. "Interview with Anthony C. Breder" (March 7, 2009).

Brewster, John P. *Action Against Enemy, Reports After/After Action Reports, Period 010001A, December, to 312400A, December 1944, 333rd Field Artillery Group.* After Action Report, College Park, MD: Department of the Army, 1944.

Brooks, John. "Letter of John Brooks, January 5, 1778." *The Administration of the American Revolutionary Army.* New York: Longmans, Green and Co., 1904.

Brown, Stuart H. *Oprep A No. D23B (2nd of 4 missions) for 24 hours ending sunset 23 December 1944. Mission No. 290. IX Fighter Command Operations Order No. W51-5.* Operation Report, Maxwell Airforce Base, Alabama: Department of the Army, 1944.

———. *Oprep A No. D23D (4th of 4 missions) for 24 hours ending sunset 23 December 1944. Mission No. 292. IX Fighter Command Operations Order No. W51-2.* Operations Report, Maxwell AFB, Alabama: Department of the Army, 1944.

Brownfield, AR. "History of the 811th Tank Destroyer Battalion." www.tankdestroyer .net. 1959. http://www.tankdestroyer.net/images/stories/ArticlePDFs/811th-Tank -Destroyer-Battalion-History_Part_2.pdf (accessed July 9, 2011).

Brubaker, W. E. *S-3 Report from: 1200 December 22, 1944, to: 1200 December 23, 1944, Unit: 377th Parachute Field Artillery Battalion.* S-3 Report, College Park, MD: Department of the Army, 1944.

———. *S-3 Report from: 1200 December 23, 1944, to: 1200 December 24, 1944, Unit: 377th Parachute Field Artillery Battalion.* S-3 Report, College Park, MD: Department of the Army, 1944.

———. *S-3 Report from: 1200 December 24, 1944, to: 1200 December 25, 1944, Unit: 377th Parachute Field Artillery Battalion.* S-3 Report, College Park, MD: Department of the Army, 1944.

Buechs, Herbert, interview by Captain L. H. Clark and First Lieutenant Robert E. Merriam. *The Ardennes Offensive (Sep.–Dec. 1944) with Major Herbert Buechs, the Luftwaffe aide to General Alfred Jodl, Chief of Operations Staff, Oberkommando der Wehrmacht, ETHINT 34* (August 31, 1945).

Cassidy, Patrick J., and Steven A. Chappuis, interview by Colonel S. L. A. Marshall. *502nd Regiment at Bastogne* (January 4–10, 1945).

Cercle d'Histoire de Bastogne. *De témoignent civil, Bastogne, Hiver 44-45.* Translated by Jeanette Angell Cezanne. Bastogne: Cercle d'Histoire de Bastogne, 1994.

Chadwick, Bruce. *George Washington's War: the Forging of a Revolutionary leader and the American Presidency*. Napierville, IL: Sourcebooks, Inc., 2004.

Chappuis, Charles W., interview by Don Cygan. "Conversation with Charles W. Chappuis, senior brother of Steven Chappuis" (July 2010).

Chappuis, Steven A. *Historical Narrative of the 502nd PIR, 1–31 December 1944*. Historical Narrative, Department of the Army, 1945.

———. *Historical Record 502nd Parachute Infantry Regiment, December 1944*. Historical Record, College Park, MD: Department of the Army, 1944.

Chappuis, Steven A., interview by Mary Hebert. *Transcript of Interview with General Steve Chappuis*. Louisiana State University: T. Harry Williams Center for Oral History Collection (November 30, 1995).

Chernak, Wasil, Ebner Datz, and Francis Walsh, interview by A. J. Webber. *3rd Platoon, Reconnaissance Company, 705th Tank Destroyer Battalion* (January 1945).

Clark, L. B. *Narrative Summary of Operations of the 4th Armored Division in the relief of Bastogne, 22–29 December*. Narrative Summary, College Park, MD: Department of the Army, 1944.

Cleaver, Frank A. *Unit Narrative—377th Parachute Field Artillery Battalion*. After Action Report, College Park, MD: Department of the Army, 1944.

Cole, Hugh M. *U.S. Army in World War II: European Theater of Operations, The Ardennes: Battle of the Bulge*. Washington, D.C.: Office of the Chief of Military History, Department of the Army, 1965.

Commune de Bastogne. "Histoire." *Commune de Bastogne*. 2011. http://www.bastogne.be/loisirs/tourisme/histoire (accessed March 26, 2011).

Cooper, John T., interview by George Koskimaki. "Interview with Colonel John T. Cooper" (Unknown).

Cox, X. B. *After Action Report for the Month of December 1944, 81st Airborne Anti-Aircraft Battalion*. After Action Report, College Park, MD: Department of the Army, 1944.

Danahy, Paul A. *G-2 Periodic Report No. 7 from 25 December 1944*. Periodic Report, Bastogne: Department of the Army, 1944.

———. *G-2 Periodic Reports No. 2, from: 200001 to 202400, December*. G-2 Intelligence Summary, College Park, MD: Department of the Army, 1944.

———. *G-2 Periodic Reports No. 4, from: 220001 to 222400, December*. G-2 Intelligence Summary, College Park, MD: Department of the Army, 1944.

———. *G-2 Periodic Reports No. 5, from: 230001 to 232400, December*. G-2 Periodic Report, College Park, MD: Department of the Army, 1944.

———. *G-2 Periodic Reports No. 6, from: 240001 to 242400, December*. G-2 Periodic Report, College Park, MD: Department of the Army, 1944.

D'Angelo, Anthony, interview by Don Cygan. "Interview with Tony D'Angelo" (January 3, 2009).

D'Angelo, Anthony, interview by Don Cygan. "Phone interview with Anthony D'Angelo" (March 4, 2009).

D'Angelo, Anthony. "Interview of Sergeant Anthony D'Angelo C Company, 24–25 December 1944." In *History of the 705th Tank Destroyer Battalion*. Lois Pawley Wick and James G. Wick. University Place, WA: 2001, JI-LO Publications, 2001. 962–68.

D'Angelo, Anthony "Tony," interview by Don Cygan. "Interview with Sergeant Anthony "Tony" D'Angelo" (June 8, 2009).

D'Angelo, Anthony "Tony," interview by Don Cygan. "Interview with Sergeant Anthony "Tony" D'Angelo (June 4, 2009).

Duvall, Claude W., interview by A. J. Webber. *Interview with First Lieutenant Claude W. Duvall* (January 1945).

Eisenhower, Dwight D. *Crusade in Europe*. Baltimore: John Hopkins University Press, 1997.

Eisenhower, John S. D. *The Bitter Woods: The Battle of the Bulge*. New York: G. P. Putnam's Sons, 1969.

Elson, Aaron. "Mixed 'Nuts': Interview with Bill Druback, John Miller, Frank Miller, Len Goodgal, and Mickey Cohen. West Point, NY, December 3, 1994." In *A Mile in Their Shoes*, by Aaron Elson, 48–69. Maywood, NJ: Chi Chi Press, 1998.

Ewell, Julian, interview by S. L. A. Marshall. *Action of the 501st Regiment at Bastogne* (January 6, 1945).

Ezell, Bert P., and Skauber, C. J., interview by L. B. Clark and William J. Dunkerly. *Relief of Bastogne—8th Tank Battalion, 4th Armored Division* (January 7, 1945).

Felkin, S. D. *A.D.I. (K) Report No. 142/1945*. A.D.I. (K) and U.S. Air Interrogation 1st February 1945, England: Department of the Army, 1945.

———. *A.D.I. (K) Report No. 175/1945 Further Report on the Crew of the Ju.88 S-3, Z6 + FH, of 1/K.G.66, shot down by A.A. 5 miles N.W. of Alost on 23rd January 1945*. A.D.I. (K) U.S. Air Interrogation Report, England: Department of the Army, 1945.

Ferretti, Fred. "Interview with Schuyler Jackson." *Stars and Stripes*, August 9, 1984: 1–2.

Flanagan, James W. "Letter to George Koskimaki." Newcastle, CA, August 9, 1990.

Fowler, Willis, interview by Don Cygan. "2nd Interview with Corporal Willis Fowler" (February 7, 2010).

Fowler, Willis, interview by Don Cygan. "Interview with Corporal Willis Fowler" (March 27, 2009).

Fradin, Dennis Brindell. *The Battle of Yorktown*. New York: Marshall Cavendish Benchmark, 2009.

Frank R. Brower, Jr. *After Action Report: December 1944, G1 101st Airborne Division*. After Action Report, College Park, MD: Department of the Army, 1945.

Gardner, Richard S., and James McDonough, *Sky Riders: History of the 327/401 Glider Infantry*. Battery Press, 1980.

Garrett, Victor E. "Letter to George Koskimaki."

Garrett, Victor E. *S-3 Report from: 192400, December 1944, to: 202400, December 1944, 463rd Parachute Field Artillery Battalion No. 205*. S-3 Report, College Park, MD: Department of the Army, 1944.

———. *S-3 Report from: 182400, December 1944, to: 192400, December 1944, 463rd Parachute Field Artillery Battalion No. 204*. S-3 Report, College Park, MD: Department of the Army, 1944.

———. *S-3 Report from: 202400, December 1944, to: 212400, December 1944, Unit: 463 Parachute Field Artillery Battalion. No. 206*. S-3 Report, College Park, MD: Department of the Army, 1944.

———. *S-3 Report from: 212400, December 1944, to: 222400, December 1944, Unit: 463 Parachute Field Artillery Battalion. No. 207*. S-3 Report, College Park, MD: Department of the Army, 1944.

———. *S-3 Report from: 222400, December 1944, to: 232400, December 1944, Unit: 463 Parachute Field Artillery Battalion. No. 208*. S-3 Report, College Park, MD: Department of the Army, 1944.

———. *S-3 Report from: 242400, December 1944, to: 252400, December 1944, Unit: 463 Parachute Field Artillery Battalion. No. 210*. S-3 Report, College Park, MD: Department of the Army, 1944.

Gerhold, William H. "Letter to George Koskimaki." September 21, 1991.

Gibney, J. L. "Books and Documents." *Office of Medical History. Office of the Surgeon General*. January 15, 1945. http://history.amedd.army.mil/booksdocs/wwii/bulge/28thIDUnitRpt6Dec44.htm (accessed October 8, 2009).

Gisi, Carmen "Geese," interview by Don Cygan. "Interview with PFC Carmen Gisi" (June 2, 2009).

Gisi, Carmen, interview by Don Cygan. "4th Interview with Carmen Gisi" (June 16, 2011).

Gisi, Carmen, interview by Don Cygan. "Interview with PFC Carmen Gisi" (April 12, 2009).

———. "Notes for George Koskimaki about Carmen Gisi."

Gisi, Carmen, interview by Don Cygan. "Phone Interview with Carmen Gisi" (June 1, 2011).

Gisi, Carmen, interview by Don Cygan. "Questionnaire for Carmen Gisi" (2009).

Goldmann, Ted B. "Letter to George Koskimaki." Northville, Michigan, March 25, 1993.

———. "Letter to Mrs. Ballard." Pusendorf, Austria, June 21, 1945.

Graves, Richard D. "Individual Flight Record Howard W. Parks." Department of the Army, December 31, 1944.

Guttman, Joachim. *MS# P109e Ardennes Follow-up: 2nd Panzer Division 16–20 December 1944 & 13–17 January 1945*. Correction Sheer, College Park, MD: Department of the Army, 1952.

Handbook on German Military Forces TM-E 30-451. Washington, D.C.: U.S. War Department, 1945.

Hanlon, John. "A Bell Rings in Hemroulle." *Reader's Digest*, December 1962: 8–10.

Harper, Joseph, interview by Colonel S. L. A. Marshall. *327th Regiment at Bastogne* (January 8–10, 1945).

———. "Bastogne Speech." Fort Campbell, July 2, 1975.

———. "Letter to George Koskimaki." *Letter to George Koskimaki*. Compiled by COL John Antal and Melissa Marr. Plano, TX: United States Army Military History Institute, August 3, 1969.

Harris, Mason. *No. 116, S-3 Report from 242400, December 1944, to 252400, December 1944, 705th Tank Destroyer Battalion*. S-3 Report, Bastogne: Department of the Army, 1944.

———. *S-3 Report from 182400, December 1944, to 192400, December 1944, No. 110 705th Tank Destroyer Battalion*. S-3 Daily Report, College Park, MD: Department of the Army, 1944.

———. *S-3 Report from 192400, December 1944, to 202400, December 1944, No. 111 705th Tank Destroyer Battalion*. S-3 Daily Report, College Park, MD: Department of the Army, 1944.

———. *S-3 Report from 212400, December 1944, to 222400, December 1944, No. 113 705th Tank Destroyer Battalion*. S-3 Daily Report, College Park, MD: Department of the Army, 1944.

———. *S-3 Report from 222400, December 1944, to 232400, December 1944, No. 114 705th Tank Destroyer Battalion*. S-3 Daily Report, College Park, MD: Department of the Army, 1944.

Hatch, James J. "Letter to George Koskimaki." Banner Elk, NC, January 26, 1991.

Hayes, Bill. "Letter from Bill Hayes." July 24, 1994.

Hazzard, Gus. "Letter to George Koskimaki—Concerning the Events of Christmas Morning, 1944." December 15, 1988.

Headquarters, 327th Glider Infantry. *Narrative of Action in Belgium, December 1944.* Narrative, College Park, MD: Department of the Army, 1944.

Heilmann, Ludwig. *5th Parachute Division (1 December 1944–12 January 1945).* After Action Report, College Park, MD: Foreign Military Studies, 1946.

Heintz, Joss. *In the Perimeter of Bastogne: December 1944–January 1945.* Bastogne: Self-published, 1984.

Herrmann, Dr., staff meterologist for the German High Command. *To be submitted to the Chief of the General Staff Notes on the probable weather development during the month of December.* Planning Paper, Berlin: OB West KTB, Anlage 50, 1944.

Hesler, Ken, interview by Don Cygan. "Interview with Ken Hesler" (April 4, 2009).

———. "Notes on the 463rd PFA and the Battle of Bastogne." October 1, 1990.

Hesler, Ken, interview by Don Cygan. "Second Interview with Ken Hesler" (April 17, 2010).

———. "World War II Historical Summary of the 463rd Parachute Field Artillery." *Official Homepage of the WWII 463rd Parachute Field Artillery.* June 2003. http://www.ww2airborne.net/463pfa/463_offstory.html (accessed March 15, 2010).

Hodge, George J., Jr., interview by Gary W. Swanson. *George Hodge Collection (AFC/2001/001/9271),* Veterans History Project, American Folklife Center, Library of Congress (2001).

Hooper, William. "Letter of William Hooper to Joseph Hewes." In *Letters of Delegates to Congress, 1774–1789, Volume 5.*

Howard M. Park. "Biographical Sketch of Editor: Howard M. Park."

Husken, J. "Letter to Mrs. Anton Adorf." Translated by Dieter Stenger. January 25, 1945.

Jodl, General Alfred, interview by Major Kenneth W. Hechler. *Interview on Planning the Ardennes Offensive with Genobst Alfred Jodl ETHINT 50* (July 26, 1945).

Johnson, Robert, and Ambrose Wyzlic, interview by A. J. Webber. *2nd Platoon, Company "A" 705th Tank Destroyer Battalion* (January 1945).

Johnson, Martin A. *Annex No. 3 to accompany Unit Report No. 207. From: 2400 hours 21 December 1944, to: 2400 hours 22 December 1944, 463rd Parachute Field Artillery Battalion.* S-4 Daily Report, College Park, MD: Department of the Army, 1944.

King, Martin. "African Nurse saved GIs at Battle of the Bulge." December 2011. http://www.army.mil/article/52148 (accessed January 18, 2012).

Kinnard, Harry W., interview by S. L. A. Marshall. *G-3 Account of Bastogne Operation.* National Archives, College Park, MD: U.S. Army Combat Interviews (January 3–11, 1945).

———. *G-3 Report No. 2, from: 192400A to: 202400, December.* G-3 Report, College Park, MD: Department of the Army, 1944.

———. *G-3 Report No. 3, from: 202400A to: 212400, December.* G-3 Report, College Park, MD: Department of the Army, 1944.

———. *G-3 Report No. 5, from: 222400A to: 232400, December.* G-3 Report, College Park, MD: Department of the Army, 1944.

———. "Letter to Thomas Potter." *Brave Men of World War II.* January 16, 2003. http://www.506infantry.org/his2ndbnwwiiarticle08.html (accessed January 2012).

Knecht, Wolfgang. *Die Geschichte des Inf. Rgts. 77.* Translated by Dieter Stenger. Koln: Self-published, 1964.

Knight's Cross, Deutsche Wehrmacht and Waffen SS. *Ritterkreuzträger Adam Dyroff Major, Panzergrenadiere.* 2005. http://www.ritterkreuztraeger-1939-45.de/Infanterie/D/Dy/Dyroff-Franz-Adam.htm (accessed September 25, 2011).

Kokott, Heinz. *Ardennes Offensive—Battle of Bastogne.* College Park, MD: Foreign Military Studies National Archives (August 28, 1950).

———. *Ardennes Offensive—Battle of Bastogne MS #B-040.* Foreign Military Studies Historical Division, College Park, MD: Department of the Army, 1950.

———. *Employment of the 26th Volksgrenadier Division from 16 to 31 December 1944.* After Action Report, Wehrmacht, 1945.

Koskimaki, George. *The Battered Bastards of Bastogne.* Havertown, PA: Casemate, 2003.

Lamke, Edward R. "Lamke Interview." In *History of the 705th Tank Destroyer Battalion.* Lois Pawley Wick and James G. Wick. University Place, WA: 2001, JI-LO Publications, 2001.

Lindemann, Ludwig, interview by Don Cygan. "Interview with Ludwig Lindemann" (Spring 2010).

Lindemann, Ludwig, interview by Don Cygan. "Interview with Ludwig Lindemann, concerning the Battle of Champs on 25 December 1944 (June 25, 2010).

Lindemann, Ludwig, interview by Don Cygan. "My Experience during the Ardennes Offensive" (June 6, 2010).

Lindemann, Ludwig, interview by Don Cygan. "Questionnaire to Ludwig Lindemann" (June 2010).

Lindemann, Ludwig, interview by Don Cygan. "Second Interview with Ludwig Lindemann" (June 25, 2010).

Long, Paul, and Donald Williams interview by Lieutenant A. J. Webber. *3rd Platoon Company "C" 705th Tank Destroyer Battalion* (January 1945).

Lott, Robert D., interview by Don Cygan. "Interview with Robert D. Lott" (April 25, 2009).

Luettwitz, Heinrich von, interview by S. L. A. Marshall. *ETHINT 41, An Interview with General Panzertruppen Heinrich von Luettwitz: XLVII Panzer Corps (16 December to 24 December 1944),* (October 13, 1945).

Luettwitz, Heinrich von, interview by Department of the Army Historical Section. *Item No. 5: Answers to Questions by Gen d Pz Tr v. Luettwitz MS A-938.* College Park, MD: Foreign Military Studies, National Archives (October 19, 1945).

Luettwitz, Heinrich von, interview by Alfred Zerbel. *The Assignment of the XLVII Panzer Corps in the Ardennes MS A-939.* College Park, MD: Department of the Army (June 13, 1950).

Luettwitz, Heinrich von, interview by S. L. A. Marshall. *XLVII Panzer Corps (16 December–24 December 44), ETHINT 41.* National Archives, College Park, MD: Department of the Army (October 13, 1945).

Luettwitz, Heinrich von. *XXXXVII Panzer Corps in the Battle of the Ardennes Manuscript A-940.* Foreign Military Studies, College Park, MD: Department of the Army, 1946.

Lyons, Joseph. "Joseph Lyons: 463rd Parachute Field Artillery Battalion, Attached to the 101st Airborne Division." In *Beyond Valor: World War II's Ranger and Airborne Veterans Reveal the Heart of Combat,* by Patrick K. O'Donnell, 258–60. New York: The Free Press, A Division of Simon and Schuster Inc., 2001.

MacDonald, Charles B. *A Time for Trumpets: The Untold Story of the Battle of the Bulge.* New York: Perennial Publishers, 2002.

MacDonald, Robert J. *Another Von Rundstedt Blunder—Bastogne.* Military Monograph, Advanced Officers Class No. 1, Fort Benning, GA: Department of the Army, 1948.

MacKenzie, Fred. *The Men of Bastogne.* New York: Ace Books, 1968.

Manteuffel, Hasso von, interview by Robert S. Merriam. *An Interview with General Panzer Hasso von Manteuffel: Fifth Panzer Army Nov 44–Jan 45 ETHINT 46.* College Park, MD: Department of the Army (October 29–31, 1945).

Manteuffel, Hasso von, interview by unknown. *Fifth Panzer Army (11 Sep 44–Jan 45) ETHINT 45.* College Park, MD: Department of the Army (June 21, 1945).

Manteuffel, Hasso von. "The Fifth Panzer Army during the Ardennes Offensive." In *Hitler's Ardennes Offensive: The German View of the Battle of the Bulge,* by Danny S. Parker, 71–161. St. Paul: Greenhill Books, 2006.

Marcus Wendel. "82. Infanterie-Division." *Axis History.* May 23, 2005. http://www.axis history.com/index.php?id=1514 (accessed March 25, 2011).

Margry, Karel. *Operation Market Garden, Then and Now, Volume 1.* London: Battle of Britain International Limited, 2002.

Marshall, S. L. A. "Men Against Armor." *Armored Cavalry Journal,* May–June 1950, 1948: 4–7.

———. *Bastogne: The First Eight Days.* Washington, D.C.: Infantry Journal Press, 1946.

Martin, Darryl R. "Deathtrap for Panzers: An Interview with Colonel Ray Allen (Ret)." *World War II,* 2004: 50–58.

Martin, Darryl. "Unexpected Trap for the Panzers: Interview with LTC Ray Allen." *Military History,* 1989: 47–53.

Martin, James L. "Letter to George Koskimaki." Chamblee, Georgia, 1989.

Maucke, Wolfgang. *Report Over the 15th Panzer-Grenadier-Division during the Ardennes Offensive from 16 December 1944 to 2 February 1945: MS P-032c.* After Action Report, College Park, MD: Department of the Army, 1949.

Maus, Bernard, interview by Don Cygan. "Interview with Bernard Maus" (July 2010).

McAuliffe, Anthony C., interview by S. L. A. Marshall. *Commander's View of the Situation* (January 5, 1945).

McAuliffe, Anthony C. *Merry Christmas.* From the collection of the 901st Glider Field Artillery Battalion, College Park, MD: Department of the Army, 1944.

———. "Merry Christmas." Bastogne: Headquarters of 101st Airborne Division, December 24, 1944.

McMorrow, Merle W. "Letter to George Koskimaki."

Mesko, Jim. *U.S. Tank Destroyers in Action, Armor Number 36.* Carrollton, TX: Squadron, Signal Publications, Inc., 1998.

———. *Walk Around: U.S. Tank Destroyers, Armor Walk around Number 3.* Carrollton, TX: Squadron/Signal Publications, Inc., 2003.

Meyer, Kennan J. "The Rise of Eduardo Alberto Peniche." *CVCC The Alumni Magazine of Central Virginia Community College,* 2007: 18–23, 31.

Middleton, Troy H., interview by L. B. Clark. *Interview with Troy H. Middleton* (January 19, 1945).

Middleton, Troy H., interview by Theater Historian. *Questions Answered by Lieutenant General Troy H. Middleton* (July 30, 1945).

Middleton, Troy H. *SITREP No. 505, HQ VIII Corps: for Period 152400A, December, to 161200 December 1944.* Situation Report, College Park, MD: Department of the Army, 1944.

Middough, Bruce. "Letter to George Koskimaki." Manhattan Beach, CA, September 17, 1990.

Military Intelligence Division. *Company Officer's Handbook of the German Army.* Washington, D.C.: Military Intelligence Division of the War Department, 1944.

Miller, Richard B., interview by Lieutenant A. J. Webber. *1st Platoon, Reconnaissance Company, 705th Tank Destroyer Battalion* (January 1945).

Mitcham, Samuel, Jr. *German Order of Battle: Volume 3: Panzer, Panzer Grenadier and Waffen SS Divisions in WWII.* Mechanicsburg, PA: Stackpole Military History Series, 2007.

Mitcham, Samuel W., Jr. *Panzer Commanders of the Western Front.* Mechanicsburg, PA: Stackpole Books, 2008.

———. *Panzers in Winter: Hitler's Army and the Battle of the Bulge.* Mechanicsburg, PA: Stackpole Books, 2006.

Mockabee, John. "Hand-Drawn Map to George Koskimaki."

———. "John Mockabee 'D' Battery, 463rd Parachute Field Artillery—Letter to George Koskimaki." January 19, 1989.

Moore, Ned D. *Action Report, 17 December 1944 to 27 December 1944.* After Action Report, College Park, MD: Department of the Army, 1944.

Moran, Donald N. "Colonel Johann Gottleib Rall: Guilty of Tactical Negligence or Guiltless Circumstances." *Liberty Tree Newsletter, Sons of Liberty Chapter Sons of the American Revolution*, 2007. www.revolutionarywararchives.org (accessed January 18, 2012).

———. "Colonel Johann Gottlieb Rall: Guilty of Tactical Negligence or Guiltless Circumstances?" *Revolutionary War Archives.* 2011. http://www.revolutionarywararchives.org/rall.html (accessed October 7, 2011).

Moran, Timothy. *Location of 463 Parachute Field Artillery Battalion to Accompany S-2 Report 207, 22 December.* Disposition Overlay, College Park, MD: Department of the Army, 1944.

———. *No. 206 S-2 Report for the 463rd Parachute Field Artillery Battalion from: 2400, 20 December 1944, to: 2400, 21 December 1944.* S-2 Report, College Park, MD: Department of the Army, 1944.

———. *S-2 Report 463rd Parachute Field Artillery Battalion from: 2400, 24 December 1944, to: 2400, 25 December 1944.* S-2 Report, Bastogne: Department of the Army, 1944.

———. *No. 208 S-2 Report for the 463rd Parachute Field Artillery Battalion, from: 2400, 22 December 1944, to: 2400, 23 December 1944.* S-2 Report, College Park, MD: Department of the Army, 1944.

Morris, Richard B., and Henry Steele Commager. *The Spirit of Seventy-Six: The Story of the American Revolution as Told by Participants.* New York: De Capo Press, 1958.

Nelson. *G-2, 1420A 16 December 44.* G-2 Report, 28th Infantry Division, College Park, MD: Department of the Army, 1944.

Nelson, C. F., interview by S. L. A. Marshall. *Artillery in the Neffe Action* (January 1945).

Nelson, Ralph, interview by George Koskimaki. *Lieutenant Nelson's Account of the Siege of Bastogne* (unknown).

Nichols, Forrest J. "Letter to George Koskimaki." Lakeland, FL, July 3, 1990.

Niland, Thomas J., interview by George Koskimaki. *Individual Action Report for Bastogne.*

Northwood, Arthur, and Leonard Rapport. *Rendezvous with Destiny.* Fort Campbell, KY: One Hundred First Airborne, 1977.

Office of the Intelligence Officer. *Unit History of 513th Fighter Squadron: Report for period ending 30 November, 1944.* Unit History, Maxwell AFB, AL: Department of the Army, 1944.

———. *Unit History of the 513th Fighter Squadron: Report for period ending 31 October 1944.* Unit History, Maxwell AFB, AL: Department of the Army, 1944.

O'Halloran, John T. *The Operations of 1st Platoon, Company "B," 401st Glider Infantry (101st Airborne Division) in the Battle of Bastogne, Belgium, 25 December 1944.* Military Monograph, Advanced Officer Class No. 2, Fort Benning, GA: Department of the Army, 1948.

O'Mara, Robert, interview by Leo G. Barron. *Interview with Robert O'Mara* (January 24, 2011).

Operations Section. *Unit Journal for the 115th Panzergrenadier Regiment.* Daily Unit Journal, Freiburg, Germany: Wehrmacht, 1944.

Operations, 26th Volksgrenadier Division. *Ia, Durchburch und Vormarsch auf Bastogne Dec 16-31, 1944.* Captured German Military Records, National Archives Microfilm Publication T733. Item #77584, Roll 828, 1st Frame 428.

Pallud, Jean Paul. *Battle of the Bulge: Then and Now.* Hobbs Cross, Essex: Battle of Britain International Ltd., 2007.

Park, Howard. "Letter to Danny Parker." October 4, 1993.

Parker, James E. "Bastogne Notes." *406th Occupier*, 1945: 24.

Parker, Danny S. *Battle of the Bulge: Hitler's Ardennes Offensive, 1944–1945.* Cambridge, MA: Da Capo Press, 1994.

Parker, Ken. "Bastogne's Bedsheets." *WW II History*, December 2009: 22–25.

Peniche, Eduardo. "A Journal by Prof. Eduardo A. Peniche, Combat Veteran of the 101st Airborne." *Lonestar College Kingwood.* May 2009. http://www.lonestar.edu/research-guides-kingwood.htm (accessed April 16, 2011).

Peplowski, Walter J. "Walter J. Peplowski—B Battery, 463rd Parachute Field Artillery Battalion—Letter to George Koskimaki." December 21, 1988.

Perry, Basil H. *Citation for War Department Distinguished Unit Citation for 110th Infantry Regiment, 28th Infantry Division Period Concerned—16th to 23rd December 1944.* Awards Citation, College Park, MD: Department of the Army, 1945.

Phillips, Ivan G. *The Operations of the 502nd Parachute Infantry Regiment, 101st Airborne Division, in the Defense of Bastogne (Ardennes Campaign) 24 to 25 December 1944 (Personal Experience of a Regimental Communications Officer).* Regiment in Defense Advanced Infantry Officers Class No 1, Fort Benning, GA: Department of the Army, 1948.

"Photo of Panzer Lustmolch." Hemroulle: Department of the Army, December 25, 1944.

"Photo of StuG III outside Hemroulle." Bastogne, December 1944.

Pierce, Frank James. *Troy H. Middleton: A Biography.* Baton Rouge: Louisiana State University Press, 1974.

Prior, Jack T. "The Night Before Christmas—Bastogne, 1944." *More Than Medicine—Weekly Thoughts from Tom Quinn.* November 24, 2007. http://morethanmedicine.blogspot.com/2007/11/night-before-christmas-bastogne-1944-by.html (accessed July 14, 2011).

Quarrie, Bruce. *The Ardennes Offensive: U.S. VII and VIII Corps and British XXX Corps.* Oxford: Osprey Publishing, 2000.

Radio Journal of the Combat Command B, 10th Armored Division, December. Radio Journal, Bastogne: Department of the Army, 1944.

Reeves, Andrew J., interview by Captain Clark. *Miscellaneous Notes on VIII Corps and Ardennes Operation* (January 18, 1945).

Revolutionary War and Beyond. http://www.revolutionary-war-and-beyond.com/george -washington-quotes-6.html, 2008–2011 (accessed July 12, 2011).

Robbins, Jack E. *Report on Air Supply to 101st Airborne Division at Bastogne.* After Action Report, College Park, MD: Department of the Army, January 11, 1945.

Roberts, William L., interview by John Westover. *Combat Command B, 10th Armored Division* (January 12, 1945).

Robinson, George. "Leibgarde Kaserne." *Veteran's Memorial Museum Online.* February 3, 2010. http://vetsmemorialmuseum.com/id6.html (accessed June 28, 2011).

Rome, Irvin J. "More on the 101st—406th Appreciation Society." *Starduster* Vol III No I, 199: 9–10.

Rundstedt, Gerhard von, interview by unknown. *An Interview with Genfldm Gerd von Rundstedt: The Ardennes Offensive.* Edited by Kenneth W. Hechler. National Archives, College Park, MD: Foreign Military Studies (August 3, 1945).

Ryan, Clarence J. "Letter to Carmen Gisi." April 2009.

rzecznik@502-101airborne.pl. *Dowódcy 502nd PIR, 101st Airborne.* 2011. http://502-101 airborne.pl/dowodcy-502nd-pir (accessed October 1, 2011).

S-1 Section. *S-1 Journal for Month of December, 327th Glider Infantry.* S-1 Journal, College Park, MD: Department of the Army, 1944.

S-1, 327th GIR. *327th Glider Infantry Casualty Report, December 1944.* Casualty Report, College Park, MD: Department of the Army, 1944.

S-2 Section, 327th Glider Infantry Regiment. *Keepsake S-2 Journal covering period 18 December 1944 to 31 December 1944.* Radio Log, College Park, MD: Department of the Army, 1944.

S-2 Section, 502nd Parachute Infantry Regiment. *S2 Journal, 502nd Parachute Infantry Regiment.* S2 Radio Log, College Park, MD: Department of the Army, 1944.

S-3 Operations Section, 327th GIR. *327th Narrative Report.* Narrative Operations Report, College Park, MD: Department of the Army, 1944.

S-3 . *S3 Journal—506th Parachute Infantry Regiment, December 1944.* Daily Journal, College Park, MD: Department of the Army, 1944.

S-3 Operations Section, 327th Glider Infantry Regiment. *Disposition of Keepsake as of 21 1800 December 1944.* Operations Overlay, College Park, MD: Department of the Army, 1944.

S-3 Report. *S-3 Gun Log 463rd Parachute Field Artillery Battalion, December 18, 2400, to December 19, 2400, 1944.* S-3 Report Gun Log, College Park, MD: Department of the Army, 1944.

S-3 Report. *S-3 Gun Log 463rd Parachute Field Artillery Battalion, December 22, 2400, to December 23, 2400, 1944.* Gun Log, College Park, MD: Department of the Army, 1944.

S-3 Section. *S-3 Journal of the 506th Parachute Infantry Regiment, December.* Journal, College Park, MD: Department of the Army, 1944.

S-3 Section, CCB 10th Armored Division. *S-3 Journal, December 1944.* S-3 Journal, College Park, MD: Department of the Army, 1944.

S-3, 327th Glider Infantry Regiment. "Disposition of Keepsake (327th GIR) as of 20 1800 December 1944." College Park, MD: Department of the Army, December 20, 1944.

S-3, 3rd Tank Battalion, Combat Command B, 10th Armored Division. *Team Cherry Strength Reports.* Strength Report, College Park, MD: Department of the Army, 25 December, 1944.

Schramm, Percy Ernst. *Preparation of the German Offensive in the Ardenne,s September to 16 December 1944, MS # A-862.* War Diary of the Wehrmacht Operations Staff, College Park, MD: Department of the Army, 1945.

Schriefer, Martin. *Order for the Attack by this Regiment (77th) on 25.12.44 on Town of Bastogne.* Operations Order, College Park, MD: Wehrmacht, 1944.

Schrijvers, Peter. *The Unknown Dead: Civilians in the Battle of the Bulge.* Lexington, KY: The University Press of Kentucky, 2005.

Seaton, Stuart M. *Casualty Report for December 1944.* Casualty Report, College Park, MD: Department of the Army, 1944.

———. *Historical Narrative 463rd Parachute Field Artillery Battalion.* Historical Narrative, College Park, MD: Department of the Army, 1944.

Shell Report for the 463rd Parachute Field Artillery Battalion, 25 December 1944. Shell Report, College Park, MD: Department of the Army, 1944.

Sherburne, Thomas P. *Subject: Enemy Tanks. To: Commanding Officer, 463rd Parachute Field Artillery Battalion, APO 472, U.S. Army.* Memorandum for Record, College Park, MD: Department of the Army, 1944.

Sink, Robert F. *After Action Report for Month of December for the 506th Parachute Infantry Regiment.* After Action Report, College Park, MD: Department of the Army, 1945.

Sledzik, Bernard J. "Battle of the Bulge." Letter submitted by Stanley J. Wyglendowski, November 2, 1992.

———. "Memories of a World War II Fighter Pilot." *406th WWII Fighter Group.* 2011. http://406thfightergroup.org/bernard-sledzik.php (accessed August 3, 2011).

Smith, Claude D. "Letter to Joseph Lyons." Hollywood, FL, 1980.

Smith, Collie. "Bastogne: American Epic." *Saturday Evening Post*, February 17, 1945: 18–19 and then 91–92.

Spielberger, Walter. *Panzer IV and Its Variants.* Atglen, PA: Schiffer Military History, 1993.

Staff, XXXXVII Panzer Corps. *Ia, Kriegstagebuch "Christrose" mit Anlagen. War journal with orders and reports pertaining to preparations for Operations "Christrose" and "Rheingold" (operations during the Ardennes offensive in the Monschau sector) Dec 2-15, 1944.* Captured German Military Records, National Archives Microfilm Publication T733. Item # 64174, Roll 1133, 1st Frame 464.

Stevens, Ruth. "Stations of the Cross Painting." *St. Mary's Parish Family.* 2011. http://www.stmary-winchester.org/stations-cross-painting/ (accessed November 2011).

Stoling, Paul. Interview by Don Cygan. "Interview with Sergeant Paul Stoling" (March 5, 2009).

Stolmeier, Joseph F. "Letter to Richard Carroll." California, July 30, 2002.

Streeter, Timothy S. "75mm Pack Howitzer M8 (Airborne)." *Modeling the U.S. Army in WWII.* 2008. http://www.usarmymodels.com/AFV%20PHOTOS/75mm%20PACK%20HOWITZER/75mm%20Howitzer.html (accessed October 22, 2011).

Stronach, George H., interview by A. J. Webber. *3rd Platoon, Company "B," 705th Tank Destroyer Battalion* (January 1945).

Stryker, William S. *The Battles of Trenton and Princeton.* Boston and New York: Houghton Mifflin and Company, 1898.

Sutton, James D. "World War II: Interview with 101st Airborne Trooper James Flanagan about D-Day." *WW II*, June 2004.

Team 9, Interrogation Prisoner of War. *Translation of Diary found on 1st Lt. WALCHEN,*

901st Panzer Lehr Grenadier Regiment. Interrogation Report, College Park, MD: U.S. Army, 1944.

Templeton, Clifford D., interview by A. J. Webber. *705th Tank Destroyer Battalion* (January 1945).

Tennant, Wayne E., interview by Don Cygan. "E-mail Interview from Wayne E. Tennant" (December 27, 2007).

Thompson, Royce L. *Air Supply to Isolated Units, Ardennes Campaign, 16 December 1944–27 January 1945*. After Action Report, College Park, MD: Department of the Army, 1951.

Tofany, Victor J., interview by George Koskimaki. Questionnaire for Victor J. Tofany.

Tolhurst, Michael. *Bastogne*. Barnsley, South Yorkshire: Pen & Sword Books Limited, 2001.

Tourist Federation of Belgian Luxembourg. "Château de Roumont (Libin), Ochamps—Ochamps." *L'Ardenne Authentique!* 2011. http://www.ftlb.be/fr/attractions/architecture/fiche.php?avi_id=965 (accessed July 16, 2011).

Turbiville, G. H. *Narrative of the 326th Airborne Engineer Battalion Activities from 16 December thru 31 December 1944*. After Action Report, Bastogne: Department of the Army, 1945.

University of New Hampshire. "The University of New Hampshire Army and Air Force ROTC Hall of Fame: Lieutenant Colonel John D. Hanlon, U.S. Army." *University of New Hampshire*. 2011. http://www.unh.edu/army/alumni/hanlon.html (accessed July 17, 2011).

Unknown. "Photograph of Christmas Dinner." December 25, 1944.

Vining, Ralph "Shorty." "Account of Ralph 'Shorty' Vining." In *History of the 705th Tank Destroyer Battalion Heavy: One Round Was Enough, Volume Number Three: Battle of the Bulge and after the Bulge*, by James G. Wick and Lois Pawley, 935–39. University Place, WA: JI-LO Publications, 1999.

Wagener, Carl, interview by Alfred Zerbel. *Fifth Panzer Army—Special Questions (Ardennes)*. National Archives, College Park, MD (October 18, 1945).

Wagener, Carl, interview by Alfred Zerbel. *Fifth Panzer Army, Ardennes Offensive, General Comments, MS #A-962* (December 8, 1945).

Wagener, Carl, interview by Alfred Zerbel. *Main Reasons for the Failure of the Ardennes Offensive MS #A-963* (December 1945).

Waldo, Albigence. "Life at Valley Forge (1777–1778)." In *American History Told by Contemporaries, Vol. II: Building of the Republic*, Albert Bushnell Hart, ed., 568–72. New York: Macmillan, 1899.

Walsh, Francis Edward, interview by Jerri R. Donohue. *Francis Walsh Collection (AFC/2001/001/64192)*, Veterans History Project, American Folklife Center, Library of Congress (September 11, 2008).

———. "Letter to George Koskimaki: The 705 Tank Destroyer Battalion to Bastogne, Belgium." Unknown.

War Department. "CHAPTER II Organization of the Field Forces." *TM E 30 451 Handbook on German Military Forces*. March 15, 1945. http://www.ibiblio.org/hyperwar/Germany/HB/HB-2.html#VII (accessed September 24, 2011).

———. *TM 9-1326: Ordnance Maintenance 105mm Howitzer M3 and Howitzer Carriages M3 and M3A1*. Washington, D.C.: War Department, 1944.

Warburg, E. M. *APWIU No. 90/1944 Two German Bombing Units Return to the Fight*. Intelligence Report No. 90/1944, England: Department of the Army, 1944.

Wehrmacht, Oberkommando der. "Befehl Fur Die OPERATION "RHEINGOLD,"
    Preparations for the Ardennes Offensive." *Preparations for the Ardennes Offensive,
    LVIII Panzer Corps.* Berlin: National Archives, College Park, MD, December 7,
    1944.

Weinberg, Jerome M. *OPREP A No. D17B (2nd of 3 missions) for 24 hours ending sunset
    17 December 1944. Mission No. 287. Ninth Fighter Command Operations Order No.
    1/21-3.* Operations Report, Maxwell AFB, AL: Department of the Army, 1944.

———. *OPREP A No. D17B (3rd of 3 missions) for 24 hours ending sunset 17 December
    1944. Mission No. 287. Ninth Fighter Command Operations Order No. 1/21-3.* Opera-
    tions Report, Maxwell AFB, AL: Department of the Army, 1944.

Weiss, Wilhelm. *Ardennen 44. Der Einsatz der 26. Volksgrenadier Division, ehemalige
    Rheinisch-Westfälische 26. Inf. Div. bei den Kampfen um Bastogne.* Aachen: Helios,
    2011.

Weiz, Ruediger, interview by unknown. *The 2nd Panzer Division (from 21 December–26
    December 1944) in the Ardennes Offensive (Thrust on Dinant) MS #B-456* (unknown).

Wendel, Marcus. "26th Volksgrenadier Division." *Axis History Factbook.* September 17,
    2009. http://www.axishistory.com/index.php?id=828 (accessed June 4, 2011).

Weyland, O. P. "Citation for Bastogne." *406th Occupier,* 1945: 24.

Wick, Lois Pawley, and James G. Wick. *History of the 705th Tank Destroyer Battalion: One
    Round Was Enough, Volume Number Three: Battle of the Bulge and After the Bulge.*
    University Place, WA: JI-LO Publications, 1999.

Willems, Filips. "Interview with Ken Hesler." *The 463rd Parachute Field Artillery Official
    Website.* 2011. www,ww2airborne.net/463pfa/index.html (accessed May 2011).

Wise, Andrew J. "Letter to Major Ivan Phillips." Fort Benning, GA, January 29, 1948.

Wright, Ben, interview by George Koskimaki. *Interview Ben Wright.* www.ritterkreuz
    traeger-1939-45.de. "Ritterkreuzträger Anton Becker." *Die Ritterkreuzträgerder
    Deutschen Wehrmacht und Waffen-SS 1939-1945.* 2011. http://www.ritterkreuztrae
    ger-1939-45.de/Infanterie/B/Be/Becker-Anton.htm (accessed March 25, 2011).

XIX Tactical Air Force. "25 December, 1944." In *Tactical Air Phase of Ardennes Campaign,
    16 December 1944–28 January 1945,* by Royce L. Thompson. College Park, MD: Of-
    fice of the Chief of Military History, Department of the Army, 1950.

Zaloga, Steven J. *M18 Hellcat Tank Destroyer 1943–1997.* New York: Osprey Publishing,
    2004.

———. *U.S. Airborne Divisions in the ETO 1944–5.* New York: Osprey Publishing, 2007.

———. *U.S. Field Artillery of World War II.* Oxford: Osprey Publishing, 2007.

Zwonitzer, Mark, and Thomas Lennon. *The American Experience, Battle of the Bulge.*
    Directed by Thomas Lennon and Mark Zwonitzer. Produced by Thomas Lennon.
    Performed by Guy Franz Arend. 1994.

ENDNOTES

Epigraph

1 "Möge die Welt nie mehr solche Weihnachtsnacht erleben!" . . . "At the sight of ruins, of blood and death, universal fraternity will rise" (Heintz 1984, 75).

Introduction

1 "The following is based on a report from A.P./W.I.U. (2nd T.A.F.) dated 25 January
1945 and on subsequent interrogation of P/W in England . . ." (Felkin, A.D.I. (K)
Report No. 142/1945 1945, 1,3) The JU 88 Struhs flew in was a modified variant, the
S-3, which had two Jumo 213A engines that could provide 2,200 horsepower to each
of the bomber's engines. This gave the Z6 FH more speed and, therefore, more
survivability against the ever-present Allied fighters.

2 "I/K.G.66. 2. It is confirmed that I/K.G.66 based at Dedelstorf has reverted to its old
duties as a specialized pathfinder unit. It is organized in the same way when it operated against England in the spring of 1944, that is to say with the 1st Staffel using
the 'Y' procedure . . . this was a weather reconnaissance over an area of the North
Sea of the Thames estuary . . ." (Felkin, A.D.I. (K) Report No. 175/1945 Further
Report on the Crew of the Ju.88 S-3, Z6 + FH, of 1/K.G.66, shot down by A.A.
5 miles N.W. of Alost on 23rd January 1945, 1); "Once again I/K.G.66 had been organized as a specialist pathfinder unit as it was in the spring of 1944 when operating
against England from Montdidier. Each Staffel now has a strength of 6/8 Ju.88 S-3's
and crews" (Felkin, A.D.I. (K) Report No. 142/1945 1945). "Present composition of
the I. Gruppe is as follows: Unit 1st Staffel Planes 8 Ju 88 S3 [AND] 1 Ju 88 A4 Crews
about 10 . . ." (Warburg 1944, 3).

3 "At the beginning of VON RUNDSTEDT's offensive a number of aircraft of
K.G.66 were detailed to mark an area near Eupen where paratroops were to be
dropped. The operation was kept a close secret and members of the unit were forbidden to write home until the flight had been completed" (Felkin, A.D.I. (K) Report

No. 175/1945 Further Report on the Crew of the Ju.88 S-3, Z6 + FH, of 1/K.G.66, shot down by A.A. 5 miles N.W. of Alost on 23rd January 1945 1945, 2).

4   "At about Christmastime some 12 aircraft of I/K.G.66, six of them acting as path-finders and illuminators and the remainder as normal bombers, flew another sorties to the Bastogne area . . . 1st Staffel. Staffelkapitän . . . Oberleutnant PIOTA. Ia (Op-erations Officer) . . . Oberleutnant HEBERSTREIT" (Felkin, A.D.I. (K) Report No. 175/1945 Further Report on the Crew of the Ju.88 S-3, Z6 + FH, of 1/K.G.66, shot down by A.A. 5 miles N.W. of Alost on 23rd January 1945 1945, 2,8); "Major SCHMIDT . . . is still the Kommandeur of the I. Gruppe of K.G. 66" (Warburg 1944, 4).

Chapter One

1   Hooper, n.d.

2   "Division command post in Waxweiler" (H. Kokott, Ardennes Offensive—Battle of Bastogne 1950, 3).

3   Mitcham Jr., *Panzers in Winter: Hitler's Army and the Battle of the Bulge*, 2006, 190.

4   "The period of reorganization lasted five weeks. . . . Commitment in Westwall. Early in November 1944, the division—without the Anti-tank Battalion's anti-aircraft company and assault gun company which followed later—was moved to the West" (H. Kokott, Ardennes Offensive—Battle of Bastogne 1950, 1–2); "The 26th Volks Gren Div was fully filled and had disposal of seasoned commanders, but in its present condition had no experience in offensive warfare . . ." (H. V. Luettwitz, XXXXVII Panzer Corps in the Battle of the Ardennes Manuscript A-940 1946, 2); "26. Volks-Gren.Div. 14 from the Army on 2 Zeugamt Nov. 1944 - Pz.Jg.Kp.1026" (Andreas Altenburger 2011).

5   "The enemy picture was as follows. . . . Although this was declined, the division took it upon itself to keep those sentries, led by seasoned NCO's and officers, beyond the front, after they had turned in all documents, papers and their paybooks" (H. Ko-kott, Ardennes Offensive—Battle of Bastogne 1950, 2–4); "At the end of November new divisions were announced . . . to the conjecture that some major operation was being planned" (H. Kokott, Ardennes Offensive—Battle of Bastogne 1950, 4).

6   "Hitler was now ready to gamble the lives of thousands. . . . A giant offensive might turn the trick." (J. S. Eisenhower, 1969, 111); "During the first days of December 1944 . . . The Ia (operations officer) of the division was at the beginning not to be fa-miliarized with the plans" (H. Kokott, Ardennes Offensive—Battle of Bastogne 1950, 5).

7   "With rigid regulations for secrecy . . . Minefields beyond and along the front were cleared or shifted" (H. Kokott, Ardennes Offensive—Battle of Bastogne 1950, 5-6); "Since mid November the Army . . . It was obvious something big was about to take place" (Lindemann, Interview with Ludwig Lindemann, 2010); "We thought it would take . . . It took nearly 900 trains to bring troops and supplies up to the assembly area" (Buechs, 1945, 1–2); "I heard for the first time of the planned offensive . . . Present were: General Manteuffel, General Krueger of the LVIII Pan-zer Corps, the commanders of the Panzer Lehr, 2 Panzer and 26 Volksgrenadier Divisions" (Bayerlein, Bayerlein: After Action Reports of the Panzer Lehr Division Commander, From D-Day to the Ruhr, 2005, 66); "At the end of the first week of in December . . . the division was subordinated to the latter—detailed information was

given with regards to the planned offensive . . ." (H. Kokott, Ardennes Offensive—Battle of Bastogne 1950, 6); (Meinrad von Lauchert would replace Schönfeld as the commander of the 2nd Panzer on 15 December).

8   Berger, 2006.

9   Mitcham Jr., *Panzer Commanders of the Western Front*, 2008, 113–41.

10   Ibid., 207.

11   See chart (Schramm 1945, 197); "To plug the forested Ardennes . . . employ every available division in the November offensive to kill Germans" (Bradley, *A Soldier's Story*, 1999, 437–38); "On 6 Nov 44 . . . The most important factors will be first—SURPRISE, and next—SPEED!'" (Brandenberger, 1946, 14–16).

12   See Figure 21, on page II-26 (Handbook on German Military Forces TM-E, 1945. 30–451).

13   "Although the numerical strength . . . their artillery was more mobile" (Schramm 1945, 200–01).

14   ". . . the Offensive therefore got underway with approximately 850-900 tanks and assault guns. 80% of these were to be considered as ready for immediate commitment" (Schramm, 1945, 200).

15   See Figure 5 on II-8 (Handbook on German Military Forces TM-E, 1945, 30–451).

16   "OKW expected . . . thus, altogether four days" (Schramm, 1945, 184–85).

17   ". . . the Luftwaffe could be expected to accomplish 8 to 900 sorties a day, 60 of which would be made by the new rocket planes (Messerschmitt 262 and Arado); this would mean a considerable relief for the ground forces" (Schramm, 1945, 175–76); "The Fuehrer informed . . . a number which will guarantee a really noticeable relief" (Schramm, 1945, 209); "After 24 Dec 44 heavy air attacks made impossible almost all daytime transport, either of troops or of their supplies. Even regrouping of troops in occupied positions was rendered extremely difficult by the bombardment" (Rundstedt, 1945, 8).

18   "For the period 10–20 December . . . is extremely rare in December" (Dr. Herrmann, 1944, 2); "'The Luftwaffe meteorologists played a big part in 1940, in the campaign in the West. . . . Mid-Dec 44 was a very foggy, high-pressure period, and on 13 Dec 44, an extended period of fog was predicted, broken only about midday" (Jodl, 1945).

19   "XLVII Panzer Corps . . . *Südflanke gegen Feindeinwirkung über Linie Brüssel—Dinant—Givet einzusetzen*" (Wehrmacht, 1944, 3–4); "66 Corps (18 and 62 VG Divs) to encircle from both sides . . . and to be employed for a quick thrust to the Meuse" (C. Wagener, Fifth Panzer Army—Special Questions (Ardennes), 1945, 2–3); "The 26 VGD was to cross the Our . . . so as to free the Pz Lehr Division to reach the Meuse quickly" (Manteuffel, The Fifth Panzer Army during the Ardennes Offensive, 2006, 86); "In my opinion . . . whose commanders had neither adequate tactical nor strategic qualifications" (Manteuffel, Fifth Panzer Army (11 Sep 44–Jan 45), ETHINT 45, 1945, 8–9).

20   "3.) XXXXVII Panzer Corps crosses with spearheads the Our (River) . . . The Maas bridges between Namur and Dinant are able to be captured and kept open by way of a lightning strike (surprise attack)" (Staff, 1944); "For the Breakthrough: right: reinforced 2nd Panzer Division left: reinforced 26th Volks-Grenadier Division Corps reserve: Panzer Lehr Division" (Staff, 1944); "After Crossing the Clerf: right: reinforced 2nd Panzer Division left: Panzer Lehr Division behind (following): 26th Volks-Grenadier Division" (Staff, 1944); "26th VGD: Following entry into prepara-

tory positions east of Fischbach . . . for further use by the general headquarters" (Staff, 1944); "a) Forward Battalion in the area of Karlshausen . . . hold open and defend the Maas and Sambre River bridges" (Staff, 1944); Though the order mentioned Waxweiler, I believe the authors meant Eschweiler, which is along the Dasburg/ Eisenbach axis to Bastogne. This is confirmed in the book *Bayerlein: The After Action Reports of the Panzer Lehr Division Commander; From D-Day to the Ruhr.*

21 "The Staff of the XXXXVII Pz Corps arrived on 7 Dec at KYLLBURG/EIFEL . . . Bastogne is to be mopped up first, then the bulk of the Corps continues its advance" (H. V. Luettwitz, The Assignment of the XLVII Panzer Corps in the Ardennes MS A-939, 1950, 3–4).

22 "After Field Marshal von Rundstedt . . . placed a manuscript before him and put on his glasses" (H. V. Luettwitz, XLVII Panzer Corps (16 Dec–24 Dec 44), ETHINT 41, 1945, 12).

23 "As usual Hitler began with the general phrases of the Nazi party attainments . . . who was not completely acquainted with the real situation at the front" (Heilmann, 1946, 13).

24 "Hitler presented the offensive plan . . . war would be largely dependent on the success of the offensive" (Bayerlein, *Bayerlein: After Action Reports of the Panzer Lehr Division Commander, From D-Day to the Ruhr,* 2005, 70).

25 "At the end of his speech Hitler pointed out . . . With these words. Hitler closed his speech" (Heilmann, 1946, 16).

26 "The plan of attack for the Division was as follows . . . The Army Group strictly declined these proposals" (H. Kokott, Ardennes Offensive—Battle of Bastogne, 1950, 9).

27 See Wolfgang Knecht's book *Die Geschichte des Inf. Rgts. 77* for the history of the 77th Volksgrenadier Regiment. Also, for a more succinct history, see http:// infanterie-regiment77.org/. "At the end of September . . . Were it not for the steel faith that became hardened; the tears of disappointment, grief, and anger should have flowed" (Knecht, Die Geschichte des Inf. Rgts. 77, 1964, 155).

28 "The commander of the Volksgrenadier Regiment 77 was Lieutenant Colonel Schriefer. . . . Captain Raab, who led the battalion until the end" (Knecht, Die Geschichte des Inf. Rgts. 77, 1964, 155); "Anton Becker . . . Anton Becker verstarb am 13.08.1995 in Lohmar-Wahlscheid" (www.ritterkreuztraeger-1939-45.de 2011); For Martin Schriefer's Iron Cross, see *Axis History Forum* (Marcus Wendel, 2005); For Raab's Iron Cross citations see *Lexikon Der Wehrmacht* (Andreas Altenburger, 2011).

29 "Against instructions by Army Group and Army . . . as soon as the bridge near Gemuend would be passable" (H. Kokott, Ardennes Offensive—Battle of Bastogne 1950, 9–10); "For the performance of its mission, the Battalion further had the following . . . a. The Pursuit Tank Company and an anti-aircraft platoon from the Anti-tank Battalion. b. A motorized engineer platoon of the Engineer Battalion. c. A caterpillar tractor 'East' motorized battery of the First Anti-tank Gun Battalion Regiment 26. d. A motorized platoon of heavy 12cm mortars" (H. Kokott, Ardennes Offensive—Battle of Bastogne, 1950, 12); Kokott's memory was a little off. According to the order of battle from the actual operations order, the reconnaissance battalion had a towed battery of 10.5-cm light howitzers, and not antitank guns. The AA platoon comprised tracked vehicles with mounted 37mm AA guns. (Staff, 1944, Frame 620).

30   "Regiments 77 and 39 ... the thrust was then to be continued west over the Hosingen road" (H. Kokott, Ardennes Offensive—Battle of Bastogne, 1950, 10).

31   "The bulk of Regiment 77 ... to the bridge near Drauffeld" (H. Kokott, Ardennes Offensive—Battle of Bastogne 1950, 10–11); "The division artillery was to form a solid group in the area west of Herbstmuehle, participate in the preparatory fire together with the artillery reinforcements (I. Volks Artillery Corps and 1st Volks Projector Brigade) and keep their limbers nearby so that they could move across the Our River as soon as the GHQ engineers completed a bridge near Gemuend" (H. Kokott, Ardennes Offensive—Battle of Bastogne, 1950, 9).

32   "The Reconnaissance Battalion of Panzer Lehr (ALA) ... via Nieder Wampach or Doncols–Bras toward Bastogne" (Bayerlein, Bayerlein: After Action Reports of the Panzer Lehr Division Commander, From D-Day to the Ruhr, 2005, 90–93).

33   "My experiences during the Ardennes Offensive in Kingdom of Luxembourg ... In September 44 we came north of Posen in a holding camp, part of the military training grounds" (Lindemann, Questionaire to Ludwig Lindemann, 2010); "Joined Army 10/3/41 as was required compulsory service ... close combat sword in silver, at age 22" (Lindemann, Interview with Ludwig Lindemann, 2010).

34   "Again we were mixed into [an] existing division. . . . By sending via radio the enemy may intercept data" (Lindemann, Questionaire to Ludwig Lindemann, 2010); "Only two commanding officers knew of the mission [Ardennes Offensive]. . . . I was in charge of 6th company IR 77" (Lindemann, Interview with Ludwig Lindemann, 2010).

35   "During the evening hours of 15 December ... After dark, the commanders informed the attack troops of the attack order" (H. Kokott, Ardennes Offensive—Battle of Bastogne, 1950, 13–14).

36   C. B. MacDonald, 2002, 97.

37   "Yes, in December 1944 I thought it was a good idea to fight this battle and to win the war" (Lindemann, Interview with Ludwig Lindemann—Second Interview, 2010).

38   "The troops accepted it with utmost seriousness ... were directed to their assembly areas through special leaders" (H. Kokott, Ardennes Offensive—Battle of Bastogne, 1950, 13–14).

39   "Many were *ersatz* [replacement] soldiers and were from flak [antiaircraft crews], naval, [and] excess personnel from the Luftwaffe ... " (Lindemann, Interview with Ludwig Lindemann, 2010).

40   "Around midnight on 16th ... we were laying on the ground freezing and very tense for the next move" (Lindemann, Questionaire to Ludwig Lindemann, 2010); "The evening before ... with MG-44 Sturmgewehr automatic rifles" (Lindemann, Interview with Ludwig Lindemann, 2010).

41   "At 0500 hours on 16 December ... The nocturnal silence was interrupted only by the occasional salvo of an enemy battery or the sound of some individual guns on our own in normal harassing fire" (H. Kokott, Ardennes Offensive—Battle of Bastogne, 1950, 15); "At 0500 hours on 16 December 1944 ... located along the heights where previous combat outposts [listening posts] were stationed" (Operations, 1945).

42   "At 0530 hours—suddenly—all of the German barrels roared out with a raging fire. . . . After a short period of time, the forward enemy line was torn open at many points along a broad front" (H. Kokott, Ardennes Offensive—Battle of Bastogne,

1950, 15–16); "Under the cover of a tremendous 17-minute preparatory artillery barrage . . . capturing the surprised enemy positions" (Operations, 1945).

43   "Around 0530 artillery and *nebelwerfers* [rocket launchers] fired for about half an hour. We were woken up at 0600 and our company was ordered to march to engage the enemy. Our goal was to take over Hosingen" (Lindemann, Interview with Ludwig Lindemann, 2010); "After 30 minutes of heavy artillery . . . We all spread out and headed towards a forest and road which led to Bockholz-Enscheringen" (Lindemann, Questionaire to Ludwig Lindemann, 2010).

Chapter Two

1   "Head Quarters, at the Gulph, December 17, 1777 . . . October 3, 1777" (Chadwick, 2004, 198).

2   Pierce, 1974, 1–209.

3   "Divisions operations centered in the barracks area at the northern edge of Bastogne. . . . Close against the north end of it, aimed at the gate to deal with armor, a self-propelled gun squatted" (MacKenzie, 1968, 72); To this day, there is still German writing faintly visible on some of the sheds and buildings.

4   Pierce, 1974, 215; 28th Infantry Division Headquarters, 1944.

5   "28th Inf Div: Enemy patrols reached vic of (P 795583) and (P 801628) at 1015A in Z of 110th Inf. Co A 707 TK Bn and Co B 110th Inf committed to clear the area. 2d Bn 112th Inf committed to restore the line of 3d Bn 112th Inf penetrated by estimated 3 Bns enemy inf" (Middleton, SITREP No. 505, HQ VIII Corps: For Period 152400A DEC to 161200 DEC 44, 1944).

6   "Estimated before breakthrough that there were 2 VG and 2 Pz Divs in the BITBURG-TRIER area . . . which he said was extremely optimistic about the situation on the Corps front" (Reeves, 1945, 17); "Captured 1 PW Lt . . . This information is from captured document—IPW will look it over for further information—they have not seen it yet" (Nelson, 1944); Though Reeves claimed he received the information from Slayden, judging by the similarities in the 112th Infantry Report, it was likely he got it from them.

7   "The high command could not have been alarmed . . . that a German attack would be made on VIII Corps' front" (Middleton, Questions Answered by Lieutenant General Troy H. Middleton, 1945, 1–2).

8   "162035 Msg from CG VIII Corps . . . which will be held at all costs. Letter of instr. follows" (28th Infantry Division Headquarters, 1944).

9   "In my questions about the decision . . . He felt that ST VITH and BASTOGNE were the critical road centers in the Corps zone and worth almost any sacrifice to hold" (Middleton, Interview with Troy H. Middleton, 1945).

10   Tolhurst, 2001, 8–9; "Origins in the early Middle Ages: Bastogne Plateau has been inhabited since the prehistoric period. . . . We must recognize that the choice of Hitler was wise" (Commune de Bastogne, 2011); Guy Franz Arend: (through interpreter) "The town of Bastogne had no military importance. The proof of it was in the plan of attack. There wasn't even a plan to take the town itself. The Germans got taken into the game. Once they saw Bastogne was becoming for America a symbol of resistance, then the Germans set out to destroy that symbol" (Zwonitzer, 1994).

11   "Bastogne was a particularly indispensable point. . . . Basic order for the sudden

capture of Bastogne by a coup-de-main within the framework of the whole offensive" (Bayerlein, Bayerlein: After Action Reports of the Panzer Lehr Division Commander, From D-Day to the Ruhr, 2005, 75).

12   "The still resistance of the Americans at Hosingen . . . That was decisive for the battle of Bastogne" (Bayerlein, *Bayerlein: After Action Reports of the Panzer Lehr Division Commander, From D-Day to the Ruhr*, 2005, 93); "The combat strength of the 110th Inf Regt during the period 16–23 December . . . and reflect the highest traditions of the Armed Forces" (Perry, 1945, 2–3).

13   "On December 16, 1944 . . . Bradley and I discussed the probable meaning" (D. D. Eisenhower, 1997, 342).

14   "I was immediately convinced that this was no local attack. . . . It seemed likely to Bradley and me that they were now starting this kind of attack" (D. D. Eisenhower, 1997, 342).

15   "Operative: The quick reaction of the American Command, following the German assault . . . because it is always the greater, which licks the smaller" (C. Wagener, Main Reasons for the Failure of the Ardennes-Offensive MS #A-963, 1945, 5–6).

16   "We called a number of SHAEF staff into our conference room . . . the 82nd and the 101st. Both had been assembled at Reims for refitting after Arnhem" (Bradley, *A Soldier's Story*, 1999, 464).

17   "As early as December 17 the 82nd and 101st Airborne Divisions were released from SHAEF Reserve to General Bradley" (D. D. Eisenhower, 1997, 348).

18   Zaloga, U.S. Airborne Divisions in the ETO 1944-5, 2007, 24; The division had a nominal strength of 824 officers and 12,211 enlisted men. They left for Bastogne with 805 officers and 11,035 enlisted men (Frank R. Brower, 1945, 6).

19   Zaloga, U.S. Airborne Divisions in the ETO 1944-5, 2007, 24.

20   "The 101st Airborne was told to go to Bastogne at 0800 on 17 Dec . . . by personal conversation in a few minutes" (H. W. Kinnard, G-3 Account of Bastogne Operation, 1945, 1).

21   "Danahy and Kinnard both were 29 years old. . . . Kinnard was Army brat: born on a military post, son of a professional soldier, West Point–trained and graduated five years before" (MacKenzie, 1968, 10, 16).

22   "The G-2 was a volunteer from civilian life . . . lived in a Buffalo, NY, neighborhood where Danahy was reared" (MacKenzie, 1968, 14).

23   "The party was going along so well under its own steam around 6 o'clock. . . . Dismissed by the General, Danahy returned to his billet, where the guests remaining at his and Kinnard's housewarming party were watching the old Gary Cooper movie" (MacKenzie, 1968, 11, 13–15).

24   Pigalle, or "Pig Alley," as it was known by several generations of GIs, was named after the eighteenth-century sculptor Jean-Baptiste Pigalle. For most of the war years, Pigalle was known in various nightclubs, such as the famous Moulin Rouge, as well as a variety of brothels.

25   Koskimaki, 2003, 26–27.

26   An interesting side note on the famous pre-Christmas game: Depending on who you ask, the answer differs on who actually won the game. Not surprisingly, Army Air Corps veterans say they won, while the 101st swears they won the game. Obviously some of the confusion involved in the interruptions that day may have led to a misconception on one part or the other, or perhaps on memory.

27   "Captain Wallace Swanson, CO of Company A, 502nd Parachute Regiment of the

Screaming Eagles . . . But like France, it involved offensive and defensive maneuver-
ing for the best position against an enemy trying to regroup and push out" (Astor,
1994, 215–18).

28   "As a boy on the farm I'd spent untold hours passing a football back and forth
through an old rubber tire hanging from a limb of a giant elm tree. . . . That's how
I heard about the German breakthrough" (Black, *The Last First Sergeant*, 1998,
225–27); Black, The Unedited Manuscript of Layton Black's Memoirs to George
Koskimaki, n.d.

29   "McAuliffe set up a General and Special Staff meeting at 2100 and in briefing his
assistants on the situation his words were these, 'All I know of the situation is that
there has been a breakthrough and that we have got to get up there" (H. W. Kinnard,
G-3 Account of Bastogne Operation, 1945, 3); "Without any preliminaries . . . to Werbomont, Belgium" (MacKenzie, 1968, 15); "At 2030 on 17 December 1944 . . . for
immediate action" (Moore, 1944, 1).

30   "He [McAuliffe] started to ask rapid fire questions . . . and a representative from each
major unit . . ." (H. W. Kinnard, G-3 Account of Bastogne Operation, 1945, 1–2).

31   "General McAuliffe was 46 years old. . . . McAuliffe sometimes referred to himself
in the presence of his younger companions as 'Old Crock'" (MacKenzie, 1968, 18).

32   "17 December 1944 2230 Lt. Col Chase notified unit is alerted for possible move, and
is in command of regiment . . . 18 December 1944 1638 Departed Camp Mourmelon
by truck convoy. Colonel Sink returned—now in command of regiment" (S3, 1944).

33   All five of the boys, Steven, Richard, Donald, Jack, and Charles, served in the military during World War II, according to the youngest of the brothers, Charles, during
an interview in 2010 (S. A. Chappuis, Transcript of Interview with General Steve
Chappuis, 1995).

34   "I remember . . . Calm and decisive" (Hayes, Letter from Bill Hayes, 1994).

35   "Steven was very smart and down to earth. He was a more of a thinker and doer,
not a talker. For one thing, even after the war was over he didn't want to talk about
it" (C. W. Chappuis, 2010). Bill Hayes, a trooper in the 502nd, witnessed Chappuis'
icy calm demeanor during a fierce firefight in Normandy. In a letter he wrote to the
Chappuis family after the war, Hayes remarked: "I remember however when we
were attacking Carentan of seeing Colonel Chappuis' mini command post in a ditch,
next to the road that led next to or thru a woody area. The enemy was in the woods.
I believe it was part of the German 6th airborne Div. or regiment. His command
post seemed quite calm—which I think reflected the Colonel's projected personality.
Calm and decisive."

36   "If Chappuis says he's in trouble, you'd better believe it and do something about it
fast, because Silent Steve will be in real big trouble and he won't call back to tell you
again" (Arend, 1987, 137).

37   "Upon arriving in Camp Mourmelon . . . to find exactly what his particular unit
needed most in the manner of training" (S. A. Chappuis, Historical Record 502nd
Parachute Infantry Regiment, December 1944, 1).

38   "Upon arrival I made a call on Division Headquarters and met General
McAuliffe. . . . As we passed the ammo dump I turned and took the whole battalion
through with orders to load as much 75mm ammo as we could carry in any vehicle,
regardless of how crowded they were" (Cooper, Interview with Colonel John T.
Cooper, unknown).

39   "It was just after midnight on Monday, December 18, 1944. . . . Because our two

divisions are the *only* reserve. Everyone else is on the line" (Black, *The Last First Sergeant*, 1998, 227–28).

40 "My first information . . . Our movement to Bastogne was quick and decisive" Although Swanson claims this happened after the game, the historical record does not match his account. Colonel Chappuis did not learn of the deployment orders until the night of the seventeenth, while he was still in Mourmelon. In addition, Black mentions his account that Swanson left the morning of the eighteenth, which makes more sense. (Astor, 1994, 216).

41 "At 1215, 18 December 1944 . . . At 1400, 18 December 1944 the division began the motor march with units in the following order: 501 Parachute Infantry, 907th Glider Field Artillery . . . " (Moore 1944, 1); "Early in December . . . Talk about a letdown!" (J. W. Flanagan, 1990).

42 "I was born and raised in Sioux City, Iowa. . . . I jumped 18th man as I had to make sure everybody followed the lieutenant out the door" (Asay, 2009).

43 "Huge trucks, we called them cattle cars, were showing up and we all were trucked to the Ardennes" (Asay, 2009).

44 "As we loaded onto the trailer trucks . . . how valuable our living and existing in freedom really was" (Koskimaki, 2003, 32).

45 "Troops of the Regiment loaded into ten ton trucks at Camp Mourmelon at about 1800 hours, 18 December 1944 and began the trip which was to end at Bastogne" (S. A. Chappuis, Historical Record 502nd Parachute Infantry Regiment, December 1944, 2).

46 "18 December, 1944, the 327th Glider Infantry and attached First Battalion, 401st Glider Infantry (referred to in reports and herein as Third Battalion), with the 463rd Field Artillery Battalion attached, left Camp Mourmelon, France, in truck convoys at 1955 hours headed toward Belgium" (Headquarters, 327th Glider Infantry, 1944, 1).

47 "I always wanted to go to West Point. . . . General Bill Lee said my battalion was the best one in the 101st—and that meant we were the best battalion in the U.S. Army" (D. Martin, 1989, 47–48).

48 Ibid.

49 See Gardner, 1980.

50 "When young MacDonald stood up straight . . . MacDonald had learned his lessons well in combat in Normandy and Holland" (MacKenzie, 1968, 179).

51 S. Marshall, 1948, 4.

52 "The 3rd Battalion of 327th Glider Infantry [1/401] was in a rest area in the vicinity of Mourmelon, France. . . . "Carry with you what equipment you came out of Holland with" (R. J. MacDonald, Another Von Rundstedt Blunder—Bastogne, 1948, 3–4).

53 "We got as much ammo and gear as we could, and then loaded up in trucks for the drive north to Belgium. . . . After we heard about the American troops getting beat up, our attitudes changed." (C. Gisi, Interview with PFC Carmen Gisi, 2009).

54 "I happened to be in England. . . . We got a C-47 airplane and flew back" (Harper, Bastogne Speech, 1975).

55 "Some of our trucks were not unloaded from the trip up from Southern France . . . regardless of how crowded they were" (Cooper, Interview with Colonel John T. Cooper, unknown).

56 "While in Mourmelon . . . We were well-supplied prior to setting out for Bastogne" (Hesler, Interview with Ken Hesler, 2009).

57 Courtesy of Filip Willems, author and web designer of The 463rd Parachute Field

Artillery Official Website: www.ww2airborne.net/463pfa/index.html, and Ken Hesler interview and permission, May 2011 (Willems, 2011).

58   "This alert was ordered into execution and this organization departed from Mourmelon, France at about 2130 hour 18 December . . ." (Seaton, 1944, 1).

59   "I [Anthony McAuliffe] met the author on or about December 14, 1944, at the Scribe Hotel in Paris. . . . Thus, he became the only correspondent with us during the Siege of Bastogne" (MacKenzie, 1968, Foreword).

60   "A realist, methodical and chary of haphazard adventures . . . They were approaching the Bois de Herbaimont 30 miles or so southwest of Werbomont" (MacKenzie, 1968, 26, 29); "As it was about to take off the advance party got a call from 18th Corps. . . . The advance party proceeded to the crossroads at Werbomont" (H. W. Kinnard, G-3 Account of Bastogne Operation, 1945, 2).

61   "Entering the town over a road fairly free of travel . . . men in disheveled and dirty battle dress carrying weapons with the unconscious ease headquarter troops do not attain" (MacKenzie, 1968, 30–31).

62   "Fortunately Gen McAuliffe, Lt Col H.W. D. Kinnard and Lt F.D. Starett took for Bastogne only 15 minutes . . . We saw the possibility that the column might be hit while it was still on the road or that it might even be caught by the air while it was moving along in column" (H. W. Kinnard, G-3 Account of Bastogne Operation, 1945, 3–4).

63   "Upon reaching Bastogne . . . He then said these words, "The enemy is just out of town" (H. W. Kinnard, G-3 Account of Bastogne Operation, 1945, 2); "The situation is best described as "confused" . . . He told me that he thought 10 CCB had 3 RBs to NE, E, and SE of the city" (A. C. McAuliffe, Commander's View of the Situation, 1945); "General McAULIFFE arrived at VIII Corps CP where he was informed that the Division was attached to the VIII Corps. He was given the mission of stemming the German offense in the vicinity of Bastogne" (Moore, 1944, 1); "He said at one time . . . He said that Gen Bradley told him over the phone it was 'OK' to hold BASTOGNE" (Middleton, Interview with Troy H. Middleton, 1945, 4); "I do not recall . . . I talked to Bradley because of the difficulty in communicating with First Army" (Middleton, Questions Answered by Lieutenant General Troy H. Middleton, 1945, 1).

64   "I realized . . . I didn't know where we were likely to be hit and nobody could help me much on that point" (A. C. McAuliffe, 1945, 2).

Chapter Three

1   "Associate yourself with men of good quality if you esteem your own reputation; for 'tis better to be alone than in bad company" (Quote DB: Interactive Database of Famous Quotations, http://quotedb.com/quotes/4137), 3, 1777 (Chadwick, 2004, 198).

2   "November saw the 406th Group still warmly sheltered at Camp Mourmelon—and not very anxious to move" (Office of the Intelligence Officer, 1944, 1–2) See officer and enlisted strengths.

3   "Howard M. Park: born International Falls, Minnesota 27 January 1922, Elementary School Minnesota" (Howard M. Park, n.d.); "After my wounding . . . was given 10 days convalescent leave effective on or about 7 October" (Office of the Intelligence Officer, 1944, 6); "Stationed with the 406th Fighter Group . . . C-47's used to fly in equipment to them and landed at our strip" (*The 406th Occupier*, 1945, 16).

4   "This was a slow month for me. . . . It is difficult for new pilots to disregard their own instruments and just fly close formation in heavy cloud" (Office of the Intelligence Officer, 1944, 4).

5   "16 P-47 a/c of the 513th Sq TO 0945 from Site A-80 (Mourmelon) on a close support mission of the 8th Division . . . TD 1230 at Site A-80" (Weinberg, 1944).

6   "12 P-47 a/c of the 513th Sq TO 1415 from Site A-80 on a close support mission of the 8th Division . . . Base 12,000,' Visual" (Weinberg, OPREP A No. D17B (3rd of 3 missions) for 24 hours ending sunset, 17 December 1944. Mission No. 287. Ninth Fighter Command Operations Order No. 1/21–3, 1944).

7   "I was on the second mission of 17th December . . . I wanted to get into the thick of it but only got off a few long-range bursts in my situation" (Park, 1993).

8   "The M18 was one of the better armored designs produced in the United States during the war . . . the crew had the ability to fire and run rather than sit and try and slug it out with the opposition." (Mesko, U.S. Tank Destroyers in Action, Armor Number 36, 1998, 21); (Mesko, Walk Around: U.S. Tank Destroyers, Armor Walk Around Number 3, 2003, 58); The Panzerkampfwagen Mark IV and the Sturmgeschutz III also had a top road speed in the mid-twenties. Tests done by current owners of restored M18s (Josh Coates of Salt Lake City, Utah, 2010) show that under ideal road conditions, fuel, and maintenance, the M18 could reach speeds of sixty mph, making it almost fifteen mph faster than the current main battle tank of the U.S. Army, the M1A2 Abrams.

9   Spielberger, 1993, 59. Armor specs on the later-war versions (Ausf. H and J) of the German Panzerkampfwagen Mk IV, vary, since additional armor was sometimes bolted or welded onto the vehicle, including spare track links and the side-skirt armor, known as *schuerzen*.

10 "We started with the M3s and by the time we got to England we got the new M18s. . . . If a German gun shot at you it went right through that armor like paper" (Breder, 2009).

11 "0001—Enroute—location Liege (Coord. VK 4828)" (Harris, S-3 Report from 182400 December 1944 to 192400 December 1944, No. 110 705th Tank Destroyer Battalion, 1944).

12 "First Lieutenant Richard B. Miller, leader of the reconnaissance platoon . . . Templeton set out to find VIII Corps headquarters and learn what the score was" (MacKenzie, 1968, 53–54); "0830—Head Advance Guard CR (Coord. VP 575835). Route changed to west" (Harris, S-3 Report from 182400 December 1944 to 192400 December 1944, No. 110 705th Tank Destroyer Battalion, 1944).

13 "The 1st section of the 2nd Recon Platoon was ordered to make contact with the advance guard because communication had been lost. . . . Captain Fred Hamilton Jr, the CO of Recon Co. to return to the bn. immediately at its positions 6 miles south of LAROCHE." (Duvall, 1945, 1–2); "0930—2nd Plat Rcn. Contact enemy armor Houffalize (Coord. VP 610720)" (Harris, S-3 Report from 182400 December 1944 to 192400 December 1944, No. 110 705th Tank Destroyer Battalion, 1944).

14 "3rd Plat. Co A organized defensive block La Roche" (Harris, S-3 Report from 182400 December 1944 to 192400 December 1944, No. 110 705th Tank Destroyer Battalion, 1944).

15 "1130—Bn C.O, report CG VIII Corps at Neufchateau . . . 705 TD Bn. attached 101st Airborne Division. Directed to proceed to Bastogne" (Harris, S-3 Report from 182400 December 1944 to 192400 December 1944, No. 110 705th Tank Destroyer Battalion, 1944).

16 These elements joined the rest of the battalion in Bastogne on December 28.

17 "We were ordered to Bastogne 12/18/44. . . . Looked like the fires of Hell to me." (A. D'Angelo, Interview with Tony D'Angelo, 2009); Name of D'Angelo's Hellcat, also Interview with Tony D'Angelo, 2009. (The song "No Love, No Nothin'" was recorded by several popular artists during the war. In the 1943 Busby Berkeley movie *The Gang's All Here*, the song was covered by Alice Faye.)

18 "With the security of the unit temporarily established . . . Recon Co reconnoitered the routes over which the column would pass" (Templeton, 1945, 1–2); "1500—Battalion COs party contact enemy armoured road block Bertogne (Coord VP 520666) and withdrew to Bastogne." The German unit was most probably an advance unit from 2nd Panzer, trying to skirt far to the north and close up the gap around Bastogne. (Harris, S-3 Report from 182400 December 1944 to 192400 December 1944, No. 110 705th Tank Destroyer Battalion, 1944).

19 "The morning of 16 Dec. 44 . . . As I was only a PFC I did not know what our missions were, and I would follow our platoon leader Lt. Vorboril" (Walsh, Letter to George Koskimaki: The 705 Tank Destroyer Battalion to Bastogne, Belgium, unknown); "2100—Battalion (-) closed Bastogne" (Harris, S-3 Report from 182400 December 1944 to 192400 December 1944, No. 110 705th Tank Destroyer Battalion, 1944).

20 "I remember we arrived at Bastogne at night. . . . Only part of our Battalion got in there" (A. D'Angelo, Interview with Tony D'Angelo, 2009); "I was the company commander of C Company. . . . I was in the hospital" (Tennant, 2007). Tennant was wounded and was one of the last casualties to be evacuated to France prior to Bastogne being completely surrounded after December 20. Wayne (Tolhurst, 2001, 69–70).

21 "By means of officers guides the Division . . . largely during darkness and during rain and snow squalls" (Moore, 1944, 1).

22 "The whole trip was miserable . . . while the remainder stood and took it" (R. J. MacDonald, Another Von Rundstedt Blunder—Bastogne, 1948, 7).

23 "Corps had pulled out during the night" (A. C. MacAuliffe, 1945, 2).

24 "Ewell [CDR 501st RCT] told Kinnard . . . 327 on its area at 1015, 326th Engr on its area at 1030, thus completing the Div assembly" (H. W. Kinnard, G-3 Account of Bastogne Operation, 1945, 7, 10).

25 "Divisions operations centered in the barracks . . . Close against the north end of it, aimed at the gate to deal with armor, a self-propelled gun squatted" (MacKenzie, 1968, 72); The last members of the staff [corps] had departed by 1200 on 19 Dec and the 101st then decided to take over the Corps CP, along with a cub airplane, a great deal of medical stores, and a 'very large' supply of cognac" (H. W. Kinnard, G-3 Account of Bastogne Operation, 1945, 8–9).

26 "Danahy was the last member of the staff to arrive from the bivouac at Mande St. Etienne . . . moreover there was no markings at all to show that a defense of Bastogne was taking shape . . . " (MacKenzie, 1968, 72–74).

27 "1000—Received enemy situation from G-2 . . . East and directed primarily at BASTOGNE" (S2 Section, 327th Glider Infantry Regiment, 1944).

28 "Between 0800 and 0900 [19 DEC] . . . and see men moving at a distance of 2½ or 3 miles" (501st Parachute Infantry Regiment, 1945).

29 "19 DEC 1400 1st Bn. to launch an attack with limited objectives north of Noville" (S-3 Section, 1944); "Somewhere between 1100 and 1400 on 19 Dec . . . send a bat-

talion to Noville to relieve the road block of Team Desobry" (H. W. Kinnard, G-3 Account of Bastogne Operation, 1945, 10).

30   "Kinnard had contact with Ewell only by radio . . . was holding his own although the enemy were all around him" (H. W. Kinnard, G-3 Account of Bastogne Operation, 1945, 9).

31   "G-2 interpreters examined letters . . . the rest of the material had been collected from the dead" (MacKenzie, 1968, 74).

32   "1700—19 Dec—Received word from Division that our Regiment [502] will move up on a defensive position" (S2 Section, 502nd Parachute Infantry Regiment, 1944).

33   "At about 1800 hours . . . Contact with the 506th Parachute Infantry at this time was maintained by patrols" (S. A. Chappuis, Historical Record 502nd Parachute Infantry Regiment, December 1944, 2); "1930—19 Dec—Regimental CP now located at ROLLE (534–618)" (S2 Section, 502nd Parachute Infantry Regiment, 1944); "At about 1500 on 19 Dec . . . There was no action anywhere along the regtl front that night" (Cassidy, 1945, 1).

34   "The week of Dec 11-16th Johnnie [Private Ballard] and I [Goldmann] attended bazooka school . . . set one at a time on guard and to hell with the Germans [and] went to sleep" (Goldmann, Letter to Mrs. Ballard, 1945).

35   "19 Dec 44 Arrive vicinity of Bastogne . . . Able in reserve. 2-AT guns attch—57mm. 4 LMGs attchd to Able from Red [1st BN]. Able Attch to White Bn [2nd]. 'Dog' on left 'Easy" on right' (A Co Headquarters Section, 502nd Parachute Infantry, 1945); "A few miles to our right . . . the Screaming Eagles are here to fight" (Peniche, 2009).

36   "The CP and Fire Direction Center was located in a house in Hemroulle, with the Aid Station in a chapel across the street" (Hesler, Notes on the 463rd PFA and the Battle of Bastogne, 1990, 2).

37   "The 463rd Prcht. F.A. Bn., enroute from Mourmelon . . . Battalion fired in support of the 327th Glider Infantry Regiment" (V. E. Garrett, S-3 Report from: 182400 Dec 1944 to: 192400 Dec 1944, 463rd Parachute Field Artillery Battalion No. 204, 1944); ". . . with the command post established in the town of Hemroulle, Belgium . . ." (Seaton, 1944, 1); "At 9 am . . . Btry B was to the north of the road a short distance beyond" (Hesler, Notes on the 463rd PFA and the Battle of Bastogne, 1990); (S-3 Report, 1944).

38   "At 1630 it was reported that German . . . especially from the East and Northeast" (Abernathy, S-2 Periodic Report for the 327th GIR—from December 181800 to December 191800, 1944); "19 December . . . 2245—a negro supply convoy has been ambushed . . . area occupied by Div. Ordnance and the 326th Medical Co" (S2 Section, 327th Glider Infantry Regiment, 1944).

39   "The reconnaissance detachment took at about midnight [20/21] the undamaged bridge across the OURTHE at OURTHEVILLE. During the advance on OURTHEVILLE an enemy attack from FLAMIERGE was repulsed" (H. V. Luettwitz, The Assignment of the XLVII Panzer Corps in the Ardennes MS A-939, 1950, 8).

40   "It was late Tuesday night . . . the Germans had thrown up in the last stages of the journey" (MacKenzie, 1968, 87–88); "2200—Battalion ordered by Bn C.O. to immediately occupy defensive positions about the town of Bastogne. 2300—All assigned positions occupied" (Harris, S-3 Report from 182400 December 1944 to 192400 December 1944, No. 110, 705th Tank Destroyer Battalion, 1944).

41 "Enemy Front Lines . . . There is no indication of a slackening up of his present counter-offensive" (P. A. Danahy, G-2 Periodic Reports No. 4 from: 220001 to 222400 December 1944).

42 See March Column list (Moore, 1944, 1).

43 "CCB 10 Armd Div attached to 101 AB Div effective 201100 A . . . 333 FA Group attached to 101 AB Div effective 200945 A. 755 Armd FA Bn attached to 101 AB Div effective 191600 A" (H. W. Kinnard, G-3 Report No. 2, from: 192400A to: 202400 December 1944).

44 "I estimate that half of the enemy attacks . . . It was our arty situation which gave me my chief reason for optimism" (A. C. McAuliffe, 1945).

45 "This order was issued . . . McAuliffe's desire to harbor his reserve to the limit" (H. W. Kinnard, G-3 Account of Bastogne Operation, 1945, 11); "We used the armor defensively . . . which got through the infantry line" (A. C. McAuliffe, 1945).

46 "The Div evacuation center was located at a cross roads . . . this put the hospital on the Div rear . . . " (H. W. Kinnard, G-3 Account of Bastogne Operation, 1945, 10).

Chapter Four

1 "On Dec. 17th, Washington wrote as follows . . . and in that position we must make ourselves the best shelter in our power." (Anderson, 2010).

2 "Xavier Gaspard, pharmacist at Bastogne . . . which was never once looted" (Cercle d'Histoire de Bastogne, 1994, 385).

3 "So cruel was the irony . . . what was happening the following morning found the GIs reticent and irritable . . ." (Schrijvers, 2005, 112).

4 "Unsubstantiated rumors flew about until . . . Other schools continued their routine, too" (Schrijvers, 2005, 112–13).

5 "By noon . . . But the opportunity for flight was disappearing fast" (Schrijvers, 2005, 113); "Toward 15 hours, three shells exploded near the Chapel Ste-Thérèse, throwing the inhabitants into confusion" (Heintz, 1984, 57).

6 "On Tuesday GIs and gendarmes began manning checkpoints . . . The Récollets offered enough room for another 100 civilians in the vaulted cellars of their seventeenth-century monastery" (Schrijvers, 2005, 114–15); "More than six hundred refugees filled the underground corridors of the Pensionnat des Soeurs de Notre Dame . . . a shelter set up beneath the chapel's choir" (Heintz, 1984, 58–59).

7 "With most town officials gone . . . Léon Jacqmin, a respected businessman and veteran of the Great War" (Schrijvers, 2005, 115); "The Burgomaster appointed by the Americans . . . the Bastogne people did not suffer too much of hunger" (Heintz, 1984, 59).

8 "Xavier Gaspard, pharmacist at Bastogne . . . which was never once looted" (Cercle d'Histoire de Bastogne, 1994, 385).

9 "1300 21 Dec. S-2 patrol crossed 2nd phase line no contact made with the enemy . . . 1630 S-2 patrol will come in with our TD Rcn. Outfit" (S2 Section, 502nd Parachute Infantry Regiment, 1944, 4); "A number of S-2 patrols were launched from here [Rolle] . . . Coming back toward Ruette [Rouette] the S-2 men hitched a ride with a column from the 705th Tank Destroyer Battalion recon outfit" (Bando, Vanguard of the Crusade: The 101st Airborne Division in World War II, 2003, 237); "From 20 December to 24 December most of the activity in the Regiment was limited to patrols to Givry . . . Rouette . . . and Givroulle. . . . Numerous patrols were sent from

the battalions to determine the enemy positions and installations" (S. A. Chappuis, Historical Record 502nd Parachute Infantry Regiment, December 1944, 3); "When the 502nd arrived at Bastogne, Captain Robert Clements, former CO of George Co, was the regimental S-2. David White was his assistant" (Mark Bando, E-mail from Mark Bando, 2011); "Lt. Vorboril, with Pvt (now sgt) Francis Walsh and Pvt. Hunis Peacock, left the platoon area at 0400 (21 Dec). . . . One jeep, with S/Sgt Kermit Gunderson and the M8 with Chernak in command remained behind after the other vehicles pulled out to make certain everyone had a ride" (Wasil Chernak, 1945); "Germain Gaspard—At Rouette, a small group got together at the intersection, looking for news . . . and when a great many Germans arrived that evening it was less than reassuring" (Cercle d'Histoire de Bastogne, 1994, Chapter 14); "Dick Ladd rode facing backward on the last M-8. . . . Ladd wound up in an aid station west of Bastogne" (Mark Bando, *Vanguard of the Crusade: The 101st Airborne Division in World War II*, 2003, 237); "As the two vehicles were leaving town . . . The two Recon vehicles went on to FLAMIERGE, while the riding infantry drove to their CP" (Wasil Chernak, 1945, 2); "1715 S-2 patrol reported into our Regimental Cp. They killed 3 enemy and captured a Volkswagen at 480-645" (S2 Section, 502nd Parachute Infantry Regiment, 1944, 4).

10   "At 2030 hours a Captain and six enlisted men from the 28th Division . . . The order was to move the company out immediately and to recapture and clear the road junction" (R. J. MacDonald, Another Von Rundstedt Blunder—Bastogne, 1948, 9); "2300 saw us on the move towards the objective. . . . With this information fragmentary orders were issued and the following plan was executed" (R. J. MacDonald, Another Von Rundstedt Blunder—Bastogne, 1948, 9–10); "20 December 0045 . . . He saw 2 German halftracks at the crossroads and heard several tracked vehicles in the 326th Medical Co.'s area" (S2 Section, 327th Glider Infantry Regiment, 1944); "We could actually see them (the German soldiers) pretty well. . . . We could hear them talking in German and their hobnails on their boots as they walked back and forth on the road." (C. Gisi, Phone Interview with Carmen Gisi, 2011); "I remember going thru a swamp. When we got to the top of the ridge overlooking the crossroads, we saw trucks burning, horns stuck, and Germans talking" (C. Gisi, Questionnaire for Carmen Gisi, 2009); "1st Lt. (now Ret.-Dis.) Selvan E. Shields platoon established a block down the South West. . . . This was the prearranged signal for the remainder of the company to open up on the Germans" (R. J. MacDonald, Another Von Rundstedt Blunder—Bastogne, 1948, 10–11); "The Krauts had ambushed an American truck convoy . . . shouts of Germans were heard and the clatter of equipment added to the din" (Koskimaki, 2003, 144); "My platoon, the 3rd platoon . . . fire 2 shots as a signal for the rest of the company, to come down firing" (C. Gisi, Questionnaire for Carmen Gisi, 2009); "We got to our feet and began to fire. . . . Platoon sergeant Mike Campana was nicked with a bullet, pierced ear lobe" (Koskimaki, 2003, 145); "One hundred percent surprise . . . This action was completed by 0445 the 21st of December [it was the twentieth]" (R. J. MacDonald, Another Von Rundstedt Blunder—Bastogne, 1948, 11); "Those Germans were close. They came right in front of our company when we hit them. I know when we [he and Sawyer] fired, we killed a few of them, we even threw some grenades, but it was a short fight" (C. Gisi, Phone Interview with Carmen Gisi, 2011); "Charlie and I . . . Mike Campana our platoon sergeant caught a German bullet that hit the buckle of his ammo belt but it did not penetrate" (C. Gisi, Questionnaire for Carmen Gisi, 2009); "This

action was completed by 0445 the 21st [20] of December. . . . Not a sign of a doctor or aid man was to be found" (R. J. MacDonald, Another Von Rundstedt Blunder— Bastogne, 1948, 11); "Bodies were lying all over the place. . . . We regrouped and returned to the top of the hill from which we had attacked" (Koskimaki, 2003, 145); "I think the Germans did that because they were too badly injured—to put them out of their misery" (C. Gisi, Phone Interview with Carmen Gisi, 2011); ". . . and then on the other side of the road was the field hospital. . . . I took a picture of the tents at the hospital and later took some combat pictures of us guys" (C. Gisi, Questionnaire for Carmen Gisi, 2009). Interestingly, sixty-five years later, Carmen Gisi met Hank Skowronski, a member of the 326th Medical Company, who was captured that day near Crossroads X. The two veterans met at a dedication for a new memorial for the 326th outside of Bastogne. Hank had been missing a camera that he left in his fox-hole when he was attacked. Gisi told Skowronski that it was most certainly his cam-era that he found that morning. "WWII prisoner of war returns to site of capture," Vanover, Christie (USAG Benelux), www.army.mil, The Official Homepage of the United States Army, Dec. 15, 2009 (C. Gisi, Interview with PFC Carmen Gisi, 2009); "By 0800 . . . but offered his services in any way he could help" (R. J. MacDonald, Another Von Rundstedt Blunder—Bastogne, 1948, 11); "The 3rd platoon of Co. 'B' was attached to the 502 at 0700 20 December. . . . Subsequently, the platoon returned to BASTOGNE and to Division Reserve" (Stronach, 1945, 1); "After such a humili-ating counter-ambush . . . we were still at the junction or not after taking such a sound shellacking the night before" (R. J. MacDonald, Another Von Rundstedt Blunder—Bastogne, 1948, 13); "We covered a 10-mile wide front, almost one-half of the perimeter defense of Bastogne . . . we seldom knew what was happening behind us at Bastogne" (D. Martin, 1989, 53); "20 December cont'd. 0530—Blue Able killed 10 enemy, 9 of which were in civilian clothes and one in German uniform, in vicin-ity of 448629 . . . 0715—Three tanks with infantry attacking Blue Able from the NW. 1015—Enemy attack repulsed by Blue Able and are withdrawing to the NE" (S2 Section, 327th Glider Infantry Regiment, 1944); "The battalion organized to defend from the North West . . . Peace and quiet prevailed as we dug in deeper to defend our area" (R. J. MacDonald, Another Von Rundstedt Blunder—Bastogne, 1948, 7); See overlay (S-3, 327th Glider Infantry Regiment, 1944); (Quarrie, 2000, 87).

11   "20 Dec 44 0600 Able still in Defense of Monaville Belgium, we are defending from the north n-east. Lines shifted to tighten defense able 3 committed as center unit on line. Contact by sound only. 1—patrol 3 men sent out a contacted 1—LMG—34 belonging to the enemy. No action this date. D on left E on right" (A Co Headquar-ters Section, 502nd Parachute Infantry, 1945); (H. V. Luettwitz, XLVII Panzer Corps (16 Dec–24 Dec 44), ETHINT 41, 1945); "On 20 Dec, 2nd Bn remained in position with Co A attached to fill out the line. 1st Bn remained in reserve at the position shown" (Cassidy, 1945, 2); "On the morning of 20 December 1944 . . . with Company 'A' attached, was still defending Longchamps" (S. A. Chappuis, Historical Record 502nd Parachute Infantry Regiment, December 1944, 3); "1130 The 3rd Bn moved off on attack and seized ground North of their positions . . . 1330 . . . 1600 3rd Bn reports they have captured 25 prisoners. PWs have been turned over to the IPW enclosure" (S2 Section, 502nd Parachute Infantry Regiment, 1944); "Stopka's Bn had not been badly hit during the advance to Recogne and it stayed on a line running through Recogne where 502 had patrolled the night before, and it extended its left flank westward to contact Second Bn" (Cassidy, 1945, 3); "As we went up the westerly

road, there suddenly appeared a big Kraut tank on the east road. If it got to the town before we could get back, it would cut us off from our jeep. We ran—I mean really ran—we made it and got out of there fast" (Koskimaki, 2003, 165); "20 December 1944 (Continued) . . . Lt. Jack J. Price, 0-1176469, of Oklahoma, an 'A' Battery forward observer, returned from near Gives [Givry] and reported that Germans are using American tanks and trucks" (Cleaver, 1944); "1100 The S-2 patrol moved out on a patrol to GIVRY (50-60) . . . 304th Pz Grenadiers Regt. 26th Reconnaissance Bn. 2nd Bn. 902 Pz Grenadier Regt" (S2 Section, 502nd Parachute Infantry Regiment, 1944); See map (P. A. Danahy, G-2 Periodic Reports No 2 from: 200001 to 202400, December 1944); "I could see them through my glasses. . . . They were used to bolster weak spots in our defense line" (Bowen, *Fighting with the Screaming Eagles: With the 101st Airborne from Normandy to Bastogne*, 2001, 165); "The following morning (0900) the platoon was attached without BN to the 1st Bn 502nd Regt. . . . As the infantry withdrew, at 1700, to the higher ground to the west of RECOGNE, the TDs went with them" (Long, 1945, 1–2); "1100—Rcn. Co. and elements of Co C support two companies Prcht Inf in attack of Recogne" (Harris, S-3 Report from 192400 December 1944 to 202400 December 1944, No. 111 705th Tank Destroyer Battalion, 1944); "After the infantry took the town at noon . . . they dug in along the woods to the south and along the road" (Duvall, 1945, 2–3).

12   "In the Division Operations Room . . . map spread on Kinnard's and Danahy's desks" (MacKenzie, 1968, 106).

13   "506th Parachute Infantry: 1st Bn withdrew from NOVILLE . . . at 201400 A. Regimental Reserve" (H. W. Kinnard, G-3 Report No. 2, from: 192400A to: 202400, December 1944); "At 1115 enemy . . . White occupied the town of MAR-VIE" (Abernathy, S-2 Periodic Report for the 327th GIR—from December 191800 to December 201800, 1944); "201420—Fr[om] 20th. Have effected withdrawal in part of Noville. Fought way out. Tks were interspersed with inf. 13 en tks knocked out. AB put up fine exhibition" (S-3 Section, CCB 10th Armored Division, 1944).

14   "This weapon is designed to provide for direct or indirect fire (figs. 1, 2, 3, 4, 5, and 6). . . . For prolonged periods, the rate may be two rounds per minute" (War Department, 1944, 4); (Zaloga, U.S. Field Artillery of World War II, 2007, 16–17).

15   "In the Division Operations Room . . . I could be in better shape fairly soon" (MacKenzie, 1968, 106–11): "The Bn had 1700 rounds of ammunition at this time . . . to bring back the only resupply of ammunition which was had by the Div until the air resupply came in" (C. Nelson, 1945).

16   "The tenor of the General's voice marked . . . The bit of drama that General McAuliffe had furnished was needed . . ." (MacKenzie, 1968, 110).

17   "On 20 December 1944, the tank divisions already moved forward north of Bastogne and their spearheads moved quickly on the Maas River. . . . However, he captured the important villages of Sibret and Senonchamps, along with additional war materiel" (H. Kokott, Employment of the 26th Volksgrenadier Division from 16 to 31 Dec 1944, 1945); For list of German Knight Cross Winners in the 26th Volksgrenadier Division, see Axis History Factbook (Wendel, 2009); "Carrying out his plan to consult with General Middleton . . . if the Bastogne garrison held out" (MacKenzie, 1968, 113); ". . . but if the road was cut . . . beginning with A, B, C. Bastogne was K" (MacKenzie, 1968, 114); "General McAuliffe, fearful that he would have trouble getting back to his C.P., moved toward the door. General Middleton said, 'Now don't get yourself surrounded Tony'" (MacKenzie, 1968, 114); "Middleton sent for me on

20 December. . . . I got back to Bastogne as quickly as I could" (A. C. McAuliffe, Commander's View of the Situation, 1945, 3); "I do not recall having received orders to hold Bastogne. . . . Supply by air was discussed" (Middleton, Questions Answered by Lieutenant General Troy H. Middleton, 1945, 1); "McAuliffe returned to Bastogne without mishap, his jeep passing through his own lines by prearrangement long after the misty darkness had settled to cloak his movement on the battlefield" (MacKenzie, 1968, 114).

18   "First impressions? I remember that at Bastogne, the fog was so heavy and thick it would lift off the ground and you could see legs but not bodies" (Hesler, Interview with Ken Hesler, 2009); Time 0100 Source FO 2 Baker Location 443-657 Installation Ey tank firing was fired on by Keynote with good effect" (T. Moran, No. 206, S-2 Report for the 463rd Parachute Field Artillery Battalion from: 2400 20 December 1944 to: 2400 21 December 1944); "Well, we went down to see what we'd hit. . . . That made us mad, you know" (C. Gisi, Fourth Interview with Carmen Gisi, 2011); "21 December . . . 0900 Blue Baker reports they have knocked out a total of 9 enemy vehicles at 448630 . . . personnel trying to escape are being fired on by small arms fire" (S2 Section, 327th Glider Infantry Regiment, 1944); "The 2 Pz Div, after attacking and taking Noville . . . These reconnaissance forces then turned northwest of the roadblock" (H. V. Luettwitz, ETHINT 41 An Interview with General Panzertruppen Heinrich von Luettwitz: XLVII Panzer Corps (16 December to 24 December, 1944), 1945, 4); "21 Dec, 2d Panzer Division . . . against the important bridge of the OURTHE at OURTHEVILLE" (H. V. Luettwitz, The Assignment of the XLVII Panzer Corps in the Ardennes MS A-939, 1950, 9); "Dawn brought forth a dirty, grey misting day. . . . He was jubilant as was General McAuliffe when he got the news" (R. J. MacDonald, Another Von Rundstedt Blunder—Bastogne, 1948, 13–14); "Captain Robert MacDonald and Company B . . . That superior force was just one little glider company" (D. R. Martin, 2004, 53–54); "It was a miserable night. . . . Once they were hit, they kept hitting them and we opened fire, too" (C. Gisi, Fourth Interview with Carmen Gisi, 2011); "At 0700, 21 Dec . . . The guns were therefore destroyed by placing some of the recovered explosives in the tubes and blowing them" (Allen, 1945, 3). I think this is a case where the initial report was wrong and then Allen sort of added to the story. We know from Carmen Gisi, who was there, that it was about seven vehicles, and only one was towing some kind of artillery piece. McDonald showed up afterward and counted nine, but his account doesn't differ too much from Gisi's. Allen based his account on the initial radio reports, which were probably wrong. "21 December . . . 0900 Blue Baker reports . . . and the personnel trying to escape are being fired on by small arms fire" (S2 Section, 327th Glider Infantry Regiment, 1944).

19   "Well, I know there were no tanks . . . but not before one of our AT guys got one of the tanks with a bazooka" (C. Gisi, Fourth Interview with Carmen Gisi, 2011); "The tank was knocked out by Pvt. George Karpac. . . . He laid on the road and knocked the tank out with his bazooka" (C. Gisi, Notes for George Koskimaki about Carmen Gisi, n.d.); "One hour later two tanks approached from the direction of Marche. . . . I think it is quite an amazing feat that they knocked out the leading tank on the third round" (R. J. MacDonald, Another Von Rundstedt Blunder—Bastogne, 1948, 14); "21 December . . . 1245 Two tanks reported at 572624. Tanks also reported at 448630" (S2 Section, 327th Glider Infantry Regiment, 1944); I figured, using McDonald's account that the third shot killed the tank, and using the rotation

described by McDonald, Karpac had to be first in order to be third. Soon two tanks and some infantry tried to flank the position from the NW . . . backed by artillery was turned on them" (Allen, 1945, 6–7); "See map (S-3 Operations Section, 327th Glider Infantry Regiment, 1944); "Captain Robert McDonald and Company B . . . but not to jeopardize my men any longer than necessary" (D. R. Martin, 2004, 53–54); "Shortly after 1200 we repulsed another probing infantry tank attack with severe losses to the enemy infantry. At this time we were ordered to pull back to the battalion perimeter some three miles to the rear. This was accomplished in thirty minutes by using the transportation we had captured at the road block" (R. J. Mac-Donald, Another Von Rundstedt Blunder—Bastogne, 1948, 14); "At 1600 . . . The Bn position [1/401st] thus became the out-post line to the westward for the Div" (Harper, 327th Regiment at Bastogne, 1945, 6); "At 1400 Company B (3rd Bn) was attacked by a patrol from their east. After the enemy had been driven off Company B began to move southwest to 3rd Battalion. This movement was made on orders from Division" (S3—Operations Section, 327th Glider Infantry Regiment, 1944, 1); "21 December . . . 1410 Blue reports rocket fire along road vicinity of 472608" (S2 Section, 327th Glider Infantry Regiment, 1944, 3–4); Though there is no mention of Allen's whereabouts at this time, we know no other account mentions his presence elsewhere, and judging by the level of activity, it is likely he was at the command post during this time. Gisi had great respect for MacDonald, as mentioned, but said he was a "tough commander with the occasional temper." According to Gisi, he recalled an incident late in the war where MacDonald stepped out of his headquarters building and threw a coffee cup at a group of German POWs working on the street, yelling at them to clean it up afterward. (C. Gisi, Fourth Interview with Carmen Gisi, 2011); "When young MacDonald stood up straight . . . Only 23 years old, Mac-Donald had learned his lessons well in combat in Normandy and Holland" (Mac-Kenzie, 1968, 179); "(3) 3rd Bn 'B' Company repulsed enemy mechanized attack at RJ 449630 at 210900A. 'B' Company withdrew to Bn area at 211600 A" (H. W. Kinnard, G-3 Report No. 3, from: 202400A to: 212400, December 1944); "Shortly after 1200 . . . that a battalion commander has little or no time for issuing plans like these immediately before they are to be executed" (R. J. MacDonald, Another Von Rundstedt Blunder—Bastogne, 1948, 14–16); "The hope for resupply by an overland route disappeared when B Company patrols reported that bridges on every road entering the area were blown to make the highways impassable for trucks" (Mac-Kenzie, 1968, 145); "As the Bn was greatly extended . . . A would then withdraw through B and C and go into a reserve position" (Allen, 1945, 1).

20   "Company C held . . . Marche 18 miles or so to the north-west" (Bowen, *Fighting with the Screaming Eagles: With the 101st Airborne Division from Normandy to Bastogne*, 2004, 164).

21   "The battalion organized to defend from the North West . . . as we dug in deeper to defend our area" (R. J. MacDonald, Another Von Rundstedt Blunder—Bastogne, 1948, 7); (Quarrie, 2000, 87); Also, (S. Marshall, 1946, 153).

22   "The exec was 1st Lt. Preston E. Towns, a lanky six foot seven beanpole from Atlanta who could curse like a sailor and who took no guff from anyone . . ." (Bowen, *Fighting with the Screaming Eagles: With the 101st Airborne Division from Normandy to Bastogne*, 2004, 24); "The CP was in the garage. . . . I could see nothing through my binoculars" (Bowen, *Fighting with the Screaming Eagles: With the 101st Airborne Division from Normandy to Bastogne*, 2004, 163–65).

23   "A 37mm anti-tank gun was set in the trees facing down the road . . . to stop any-
       thing coming down the road" (Bowen, *Fighting with the Screaming Eagles: With the
       101st Airborne Division from Normandy to Bastogne*, 2004, 164).

24   "Besides the financial incentive . . . He had not, and John received the Purple Heart
       for the wound" (K. Parker, 2009, 22–25); "On 21 December, Company 'A' . . . which
       successfully beaten off" (S. A. Chappuis, Historical Record, 502nd Parachute Infan-
       try Regiment, December 1944, 3); "21 Dec . . . 0740 Division orders our 1st Bn. to
       move to 555-619 . . . to fill in gap between the 506 and the 502 lines" (S2 Section,
       502nd Parachute Infantry Regiment, 1944, 3); "On 21 Dec pressure continued
       against the 506th flank . . . to back-stop anything coming that way" (Cassidy, 1945,
       3–5); "21 Dec . . . 1130 An S-2 patrol will move out to an known objective and estab-
       lish an OP. They will report into Regiment by 300 radio every 30 min . . . 1215 S-2
       patrol crossed 1st phase line. No contact made with the enemy" (S2 Section, 502nd
       Parachute Infantry Regiment, 1944, 4).

25   "CC 901 with two companies of tanks and one battalion of artillery still engaged
       southeast of Bastogne and attached to the 26 Volksgrenadier Division" (Bayerlein,
       *Bayerlein: After Action Reports of the Panzer Lehr Division Commander, From D-Day
       to the Ruhr*, 2005, 81); "At dusk . . . as long as there was no shortage of ammunition
       and supply" (H. V. Luettwitz, The Assignment of the XLVII Panzer Corps in the
       Ardennes MS A-939, 1950, 10).

26   "The losses for the day (21 December) amounted for the division to 300 to 350 men
       (including officers) killed, wounded, and missing . . . for the final closing of the gap
       between Senonchamps and Champs" (H. Kokott, Ardennes Offensive—Battle of
       Bastogne, MS # B-040, 1950 , 90–93) .

27   "The snow began covering the ground and quickly got deeper . . . shelter halves and
       sleeping bags and still cold" (Bowen, *Fighting with the Screaming Eagles: With the
       101st Airborne Division from Normandy to Bastogne*, 2004, 166–67); "22 December . . .
       0050 Blue Able heard . . . 0730 Blue reports an increase in enemy activity and move-
       ment during the night" (S2 Section, 327th Glider Infantry Regiment, 1944, 4); "I
       plowed through the knee-deep snow. . . . I decided to check with Felker to get an
       idea of the dispositions of the enemy" (Bowen, *Fighting with the Screaming Eagles:
       With the 101st Airborne Division from Normandy to Bastogne*, 2004, 167); "0825 Blue
       reports 2 half-tracks and two other vehicles approaching their positions in the vicin-
       ity of 498589, about 30 personnel with the vehicles" (S2 Section, 327th Glider Infan-
       try Regiment, 1944, 5); "To the Northeast in Blue's sector . . . about 30 men
       approaching their positions from 498589" (Abernathy, S-2 Periodic Report for the
       327th GIR—from December 211800 to December 221800, 1944); "Company A had
       two squads dug in. . . . 'I've been in shit since D-Day plus 12 and seen a lot of things.
       But I never saw anything like this. You guys are tops in my books" (Bowen, *Fighting
       with the Screaming Eagles: With the 101st Airborne Division from Normandy to Bas-
       togne*, 2004, 166–71); ". . . at 0825 Blue reported two half-tracks and a jeep with
       trailer . . . and clearing the area of the enemy" (Abernathy, S-2 Periodic Report for
       the 327th GIR—from December 211800 to December 221800, 1944); "0910 Blue
       reports 30 enemy troops . . . the jeep and trailer were left on the road" (S2 Section,
       327th Glider Infantry Regiment, 1944); "Thereupon they discovered that what had
       been reported as a jeep and a trailer. . . . 'Good. We've got two or three jeeps holding
       for us out there'" (Harper, 327th Regiment at Bastogne, 1945).

28   In an experiment conducted by author Don Cygan, a standard one-man-size foxhole

was dug in the frozen and snow-covered ground in a forest in Colorado in January of 2011. Two adult males working on the three-foot-deep-by-six-by-four-foot-wide position took approximately four hours and almost destroyed the WWII–era M1910 entrenching tool that was used. Both author and comrade were exhausted when finished.

29 "So they've got us surrounded, the poor bastards!" (Prior, 2007).

30 "The 20th dawned without incident and we spent the morning digging in . . . but shared willingly again, bread, butter, and chicory [coffee substitute]" (Goldmann, Letter to Mrs. Ballard, 1945).

31 "22 Dec . . . 1015 'A' Co is now in position at Regimental road-block" (S2 Section, 502nd Parachute Infantry Regiment, 1944, 5); "22 Dec 44 0935 Able attached to Kickoff. Move in defense of CHAMPS, Able 2 on left, Able 1 on right and Able 3 in center. Three TD's and crews attached. One forward observer and two EM from 377th. One 57 AT gun and crew. Artillery fire on F.O. orders" (A Co Headquarters Section, 502nd Parachute Infantry, 1945).

32 "The next day (21 Dec), Hill and Ortega continued their performance as an evacuation team with great success . . . by the church to cover the high ground to the NW and the N road" (Duvall, 1945, 2); "On 14 December 1944 Company C, 811th TD Bn . . . This position was held for 3 days and nights" (Brownfield, 1959).

33 "The M-8's position was on the NW side of town near the CR (520621) . . . where it could affect fire for 270 degrees and fire down three roads" (Duvall, 1945, 2); "22 Dec . . . 1050 1 TD-2 M-8's and a few jeeps will support 'A' Co. for a possible enemy attack" (S2 Section, 502nd Parachute Infantry Regiment, 1944, 5); "While the 1st section remained with Co. 'H' on the high ground near RECOGNE . . . Movement would be undertaken under the cover of darkness" (Long, 1945, 2).

34 "Besides the financial incentive . . . and John received the Purple Heart for the wound" (K. Parker, 2009, 22–25).

35 See the University of New Hampshire, 2011

36 "It was just an ordinary bed sheet . . . but they were well concealed" (Hanlon, 1962).

37 "I was commander of the 115th Pz. Gren. Regiment of the 15th Pz. Gren. Div . . . I returned to my post as the regimental commander" (Maucke, Report Over the 15th Panzer-Grenadier-Division during the Ardennes Offensive from 16 December 1944 to 2 February 1945: MS P-032c, 1949).

38 "20.12.44 0715 Hours Call from the 01 . . . and regimental units travel into the new area eastward of Prüm" (Operations Section, 1944).

39 "The 15th Pz.Gren.Div . . . in the area of Wassenberg-Erkelenz" (Maucke, Report Over the 15th Panzer-Grenadier-Division during the Ardennes Offensive from 16 December 1944 to 2 February 1945: MS P-032c, 1949); See order of battle for the 15th Panzergrenadier Division (Maucke, Report Over the 15th Panzer-Grenadier-Division during the Ardennes Offensive from 16 December 1944 to 2 February 1945: MS P-032c, 1949, Anlage 1).

40 Samuel Mitcham, 2007, 104–06; "I was the commander of the 115th Pz.Gren. Regiment of the 15th Pz.Gren.Div . . . I returned to my post as the regimental commander" (Maucke, Report Over the 15th Panzer-Grenadier-Division during the Ardennes Offensive from 16 December 1944 to 2 February 1945: MS P-032c, 1949); To find his age, see www.das-ritterkreuz.de (Andreas Düfel, 2006).

41 "Around 12.12.44, under strict secrecy and camouflaged against their own troops . . . The division reached the area around Pruem in the early morning hours on 23 De-

cember" (Maucke, Report Over the 15th Panzer-Grenadier-Division during the Ardennes Offensive from 16 December 1944 to 2 February 1945: MS P-032c, 1949); "16.12.44 Circular from the headquarters regarding their own successful larger offensive . . . The regimental staff arrived at 2345 hours in Roggendorf and entered quarters" (Operations Section, 1944).

42   "On 22 Dec 44 . . . I saw to it that the people were not moved out" (H. V. Luettwitz, ETHINT 41, An Interview with General Panzertruppen Heinrich von Luettwitz: XLVII Panzer Corps (16 December to 24 December 1944), 1945, 5–6).

43   Tourist Federation of Belgian Luxembourg, 2011.

44   "Consultation about the capitulation proposals to be addressed to the garrison of Bastogne were composed by Manteuffel and Lüttwitz and transmitted by a spokesman (adjutant of the Panzer Lehr) on 22 December" (Bayerlein, *Bayerlein: After Action Reports of the Panzer Lehr Division Commander, From D-Day to the Ruhr*, 2005, 70); "Details of this adventure were relayed in detail to the author by Mr. Hellmuth Henke, Bayerlein's English speaking adjutant, and published in *Bayerlein; From Afrikakorps to Panzer Lehr*. Mr. Henke confirmed the accuracy of the events he experienced as written in Bayerlein's biography" (Bayerlein, *Bayerlein: After Action Reports of the Panzer Lehr Division Commander, From D-Day to the Ruhr*, 2005, 104) "The emissaries included two enlisted men, Maj. Wagner from the *XLVII Panzerkorps* and Lt. Helmuth Henke from the operations section of the *Panzer Lehr Division*" (D. S. Parker, 1994, 199); "In a television interview early in 1960 General von Luettwitz admitted that he was responsible for the ultimatum to the Bastogne garrison. This confirms a like statement made to Colonel Marshall in 1945 but later denied by Luettwitz" (Cole, 1965, 468); "Pz Lehr Div sent a parlementaire to Bastogne without my authorization. The demand to surrender was refused as was to be expected" (Manteuffel, Fifth Panzer Army (11 Sep 44–Jan 45), ETHINT 45, 1945, 11); "As I have stated previously, I did not authorize the surrender demand which was made of the Bastogne garrison, and I am still not sure exactly who did authorize this ultimatum" (Manteuffel, An Interview with General Panzer Hasso von Manteuffel: Fifth Panzer Army (Nov 44–Jan 45), ETHINT 46, 1945, 8); "21 Dec . . . Panzer-Lehr Division: The Division was ordered—because BASTOGNE was encircled and the Army had announced that the occupants of the SCHNEE EIFEL had surrendered after having been summoned to send a negotiator to BASTOGNE" (H. V. Luettwitz, The Assignment of the XLVII Panzer Corps in the Ardennes, MS A-939, 1950, 9); "The negotiator, who was sent out to BASTOGNE returned with the well known answer 'nuts'" (H. V. Luettwitz, The Assignment of the XLVII Panzer Corps in the Ardennes, MS A-939, 1950, 11); "In the course of the morning, corps had informed the division that, by orders of corps . . . i.e. capture of Bastogne—would be approached on that, or at least the following day" (H. Kokott, Ardennes Offensive—Battle of Bastogne, MS #B-040, 1950 , 85–86).

45   "22 December . . . 1205 A German Major with an 'Ultimatum' came to our lines with a white flag. He was received and blindfolded and brought to the Fox C.P." (S2 Section, 327th Glider Infantry Regiment, 1944, 5).

46   "The two officers were blind folded . . . who was then Acting Chief of Staff" (Harper, 327th Regiment at Bastogne, 1945, 8).

47   "The fortune of war is changing . . . would not correspond with the well known American humanity" (P. A. Danahy, G-2 Periodic Reports No. 4 from: 220001 to 222400 December 1944).

48   "Now as to the request of our surrender . . . and because they thought it was alright, I sent it along" (A. C. McAuliffe, Merry Christmas, 1944).

49   "When the two Germans arrived at the outpost . . . to deliver it to the German officers to see their reaction" (Harper, Letter to George Koskimaki, 1969), (Harper, 327th Regiment at Bastogne, 1945, 7–9).

50   "'Will you see that it's delivered?' Harper replied . . . It was then 1350" (Harper, 327th Regiment at Bastogne, 1945, 9); "They [German officers] were waiting still blindfolded in the Company F C.P. . . . I knew that as soon as the weather cleared, we'd receive more ammunition" (Harper, Letter to George Koskimaki, 1969).

51   "6. Own firing—A. Type of Fire . . . Call fire—16. B. Results—Good. 7. Ammunition expended during this period . . . M48—57 M54—152 M57—48 . . ." (V. E. Garrett, S-3 Report from: 212400 Dec 1944 to: 222400 Dec 1944, Unit: 463 Parachute Field Artillery Battalion, No. 207, 1944); "1. STATUS OF SUPPLY . . . Critical shortage of ammunition and rations with no source of supply available in present combat situation" (M. A. Johnson, 1944); "Own firing—A. Type of Fire . . . Registration -1 Call fire—25. B. Results—Good. 7. Ammunition expended during this period . . . M48—394 M54—154 M57—108 . . ." (V. E. Garrett, S-3 Report from: 202400 Dec 1944 to: 212400 Dec 1944, Unit: 463 Parachute Field Artillery Battalion, No. 206, 1944); "Own firing—A. Type of Fire . . . Registration -8 Call fire—27. B. Results—Good. 7. Ammunition expended during this period . . . M48—785 M54—102 M57—79 . . ." (V. E. Garrett, S-3 Report from: 192400 December 1944 to: 202400 December 1944, 463rd Parachute Field Artillery Battalion, No. 205, 1944); "Dec 22: the Gp established officer liaison . . . 327 Glider Inf which battalions were protecting the western and southern approaches to BASTOGNE" (Brewster, 1944, 6); "Direct support of the 502nd Prcht. Inf . . . Heavy damage could be done in [if] ammunition was available" (Brubaker, S-3 Report from: 1200 December 22, 1944, to: 1200 December 23, 1944, Unit: 377th Parachute Field Artillery Battalion, 1944); "We then got down to 10 rounds per gun . . . but no more than two rounds." (A. C. McAuliffe, Merry Christmas, 1944); "The days prior to Christmas . . . We had 20 rounds per gun of hollow charge anti-tank ammo that were never used or counted in ammo reports except to be used for direct fire" (Koskimaki, 2003, 275).

52   "Having surveyed the terrain in front of 'Silent Steve' Chappuis's 502nd Regiment on the northwestern perimeter, Higgins concluded it would be ideal for massed tank operations if the sodden fields froze" (MacKenzie, 1968, 160); "22 Dec . . . 0955 . . . He also stated that enemy is also in town of ROUETTE" (S2 Section, 502nd Parachute Infantry Regiment, 1944, 4); "0955 22 Dec Our Battalions have been alerted for possible enemy attack from GIVRY. 'A' Co. has been alerted to move up to Regimental road-block" (S2 Section, 502nd Parachute Infantry Regiment, 1944, 5); "On 22 Dec . . . A Regimental S-2 patrol was sent to Rouette to check an enemy build-up to north of Champs" (Cassidy, 1945, 5); "22 Dec . . . 1215 . . . They had American vehicles and equipment" (S2 Section, 502nd Parachute Infantry Regiment, 1944); "1520: BN NO: Div 20: DESCRIPTION COORDINATES Enemy CP (5032-6398) : REC'D FROM K'fish: TIME COMPLETED 1530 . . ." (Brubaker, S-3 Report from: 1200 December 22, 1944, to: 1200 December 23, 1944, Unit: 377th Parachute Field Artillery Battalion, 1944); "A Regimental S-2 patrol was sent to Rouette . . . and the patrol returned to our lines at 1630" (Cassidy, 1945, 5); "22 Dec 1715 Our 1st Bn. is moving up to a new position" (S2 Section, 502nd Parachute Infantry Regiment, 1944); "General Summary . . . The enemy has now sufficient forces

in the western area to attack in strength from that direction" (P. A. Danahy, G-2 Periodic Reports No. 4 from: 220001 to 222400 December 1944); See accompanying map number four with Danahy's report. He labeled on the map the report of four to five hundred Germans and forty to fifty tanks in Givry.

53   "The first message from the 4th Armored said, 'Hugh is coming' . . . for on the day before VIII Corps had told him to prepare for 'resupply tomorrow if weather permits'" (S. Marshall, 1946, 134–35); "Communications would present no major problem . . . had to be couched in ambiguous—sometimes quite meaningless— terms" (Cole, 1965, 461); "Instead of repairing old lines . . . had one line laid to the switchboard and one to the field artillery radio operator located in the servant's quarters" (Phillips, 1948, 16–17); "There was a delightfully ironic touch even to that restriction. . . . At the same time, the Bastogne defenders were running low on small- arms ammunition" (S. Marshall, 1946, 133–34); "We then got down to 10 rounds per gun. . . . (If you see four hundred Germans in a one hundred yard area and they have their heads up, you can fire artillery at them—but no more than two rounds)" (A. C. McAuliffe, Merry Christmas, 1944); "The busiest member of the staff was Colonel Kohls. . . . The G-4, his eyes inflamed, and the flesh around them swollen and red, seemed to be in constant misery" (MacKenzie, 1968, 169–70); "On 21 December 1044, the AC of S . . . was notified that the resupply mission was canceled because of bad weather" (Robbins, 11 January 1945); "For by noon of December 22 . . . he would have to ration his guns to ten rounds per day" (S. Marshall, 1946, 133); "The airdrop laid on for the 22d never reached Bastogne—bad flying weather continued as in the days past . . . to the men in the line this was heartening news" (Cole, 1965, 467).

54   "The losses of the division for 22 December amounted to about 400 men killed, wounded and missing. . . . Up to ten men temporarily had to share a loaf of bread per day" (H. Kokott, Ardennes Offensive—Battle of Bastogne, MS #B-040, 1950, 110).

55   "In the course of the morning . . . displayed by the defending forces" (H. Kokott, Ardennes Offensive—Battle of Bastogne, MS #B-040, 1950, 98).

56   "The battles between Assenois—Villeroux—Senonchamps were fluctuating all through the morning . . . was making steady progress towards Bastogne" (H. Ko- kott, Ardennes Offensive—Battle of Bastogne, MS #B-040, 1950, 97–98).

57   "During the late evening of 22 December the following picture of the situation was arrived at: . . . announced by the XXXXVII Panzer Corps, had come up" (H. Ko- kott, Ardennes Offensive—Battle of Bastogne, MS #B-040, 1950, 103).

58   "Throughout the day the enemy forces in the northern and eastern sectors had again been entirely passive. . . . There were indic[a]tions which seemed to confirm such an assumption" (H. Kokott, Ardennes Offensive—Battle of Bastogne, MS #B-040 1950, 103–05).

59   "Civilian refugees from Bastogne mentioned excitement . . . was questionable" (H. Kokott, Ardennes Offensive—Battle of Bastogne, MS #B-040 1950, 105).

60   "The intention of the division for 23 December was to close . . . for the attack against Flamierge from the west" (H. Kokott, Ardennes Offensive—Battle of Bastogne, MS #B-040, 1950, 106).

61   "The corps still seemed to be of the opinion that the enemy inside Bastogne could not be very strong . . . to assemble then for an attack on Bastogne as well" (H. Ko- kott, Ardennes Offensive—Battle of Bastogne, MS #B-040, 1950, 106–07).

62   "The losses of the division for 22 December amounted to about 400 men killed,

wounded and missing. . . . Up to ten men temporarily had to share a loaf of bread per day" (H. Kokott, Ardennes Offensive—Battle of Bastogne, MS #B-040, 1950, 110); "In the course of the morning, news arrived from corps to the effect that the commander in charge of the Bastogne forces had a declined a surrender with remarkable brevity. This response was fully in accord with the stubborn tenacity displayed by the defending forces" (H. Kokott, Ardennes Offensive—Battle of Bastogne, MS #B-040, 1950, 98); "The battles between Assenois—Villeroux—Senonchamps were fluctuating . . . was making steady progress towards Bastogne" (H. Kokott, Ardennes Offensive—Battle of Bastogne, MS #B-040 1950, 97–98); "During the late evening of 22 December . . . announced by the XXXXVII Panzer Corps, had come up" (H. Kokott, Ardennes Offensive—Battle of Bastogne, MS #B-040, 1950, 103); "Throughout the day the enemy forces in the northern and eastern sectors had again been entirely passive. . . . There were indic[a]tions which seemed to confirm such an assumption" (H. Kokott, Ardennes Offensive—Battle of Bastogne, MS #B-040, 1950, 103–05); "Civilian refugees from Bastogne mentioned excitement . . . by the enemy forces in the south, was questionable" (H. Kokott, Ardennes Offensive—Battle of Bastogne, MS #B-040, 1950, 105). In essence, Kokott was assuming a similar withdrawal might occur from Bastogne as the Americans had executed the day before from the town of St. Vith. "The intention of the division for 23 December . . . for the attack against Flamierge from the west" (H. Kokott, Ardennes Offensive—Battle of Bastogne, MS #B-040, 1950, 106); "The corps still seemed to be of the opinion . . . to assemble then for an attack on Bastogne as well" (H. Kokott, Ardennes Offensive—Battle of Bastogne, MS #B-040, 1950, 106–07).

Chapter Five

1   Brooks, 1904, 94.
2   "Prowling about Bastogne, the Civil Affairs Officer, Captain Robert S. Smith . . . to wrap around their feet where they lacked arctic overshoes." (S. Marshall, 1946, 140). If the Americans defending Bastogne had been fighting more of an offensive battle, perhaps there would have been fewer cases of frostbite, fatigue, and "trench foot." Obviously, if a human is able to get up and move around, he is more apt to keep healthy, improve circulation, and stay somewhat warmer. Unfortunately, the majority of the men were emplaced in soaking wet or freezing cold holes and trenches. The vast majority of the men sat, day after day, hour after hour, with only the occasional break to some warming barn or farmhouse behind their lines.
3   "Steve Chappuis gave an order . . . to set up company kitchens in their buildings and were eating first class" (Koskimaki, 2003, 198). McAuliffe had already directed the men to forage from the farms, and give any farmer a receipt to be paid back for the food and livestock. For the remainder of the siege, some GIs lived pretty well off of stocks of mutton, potatoes, and white beans secured from nearby farmers.
4   "All around I could hear the sounds of fighting, sometimes muffled. . . . I checked my squad several times during the night, mainly to keep warm" (Bowen, *Fighting with the Screaming Eagles: With the 101st Airborne Division from Normandy to Bastogne*, 2004, 166).
5   "When we left [Germany] we were pretty much fully supplied with ammo, gas, rations, clothes . . . like it must be Christmas" (S. A. D'Angelo, Interview with Sergeant Anthony "Tony" D'Angelo, March 4, 2009).

6   The 502nd's regimental symbol was a skull with bat wings, earning their nickname "Widowmakers." What had started out as a fearsome name in training back in the States started to take on a darker meaning when the regiment suffered many casualties after D-day and Holland. Within no time, troopers of the 502nd preferred the nicknames "Deuce," "Oh-Deuce," or "Five-Oh-Deuce" over "Widowmakers."

7   "One evening before Christmas an American sentinel . . . said old man Raviola" (Cercle d'Histoire de Bastogne, 1994, Chapter 14). Perhaps this was not a recon patrol. . . . Enemy patrol action. Cpl Nicolai shot" (A Co Headquarters Section, 502nd Parachute Infantry, 1945); "This note will attempt to correct several errors . . . and myself so no one knows their first names or hometowns" (Goldmann, Letter to George Koskimaki, 1993); "That night a six-man patrol from our platoon went out with Givry . . . with a tommy gun and wounded one which caused them to retire" (Goldmann, Letter to Mrs. Ballard, 1945).

8   "IN NOVILLE . . . But to the eastward where 506th stood guard, the boys who had prayed for morning soon wondered why" (S. Marshall, 1946, 87).

9   "The sounds of war were muffled and far off, but growing closer and closer in the east. We were waiting" (Black, *The Last First Sergeant*, 1998, 235).

10   "When I woke up in the morning in a slit-trench foxhole, water was already settling in. . . . Same Germans, same noise of war, the same dirty foxhole for a home. We were back in combat" (Black, *The Last First Sergeant*, 1998, 233–34).

11   Information provided by Bernard Maus, grandson of Dame Maus de Rolle. Only a small part of the Dreve de Mande can still be seen on the southern part of this intersection today. These are just a few of the surviving elm trees. Most of the pines died off from disease after the war.

12   "I don't know how many personnel realize . . . until we came to a road stop later in the night" (Koskimaki, 2003, 35).

13   After the war, for some unknown reason, the name of the château was changed from Rolle to Rolley (Maus, 2010).

14   "Just now, I am in a beautiful 17th century castle which also serves as my home . . . makes everything look like a Xmas postcard" (Koskimaki, 2003, 92–93). A kitchen has been added to the forward landing of the château, and the thick stone walls, easily three feet thick, are easy to see today where the room was carved into the facade.

15   "From our vantage point . . . I seem to recall at least one 6X6 truck parked just outside the main gates and under it one or two deep foxholes had been dug" (Koskimaki, 2003, 92–93).

16   Maus, 2010.

17   "In the morning, Captain Mac summoned our squad to the CP. . . . This meant being prepared to fight" (Koskimaki, 2003, 168); (Bostwick, 1946, 7); "Col. Allen ordered the platoon to retake Flamierge at 1000. A five minute artillery and mortar barrage would precede the attack" (Wasil Chernak, 1945, 3); "The Germans began to infiltrate early on the morning of the 23rd. . . . One mg from a jeep was used for the security of the M8" (Wasil Chernak, 1945, 3); "23 December 1944 During the early daylight hours of 23 December . . . were repelled with heavy fighting" (H. Kokott, Ardennes Offensive—Battle of Bastogne, MS #B-040, 1950 , 110–11).

18   "After we got back to our regular positions . . . We rode on the tanks and other vehicles up there" (C. Gisi, Questionnaire for Carmen Gisi, 2009); "A light tank was assigned to us. . . . I suspect it was WWI surplus" (Koskimaki, 2003, 168); (Bost-

wick, 1946, 7); "Col. Allen ordered the platoon to retake FLAMIERGE at 1000 . . . followed by four more jeeps, the 2 M8s and then the AG" (Wasil Chernak, 1945, 3); "On arrival at the 3rd battalion's line at Flamizoulle . . . Also please note, we have no medical support" (Walsh, Letter to George Koskimaki: The 705 Tank Destroyer Battalion to Bastogne, Belgium, unknown).

19 "Time . . . 0915 . . . Source . . . FO 5 B . . . Location . . . 475-615 . . . Remarks Ey personnel and half-tracks, effect very good . . . Time . . . 0955 . . . Source FO 5 B . . . Location . . . 4756-6165 . . . Remarks . . . Ey MG, not completed effects" (T. Moran, No. 208, S-2 Report for the 463rd Parachute Field Artillery Battalion from: 2400, 22 December 1944 to: 2400, 23 December 1944); (S-3 Report, 1944).

20 "When Gunderson and Chernak arrived at FLAMIERGE . . . the other was to the rear of the last building on the S side of town" (Wasil Chernak, 1945, 2); "Rcn. Co. Atchd 327 Gli Inf" (Harris, S-3 Report from 212400, December 1944, to 222400, December 1944, No. 113, 705th Tank Destroyer Battalion, 1944); "On 22 Dec. 44 the 3rd battalion of the 327th Glider Inf. Regt. . . . Two of the roads into Flamierge came from the Bastogne-Marche Rd. [main road], 1 km, and the other road was from the Marche-Bertgone Rd., 4 km thru Salle, Tronie, Flamierge" (Walsh, Letter to George Koskimaki: The 705 Tank Destroyer Battalion to Bastogne, Belgium, unknown); "Each patrol [in the case of a three-car patrol] marches with a radio car in the rear. . . . The commander may order the patrol either to by-pass the obstacle or to await reinforcement" (Military Intelligence Division, 1944, 11); "There was no action in FLAMIERGE until 1600, Dec 22. . . . Then one shot destroyed the truck that was parked by the building . . . " (Wasil Chernak, 1945, 2); "22 December cont'd 1720—Blue reports they knocked out a German jeep at their road block, killing three Germans. One of them escaped. This occurred at 1600 hours" (S2 Section, 327th Glider Infantry Regiment, 1944, 6); "The company stayed in reserve until the next morning when we were ordered to defend strong points in the vicinity of Flamizoulle . . . by being with him I was well abreast with the situation at all times" (R. J. MacDonald, Another Von Rundstedt Blunder—Bastogne, 1948, 17); "During the shooting a 60 mm mortar . . . That night, with 6 infantry reinforcements, the platoon with exception of the men in the M8 dug in" (Wasil Chernak, 1945, 2–3); "German troops moved into a woods just off the Marche-Bastogne Rd. between 2 roads in Flamierge. . . . We spent in the night in these positions, waiting for them to move" (Walsh, Letter to George Koskimaki: The 705 Tank Destroyer Battalion to Bastogne, Belgium, unknown).

21 "Just as we entered the outskirts of the village . . . blasting away at every building in sight" (Koskimaki, 2003, 168–69); (Bostwick, 1946, 8); "We no sooner got there and the Germans opened up on us . . . We thought that it would get hit by a machine gun bullet and hit both of us" (C. Gisi, Questionnaire for Carmen Gisi, 2009); "As the column reached the outskirts of town . . . the armored vehicles drove up the street to the positions held previous to the first withdrawal" (Wasil Chernak, 1945, 3); "On the move to reenter the town . . . we drove back to Flamizoulle, and the 3rd Bn" (Walsh, Letter to George Koskimaki: The 705 Tank Destroyer Battalion to Bastogne, Belgium, unknown).

22 "When the machine gun stopped . . . with statues of saints in them" (C. Gisi, Questionnaire for Carmen Gisi, 2009).

23 "As we passed in front of the house . . . The prisoners were herded outside without incident" (Koskimaki, 2003, 169–70); (Bostwick, 1946, 8–9); "When the foot

elements could no longer move . . . after several rounds of 37 were sent into the basement" (Wasil Chernak, 1945, 3).

24 "23 December 1050—Division reports 6 horse-drawn vehicles at 503630. . . . It came from the direction of SIBRET (495545)" (S2 Section, 327th Glider Infantry Regiment 1944, 6); "On 23 Dec at 0945 pathfinders jumped in the vicinity of Bastogne . . . Company 'B' was not in this action" (Harper, 327th Regiment at Bastogne, 1945, 10).

25 "The drop was successful . . . because the Germans would have 'honed in' on us and blasted us to bits" (Koskimaki, 2003, 224–25); "On 23 Dec at 0945 pathfinders jumped in the vicinity . . . by parachute and ammunition and food were the bulk of the cargo" (Harper, 327th Regiment at Bastogne, 1945, 10–11); "3. Early in the morning of 23rd December 1944 . . . 23 December 1944 241 planes were used between the hours of 1150 and 1606" (Robbins, 11 January 1945, 1–2).

26 "The situation at Flamierge was at first still uncertain . . . anti-aircraft forces located close by were firing rapidly at the planes" (H. Kokott, Ardennes Offensive—Battle of Bastogne, MS #B-040 1950 , 111–12); See the maps for Kokott's work in Wilhelm Weiss's book *Ardennen 44* (Weiss, 2011).

27 "The 514th Sq with 8 P-47 a/c TO 1206 from Site A-80 on an area cover mission for 36 C-47's in vicinity of Bastogne. RV at 1230 over P-545585 . . . Lt-wk-acc flak at P5454. Weather: CAVU. TD 1430 at Site A-80" (Brown, Oprep A No. D23D (4th of 4 missions) for 24 hours ending sunset, 23 December 1944. Mission No. 292. IX Fighter Command Operations Order No. W51-2, 1944).

28 "Enemy fighter bombers swooped down on Hompre and pushed their thrusts of fire into the fluctuating and congested mass . . . but ammunition and ration containers!" (H. Kokott, Ardennes Offensive—Battle of Bastogne, MS #B-040, 1950 , 112–14).

29 "The parachutes, cargo, dropping, are known as types G-2, G-3, G-4, and G-5. . . . For instance, blue canopies might designate water, red canopies, ammunition, green canopies, rations, etc" (Raymond C. Altermatt, 1945).

30 "Meanwhile, across the road near the entrance to the cellar command post . . . exulted a little soldier dancing by" (MacKenzie, 1968, 180–82).

31 "Lt. General Harry W. O. Kinnard, General McAuliffe's Assistant Chief of Staff G-3 during the siege of Bastogne . . . Many thanks and all the best, Harry Kinnard" (Kinnard, Letter to Thomas Potter, 2003).

32 "On 22 December 1944 . . . The remainder of the 1st Battalion constituted the Regimental reserve at Hemroulle (coordinates -534602)" (S. A. Chappuis, Historical Record 502nd Parachute Infantry Regiment, December 1944, 3–4); "In the morning were told to pack up our gear and prepare to move out as the division's reserve . . . we stood outside our foxholes watching those brightly colored parachutes fall softly to the ground" (Black, *The Last First Sergeant*, 1998, 238–40); "23 December 1944 241 planes were used between the hours of 1150 and 1606 . . . Rations Type 'K' 16488" (Robbins, 11 January 1945, 2).

33 "On the 23rd of Dec. after the weather cleared . . . we were yelling and screaming with joy" (C. Gisi, Questionnaire for Carmen Gisi, 2009).

34 "We had been in the village for several hours. . . . A phosphorous bomb was placed in the tank's engine to immobilize it" (Koskimaki, 2003, 170); "The tank suddenly ceased moving. The motor was again out of commission" (Wasil Chernak, 1945, 3–4).

35 "Blimp had returned inside the house and had gone upstairs when he called . . . but

the turret had frozen solid" (Koskimaki, 2003, 170); (Bostwick, 1946, 10); "Datz took the armored car . . . 1 German sniper in the church steeple was eliminated with the 37mm" (Wasil Chernak, 1945, 4); "Gunderson, trying to get to the roadblock had been killed by mg fire. Datz attempted three times to recover his body but the fire was too intense" (Wasil Chernak, 1945, 4).

36 "Meanwhile heavy enemy mortar fire was crashing into the town. . . . Although German snipers in windows made any movement hazardous" (Wasil Chernak, 1945, 4); "And then return back down to Flamierge . . . and move right back to Flamizoulle" (Walsh, Francis Walsh Collection (AFC/2001/001/64192), Veterans History Project, American Folklife Center, Library of Congress, 2008); "I left him there, and returned to Flamierge . . . Casualties this venture, 2 dead, 1 wounded" (Walsh, Letter to George Koskimaki: The 705 Tank Destroyer Battalion to Bastogne, Belgium, unknown).

37 "Datz returned to the garrison with gasoline for the AG which failed to respond to treatment . . . and to take positions with the AB roadblock" (Wasil Chernak, 1945, 4); "Our tank had run out of gas and had used up its ammunition. A phosphorous bomb was placed in the tank's engine to immobilize it" (Koskimaki, 2003, 170); (Bostwick, 1946, 10).

38 "Watson ordered the armored car to shuttle as many men as it would hold back to our lines . . . we literally stumbled into the company area" (Koskimaki, 2003, 170–71); (Bostwick, 1946, 10–11); "The wounded went first and 8 men were taken from the town . . . and 4 other men reinforced the AT defenses" (Wasil Chernak, 1945, 4); "At 1600 the 3rd Battalion was forced to give up Flamierge" (S3—Operations Section, 327th GIR, 1944, 3); "In Flamierge there was heavy fighting and some of the guys captured a few Germans. . . . We could have been captured" (C. Gisi, Questionnaire for Carmen Gisi, 2009); "1600—3rd Platoon, Rcn. Co. established road block 500 yards west of Flamierge" (Harris, S-3 Report from 222400, December 1944, to 232400, December 1944, No. 114, 705th Tank Destroyer Battalion, 1944).

39 "A burst of fire from the 2nd Platoon's roadblock, the rattle of small arms fire and the bark of cannon startled me awake on the 23rd . . . had his thumb shot off but managed to get back" (Bowen, *Fighting with the Screaming Eagles: With the 101st Airborne Division from Normandy to Bastogne*, 2004, 172); "23 December cont'd 1325—Blue being attacked by 5 tanks and an unknown number of inf. at 480602" (S2 Section, 327th Glider Infantry Regiment, 1944, 7); "At 1200 on the 23 Dec . . . They did not try to engage it" (Allen, 1945, 1).

40 "I was heating K rations when Labbe got me a message to report to Captain Towns immediately. . . . It was the last time I would ever see him" (Bowen, *Fighting with the Screaming Eagles: With the 101st Airborne Division from Normandy to Bastogne*, 2004, 172–73).

41 "One day before Christmas, I don't remember the day . . . That night, Charlie Thompson, our armor[er], crawled up to one of our knocked out tank destroyers and removed the breech block so it couldn't be fired" (Vining, 1999).

42 "1330—2nd Plat. Co. A ordered to move forward to positions around Monty. Encountered 15 enemy tanks. Mark IVs and Vs. Engaged enemy. Withdrew and occupied positions east of Monty" (Harris, S-3 Report from 222400, December 1944, to 232400, December 1944, No. 114, 705th Tank Destroyer Battalion, 1944); "In order to supplement the Division reserve, Task Force 'X' was organized . . . sided by the dismounted personnel that had accompanied the platoon" (A. W. Johnson, 1945,

1–2); "The 1st platoon of Recon Co. with the 2nd platoon of Co 'B' were attached to the 2nd Bn of the 501st Infantry at 2330, 19 December. . . . They dug in with Miller's men" (R. B. Miller, 1945, 1–2).

43   "I collected the men and their gear. . . . One of the dead lying near them was Staff Sergeant Robert Rehler, Circleville, Ohio, a young dedicated fellow who had only recently received his sergeant's stripes" (Bowen, *Fighting with the Screaming Eagles: With the 101st Airborne Division from Normandy to Bastogne*, 2004, 173–76); "The 3rd Platoon of Co. 'B' was attached to the 502 at 0700 20 December. . . . The grid that the report mentioned was actually in 327's area of operations" (Stronach, 1945, 1).

44   "At 1200 on the 23 Dec . . . and continued to fire into C for the remainder of the afternoon" (Allen, 1945, 1–2); "23 December 1944 . . . 1500 Blue Running short of mortar ammo. Send 300 rounds 81, 300 rds 50 by N route. Also small arms ammo" (S-1 Section, 1944, 3); "23 December cont'd 1325—Blue being attacked by 5 tanks and an unknown number of inf. at 480602, 1448 . . . They report twelve tanks painted white are in the area somewhere S of C CO" (S2 Section, 327th Glider Infantry Regiment, 1944, 7); "At 1350 Company C (3rd Bn) received an attack by five tanks and infantry at 48062 . . . the tanks withdrew after artillery fire had been placed on them" (S3—Operations Section, 327th GIR, 1944, 3).

45   "Time . . . 1500 . . . Source . . . FO 5 B . . . Location . . . 475-598 482-592 . . . Remarks . . . Ey tanks & personnel, effect excellent" (T. Moran, No. 208 S-2 Report for the 463rd Parachute Field Artillery Battalion from: 2400, 22 December 1944, to: 2400, 23 December 1944); "Ten Ey Tanks are taken under fire vic (4879-5930) with excellent effect . . . Type of Fire—Harassing—5 Registration—0 Call Fire—29 . . . " (V. E. Garrett, S-3 Report from: 222400, Dec 1944, to: 232400, Dec 1944, Unit: 463 Parachute Field Artillery Battalion, No. 208, 1944); "1500 . . . Description . . . 10 Ey tank + Pers . . . Information Received From . . . 5 Baker . . . Target Assigned To . . . B+D . . . Time Mission Assigned . . . 1500 . . . Time Completed . . . 1610 . . . Observed By . . . LT Smithers . . . No. Rounds . . . 58 . . . Effect . . . Excell" (S-3 Report, 1944).

46   "Date & Time Received . . . 1518 . . . Description Coordinates . . . 10 Tanks (4820 5930) . . . Rec'd from . . . Keynot . . . Time Completed . . . 1530 . . . Obs By . . . Knote . . . No Rds . . . 38 . . . " (Brubaker, S-3 Report from: 1200, December 23, 1944, to: 1200, December 24, 1944, Unit: 377th Parachute Field Artillery Battalion, 1944).

47   "I told Wagner that perhaps the gun on the disabled tank might help out and that I had some experience in artillery. . . . Then saying, 'For you the war is over'" (Bowen, *Fighting with the Screaming Eagles: With the 101st Airborne Division from Normandy to Bastogne*, 2004, 193–97).

48   "As darkness approached ALLEN was notified that the road block at FLA-MIERGE had been overrun by enemy infantry in white suits. . . . Just watching them was a hardship on the men" (Allen, 1945, 2–3); "23 December cont'd . . . 1810—Enemy tanks reported to have overrun Blue Charlie . . . 1840—Blue withdrawing from FLAMIZOULLE. (491613)" (S2 Section, 327th Glider Infantry Regiment, 1944, 7); "At 1350 Company 'C' got an attack by five tanks and one company of infantry at 480602 . . . which they held until their lines were taken over by the 17th Airborne Division on 10 Jan 45" (Harper, 327th Regiment at Bastogne, 1945, 11); "23 December 1944 . . . 2200 Blue CP at 529608 . . . White and Blue received attacks throughout the day" (S-1 Section, 1944, 3); "Then, on December 23, Company C was attacked by 14 German tanks . . . closer to Bastogne to keep them from being surrounded"

(D. R. Martin, 2004, 54); "By dusk of the 23rd the withdrawal plan that had been issued to all commanders was put into effect. . . . This forced us to abandon some of the equipment and scuttle the rest" (R. J. MacDonald, Another Von Rundstedt Blunder—Bastogne, 1948, 18–19); "The platoon was attached to 327-3, and Andrews moved to the vicinity of FLAMIZOULLE. . . . By 2230, the retrograde movement was completed and the TDs returned to the line NE of MANDE ST. ETIENNE" (Andrews, 1945, 2).

49   "The situation became less tense after some time when Reconnaissance Battalion 26 reported . . . been discovered already earlier—paratroopers, but ammunition and ration containers!" (H. Kokott, Ardennes Offensive—Battle of Bastogne, MS #B-040, 1950, 112–14); "CHAUMONT was entered twice by units of Combat Command B. The disposition for troops for the attack on the 23 December was as follows . . . a total of eleven tanks knocked out of the fight at this point" (Ezell, 1945); "Shortly after noon on the 23rd, CCB attacked CHAUMONT . . . his tanks withdrew, leaving infantry to hold the town" (Clark, 1944, 3); It was 10 o'clock, and the moonlit night was growing steadily colder . . . recalling his words at Mande St. Etienne: 'We have got to make Christians out of a lot of people around here'" (MacKenzie, 1968, 192–94); "General Summary . . . Tac R has the general impression that traffic is more to the northeast away from our position than towards it" (P. A. Danahy, G-2 Periodic Reports No. 5, from: 230001 to 232400, December 1944); "CCB, 4th Armored Division heavily engaged at CHAUMONT . . . CCB, 10th Armored Division: Half of reserve force committed in 3rd Bn, 327 Glider Infantry sector at 231850 . . . 705th TD Bn: Reserve platoon committed in 3rd Bn, 327th Glider Infantry sector at 231500 A . . . 3rd Bn, 327th Glider Infantry: 'C' Co positions overrun by enemy tanks at 231755. Bn withdrew at 231800 A to shorten lines and strengthen position. Attack repulsed" (H. W. Kinnard, G-3 Report No. 5, from: 222400A to: 232400, December 1944); "DECEMBER 23RD . . . completely surrounded them and overran this position" (S3 Operations Section, 327th GIR, 1944); "Illusions of that sort did not divert the professional soldiers: the record shows General Higgins suggested to General McAuliffe that on Christmas Day they might expect an all-out German effort to smash into Bastogne. The Germans are a sentimental people and are probably thinking about giving a present to Hitler'" (MacKenzie, 1968, 182–83).

50   "On 22 Dec 44, I installed my headquarters in Chateau Roumount. Christmas time was coming on and although under the circumstances we had to take over this installation, I saw to it that the people were not moved out" (H. V. Luettwitz, ETHINT 41, An Interview with General Panzertruppen Heinrich von Luettwitz: XLVII Panzer Corps (16 December to 24 December 1944), 1945, 5–6.

51   "23 Dec. 2nd Panzer Division . . . the situation of the endangered right flank would no longer be critical" (H. V. Luettwitz, The Assignment of the XLVII Panzer Corps in the Ardennes, MS A-939, 1950, 11–12); "My original plan was to move Pz Lehr Div through Bastogne, if Bayerlein [Commander of the Panzer Lehr Division] . . . coming along behind who could take the town" (Manteuffel, An Interview with General Panzer Hasso von Manteuffel: Fifth Panzer Army, Nov. 44–Jan. 45, ETHINT 46, 1945, 7); "The first reserves of the OKW (3rd, 15th Panzer Grenadier Divisions and 9th Panzer Division) were committed since 24 December 1944. . . . This would depend from the time of their arrival but the Army suggested to commit them on the Maas River" (C. Wagener, Fifth Panzer Army, Ardennes Offen-

sive, General Comments, MS #A-962, 1945, 1). Interesting to speculate what would have happened if von Lüttwitz had decided to direct the reinforcements to the Meuse instead of Bastogne.

Chapter Six

1   Waldo, 1899, December 14.
2   "Starting from 12/18/44, since no other officer was available, as an NCO I was put in charge of 6th company IR 77. . . . This was confirmed at a gathering of veterans at Isle near Bastogne" (Lindemann, *My Experience during the Ardennes Offensive*, 2010).
3   "Yes. The winter in Russia was stronger. Very, very cold. Minus forty degrees . . . Every day we had new orders" (Lindemann, Second Interview with Ludwig Lindemann, 2010).
4   "The preliminary march was to pass over Stadtkyll, Pruem, and onto Ulfingen. . . . The I Battalion, 115th Pz.Gren.Rgt. (I./115): Boeur; II./115: Buret; III./115: Trotten [various locations southeast of Houffalize]" (Maucke, Report Over the 15th Panzer-Grenadier-Division during the Ardennes Offensive from 16 December 1944 to 2 February 1945: MS P-032c, 1949); "2300 Hours Regimental staff and staff company begin march . . . 1730 Hours Colonel Maucke was ordered to the division" (Operations Section, 1944).
5   "Shortly after 2200 hours, the Panzer Grenadier regiment reported . . . there arrived at the division command post the reconnaissance and advance detachments of the approaching 15th Panzer Grenadier Division" (H. Kokott, Ardennes Offensive— Battle of Bastogne, MS #B-040, 1950, 116–25); "The broad front lines extended approximately 40 kilometers . . . and more advantageous positions were gained by German troops in preparations for the attack against the town" (H. Kokott, Employment of the 26th Volksgrenadier Division from 16 to 31 Dec 1944, 1945); Kokott's assessment was spot on. "Manteuffel . . . That town could then be used as a base for further operations to drive into the deep flank of our own forces" (Manteuffel, *The Fifth Panzer Army: Hasso von Manteuffel*, 2006, 113).
6   "I knew that on 24 Dec, the advance detachment of the 2 Pz Div was attacked by the 2 U.S. Armored Div. Elements of this division had already taken Buissonville and Humain. . . . The first part of the 15 Pz Gren Div arrived on 24 Dec 44 and were subordinated to the 26 Volks Gren Div to participate in the attack on Bastogne, which was to be launched on 25 Dec 44" (H. V. Luettwitz, XXXXVII Panzer Corps in the Battle of the Ardennes, Manuscript A-940, 1946, 9–10, 12–13); "24 Dec, 2nd Panzer Division: On this day started the attacks of the American 2nd Armored Division . . . which was given orders to make an attack against the town on 25 Dec, in order to take it definitely." (H. V. Luettwitz, The Assignment of the XLVII Panzer Corps in the Ardennes, MSA-939, 1950, 12–14); "Meanwhile, pressure on the forces advancing to Dinant had so increased . . . Attempts to establish contact with it from the Conneux pocket proved unsuccessful" (Weiz, unknown, 4–7); "3. The fact that Bastogne could not be captured . . . to protect past of the left flank of the army" (H. V. Luettwitz, Item No. 5: Answers to Questions by Gen d Pz Tr v. Luettwitz, MS A-938, 1945, 4).
7   "24 December 1944 160 planes were used between the hours of 0855 and 1500. The supplies recovered are listed below. Ammunition 75mm How. 3542 105mm How. M3 598 60mm 757 81mm mortar 484 Rockets, AT 182 . . . Rations, Type 'K' 9918"

(Robbins, 11 January 1945, 2–3); Eleven gliders had been able to land near Savy, at the vicinity of the "B" Battery positon of the 327th Parachute Field Artillery Battalion, carrying medical personnel including four surgeons (Arend, 1987, 197).

8   "At 0900 fighter air support arrived and remained active in the vicinity throughout the remainder of the day. During this period the enemy's activities were confined generally to passive resistance of the aircraft" (P. A. Danahy, G-2 Periodic Reports No. 6 from: 240001 to 242400, December 1944); "1345—P-47s are strafing and bombing MARVIE (5755)" (S2 Section, 327th Glider Infantry Regiment, 1944, 8).

9   "The commanders and staffs took official notice of the occasion . . . showing only in the words 'Merry Christmas' across the position held by the defenders." (S. Marshall, 1946, 156); See enemy situational template overlays.

10   "The finest Christmas present the 101st could get would be a relief tomorrow" (MacKenzie, 1968, 203).

11   J. S. Eisenhower, 1969, 328.

12   Ibid.

13   A. C. McAuliffe, Merry Christmas, 1944.

14   "First, we were with the 501st, later we were with the 502nd . . . but I wasn't injured" (A. D'Angelo, Interview with Tony D'Angelo, 2009); Author's note: During a visit in July of 2010, with the help of Bernard Maus and locals, Don was able to find the location and the religious shrine on a hill just above Longchamps. The shrine has been remodeled, but it is indeed the same location where Swanson and D'Angelo witnessed the massing of the German armor. As for the panzers, by this time, 15th Panzergrenadier Division was arriving in sector. Whether these panzers belonged to them or elements of another panzer division is more than possible, since the northern route was the main avenue of approach around Bastogne for the Germans. Still, it must've been quite a daunting sight for the two U.S. soldiers.

15   "Someone told me later . . . That's what we did Christmas Eve Day" (A. D'Angelo, Interview with Tony D'Angelo, 2009).

16   "The 24th. Sleep? Ha! Didn't sleep that night because of the bombardment and bombing. . . . We were busy just trying to stay warm and alive" (A. D'Angelo, Interview with Tony D'Angelo, 2009).

17   "What helped was when it snowed—then it got warmer. . . . We didn't have anything to camouflage our positions or TDs with, just snow. We didn't have radios per se in the TDs, just intercoms, which didn't work well" (Breder, 2009).

18   "Rations got old. But you ate what you had to. . . . We were very grateful" (A. D'Angelo, Phone Interview with Anthony D'Angelo, 2009); "That night [Dec 24] I didn't get any sleep at all" (A. D'Angelo, Interview with Tony D'Angelo, 2009).

19   "We were sleeping in this potato shed there, along the road going out of Champs . . . so it seemed like the smart thing to do" (Fowler, Interview with Corporal Willis Fowler, 2009); "The rest of the platoon was over there on my left. . . . We had men in those houses, OPs" (Fowler, 2nd Interview with Corporal Willis Fowler, 2010).

20   "We were at Champs and our company had the job of protecting the town. . . . I was a bit of mother hen" (Asay, 2009); "A few buzz bombs [V-1s] were clearly heard going over low each night. . . . We had been sleeping in hay in the barns. . . ." (Goldmann, Letter to Mrs. Ballard, 1945).

21   "At 1800 hours I arrived at the combat command post of the 26th VGD. . . . At 2200 hours I was directed to report to the command post of the 26th VGD, where I would receive my orders personally from the divisional commander" (Maucke, Report Over

the 15th Panzer-Grenadier-Division during the Ardennes Offensive from 16 December 1944 to 2 February 1945: MS P-032c, 1949); "1730 Hours Colonel Maucke was ordered to the division" (Operations Section, 1944); "While the division commander, on 24 December . . . All necessary preparations for the additional artillery were made by the senior artillery officer together with the commander of Artillery Regiment 26" (H. Kokott, Ardennes Offensive—Battle of Bastogne, MS #B-040, 1950, 125).

22   "They hadn't come at our area during the first days there. . . . It sounds terrible but he had no more use for it" (Astor, 1994, 330).

23   "24 Dec . . . 1735—Division notified our Regiment to be alert for a possible enemy attack from the West tonight" (S2 Section, 502nd Parachute Infantry Regiment, 1944); "After a section of weary, tired wiremen reported in . . . Chain antitank mines were also made available for placing across the road at both of these points" (Phillips, 1948, 18–19).

24   "Since it had become bitter cold for the first time in the Bulge, Sergeant DeWitt moved the 2nd Platoon into an old barn with a hayloft. . . . They just might have been the best cookies I ever ate" (Black, *The Last First Sergeant*, 1998, 241–42).

25   "Well, Gresh, he got sick. . . . That's about all I remember about our Christmas Eve" (Lott, 2009).

26   "We had seen the Germans building up west of our lines for two days. . . . Then they got back in their foxholes and waited" (D. R. Martin, 2004, 54–55).

27   "We talked about being surrounded, but it never changed our morale. . . . On Christmas Day from our foxholes we could see the Germans building for an attack, tanks and troops in white uniforms headed for us" (C. Gisi, Questionnaire for Carmen Gisi, 2009).

28   See overlay (T. Moran, Location of 463 Parachute Field Artillery Battalion to Accompany S-2 Report 207, 22 December 1944).

29   "One could hardly forget the night before, Christmas Eve. . . . I was thinking of everyone at home" (Koskimaki, 2003, 256).

30   "Well, on the twenty-fourth, I don't recall how, but we were alerted. . . . It was one of the more quiet evenings in between" (Hesler, Second Interview with Ken Hesler, 2010).

31   For a list of officers, see the following source: rzecznik@502-101airborne.pl 2011.

32   "I [Captain Pangerl] can just remember the Christmas Party for the kids in the Chateau Rolle through one of my letters. . . . The family house was also present, of course. I thought about you at home . . ." (Koskimaki, 2003, 255–56); "I [Captain Hatch] recall an event which went from a moment of joy to sadness . . . so they could decorate the tree and open their presents . . ." (Koskimaki, 2003, 255).

33   "General Higgins jolted Harper with the news. . . . Higgins responded, 'Do what you can with it, Bud. There isn't any other solution'" (MacKenzie, 1968, 203); "At 1800 Harper was told that he had the sector all the way from Marvie to 511610. He said to Gen Higggins, 'Look at it; this is half of the Div perimeter.' Higgins replied, 'It's all yours; do what you can with it. There isn't any other solution'" (Harper, 327th Regiment at Bastogne, 1945, 20).

34   "Catholic soldiers spread the word that a mass would be celebrated at 7 o'clock. . . . It was as though one was dying, or being born, in travail" (MacKenzie, 1968, 204).

35   "Instead, as Christmas Eve neared . . . when daylight began to fade on the battlefield" (MacKenzie, 1968, 202–03).

36   "At commencement of the offensive, on the 16th of December . . . I then returned to my Command Post" (Heintz, 1984, 64).

Chapter Seven

1   D. N. Moran, 2011.
2   "24 December . . . 1925—Unidentified aircraft over Bastogne. 1945—Enemy aircraft bombing Bastogne" (S2 Section, 327th Glider Infantry Regiment, 1944, 8).
3   "At 1955 approx 4-6 German planes believed to be Ju-88's bombed Bastogne and vicinity of CP . . . the planes were out of range and did not fire" (Cox, 1944, 3).
4   S. Marshall, 1946, 250.
5   "Suddenly, three petrifying explosions . . . Colonel Renfro strode away, followed by the other" (MacKenzie, 1968, 205–08); August Chiwy, an African nurse from the Belgian Congo, also regarded as a heroine for her work with the wounded, survived the bombing (King, 2011).
6   "At 8:30 p.m. Christmas Eve . . . It is on these grounds that I recommend the highest award possible to one, who though not a member of the armed forces of the United States, was of invaluable assistance to us" (Prior, 2007); (King, 2011).
7   "On Christmas Eve they started. . . . So we moved up right behind his CP, a place called" (Harper, Bastogne Speech, 1975). To this day, if you visit the Bastogne cemetery, you can still see many of the tombstones and vaults cracked or displaced from the bombing.
8   "That night I didn't get any sleep at all. I was banged and bounced around in my bed by them Luftwaffe bombs" (A. D'Angelo, Phone Interview with Anthony D'Angelo, 2009).
9   "Sometime after that I fell asleep. . . . that fires could be seen from outside our hayloft" (Black, *The Last First Sergeant*, 1998, 242).
10   "I would carry arms and legs from the hospital and put them in a pile. We would burn them later. It was Godawful" (Breder, 2009).
11   "I could watch the bombing of Bastogne . . . when they dove over Bastogne from the reflection of the flares" (Middough, 1990).
12   "Christmas Eve was not special . . . but I don't remember that as our goal/target [objective]" (Lindemann, Second Interview with Ludwig Lindemann, 2010): "Christmas Eve we were in a large tank dugout westerly of Bastogne. . . . I don't think it registered to us that it was Christmas" (Lindemann, Questionnaire to Ludwig Lindemann, 2010).
13   "Enemy: Bastogne has been encircled completely for days; enemy supplies munitions and food by air continuously . . . Achieved objectives are to be indicated through firing of white flares and by telephone or radio to Regtl CP" (Schriefer, 1944); See also German tactics and TO & Es in *Handbook on German Military Forces*, 1945 (War Department, 1945, Figure 51, Chapter 2); See Order of Battle for the XXXXVII Panzer Corps for the inclusion of Hetzers in 26th VGD (Staff, 1944).
14   "At the command post of the 26th VGD I received from the division commander the written order for the attack against Bastogne . . . The German troops did not know this, but later they noticed" (Maucke, Report Over the 15th Panzer-Grenadier-Division during the Ardennes Offensive from 16 December 1944 to 2 February 1945: MS P-032c, 1949).
15   Maucke's assault force, or *kampfgruppe*, was equipped with an armory of the Third

Reich's weaponry, even if some of it was slightly out-of-date. His Panzergrenadiers were mainly equipped with obsolete Mauser Kar 98k bolt-action rifles. Here and there, several NCOs carried Schmeisser MP 40 9mm submachine guns or the semi-automatic Gewehr 43, also known as the "German Garand." Many may have also carried the latest and most effective personal weapon, the Sturmgewehr 44, the first true assault rifle, firing a full magazine of thirty short-caliber 7.92mm bullets. For machine gun support, each squad of grenadiers (nine to eleven men) had an MG 42 or medium machine gun team, consisting of a gunner and spotter/ammo carrier. Many of the Germans carried the stick grenade, or Model 24 Stielhandgranate, commonly known as the "potato masher" grenade among the GIs. For camouflage, most of the soldiers had on reversible parkas and snowsuits of white. Helmets had been painted white, or white cloth covers had been attached to blend in with the snow. To strike terror in the hearts of the Americans, Maucke had specifically made sure that several squads fielded flamethrowers. The unusual devices, similar to the American version used mostly in the Pacific theater, consisted of a tank strapped to the back of the operator, carrying petrol and an oily gel similar to napalm. Another tank was filled with hydrogen as a propellant. When the operator squeezed a lever on the "gun" portion, a rubber tube attached to the tank squirted a hose of flaming liquid that could shoot some fifty or more feet. There was also a one-shot, smaller version of this device called the Einstossflammenwerfer 46, which could be carried under the arm. Although terrifying, the flamethrowers were not popular among the grenadiers. Often, these devices were more dangerous to the operator than to the enemy. A few of Maucke's soldiers carried the antitank Panzerfaust or Panzerschreck, bazookalike weapons that propelled a cone-shaped explosive charge to penetrate enemy armor plating. Of *Hauptmann* Schmidt's eleven tanks, the majority were the standard Panzerkampfwagen IV Ausf H, an aging but reliable medium tank used since 1941. Known to Americans as the Mark (Mk) IV, this veteran tank (although underarmored and undergunned compared to newer German tanks, such as the Mark V Panther and monstrous King Tigers and Jagdtigers), was still a force to be reckoned with when compared to the American M4 Sherman and M18 Hellcat. The Mk IV had long been regarded as the workhorse tank of the Wehrmacht and, in its most updated version, had supplied most of the tank companies during *Wacht am Rhein*. The crews were not happy about one recent change to the vehicle. Earlier that year, someone in the division that oversaw armament production decided to add extra gas tanks to extend the tank's range. To accommodate this change, the small motor that powered the turret was removed. Now the crew had to turn a hand crank every time to rotate the turret. The maximum speed to turn the gun 180 degrees was now about five minutes—a fatal slowness in battle. There were at least three Sturmgeschütz III Ausf G assault guns attached to Dyroff's battalion. The StuG ("Stoog"), for short, was an ungainly, bargain-basement armored vehicle that was really not supposed to serve as a tank. As a self-propelled (SP) or "assault" gun, the StuG had the same 75mm weapon as the Panzer Mk IV, yet the gun was mounted low and almost immobilized in the hull, simply pointing straight forward. The StuG III lacked a traversing turret like the Mk IV. It could really fire in only one direction—forward. This was actually a cost-effective idea—by skipping the production of a complicated rotating turret more StuGs could be manufactured in German factories compared to turreted tanks, and, at 82,500 reichsmarks, a StuG was also cheaper than a Mk IV, which cost more than double that amount to build. This may have seemed a strange concept, but originally the assault gun idea had been a great success during the early part of the war. In the open plains of Russia, the vehicle was considered simply a tracked artillery piece that could keep pace with the infantry. StuGs were originally crewed and managed by the Wehrmacht's artillery corps. Later in the war, as with the 115th Panzer, the vehicles were used simply as tanks, or tank destroyers to supplement the lack of Jagdpanthers, Jagdpanzer IVs, Panzer IVs, and Panther V medium tanks at the battalion level. With a low silhouette, the StuG III was hard to see and hard to hit. Although providing less cover without a turret, with their flat backs they were easier for soldiers to ride on. Some even came with handrails welded on for just this purpose. The 75mm KwK 40 L/48 anti-tank gun shared by both the Mk IV and StuG III was indeed an awesome weapon. With a muzzle velocity of 2,800 feet per second, the weapon was easily comparable to the more famous (infamous to the Allies) German 88mm. Especially on the mobile Mk IV, the 75mm, firing a APCBC (armor-piercing capped ballistic cap) round could cut through the armor on any American tank of the time. As described in an U.S. Army intelligence bulletin of the time, the German 75mm was capable of "defeating, in European fighting conditions [that is, up to 1,500 yards], armor 100 millimeters thick and greater thicknesses at shorter ranges"—information that was certainly not comforting to American tankers. Maucke's 33rd Panzerjäger (tank destroyer) Battalion seems to have been equipped with a motley collection of about twenty older tank destroyers of the Marder II, III, and Hetzer types. Several of the versatile StuG IIIs may have even rounded out the unit.

16   "At 2000 hours, in accordance with the card . . . Despite a bitter defense, the enemy was obviously surprised" (Maucke, Report Over the 15th Panzer-Grenadier-Division during the Ardennes Offensive from 16 December 1944 to 2 February 1945: MS P-032c, 1949); "Distribution of orders . . . The II Battalion shall be in reserve" (Operations Section, 1944).

17   "After 2100 hours on 24 December . . . The promised support had not been given any credence from the very start. Towards midnight of 24/25 December, several German planes appeared over Bastogne and dropped some bombs . . ." (H. Kokott, Ardennes Offensive—Battle of Bastogne, MS #B-040, 1950, 125–27).

18   "In Contact . . . 77th VG Regt 78th VG Regt 39th VG Regt 901 PG Regt 902 PG Regt 2 PG Regt 2 SS PG Regt, 'Der Fuhrer' . . . 123 casualties were in the aid station at the time of the bombing and 23 are still missing" (P. A. Danahy, G-2 Periodic Reports No. 6 from: 240001 to 242400, December 1944).

19   For the intelligence overlay, see Anlage 2. "At 0000 hours, orders were distributed for the attack against Bastogne. . . . The commander was temporarily assigned as a stop measure, which explains why the battalion was not committed to the difficult task in the front lines" (Maucke, Report Over the 15th Panzer-Grenadier-Division during the Ardennes Offensive from 16 December 1944 to 2 February 1945: MS P-032c, 1949); "1830 Hours Distribution of orders to the commanders and chiefs of the regimental units . . . each of the 2 battalions shall receive two forward observers. The II Battalion shall be in reserve" (Operations Section, 1944); *"Franz Adam Dyroff wurde am 06. Mai 1916 in Langstadt bei Dieburg geboren . . . Franz Adam Dyroff verstarb am 24. März 1998 und wurde auf dem Friedhof Darmstadt-Eberstadt beigesetzt"* (The Knight's Cross, Deutsche Wehrmacht and Waffen SS, 2005).

20   "The night in the basement of the Pensionnat des Soeurs de Notre-Dame . . . but also all the other passages where the hundreds of refugees were crowded" (Heintz,

1984, 65); "0300 25 Dec. Enemy planes are now bombing our entire Regimental area" (S2 Section, 502nd Parachute Infantry Regiment, 1944, 8).

Chapter Eight

1   Stryker, 1898, 70–71; D. N. Moran, Colonel Johann Gottleib Rall: Guilty of Tactical Negligence or Guiltless Circumstances, 2007.

2   Stryker, 1898, 70–71; D. N. Moran, Colonel Johann Gottleib Rall: Guilty of Tactical Negligence or Guiltless Circumstances, 2007.

3   "The unsheltered bystander [MacKenzie], too, had heard the first note of Death's Christmas Hymn . . . they expanded and rose as upright as they might until the next" (MacKenzie, 1968, 212–13).

4   "In the deep foxhole beside the main gates at the western side of the Division headquarters compound . . . 'We had better wake the Old Man,' the Chief of Staff said to the early morning crew with him in the operations room. General McAuliffe accordingly was called" (MacKenzie, 1968, 211–16, 218).

5   "0300 25 Dec. Enemy planes are now bombing our entire Regimental area" (S2 Section, 502nd Parachute Infantry Regiment, 1944, 8); "At 0300 hours attack of Regimental strength was launched. . . . Casualties were light" (Danahy, 1944); "At 0300 hours on the 25 December 1944 'A' Company's position . . . hand to hand street fighting ensued" (Chappuis, 1944, 4).

6   "25 Dec 44 Shelling has been going on for three minutes on our positions. All communication destroyed with Able 1, 3, and 3" (A Co Headquarters Section, 502nd Parachute Infantry, 1945).

7   "On December 25th, Christmas morning, shelling started about 0300 . . . but that was something we had to keep doing out of necessity" (Koskimaki, 2003, 284).

8   ". . . an all-out barrage, artillery, cannon, mortar and other firepower . . . and all connections from the front to the back and around our strongpoints" (Astor, 1994, 329–30).

9   "Well, about 2:30 in the morning there was this intense artillery barrage. . . . We knew something was up" (Fowler, Interview with Corporal Willis Fowler, 2009); "A little after 2 a.m. on the 25th . . . the Germans had broke and we scurried to our holes" (Goldmann, 1945).

10   "Mr. Hodge was born 12 Feb 1925. He was a member A/502 PIR, 101st ABN DIV. Born in Jefferson City, Missouri . . . That was his last big battle" (Hodge Jr., 2001); "The C.P. of the 2nd Platoon Co 'A' on December 24, 1944 was stationed in a farmhouse . . . as one of the men in the outpost had been severely wounded in the back by shrapnel" (Wise, 1948). Airborne platoons typically had two platoon leaders, since attrition was so high. One was designated the assistant platoon leader. In this case, Wise was the assistant.

11   "One Christmas Eve the Regt had midnight Mass in the 10th Century chapel of Rolle . . . that his men were locked in a hand-to-hand and house-to-house fight with them" (Cassidy, 1945, 7).

12   Another possibility is the explosive charges froze that night due to the frigid temperatures and damp weather.

13   "During the night, the Bastogne area was bombed . . . were rushed into position to back up the machine guns, but never had to fire as the enemy withdrew into the

woods and ceased fire on 2nd Battalion's positions" (Phillips, 1948, 20–21); "That very night, on the opposite side of our lines, the enemy activity had increased . . . in grotesque forms the death froze into eternity" (Peniche, 2009); "'I thought mostly about home in the Yucatan in southern Mexico where we never had snow,' he recorded in his journal . . . you have to be a patriot . . . you cannot shrink" (Meyer, 2007, 18).

14   This is alluded to by Asay and others in Koskimaki, but I have no direct accounts or figures.

15   "25 Dec 44 . . . 0319 Enemy attacked between Able 1 and 3. Street fighting throughout the site. Able 2 CP set on fire. Large enemy forces behind lines, TD committed" (A Co Headquarters Section, 502nd Parachute Infantry, 1945).

16   "The CP of the 2nd Platoon with 1Lt. John Harrison (I was assistant platoon leader) on December 24, 1944 was situated in a farmhouse on the outskirts of Champs . . . while we fired at the Jerries attacking the 1st Platoon CP trying to distract the enemy" (Wise, 1948).

17   "I see German soldiers starting over the ridge to our front. . . . We always thought could get attacked, so it seemed like the smart thing to do" (Fowler, Interview with Corporal Willis Fowler, 2009); "Well, my assistant gunner, Bill Emerson, he wasn't shooting when I came out of the potato shed. . . . He hadn't been firing the machine gun; I knew I had to get that gun into action. I think he just kind of froze up a bit" (Fowler, 2nd Interview with Corporal Willis Fowler, 2010).

18   There are several stories from Bastogne veterans of machinery from pistols to tanks freezing up in the cold. In a purely nonscientific experiment, I once placed an M1 Garand, a M1A1 Thompson submachine gun, and an M1 carbine in the woods overnight during a frigid Colorado winter night. Taking temperature readings each hour, I recorded temperatures from thirteen degrees at seven p.m. to minus five degrees at about four a.m. The bolts and actions on all three weapons worked fine, even with frost buildup. It is my belief that the freezing and thawing (melted ice in the action), along with grime, grease, and gun oil, were the real culprits. Most of these weapons were designed to work in freezing temperatures as long as they were routinely stripped of oil and grease and kept dry and clean, which would have been near impossible for the soldiers in their foxholes that December (Author Don Cygan).

19   "The squad on the right side of the road wasn't so lucky . . . which substantiated our beliefs" (Goldmann, 1945).

20   "The Germans hit us Christmas Eve. Fought an all-nite action at Champs. Squad on right overrun. Spent the nit directing fire and throwing hand grenades on the right to keep the Germans off our flank" (Asay, Individual Action Report for Bastogne, 1990); For list of MIAs, see A Company logs for that day (A Co Headquarters Section, 502nd Parachute Infantry, 1945).

21   "I should have gotten back to our line. . . . That was the beginning of the worst four months of my life" (Koskimaki, 2003, 286).

22   "Company 'A' had the responsibility of protecting the Champs area . . . although they didn't know if we were still around or who it was that might be on the right" (Koskimaki, 2003, 285–86).

23   "Arriving from across the fields, the first Germans reached the road which crossed the village, and infiltrated between the houses and Raviola and Ries . . . still had the courage to demand a cigarette" (Heintz, 1984, 72–73); "Witness Statements . . .

Victor Raviola, Albert Clement, Achille Denis, Madeleine Seleck, Angèle Clement-Gouvienne, Rosine Paul-Denis . . . another was put in over the staircase" (Cercle d'Histoire de Bastogne, 1994, Chapter 14).

24   "At 0330 Cassidy called Swanson again. . . . And while they were talking the line went out" (Cassidy, 1945, 7); "At 0330, Colonel Cassidy called Captain Swanson (Company A) asking him about the situation at Champs. . . . Colonel Cassidy tried the radio but failed to make contact with Captain Swanson" (Phillips, 1948, 21).

25   "Prior to Company 'A' moving to Champs there had been another road block along the road south of Champs and due west of Rolle . . . if it pushed on into town and the Germans came around it" (Cassidy, 1945, 7–8); "The Regimental Commander, Lieutenant Colonel Steve A. Chappuis, was awakened. . . . This sector was thinly held by the 3rd Battalion [1/401st] 327th Glider Regiment" (Phillips, 1948, 21–23).

26   "Chappuis called First Bn by radio and told them to get ready to move . . . . then get forward into Champs and help Swanson" (Cassidy, 1945, 7); "During the early morning hours of the 25th, the regimental command wanted to know if we could use additional help. I informed them that even though there was lots of action going on in Champs, I did not feel as though any more troops should be sent in because of the darkness" (Koskimaki, 2003, 289); "Lt. Colonel Hanlon was ordered by the Regimental Commander . . . Companies 'B' and 'C' were halted along the road from Hemroulle to Champs" (Chappuis, 1944, 4).

27   "That's when we saw those four tanks on the ridge . . . that probably would have been the end of us" (Fowler, 2nd Interview with Corporal Willis Fowler, 2010); "Then these four German tanks show up there . . . I took off my helmet and peeked over the foxhole" (Fowler, Interview with Corporal Willis Fowler, 2009).

28   "Christmas Eve was not special. . . . We had tanks come up later" (Lindemann, 2010).

29   "They shot flares into a totally dark sky and we took advantage of them. They fired haystacks and then got in between us and the blazes to form perfect silhouettes and down they went" (Goldmann, 1945).

30   "Suddenly, I heard what sounded like a moan from the direction of the machine gun. . . . The German who had fired at me from the flank made a getaway" (Koskimaki, 2003, 288).

31   "25 December 0350 from Rcn D/90—75 rds mortar and 88 from 0250 to 0305 still falling . . . 0400 Enemy is about 8 to 10 houses in North end of town. From Rcn D/90" (S-3 Section, CCB 10th Armored Division, 1944).

32   "We were in the upstairs of a farmhouse near Champs. . . . TDs not supposed to do that job for a tank, but we had to make do" (D'Angelo, 2009); "This 2nd Section maintained their two positions . . . instead of returning to their usual daylight positions" (Long, 1945, 2); "At 1000, 22 Dec the Recon section and 2 TDs reported to Captain Swanson of Co. 'A' 502 . . . canister flowing in a northwesterly direction to deny that route to the enemy" (Duvall, 1945, 3–4); "Yes. I got the tank ready. We [Vallitta and Stoling] went in and we blew up a house" (Stoling, 2009); "The other action that helped out was by the tank destroyers . . . using the tank destroyers direct firing into the enemy position even though close in contact with our men" (Koskimaki, 2003, 298).

33   "The Germans sent us Christmas Greetings when they bombed Bastogne for the first time. We were alerted at 0330 for an attack . . ." (Cleaver, 1944, 4); "DATE & TIME RECEIVED 12/25 0350: BN NO: NB : DESCRIPTION COORDI-NATES: Infantry (530-652) REC'D FROM: 41 TIME COMPLETED 0355: OBS

BY 41: NO RDS 22: EFFECT Excellent . . . DATE & TIME RECEIVED 12/25 0400: BN NO: W2 : DESCRIPTION COORDINATES: Infantry (5300-6512) REC'D FROM: 51 TIME COMPLETED 0420: OBS BY 51: NO RDS 57: EFFECT Excellent" (Brubaker, 1944).

34　"J. Huesken, Lieutenant. In the field, 25 Jan 1945 Dearest Mrs. Adorf . . . Please accept my apologies for writing to you on a typewriter" (Husken, 1945).

35　"Around 0300 AM on Christmas morning, 1944 . . . which burst in the air above the woods where his O.P. as well as some 502 listening posts had been overrun during darkness" (Bando, 2000).

36　"About 4:00 A.M. there was another lull in the firing and at this time . . . I remained at our outpost with Private Grovesnor for the remainder of the night" (Wise, 1948).

37　"Prior to Company 'A' moving to Champs there had been another road block along the road south of Champs and due west of Rolle . . . if it pushed on into town and the Germans came around it" (Cassidy, 1945, 7–8); "The Regimental Commander, Lieutenant Colonel Steve A. Chappuis, was awakened and given a resume of the situation by Colonel Cassidy . . . This sector was thinly held by the 3rd Battalion [1/401st] 327th Glider Regiment" (Phillips, 1948, 21–23); "0440 Our 1st BN is now committing its reserve Company (C Company) in support of 'A' and 'B.' We also have notified Division of our present situation" (S2 Section, 502nd Parachute Infantry Regiment, 1944, 8). It's hard to estimate when B Company sent out the additional platoon to secure the southern flank of 2nd Battalion. There are no reports with time hacks associated with the order, and it doesn't seem clear when the order was given. Phillips's account gives the impression that it was before Hanlon arrived. Unfortunately, Chappuis' account is not clear either. This is a best guess, since the only time hack we have is around 0440, when the regimental staff logged that they were bringing up other units to support 1st BN. "Christmas morning we noticed quite a bit of activity to our front . . . and we dug in" (Nichols, 1990).

38　"After giving this order by radio . . . This sector was thinly held by the 3rd Battalion [1/401st] 327th Glider Regiment" (Phillips, 1948, 22–23).

39　"We were at Champs and our company had the job of protecting the town. . . . We were clearing out house to house all day and taking prisoners" (Asay, Interview with Charles Asay, 2009).

40　"We'd be very quiet and inconspicuous. . . . I'm not sure whether I killed every one of them or not but I'm sure I killed some" (Koskimaki, 2003, 290).

41　"We were sleeping in this potato shed there, along the road going out of Champs. . . . I tell you, we had a pretty rough time there for a while" (Fowler, Interview with Corporal Willis Fowler, 2009).

42　"Look on the map. . . . There four tanks were driven off by aerial burst from the hoarded supplies of artillery ammo which we had practically none of, and by the appearance of four P-47's" (Goldmann, 1945); "At 0530 hours, 22 December 1944 . . . After their vehicle was knocked out the crew of this vehicle was used by the 609th TD bn. in relief roles at Bastogne" (Brownfield, 1959).

43　"25 December 0530 . . . Tanks . . . (5120-6345) Rec'd From: 51 . . . Time Completed . . . 0550 . . . Observed by 51 . . . Number of Rounds . . . 22 . . . Effect . . . Very Good" (Brubaker, 1944).

44　"Lovely artillery, beautiful TD's wonderful Air Corps; we had been hurting for sure and now we had won" (Goldmann, 1945).

45　We were sleeping in this potato shed there, along the road going out of Champs. . . .

I tell you, we had a pretty rough time there for a while" (Fowler, Interview with Corporal Willis Fowler, 2009).

46   "The Germans were at the end of their ropes by now; grenades and submachine gun fire were beginning to slow down. . . . Everyone was relieved, but no one dared go outside" (Cercle d'Histoire de Bastogne, 1994, Chapter 14).

47   "By 8 am Champs had been taken back from the Germans. . . . Dozens of prisoners were gathered near Raviola's farm, with an American soldier (and Mr. Raviola himself) supervising them" (Cercle d'Histoire de Bastogne, 1994, Chapter 14).

48   "The village heights resembled a necropolis. . . . Torn arms, slashed legs, gaping wounds flooded with blood the Raviola kitchen where dozens of the injured awaited aid" (Heintz, 1984, 73).

49   "0500 from Rcn D/90 fighting continuing believe line is holding same position . . . 0600 from Rcn D/90 Situation quieting down 6 or 8 Germans trapped in town will mop up at day light" (S-3 Section, CCB 10th Armored Division, 1944).

Chapter Nine

1   Morris, 1958.

2   "Shortly after midnight, a stocky young 2nd lieutenant, John Adams, of Stillwater, Oklahoma . . . These were Mk IV panzers and not Tiger tanks since the 15th panzergrenadier had no Tigers attached to it (Smith, 1945, 92); "The II./115 received resistance 1st along the Flamizoulle Stream in the small forest north of Flamizoulle" (Maucke, Report Over the 15th Panzer-Grenadier-Division during the Ardennes Offensive from 16 December 1944 to 2 February 1945: MS P-032c, 1949). Though Maucke claimed this was his 2nd battalion, his memory might have been off, which he freely admitted in the beginning of the document. His start times seemed to corroborate American sources, but once the battle started his times did not coincide with American reports.

3   "Reconnaissance had already convinced Division that this was the most likely avenue in the whole defensive circle for a thrust by enemy armor . . . which were just entering the battle" (S. Marshall, 1948, 5); "That night [Christmas Eve], we could hear the tanks and knew the Germans were up to something, near Flamierge" (C. Gisi, Interview with PFC Carmen Gisi, 2009); "We had seen the Germans building up west of our lines for two days. . . . At 10 p.m. the men on the front line could hear panzers arriving near Flamizoulle, a small village about two miles west of our line" (D. R. Martin, 2004, 54–55); "1735 [24 December] Division notified our Regiment [502] to be alert for a possible enemy attack from the West tonight" (S2 Section, 502nd Parachute Infantry Regiment, 1944); "Around 2200 hours, the battalions prepared for the attack in the following order: I./- Tank, Regimental troops, II./-, III" (Maucke, Report Over the 15th Panzer-Grenadier-Division during the Ardennes Offensive from 16 December 1944 to 2 February 1945: MS P-032c, 1949).

4   "At 2200 on Christmas Eve, on order from Division . . . But it was too late to be effective" (S. Marshall, 1948, 5–6); "The 327th reports 8 tanks at north of FLEMIERGE. Shells are falling in rear of Regimental CP and in court-yard" (S2 Section, 502nd Parachute Infantry Regiment, 1944); "Harper was called at 0500 by Company 'A' 3rd Bn who informed him that 14 tanks were forming for attack just east of Mande St. Etienne. He got this message from Lt Howard Bowles, Comdg the com-

pany." Though Harper claims the report said fourteen tanks, the radio log mentions only eight (Harper, 327th Regiment at Bastogne, 1945, 21).

5   "At 0300 hours, all the units reported entered the preparatory positions . . . which was not out of the ordinary" (Maucke, Report Over the 15th Panzer-Grenadier-Division during the Ardennes Offensive from 16 December 1944 to 2 February 1945: MS P-032c, 1949).

6   "The enemy has now sufficient forces in the western area to attack in strength from that direction" (L. C. Danahy, No. 4 G-2 Periodic Report, 22 December 1944, for the 101st Airborne Division, 1944); "At 1800 Harper was told that he had the sector all the way from Marvie to 511610 [south of Champs]. He said to Higgins, 'Look at it; this is half of the Div perimeter.' Higgins replied, 'It's all yours; do what you can with it. There isn't any other solution'" (Harper, 327th Regiment at Bastogne, 1945, 20); "At that time the 327th was holding all the way from Marvie around here to the 502, a good 8 miles—maybe a little more; it looked bigger to me" (Harper, Bastogne Speech, 1975).

7   "0430—2nd Platoon Co. A . . . Two of the four enemy tanks destroyed and enemy infantry dispersed" (Harris, No. 116, S-3 Report, 705th Tank Destroyer Battalion, 242400, December 1944, to 252400, December 1944); See map, S. Marshall, 1948, 6; "The TDs were now attached to Co 'A' 401st and at 1600 [24 Dec] moved to a position behind two wooded areas just north of their former position at the cut . . . All men dug in" (R. B. Miller 1945); "Around 0620 hours, the I./115 reported flanking fire from the south from anti-tank or tanks guns" (Maucke, Report Over the 15th Panzer-Grenadier-Division during the Ardennes Offensive from 16 December 1944 to 2 February 1945: MS P-032c, 1949). Though the time was off, this might have been 2/B/705th TD BN's flank shots at the column as it emerged from Monty.

8   "Commitment of two battalions in the forward most line . . . The tank destroyers were to follow the II./115, in order to engage and neutralize enemy tanks during the offensive or defensive situations" (Maucke, Report Over the 15th Panzer-Grenadier-Division during the Ardennes Offensive from 16 December 1944 to 2 February 1945: MS P-032c, 1949); For Maucke's Order of Battle, Concept Sketch, and Officer Chart, see the Tabs in back of his account (Maucke, Report Over the 15th Panzer-Grenadier-Division during the Ardennes Offensive from 16 December 1944 to 2 February 1945: MS P-032c, 1949, Appendix 5, Appendix 6, Tab a and b); "Distribution of orders . . . The II Battalion shall be in reserve" (Operations Section, 1944).

9   "Commitment of two battalions in the forward most line . . . The tank destroyers were to follow the II./115, in order to engage and neutralize enemy tanks during the offensive or defensive situations" (Maucke, Report Over the 15th Panzer-Grenadier-Division during the Ardennes Offensive from 16 December 1944 to 2 February 1945: MS P-032c, 1949); For Maucke's Order of Battle, Concept Sketch, and Officer Chart see the Tabs in back of his account (Maucke, Report Over the 15th Panzer-Grenadier-Division during the Ardennes Offensive from 16 December 1944 to 2 February 1945: MS P-032c, 1949, Appendix 5, Appendix 6, Tab a and b).

10   Reports from several American soldiers mention repeatedly that the Germans appeared to be acting "drunk" during the attack. Hardly a stretch, if one considers the holiday, the need for "liquid courage," and the stress on the tired and hungry German soldiers that night. "The Germans were wearing white uniforms and shooting their guns point-blank at us, yelling. I heard some say they were drunk" (C. Gisi,

Interview with PFC Carmen Gisi, 2009); "Screaming and shouting as they advanced, the grenadiers seemed to be drunk" (Arend, 1987, 213); "To the rear of the armor were men on foot. They came up the hill in an unstoppable numbers, hundreds of them, many yelling. MacDonald assumed they were drunk" (MacKenzie, 1968, 221).

11   "0405 Hours Flamizoulle free of the enemy. Both battalions made good forward progress. The enemy withdrew without a defense" (Operations Section, 1944).

12   "After crossing their preparatory lines . . . which proved especially costly for the II./115" (Maucke, Report Over the 15th Panzer-Grenadier-Division during the Ardennes Offensive from 16 December 1944 to 2 February 1945: MS P-032c, 1949, 17–18). However, Maucke makes no mention of a panzer receiving damage. Lieutenant Miller in his account reports that the Germans were towing one of their tanks, which meant that the tank suffered a mechanical failure or had sustained damage before the main assault. We assess that it had received damage because of the flank shots from 2/B/705th TD BN (S. Marshall, 1948, 6).

13   "The Chief of Staff emphasized the moment of surprise when the enemy was attacked during the early morning on the 1st day of Christmas. . . . My objections to attack without a plan were dismissed" (Maucke, Report Over the 15th Panzer-Grenadier-Division during the Ardennes Offensive from 16 December 1944 to 2 February 1945: MS P-032c, 1949).

14   "The II./115 received resistance 1st along the Flamizoulle Stream in the small forest north of Flamizoulle. . . . At this time, the regimental command post relocated Flamizoulle" (Maucke, Report Over the 15th Panzer-Grenadier-Division during the Ardennes Offensive from 16 December 1944 to 2 February 1945: MS P-032c, 1949).

15   "The attack in the direction of Isle-la-Hesse against stubborn resistance at 1st gained good ground. At the same time, the Fusilier Regiment 39 fought its way up to Isle-le Pre" (H. Kokott, Employment of the 26th Volksgrenadier Division from 16 to 31 Dec 1944, 1945); "Reconnaissance Battalion 26—starting out from the area around Mande St. Etienne . . . to capture Isle-la-Pre as its 1st objective" (G. H. Kokott, Ardennes Offensive—Battle of Bastogne, MS #B-040, 1950, 123).

16   "At 0300 hours attack of regimental strength was launched against the town of CHAMPS (5262). . . . Activity on the remainder of the Division perimeter consisted of only light probing attacks which were easily repulsed without incident" (L. C. Danahy, No. 7 G-2 Periodic Report, 25 December 1944).

17   "At 0645 hours, a radio message from the I./115 arrived, 'Standing before west rim of Bastogne!'" (Maucke, Report Over the 15th Panzer-Grenadier-Division during the Ardennes Offensive from 16 December 1944 to 2 February 1945: MS P-032c, 1949).

18   "Almost coincidentally, Private Allie Moore got back from the 2nd Platoon outpost and told Bowles that a considerable force of infantry and 'many tanks' were moving directly on his front" (S. Marshall, 1948, 6); "Battalion outpost reported enemy tanks approaching at approximately 0630 hour in area (530-605)" (C. T. Moran, 1944).

19   "Them tanks came rolling off those hills, from behind the woods, and spread out. Scary, but we had heard German tanks before and you did what we had to do" (C. Gisi, Interview with PFC Carmen Gisi, 2009).

20   "Bowles ran forward to the outpost on his left flank. . . . Bowles doubled back to his main position" (S. Marshall, 1948, 6).

21   "On reporting back, he [Lt Adams], Lt. Bowles and I decided we were in the path of attack and to withhold fire until the tanks had gone through us . . . but headed toward Hemroulle" (L. R. Nelson, unknown); "When the four tanks materialized (0830) there were eleven tanks, two armored half-tracks with 200 infantry supporting the armor . . . because the enemy was far too strong numerically to handle at this point" (A. W. Johnson, 1945).

22   "When the report was called in to Lt. Bowles at his CP . . . He phoned my CP and asked for artillery fire on the tanks" (D. R. Martin, 2004, 55).

23   "I was aleep upstairs in my CP when Bowles called . . . and I told him, No, tell the men to hold their fire" (D. R. Martin, 2004, 55-56).

24   "The nighttime was definitely to my advantage . . . they would have seen our positions and we would have been quickly wiped out" (D. R. Martin, 2004, 56).

25   See map in S. Marshall, 1948, 6.

26   "Perhaps the best measure of the fighting élan of this unit is that on the morning of the attack they were covering their ground with five .50 caliber machine guns and two light machine guns . . . its men never overlooked the chance to build up weapon power" (S. Marshall, 1948, 5); "We had two .50 caliber machine guns we had got from our scouting mission. . . . Anyway, those .50 calibers came in handy during that battle [25 December]" (C. Gisi, Interview with PFC Carmen Gisi, 2009).

27   "Christmas morning 1944 came peacefully. . . . Their gas masks clanking, other equipment rattling, and all of them screaming at the top of their lungs" (R. J. MacDonald, Another Von Rundstedt Blunder—Bastogne, 1948, 20–21).

28   "On 25 December 1944 the 1st Platoon of 'B' company, 1st Battalion, 401st Glider Infantry Regiment, theoretically in reserve. . . . Morale was superior. The troops were seasoned veterans . . ." (O'Halloran, 1948, 8).

29   "For 2nd Platoon, which was looking right down the muzzle of the enemy thrust, the 'right thing' was to fold over to the vastly better cover on the flank position held by 3rd Platoon" (S. Marshall, 1948, 6).

30   "From that time on . . . and continue firing into the enemy column" (S. Marshall, 1948, 6); "One of my men on the far left flank began firing a .50-caliber machine gun, but no one else did any firing. This added to the deception. The German tanks thought they had passed a weak outpost and kept on going. They didn't know they had passed through a well-fortified, frontline positions" (D. R. Martin, 2004, 56–57).

31   "For the CP group in the little wood . . . 4 dead and five wounded" (S. Marshall, 1948, 6).

32   "We had a close call in a wooded area when a flame thrower came in. . . . My buddy's helmet got smashed" (Koskimaki, 2003, 267).

33   Shell Report for the 463rd Parachute Field Artillery Battalion, 25 December 1944.

34   "I was on the edge of an evergreen patch just east of Hemroulle. . . . I reached over and found that he was dead" (Hesler, World War II Historical Summary of the 463rd Parachute Field Artillery, 2003); "During the early morning a strong enemy attack developed along line CHAMPS-FLAMIZOULLE . . . tanks were moving in the direction of the firing batteries' positions" (C. T. Moran, 1944).

35   "Among the 463rd artillerymen killed in an infantry mode that morning were Howard Hickenlooper and John T. Hall, both of Battery C. Hickenlooper was struck in

the neck by a burst of 9mm rounds from a MP40, while Hall caught a burst of MG42 fire through the chest" (Bando, *101st Airborne: The Screaming Eagles in World War II*, 2007, 185).

36   ". . . and it was in this group that most of the night's casualties occurred—4 dead and five wounded" (S. Marshall, 1948, 6); "Four Screaming Eagles of A Company in the path of the juggernaut were killed and five wounded" (MacKenzie, 1968, 221).

37   See map in S. Marshall, 1948, 6.

38   "Attack after attack was repulsed by a small group of men under 1st Lt. (now Capt.) John Adams of A Company. . . . The three men who were left joined our company" (R. J. MacDonald, Another Von Rundstedt Blunder—Bastogne, 1948, 21); "The German infantry was walking five or six abreast in a column . . . and we would have been quickly wiped out" (D. R. Martin, 2004, 56).

39   "I called Lt. Colonel Allen and told him the battalion had been penetrated . . . as he could not reach him with his SCR 300" (R. J. MacDonald, Another Von Rundstedt Blunder—Bastogne, 1948, 22–23).

40   "We could hold the infantry, but not the tanks, so I told the platoon leaders to let the tanks through and they would get 'em in the rear but to knock every Jerry on foot" (Ryan, 2009).

41   "We had two .50 caliber machine guns we had got from our scouting mission to where the field hospital had been attacked. . . . Anyway, those .50 calibers came in handy during that battle [25 December]" (C. Gisi, Interview with PFC Carmen Gisi, 2009).

42   "When the enemy attacks of the morning trundled over 'A' company . . . preventing him from turning northward and rolling up the flank of 'B' company" (O'Halloran, 1948, 8–9).

43   "As the German tanks slowly rolled past them . . . The German tanks slowly rumbled toward Company C" (D. R. Martin, 2004, 57).

44   "13 enemy tanks and an unknown number of infantrymen attacked. . . . All 7 tanks stopped east of the woods" (R. B. Miller, 1945); "There was a little patch of woods where they put our reconnaissance. . . . I couldn't turn the gun for the trees" (Lamke, n.d., 974).

45   "Our guards told us the Germans had bombed Bastogne at midnight. . . . By now Jerry had broken through on the east side of them in the area of our 2nd Battalion" (Black, *The Last First Sergeant*, 1998, 242).

46   "We got ready in a hurry with few words. . . . What upset me the most was that Jerry wasn't going to take Christmas off!" (Black, *The Last First Sergeant*, 1998, 242).

47   "Our 'C' Company moved about halfway up the road. My 2nd Platoon . . . Start a fire!" (Black, *The Last First Sergeant*, 1998, 242–43); "That was Christmas morning . . . when we were coming down a road, single file on each side . . ." (Elson, 1998).

48   "It was early, 6 o'clock in the morning, just getting light, it really didn't get too light until about 8 o'clock or so, till the fog cleared" (Elson, 1998, 3).

49   "It was cold, and everything was covered in snow. We were jumpy. . . . Somebody started to heat up coffee" (Black, *The Last First Sergeant*, 1998, 243).

50   "I took my time setting up my squad's machine gun at the corner of the courtyard gate. . . . They had to burn maps and papers" (Black, *The Last First Sergeant*, 1998, 243).

51   "They put us in a condominium up towards Foy. . . . He never got credit for it" (O'Mara, 2011).

52 "We were in reserve. . . . Captain Towns told me 'Bob, pass the word out—not any soldier is to take a shot'" (Lott, 2009); "He [LTC Allen] ordered me to call Captain Preston E. Towns and to tell him to counterattack in that sector as he could not reach with his SCR 300. Towns 'rogered' my instructions . . ." (R. J. MacDonald, Another Von Rundstedt Blunder—Bastogne, 1948, 21–23).

53 "We were holding our fire to let them pass through our position and then we would trap them. . . . It was definitely a miracle on Christmas Day" (Lott, 2009).

54 "I think what helped us was that the Germans split up. . . . We wondered why the Germans went in opposite directions . . ." (Lott, 2009).

55 "Around 0700 hours the II./115 reached the heights west of Hemroulle . . . required authentication" (Maucke, Report Over the 15th Panzer-Grenadier-Division during the Ardennes Offensive from 16 December 1944 to 2 February 1945: MS P-032c, 1949).

56 "The 15th panzer Grenadier Division . . . Initial objective: country road Hemroulle–Isle-la-Hesse" (G. H. Kokott, Ardennes Offensive—Battle of Bastogne, MS #B-040, 1950, 122–23).

57 "Yes, my CP was beside the road leading from Champs to Hemroulle. . . . No, I was busy, it was foggy and the tanks were coming up behind the CP" (D. R. Martin, 2004, 58); "Allen had previously got a telephone call from Capt. Preston E. Towns of Company 'C' . . . Towns replied, 'If you look out your window you will be looking down the muzzle of an 88'" (Harper, 327th Regiment at Bastogne, 1945, 21).

58 "I looked out the back window . . . He ordered me to get out and get out fast" (D. R. Martin, 2004, 58); "At 0715 Col Allen, Comdg 3rd Bn, called Harper. . . . 'My units are still in position but I've got to run.'" (Harper, 327th Regiment at Bastogne, 1945, 21).

59 "Captain James Pounders and Joseph S. Brewster had refused to leave me. . . . He said: 'No. You were definitely leading it'" (D. R. Martin, 2004, 58).

60 "At the command post of the 327th Glider Regiment's 3rd Battalion . . . I called out the order. 'Get the hell out of here! Head for the trees!' (Black, The Last First Sergeant, 1998, 243–44).

61 ". . . and we were going along this road when something started shooting. . . . And the idea is so you're not silhouetted against the snow completely" (Elson, 1998).

62 "C Company was broadside to this mess and we were ordered to fall back to the woods on the east side of the road . . . as my trusty M1 was frozen due to my dunking, I couldn't do much more than act as a cheerleader" (J. Flanagan, n.d.); "Before breakfast, German panzers began pushing through our lines . . . they would have had to be very fast" (Sutton, 2004).

63 "This farm was a split-level with the house over the horse and cow stables. . . . I could see German tracer bullets over his head" (Black, The Last First Sergeant, 1998, 244).

64 "He ran through the woods with two members of his staff . . . and he got out of it with none of his party being hurt" (Harper, 327th Regiment at Bastogne, 1945, 22).

65 "You know something? For a moment there, he looked a lot like Jesus Christ to me" (Koskimaki, 2003, 273).

66 "Captain Cody came back after seeing tanks to find one platoon already engaged in a firefight. . . . This squad was captured along with everything left by 3d Battalion CP when they evacuated" (Phillips, 1948, 24).

67 "The Colonel's run was at least two hundred yards to the 1st cover of any kind. . . . They were scattered, too, but in good shape" (Black, The Last First Sergeant, 1998, 244–45).

68 "Lt. Colonel Hanlon was ordered by the Regimental Commander . . . reached an

area 500 yards behind the Regimental CP" (S. A. Chappuis, Historical Narrative of the 502nd PIR, 1–31 December 1944, 1945, 4); "While Swanson was becoming engaged [in Champs] . . . if it pushed on into town and the Germans came around it" (Cassidy, 1945, 8); "This Regiment [77th Volksgrenadier Regiment] in its role of the left attacking force will be on alert at 0215 . . . 2nd Bn, 77th Regt in the Rau-Bachgrund 500 meters east of Rouette" (Schriefer, Order for the Attack by this Regiment (77th) on 25.12.44 on Town of Bastogne, 24 December 1944).

69   "The section left CHAMPS at 0900 [probably a lot earlier] and proceeded down the road toward HEMROULLE. . . . Williams decided that his TDs would be better off covering the cross road (527613) south of ROLLE" (Long, 1945, 3); See map from D'Angelo interview (A. D'Angelo, Interview with Tony D'Angelo, 2009).

70   "By this time all of the Regimental CP men were out on out-post duty around Rolle. . . . He had first sighted them at 523-603" (Cassidy, 1945, 8).

71   PFC Amos Almeida wrote, "On the way over [to Champs], we were shelled. . . . There was no time for us to position ourselves before we were attacked" (Koskimaki, 2003, 291).

72   "In the morning we started down the road [from Champs to Rolle] to our usual position by the trees and a German burp gun opened up on me. . . . He started swearing, calling me every name in the book" (A. D'Angelo, Interview with Tony D'Angelo, 2009); "As these two TDs moved across country . . . but Williams decided that he best get out of the line of fire of the tank and then flush it" (Long, 1945, 2).

73   "I remember the Lieutenant who threatened to court martial us. I said [if he had sent us straight at the German tanks] there, five men killed! You happy?" (Stoling, 2009).

74   "Look, Lieutenant, I told him we'll fight our way, the way we are trained. We go around behind, back in the woods, and come out on them" (A. D'Angelo, Interview with Tony D'Angelo, 2009). It is possible the unidentified officer who argued with D'Angelo was Lieutenant Nickels.

75   "Colonel Chappuis agreed this was a sound decision and gave instructions. . . . Lieutenant Nickels, S-2 of the 1st Battalion, came running into the CP with one excited sentence, 'Seven tanks and infantry coming from the left'" (Phillips, 1948, 23–24).

76   "Cooks, clerks, chaplains, and radio men were gathered up under Capt James C Stone, the Hq Comdt, and rushed west to the next hill. They saw the German tanks coming on straight toward the CP" (Cassidy, 1945, 8); "Before further details were known . . . rushed forward to command the scratch force composed of cooks, radio operators, wiremen, demolition troops, and staff personnel" (Phillips, 1948, 24).

77   "I [Barnes] dozed sitting on a parachute in a candle-lit barn while talking to the wounded. . . . We heard there were seven tanks outside with about a company of infantry" (Koskimaki, 2003, 293).

78   "Left in the CP were only Chappuis, Cassidy and one radio operator. . . . By this time, however, the tanks were coming on over the hill and every gun was blazing into Company 'C'" (Cassidy, 1945, 8–9); "While this action was going on . . . and take the tanks under fire" (Phillips, 1948, 25).

Chapter Ten

1   Aron, 2009, 196.

2   "As soon as the last tank rolled through 2nd Platoon's position . . . and in front of

the approaching infantry" (D. R. Martin, 2004, 56); "Now to get back to Second Platoon . . . following along behind the tanks, had mistaken the meaning of their easy passage" (S. Marshall, 1948, 7).

3   "Harper realizing that control of the Bn was jeopardized by these rapid developments sent his own S-3, Maj Jones. . . . 'Hold tight to your positions and fight back at them.'" (Harper, 327th Regiment at Bastogne, 1945, 22); "How the Command Post group got out of that house alive is a story in itself . . . and a good vantage point for the duration of the battle. (R. J. MacDonald, Another Von Rundstedt Blunder—Bastogne, 1948, 23).

4   "Speck, this is the time for a counterattack. . . . We can take them right where they are" (MacKenzie, 1968, 228).

5   "They were still marching in formation in the field below the ridge . . . and the infantry still didn't know where we were dug in" (D. R. Martin, 2004, 57).

6   "Bowles' one mortar (the other had been overrun by the armor) found this body immediately . . . the few survivors of the anti-climatic action came in with their hands up" (S. Marshall, 1948, 7).

7   "It was a hell of a fight. The Germans we didn't kill, we captured" (C. Gisi, Interview with PFC Carmen Gisi, 2009); "No, I don't seem to remember that. I just remember it was pure hell. A real fight on Christmas Day" (C. Gisi, 2009).

8   "You were shooting in almost every direction, it seemed" (C. Gisi, Interview with PFC Carmen Gisi, 2009).

9   "We just piled the Jerry dead up and they did a good job on us too, but we got the most in the long run" (Ryan, 2009).

10   "In effect, we had bottled up the krauts . . . and we were pouring in plenty of lead from the [right] flank" (R. J. MacDonald, Another Von Rundstedt Blunder—Bastogne, 1948, 23).

11   Finally, as dawn broke the enemy panicked and attempted to cross the 300 yards of open ground to our front. . . . The riflemen were standing out of their holes bracing their rifles against the fir trees for better aim" (R. J. MacDonald, Another Von Rundstedt Blunder—Bastogne, 1948, 24).

12   "Company 'A' captured 92 of the upcoming infantry" (Harper, 327th Regiment at Bastogne, 1945, 23).

13   "Early morning of the 24th they would break through then with their tanks and infantry and get behind them and . . . They would take care of them" (Walsh, Francis Walsh Collection (AFC/2001/001/64192), Veterans History Project, American Folklife Center, Library of Congress, 2008); Walsh confuses the dates. There was no attack on December 24, but his description easily matches the attack on the twenty-fifth, even though he said that was a second attack.

14   "0735 [25 December] to Cherry. Move strongest team to pos[ition] held 24th by Ryerson. En[emy] t[an]ks in vic. When situation in hand return to town and alert. Fr[om] Rbts. [Colonel Roberts]. 0822. Alert 2nd half of Cherry to move to NW on O" (Radio Journal of the Combat Command B, 10th Armored Division, December 1944); "I continued to warn my infantry that the tanks would break through. . . . Well, they did break through—the chief break-through coming on Christmas morning . . ." (A. C. McAuliffe, 1945, 6); Team Cherry Strength reports see (S3, 3rd Tank Battalion, Combat Command B, 10th Armored Division, 25 December 1944); ". . . but it was known in the Operations Room there that out beyond the long sweep of plain stretching westward from General McAuliffe's C.P. a tank force was pounding on

a damaged inner door at Hemroulle. . . . Captain Leo H. Schweiter, the assistant G-2, passed the word to Bernay to round up any bazookas he could find" (MacKenzie, 1968, 225).

15 "Around 0700 hours the II./115 reached the heights west of Hemroulle and encountered strong enemy resistance. . . . The II./115 made a futile attempt to entrench into the frozen ground" (Maucke, Report Over the 15th Panzer-Grenadier-Division during the Ardennes Offensive from 16 December 1944 to 2 February 1945: MS P-032c, 1949).

16 "0800 Hours I and III Battalions stand 2.5 km west of Bastogne and encounter strong enemy resistance . . . received heavy tank and machine gun fire" (Operations Section, 1944).

17 "Based on the situation that remained unclear . . . American fighter aircraft began uninterrupted attacks, which included the regimental combat command post" (Maucke, Report Over the 15th Panzer-Grenadier-Division during the Ardennes Offensive from 16 December 1944 to 2 February 1945: MS P-032c, 1949).

18 "0858 Hours Radio communiqué from the I./115 . . . The enemy reoccupied the road" (Operations Section, 1944).

19 "Grenadier Regiment 77 reported: 'Heavy fighting around Champs, to the south, penetration into the wooded sections west of Rolle . . . One had the impression that enemy resistance would have to break down now" (G. H. Kokott, Ardennes Offensive—Battle of Bastogne, MS #B-040, 1950, 129–30). Kokott mentioned these reports came into his command post at 1000, but that is doubtful, since Maucke had already called off the attack by 0900, which coincides with American reports. Kokott likely received these reports but at an earlier time than he mentioned.

20 "The artillery- and mortar fire was raging furiously on both sides . . . same as Salle, Givroulle and Gives were exposed to incessant by the bombs and aircraft armament of the fighter-bombers" (G. H. Kokott, Ardennes Offensive—Battle of Bastogne, MS #B-040, 1950, 130).

21 "At 0800, the CO of 502-1 [Hanlon] came to Andrews and asked for AT support. . . . Upon returning, he told Andrews that he had seen 2 Mk IVs and 5 SP guns. This was at 0900" (Andrews, 1945, 2).

22 "Halfway back to the farmhouse command post . . . They had made the mistake of not coming after us or not being ready for a counter attack" (Black, *The Last First Sergeant*, 1998, 245); "This had all happened within thirty minutes at the most. . . . We were all engaged in a deadly serious act" (Black, The Unedited Manuscript of Layton Black's Memoirs to George Koskimaki, n.d., 344–45); "The Germans got out of their tanks and made coffee and sat around waiting for daylight . . . they had parked in front of the only gun that had the ammo" (Cooper, Interview with Colonel John T. Cooper, unknown). We know from the radio logs that the German units overran the 401st headquarters around 0720, and then a lull occurred in the action, and fighting did not resume until 0900, after the sun had risen. This was verified by the radio logs from the 321st FA BN, CCB 10th AR DIV, and the AARs of the 705th TD BN.

23 "We [D'Angelo and his section of TDs] drove over to the woods near the road. . . . We were hidden in those woods good. That's what helped us get the Germans" (A. D'Angelo, Interview with Tony D'Angelo, 2009); "The château was on our left. . . . Some of them paratroopers told me later they didn't know we were in there" (A. D'Angelo, Interview with Tony D'Angelo, 2009); "There were a lot of paratroop-

ers around us. I sort of remember him [Black]. Of course, 'Moe' Williams was there, too. I think he'd come up in a jeep about the same time we got into positions" (A. D'Angelo, Interview with Tony D'Angelo, 2009); "He [Williams] then move back to ROLLE where he was informed that German tank was in the woods covering the road . . . the infantry flushed it out with bazookas and small arms" (Long, 1945, 2–3).

24   "Ten minutes later [0910] . . . The remaining Mk IV, the covering tank which put both TDs out of action, surrendered intact in HEMROULLE" (Andrews, 1945, 2–3); "As the Germans came over the hill . . . it was learned that they had knocked out the two tank destroyers after the running battle engagement" (Phillips, 1948, 24–27); "The two TDs with the 327th Regt had been hit and destroyed by this tank onslaught . . . at about the same moment the guns were turned against Company C's flank" (Cassidy, 1945, 10); "25 December . . . 0905 Fr[om] D/90. Quite an armed action taking place back of our daylight pos[itions]. Cherry will run into it on road" (Radio Journal of the Combat Command B, 10th Armored Division, December 1944); (Photo of StuG III outside Hemroulle 1944); The photo shows a StuG III with a significant penetration on its westward side, facing the Lane of Trees. This could have only come from Schmidt's section of Hellcats. History of 705th, TD history, Breder interview, etc. Sadly, this was the same George N. Schmidt who had put up a historic fight on the twentieth outside of Neffe. In that fight, Schmidt held off attacking German infantry with the M18 .50-caliber machine gun, firing some 2,000 rounds at the attackers. Little information is available on how Schmidt or the remaining crew of the two tank destroyers were killed or wounded on the twenty-fifth. Through a newspaper obituary, graciously given to me by Ray Bankers of the Pardeeville American Legion Post #215, I was able to verify that Schmidt was definitely the commander of one of the destroyed Hellcats. His mother was presented with his posthumous silver star in August of 1945. Also, the 705th records list the following members wounded on Christmas Day, 1944 (all were from B Company's 1st Platoon): Corporal Richard J. Ellner, Tech 4 Lawrence W. Frye, and Sergeant Phillip Hopkins. Along with Schmidt, Private First Class Manuel Rivas Jr. was reported KIA that day. Since the 705th participated in no other major actions anywhere else around the perimeter or lost any other TDs that day, it is assumed that the rest of these men were the crews of the two tank destroyers destroyed in the assault. (Although there is the remote possibility that some were wounded or killed by artillery, etc., in Bastogne, as the 705th had a great number of support personnel in the town.) Colonel John C. "Jack" Dibble Jr., of Satellite Beach, Florida, who succeeded Templeton to command the 705th after Templeton was killed March 1, 1945, said in an interview in March of 2009 that he knew of Schmidt's demise, and said only that he had heard "he [Schmidt] did it in the classic style—he got several tanks and the last one got him."

25   "And we just were in a long line more or less of guys set up . . . everybody was firing at once, and there were lots of flashes, you'd fire at flashes" (Elson, 1998, 59).

26   "The tanks were coming forward, boldly now, firing as they moved, with no effects of accuracy. . . . More enemy infantry came out of the woods to be caught in the line of American fire" (Phillips, 1948, 25).

27   "We opened up at the same time . . . as if the only thing that mattered was saving the tanks" (Black, *The Last First Sergeant*, 1998, 246).

28   Photo of Panzer *Lustmolch*, 1944; "In the first 15 minutes we [the 463rd] had disabled

8 tanks, hit ten tanks . . . but put a white undershirt on the tube and wait for me" (Cooper, Interview with Colonel John T. Cooper, unknown); ". . . the western tank defenses engaged four medium enemy tanks area (52.9-59.5). . . . This same party also captured two officers and twelve enlisted men on the same patrol" (C. T. Moran, 1944, 2); "The team leader of the German tanks escaped towards Hemroulle only to be captured. From the prisoners of this enemy tank, it was learned that they had knocked out the two tank destroyers after the running battle engagement" (Phillips, 1948, 26–27). There is a good chance, based on our research, that "*Lustmolch*" was *Hauptmann* Schmidt's command tank and crew.

29   "By now the situation took a complete turning as Company C's first fire cut among the German infantry riding on the tanks . . . the infantry riding on the tanks were cut to pieces by the automatic rifle fire" (Cassidy, 1945, 10).

30   "It was close in, immediate [the battle on Christmas morning]. . . . That private had the stuff of which good soldiers are made" (Hanlon, 1962).

31   "Two mortar crews had combined and set up one mortar near the Rolle command post . . . before Major Haire, Regimental S-4, stopped the action to keep his ammunition from being depleted of the last one hundred rounds" (Phillips, 1948, 25–26).

32   "German infantrymen rushed out of the farmhouse to catch a ride on the tanks. Many of them were cut down by our rifle fire, now crossfire of the Second, First and 3rd Platoons of 'C' Company" (Black, *The Last First Sergeant*, 1998, 246).

33   "By this time Cassidy's runner had arrived . . . they left a completely exposed flank turned toward the TDs and they went into action" (Cassidy, 1945, 10).

34   "Our platoon sergeant Don 'Moe' Williams came up. He told the paratroopers, 'Don't worry about it—we'll get those sons of bitches for you'" (A. D'Angelo, Interview with Tony D'Angelo, 2009).

35   "I was walking along near the edge of the clearing in line with the potato pile by now . . . he taught the Germans a small lesson in tank warfare" (Black, The Unedited Manuscript of Layton Black's Memoirs to George Koskimaki, n.d., 345).

36   "Saw four our five tanks coming down the road. Certain they were Mk IVs all. Had turrets" (A. D'Angelo, Interview with Tony D'Angelo, 2009); "Yes, their flanks [German panzers] were to us. . . . Our guns worked best at that close range" (A. D'Angelo, Interview with Sergeant Anthony "Tony" D'Angelo, June 4, 2009).

37   In many published accounts, the distance of D'Angelo's and Vallitta's shots has been mentioned as four hundred yards or more. Based on the location of the destroyed armor in the photographs, I believe most of the shots were much closer, almost half that distance. After all, the distance from the position of the two M18s in the woods to the Lane of Trees (which would have represented one of their farthest shots) is barely three hundred yards. Most of the destroyed armor was little more than two hundred yards from their position. See penetration ammunition tables for the M18 Hellcat in Osprey Book, *M18 Hellcat* (Zaloga, M18 Hellcat Tank Destroyer 1943–1997, 2004).

38   "Yes, their flanks were to us. That's what made it such a perfect shot. They were going by slow, I guess. Two got by" (A. D'Angelo, Interview with Sergeant Anthony "Tony" D'Angelo, June 4, 2009).

39   "I told him to take the last tank first, and then one at a time on up the line and fire when ready" (A. D'Angelo, Interview with Tony D'Angelo, 2009).

40   "He [Vallitta] told us to take the lead tanks . . ." (Stoling, 2009).

41 "And me and him stayed outside the TD . . . there was two more still coming" (A. D'Angelo, Interview with Tony D'Angelo, 2009).

42 "We backed up and repositioned the TD for a better shot. Well, I don't know how many we got. . . . Vallitta hit one . . ." (A. D'Angelo, Interview with Tony D'Angelo, 2009); "My gunner, Corporal Sam Dedio, was kind of new. He was a replacement, so he didn't really have a lot of time on the gun" (A. D'Angelo, Interview with Sergeant Anthony "Tony" D'Angelo, March 4, 2009); "I'll tell you, my gunner was a replacement. Larry had the better gunner on his TD. Clark was his name. He was one of the best shots in the battalion" (A. D'Angelo, Interview with Sergeant Anthony "Tony" D'Angelo, June 4, 2009).

43 "Vallitta hit one, had a round cook off in the breech and had to back out. They took a rammer and rammed it out" (A. D'Angelo, Interview with Tony D'Angelo, 2009); "Yes, it cooked off in the tube. We backed up and put a rammer staff down it to clear it out" (Stoling, 2009); "The second tank destroyer, Larry's tank [Vallitta] . . . It had cooked in the tube" (A. D'Angelo, n.d.).

44 "I think we fired about five to six rounds at about that many German tanks. Again, I am sure we got three, maybe four, though. Larry's gun got at least one before they had that jam" (A. D'Angelo, Interview with Sergeant Anthony "Tony" D'Angelo, 8 June 2009).

45 "The TD next to me fired six shots. Two hit big trees, four hit tanks, and four were knocked out. It was the best I ever saw" (Black, The Unedited Manuscript of Layton Black's Memoirs to George Koskimaki, n.d., 345).

46 "My gunner [Dedio], he took a shot at one of those last panzers at the treeline . . . he would have hit him in the gas tank!" (A. D'Angelo, Interview with Sergeant Anthony "Tony" D'Angelo, June 4, 2009). Though Black claims the TDs destroyed four tanks, Chappuis and Cassidy credited the TDs with three kills and an unknown bazooka man from C Company with the fourth kill. "In the next few minutes Stone's group got one tank with a bazooka [Jackson] . . . and the infantry riding on the tanks were cut to pieces by automatic rifle fire" (Cassidy, 1945, 10). Despite who killed whom, the count was four Mk IVs destroyed in vicinity of the captured 1/401st headquarters along the Champs road.

47 "Sam's [CPL Dedio] round, last one, hit the back of one of those tanks . . . but it was a German crewman engulfed in flames" (A. D'Angelo, Interview with Sergeant Anthony "Tony" D'Angelo, June 4, 2009).

48 "We [Jackson and others] had originally put mines in the road but . . . They drove off on the side and exploded our mines" (Astor, 1994, 330–31).

49 "A second German tank making a break to follow the first one met its doom near the Rolle crossroads as Sergeant Schuyler Jackson (Demolition Platoon) made a cleancut hit when he rushed forward to fire his loaded bazooka" (Phillips, 1948, 26); "Sgt. Schuyler Jackson was in the barn cellar . . . killed all the infantrymen. I got the Silver Star for that one . . ." (Ferretti, 1984, 1); "There was a bridge in front of us. . . . We had to shoot them" (Astor, 1994, 330).

50 "We [Jackson and others] had enough ammo at our spot. . . . Somebody else destroyed it" (Astor, 1994, 331); "One Mark IV tank made a break for Champs. . . . This gave the Mark IV tank a clear run into Champs" (Phillips, 1948, 26). Phillips did not identify the failed bazooka gunner, but it was likely Jackson, since the stories are so similar—the biggest difference being that the surviving tank escaped before the

second tank failed to make it past the crossroads. Jackson claims the story was reversed.

51   Some of the veterans I interviewed (D'Angelo, Asay, Stoling, etc.) speculated that the "rogue tank" may have found a temporary haven in the wood plantation between Champs and Rolle. Both authors have traveled through the woodlots in these woods, including the area known as "Aviator Woods," and have been amazed at the myriad maze of clearings, trails, and clumps of trees where it is entirely possible to hide a full-size tank.

52   "Four German tanks were in sight . . . and all that happened was a loud clang when it hit the tank" (Ferretti, 1984).

53   "0928 [25 December] Sit[uation] improving. Inf[antry] trying to regain positions. En[emy] t[an]ks have pulled off OP" (Radio Journal of the Combat Command B, 10th Armored Division, December 1944).

54   "Some of the guys went to go check out the knocked out German tanks. I didn't want to see that. I mean, that's still some mother's son" (A. D'Angelo, Interview with Sergeant Anthony "Tony" D'Angelo, June 4, 2009).

55   "After the fight, we 'mopped up' the battleground area . . . not that he had done so" (Black, *The Last First Sergeant*, 1998, 247). Although this incident was certainly callous and cruel, it is by no means unique. After Americans got word of the Malmedy massacre—where SS troops had gunned down unarmed American prisoners on Dec. 17—many soldiers had made personal vows not to take any German prisoners.

56   "Our 'C' Company took thirty-five prisoners and killed sixty-seven Germans for our part in that Christmas morning fight" (Black, *The Last First Sergeant*, 1998, 246–47).

57   "Well, I [D'Angelo] felt relieved" (A. D'Angelo, Interview with Tony D'Angelo, 2009).

58   "We were great marksmen [705th TD BN] and Templeton had trained us well when we were back in the States" (A. D'Angelo, Interview with Sergeant Anthony "Tony" D'Angelo, March 4, 2009).

59   "By the grace of God, we got our rounds off before the Germans, or it would have been a different story" (A. D'Angelo, Interview with Tony D'Angelo, 2009).

60   "Colonel Templeton came up to me and said, 'Job well done . . . As a matter of fact, I had a good [Christmas] day after that" (A. D'Angelo, Interview with Tony D'Angelo, 2009).

Chapter Eleven

1   Fradin, 2009, 32.

2   "I think it was about 6-7 Christmas morning . . . we only had rifles" (Hesler, 2009).

3   "The days prior to Christmas began to pass about . . . we had another gun that would have a side shot at the tank" (Cooper, unknown).

4   "There were generally four to a crew . . . but I don't know for sure" (Hesler, Second Interview with Ken Hesler, 2010).

5   This data (total number of enemy tanks destroyed during the battle near both Rolle and Hemroulle) comes from many different sources, reports, and claims, and many of those sources are at odds with one another. It may truly be impossible, in all certainty, to determine who was responsible for destroying how many and which enemy vehicles, especially since many of the accounts are contradictory, even from the same unit. "During the fire fight in the battalion's northern sector, at approximately

0730 hours . . . where it was captured by Battalion Tank Stalking party . . ." (Moran, 1944, 2).

6 "Everyone was prepared for the worst . . . in case we were overrun by the enemy" (Tofany, n.d.).

7 "A little after dawn on Christmas morning . . . we could have guns covering any field of fire" (Lyons, 2001, 259).

8 Positions ascertained from a letter and hand-drawn map supplied by John Mockabee, D Btry, 463rd PFAB, after the war (Mockabee, n.d.).

9 Streeter, 2008.

10 "There were generally four to a crew . . . but I don't know for sure" (Hesler, Second Interview with Ken Hesler, 2010).

11 "The number 3 pack howitzer with [Clifford] Wolfenberger, Silvas and Peplowksi . . . We wait knowing to fire now would invite disaster, powder snow, smoke, a real give away" (Peplowski, 1988).

12 "The Germans got out of their tanks and made coffee . . . they were being observed through the tube of a 75 pack howitzer . . ." (Cooper, unknown). He said that guys like Childress (who were closer to the Germans" told him the Germans were cooking. Hesler, though, was not there himself, said that he believed the Germans had "gone to ground while it was still somewhat dark." The breakfast story he heard from a few other guys afterward besides Childress, but he said it is "one of those things that I can't testify to," since he didn't witness it.

13 "Our Battery Commander was Capt. Ardel E. Cole and our Executive Officer was a young Lt. by the name of Joseph Lyons. . . . Capt Cole called again and said, 'Sgt. Smith, if you are going to get up it had better be now'" (Smith, 1980).

14 Moran, 1944, 3.

15 "I was not in a gun section . . . and the gun had to be moved down the slope slightly to get the tube depressed sufficiently to get the tanks in the gun sight" (McMorrow, n.d.); "The mission of the First Airborne Task Force was completed. . . . General Eisenhower presented the Division with the Presidential Unit Citation" (Barrett, 2012).

16 "Once the tanks got in range . . . We waited about three or four minutes and then started to fire" (Lyons, 2001, 259).

17 "Once the tanks came into view . . . we knew we were facing German tanks" (Lyons, 2001, 259); "Then I heard the tanks west of me . . . they might be Patton's tanks" (Gerhold, 1991).

18 "The enemy infantry action to the right indicates that a tank swing to the left is inevitable to make a fire team. . . . Wolfenberger is gunner, a cool, calm, efficient and accurate one" (Peplowski, 1988).

19 "On Christmas Day, at daybreak . . . His burns were minor" (Koskimaki, 2003, 277); (Bellaza, 1988).

20 "I came out of my foxhole on the run. . . . We destroyed three tanks and dispatched a ground crew out and captured the tank's crew" (Smith, 1980).

21 "As the Germans began to make a move . . . The S-3 gave the order, 'Let the shit hit the fan!'" (Cooper, unknown); "About daylight Capt. Ardelle E. Cole advised me . . . which was the code for direct fire" (Garrett, Letter to George Koskimaki, n.d.).

22 "No, I did not, but we could hear it . . . so I could make out our guns firing" (Hesler, Second Interview with Ken Hesler, 2010).

23 "Well, we were taught that the back of the German tanks were greasy. . . . I can also

get you the numbers for how much WP was fired in that action" (Hesler, Second Interview with Ken Hesler, 2010).

24   "During the battle word came that tanks were coming up from the rear. . . . I was a member of that 50 caliber machine gun team" (Mockabee, n.d.); (Mockabee, John Mockabee "D" Battery, 463rd Parachute Field Artillery—Letter to George Koski-maki, 1989).

25   "In the predawn hours of 25 December 1944, T/4 Corsen 'Booger' Childress, Joe Pimlott and myself were assigned as supporting infantry . . . the tanks were driven back to our lines by Childress, Pimlott and myself" (Hazzard, 1988); (Koskimaki, 2003, 278); "(1) Destroyed with AP and WP two medium tanks, proven by line of hits . . . (4) Captured fourteen assorted infantry and tank crew members" (Sher-burne, 1944); " . . . destroying two and damaging one to such an extent that it with-drew to a hull down position . . . capturing eight enlisted men who were turned over to the 502nd Parachute Infantry" (Moran, 1944); "The positions remained the same until 25 December 1944 . . . and by these actions repelled the attack on Hemroulle" (Seaton, 1944, 1–2); (Mockabee, Hand-drawn Map to George Koskimaki, n.d.); "In the first 15 minutes we had disabled 8 tanks . . . but put a white undershirt on the tube and wait for me" (Cooper, unknown). Again, there is a good chance the wounded German tank commander was *Hauptmann* Schmidt.

26   "Upon returning, he [Schmidt] told Andrews that he had seen 2 Mk IVs and 5 SP guns . . . and Cpl. Richard Ellner was seriously wounded" (Andrews, 1945, 2–3); See photos from Donald Pratt Museum.

27   "Christmas morning I had been making my usual rounds to the different gun positions. . . . A-Btry took no prisoners" (Gerhold, 1991).

28   "We had a real Christmas Day Turkey Shoot . . . unless you see his boots go up higher than his head" (Stolmeier, 2002).

29   "After the shooting was over . . . to check on our mess crew" (Smith, 1980).

30   "As the Germans began to make a move . . . and one getting in" (Cooper, unknown).

31   "Our machine gun section drove the captured tank near our positions. . . . Lyons looked him in the eye and replied, 'You're the prisoner, I'm not'" (Lyons, 2001, 260).

32   "In the first 15 minutes we had disabled 5 tanks . . . and parked it outside my HQ" (Cooper, unknown).

33   Seaton, Casualty Report for December 1944.

34   See ammunition expended in Garrett, S-3 Report from: 242400, Dec 1944, to: 252400, Dec 1944, Unit: 463 Parachute Field Artillery Battalion, No. 210, 1944).

35   ". . . there was a German tank burned to a crisp hanging upside down on the right side of the tank . . . until it hit a bank about 4 feet high at a 45 degree angle" (J. L. Martin, 1989).

36   "By this time, about 45 minutes had passed. . . . No American anti-tank guns and or tanks were involved in our battle" (Cooper, unknown).

37   Asay took an Iron Cross dated 1939 off of one of the Germans, which he still has to this day. "We (my squad and I) went after them. . . . We were clearing out house to house all day and taking prisoners" (Asay, Interview with Charles Asay, 2009).

38   "Well, I took a patrol up the Givry road, the last house up to Givry. . . . I was taken to the American field hospital and took me four months to mend" (Asay, Interview with Charles Asay, 2009).

39   "In an interesting action in Champs . . . when I brought a German officer from the church steeple area" (Koskimaki, 2003, 297).

40 "0805 . . . Contact made with all by runners" (A Co Headquarters Section, 502nd Parachute Infantry, 1945).

41 "As the day continued on with fighting in and around Champs . . . and destroyed the tank crew by small arms fire by our men" (Koskimaki, 2003, 299); "I did talk to him [Swanson] . . . and they couldn't move it" (Hatch, 1991).

42 ". . . I was telephoning with my back to the door, looking out of the window . . . but of course not doing any damage" (Koskimaki, 2003, 299).

43 "Well, you know we had that one German tank come up through Champs. . . . The other guys took care of the crew" (Fowler, second Interview with Corporal Willis Fowler, 2010).

44 "Food and bragging and post mortem of the battle were the order of the day now . . . his pants shot off and the radio gone" (Goldmann, Letter to Mrs. Ballard, 1945).

45 See A Company log (A Co Headquarters Section, 502nd Parachute Infantry, 1945).

46 "Suddenly, as if on signal, the fighting ended; and eerie calm broken only by the crackling of burning tanks, came over the field" (Hanlon, 1962).

47 "The attack by the enemy soldiers advancing under cover of darkness on the 'A' Company positions north and west of Champs . . . and were engaged with the enemy until dark" (Koskimaki, 2003, 301).

48 "A new line was laid to Company A and the 2d Battalion . . . but was stopped before it could materialize" (Phillips, 1948, 27–28); "The wire maintenance men had continued their work right through the fire fight. . . . Christmas Day closed with Cassidy and Chappuis eating a can of sardines and some crackers for their dinner" (Cassidy, 1945, 11–12).

49 "Information contained in captured documents showed the 115th Panzergrenadier Regiment (recently brought up from Italy) and two battalions of the 77th Volksgrenadier Regiment supported by the 26th Volksgrenadier Division Artillery had participated in the German attack" (Phillips, 1948, 28).

50 "Prisoners take during period: [FROM DEC 241800 TO DEC 251800] 117" (Abernathy, Journal of the 327th Glider Infantry Regiment, December 1944).

51 "1020—The attack upon Red (1st BN) along the RR turned out to be an enemy reconnaissance in force . . . 1500—PW's from 1st Bn, 77th Regt state that their Regimental staff is at 513634" (S2 Section, 327th Glider Infantry Regiment, 1944, 9).

52 S1, 327th GIR, 1944; "Upon reaching the OP, the company commander [McDonald] without formality began orienting the platoon leader [Halloran]. . . . The massing of these enemy troops indicated a probable night attack" (O'Halloran, 1948, 9); "A little more than a hundred yards from the farm buildings . . . cautiously continued their advance" (O'Halloran, 1948, 13); "Near the farm buildings . . . The enemy fire appeared to come from one of the farmhouse's basement windows" (Koskimaki, 2003, 244); "At this time the platoon leader directed . . . yet immobility would eventually spell annihilation" (O'Halloran, 1948, 13–14); "Signalling for increased rates of fire the squads were ordered to move forward. . . . Ammunition supply was more than adequate" (O'Halloran, 1948, 14); "The rest of us made a wild dash to the barn and stood there against a stone wall, out of the gunner's sight" (Koskimaki, 2003, 244); "Two riflemen had taken up a position behind a small tree . . . unable to persist in the attack" (O'Halloran, 1948, 14); "Blimp and I became separated . . . hay hanging above my head" (Koskimaki, 2003, 244); "The platoon . . . and four men had received slight wounds" (O'Halloran, 1948, 11, 15, 18); "Lt. O'Halloran led a platoon backed up by TD in an attack on the buildings. . . . S/Sgt Joseph Sopcyzk was

killed in the operation" (Koskimaki, 2003, 243); "Minutes later, as twilight faded into darkness . . . The squad leaders were ordered to prepare for withdrawal" (O'Halloran, 1948, 17); (S1, 327th GIR, 1944).

53   "Stationed with the 406th Fighter Group at Mourmelon-le-Grand in the French area of the installation was the 101st Airborne Division . . . there began the most intensive period of activity and destruction in the history of the organization" (Bastogne and the 101st Division, 1945).

54   "Intelligence informed us that about 700 four-barrel . . . And I had been on flak-busting missions before Bastogne" (Park, 1993, 1–2).

55   "Yes—I flew each of the days from 23rd thru 27th . . . conferring with crew chief on return, and debriefing" (Park, 1993); (Graves, 1944).

56   ". . . we attacked targets within 400 yards of our own perimeter . . . Despite skill, a lot of luck was needed to escape unscathed" (Park, 1993).

57   "Captain Parker of the Ninth Air Force stationed his radio-equipped jeep in the central courtyard, the better to operate as ground controller . . . that it was in fact an enemy ruse designed to get a body of armor past the aerial screen and into Bastogne" (MacKenzie, 1968, 230–31); "On December 19 Capt. James E. Parker. . . . were given to Captain Parker" (Rome, 199).

58   "406th Ftr. Grp. (OPREP only [25 December 1944] 115 sorties, all in battlefield. Supported by VIII Corps, according to OPREP . . . 'At 151, 6 mi. E of Bastogne, "Roscoe" repeated request of Maestro to bomb Bastogne'" (XIX Tactical Air Force, 1950, 15–17).

59   "Such was the execution that one of the pilots later said to General McAuliffe, 'This was better hunting than the Falaise pocket and that was the best I ever expected to see'" (Rome, 199).

60   "25 December—1st Lt. MYRON A. STONE failed to return from ground support . . . failed to return from ground support dive bomb mission to Bastogne" (Office of the Intelligence Officer, 1944).

61   "Actually we lost five of the 513th in three days . . . contributed to longevity in this instance" (Park,1993).

62   "All the pots and pans had holes in them. Sgt. Thomas Spivey [the mess sergeant] was mad as a wet hen" (C. D. Smith, 1980).

63   "On the morning of the 26th we were ordered to take a hill in front of us. . . . Can you believe it?" (Lott, 2009). A classic story to relate Towns's courage is related in Karel Margry's *Operation Market-Garden, Then and Now*. During the Holland drop, Towns's glider tug, a C-47, was hit by flak and started to dive to the ground, dragging the Waco glider with it. Towns smashed the Plexiglas windshield of the glider and, reaching out with his combat knife, cut the tow rope, freeing the glider and allowing it to land safely complete with Towns and his men (Margry, 2002, 265).

64   ". . . the pilots of the 406th Fighter Group pressed home their attacks . . . and 13 ammunition and fuel dumps" (Weyland, 1945).

65   "According to Intelligence of the 101st . . . The Thunderbolts flew in above the tree tops and tackled every target assigned to them" (C. J. Parker, 1945).

66   "We went out on the mission determined to help our ground forces. . . . Summing up, the Bastogne period was the most significant time in my combat experience of [the] 11½ months and two Purple Hearts" (Park, 1993).

67   "In the morning, dozens of wounded men filled the Féron house . . . eight families were left with nothing" (Heintz, 1984, 77).

68 "By early afternoon of 25 December, the division command . . . to bring the exhausted attacking forces to a 'halt'" (G. H. Kokott, 1950, 134–35).

69 "Only one thing was certain: the 5th Parachute Division . . . attacking from the southwest" (G. H. Kokott, 1950, 136).

70 "In the afternoon, the division . . . Reconnaissance Battalion 26 and Rifle Regiment 39 stuck to their positions" (G. II. Kokott, 1950, 135).

71 "Around 0900 hours . . . and directed to dig in and hold the gained ground" (Maucke, 1949); "At first light . . . along the outskirts of Bastogne" (H. Kokott, Employment of the 26th Volksgrenadier Division from 16 to 31 Dec 1944, 1945).

72 The 463rd PFA BN conducted nine separate fire missions. . . . They fired exactly 208 shells" (Shell Report for the 463rd Parachute Field Artillery Battalion, 25 December 1944).

73 "The enemy reacted with very powerful and effective fire concentrations. Pursuits of the retreating German forces did not take place" (G. H. Kokott, 1950, 135).

74 "By afternoon, however, the troops had checked all enemy attacks along a line extending as follows: road fork 2 kilometers north of Nives–Remoiville-Hollange" (G. H. Kokott, 1950, 136).

75 "All efforts by 'Baker' Company to drive the Germans . . . converged on the target" (Koskimaki, 2003, 301–02); "On the Christmas Day attack . . . We did inflict several on the Jerries" (Wise, 1948).

76 "During this Christmas Day encounter with the enemy, the field artillery observer . . . firing into the enemy position even though close in contact with our men" (Koskimaki, 2003, 298).

77 "Yes, in December 1944 I thought it was a good idea to fight this battle and to win the war. . . . By Christmas Day I had less than 30 in my company" (Lindemann, Interview with Ludwig Lindemann concerning the Battle of Champs on 25 December 1944 [2010]).

78 "On 22 December . . . I was able to issue two K rations to every member of my staff and to each of the Belgian children" (Luettwitz, XLVII Panzer Corps (16 Dec–24 Dec 44), ETHINT 41, 1945, 5–6); "The advance detachment of the 2d Pz Division had no gasoline . . . in order to take it definitively" (Luettwitz, The Assignment of the XLVII Panzer Corps in the Ardennes MS A-939, 1950, 14); "In this offensive, Bastogne was the key point of communications behind our front lines, which we needed to be able to bring in supplies for the divisions" (Buechs, 1945, 4).

79 "Christmas Eve was rather melancholy for the Corps. . . . The Division continued to be in a critical situation. During the day CHAVANNE was lost" (Luettwitz, The Assignment of the XLVII Panzer Corps in the Ardennes, MS #A-939, 1950, 14–15); "On 24 December Rochefort was captured by Panzer Lehr. . . . Humain and Havrenne were taken on 25 December at noon" (Bayerlein, 2005, 98); "I [Luettwitz] knew that on 24 Dec 44, the advance detachment of the 2 Pz Div was attacked by the 2 US Armored Div" (Luettwitz, XXXXVII Panzer Corps in the Battle of the Ardennes, MS #A-940, 1946, 9).

80 "25 December: 0900. Humain taken by 902. Havrenne captured by Lehr Recon . . . Only a few escaped" (Bayerlein, 2005, 82).

81 "The situation had developed as expected . . . so that the available forces were not strong enough for the definite mopping up of BASTOGNE" (Luettwitz, The Assignment of the XLVII Panzer Corps in the Ardennes, MS #A-939, 1950, 15–16).

82 "The Chief of Staff emphasized the moment of surprise when the enemy was at-

tacked during the early morning on the first day of Christmas. . . . Without objections, the courageous regiment prepared for an attack on Christmas Eve" (Maucke, 1949).

83   "The III./115 was designated the reserve . . . why the battalion was not committed to the difficult task in the front lines" (Maucke, 1949); "1535 Hours Colonel Maucke traveled to the III Battalion. . . . The III./115 was attached" (Operations Section, 1944). The AAR that Maucke wrote after the war was a day off. The artillery strike hit the 3rd Battalion—not the 2nd. Dyroff was injured. "1600 Hours Enemy assault troops with two tanks at the path-crossing . . . and deliver the new orders" (Operations Section, 1944).

84   "No reports from the I./115 were received until evening. . . . At the heights at Isle-La-Hesse I encountered strong enemy resistance" (Maucke, 1949).

85   "Estimated Enemy Casualties: PWs evacuated to PWE, 222. Total to date, 616. Tracked vehicles destroyed this date—Tanks, 27; half-tracks. 1. Total to date: Tanks, 144; half-tracks, 25" (Danahy, G-2 Periodic Reports No. 7 from: 250001 to 252400, December 1944).

86   "The kitchen of the Signal Company was strafed. . . . Friendly armor that had been attacking the Germans south of the town was 1,000 yards from the outer defense lines, he said" (MacKenzie, 1968, 231–32); (Unknown, 1944).

87   "With the massing of troops and tanks on Christmas Day. . . . He said, 'Hell, I know that! I want to know where the 4th Armored is'" (Wright, n.d.).

88   "I saw a large pillbox ahead and ordered Dickerman to throw several rounds into it—it was demolished. . . . Time 1640, December 26, 1944" (Boggess, 1984, 7–8).

89   Koskimaki, 2003, 339.

90   Copy of letter from Templeton (Wick, 1999, 990–91).

91   "All 7 tanks stopped E of the woods. . . . They were burning before Love left them" (R. B. Miller, 1945, 2); "However, Sgt. Love (Co. B) got 2 MkIV's with four shots as the enemy passed his position" (A. W. Johnson, 1945, 3); "Someone contacted the tank destroyers. . . . They jumped and went down into the woods" (Lamke, n.d., 974–75); "Instantly, the four tank destroyers raced into position behind the tanks and opened fire. Five of the tanks exploded as their thin, unprotected backsides took direct hits" (D. R. Martin, 2004, 58); "25 December 1944 H&S COMPANY . . . The remaining two escaped temporarily to the woods to our north" (Turbiville, 1945, 4); Captain William J. Nancarrow; Privates Joe J. Berra, Stanley W. Wieczorek, Romer L. Williams, Joe H. Douglas, Jacques Levan, and Cort L. Paine; and Technician Fifth Grade William H. Hussey all received a Bronze Star for their action on 25 December 1944, Order 4, Dated 10 January 1945. See Awards and Decorations for the 326th Airborne Engineer Battalion, 1945; "On 25 December a German force was approaching our area. . . . We all received the Bronze Star" (Berra, n.d.). From the accounts, it is more likely that Miller's TD section (Love, et al.) and Nancarrow's men stopped or disabled three tanks and possibly drove two more off.

92   "I wasn't a member of your Battalion. . . . You may have heard from others from our outfit. If not here's a tribute to you," Copy of letter from Bob Johnston, Machine Gunner, Co. C., 327 Glider Infantry, 101st Airborne Division. (Wick, 1999, 1001).

93   "I [Jackson] got the Silver Star for that one [shooting the tank on Christmas Day]" (Ferretti, 1984, 2).

Epilogue

1   This story comes courtesy of Bernard Maus, the grandson of Madame Maus de Rolle. Again, Mr. Cygan and Mr. Barron are in great debt to Mr. Maus for all of the help he has given the authors in researching the events during the battle at and around Rolle Château. On another note, Cygan and Maus were quite surprised to discover a live U.S. hand grenade while touring the Rolle Château outbuildings in July of 2010. The item was carefully disposed of by local Belgian military ordnance experts (Maus, 2010).

2   In July of 2010, author Don Cygan and Bernard Maus also discovered several stacks of what are most certainly the Winchester bedsheets in the attic of the Rolle Château. Evidently, there were several left over, as so many had been given to the residents of Hemroulle to make good their losses, that they didn't know what to do with the remainder. As far as we know, they are still there today.

3   Parker, 2009, 22–25.

4   This information was provided in November of 2010 by Donna Humphrey, secretary at St. Mary's Church in Winchester, Massachusetts. The authors are greatly in her debt for providing the information and relating the story of the stations of the cross. "You may observe a painting. . . . The painting in St. Mary's was restored in July 1998 under the pastorate of Rev. Richard Messina" (Stevens, 2011).

INDEX

ABOUT THE AUTHORS

Leo Barron works for General Dynamics as an instructor of military intelligence officers for the U.S. Army. He holds undergraduate and graduate degrees in history and has served with the 101st Airborne. Barron has seen two tours of active duty in Iraq as an infantry and intelligence officer. His articles about Bastogne and other WWII-related military topics have appeared in *Infantry Magazine*, *Military Intelligence Professional Bulletin*, *WWII History Magazine*, and *WWII Magazine*. He has used some of his research on Bastogne and the Christmas battle to teach his students about intelligence preparation of the battlefield.

Don Cygan has studied military history for decades. Cygan has also worked as a reporter for the *Douglas County Daily News–Press*. In addition, he has worked as a freelance writer for several years in Colorado, with articles published in *The Parker Chronicle*, the *Denver Business Journal*, and other publications. During Operation Desert storm, Cygan performed public relations for the U.S. Army. His degrees are in journalism and communication.

CONNECT ONLINE

www.nosilentnight.com